Twentieth-Century American Poetics

Poets on the Art of Poetry

Edited by

Dana Gioia

David Mason
The Colorado College

Meg Schoerke
San Francisco State University

with D. C. Stone

Boston Burr Ridge, IL Dubuque, IA M
San Francisco St. Louis Bangkok Bogotá
Lisbon London Madrid Mexico City Mil
Santiago Seoul Singapore Sydne

McGraw-Hill Higher Education

*A Division of The **McGraw-Hill** Companies*

TWENTIETH-CENTURY AMERICAN POETICS:
POETS ON THE ART OF POETRY
Published by McGraw-Hill, a business unit of The McGraw-Hill Companies, Inc.,
1221 Avenue of the Americas, New York, NY, 10020. Copyright © 2004, by
Dana Gioia, David Mason, and Meg Schoerke. All rights reserved. No part of this
publication may be reproduced or distributed in any form or by any means, or stored
in a database or retrieval system, without the prior written consent of The McGraw-
Hill Companies, Inc., including, but not limited to, in any network or other electronic
storage or transmission, or broadcast for distance learning.
Some ancillaries, including electronic and print components, may not be available to
customers outside the United States.

This book is printed on acid-free paper.

1 2 3 4 5 6 7 8 9 0 FGR/FGR 0 9 8 7 6 5 4 3

ISBN   0-07-241472-3

President of McGraw-Hill Humanities/Social Sciences: *Steve Debow*
Executive editor: *Lisa Moore*
Senior developmental editor: *Jane Carter*
Executive marketing manager: *David S. Patterson*
Senior media producer: *Todd Vaccaro*
Senior project manager: *Jean Hamilton*
Production supervisor: *Janean A. Utley*
Senior designer: *Gino Cieslik*
Lead supplement producer: *Marc Mattson*
Permissions: *Marty Granahan*
Cover design: *Gino Cieslik*
Cover photo: *Elsie Driggs 1898–1992. Pittsburgh. 1927. Oil on canvas. Gift
          of Gertrude Vanderbilt. Photograph copyright © 1996: Whitney
          Museum of American Art, New York.*
Typeface: *9.5/11.5 Sabon*
Compositor: *Thompson Type*
Printer: *Quebecor World Fairfield Inc.*

Library of Congress Cataloging-in-Publication Data
Twentieth-century American poetics : poets on the art of poetry / edited by Dana Gioia,
    David Mason, Meg Schoerke.
      p. cm.
    Includes index.
    ISBN 0-07-241472-3 (soft cover : alk. paper)
    1. American poetry--20th century--History and criticism--Theory, etc. 2.
    Poetry--Authorship. 3. Poetics. I. Gioia, Dana. II. Mason, David, 1954– III.
    Schoerke, Meg.
PS323.5.T87 2004
808.1--dc21

                                                                2003045926

www.mhhe.com

*To our teachers,
living and dead,
including a few immortals*

About the Editors

Born in Los Angeles in 1950, **Dana Gioia** attended Stanford University and Harvard University, where he studied with Elizabeth Bishop and Robert Fitzgerald, earning an M.A. in comparative literature. Returning to Stanford for his M.B.A., he then worked in New York for fifteen years, writing on nights and weekends, before giving up business to write full time. Gioia has published three books of poems—*Daily Horoscope* (1986), *The Gods of Winter* (1991), and *Interrogations at Noon* (2001), which won the American Book Award—and has edited a dozen anthologies of poetry and fiction, including two anthologies of Italian poetry and a translation of *Mottetti* (1990) by the Italian Nobel laureate Eugenio Montale. He is also the author of "Can Poetry Matter?" (originally published in *Atlantic* in 1991 and collected in *Can Poetry Matter?: Essays on Poetry and American Culture*, 1992). Reissued in honor of its tenth anniversary, this essay continues to stimulate debate over the role poetry plays in the United States today. A prolific critic and reviewer, Gioia is a frequent commentator on American culture for BBC Radio. He has also written *Nosferatu* (2001), an opera libretto, for composer Alva Henderson. In 2003 he became Chairman of the National Endowment for the Arts.

David Mason grew up in Washington State and has lived in many other places, including Greece, New York, Minnesota, and Colorado. He received his B.A. at the Colorado College and his Ph.D. from the University of Rochester. Among his collections of poems are two award-winning books—*The Buried Houses* and *The Country I Remember*—and two chapbooks—*Small Elegies* and *Land Without Grief*. With Mark Jarman he coedited *Rebel Angels: Twenty-five Poets of the New Formalism*, and with the late John Frederick Nims, *Western Wind: An Introduction to Poetry*. He is also author of a collection of essays entitled *The Poetry of Life and the Life of Poetry*. His poems, stories, translations, essays, and memoirs have appeared in a variety of periodicals, including the *New York Times, Hudson Review, Sewanee Review, Poetry, Irish Times, American Scholar, Grand Street*, and *Shenandoah*. Mason has been a Fulbright Fellow to Greece and currently teaches at the Colorado College. He lives in the mountains outside Colorado Springs.

Raised in the Philadelphia and Chicago areas, **Meg Schoerke** did undergraduate work at Northwestern University and earned M.A., M.F.A., and Ph.D degrees from Washington University in St. Louis. Her poems and reviews have appeared in journals such as the *American Scholar, TriQuarterly*, and *Hudson Review*. She has also published a book of poetry, *Anatomical Venus* (2004), and a poetry chapbook, *Beyond Mourning;* and she has contributed essays to a variety of books on twentieth-century American poetry. She is Associate Professor of English at San Francisco State University and lives in San Francisco.

Contents

Preface

WHY POET-CRITICS?

*"Any general statement is like a cheque drawn on a bank.
Its value depends on what is there to meet it."*
— *Ezra Pound*

Practitioners of any art will often feel compelled to explain it, and poets are no exception. Although the poet-critic may seem a modern phenomenon—a creature of little magazines or university lecture halls—the role dates back to antiquity. The Western tradition documents over two thousand years of poets discussing and debating the nature of their art. The Roman poet Horace, for example, wrote a series of witty and memorable verse letters, traditionally known as *Ars Poetica* or *The Poetic Art* (c. 19 BCE), which offered his views on literary aesthetics. Dante composed a prose treatise, *De Vulgari Eloquentia* or *On the Eloquence of the Vernacular* (c. 1304)—written ironically in Latin—to justify his decision to write poetry in Italian. Milton attached a preface to *Samson Agonistes* (1671) to explain his approach to the tragic Biblical subject, and William Wordsworth provided a long defense of his poetic aims and ambitions to introduce the second edition of his *Lyrical Ballads* (1800), which had received an indifferent reception in its first printing.

Statements of aesthetic value have been made by poets in prefaces, letters, essays, conversations, interviews, and even poems. All of these expressions attempt, as Wordsworth put it, to create "the taste by which" poets "are to be enjoyed." While some readers feel no special curiosity about Shakespeare's authorial intentions or creative process, it would nonetheless be illuminating to have an essay from him on poetic drama to supplement the plays. Alas, no scrap of critical prose survives—if any ever existed—from the Bard of Avon, but readers of modern literature enjoy a wealth of critical material from the period's writers. Anyone seeking to understand and appreciate twentieth-century American poetry will eventually be glad to discover that many of the period's most important poets wrote illuminating, sometimes challenging prose.

Despite the long tradition of poet-critics writing in English, there does seem to have been something unprecedented about the prominence of poet-critics in twentieth-century American literature. Never before had poets exercised such powerful influence on both practical criticism and literary theory. Confronting a historical moment in which the aesthetic, social, and political notions of the art were being brought into question by frenetic innovation and experiment, poet-critics played an active and ambitious role in defining and promoting the standards by which this new art would be experienced, understood, judged, and discussed.

Often the poet-critic sought to introduce new writers to an audience, as in James Weldon Johnson's introduction to *The Book of American Negro Poetry* (1922), which also explored the importance of music and other cultural matters. Sometimes they were implicitly commenting on their own poetic aims, as in Robert Frost's "The Figure a Poem Makes," which served as the preface to his *Collected Poems* (1939). Modern American poets have also needed to explain the bewildering array of revolutionary changes in poetic practice from Modernism in forms as diverse as Imagism, Vorticism, Surrealism, and Objectivism to such post-modern movements as Confessionalism, the Beats, Black Arts, Language Poetry, New Formalism, and Identity Poetics. They have needed to relate their art to social issues of their time, such as Marxism, feminism, gay rights, and multiculturalism. And sometimes poets have written prose to explain the art to themselves.

Early in the twentieth century, poet-critics felt that they were acquiring and educating new readers for novel kinds of poetry. These arguments were often contentious. (The British critic Cyril Connolly caustically observed in 1944, "Poets arguing about modern poetry: jackals snarling over a dried-up well.") Since much of the new poetry was difficult or challenging to readers, the role of the critic or interpreter became even more important. By mid-century, the New Criticism had canonized methods of reading, largely based upon the technical practices of poets, that dominated American college classrooms and also contributed to various anti-academic reactions such as Beat poetry.

In the last decades of the century, however, poet-critics lost their allure on college campuses. Academic criticism was often concerned with theories of reading, sometimes subverting the explanations of poets in favor of philosophically or politically charged readings that broke down literary canons. One result of such cultural change was that it helped make a variety of new writers available to us who might not have been discussed by a previous generation. Another was that the culture of poetry itself changed. Some poets adapted their practice to make it attractive to such critics, while others sought a sometimes-elusive audience among "common readers." American poetry and criticism had always exhibited a split between elitists and populists, but these divisions became even more pronounced.

Certainly the fact that after World War II so many American poets found work as college teachers contributed to these phenomena. As the emphases of English departments changed in the last decades of the century, some poets found themselves less than enamored of the literary criticism being practiced there. Poets who obsessed over the value of their own and others' work found it dispiriting when colleagues announced that one text could not be said to have more value than another. Others found such assertions liberating. More troubling to some was the increasingly prevalent belief that criticism could only speak to a class of trained professionals, not to alert and intelligent readers outside the university.

Such conflicts will no doubt be visible in the essays we have chosen here, along with questions about just what poetry *is* and why it holds the attention of communities of people. Since anthologies exist that are specifically designed only for academic communities, we wanted ours to speak in a greater variety of voices, more often than not in beautiful, lucid prose. This anthology was designed for the classroom, but we hope it will prove equally useful and provocative elsewhere.

Of course, twentieth-century poetry did not lose its audience, or its variety of audiences, and poets continue to explain themselves and their work, increasingly in terms of social identity. The art form has remained both vital and diverse, and the prose that poets write plays a part in that vitality. Perhaps because of their investment in their art, poets often lend special urgency and vitality to critical prose. As T. S. Eliot wrote, the poet "is always trying to defend the kinds of poetry he is writing, or to formulate the kinds he wants to write." This lack of disinterestedness proves a virtue when the criticism entertains and illuminates. Ezra Pound wrote that the modern era was "an age of science and abundance" in which books too easily proliferated. The critic was the "weeder" who was "supremely needed if the Garden of the Muses is to persist as a garden." For other critics the garden of American poetry would need to include a greater variety of plants less stringently weeded. The growing diversity of American society should be reflected in what was allowed to remain and grow of its poetry.

These social changes, however, cannot absolve us from trying to understand aesthetic values. "Criticism should animate the imagination," wrote Marianne Moore. Important essays are important for their qualities of writing as well as their ideas. Pound was able to write,

> A classic is classic not because it conforms to certain structural
> roles, or fits certain definitions. . . . It is classic because of a certain
> eternal and irrepressible freshness.

These days, it is very hard to say what a "classic" might be, but Pound's definition is usefully subversive. He sought vitality, not mere canonization. While none of us can be sure of eternity, we can at least celebrate the fact that poets often bring "irrepressible freshness" to their critical prose. They help us understand their art and its place in our society, and give us the added pleasure of language used with exactitude and imagination.

ORGANIZATION OF THIS BOOK

> "The critic, unless he is one in a thousand, reads to
> criticize; the reader reads to read."
> — Randall Jarrell

Twentieth-Century American Poetics is designed to provide students and general readers a comprehensive overview of the major issues influencing the art over the past century as they were seen, articulated, and debated by the poets themselves. Every essay in the book was written by a poet of substantial reputation. The volume is, therefore, both a survey of modern American poetics and a representative history of the poet-critic in contemporary letters. Twentieth-Century American Poetics is the largest and most inclusive historical anthology of its kind ever published, representing fifty-three authors and fifty-eight essays. The book could have been (and indeed was originally planned to be) even larger, but the editors wanted an ample and diverse volume, not an overwhelming one.

Twentieth-Century American Poetics can be read independently as an anthology of critical prose, or it can be used as a companion volume to our anthology, Twentieth-Century American Poetry. Most of the writers collected here are represented by poems in the other book, which groups poets both by chronology and by literary "school" or inclination. In this book, however, simple chronological order is used. For each author we have also written a substantial biographical and critical headnote to provide some context for the selection. Selected bibliographies can also be found in the back of the volume.

In selecting the essays represented in this anthology, the editors have limited themselves to pieces on general topics of poetics rather than considerations of particular writers. Covering those broad issues with a diversity of opinions was the essential business of *Twentieth-Century American Poetics*—a task that no other volume adequately attempted—whereas single author studies were widely available elsewhere. Consequently, certain poet-critics were omitted since their work consists entirely or primarily of critical essays on particular writers rather than explorations of general ideas. We have also avoided reprinting literary memoirs, another popular genre, since for the purposes of this book we preferred analytical discussion of ideas to personal testimony. A few essays in the book contain elements of memoir, but these pieces quickly expand their focus beyond the personal.

As poets and teachers, we felt, first of all, that such a comprehensive book would be useful to students of modern American poetry. Other anthologies of critical prose we had read were mostly focused on one movement or generation—or a single race, gender, ideology, or subject. We wanted *Twentieth-Century American Poetics* to provide broad and fair coverage, so that each major school or movement was represented at least by some of its high points. Obviously, we cannot claim to have included every significant essay published by American poets in the twentieth century, but we did try to include a substantial number of the most influential and widely cited critical essays of the period.

There is no single viewpoint running through the selections. *Twentieth-Century American Poetics* contains essays of differing and even irreconcilable opinions because there is no other way to represent the period faithfully. The history of poetics has less to do with conclusions than with questions—and never was this truer than in modern America. The editors have collected the last century's various and divergent definitions of poetic theory and practice in the spirit of Walt Whitman's quintessentially American pronouncement:

Do I contradict myself?
Very well then. . . . I contradict myself;
I am large. . . . I contain multitudes.

We have sought to provide readers of all stripes with the best available selection of essays by poets. We still believe that poets write better about the art than most other critics have done, usually because they hope to be understood by a variety of readers. As with the poetry book, we have had many discussions and consulted many friends and colleagues about our contents. If Jarrell's distinction between critics and readers still makes any sense, we hope this volume will prove useful to both groups. We base it on the assumption that poetry is primary, criticism secondary, but both can provide the pleasure and fascination of art.

ACKNOWLEDGMENTS

Mary Gioia played as important a role in creating this anthology as any of the editors. She not only organized the contents and managed the editorial process, but she also meticulously fact-checked the critical notes and biographies—a grueling task too often neglected in anthologies. An astute and common-sensical critic, she also suggested hundreds of small changes—additions, deletions, expansions, or revisions—that have made *Twentieth-Century American Poetics* a more useful and reliable book.

D. C. Stone worked tirelessly checking facts, texts, and bibliographies, as well as helping to draft some of the biographical notes. His contributions were so substantial that we felt it appropriate to mention his important supporting role on the title page.

David Mason wishes especially to thank The Colorado College for assistance that made his work on these books possible. His department chair, Barry Sarchett, and colleagues such as Claire Garcia, Daniel Tynan, John Simons, and Jane Hilberry provided invaluable help. Colby Cedar Smith helped immensely with research.

Meg Schoerke is grateful for the computer expertise and critical eye of Mark Seiden, the last-resort aid of Purdue University reference librarian Robert Freeman, and the inspiring example of feminist anthologist Susan Koppelman. She also thanks her mother, Donna S. White, for keeping the faith, and Anne-Marie Cusac, Brighde Mullins, Catherine Rankovic, and Loretta Stec, for their sustaining support and friendship.

In creating this book the editors received the help of a considerable number of scholars, critics, poets, and instructors, including: Mark Bauerlein; Rosemary Catacalos; Annie Finch; H. L. Hix; April Lindner; Lois Lyles; Cristina Ruotolo; Dorothy Barresi, California State University—Northridge; James Bobrick, University of Massachusetts—Dartmouth; Kim Bridgford, Fairfield University; Kenneth Chamlee, Brevard College; Tricia Cherin, California State University—Dominguez Hills; Martha Crowe, Eastern Tennessee State University; William Virgil Davis, Baylor University; Anthony Farrow, Saint Bonaventure University; Henry Herring, The College of Wooster; Hilary Holladay, University of Massachusetts—Lowell; James Kimbrell, Florida State; Miriam N. Kotzin, Drexel University; David McAleavey, George Washington University; Mark Morrisson, Penn State University; Kay Murphy, University of New Orleans; Russell E. Murphy, University of Arkansas—Little Rock; John T. Newcomb, West Chester College; Suzanne Paola, Western Washington University; Robert M. Randolph, Southwest Texas State University; Ira Sadoff, Colby College; Reginald Shepherd, Cornell University; Ernest Smith, University of Central Florida; Jon Thompson, North Carolina State University; and Mark Vinz, Minnesota State University—Moorhead.

We would also like to thank the editorial and production team at McGraw-Hill: to our editors—Sarah Touborg and Lisa Moore—we offer our heartfelt appreciation for their support of this project. We also thank: Jane Carter, Senior Development Editor, who helped us finetune our biographical headnotes and prepare the manuscript for production; Marty Granahan, McGraw-Hill Higher Education's permissions editor, who oversaw the tracking down of permissions holders and handled the myriad permissions details that a book of this nature generates; Jean Hamilton, Senior Project Manager, who saw the manuscript safely through production, turning our manuscript into the book you now hold in your hands; and Gino Cieslik, whose talent as a designer of interiors and covers more than speaks for itself.

Dana Gioia
David Mason
Meg Schoerke

JAMES WELDON JOHNSON
(1871–1938)

In his preface to *The Book of American Negro Poetry* (1922), James Weldon Johnson celebrates "this power of the Negro to suck up the national spirit from the soil and create something artistic and original, which, at the same time, possesses the note of universal appeal," and he credits the achievement to "a remarkable racial gift of adaptability; . . . it is a transfusive quality." In his life and work, Johnson himself was remarkably adaptable, skilled in fusing a variety of styles in his poetry and successful in pursuing careers as a poet, novelist, autobiographer, journalist, songwriter, teacher, lawyer, diplomat, and leader of the National Association for the Advancement of Colored People (NAACP).

Born in Jacksonville, Florida, in 1871, Johnson grew up in a middle-class African American family and attended the Stanton school, one of the largest public schools in the state. At the age of sixteen, he matriculated at Atlanta University and after graduating returned to Stanton in 1894 to serve as principal. While directing the school, he studied law and became the first African American to pass the Florida bar examination. He also started a newspaper, the *Daily American,* which served the Jacksonville African American community from 1895 to 1896. In 1897, Johnson began collaborating with his brother Rosamond, a graduate of the New England Conservatory of Music, and wrote a number of popular songs, including "Lift Ev'ry Voice and Sing," which became known as the "Negro National Anthem." After moving to New York in 1901, Johnson continued to write songs, and several became national hits. Diplomatic appointments to serve as the U.S. Consul to Venezuela (1906–1909) and to Nicaragua (1909–1912) gave him time to pursue literary endeavors. In Central America he completed a novel, *Autobiography of an Ex-Colored Man,* which was published anonymously in 1912. Returning to the United States in 1913, Johnson again turned to journalism, writing editorials for *New York Age.* He also wrote poetry, which appeared in *Fifty Years and Other Poems* (1917). Beginning in 1916, as field secretary for the NAACP, Johnson became adept at political organizing; from 1920 to 1930, as general secretary, he refined the NAACP into a catalyst for legal action and public protest against racism.

Johnson's political commitments, however, did not diminish his literary energy. By the end of the 1920s he had become a leading figure of the Harlem Renaissance through his poetry, anthologies, reviews, and his mentorship of younger writers. In a series of anthologies, *The Book of American Negro Poetry* (1922), *The Book of American Negro Spirituals* (1925), and *The Second Book of American Negro Spirituals* (1926), Johnson showcased the vitality of African American poetry, particularly its roots in music. His own poetry of this period, *God's Trombones: Seven Negro Sermons in Verse* (1927), pays homage to spirituals and adopts the colloquial language and rolling rhythms of African American preaching. These poems, which achieved great popularity at the time, also participate in the Modernist trend toward loosened form, for Johnson turns from the rhyme and meter and dialect poetry of his first collection to a supple vernacular speech that builds momentum through incremental repetitions and varied line lengths. *God's Trombones* fulfills the challenge Johnson proposes in his preface to *The Book of American Negro Poetry*:

> What the colored poet in the United States needs to do is something like what Synge did for the Irish; he needs to find a form that will express the racial spirit by symbols from within rather than by symbols from without. . . . He needs a form that is freer and larger than dialect, but which will still hold the racial flavor; a form expressing the imagery, the idioms, the peculiar turns of thought, and the distinctive humor and pathos, too, of the Negro, but which will also be capable of voicing the deepest and highest human emotions and aspirations, and allow of the widest range of subjects and the widest scope of treatment.

In 1930, Johnson accepted a professorship at Fisk University, where he completed his autobiography, *Along This Way* (1933); a call for integration, *Negro Americans, What Now?* (1934); and *Saint Peter Relates an Incident: Selected Poems* (1935). He died in an automobile accident in June 1938.

◆

FROM PREFACE TO THE BOOK OF AMERICAN NEGRO POETRY

There is, perhaps, a better excuse for giving an Anthology of American Negro Poetry to the public than can be offered for many of the anthologies that have recently been issued. The public, generally speaking, does not know that there are American Negro poets—to supply this lack of information is, alone, a work worthy of somebody's effort.

Moreover, the matter of Negro poets and the production of literature by the colored people in this country involves more than supplying information that is lacking. It is a matter which has a direct bearing on the most vital of American problems.

Originally published as the preface to *The Book of American Negro Poetry* (New York: Harcourt, Brace and Company, 1922).

A people may become great through many means, but there is only one measure by which its greatness is recognized and acknowledged. The final measure of the greatness of all peoples is the amount and standard of the literature and art they have produced. The world does not know that a people is great until that people produces great literature and art. No people that has produced great literature and art has ever been looked upon by the world as distinctly inferior.

The status of the Negro in the United States is more a question of national mental attitude toward the race than of actual conditions. And nothing will do more to change that mental attitude and raise his status than a demonstration of intellectual parity by the Negro through the production of literature and art.

Is there likelihood that the American Negro will be able to do this? There is, for the good reason that he possesses the innate powers. He has the emotional endowment, the originality and artistic conception, and, what is more important, the power of creating that which has universal appeal and influence.

I make here what may appear to be a more startling statement by saying that the Negro has already proved the possession of these powers by being the creator of the only things artistic that have yet sprung from American soil and been universally acknowledged as distinctive American products.

These creations by the American Negro may be summed up under four heads. The first two are the Uncle Remus stories, which were collected by Joel Chandler Harris, and the "spirituals" or slave songs, to which the Fisk Jubilee Singers made the public and the musicians of both the United States and Europe listen. The Uncle Remus stories constitute the greatest body of folk lore that America has produced, and the "spirituals" the greatest body of folk song. I shall speak of the "spirituals" later because they are more than folk songs, for in them the Negro sounded the depths, if he did not scale the heights, of music.

The other two creations are the cakewalk and ragtime. We do not need to go very far back to remember when cakewalking was the rage in the United States, Europe and South America. Society in this country and royalty abroad spent time in practicing the intricate steps. Paris pronounced it the "poetry of motion." The popularity of the cakewalk passed away but its influence remained. The influence can be seen today on any American stage where there is dancing.

. . .

This power of the Negro to suck up the national spirit from the soil and create something artistic and original, which, at the same time, possesses the note of universal appeal, is due to a remarkable racial gift of adaptability; it is more than adaptability, it is a transfusive quality. And the Negro has exercised this transfusive quality not only here in America, where the race lives in large numbers, but in European countries, where the number has been almost infinitesimal.

Is it not curious to know that the greatest poet of Russia is Alexander Pushkin, a man of African descent; that the greatest romancer of France is Alexandre Dumas, a man of African descent; and that one of the greatest musicians of England is Coleridge-Taylor, a man of African descent?

The fact is fairly well known that the father of Dumas was a Negro of the French West Indies, and that the father of Coleridge-Taylor was a native-born African; but the facts concerning Pushkin's African ancestry are not so familiar.

When Peter the Great was Czar of Russia, some potentate presented him with a full-blooded Negro of gigantic size. Peter, the most eccentric ruler of modern times, dressed this Negro up in soldier clothes, christened him Hannibal, and made him a special body-guard.

But Hannibal had more than size, he had brain and ability. He not only looked picturesque and imposing in soldier clothes, he showed that he had in him the making of a real soldier. Peter recognized this, and eventually made him a general. He afterwards ennobled him, and Hannibal, later, married one of the ladies of the Russian court. This same Hannibal was great-grandfather of Pushkin, the national poet of Russia, the man who bears the same relation to Russian literature that Shakespeare bears to English literature.

I know the question naturally arises: If out of the few Negroes who have lived in France there came a Dumas; and out of the few Negroes who have lived in England there came a Coleridge-Taylor; and if from the man who was at the time, probably, the only Negro in Russia there sprang that country's national poet, why have not the millions of Negroes in the United States with all the emotional and artistic endowment claimed for them produced a Dumas, or a Coleridge-Taylor, or a Pushkin?

The question seems difficult, but there is an answer. The Negro in the United States is consuming all of his intellectual energy in this grueling race-struggle. And the same statement may be made in a general way about the white South. Why does not the white South produce literature and art? The white South, too, is consuming all of its intellectual energy in this lamentable conflict. Nearly all of the mental efforts of the white South run through one narrow channel. The life of every Southern white man and all of his activities are impassably limited by the ever present Negro problem. And that is why, as Mr. H. L. Mencken puts it, in all that vast region, with its thirty or forty million people and its territory as large as a half dozen Frances or Germanys, there is not a single poet, not a serious historian, not a creditable composer, not a critic good or bad, not a dramatist dead or alive.

. . .

It may be surprising to many to see how little of the poetry being written by Negro poets today is being written in Negro dialect. The newer Negro poets show a tendency to discard dialect; much of the subject-matter which went into the making of traditional dialect poetry, 'possums, watermelons, etc., they have discarded altogether, at least, as poetic material. This tendency will, no doubt, be regretted by the majority of white readers; and, indeed, it would be a distinct loss if the American Negro poets threw away this quaint and musical folk speech as a medium of expression. And yet, after all, these poets are working through a problem not realized by the reader, and, perhaps, by many of these poets themselves not realized consciously. They are trying to break away from, not Negro dialect itself, but the limitations on Negro dialect imposed by the fixing effects of long convention.

The Negro in the United States has achieved or been placed in a certain artistic niche. When he is thought of artistically, it is as a happy-go-lucky, singing, shuffling, banjo-picking being or as a more or less pathetic figure. The picture of him is in a log cabin amid fields of cotton or along the levees. Negro dialect is naturally and by long association the exact instrument for voicing this phase of Negro life; and by that very exactness it is an instrument with but two full stops, humor and pathos. So even when he confines himself to purely racial themes, the Aframerican poet realizes that there are phases of Negro life in the United States which cannot be treated in the dialect either adequately or artistically. Take, for example, the phases rising out of life in Harlem, that most wonderful Negro city in the world. I do not deny that a Negro in a log cabin is more picturesque than a Negro in a Harlem flat, but the Negro in the Harlem flat is here, and he is but part of a group growing everywhere in the country, a group whose ideals are becoming increasingly more vital than those of the traditionally artistic group, even if its members are less picturesque.

What the colored poet in the United States needs to do is something like what Synge did for the Irish; he needs to find a form that will express the racial spirit by symbols from within rather than by symbols from without, such as the mere mutilation of English spelling and pronunciation. He needs a form that is freer and larger than dialect, but which will still hold the racial flavor; a form expressing the imagery, the idioms, the peculiar turns of thought, and the distinctive humor and pathos, too, of the Negro, but which will also be capable of voicing the deepest and highest emotions and aspirations, and allow of the widest range of subjects and the widest scope of treatment.

Negro dialect is at present a medium that is not capable of giving expression to the varied conditions of Negro life in America, and much less is it capable of giving the fullest interpretation of Negro character and psychology. This is no indictment against the dialect as dialect, but against the mold of convention in which Negro dialect in the United States has been set. In time these conventions may become lost, and the colored poet in the United States may sit down to write in dialect without feeling that his first line will put the general reader in a frame of mind which demands that the poem be humorous or pathetic. In the meantime, there is no reason why these poets should not continue to do the beautiful things that can be done, and done best, in the dialect.

In stating the need for Aframerican poets in the United States to work out a new and distinctive form of expression I do not wish to be understood to hold any theory that they should limit themselves to Negro poetry, to racial themes; the sooner they are able to write *American* poetry spontaneously, the better. Nevertheless, I believe that the richest contribution the Negro poet can make to the American literature of the future will be the fusion into it of his own individual artistic gifts.

1922

◦➤◄ ROBERT FROST ►◄◦
(1874–1963)

Robert Frost stands as the preeminent contrarian of twentieth-century American poetry. His achievement contradicts most easy definitions of modern poetry, and yet no satisfactory explanation of American Modernism can afford to ignore his work. Aside from a few parodies of his friend Ezra Pound, Frost wrote exclusively in meter and mastered traditional forms like the sonnet, ballad, couplet, and blank verse. "I'd as soon write free verse," he famously quipped, "as play tennis with the net down." His use of poetic language was spare and understated, but like his masters—Henry Wadsworth Longfellow, Thomas Hardy, and E. A. Robinson—Frost wrote for the ear. His poems were composed to be spoken and heard, and even memorized. Yet Frost's worldview is indisputably modern. An agnostic, he saw humanity as alone in a universe seemingly devoid of meaning yet fraught with the terror of pain or extinction.

Robert Lee Frost, the great poet of rural New England, was born in San Francisco in 1874. His childhood was not only West Coast but urban. The future farmer grew up in the apartments and hotels of California's biggest city, within sight of the Pacific Ocean. He spent his first eleven years in San Francisco's extraordinarily constant climate where he never saw snow or dramatic seasons. Frost's mother, Isabelle Moodie, was a Scottish immigrant. Born near Edinburgh, she had been raised with relations in Ohio, but she never lost her Scottish accent. The future Poet Laureate of Vermont's only connection to New England came from his father, William Prescott Frost, who had been born in New Hampshire, but had fled the state at an early age. During the Civil War he had traveled south to fight under Robert E. Lee for the Confederacy, but had been arrested in Philadelphia and sent home. He remained a Copperhead Rebel sympathizer until the end and christened his only son Robert Lee Frost, an ironic name for the great bard of Yankee New England. In California the hard-drinking temperamental William Frost worked in journalism and politics but achieved little success in either field.

Frost's California childhood came abruptly to an end in 1885 when his father died at thirty-four from tuberculosis. The elder Frost left no insurance. The poet's mother had nowhere to turn except her husband's family. Taking William Frost's body with them, she and her children travelled by train to Lawrence, Massachusetts, where the young poet spent the next decade in poverty, moving between a series of dreary mill towns in pursuit of financial security.

When the eleven-year-old Frost followed his father's body to Massachusetts, he saw the region with fresh eyes. He took nothing in this new landscape for granted—the flora, fauna, weather, and folkways of the Northeast were new to him—and their connection to his dead father gave them a deep resonance. Frost's position was, therefore, half inside and half outside the region. As a newcomer, he had to make conscious sense of a place in ways that a native never bothers. Frost was an elective New Englander, and a convert is always more passionate about a new faith than someone born to the religion.

The young Frost was a brilliant student—a relentless competitor both in the classroom and on the playing field. He graduated from high school at the top of his class (he was co-valedictorian with Elinor White, whom he married in 1895) and won a scholarship to nearby Dartmouth College. At this point something happened to Frost that no biographer has ever adequately explained. His ferociously competitive instincts suddenly turned inward. He no longer cared much for external measures of success and set his eyes on literary greatness, which he instinctively knew would take decades of dedication to achieve.

Within a few weeks, Frost dropped out of Dartmouth (as he would leave Harvard five years later). The academic work was easy for him, but he found it uncongenial. Instead he devoted himself to courting the wary and often reluctant Elinor. It took three years to convince her to marry him. Whatever his faults as a husband, Frost never wavered in his love for his wife. They were married forty-three years and had six children together.

For the next sixteen years, he eked out a living mostly as a chicken farmer with a few short stints as a schoolteacher. (His grandfather gave him a small farm under the condition that he would work it for ten years.) Frost published almost nothing, but he wrote constantly. He liked farming, but he wasn't very good at it (especially since he often slept till noon). He was an excellent—if unorthodox—teacher, but he refused to stay in the profession for very long since it made writing difficult.

The turning point in Frost's public life occurred in 1912 when he sold his farm and took his family to England. The Frosts settled in Beaconsfield outside London. After twenty years of writing in isolation, Frost felt the time had finally come to make his mark on the literary world. He was thirty-eight years old, he had no poetic reputation, and he had never published a book. But Frost had long wagered his life for just this moment. Almost immediately the wager paid off. Frost had his first book of poems, *A Boy's Will* (1913), accepted by a small but established London firm. (It was reprinted two years later in the United States.) He also met many writers at the newly opened Poetry Bookshop on Devonshire Street in London, including the American Modernist Ezra Pound, who championed his fellow expatriate and helped make Frost's debut volume a critical success. He also met W. B. Yeats, Ford Madox Ford, and Robert Bridges. Most importantly, he met Edward Thomas, with whom he would have the closest literary friendship of his life. He inspired Thomas to shift from nature writing to poetry, and

Thomas's friendship helped Frost mature and deepen as a poet. During his two years in England, Frost not only wrote some of the best poems of his life but paradoxically some of the most American—like "Birches," "Home Burial," "Mending Wall," "After Apple Picking," and "The Road Not Taken." Living in England somehow gave him the clarity to understand his homeland. In 1914 his second book, *North of Boston,* appeared, and the forty-year-old poet was now established. When a New York publisher offered to print a U.S. edition, Frost told his wife, "Now we can go home." He returned to America a celebrated poet. His public reputation would never stop growing. But his private sorrows had only just begun.

If Frost was by nature a family man, his domestic life was marked by enormous suffering and loss. The couple's first son died of typhoid fever in childhood. Another daughter died at birth. Frost's only sister went insane, a fate later shared by one of his daughters. His youngest daughter died agonizingly in childbirth. His second son committed suicide. Only one of his six children—his daughter Lesley—lived out a natural and healthy life. Under the burden of such private sorrow, it hardly seems surprising that Frost would carefully create a happier public image. Literary fame gradually became his refuge from personal agony. The poet's later years were marked by public fame and increasing emotional isolation. He died at eighty-eight in 1963.

Frost never allowed the public to view his suffering. His poetry seems so compellingly personal that one forgets how seldom it is overtly autobiographical. His most painful poems, like "Home Burial" or "'Out, Out—,'" are mostly narratives, which distance their tragedies by placing them in fictive lives. Fear, guilt, and suffering cast their shadows everywhere across his poetry, but in art, as in life, Frost kept those dark themes in such careful balance that they did not overwhelm him.

Frost's greatness as a lyric poet has never been seriously questioned. He perfected a compressed but accessible style that combined evocative musicality with spiritual profundity. His best work has an extraordinarily meaningful complexity in which he often explores two opposing ideas with balanced intelligence, intensity, and invention. Frost's great preeminence, however, rests on the breadth of his accomplishment. He did distinguished work in lyric, narrative, and didactic poetry, and he mastered the tragic, comic, pastoral, and satiric modes with equal genius. No other major modern American poet matched his versatility. Only in dramatic verse did his genius falter to the level of mere talent as in his verse plays *A Masque of Reason* (1945) and *A Masque of Mercy* (1947).

Frost was the most famous and popular American poet of the twentieth century. Alone among his poetic contemporaries, he achieved the difficult feat of combining immense popularity with nearly universal critical esteem. No modern American poet was so abundantly honored in his own lifetime. Frost won every prize the nation had to offer, including four Pulitzer Prizes—a record no other poet or novelist has ever matched and an achievement all the more remarkable since he did not win his first Pulitzer until he was forty-nine. By the end of his long life, Frost had become a national icon: his later books became best-sellers; universities competed for his presence; buildings were named in his honor; and his poems entered the curriculum at every level of education from grammar school to graduate school.

The height of his celebrity came when the eighty-six-year-old poet read at John F. Kennedy's 1961 presidential inauguration. Televised live, it became the most famous public appearance by any American writer.

While Frost's importance as a poet is undisputed, his importance as a critic has often been underestimated because his modes of discourse had so little in common with the conventional literary criticism of his period. The condescension of academic critics is illustrated in the harsh assessment of Richard Ellmann and Robert O'Clair in their once influential *Norton Anthology of Modern Poetry* (1973) which declared that "Unlike Yeats and Eliot, [Frost] has almost nothing to say in prose, whether from guardedness or economy, except some gnomic and highly quotable statements." Today this summary judgment seems a parochial charge to level against the author of "The Figure a Poem Makes" or "Education by Poetry."

As a critic, Frost had little interest in current poetic trends or formal critical methods. His central concern was mostly the broader human purposes of poetry about which he wrote with wit, insight, and originality. Although not a prolific critic, Frost left behind some of the most eloquent and profound statements ever written about poetry, often couched in extraordinary metaphors. In the two pieces that follow—one from a letter, the other a preface to one of his collections—notice the way he illustrates his points with examples from life.

◄●━━◄ ▮ ►━━●►

THE SOUND OF SENSE

A Letter to John T. Bartlett

Fourth of July [1913] Beaconsfield

Dear John:-

Those initials you quote from T.P.'s belong to a fellow named Buckley and the explanation of Buckley is this that he has recently issued a book with David Nutt, but at his own expense, whereas in my case David Nutt assumed the risks. *And* those other people Buckley reviewed are his personal friends or friends of his friends or if not that simply examples of the kind of wrong horse most fools put their money on. You will be sorry to hear me say so but they are not even craftsmen. Of course there are two ways of using that word the good and the bad one. To be on the safe side it is best to call such dubs mechanics. To be perfectly frank with you I am one of the most notable craftsmen of my time. That will transpire presently. I am possibly the only person going who works on any but a worn out theory (principle I had better say) of versification. You see the great successes in recent poetry have been made on the assumption that the music of words was a matter of harmonised vowels and consonants. Both Swinburne and Tennyson arrived largely at effects in assonation. But they were on the wrong track or at any rate on a short track. They went the length of it. Any one else who goes that way must go after them. And that's where most are going. I alone of English writers have consciously

Originally published in *Selected Letters of Robert Frost*, ed. Lawrance Thompson (New York: Holt, Rinehart, and Winston, 1964).

set myself to make music out of what I may call the sound of sense. Now it is possible to have sense without the sound of sense (as in much prose that is supposed to pass muster but makes very dull reading) and the sound of sense without sense (as in Alice in Wonderland which makes anything but dull reading). The best place to get the abstract sound of sense is from voices behind a door that cuts off the words. Ask yourself how these sentences would sound without the words in which they are embodied:

> You mean to tell me you can't read?
> I said no such thing.
> Well read then.
> You're not my teacher.
>
> *
>
> He says it's too late.
> Oh, say!
> Damn an Ingersoll watch anyway.
>
> *
>
> One-two-three—go!
> No good! Come back————come back.
> Haslam go down there and make those kids get out of the track.

Those sounds are summoned by the audile [audial] imagination and they must be positive, strong, and definitely and unmistakeably indicated by the context. The reader must be at no loss to give his voice the posture proper to the sentence. The simple declarative sentence used in making a plain statement is one sound. But Lord love ye it mustn't be worked to death. It is against the law of nature that whole poems should be written in it. If they are written they won't be read. The sound of sense, then. You get that. It is the abstract vitality of our speech. It is pure sound—pure form. One who concerns himself with it more than the subject is an artist. But remember we are still talking merely of the raw material of poetry. An ear and an appetite for these sounds of sense is the first qualification of a writer, be it of prose or verse. But if one is to be a poet he must learn to get cadences by skillfully breaking the sounds of sense with all their irregularity of accent across the regular beat of the metre. Verse in which there is nothing but the beat of the metre furnished by the accents of the polysyllabic words we call doggerel. Verse is not that. Neither is it the sound of sense alone. It is a resultant from those two. There are only two or three metres that are worth anything. We depend for variety on the infinite play of accents in the sound of sense. The high possibility of emotional expression all lets in this mingling of sense-sound and word-accent. A curious thing. And all this has its bearing on your prose me boy. Never if you can help it write down a sentence in which the voice will not know how to posture *specially*.

That letter head shows how far we have come since we left Pink. Editorial correspondent of the Montreal Star sounds to me. Gad, we get little mail from you.

Affectionately R.F.

Maybe you'll keep this discourse on the sound of sense till I can say more on it.

THE FIGURE A POEM MAKES

Abstraction is an old story with the philosophers, but it has been like a new toy in the hands of the artists of our day. Why can't we have any one quality of poetry we choose by itself? We can have in thought. Then it will go hard if we can't in practice. Our lives for it.

Granted no one but a humanist much cares how sound a poem is if it is only *a* sound. The sound is the gold in the ore. Then we will have the sound out alone and dispense with the inessential. We do till we make the discovery that the object in writing poetry is to make all poems sound as different as possible from each other, and the resources for that of vowels, consonants, punctuation, syntax, words, sentences, meter are not enough. We need the help of context—meaning—subject matter. That is the greatest help towards variety. All that can be done with words is soon told. So also with meters—particularly in our language where there are virtually but two, strict iambic and loose iambic. The ancients with many were still poor if they depended on meters for all tune. It is painful to watch our sprung-rhythmists straining at the point of omitting one short from a foot for relief from monotony. The possibilities for tune from the dramatic tones of meaning struck across the rigidity of a limited meter are endless. And we are back in poetry as merely one more art of having something to say, sound or unsound. Probably better if sound, because deeper and from wider experience.

Then there is this wildness whereof it is spoken. Granted again that it has an equal claim with sound to being a poem's better half. If it is a wild tune, it is a poem. Our problem then is, as modern abstractionists, to have the wildness pure; to be wild with nothing to be wild about. We bring up as aberrationists, giving way to undirected associations and kicking ourselves from one chance suggestion to another in all directions as of a hot afternoon in the life of a grasshopper. Theme alone can steady us down. Just as the first mystery was how a poem could have a tune in such a straightness as meter, so the second mystery is how a poem can have wildness and at the same time a subject that shall be fulfilled.

It should be of the pleasure of a poem itself to tell how it can. The figure a poem makes. It begins in delight and ends in wisdom. The figure is the same as for love. No one can really hold that the ecstasy should be static and stand still in one place. It begins in delight, it inclines to the impulse, it assumes direction with the first line laid down, it runs a course of lucky events, and ends in a clarification of life—not necessarily a great clarification, such as sects and cults are founded on, but in a momentary stay against confusion. It has denouement. It has an outcome that though unforeseen was predestined from the first image of the original mood—and indeed from the very mood. It is but a trick poem and no poem at all if the best of it was thought of first and saved for the last. It finds its own name as it goes and discovers the best waiting for it in some final phrase at once wise and sad—the happy-sad blend of the drinking song.

No tears in the writer, no tears in the reader. No surprise for the writer, no surprise for the reader. For me the initial delight is in the surprise of remembering

Originally published in *Collected Poems of Robert Frost* (New York: Holt, Rinehart, and Winston, 1939).

something I didn't know I knew. I am in a place, in a situation, as if I had materialized from cloud or risen out of the ground. There is a glad recognition of the long lost and the rest follows. Step by step the wonder of unexpected supply keeps growing. The impressions most useful to my purpose seem always those I was unaware of and so made no note of at the time when taken, and the conclusion is come to that like giants we are always hurling experience ahead of us to pave the future with against the day when we may want to strike a line of purpose across it for somewhere. The line will have the more charm for not being mechanically straight. We enjoy the straight crookedness of a good walking stick. Modern instruments of precision are being used to make things crooked as if by eye and hand in the old days.

I tell how there may be a better wildness of logic than of inconsequence. But the logic is backward, in retrospect, after the act. It must be more felt than seen ahead like prophecy. It must be a revelation, or a series of revelations, as much for the poet as for the reader. For it to be that there must have been the greatest freedom of the material to move about in it and to establish relations in it regardless of time and space, previous relation, and everything but affinity. We prate of freedom. We call our schools free because we are not free to stay away from them till we are sixteen years of age. I have given up my democratic prejudices and now willingly set the lower classes free to be completely taken care of by the upper classes. Political freedom is nothing to me. I bestow it right and left. All I would keep for myself is the freedom of my material—the condition of body and mind now and then to summons aptly from the vast chaos of all I have lived through.

Scholars and artists thrown together are often annoyed at the puzzle of where they differ. Both work for knowledge; but I suspect they differ most importantly in the way their knowledge is come by. Scholars get theirs with conscientious thoroughness along projected lines of logic; poets theirs cavalierly and as it happens in and out of books. They stick to nothing deliberately, but let what will stick to them like burrs where they walk in the fields. No acquirement is on assignment, or even self-assignment. Knowledge of the second kind is much more available in the wild free ways of wit and art. A school boy may be defined as one who can tell you what he knows in the order in which he learned it. The artist must value himself as he snatches a thing from some previous order in time and space into a new order with not so much as a ligature clinging to it of the old place where it was organic.

More than once I should have lost my soul to radicalism if it had been the originality it was mistaken for by its young converts. Originality and initiative are what I ask for my country. For myself the originality need be no more than the freshness of a poem run in the way I have described: from delight to wisdom. The figure is the same as for love. Like a piece of ice on a hot stove the poem must ride on its own melting. A poem may be worked over once it is in being, but may not be worried into being. Its most precious quality will remain its having run itself and carried away the poet with it. Read it a hundred times: it will forever keep its freshness as a metal keeps its fragrance. It can never lose its sense of a meaning that once unfolded by surprise as it went.

1939

AMY LOWELL
(1874–1925)

The youngest of five children, Amy Lowell was born into an elite Boston family whose ancestors included nineteenth-century textile magnates and the poet James Russell Lowell. She grew up on her family's Brookline estate, Sevenels, which she inherited after her father's death in 1900. She was educated at home by governesses and then attended private schools; but, disdaining rote curriculum, she mostly pursued her own course of reading in her family's extensive private library. At age seventeen she entered Boston social life as a debutante, attending sixty dinners given in her honor. Entranced by the theater, she considered becoming an actress in her early twenties, but a severe weight problem that was glandular in origin made a stage career impossible.

Until 1910, Lowell engaged in activities typical of an upper-class woman—travel to Europe, projects for civic improvement, and party hosting at Sevenels. But she also devoted an increasing number of hours to writing poetry. In 1910, the *Atlantic Monthly* accepted four sonnets, and in 1912 she published her first collection, *A Dome of Many-Coloured Glass*, whose poems reflect her immersion in the work of Keats and Shelley.

1912 was a landmark year for Lowell not only because of the publication of her first book, but also because she met the woman who became her life-long companion, Ada Dwyer Russell, a professional actress who gave up her career to live with Lowell at Sevenels. Lowell's prolific production over the next decade, in which she averaged a book per year, is due in part to her sustaining relationship with Russell, who helped manage Sevenels and offered supportive criticism.

The year 1912 was also important for American letters, for Harriet Monroe founded the journal *Poetry* in Chicago. Inspired by the magazine's ad-vocacy of "the New Poetry," especially the poems of H. D. (Hilda Doolittle) and the expositions of the new movement, Imagism, contributed by F. S. Flint and Ezra Pound, Lowell experienced a shift of sensibility as powerful as a religious conversion. In the summer of 1913, she traveled to Chicago to meet Monroe, then set off for London to introduce herself to Pound, H. D., Flint, and their Imagist cohorts. By the time she returned to the United States

13

in midsummer, the conversion was complete: her new poems were spare and direct, written in end-stopped free verse whose lines were carefully aligned to match the clauses of her sentences. The next year, Lowell's new poems appeared in *Poetry*, the *Egoist*, and in Pound's anthology, *Des Imagistes*, as well as in her second book, *Sword Blades and Poppy Seed*. But when she took a second trip to London in July 1914, Pound had christened a new movement, Vorticism. Lowell felt that in calling for a poetry of explosive energy Pound had abandoned the smooth perfection of Imagism. Concerned that the cause would lapse, Lowell decided to edit further Imagist anthologies herself. By the time she left England in September 1914, she had secured the support of the other Imagist poets—with the exception of Pound, who scoffed at Lowell's determination to promote a movement he considered moribund. Lowell went on to edit three more Imagist anthologies.

Through her poetry collections, anthologies, extensive public appearances, and two books of criticism, *Six French Poets* (1915) and *Tendencies in Modern American Poetry* (1917), Lowell helped popularize the Modernist movement in the United States—so much so that by the late teens *vers libre,* or free verse, had become so commonplace that it could be found not just in bohemian literary journals but also in mainstream magazines. Although Pound disparaged Lowell's version of the movement as "Amygism," her advocacy made modern poetry palatable to large numbers of readers.

Despite her championship of Imagism, her nine books of poetry contain a wide spectrum of styles: narrative poems, experiments in the rhythmical prose that she called "polyphonic," haiku, long-lined descriptive poems in the mode of Whitman and Sandburg, and lyric monologues. Lowell's many evocations of female beauty place her in a tradition of lesbian love poets.

Despite the coded eroticism of some of her love poetry, her books were accessible to a wide audience, which set her work apart from the dense and allusive poetry that Pound, Marianne Moore, and other Modernists went on to write. By the early twenties, she and Pound had become such implacable foes that she automatically dismissed writers he supported, such as T. S. Eliot and James Joyce. By then she had turned her critical energy back to her first inspiration, John Keats, and wrote a two-volume biography of the poet based in part on an extensive selection of his manuscripts that she had purchased over the years.

At the time of her death in 1925 from a cerebral hemorrhage, she was recognized as an important woman of letters, a status she had achieved through a brief thirteen years of hard work and energetic self-promotion. In 1926, she was awarded the Pulitzer Prize posthumously, for *What's O'Clock*. After her death, Lowell was remembered more for biographical details, such as her obesity and fondness for cigars, than for her poetry. By the close of the century, however, feminist scholars had drawn attention to her role in the development of modern American poetry, and some of Lowell's work was restored to the canon.

What follows is her preface to the second anthology of imagist poetry. It contains Lowell's argument for the continuing validity of the movement, including her response to criticisms that had been leveled against free verse.

PREFACE TO SOME IMAGIST POETS

In bringing the second volume of *Some Imagist Poets* before the public, the authors wish to express their gratitude for the interest which the 1915 volume aroused. The discussion of it was widespread, and even those critics out of sympathy with Imagist tenets accorded it much space. In the Preface to that book, we endeavoured to present those tenets in a succinct form. Bt the very brevity we employed has led to a great deal of misunderstanding. We have decided, therefore, to explain the laws which govern us a little more fully. A few people may understand, and the rest can merely misunderstand again, a result to which we are quite accustomed.

In the first place "Imagism" does not mean merely the presentation of pictures. "Imagism" refers to the manner of presentation, not to the subject. It means a clear presentation of whatever the author wishes to convey. Now he may wish to convey a mood of indecision, in which case the poem should be indecisive; he may wish to bring before his reader the constantly shifting and changing lights over a landscape, or the varying attitudes of mind of a person under strong emotion, then his poem must shift and change to present this clearly. The "exact" word does not mean the word which exactly describes the object in itself, it means the "exact" word which brings the effect of that object before the reader as it presented itself to the poet's mind at the time of writing the poem. Imagists deal but little with similes, although much of their poetry is metaphorical. The reason for this is that while acknowledging the figure to be an integral part of all poetry, they feel that the constant imposing of one figure upon another in the same poem blurs the central effect.

The great French critic, Remy de Gourmont, wrote last Summer in *La France* that the Imagists were the descendants of the French *Symbolistes*. In the Preface to his *Livre des Masques,* M. de Gourmont has thus described *Symbolisme:* "Individualism in literature, liberty of art, abandonment of existing forms . . . The sole excuse which a man can have for writing is to write down himself, to unveil for others the sort of world which mirrors itself in his individual glass . . . He should create his own aesthetics—and we should admit as many aesthetics as there are original minds, and judge them for what they are and not what they are not." In this sense the Imagists are descendants of the *Symbolistes;* they are Individualists.

The only reason that Imagism has seemed so anarchaic and strange to English and American reviewers is that their minds do not easily and quickly suggest the steps by which modern art has arrived at its present position. Its immediate prototype cannot be found in English or American literature, we must turn to Europe for it. With Debussy and Stravinsky in music, and Gauguin and Matisse in painting, it should have been evident to every one that art was entering upon an era of change. But music and painting are universal languages, so we have become accustomed to new idioms in them, while we still find it hard to recognize a changed idiom in literature.

The crux of the situation is just here. It is in the idiom employed. Imagism asks to be judged by different standards from those employed in Nineteenth-Century art. It is small wonder that Imagist poetry should be incomprehensible to men whose sole touchstone for art is the literature of one country for a period of four centuries. And it is an illuminating fact that among poets and men conversant with

Originally published as the preface to *Some Imagist Poets* (Boston: Houghton Mifflin, 1916).

many poetic idioms, Imagism is rarely misconceived. They may not agree with us, but they do not misunderstand us.

This must not be misconstrued into the desire to belittle our forerunners. On the contrary, the Imagists have the greatest admiration for the past, and humility towards it. But they have been caught in the throes of a new birth. The exterior world is changing, and with it men's feelings, and every age must express its feelings in its own individual way. No art is any more "egoistic" than another; all art is an attempt to express the feelings of the artist, whether it be couched in narrative form or employ a more personal expression.

It is not what Imagists write about which makes them hard of comprehension; it is the way they write it. All nations have laws of prosody, which undergo changes from time to time. The laws of English metrical prosody are well known to every one concerned with the subject. But that is only one form of prosody. Other nations have had different ones: Anglo-Saxon poetry was founded upon alliteration, Greek and Roman was built upon quantity, the Oriental was formed out of repetition, and the Japanese Hokku got its effects by an exact and never-to-be-added-to series of single syllables. So it is evident that poetry can be written in many modes. That the Imagists base much of their poetry upon cadence and not upon meter makes them neither good nor bad. And no one realizes more than they that no theories nor rules make poetry. They claim for their work only that it is sincere.

It is this very fact of "cadence" which has misled so many reviewers, until some have been betrayed into saying that the Imagists discard rhythm, when rhythm is the most important quality in their technique. The definition of *vers libre* is—a verse-form based upon cadence. Now cadence in music is one thing, cadence in poetry quite another, since we are not dealing with tone but with rhythm. It is the sense of perfect balance of flow and rhythm. Not only must the syllables so fall as to increase and continue the movement, but the whole poem must be as rounded and recurring as the circular swing of a balanced pendulum. It can be fast or slow, it may even jerk, but this perfect swing it must have, even its jerks must follow the central movement. To illustrate: Suppose a person were given the task of walking, or running, round a large circle, with two minutes given to do it in. Two minutes which he would just consume if he walked round the circle quietly. But in order to make the task easier for him, or harder, as the case might be, he was required to complete each half of the circle in exactly a minute. No other restrictions were placed upon him. He might dawdle in the beginning, and run madly to reach the half-circle mark on time, and then complete his task by walking steadily round the second half to goal. Or he might leap, and run, and skip, and linger in all sorts of ways, making up for slow going by fast, and for extra haste by pauses, and varying these movements on either lap of the circle as the humor seized him, only so that he were just one minute in traversing the first half-circle, and just one minute in traversing the second. Another illustration which may be employed is that of a Japanese wood-carving where a toad in one corner is balanced by a spray of blown flowers in the opposite upper one. The flowers are not the same shape as the toad, neither are they the same size, but the balance is preserved.

The unit in *vers libre* is not the foot, the number of the syllables, the quantity, or the line. The unit is the strophe, which may be the whole poem, or may be only a part. Each strophe is a complete circle: in fact, the meaning of the Greek word "strophe" is simply that part of the poem which was recited while the chorus were making a turn round the altar set up in the center of the theater. The simile of the circle is more than a simile, therefore; it is a fact. Of course the circle need not always be the same size, nor need the times allowed to negotiate it be always the same. There is room here for an infinite number of variations. Also, circles can be added to circles, movement upon movement, to the poem, provided each movement completes itself, and ramifies naturally into the next. But one thing must be borne in mind: a cadenced poem is written to be read aloud, in this way only will its rhythm be felt. Poetry is a spoken and not a written art.

The *vers libristes* are often accused of declaring that they have discovered a new thing. Where such an idea started, it is impossible to say, certainly none of the better *vers libristes* was ever guilty of so ridiculous a statement. The name *vers libre* is new, the thing, most emphatically, is not. Not new in English poetry, at any rate. You will find something very much like it in Dryden's *Threnodia Augustalis;* a great deal of Milton's *Samson Agonistes* is written in it; and Matthew Arnold's *Philomela* is a shining example of it. Practically all of Henley's *London Voluntaries* are written in it, and (so potent are names) until it was christened *vers libre,* no one thought of objecting to it. But the oldest reference to *vers libre* is to be found in Chaucer's *House of Fame,* where the Eagle addresses the Poet in these words:

And nevertheless hast set thy wyt
Although that in thy heed full lyte is
To make bookes, songes, or dytees
In rhyme or elles in cadence.

Commentators have wasted reams of paper in an endeavor to determine what Chaucer meant by this. But is it not possible that he meant a verse based upon rhythm, but which did not follow the strict metrical prosody of his usual practice?

One of the charges frequently brought against the Imagists is that they write, not poetry, but "shredded prose." This misconception springs from the almost complete ignorance of the public in regard to the laws of cadenced verse. But, in fact, what is prose and what is poetry? Is it merely a matter of typographical arrangement? Must everything which is printed in equal lines, with rhymes at the ends, be called poetry, and everything which is printed in a block be called prose? Aristotle, who certainly knew more about this subject than any one else, declares in his *Rhetoric* that prose is rhythmical without being metrical (that is to say, without insistence on any single rhythm), and then goes on to state the feet that are employed in prose, making, incidentally, the remark that the iambic prevailed in ordinary conversation. The fact is, that there is no hard and fast dividing line between prose and poetry. As a French poet of distinction, Paul Fort, has said: "Prose and poetry are but one instrument, graduated." It is not a question of typography; it is not even a question of rules and forms. Poetry is the vision in a man's soul which he translates as best he can with the means at his disposal.

We are young, we are experimentalists, but we ask to be judged by our own standards, not by those which have governed other men at other times.

1916

GERTRUDE STEIN
(1874–1946)

Born in Allegheny, Pennsylvania, Gertrude Stein was the youngest of the five children of Daniel Stein, a prosperous Jewish businessman, and his wife Amelia Keyser Stein. The family moved to Europe in 1875, and Stein was raised first in Vienna and then in Passy, France; consequently, she first spoke German and French, rather than English, which she did not learn until the family returned to the United States in 1879. After a year in Baltimore, they relocated to Oakland, California, where Daniel Stein became vice president of the Omnibus Cable Company, which operated San Francisco's streetcars. His profits allowed him to rent a ten-acre farm just outside Oakland and to pamper his children. Before her college years, Stein's formal education was uneven, divided between studying with governesses and sporadic attendance at various schools; she never officially graduated from high school. In 1888 her mother died of cancer, and when Daniel Stein died three years later, Gertrude's oldest brother, Michael, took over the care of his four siblings. After discovering that his father had left the family in debt, Michael took a job as a branch manager of the Central Pacific Railway, eventually earning enough money to ensure that his brothers and sisters would never have to work for a living.

In 1892 Stein moved to Baltimore to live with an aunt, and a year later entered Radcliffe College, choosing to be near her brother Leo, who was studying at Harvard with the psychologist William James. Gertrude found James's ideas cogent and attractive. His calls for detailed empirical observation and for open-minded attitudes would serve as core principles that enabled her to question poetic conventions. In 1898 she began studies in medicine at Johns Hopkins University, a prerequisite for advanced work in psychology. She left Hopkins in 1901, having failed four courses, and began to travel with Leo, visiting Morocco, Spain, France, Italy, and England. In 1903, Stein decided to make France her permanent home and settled in Paris with Leo, who had become a patron of the arts.

In 1907 Stein met and fell in love with Alice B. Toklas, an American visitor, who, recognizing genius, decided to dedicate her life to Stein. In 1910 Toklas moved into Gertrude and Leo's Paris apartment, and three years later, Leo moved out, taking his half of the art collection. For the next thirty-six

do not have to accept it for any reason. They themselves that is everybody in their entering the modern composition and they do enter it, if they do not enter it they are not so to speak in it they are out of it and so they do enter it; but in as you may say the non-competitive efforts where if you are not in it nothing is lost except nothing at all except what is not had, there are naturally all the refusals, and the things refused are only important if unexpectedly somebody happens to need them. In the case of the arts it is very definite. Those who are creating the modern composition authentically are naturally only of importance when they are dead because by that time the modern composition having become past is classified and the description of it is classical. That is the reason why the creator of the new composition in the arts is an outlaw until he is a classic, there is hardly a moment in between and it is really too bad very much too bad naturally for the creator but also very much too bad for the enjoyer, they all really would enjoy the created so much better just after it has been made than when it is already a classic, but it is perfectly simple that there is no reason why the contemporaries should see, because it would not make any difference as they lead their lives in the new composition anyway, and as every one is naturally indolent why naturally they don't see. For this reason as in quoting Lord Grey it is quite certain that nations not actively threatened are at least several generations behind themselves militarily so æsthetically they are more than several generations behind themselves and it is very much too bad, it is so very much more exciting and satisfactory for everybody if one can have contemporaries, if all one's contemporaries could be one's contemporaries.

There is almost not an interval.

For a very long time everybody refuses and then almost without a pause almost everybody accepts. In the history of the refused in the arts and literature the rapidity of the change is always startling. Now the only difficulty with the *volte-face* concerning the arts is this. When the acceptance comes, by that acceptance the thing created becomes a classic. It is a natural phenomena a rather extraordinary natural phenomena that a thing accepted becomes a classic. And what is the characteristic quality of a classic. The characteristic quality of a classic is that it is beautiful. Now of course it is perfectly true that a more or less first rate work of art is beautiful but the trouble is that when that first rate work of art becomes a classic because it is accepted the only thing that is important from then on to the majority of the acceptors the enormous majority, the most intelligent majority of the acceptors is that it is so wonderfully beautiful. Of course it is wonderfully beautiful, only when it is still a thing irritating annoying stimulating then all quality of beauty is denied to it.

Of course it is beautiful but first all beauty in it is denied and then all the beauty of it is accepted. If every one were not so indolent they would realise that beauty is beauty even when it is irritating and stimulating not only when it is accepted and classic. Of course it is extremely difficult nothing more so than to remember back to its not being beautiful once it has become beautiful. This makes it so much more difficult to realise its beauty when the work is being refused and prevents every one from realising that they were convinced that beauty was denied, once the work is accepted. Automatically with the acceptance of the time-sense comes the recognition of the beauty and once the beauty is accepted the beauty never fails any one.

Beginning again and again is a natural thing even when there is a series.

Beginning again and again and again explaining composition and time is a natural thing.

It is understood by this time that everything is the same except composition and time, composition and the time of the composition and the time in the composition.

Everything is the same except composition and as the composition is different and always going to be different everything is not the same. Everything is not the same as the time when of the composition and the time in the composition is different. The composition is different, that is certain.

The composition is the thing seen by every one living in the living they are doing, they are the composing of the composition that at the time they are living is the composition of the time in which they are living. It is that that makes living a thing they are doing. Nothing else is different, of that almost any one can be certain. The time when and the time of and the time in that composition is the natural phenomena of that composition and of that perhaps every one can be certain.

No one thinks these things when they are making when they are creating what is the composition, naturally no one thinks, that is no one formulates until what is to be formulated has been made.

Composition is not there, it is going to be there and we are here. This is some time ago for us naturally.

The only thing that is different from one time to another is what is seen and what is seen depends upon how everybody is doing everything. This makes the thing we are looking at very different and this makes what those who describe it make of it, it makes a composition, it confuses, it shows, it is, it looks, it likes it as it is, and this makes what is seen as it is seen. Nothing changes from generation to generation except the thing seen and that makes a composition.

Now the few who make writing as it is made and it is to be remarked that the most decided of them are those that are prepared by preparing, are prepared just as the world around them is prepared and is preparing to do it in this way and so if you do not mind I will again tell you how it happens. Naturally one does not know how it happened until it is well over beginning happening.

Each period of living differs from any other period of living not in the way life is but in the way life is conducted and that authentically speaking is composition. After life has been conducted in a certain way everybody knows it but nobody knows it, little by little, nobody knows it as long as nobody knows it. Any one creating the composition in the arts does not know it either, they are conducting life and that makes their composition what it is, it makes their work compose as it does.

Their influence and their influences are the same as that of all of their contemporaries only it must always be remembered that the analogy is not obvious until as I say the composition of a time has become so pronounced that it is past and the artistic composition of it is a classic.

And now to begin as if to begin. Composition is not there, it is going to be there and we are here. This is some time ago for us naturally. There is something to be added afterwards.

Just how much my work is known to you I do not know. I feel that perhaps it would be just as well to tell the whole of it.

In beginning writing I wrote a book called *Three Lives* this was written in 1905. I wrote a negro story called *Melanctha*. In that there was a constant recurring and beginning there was a marked direction in the direction of being in the present although naturally I had been accustomed to past present and future, and why, because the composition forming around me was a prolonged present. A composition of a prolonged present is a natural composition in the world as it has been these thirty years it was more and more a prolonged present. I created then a prolonged present naturally I knew nothing of a continuous present but it came naturally to me to make one, it was simple it was clear to me and nobody knew why it was done like that, I did not myself although naturally to me it was natural.

After that I did a book called *The Making of Americans* it is a long book about a thousand pages.

Here again it was all so natural to me and more and more complicatedly a continuous present. A continuous present is a continuous present. I made almost a thousand pages of a continuous present.

Continuous present is one thing and beginning again and again is another thing. These are both things. And then there is using everything.

This brings us again to composition this the using everything. The using everything brings us to composition and to this composition. A continuous present and using everything and beginning again. In these two books there was elaboration of the complexities of using everything and of a continuous present and of beginning again and again and again.

In the first book there was a groping for a continuous present and for using everything by beginning again and again.

There was a groping for using everything and there was a groping for a continuous present and there was an inevitable beginning of beginning again and again and again.

Having naturally done this I naturally was a little troubled with it when I read it. I became then like the others who read it. One does, you know, excepting that when I reread it myself I lost myself in it again. Then I said to myself this time it will be different and I began. I did not begin again I just began.

In this beginning naturally since I at once went on and on very soon there were pages and pages and pages more and more elaborated creating a more and more continuous present including more and more using of everything and continuing more and more beginning and beginning and beginning.

I went on and on to a thousand pages of it.

In the meantime to naturally begin I commenced making portraits of anybody and anything. In making these portraits I naturally made a continuous present an including everything and a beginning again and again within a very small thing. That started me into composing anything into one thing. So then naturally it was natural that one thing an enormously long thing was not everything an enormously short thing was also not everything nor was it all of it a continuous present thing nor was it always and always beginning again. Naturally I would then begin again. I would begin again I would naturally begin. I did naturally begin. This brings me to a great deal that has been begun.

And after that what changes what changes after that, after that what changes and what changes after that and after that and what changes and after that and what changes after that.

The problem from this time on became more definite.

It was all so nearly alike it must be different and it is different, it is natural that if everything is used and there is a continuous present and a beginning again and again if it is all so alike it must be simply different and everything simply different was the natural way of creating it then.

In this natural way of creating it then that it was simply different everything being alike it was simply different, this kept on leading one to lists. Lists naturally for a while and by lists I mean a series. More and more in going back over what was done at this time I find that I naturally kept simply different as an intention. Whether there was or whether there was not a continuous present did not then any longer trouble me there was or there was not, and using everything no longer troubled me if everything is alike using everything could no longer trouble me and beginning again and again could no longer trouble me because if lists were inevitable if series were inevitable and the whole of it was inevitable beginning again and again could not trouble me so then with nothing to trouble me I very completely began naturally since everything is alike making it as simply different naturally as simply different as possible. I began doing natural phenomena what I call natural phenomena and natural phenomena naturally everything being alike natural phenomena are making things be naturally simply different. This found its culmination later, in the beginning it began in a center confused with lists with series with geography with returning portraits and with particularly often four and three and often with five and four. It is easy to see that in the beginning such a conception as everything being naturally different would be very inarticulate and very slowly it began to emerge and take the form of anything, and then naturally if anything that is simply different is simply different what follows will follow.

So far then the progress of my conceptions was the natural progress entirely in accordance with my epoch as I am sure is to be quite easily realised if you think over the scene that was before us all from year to year.

As I said in the beginning, there is the long history of how every one ever acted or has felt and that nothing inside in them in all of them makes it connectedly different. By this I mean all this.

The only thing that is different from one time to another is what is seen and what is seen depends upon how everybody is doing everything.

It is understood by this time that everything is the same except composition and time, composition and the time of the composition and the time in the composition.

Everything is the same except composition and as the composition is different and always going to be different everything is not the same. So then I as a contemporary creating the composition in the beginning was groping toward a continuous present, a using everything a beginning again and again and then everything being alike then everything very simply everything was naturally simply different and so I as a contemporary was creating everything being alike was creating everything naturally being naturally simply different, everything being alike. This then was the period that brings me to the period of the beginning of 1914. Everything being alike everything naturally would be simply different and war came and everything being alike and everything being simply different brings everything being simply different brings it to romanticism.

Romanticism is then when everything being alike everything is naturally simply different, and romanticism.

Then for four years this was more and more different even though this was, was everything alike. Everything alike naturally everything was simply different and this is and was romanticism and this is and was war. Everything being alike everything naturally everything is different simply different naturally simply different.

And so there was the natural phenomena that was war, which had been, before war came, several generations behind the contemporary composition, because it became war and so completely needed to be contemporary became completely contemporary and so created the completed recognition of the contemporary composition.

Every one but one may say every one became consciously became aware of the existence of the authenticity of the modern composition. This then the contemporary recognition, because of the academic thing known as war having been forced to become contemporary made every one not only contemporary in act not only contemporary in thought but contemporary in self-consciousness made every one contemporary with the modern composition. And so the art creation of the contemporary composition which would have been outlawed normally outlawed several generations more behind even than war, war having been brought so to speak up to date art so to speak was allowed not completely to be up to date, but nearly up to date, in other words we who created the expression of the modern composition were to be recognized before we were dead some of us even quite a long time before we were dead. And so war may be said to have advanced a general recognition of the expression of the contemporary composition by almost thirty years.

And now after that there is no more of that in other words there is peace and something comes then and it follows coming then.

And so now one finds oneself interesting oneself in an equilibration, that of course means words as well as things and distribution as well as between themselves between the words and themselves and the things and themselves, a distribution as distribution. This makes what follows what follows and now there is every reason why there should be an arrangement made. Distribution is interesting and equilibration is interesting when a continuous present and a beginning again and again and using everything and everything alike and everything naturally simply different has been done.

After all this, there is that, there has been that that there is a composition and that nothing changes except composition the composition and the time of and the time in the composition.

The time of the composition is a natural thing and the time in the composition is a natural thing it is a natural thing and it is a contemporary thing.

The time of the composition is the time of the composition. It has been at times a present thing it has been at times a past thing it has been at times a future thing it has been at times an endeavour at parts or all of these things. In my beginning it was a continuous present a beginning again and again and again and again, it was a series it was a list it was a similarity and everything different it was a distribution and an equilibration. That is all of the time some of the time of the composition.

Now there is still something else the time-sense in the composition. This is what is always a fear a doubt and a judgment and a conviction. The quality in the creation of expression the quality in a composition that makes it go dead just after it has been made is very troublesome.

The time in the composition is a thing that is very troublesome. If the time in the composition is very troublesome it is because there must even if there is no time at all in the composition there must be time in the composition which is in its quality of distribution and equilibration. In the beginning there was the time in the composition that naturally was in the composition but time in the composition comes now and this is what is now troubling every one the time in the composition is now a part of distribution and equilibration. In the beginning there was confusion there was a continuous present and later there was romanticism which was not a confusion but an extrication and now there is either succeeding or failing there must be distribution and equilibration there must be time that is distributed and equilibrated. This is the thing that is at present the most troubling and if there is the time that is at present the most troublesome the time-sense that is at present the most troubling is the thing that makes the present the most troubling. There is at present there is distribution, by this I mean expression and time, and in this way at present composition is time that is the reason that at present the time-sense is troubling that is the reason why at present the time-sense in the composition is the composition that is making what there is in composition.

And afterwards.

Now that is all.

1926

◦─◄ WALLACE STEVENS ►─◦
(1879–1955)

Wallace Stevens was born in Reading, Pennsylvania, the second of five children in a family of Dutch-German ancestry. His father was a prosperous and practical lawyer, his mother a former schoolteacher who loved poetry and read the Bible to her children each night. Although in later life Stevens became passionately interested in genealogy, he rarely mentioned his own childhood, which seems to have been conventional, middle-class, Presbyterian, and provincial. In high school he played football, took the classical curriculum, which included Greek and Latin, and failed to pass one year. Finally graduating in 1897 (in the same class as his younger brother), Stevens entered Harvard University as a special student, which allowed him to attend classes at a reduced tuition but not qualify for a degree. At Harvard he studied French, German, and English literature while also publishing stories and poems in campus magazines. ("Some of one's early things give one the creeps," he later commented on his undergraduate writing.) In his third and last year Stevens was elected president of the *Harvard Advocate,* the college literary magazine. A formative experience in his Cambridge years was meeting the Spanish-born and Harvard-educated philosopher and poet, George Santayana (1863–1952). Stevens never took a course from Santayana, but he visited the brilliant man of letters numerous times and even read early poems to him. Santayana's ideas on aesthetics, philosophy, and religion influenced Stevens throughout his life.

Stevens was an intensely private man who avoided publicity and preferred to speak in abstract universal terms. (His published poetry and prose never indulges in direct autobiography.) In later life he seemed a remote and Olympian figure in American poetry—working in a corporate office in commercial Hartford, Connecticut, avoiding literary circles, and hardly socializing even with business associates. Not surprisingly, a mythology arose about Stevens as the businessman-poet, a unique and solitary figure, half-playful aesthete and half-stolid burgher. While there is some truth to this image of the mysteriously divided man, it describes the staid and narrow life of the older Stevens, not the unsettled and urban existence of the aspiring poet.

When Stevens left Harvard in 1900, he intended to be a writer. Moving to New York, he started first as a reporter for the *New York Tribune* and then as an editor for *World's Work*. He fell in love with the cosmopolitan life of New York, which always remained his favorite city. His father strongly disapproved of Stevens's artistic aspirations. When the young poet wrote home suggesting he should quit journalism and dedicate himself solely to literature, his father returned the letter torn in half. Family pressure continued until 1901 when the young poet reluctantly agreed to enter New York Law School from which he graduated two years later.

Now began a crucial period of Stevens's life that was not well understood by early critics who viewed the poet only in his reclusive later years. Between 1903 and 1916 Stevens lived mostly in Manhattan, worked at various legal jobs, and actively mixed in bohemian cultural life. In the salons of Manhattan, Stevens met many major Modernists, including fellow poet William Carlos Williams, the artist Marcel Duchamp, and the composer Edgard Varèse. During this period Stevens's business career was not successful; he drifted through five law firms and four insurance companies in fourteen years. He did, however, begin writing the brilliantly original poems that would eventually fill his book, *Harmonium*.

The other major event of the New York years was Stevens's long courtship, troubled engagement, and difficult marriage to Elsie Viola Kachel Moll. He met the eighteen-year-old salesclerk on a visit home in 1904 and quickly fell in love with "the prettiest girl in Reading." Over the next four years he courted her through letters and occasional visits. When they became formally engaged on Christmas, 1908, his father objected to Elsie's social background. (She had only a grammar school education, and the elder Stevens suspected that she had been born illegitimately.) The young poet stood loyally by his fiancée and cut off relations with his family. He never spoke to his father again. The couple was married in 1909, but differences in their temperaments and tastes soon caused difficulties. They never enjoyed a happy relationship, although the exact nature of their problems remains obscure since both husband and wife displayed a discretion that bordered on secrecy. In later years they lived in separate sections of their large Hartford house. They also delayed their first and only child for fifteen years—until Stevens had published his first book.

Stevens tasted failure often in these early years, and in 1916 the thirty-six-year-old found himself once again without a job when his employer went bankrupt. Reluctantly leaving New York, he accepted a position in Connecticut at Hartford Accident and Indemnity to head their surety claims department. He now settled into the second and final phase of his professional and artistic life. He would never leave the city or the company. Hartford would nourish the reclusive and meditative side of his personality, and his new career was so secure and remunerative that it sheltered him from economic worry, even during the harsh Depression years. Stevens now focused more seriously on his writing, and in 1923 at the age of forty-three, published his first book, *Harmonium*.

Harmonium is not merely the most astonishing and ample first book by any American Modernist poet; it ranks with Walt Whitman's *Leaves of Grass* as one of the greatest poetic debuts in American literature—with both eccentricities and originality equal to Whitman's. Simply to list some of the poems from *Harmonium* gives an idea of the book's extraordinary level of achievement—"The Snow Man," "The Emperor of Ice-Cream," "Disillusionment at Ten O'Clock," "Sunday Morning," "Anecdote of a Jar," "Peter Quince at the Clavier," and "Thirteen Ways of Looking at a Blackbird."

Harmonium was a commercial failure, earning Stevens only $6.70 in his first royalty check, but it announced him as a major poet. The poet was not immune to the disappointment of *Harmonium*'s modest impact, but he was supremely confident of his own artistic development. Always cautious, he waited until he was fifty-five to publish a second volume, *Ideas of Order* (1935), which appeared first in a small limited edition that he expanded into a full-length trade book the next year. His business career and family life now firmly settled, Stevens finally began publishing regularly. Over the remaining twenty years of his life he issued a series of books of notable artistic ambition, intellectual seriousness, and poetic distinction—*Owl's Clover* (1936), *The Man with the Blue Guitar* (1937), *Parts of a World* (1942), *Notes Toward a Supreme Fiction* (1942), *Esthétique du Mal* (1945), *Transport to Summer* (1947), *Auroras of Autumn* (1950), *The Collected Poems* (1954), as well as *The Necessary Angel* (1951), a volume of "Essays on Reality and the Imagination." There was no falling off in his later years—a common fault among poets—and his last poems rank among his finest work. Some of these volumes appeared only in limited editions, but having already waited so long to pursue a public literary career, Stevens was indifferent to fame and expected no financial reward from poetry.

Until his final years, he declined most invitations for readings, lectures, recordings, and interviews. Literary honors came too late to matter greatly—a Bollingen Prize (1950), two National Book Awards (1951 and 1955), and a Pulitzer Prize (1955) that was announced a few weeks after he had been diagnosed with incurable stomach cancer.

Stevens's later years revealed a well-ordered life of artistic dedication, personal prosperity, and self-imposed emotional deprivation. Inured to his joyless marriage, Stevens led a reclusive life outside the office. He and his wife were never seen together in public, and he drank mostly at his club to avoid her censure. He had no intimate friends, and almost none of his acquaintances were allowed in his house. His copious correspondence shows how few people, including old friends, he addressed on a first-name basis. The office provided him with his social existence, and he did not retire until his final illness. On his deathbed he had several conversations with the hospital's Catholic chaplain and reportedly requested and received baptism—an incident which his daughter disputed, but which, if true, can be interpreted (depending on the critic) as either a denial or vindication of his lifelong obsession with the idea of God in an apparently godless universe.

Stevens is the most romantic of the high Modernists. His sensibility was fixated on the central themes of Wordsworth and Coleridge—the relation between intellect and reality, the growth of poetic imagination as an instrument of perception and creativity, and the correspondence between the mind and the natural world. Although some early poems—like "Thirteen Ways of Looking at a Blackbird" reflect the methods of Imagism, Stevens was never a true member of that school. His imagination was too expansive and abundant, his need to pursue intellectual development too strong. From first to last Stevens was also fascinated with the long poem. *Harmonium* contains three extended poems—the briefest, "Sunday Morning," resembles one of Keats or Wordsworth's great Romantic odes, and the others, "Le Monocle de Mon Oncle" and "The Comedian as the Letter C" presage the long poems he would regularly publish across his career culminating in *Notes Toward a Supreme Fiction,* perhaps the greatest *ars poetica* of American Modernism.

Although he wrote relatively little formal criticism, publishing only a single volume of lectures, Stevens intermittently kept notebooks from his college years into which he wrote ideas and observations usually in compressed and epigrammatic form. A selection of these playful, gnomic, and revelatory adages were collected after his death as "Adagia" in *Opus Posthumous* (1957). These provocative remarks seem closer to the spirit of his poetry than his formal essays:

> The poem reveals itself only to the ignorant man.
>
> *
>
> All poetry is experimental poetry.
>
> *
>
> The poet is the priest of the invisible.
>
> *
>
> There is no difference between god and his temple.
>
> *
>
> Money is a kind of poetry.
>
> *
>
> The theory of poetry is the theory of life.

Most of Stevens's formal criticism was written late in life to be delivered as academic lectures. On such occasions the poet adopted a serious and intellectually intricate style. "The Noble Rider and the Sound of Words" was first delivered by Stevens as a lecture at Princeton University in May 1941. In it he set forth the importance of the imagination as a counter to "reality," which was then full of the horror of war. This tension between reality and imagination was, for Stevens, a defining factor in poetry itself and more broadly in human experience. The "sound of words" so important to Stevens as a poet can be compared to other imaginative activities that elevate humanity from a barbarous state.

--◦━━◖▶━◦--

THE NOBLE RIDER AND THE SOUND OF WORDS

In the *Phaedrus*, Plato speaks of the soul in a figure. He says:

> *Let our figure be of a composite nature—a pair of winged horses and a charioteer. Now the winged horses and the charioteer of the gods are all of them noble, and of noble breed, while ours are mixed; and we have a charioteer who drives them in a pair, and one of them is noble and of noble origin, and the other is*

Originally delivered as a lecture at Princeton University in 1941. Collected in *The Necessary Angel* (New York: Knopf, 1951).

ignoble and of ignoble origin; and, as might be expected, there is a great deal of trouble in managing them. I will endeavor to explain to you in what way the mortal differs from the immortal creature. The soul or animate being has the care of the inanimate, and traverses the whole heaven in divers forms appearing;—when perfect and fully winged she soars upward, and is the ruler of the universe; while the imperfect soul loses her feathers, and drooping in her flight at last settles on the solid ground.

We recognize at once, in this figure, Plato's pure poetry; and at the same time we recognize what Coleridge called Plato's dear, gorgeous nonsense. The truth is that we have scarcely read the passage before we have identified ourselves with the charioteer, have, in fact, taken his place and, driving his winged horses, are traversing the whole heaven. Then suddenly we remember, it may be, that the soul no longer exists and we droop in our flight and at last settle on the solid ground. The figure becomes antiquated and rustic.

1

What really happens in this brief experience? Why does this figure, potent for so long, become merely the emblem of a mythology, the rustic memorial of a belief in the soul and in a distinction between good and evil? The answer to these questions is, I think, a simple one.

I said that suddenly we remember that the soul no longer exists and we droop in our flight. For that matter, neither charioteers nor chariots any longer exist. Consequently, the figure does not become unreal because we are troubled about the soul. Besides, unreal things have a reality of their own, in poetry as elsewhere. We do not hesitate, in poetry, to yield ourselves to the unreal, when it is possible to yield ourselves. The existence of the soul, of charioteers and chariots and of winged horses is immaterial. They did not exist for Plato, not even the charioteer and chariot; for certainly a charioteer driving his chariot across the whole heaven was for Plato precisely what he is for us. He was unreal for Plato as he is for us. Plato, however, could yield himself, was free to yield himself, to this gorgeous nonsense. We cannot yield ourselves. We are not free to yield ourselves.

Just as the difficulty is not a difficulty about unreal things, since the imagination accepts them, and since the poetry of the passage is, for us, wholly the poetry of the unreal, so it is not an emotional difficulty. Something else than the imagination is moved by the statement that the horses of the gods are all of them noble, and of noble breed or origin. The statement is a moving statement and is intended to be so. It is insistent and its insistence moves us. Its insistence is the insistence of a speaker, in this case Socrates, who, for the moment, feels delight, even if a casual delight, in the nobility and noble breed. Those images of nobility instantly become nobility itself and determine the emotional level at which the next page or two are to be read. The figure does not lose its vitality because of any failure of feeling on Plato's part. He does not communicate nobility coldly. His horses are not marble horses, the reference to their breed saves them from being that. The fact that the horses are not marble horses helps, moreover, to save the charioteer from being, say, a creature of cloud. The result is that we recognize, even if we cannot realize, the feelings of the robust poet clearly and fluently noting the images in his mind and by means of his robustness, clearness and fluency communicating much more than the images themselves. Yet we do not quite yield. We cannot. We do not feel free.

In trying to find out what it is that stands between Plato's figure and ourselves, we have to accept the idea that, however legendary it appears to be, it has had its vicissitudes. The history of a figure of speech or the history of an idea, such as the idea of nobility, cannot be very different from the history of anything else. It is the episodes that are of interest, and here the episode is that of our diffidence. By us and ourselves, I mean you and me; and yet not you and me as individuals but as representatives of a state of mind. Adams in his work on Vico makes the remark that the true history of the human race is a history of its progressive mental states. It is a remark of interest in this relation. We may assume that in the history of Plato's figure there have been incessant changes of response; that these changes have been psychological changes, and that our own diffidence is simply one more state of mind due to such a change.

The specific question is partly as to the nature of the change and partly as to the cause of it. In nature, the change is as follows: The imagination loses vitality as it ceases to adhere to what is real. When it adheres to the unreal and intensifies what is unreal, while its first effect may be extraordinary, that effect is the maximum effect that it will ever have. In Plato's figure, his imagination does not adhere to what is real. On the contrary, having created something unreal, it adheres to it and intensifies its unreality. Its first effect, its effect at first reading, is its maximum effect, when the imagination, being moved, puts us in the place of the charioteer, before the reason checks us. The case is, then, that we concede that the figure is all imagination. At the same time, we say that it has not the slightest meaning for us, except for its nobility. As to that, while we are moved by it, we are moved as observers. We recognize it perfectly. We do not realize it. We understand the feeling of it, the robust feeling, clearly and fluently communicated. Yet we understand it rather than participate in it.

As to the cause of the change, it is the loss of the figure's vitality. The reason why this particular figure has lost its vitality is that, in it, the imagination adheres to what is unreal. What happened, as we were traversing the whole heaven, is that the imagination lost its power to sustain us. It has the strength of reality or none at all.

2

What has just been said demonstrates that there are degrees of the imagination, as, for example, degrees of vitality and, therefore, of intensity. It is an implication that there are degrees of reality. The discourse about the two elements seems endless. For my own part, I intend merely to follow, in a very hasty way, the fortunes of the idea of nobility as a characteristic of the imagination, and even as its symbol or alter ego, through several of the episodes in its history, in order to determine, if possible, what its fate has been and what has determined its fate. This can be done only on the basis of the relation between the imagination and reality. What has been said in respect to the figure of the charioteer illustrates this.

I should like now to go on to other illustrations of the relation between the imagination and reality and particularly to illustrations that constitute episodes in the history of the idea of nobility. It would be agreeable to pass directly from the charioteer and his winged horses to Don Quixote. It would be like a return from what Plato calls "the back of heaven" to one's own spot. Nevertheless, there is Verrocchio (as one among others) with his statue of Bartolommeo Colleoni, in Venice, standing in the way. I have not selected him as a Neo-Platonist to relate us back from a modern time to Plato's time, although he does in fact so relate us, just as through Leonardo, his pupil, he strengthens the relationship. I have selected him because there, on the edge of the world in which we live today, he established a form of such nobility that it has never ceased to magnify us in our own eyes. It is like the form of an invincible man, who has come, slowly and boldly, through every warlike opposition of the past and who moves in our midst without dropping the bridle of the powerful horse from his hand, without taking off his helmet and without relaxing the attitude of a warrior of noble origin. What man on whose side the horseman fought could ever be anything but fearless, anything but indomitable? One feels the passion of rhetoric begin to stir and even to grow furious; and one thinks that, after all, the noble style, in whatever it creates, merely perpetuates the noble style. In this statue, the apposition between the imagination and reality is too favorable to the imagination. Our difficulty is not primarily with any detail. It is primarily with the whole. The point is not so much to analyze the difficulty as to determine whether we share it, to find out whether it exists, whether we regard this specimen of the genius of Verrocchio and of the Renaissance as a bit of uncommon panache, no longer quite the appropriate thing outdoors, or whether we regard it, in the language of Dr. Richards, as something inexhaustible to meditation or, to speak for myself, as a thing of a nobility responsive to the most minute demand. It seems, nowadays, what it may very well not have seemed a few years ago, a little overpowering, a little magnificent.

Undoubtedly, Don Quixote could be Bartolommeo Colleoni in Spain. The tradition of Italy is the tradition of the imagination. The tradition of Spain is the tradition of reality. There is no apparent reason why the reverse should not be true. If this is a just observation, it indicates that the relation between the imagination and reality is a question, more or less, of precise equilibrium. Thus it is not a question of the difference between grotesque extremes. My purpose is not to contrast Colleoni with Don Quixote. It is to say that one passed into the other, that one became and was the other. The difference between them is that Verrocchio believed in one kind of nobility and Cervantes, if he believed in any, believed in another kind. With Verrocchio it was an affair of the noble style, whatever his prepossession respecting the nobility of man as a real animal may have been. With Cervantes, nobility was not a thing of the imagination. It was a part of reality, it was something that exists in life, something so true to us that it is in danger of ceasing to exist, if we isolate it, something in the mind of a precarious tenure. These may be words. Certainly, however, Cervantes sought to set right the balance between the imagination and reality. As we come closer to our own times in Don Quixote and as we are drawn together by the intelligence common to the two periods, we may derive so much satisfaction from the restoration of reality as to become wholly prejudiced against the imagination. This is to reach a conclusion prematurely, let alone that it may be to reach a conclusion in respect to something as to which no conclusion is possible or desirable.

There is in Washington, in Lafayette Square, which is the square on which the White House faces, a statue of Andrew Jackson, riding a horse with one of the most beautiful tails in the world. General Jackson is raising his hat in a gay gesture, saluting the ladies of his generation. One looks at this work of Clark Mills and thinks of the remark of Bertrand Russell that to acquire immunity to eloquence is of the utmost importance to the citizens of a democracy. We are bound to think that Colleoni, as a mercenary, was a much less formidable man than General Jackson, that he meant less to fewer people and that, if Verrocchio could have applied his prodigious poetry to Jackson, the whole American outlook today might be imperial. This work is a work of fancy. Dr. Richards cites Coleridge's theory of fancy as opposed to imagination. Fancy is an activity of the mind which puts things together of choice, *not* the will, as a principle of the mind's being, striving to realize itself in knowing itself. Fancy, then, is an exercise of selection from among objects already supplied by association, a selection made for purposes which are not then and therein being shaped but have been already fixed. We are concerned then with an object occupying a position as remarkable as any that can be found in the United States in which there is not the slightest trace of the imagination. Treating this work as typical, it is obvious that the American will as a principle of the mind's being is easily satisfied in its efforts to realize itself in knowing itself. The statue may be dismissed, not without speaking of it again as a thing that at least makes us conscious of ourselves as we were, if not as we are. To that extent, it helps us to know ourselves. It helps us to know ourselves as we were and that helps us to know ourselves as we are. The statue is neither of the imagination nor of reality. That it is a work of fancy precludes it from being a work of the imagination. A glance at it shows it to be unreal. The bearing of this is that there can be works, and this includes poems, in which neither the imagination nor reality is present.

The other day I was reading a note about an American artist who was said to have "turned his back on the aesthetic whims and theories of the day, and established headquarters in lower Manhattan." Accompanying this note was a reproduction of a painting called *Wooden Horses*. It is a painting of a merry-go-round, possibly of several of them. One of the horses seems to be prancing. The others are going lickety-split, each one struggling to get the bit in his teeth. The horse in the center of the picture, painted yellow, has two riders, one a man, dressed in a carnival costume, who is seated in the saddle, the other a blonde, who is seated well up the horse's neck. The man has his arms under the girl's arms. He holds himself stiffly in order to keep his cigar out of the girl's hair. Her feet are in a second and shorter set of stirrups. She has the legs of a hammer-thrower. It is clear that the couple are accustomed to wooden horses and like them. A little behind them is a younger girl riding alone. She has a strong body and streaming hair. She wears a short-sleeved, red waist, a white skirt and an emphatic bracelet of pink coral. She has her eyes on the man's arms. Still farther behind, there is another girl. One does not see much more of her than her head. Her lips are painted bright red. It seems that it would be better if someone were to hold her on her horse. We, here, are not interested in any aspect of this picture except that it is a picture of ribald and hilarious reality. It is a picture wholly favorable to what is real. It is not without imagination and it is far from being without aesthetic theory.

3

These illustrations of the relation between the imagination and reality are an outline on the basis of which to indicate a tendency. Their usefulness is this: that they help to make clear, what no one may ever have doubted, that just as in this or that work the degrees of the imagination and of reality may vary, so this variation may exist as between the works of one age and the works of another. What I have said up to this point amounts to this: that the idea of nobility exists in art today only in degenerate forms or in a much diminished state, if, in fact, it exists at all or otherwise than on sufferance; that this is due to failure in the relation between the imagination and reality. I should now like to add that this failure is due, in turn, to the pressure of reality.

A variation between the sound of words in one age and the sound of words in another age is an instance of the pressure of reality. Take the statement by Bateson that a language, considered semantically, evolves through a series of conflicts between the denotative and the connotative forces in words; between an asceticism tending to kill language by stripping words of all association and a hedonism tending to kill language by dissipating their sense in a multiplicity of associations. These conflicts are nothing more than changes in the relation between the imagination and reality. Bateson describes the seventeenth century in England as predominately a connotative period. The use of words in connotative senses was denounced by Locke and Hobbes, who desired a mathematical plainness; in short, perspicuous words. There followed in the eighteenth century an era of poetic diction. This was not the language of the age but a language of poetry peculiar to itself. In time, Wordsworth came to write the preface to the second edition of the *Lyrical Ballads* (1800), in which he said that the first volume had been published, "as an experiment, which, I hoped, might be of some use to ascertain how far, by fitting to metrical arrangement a selection of the real language of man in a state of vivid sensation, that sort of pleasure and that quantity of pleasure may be imparted, which a Poet may rationally endeavour to impart."

As the nineteenth century progressed, language once more became connotative. While there have been intermediate reactions, this tendency toward the connotative is the tendency today. The interest in semantics is evidence of this. In the case of some of our prose writers, as, for example, Joyce, the language, in quite different ways, is wholly connotative. When we say that Locke and Hobbes denounced the connotative use of words as an abuse, and when we speak of reactions and reforms, we are speaking, on the one hand, of a failure of the imagination to adhere to reality, and, on the other, of a use of language favorable to reality. The statement that the tendency toward the connotative is the tendency today is disputable. The general movement in the arts, that is to say, in painting and in music, has been the other way. It is hard to say that the tendency is toward the connotative in the use of words without also saying that the tendency is toward the imagination in other directions. The interest in the subconscious and in surrealism shows the tendency toward the imaginative. Boileau's remark that Descartes had cut poetry's throat is a remark that could have been made respecting a great many people during the last hundred years, and of no one more aptly than of Freud, who, as it happens, was familiar with it and repeats it in his *Future of an Illusion*. The object of that essay was to suggest a surrender to reality. His premise was that it is the unmistakable character of the present situation not that the promises of religion have become smaller but that they appear less credible to people. He notes the decline of religious belief and disagrees with the argument that man cannot in general do without the consolation of what he calls the religious illusion and that without it he would not endure the cruelty of reality. His conclusion is that man must venture at last into the hostile world and that this may be called education to reality. There is much more in that essay inimical to poetry and not least the observation in one of the final pages that "The voice of the intellect is a soft one, but it does not rest until it has gained a hearing." This, I fear, is intended to be the voice of the realist.

A tendency in language toward the connotative might very well parallel a tendency in other arts toward the denotative. We have just seen that that is in fact the situation. I suppose that the present always appears to be an illogical complication. The language of Joyce goes along with the dilapidations of Braque and Picasso and the music of the Austrians. To the extent that this painting and this music are the work of men who regard it as part of the science of painting and the science of music it is the work of realists. Actually its effect is that of the imagination, just as the effect of abstract painting is so often that of the imagination, although that may be different. Busoni said, in a letter to his wife, "I have made the painful discovery that nobody loves and feels music." Very likely, the reason there is a tendency in language toward the connotative today is that there are many who love it and feel it. It may be that Braque and Picasso love and feel painting and that Schönberg loves and feels music, although it seems that what they love and feel is something else.

A tendency toward the connotative, whether in language or elsewhere, cannot continue against the pressure of reality. If it is the pressure of reality that controls poetry, then the immediacy of various theories of poetry is not what it was. For instance, when Rostrevor Hamilton says, "The object of contemplation is the highly complex and unified content of consciousness, which comes into being through the developing subjective attitude of the percipient," he has in mind no such "content of consciousness" as every newspaper reader experiences today.

By way of further illustration, let me quote from Croce's Oxford lecture of 1933. He said: "If . . . poetry is intuition and expression, the fusion of sound and imagery, what is the material which takes on the form of sound and imagery? It is the whole man: the man who thinks and wills, and loves, and hates; who is strong and weak, sublime and pathetic, good and wicked; man in the exultation and agony of living; and together with the man, integral with him, it is all nature in its perpetual labour of evolution. . . . Poetry . . . is the triumph of contemplation. . . . Poetic genius chooses a strait path in which passion is calmed and calm is passionate."

Croce cannot have been thinking of a world in which all normal life is at least in suspense, or, if you like, under blockage. He was thinking of normal human experience.

Quite apart from the abnormal aspect of everyday life today, there is the normal aspect of it. The spirit of negation has been so active, so confident and so intolerant that the commonplaces about the romantic provoke us to wonder if our salvation, if the way out, is not the romantic. All the great things have been denied and we live in an intricacy of new and local mythologies, political, economic, poetic, which are asserted with an ever-enlarging incoherence. This is accompanied by an absence of any authority except force, operative or imminent. What has been called the disparagement of reason is an instance of the absence of authority. We pick up the radio and find that comedians regard the public use of words of more than two syllables as funny. We read of the opening of the National Gallery at Washington and we are convinced, in the end, that the pictures are counterfeit, that museums are impositions and that Mr. Mellon was a monster. We turn to a recent translation of Kierkegaard and we find him saying: "A great deal has been said about poetry reconciling one with existence; rather it might be said that it arouses one against existence; for poetry is unjust to men . . . it has use only for the elect, but that is a poor sort of reconciliation. I will take the case of sickness. Aesthetics replies proudly and quite consistently, 'That cannot be employed, poetry must not become a hospital.' Aesthetics culminates . . . by regarding sickness in accordance with the principle enunciated by Friedrich Schlegel: 'Nur Gesundheit ist liebenswürdig.' (Health alone is lovable.)"

The enormous influence of education in giving every one a little learning, and in giving large groups considerably more: something of history, something of philosophy, something of literature; the expansion of the middle class with its common preference for realistic satisfactions; the penetration of the masses of people by the ideas of liberal thinkers, even when that penetration is indirect, as by the reporting of the reasons why people oppose the ideas that they oppose,—these are normal aspects of everyday life. The way we live and the way we work alike cast us out on reality. If fifty private houses were to be built in New York this year, it would be a phenomenon. We no longer live in homes but in housing projects and this is so whether the project is literally a project or a club, a dormitory, a camp or an apartment in River House. It is not only that there are more of us and that we are actually close together. We are close together in every way. We lie in bed and listen to a broadcast from Cairo, and so on. There is no distance. We are intimate with people we have never seen and, unhappily, they are intimate with us. Democritus plucked his eye out because he could not look at a woman without thinking of her as a woman. If he had read a few of our novels, he would have torn himself to pieces. Dr. Richards has noted "the widespread increase in the aptitude of the average mind for self-dissolving introspection, the generally heightened awareness of the goings-on of our own minds, *merely as goings-on.*" This is nothing to the generally heightened awareness of the goings-on of other people's minds, *merely as goings-on.* The way we work is a good deal more difficult for the imagination than the highly civilized revolution that is occurring in respect to work indicates. It is, in the main, a revolution for more pay. We have been assured, by every visitor, that the American businessman is absorbed in his business and there is nothing to be gained by disputing it. As for the workers, it is enough to say that the word has grown to be literary. They have become, at their work, in the face of the machines, something approximating an abstraction, an energy. The time must be coming when, as they leave the factories, they will be passed through an air-chamber or a bar to revive them for riot and reading. I am sorry to have to add that to one that thinks, as Dr. Richards thinks, that poetry is the supreme use of language, some of the foreign universities in relation to our own appear to be, so far as the things of the imagination are concerned, as Verrocchio is to the sculptor of the statue of General Jackson.

These, nevertheless, are not the things that I had in mind when I spoke of the pressure of reality. These constitute the drift of incidents, to which we accustom ourselves as to the weather. Materialism is an old story and an indifferent one. Robert Wolseley said: "True genius . . . will enter into the hardest and dryest thing, enrich the most barren Soyl, and inform the meanest and most uncomely matter . . . the baser, the emptier, the obscurer, the fouler, and the less susceptible of Ornament the subject appears to be, the more is the Poet's Praise . . . who, as Horace says of Homer, can fetch Light out of Smoak, Roses out of Dunghills, and give a kind of Life to the Inanimate . . ." (Preface to Rochester's *Valentinian,* 1685, *English Association Essays and Studies* 1939). By the pressure of reality, I mean the pressure of an external event or events on the consciousness to the exclusion of any power of contemplation. The definition ought to be exact and, as it is, may be merely pretentious. But when one is trying to think of a whole generation and of a world at war, and trying at the same time to see what is happening to the imagination, particularly if one believes that that is what matters most, the plainest statement of what is happening can easily appear to be an affectation.

For more than ten years now, there has been an extraordinary pressure of news—let us say, news incomparably more pretentious than any description of it, news, at first, of the collapse of our system, or, call it, of life; then of news of a new world, but of a new world so uncertain that one did not know anything whatever of its nature, and does not know now, and could not tell whether it was to be all-English, all-German, all-Russian, all-Japanese, or all-American, and cannot tell now; and finally news of a war, which was a renewal of what, if it was not the greatest war, became such by this continuation. And for more than ten years, the consciousness of the world has concentrated on events which have made the ordinary movement of life seem to be the movement of people in the intervals of a storm. The disclosures of the impermanence of the past suggested, and suggest, an impermanence of the future. Little of what we have believed has been true. Only the prophecies are true. The present is an opportunity to repent. This is familiar enough. The war is only a part of a war-like whole. It is not possible to look backward and to see that the same thing was true in the past. It is a question of pressure, and pressure is incalculable and eludes the historian. The Napoleonic era is regarded as having had little or no effect on the poets and the novelists who lived in it. But Coleridge and Wordsworth and Sir Walter Scott and Jane Austen did not have to put up with Napoleon and Marx and Europe, Asia and Africa all at one time. It seems possible to say that they knew of the events of their day much as we know of the bombings in the interior of China and not at all as we know of the bombings of London, or, rather, as we should know of the bombings of Toronto or Montreal. Another part of the war-like whole to which we do not respond quite as we do to the news of war is the income tax. The blanks are specimens of mathematical prose. They titillate the instinct of self-preservation in a class in which that instinct has been forgotten. Virginia Woolf thought that the income tax, if it continued, would benefit poets by enlarging their vocabularies and I dare say that she was right.

If it is not possible to assert that the Napoleonic era was the end of one era in the history of the imagination and the beginning of another, one comes closer to the truth by making that assertion in respect to the French Revolution. The defeat or triumph of Hitler are parts of a war-like whole but the fate of an individual is different from the fate of a society. Rightly or wrongly, we feel that the fate of a society is involved in the orderly disorders of the present time. We are confronting, therefore, a set of events, not only beyond our power to tranquillize them in the mind, beyond our power to reduce them and metamorphose them, but events that stir the emotions to violence, that engage us in what is direct and immediate and real, and events that involve the concepts and sanctions that are the order of our lives and may involve our very lives; and these events are occurring persistently with increasing omen, in what may be called our presence. These are the things that I had in mind when I spoke of the pressure of reality, a pressure great enough and prolonged enough to bring about the end of one era in the history of the imagination and, if so, then great enough to bring about the beginning of another. It is one of the peculiarities of the imagination that it is always at the end of an era. What happens is that it is always attaching itself to a new reality, and adhering to it. It is not that there is a new imagination but that there is a new reality. The pressure of reality may, of course, be less than the general pressure that I have described. It exists for individuals according to the circumstances of their lives or according to the characteristics of their minds. To sum it up, the pressure of reality is, I think, the determining factor in the artistic character of an era and, as well, the determining factor in the artistic character of an individual. The resistance to this pressure or its evasion in the case of individuals of extraordinary imagination cancels the pressure so far as those individuals are concerned.

4

Suppose we try, now, to construct the figure of a poet, a possible poet. He cannot be a charioteer traversing vacant space, however ethereal. He must have lived all of the last two thousand years, and longer, and he must have instructed himself, as best he could, as he went along. He will have thought that Virgil, Dante, Shakespeare, Milton placed themselves in remote lands and in remote ages; that their men and women were the dead—and not the dead lying in the earth, but the dead still living in their remote lands and in their remote ages, and living in the earth or under it, or in the heavens—and he will wonder at those huge imaginations, in which what is remote becomes near, and what is dead lives with an intensity beyond any experience of life. He will consider that although he has himself witnessed, during the long period of his life, a general transition to reality, his own measure as a poet, in spite of all the passions of all the lovers of the truth, is the measure of his power to abstract himself, and to withdraw with him into his abstraction the reality on which the lovers of truth insist. He must be able to abstract himself and also to abstract reality, which he does by placing it in his imagination. He knows perfectly that he cannot be too noble a rider, that he cannot rise up loftily in helmet and armor on a horse of imposing bronze. He will think again of Milton and of what was said about him: that "the necessity of writing for one's living blunts the appreciation of writing when it bears the mark of perfection. Its quality disconcerts our hasty writers; they are ready to condemn it as preciosity and affectation. And if to them the musical and creative powers of words convey little pleasure, how out of date and irrelevant they must find the . . . music of Milton's verse." Don Quixote will make it imperative for him to make a choice, to come to a decision regarding the imagination and reality; and he will find that it is not a choice of one over the other and not a decision that divides them, but something subtler, a recognition that here, too, as between these poles, the universal interdependence exists, and hence his choice and his decision must be that they are equal and inseparable. To take a single instance: When Horatio says,

> Now cracks a noble heart. Good night, sweet prince,
> And flights of angels sing thee to thy rest!

are not the imagination and reality equal and inseparable? Above all, he will not forget General Jackson or the picture of the *Wooden Horses*.

I said of the picture that it was a work in which everything was favorable to reality. I hope that the use of that bare word has been enough. But without regard

to its range of meaning in thought, it includes all its natural images, and its connotations are without limit. Bergson describes the visual perception of a motionless
object as the most stable of internal states. He says: "The object may remain the
same, I may look at it from the same side, at the same angle, in the same light; nevertheless, the vision I now have of it differs from that which I have just had, even if
only because the one is an instant later than the other. My memory is there, which
conveys something of the past into the present."

Dr. Joad's comment on this is: "Similarly with external things. Every body,
every quality of a body resolves itself into an enormous number of vibrations,
movements, changes. What is it that vibrates, moves, is changed? There is no answer. Philosophy has long dismissed the notion of substance and modern physics
has endorsed the dismissal. . . . How, then, does the world come to appear to us
as a collection of solid, static objects extended in space? Because of the intellect,
which presents us with a false view of it."

The poet has his own meaning for reality, and the painter has, and the musician has; and besides what it means to the intelligence and to the senses, it means
something to everyone, so to speak. Notwithstanding this, the word in its general
sense, which is the sense in which I have used it, adapts itself instantly. The subject-
matter of poetry is not that "collection of solid, static objects extended in space"
but the life that is lived in the scene that it composes; and so reality is not that external scene but the life that is lived in it. Reality is things as they are. The general
sense of the word proliferates its special senses. It is a jungle in itself. As in the
case of a jungle, everything that makes it up is pretty much of one color. First,
then, there is the reality that is taken for granted, that is latent and, on the whole,
ignored. It is the comfortable American state of life of the eighties, the nineties
and the first ten years of the present century. Next, there is the reality that has
ceased to be indifferent, the years when the Victorians had been disposed of and
intellectual minorities and social minorities began to take their place and to convert our state of life to something that might not be final. This much more vital reality made the life that had preceded it look like a volume of Ackermann's colored
plates or one of Töpfer's books of sketches in Switzerland. I am trying to give the
feel of it. It was the reality of twenty or thirty years ago. I say that it was a vital
reality. The phrase gives a false impression. It was vital in the sense of being tense,
of being instinct with the fatal or with what might be the fatal. The minorities
began to convince us that the Victorians had left nothing behind. The Russians
followed the Victorians, and the Germans, in their way, followed the Russians.
The British Empire, directly or indirectly, was what was left and as to that one
could not be sure whether it was a shield or a target. Reality then became violent
and so remains. This much ought to be said to make it a little clearer that in speaking of the pressure of reality, I am thinking of life in a state of violence, not physically violent, as yet, for us in America, but physically violent for millions of our
friends and for still more millions of our enemies and spiritually violent, it may be
said, for everyone alive.

A possible poet must be a poet capable of resisting or evading the pressure of
the reality of this last degree, with the knowledge that the degree of today may
become a deadlier degree tomorrow. There is, however, no point to dramatizing
the future in advance of the fact. I confine myself to the outline of a possible poet,
with only the slightest sketch of his background.

5

Here I am, well-advanced in my paper, with everything of interest that I started out to say remaining to be said. I am interested in the nature of poetry and I have stated its nature, from one of the many points of view from which it is possible to state it. It is an interdependence of the imagination and reality as equals. This is not a definition, since it is incomplete. But it states the nature of poetry. Then I am interested in the role of the poet and this is paramount. In this area of my subject I might be expected to speak of the social, that is to say sociological or political, obligation of the poet. He has none. That he must be contemporaneous is as old as Longinus and I dare say older. But that he *is* contemporaneous is almost inevitable. How contemporaneous in the direct sense in which being contemporaneous is intended were the four great poets of whom I spoke a moment ago? I do not think that a poet owes any more as a social obligation than he owes as a moral obligation, and if there is anything concerning poetry about which people agree it is that the role of the poet is not to be found in morals. I cannot say what that wide agreement amounts to because the agreement (in which I do not join) that the poet is under a social obligation is equally wide. Reality is life and life is society and the imagination and reality; that is to say, the imagination and society are inseparable. That is pre-eminently true in the case of the poetic drama. The poetic drama needs a terrible genius before it is anything more than a literary relic. Besides the theater has forgotten that it could ever be terrible. It is not one of the instruments of fate, decidedly. Yes: the all-commanding subject-matter of poetry is life, the never-ceasing source. But it is not a social obligation. One does not love and go back to one's ancient mother as a social obligation. One goes back out of a suasion not to be denied. Unquestionably if a social movement moved one deeply enough, its moving poems would follow. No politician can command the imagination, directing it to do this or that. Stalin might grind his teeth the whole of a Russian winter and yet all the poets in the Soviets might remain silent the following spring. He might excite their imaginations by something he said or did. He would not command them. He is singularly free from that "cult of pomp," which is the comic side of the European disaster; and that means as much as anything to us. The truth is that the social obligation so closely urged is a phase of the pressure of reality which a poet (in the absence of dramatic poets) is bound to resist or evade today. Dante in Purgatory and Paradise was still the voice of the Middle Ages but not through fulfilling any social obligation. Since that is the role most frequently urged, if that role is eliminated, and if a possible poet is left facing life without any categorical exactions upon him, what then? What is his function? Certainly it is not to lead people out of the confusion in which they find themselves. Nor is it, I think, to comfort them while they follow their readers to and fro. I think that his function is to make his imagination theirs and that he fulfills himself only as he sees his imagination become the light in the minds of others. His role, in short, is to help people to live their lives. Time and time again it has been said that he may not address himself to an élite. I think he may. There is not a poet whom we prize living today that does not address himself to an élite. The poet will continue to do this: to address himself to an élite even in a classless society, unless, perhaps, this exposes him to imprisonment or exile. In that event he is likely not to address himself to anyone at all. He may, like Shostakovich, content himself with pretence. He will, nevertheless, still be addressing himself to an élite, for all poets address themselves to someone and it is of the essence of that instinct, and it seems to amount to an instinct, that it should be to an élite, not to a drab but to a woman with the hair of a pytheness, not to a chamber of commerce but to a gallery of one's own, if there are enough of one's own to fill a gallery. And that élite, if it responds, not out of complaisance, but because the poet has quickened it, because he has educed from it that for which it was searching in itself and in the life around it and which it had not yet quite found, will thereafter do for the poet what he cannot do for himself, that is to say, receive his poetry.

I repeat that his role is to help people to live their lives. He has had immensely to do with giving life whatever savor it possesses. He has had to do with whatever the imagination and the senses have made of the world. He has, in fact, had to do with life except as the intellect has had to do with it and, as to that, no one is needed to tell us that poetry and philosophy are akin. I want to repeat for two reasons a number of observations made by Charles Mauron. The first reason is that these observations tell us what it is that a poet does to help people to live their lives and the second is that they prepare the way for a word concerning escapism. They are: that the artist transforms us into epicures; that he has to discover the possible work of art in the real world, then to extract it, when he does not himself compose it entirely; that he is *un amoureux perpétuel** of the world that he contemplates and thereby enriches; that art sets out to express the human soul; and finally that everything like a firm grasp of reality is eliminated from the aesthetic field. With these aphorisms in mind, how is it possible to condemn escapism? The poetic process is psychologically an escapist process. The chatter about escapism is, to my way of thinking, merely common cant. My own remarks about resisting or evading the pressure of reality mean escapism, if analyzed. Escapism has a pejorative sense, which it cannot be supposed that I include in the sense in which I use the word. The pejorative sense applies where the poet is not attached to reality, where the imagination does not adhere to reality, which, for my part, I regard as fundamental. If we go back to the collection of solid, static objects extended in space, which Dr. Joad posited, and if we say that the space is blank space, nowhere, without color, and that the objects, though solid, have no shadows and, though static, exert a mournful power, and, without elaborating this complete poverty, if suddenly we hear a different and familiar description of the place:

> This City now doth, like a garment, wear
> The beauty of the morning, silent bare,
> Ships, towers, domes, theatres, and temples lie
> Open unto the fields, and to the sky;
> All bright and glittering in the smokeless air;

if we have this experience, we know how poets help people to live their lives. This illustration must serve for all the rest. There is, in fact, a world of poetry indistinguishable from the world in which we live, or, I ought to say, no doubt, from the world in which we shall come to live, since what makes the poet the potent figure that he is, or was, or ought to be, is that he creates the world to which we turn incessantly and without knowing it and that he gives to life the supreme fictions without which we are unable to conceive of it.

**un amoureux perpétuel*: a perpetual lover.

And what about the sound of words? What about nobility, of which the fortunes were to be a kind of test of the value of the poet? I do not know of anything that will appear to have suffered more from the passage of time than the music of poetry and that has suffered less. The deepening need for words to express our thoughts and feelings which, we are sure, are all the truth that we shall ever experience, having no illusions, makes us listen to words when we hear them, loving them and feeling them, makes us search the sound of them, for a finality, a perfection, an unalterable vibration, which it is only within the power of the acutest poet to give them. Those of us who may have been thinking of the path of poetry, those who understand that words are thoughts and not only our own thoughts but the thoughts of men and women ignorant of what it is that they are thinking, must be conscious of this: that, above everything else, poetry is words; and that words, above everything else, are, in poetry, sounds. This being so, my time and yours might have been better spent if I had been less interested in trying to give our possible poet an identity and less interested in trying to appoint him to his place. But unless I had done these things, it might have been thought that I was rhetorical, when I was speaking in the simplest way about things of such importance that nothing is more so. A poet's words are of things that do not exist without the words. Thus, the image of the charioteer and of the winged horses, which has been held to be precious for all of time that matters, was created by words of things that never existed without the words. A description of Verrocchio's statue could be the integration of an illusion equal to the statue itself. Poetry is a revelation in words by means of the words. Croce was not speaking of poetry in particular when he said that language is perpetual creation. About nobility I cannot be sure that the decline, not to say the disappearance of nobility is anything more than a maladjustment between the imagination and reality. We have been a little insane about the truth. We have had an obsession. In its ultimate extension, the truth about which we have been insane will lead us to look beyond the truth to something in which the imagination will be the dominant complement. It is not only that the imagination adheres to reality, but, also, that reality adheres to the imagination and that the interdependence is essential. We may emerge from our *bassesse** and, if we do, how would it happen if not by the intervention of some fortune of the mind? And what would that fortune of the mind happen to be? It might be only commonsense but even that, a commonsense beyond the truth, would be a nobility of long descent.

The poet refuses to allow his task to be set for him. He denies that he has a task and considers that the organization of materia poetica is a contradiction in terms. Yet the imagination gives to everything that it touches a peculiarity, and it seems to me that the peculiarity of the imagination is nobility, of which there are many degrees. This inherent nobility is the natural source of another, which our extremely headstrong generation regards as false and decadent. I mean that nobility which is our spiritual height and depth; and while I know how difficult it is to express it, nevertheless I am bound to give a sense of it. Nothing could be more evasive and inaccessible. Nothing distorts itself and seeks disguise more quickly. There is a shame of disclosing it and in its definite presentations a horror of it. But there it is. The fact that it is there is what makes it possible to invite to the reading and writing of poetry men of intelligence and desire for life. I am not

---

*bassesse: baseness; vileness.

thinking of the ethical or the sonorous or at all of the manner of it. The manner of it is, in fact, its difficulty, which each man must feel each day differently, for himself. I am not thinking of the solemn, the portentous or demoded. On the other hand, I am evading a definition. If it is defined, it will be fixed and it must not be fixed. As in the case of an external thing, nobility resolves itself into an enormous number of vibrations, movements, changes. To fix it is to put an end to it. Let me show it to you unfixed.

Late last year Epstein exhibited some of his flower paintings at the Leicester Galleries in London. A commentator in *Apollo* said: "*How with this rage can beauty hold a plea* . . . The quotation from Shakespeare's 65th sonnet prefaces the catalogue. . . . It would be apropos to any other flower paintings than Mr. Epstein's. His make no pretence to fragility. They shout, explode all over the picture space and generally oppose the rage of the world with such a rage of form and color as no flower in nature or pigment has done since Van Gogh."

What ferocious beauty the line from Shakespeare puts on when used under such circumstances! While it has its modulation of despair, it holds its plea and its plea is noble. There is no element more conspicuously absent from contemporary poetry than nobility. There is no element that poets have sought after, more curiously and more piously, certain of its obscure existence. Its voice is one of the inarticulate voices which it is their business to overhear and to record. The nobility of rhetoric is, of course, a lifeless nobility. Pareto's epigram that history is a cemetery of aristocracies easily becomes another: that poetry is a cemetery of nobilities. For the sensitive poet, conscious of negations, nothing is more difficult than the affirmations of nobility and yet there is nothing that he requires of himself more persistently, since in them and in their kind, alone, are to be found those sanctions that are the reasons for his being and for that occasional ecstasy, or ecstatic freedom of the mind, which is his special privilege.

It is hard to think of a thing more out of time than nobility. Looked at plainly it seems false and dead and ugly. To look at it at all makes us realize sharply that in our present, in the presence of our reality, the past looks false and is, therefore, dead and is, therefore, ugly; and we turn away from it as from something repulsive and particularly from the characteristic that it has a way of assuming: something that was noble in its day, grandeur that was, the rhetorical once. But as a wave is a force and not the water of which it is composed, which is never the same, so nobility is a force and not the manifestations of which it is composed, which are never the same. Possibly this description of it as a force will do more than anything else I can have said about it to reconcile you to it. It is not an artifice that the mind has added to human nature. The mind has added nothing to human nature. It is a violence from within that protects us from a violence without. It is the imagination pressing back against the pressure of reality. It seems, in the last analysis, to have something to do with our self-preservation; and that, no doubt, is why the expression of it, the sound of its words, helps us to live our lives.

1941

WILLIAM CARLOS WILLIAMS
(1883–1963)

With the exception of a few sojourns in Europe and an education pursued in New York City and Philadelphia, William Carlos Williams spent his life in the town of his birth—Rutherford, New Jersey. Yet his background was quite cosmopolitan. He was the son of William George Williams, a cultured businessman who was born in England and came to the United States with his mother at the age of five, but chose never to abandon his British citizenship. Because his father's work as an advertising manager for a perfume manufacturer required long stretches of travel abroad, the poet was raised in Rutherford by his British grandmother, Emily Dickinson Wellcome, and his mother, Raquel Hélène Rose Hoheb Williams, a woman of Basque, Spanish, Dutch, and Jewish ancestry whom his father had met in Puerto Rico. Although she acquired some English, she preferred to speak Spanish, especially at home, and to practice the French she had learned while studying art in Paris. Williams's interest in celebrating an American language whose vigor derives from actual speech was perhaps initiated in his childhood home listening intently to the blend of languages around him. Despite his later emphasis on his American identity, he imbibed significant doses of European culture during his childhood. In 1897, when Williams was fourteen, his mother took him and his younger brother to Europe for a year-long stay and sent them to private schools, first in Geneva and then in Paris.

After their return to the United States in 1899, Williams attended Horace Mann High School, a prestigious private school in New York City. Although Williams's parents enrolled him in a course of study that emphasized science, he excelled in his English courses, for which he read poetry from Chaucer to Tennyson and discovered the Romantics, especially John Keats, whose work he began to imitate. Along with Keatsian imitations, he also filled notebooks with long-lined, cadenced effusions in the style of Whitman: "I wrote my immortal thoughts in those books, whatever they were. If I had an opinion about things about me, I'd jot it down, and occasionally it would take the loose form of verse. I was reading Keats at the time. Keats was my favorite." The pleasure he found in writing determined the course he would take for the rest of his life. In addition to the career in medicine that his parents expected, he would become a poet.

In 1902 he enrolled in the school of dentistry at the University of Pennsylvania but soon switched to the medical school. Even in the midst of his demanding studies, he continued to write. His commitment to poetry was encouraged by his new friend Ezra Pound, whom he met during his first semester. The friendship, though strained at times, lasted for sixty years until Williams's death. Pound introduced Williams to other poets, such as Hilda Doolittle (H. D.), and, above all, offered astringent criticism that helped Williams drop the nineteenth-century affectations clogging his early poetry. After finishing his course work at Penn in 1906, Williams interned in New York City for two years. Despite a grueling schedule, he produced a blank verse epic, modeled on Keats's *Endymion*. Although Williams never published his pseudo-Romantic epic, he subsidized a short collection simply entitled *Poems* (1909), containing twenty-seven poems, a third of them in blank verse, the rest in rhymed stanzas. After Williams sent him a copy of the book, Pound wrote back from London, declaring, "Individual, original it is not. Great art it is not. . . . There are fine lines in it, but nowhere I think do you add anything to the poets you have used as models. . . . You are out of touch." Urging him to update his reading, in subsequent letters Pound alerted Williams to the incipient Imagist movement. Williams soon changed his style so radically—going on to champion what Pound advocated in a 1913 letter as "the simple order of natural speech"— that he dumped the remaining copies of the book and never republished any of the poems. In old age he remarked that there was nothing "of the slightest value in the whole thin booklet—except the intent."

Williams's intent held firm through studies in pediatrics undertaken during the winter of 1909 and 1910 in Germany and through the work of establishing a private practice in Rutherford after his return. Even marriage in 1912 to Florence ("Flossie") Herman, and the birth of his two sons soon after, did not diminish his efforts. His poems appeared in several of the Imagist anthologies and in little magazines such as *Poetry, Others,* and the *Egoist.* His second book, *The Tempers* (1913), was transitional, but his third book, *Al Que Quiere!* (1917), established the parameters he would explore for the rest of his career: a style grounded not on traditional metrics but on the vigor of American speech and a celebration of the particular, of quotidian details that his critics would call antipoetic but that Williams saw as the essence of poetry; and an emphasis on the mind and the imagination.

Williams's lifelong fascination with painting, prompted by his mother's background in the arts and his own amateur forays into painting, carried over into his poetry. He later remarked that "because of my interest in painting, the Imagists appealed to me. It was an image that I was seeking, and when Pound came along with his drive for the image it appealed to me very strongly." His friendship with the artist Charles Demuth, whom he had met in Philadelphia, helped attune him to the Modernist revolution in painting, as did his visits to the 1913 Armory Show and New York galleries. His engagement with the work of painters such as Cézanne, Matisse, Duchamp, and the Cubists taught him to think of poetry not as representational, but as a form of design that forces readers to look at both the world and their own habits of perception differently. Thus, Williams's focus on "things" in his poetry (and his well-known aphorism "no ideas but in things") involves not static depiction, but active processes of observation: the mind in motion.

Williams's work in medicine also nourished his poetry. In interviews and essays, he sometimes made analogies between the habits of observation he developed as a doctor and his aims as a poet, claiming that the poet's business is "not to talk in vague categories, but to write particularly, as a physician works, upon a patient, upon the thing before him, in the particular to discover the universal." In the midst of a thriving medical practice—between house calls, hospital visits, seeing patients in his office, and delivering babies—he claimed time to write not only poetry, but also novels, short stories, essays, plays, experimental prose, and autobiography, publishing almost fifty books during his lifetime. In the introduction to his *The Autobiography* (1951) he described his method:

> Five minutes, ten minutes, can always be found. I had my typewriter in my office desk. All I needed to do was pull up the leaf to which it was fastened and I was ready to go. I worked at top speed. If a patient came in at the door while I was in the middle of a sentence, bang would go the machine—I was a physician. When the patient left, up would come the machine. . . . Finally, after eleven at night, when the last patient had been put to bed, I could always find the time to bang out ten or twelve pages. In fact, I couldn't rest until I had freed my mind from the obsessions that had been tormenting me all day.

As Williams neared forty, he published two books of improvisatory, experimental prose, *Kora in Hell* (1920) and *The Great American Novel* (1923), a book of new poetry, *Sour Grapes* (1921), and *Spring and All* (1923), a remarkable series of poems interspersed with brusque, annunciatory, and sometimes contradictory prose meditations on his goals as an artist. Seeking "to refine, to clarify, to intensify that eternal moment in which we alone live," he concluded that "there is but a single force—the imagination." Yet Williams also celebrated poetry's potential to "affirm reality," for he argued that the imagination's "unique power is to give created forms reality, actual existence." At the same time he stressed that the imagination does not "avoid reality, nor is it a description nor an evocation of objects or situations[;] . . . poetry does not tamper with the world but moves it—it affirms reality most powerfully." The *Spring and All* poems test these ideas. The urgency of Williams's voice, moreover, moves the poems forward through feeling, a passion for discovery similar to the enthusiasm he attributed in the essays of his next book, *In the American Grain* (1925), to the men who explored the New World.

Williams thought of himself as akin to those explorers, for he aimed to chart a "New World" in his poetry: American subjects and American speech. For him, dedication to American themes was a moral choice, and he set himself against the expatriate Modernism of T. S. Eliot, whom he thought had turned poetry in the wrong direction:

> I had a violent feeling that Eliot had betrayed what I believed in. He was looking backward; I was looking forward. He was a conformist, with wit, learning I did not possess. He knew French,

> Latin, Arabic, God knows what. I was interested in that. But I felt
> he had rejected America and I refused to be rejected. . . . I realized
> the responsibility that I must accept. . . . I had envisaged a new
> form of poetic composition, a form for the future.

Although Williams's opposition to Eliot sprung from profound philosophical and temperamental differences, it also arose, as Williams freely acknowledged, from professional jealousy. After *The Waste Land* (1922), critics had canonized Eliot as the premier Modernist poet, and Williams felt overlooked. But Williams's "violent reaction" was also grounded on his opposition to what he saw as Eliot's pessimism, dependence on European traditions, and adherence (even in his free verse) to an iambic norm.

During the Great Depression conditions worsened for Williams, as they did for most Americans. In the 1920s he had invested in the stock market, hoping that his profits would enable him to retire early. The crash of 1929 ended those hopes. As the depression deepened, his medical practice grew even more burdensome. He often waived his fees for patients who were unable to pay, and he had to put in additional hours to make ends meet. Like many writers of the era, he grew interested in the possibilities for political poetry, and he wrote a number of poems, such as "The Yachts," that implicitly attack class injustices in America. Yet he also drew fire in leftist journals for his refusal to commit himself unreservedly to radical causes, and he remained skeptical of poetry about public events. By the middle of the decade, just after he had turned fifty, he found new opportunities for publication. In 1934, the poet Louis Zukofsky arranged for the Objectivist Press to publish Williams's *Collected Poems 1921–1931*. Although the book appeared under the imprint of yet another small press, it gave Williams the chance both to consolidate his mature work and to receive homage from the Objectivists, a group of young writers led by Zukofsky, who considered Williams a crucial Modernist poet and credited him for inspiring their own poetry of concrete particulars. Only in 1938, however, when James Laughlin's New Directions press published *The Complete Collected Poems,* did Williams's work become widely available. "All my life I've been hoping to get a regular publisher to put my stuff out in a more or less uniform style," Williams wrote at the time. He found that publisher in Laughlin, who considered him the cornerstone of New Directions.

Among the many volumes that Williams published with New Directions was his long poem *Paterson,* which was released in five books, the first appearing in 1946, the last in 1958. Setting himself against *The Waste Land* and Pound's *Cantos,* yet also borrowing collage techniques from these two poems, Williams looked back to Whitman in hopes of writing an American epic both local and inclusive. His solution was to focus on a particular place, the city of Paterson, New Jersey, and to fuse that place with an Everyman figure, Dr. Paterson. Williams explained: "*Paterson* is a long poem in four parts—that a man in himself is a city, beginning, seeking, achieving and concluding his life in ways which the various aspects of a city may embody—any city, all the details of which may be made to voice his most intimate convictions." Those details include not only the characteristically rapid movements of Williams's own verse and prose, but extracts from newspapers, historical documents, and private letters from friends.

Williams struggled to create the right form not only for a long poem but also for a prosody (or "measure," as he preferred to call it) responsive to American language, for he associated traditional accentual syllabic prosody with British English. Throughout his career Williams argued that no verse is free and strove to articulate a prosodic system that matched the rhythms of American speech. Yet his impulse for invention and novelty chafed against his wish to develop a quantifiable system. As he aged and attracted followers, he increased his efforts to discover a specifically American prosody, and, in essays such as "The Poem as a Field of Action" (1948), he envisioned an elastic system that allowed room for change. While writing *Paterson,* he hit on a concept that he would call "the variable foot," a triadic, step-down line that first emerged in "The Descent," a poem that was originally part of Book 2 and that he fully developed in late poems such as "Asphodel, That Greeny Flower." Although the step-down line seems more a style of free verse than a new system of prosody, Williams's emphasis on process and motion, on capturing the subtleties of American speech, and on using the whole page as an active "field" of composition influenced a wide range of poets, including Zukofsky, George Oppen, Lorine Niedecker, Charles Olson, Robert Duncan, Robert Creeley, Allen Ginsberg, Denise Levertov, and Robert Lowell.

Due in part to the advocacy of this new generation of poets, toward the end of his life Williams began to gain institutional recognition: honorary degrees, invitations to lecture, a book contract with Random House, the 1953 Bollingen Prize (shared with Archibald MacLeish), and the 1963 Pulitzer Prize, awarded posthumously for *Pictures from Brueghel* (1962). Yet his later years involved hardship. Forced to give up his medical practice after a series of debilitating strokes, Williams fought to continue writing, teaching himself to type with his left hand because his right hand was incapacitated. He was offered the post of poetry consultant to the Library of Congress in 1952, but the appointment was revoked after the librarian of Congress received protests from literary editors complaining about both Williams's purported communist sympathies and his public defense of Ezra Pound. His wife's devoted care during these difficult years also prompted the poet to feel intense remorse over extramarital affairs he had had during the course of their marriage. His late poems, published in *The Desert Music* (1954) and *Pictures from Brueghel* often contemplate renewal, both of love and of the power to write. These poems, the publication of a single-volume edition, *Paterson* (1963), and increased attention to his early lyrics contributed to the marked rise in Williams's literary fortunes after his death.

A NEW MEASURE

I have never been one to write by rule, even by my own rules. Let's begin with the rule of counted syllables, in which all poems have been written hitherto. That has become tiresome to my ear.

From a letter written to Richard Eberhart, May 23, 1954. Published in *The Selected Letters of William Carlos Williams,* ed. John C. Thirlwall (New York: McDowell, Obolensky, 1957).

Finally, the stated syllables, as in the best of present-day free verse, have become entirely divorced from the beat, that is the measure. The musical pace proceeds without them.

Therefore the measure, that is to say, the count, having got rid of the words, which held it down, is returned to the *music*.

The words, having been freed, have been allowed to run all over the map, "free," as we have mistakenly thought. This has amounted to no more (in Whitman and others) than no discipline at all.

But if we keep in mind the *tune* which the lines (not necessarily the words) make in our ears, we are ready to proceed.

By measure I mean musical pace. Now, with music in our ears the words need only be taught to keep as distinguished an order, as chosen a character, as regular, according to the music, as in the best of prose.

By its *music* shall the best of modern verse be known and the *resources* of the music. The refinement of the poem, its subtlety, is not to be known by the elevation of the words but—the words don't so much matter—by the resources of the *music*.

To give you an example from my own work—not that I know anything about what I have myself written:
(count):—not that I ever count when writing but, at best, the
        lines must be capable of being counted, that is to say,
        measured—(believe it or not).—At that I may, half
        consciously, even count the measure under my breath
        as I write.—
(approximate example)
    (1)   The smell of the heat is boxwood
        (2) when rousing us
           (3) a movement of the air
    (4)   stirs our thoughts
        (5) that had no life in them
           (6) to a life, a life in which
(or)
    (1)   Mother of God! Our Lady!
        (2) the heart
           (3) is an unruly master:
    (4)   Forgive us our sins
        (5) as we
           (6) forgive
    (7)   those who have sinned against

Count a single beat to each numeral. You may not agree with my ear, but that is the way I count the line. Over the whole poem it gives a pattern to the meter that can be felt as a new measure. It gives resources to the ear which result in a language which we hear spoken about us every day.

1954

THE POEM AS A FIELD OF ACTION

Let's begin by quoting Mr. Auden—(from The Orators): "Need I remind you that you're no longer living in ancient Egypt?"

I'm going to say one thing to you—for a week! And I hope to God when I'm through that I've succeeded in making you understand me. It concerns the poem as a field of action, at what pitch the battle is today and what may come of it.

As Freud says bitterly in the first chapter of his *The Interpretation of Dreams*, speaking of the early opposition to his theory:

—the aversion of scientific men to
learning something new

we shall learn that is a characteristic quite as pronounced in literature—where they will *copy* "the new"—but the tiresome repetition of this "new," now twenty years old, disfigures every journal: I said a field of action. I can see why so many wish rather, avoiding thought, to return to the classic front of orthodox acceptance. As Anatole France put it in Freud's time, *"Les savants ne sont pas curieux."* *

It is next to impossible to bring over the quantitative Greek and Latin texts into our language. But does anyone ever ask *why* a Latin line in translation tends to break in half in our language? *Why* it cannot be maintained in its character, its quantitative character as against our accented verse? Have *all* the equivalents been exhausted or even tried? I doubt it.

I offer you then an initiation, what seems and what is actually only a half-baked proposal—since I cannot follow it up with proofs or even *final* examples—but I do it with at least my eyes open—for what I myself may get out of it by presenting it as well as I can to you.

I propose sweeping changes from top to bottom of the poetic structure. I said structure. So now you are beginning to get the drift of my theme. I say we are *through* with the iambic pentameter as presently conceived, at least for dramatic verse; through with the measured quatrain, the staid concatenations of sounds in the usual stanza, the sonnet. More has been done than you think about this though not yet been specifically named for what it is. I believe something can be said. Perhaps all that I can do here is to call attention to it: a revolution in the conception of the poetic foot—pointing out the evidence of something that has been going on for a long time.

At this point it might be profitable (since it would bring me back to my subject from a new point of view) to turn aside for a brief, very brief discussion (since it is not in the direct path of my essay) of the materials—that is to say, the subject matter of the poem. In this let me accept all the help I can get from Freud's theory of the dream—as a fulfillment of the wish—which I accept here holus-bolus. The poem is a dream, a daydream of wish fulfillment but not by any means a field of action and purposive action of a less high order because of that.

It has had in the past a varying subject matter—almost one might say a progressively varying choice of subject matter as you shall see—I must stress here that we are talking of the *recent* past.

Originally delivered as a lecture at the University of Washington in 1948. Collected in *Selected Essays of William Carlos Williams* (New York: Random House, 1954).
* *Les savants ne sont pas curieux:* the scholars are not curious.

And let me remind you here to keep in your minds the term reality as contrasted with phantasy and to tell you that the *subject matter* of the poem is always phantasy—what is wished for, realized in the "dream" of the poem—but that the structure confronts something else.

We may mention Poe's dreams in a pioneer society, his dreams of gentleness and bliss—also, by the way, his professional interest in meter and his very successful experiments with form. Yeats's subject matter of faery. Shakespeare—the butcher's son dreaming of Caesar and Wolsey. No need to go on through Keats, Shelley to Tennyson. It is all, the subject matter, a wish for aristocratic attainment—a "spiritual" bureaucracy of the "soul" or what you will.

There was then a subject matter that was "poetic" and in many minds that is still poetry—and exclusively so—the "beautiful" or pious (and so beautiful) wish expressed in beautiful language—a dream. That is still poetry: full stop. Well, that was the world to be desired and the poets merely expressed a general wish and so were useful each in his day.

But with the industrial revolution, and steadily since then, a new spirit—a new *Zeitgeist* has possessed the world, and as a consequence new values have replaced the old, aristocratic concepts—which had a pretty seamy side if you looked at them like a Christian. A new subject matter began to be manifest. It began to be noticed that there could be a new subject matter and that that was not in fact the poem at all. Briefly then, money talks, and the poet, the modern poet has admitted new subject matter to his dreams—that is, the serious poet has admitted the whole armamentarium of the industrial age to his poems—

Look at Mr. Auden's earlier poems as an example, with their ruined industrial background of waste and destruction. But even that is passing and becoming old-fashioned with the new physics taking its place. All this is a subject in itself and a fascinating one which I regret to leave, I am sorry to say, for a more pressing one.

Remember we are still in the world of fancy if perhaps disguised but still a world of wish-fulfillment in dreams. The poet was not an owner, he was not a money man—he was still only a poet; a wisher; a word man. The best of all to my way of thinking! Words are the keys that unlock the mind. But is that all of poetry? Certainly not—no more so than the material of dreams was phantasy to Dr. Sigmund Freud.

There is something else. Something if you will listen to many, something permanent and sacrosanct. The one thing that the poet has not wanted to change, the one thing he has clung to in his dream—unwilling to let go—the place where the time-lag is still adamant—is structure. Here we are unmovable. But here is precisely where we come into contact with reality. Reluctant, we waken from our dreams. And what is reality? How do we know reality? The only reality that we can know is MEASURE.

Now to return to our subject—the structure of the poem. Everything in the social, economic complex of the world at any time-sector ties in together—

(Quote Wilson on Proust—modern physics, etc.)

But it might at this time be a good thing to take up first what is spoken of as free verse.

How can we accept Einstein's theory of relativity, affecting our very conception of the heavens about us of which poets write so much, without incorporating its essential fact—the relativity of measurements—into our own category of activity: the poem. Do we think we stand outside the universe? Or that the Church of England does? Relativity applies to everything, like love, if it applies to anything in the world.

What, by this approach I am trying to sketch, what we are trying to do is not only to disengage the elements of a measure but to seek (what we believe is there) a new measure or a new way of measuring that will be commensurate with the social, economic world in which we are living as contrasted with the past. It is in many ways a different world from the past calling for a different measure.

According to this conception there is no such thing as "free verse" and so I insist. Imagism was not structural: that was the reason for its disappearance.

The impression I give is that we are about to make some discoveries. That they will be far-reaching in their effects.— This will depend on many things. My address (toward the task) is all that concerns me now: That we do approach a change.

What is it? I make a clear and definite statement—that it lies in the structure of the verse. That it may possibly lie elsewhere I do not for a moment deny or care—I have here to defend that only and that is my theme.

I hope you will pardon my deliberation, for I wish again to enter a short by-path: It may be said that I wish to destroy the past. It is precisely a service to tradition, honoring it and serving it that is envisioned and intended by my attack, and not disfigurement—confirming and *enlarging* its application.

Set the overall proposal of an enlarged technical means—in order to liberate the possibilities of depicting reality in a modern world that has seen more if not felt more than in the past—in order to be *able* to feel more (for we know we feel less, or surmise that we do. Vocabulary opens the mind to feeling). But modern in that by psychology and all its dependencies we *know,* for we have learned that to feel more we have to have, in our day, the means to feel *with*—the tokens, the apparatus. We are lacking in the means—the appropriate paraphernalia, just as modern use of the products of chemistry for *refinement* must have means which the past lacked. Our poems are not subtly enough made, the structure, the staid manner of the poem cannot let our feelings through.

(Note: Then show (in what detail I can) what we may do to achieve this end by a review of early twentieth-century literary accomplishments. Work done.)

We seek profusion, the Mass—heterogeneous—ill-assorted—quite breathless—grasping at all kinds of things—as if—like Audubon shooting some little bird, really only to look at it the better.

If any one man's work lacks the distinction to be expected from the finished artist, we might well think of the *profusion* of a Rabelais—as against a limited output. It is as though for the moment we should be profuse, we Americans; we need to build up a mass, a conglomerate maybe, containing few gems but bits of them—Brazilian brilliants—that shine of themselves, uncut as they are.

Now when Mr. Eliot came along he had a choice: 1. Join the crowd, adding his blackbird's voice to the flock, contributing to the conglomerate (or working over it for his selections) or 2. To go where there was already a mass of more ready distinction (to turn his back on the first), already an established literature in what to him was the same language (?) an already established place in world literature—a short cut, in short.

Stop a minute to emphasize our own position: It is *not* that of Mr. Eliot. We are making a modern bolus: That is our somewhat undistinguished burden; profusion, as, we must add in all fairness, against his distinction. His is a few poems beautifully phrased—in his longest effort thirty-five quotations in seven languages. We, let us say, are the Sermons of Launcelot Andrewes from which (in time) some selector will pick *one* phrase. Or say, the *Upanishad* that will contribute a single word! There are summative geniuses like that—they shine. We must value them—the extractors of genius—for what they do: extract. But they are there; we are here. It is not possible for us to imitate them. We are in a different phase—a new language—we are making the mass in which some other later Eliot will dig. We must *see* our opportunity and increase the hoard others will find to use. We must find our *pride* in *that*. We must have the pride, the humility and the thrill in the making. (Tell the story of Bramante and the building of the dome of the Duomo in Florence.)

The clearness we must have is first the clarity of knowing what we are doing— what we may do: Make anew—a reexamination of the means—on a fresh—basis. Not at *this* time an analysis so much as an accumulation. You couldn't expect us to be as prominent (as *read* in particular achievements—outstanding single poems). We're not doing the same thing. We're not putting the rose, the single rose, in the little glass vase in the window—we're digging a hole for the tree—and as we dig have disappeared in it.

(Note: Pound's story of my being interested in the loam whereas he wanted the finished product.)

(Note: Read Bridges—two short pieces in the anthology: 1. The Child 2. Snow.)

We begin to pick up what so far is little more than a feeling (a feeling entirely foreign to a Mr. E. or a Mr. P.—though less to them than to some others) that something is taking place in the accepted prosody or ought to be taking place. (Of course we have had Whitman—but he is a difficult subject—prosodically and I do not want to get off into that now.) It is similar to what must have been the early feelings of Einstein toward the laws of Isaac Newton in physics. Thus from being fixed, our prosodic values should rightly be seen as only relatively true. Einstein had the speed of light as a constant—his only constant—What have we? Perhaps our concept of musical time. I think so. But don't let us close down on that either at least for the moment.

In any case we as loose, disassociated (linguistically), yawping speakers of a new language, are privileged (I guess) to sense and so to seek to discover that possible thing which is disturbing the metrical table of values—as unknown elements would disturb Mendelyeev's table of the periodicity of atomic weights and so lead to discoveries.

And we had better get on the job and make our discoveries or, quietly, someone else will make them for us—covertly and without acknowledgment—(one acknowledges one's indebtedness in one's notes only to dead writers—preferably long dead!).

We wish to find an objective way at least of looking at verse and to redefine its elements; this I say is the theme (the radium) that underlies Bridges' experiments as it is the yeast animating Whitman and all the "moderns."

That the very project itself, quite apart from its solutions, is not yet raised to consciousness, to a clear statement of purpose, is our fault. (Note: the little Mag: Variegations) But one thing, a semiconscious sense of a rending discovery to be made is becoming apparent. For one great thing about "the bomb" is the awakened sense it gives us that catastrophic (but why?) alterations are also possible in the human *mind,* in art, in the arts. . . . We are too cowed by our fear to realize it fully. But it is *possible.* That is what we mean. This isn't optimism, it is chemistry: Or better, physics.

It appears, it disappears, a sheen of it comes up, when, as its shattering implications affront us, all the gnomes hurry to cover up its traces.

> Note: Proust: (Wilson) He has supplied for the first time in literature an equivalent on the full scale for the new theory of modern physics—I mention this merely to show a possible relationship—between a style and a natural science—intelligently considered.

Now for an entirely new issue: Mr. Auden is an interesting case—in fact he presents to me a deciding issue. His poems are phenomenally worth studying in the context of this theme.

There is no modern poet so agile—so impressive in the use of the poetic means. He can do anything—except one thing. He came to America and became a citizen of this country. He is truly, I should say, learned. Now Mr. Auden didn't come here for nothing or, if you know Auden, without a deep-seated conviction that he *had* to come. Don't put it down to any of the superficial things that might first occur to you—that he hates England, etc. He came here because of a crisis in his career—his career as a writer, as a poet particularly I should say. Mr. Auden may disagree with me in some of this but he will not disagree, I think, when I say he is a writer to whom writing is his life, his very breath which, as he or any man goes on, in the end absorbs *all* his breath.

Auden might have gone to France or to Italy or to South America or following Rimbaud to Ceylon or Timbuctoo. No! He came to the United States and became a citizen. Now the crisis, the only crisis which could drive a man, a distinguished poet, to that would be that he had come to an end of some sort in his poetic means—something that England could no longer supply, and that he came here implicitly to find an answer—in another language. As yet I see no evidence that he has found it. I wonder why? Mind you, this is one of the cleverest, most skilled poets of our age and one of the most versatile and prolific. He can do anything.

But when he writes an ode to a successful soccer season for his school, as Pindar wrote them for the Olympic heroes of his day—it is in a classic meter so successful in spite of the subject, which you might think trivial, that it becomes a serious poem. And a bad sign to me is always a religious or social tinge beginning to creep into a poet's work. You can put it down as a general rule that when a poet, in the broadest sense, begins to devote himself to the *subject matter* of his poems, *genre,* he has come to an end of his poetic means.

What does all this signify? That Auden came here to find a new way of writing— for it looked as if this were the place where one might reasonably expect to find that instability in the language where innovation would be at home. Remember even Mr. Eliot once said that no poetic drama could any longer be written in the iambic pentameter, but that perhaps jazz might offer a suggestion. He even wrote something about "My Baby," but it can't have been very successful for we seldom hear any more of it.

I wish I could enlist Auden in an attack, a basic attack upon the whole realm of structure in the poem. I have tried but without success so far. I think that's what he came here looking for, I think he has failed to find it (it may be constitutional with him). I think we have disappointed him. Perhaps he has disappointed himself. I am sure the attack must be concentrated on the *rigidity of the poetic foot*.

This began as a basic criticism of Auden's poems—as a reason for his coming to America, and has at least served me as an illustration for the *theory* upon which I am speaking.

Look at his poems with this in view—his very skill seems to defeat him. It need not continue to do so in my opinion.

Mr. Eliot, meanwhile, has written his *Quartets*. He is a very subtle creator—who knows how to squeeze the last ounce of force out of his material. He has done a good job here though when he speaks of developing a new manner of writing, new manners following new manners only to be spent as soon as that particular piece of writing has been accomplished—I do not think he quite knows what he is about.

But in spite of everything and completely discounting his subject matter, his *genre*, Eliot's experiments in the *Quartets* though limited, show him to be more American in the sense I seek than, sad to relate, Auden, with his English ears and the best will in the world, will ever be able to be.

It may be the tragedy of a situation whose ramifications we are for the moment unable to trace: That the American gone over to England might make the contribution (or assist in it) which the Englishman come to America to find it and with the best will in the world, is unable to make.

Thus the Gallicized American, D'A——, according to Edmund Wilson in *Axel's Castle,* with the iambic pentameter in his brain, was able, at the beginning of the symbolist movement in Paris to break the French from their six-syllable line in a way they had of themselves never been able to do. There is Ezra Pound also to be thought of—another entire thesis—in this respect. I see that I am outlining a year's or at least a semester's series of lectures as I go along.

Now we come to the question of the origin of our discoveries. Where else can what we are seeking arise from but speech? From speech, from American speech as distinct from English speech, or presumably so, if what I say above is correct. In any case (since we have no body of poems comparable to the English) from what we *hear* in America. Not, that is, from a study of the classics, not even the American "Classics"—the *dead* classics which—may I remind you, we have *never heard* as living speech. No one has or can *hear* them as they were written any more than we can *hear* Greek today.

I say this once again to emphasize what I have often said—that we here must *listen* to the language for the discoveries we hope to make. This is not the same as the hierarchic or tapeworm mode of making additions to the total poetic body: the mode of the schools. This will come up again elsewhere.

That being so, what I have presumed but not proven, concerning Auden's work, can we not say that there are many more *hints* toward literary composition in the American language than in English—where they are inhibited by classicism and "good taste." (Note the French word *tête*, its derivation from "pot.") I'd put it much stronger, but let's not be diverted at this point, there are too many more important things pressing for attention.

In the first place, we have to say, following H. L. Mencken's *The American Language,* which American language? Since Mencken pointed out that the American student (the *formative* years—very important) is bilingual, he speaks English in the classroom but his own tongue outside of it.

We mean, then, American—the language Mr. Eliot and Mr. Pound carried to Europe *in their ears*—willy-nilly—when they left here for their adventures and which presumably Mr. Auden came here to find—perhaps too late. A language full of those hints toward newness of which I have been speaking. I am not interested in the history but these things offer a point worth making, a rich opportunity for development lies before us at this point.

I said "hints toward composition." This does not mean realism in the language. What it does mean, I think, is ways of managing the language, new ways. Primarily it means to me opportunity to expand the structure, the basis, the actual making of the poem.

It is a chance to attack the language of the poem seriously. For to us our language is serious in a way that English is not. Just as to them English is serious—too serious—in a way no dialect could be. But the dialect is the mobile phase, the changing phase, the productive phase—as their languages were to Chaucer, Shakespeare, Dante, Rabelais in their day.

It is there, in the mouths of the living, that the language is changing and giving new means for expanded possibilities in literary expression and, I add, basic structure—the most important of all.

To the English, English is England: "History is England," yodels Mr. Eliot. To us this is not so, not so *if* we prove it by writing a poem built to refute it—otherwise he wins!! But that leads to mere controversy. For us rehash of rehash of hash of re-hash is *not* the business.

A whole semester of studies is implicit here. Perhaps a whole course of post-graduate studies—with theses—extending into a life's work!! But before I extol too much and advocate the experimental method, let me emphasize that, like God's creation, the objective is not experimentation but *man.* In our case, poems! There were enough experiments it seems, from what natural history shows, in that first instance but that was not the culmination. The poem is what we are after.

And again let me emphasize that this is something that has been going on, unrecognized for years—here *and* in England. What we are at is to try to discover and isolate and *use* the underlying element or principle motivating this change which is trying to speak outright. Do you not see now why I have been inveighing against the sonnet all these years? And why it has been so violently defended? Because it is a form which does not admit of the slightest structural change in its composition.

1948

━━━━◦►◄ EZRA POUND ►━◦━━━━
(1885–1972)

Ezra Loomis Pound, the central genius and tragic figure of Modernist poetry, was born in the remote mining town of Hailey, Idaho, five years before the territory was admitted to the Union. The poet's father, Homer Pound, had obtained a political appointment from his own father, a congressman from Wisconsin, as local assayer of gold and silver and register of mining claims. The poet's mother, Isabel Weston Pound, a relative of Henry Wadsworth Longfellow, disliked Hailey, and by late 1887 the family moved back east, eventually settling in Philadelphia where Homer worked for the U.S. Mint. In 1901 the sixteen-year-old Pound enrolled at the University of Pennsylvania where the next year he met William Carlos Williams, who was starting medical school. In 1903 Pound transferred to Hamilton College, a smaller college with a superior language program, so that he could study Italian and Spanish in addition to Greek, Latin, French, German, Portuguese, and Anglo Saxon. (He later studied Provençal and Chinese.) Linguistics was an exciting field at that time, as European philologists documented and analyzed the Continent's complex language families. Pound became fascinated with the Romance languages and in 1906 returned to Penn to earn a master's degree in the field. Later specialists have sometimes criticized Pound's command of foreign languages. While it is true that he did not know all these languages equally well, his range was impressive. Pound not only translated widely from eight languages, he also published in Italian and French and even composed two cantos in Italian.

Pound's academic studies proved crucial to his artistic development. His immersion in linguistics gave his own work an international orientation, and it led him to become the most influential translator of poetry in American literature. But equally important were the human relationships he cultivated. Pound had an indisputable genius not only for identifying artistic talent but also for encouraging, shaping, and promoting it. He was the great literary mentor of Modernism, often serving in important advisory roles even to his elders, like William Butler Yeats. While still a teenager he formed lifelong friendships with William Carlos Williams and Hilda Doolittle (H.D.). (Pound had even hoped to marry Doolittle but was prevented by her father who was suspicious of the brash, young bohemian.) Pound was not satisfied merely with articulating a new aesthetic in his own poetry and criticism. He wanted to create a new literary culture that embodied these values. He understood that meant convincing the most talented writers of his time to pursue Modernism and then shaping and supporting their efforts.

No writer of his time proved more influential. Pound was a decisive figure in the literary careers of T. S. Eliot, James Joyce, William Carlos Williams, H. D., the later W. B. Yeats, and the younger poets who gathered under the "Objectivist" banner (most notably Basil Bunting, George Oppen, and Louis Zukofsky). His role in Eliot's career was crucial. He took the draft of Eliot's poem "He Do the Police in Different Voices," drastically cut and reshaped it, and remarkably retitled it "The Waste Land." Pound's compressed and elliptical version of Eliot's poem became the poetic touchstone of the Modernist movement. He also influenced and championed visual artists like Jacob Epstein, Henri Gaudier-Brzeska, and Constantine Brancusi as well as the avant-garde composer George Antheil, the so-called Bad Boy of Music. Few major writers have ever been so generous—not only with attention and energy but also with money. Although Pound lived a bohemian life of voluntary poverty, he was always ready to pass on whatever funds he had to needy friends. As Pound's lifelong mistress Olga Rudge commented, "He didn't talk about things—He wanted something *done.*"

Pound first traveled to Europe on a tiny fellowship in 1906. After touring Spain and France, he returned to Penn to work on his doctorate and study Provençal and Sicilian. In the autumn of 1907, the twenty-one-year-old poet began teaching at Wabash College in Crawfordsville, Indiana. The flamboyant young bohemian was not destined to stay long in such a conservative milieu. (Tobacco and alcohol were forbidden by local law.) In February he was dismissed by the college authorities for allowing a stranded actress to spend the night in his room (while he slept on the floor). The trustees could not prove immorality, but they wanted the cigarette-smoking, free-speaking "Latin Quarter type" off campus. They offered to pay his full year's salary if he left. Pound took the money and sailed to Europe. He would spend the next thirty-seven years as an émigré in England, France, and Italy. Indiana lost a fine professor of comparative literature, and America gained a great Modernist poet.

After privately publishing his first book of poems in Venice, *A Lume Spento* ("With Candles Quenched") (1908), Pound settled in London where he soon became the central figure in the new experimental movement that would become known as Modernism. At that time Pound believed that English-language poetry was moribund, stuck in stale Romantic clichés, and unable to reflect the complex reality of the modern world. Only Yeats, he felt, was a great living poet, although even he needed to develop a more contemporary idiom. In both poetry and criticism, the young Pound proclaimed a program of artistic modernization. *Make It New,* the title of his 1934 critical collection, aptly summarizes the artistic battle cry of Pound's London years.

In 1912 Pound created his first and most influential literary movement, Imagism, or to use the French term initially employed, *Imagisme.* Joining Richard Aldington, T. E. Hulme, F. S. Flint, and Hilda Doolittle (whom he renamed "H. D., Imagiste"), Pound announced a new poetic credo of

intensity, concision, and directness. In *Poetry* (March 1913) Pound published
a manifesto, "A Few Don'ts by an Imagist," which remains one of the generative Modernist texts.

Pound soon published an anthology, *Des Imagistes* (1914), containing
work by eleven poets, including H. D., Amy Lowell, William Carlos Williams,
and James Joyce. In his introduction he elaborated on the principles of the
new experimental poetry to include "to use the language of common speech,
but always the exact word—not the almost exact one" and "to create new
rhythms." As a distinct and unified movement, Imagism lasted only two
years. By 1914 Pound was plotting his next movement, Vorticism, with
writer-artist Wyndham Lewis. Amy Lowell soon issued rival Imagist anthologies, which led Pound to dismiss her efforts as "Amygisme." Vorticism, however, never clearly articulated a distinct aesthetic and soon faltered, leaving
behind two issues of *BLAST* (1914 and 1915)—a rudely exuberant, oversized
arts journal—as its chief memorial.

Pound's attention now turned to Chinese and Japanese verse—an artistic
enterprise that would have profound influence on modern poetry. Pound had
always been interested in poetic translation, though his early efforts had focused mostly on Italian, French, and Provençal work, a natural consequence
of his training in Romance languages. Significantly, Pound had rejected the
Romantic assertion—found in Coleridge, Shelley, and others—that poetry is
essentially untranslatable. Instead, Pound reasserted the Renaissance notion
of poetic translation as a creative art that expands a national literature by
introducing foreign works. Translation is not a doomed enterprise but a necessary part of literary culture. "A great age of literature," he asserted, "is
perhaps always a great age of translation; or follows it." Translation became
central to both Pound's own poetic development and his cultural program to
modernize and reform English-language verse.

In London Pound also pioneered what would become perhaps the major
Modernist long poetic form, the sequence. Pound, like most American Modernists, rejected the narrative mode as the organizing structure for longer
poems. He became fascinated with the concept of creating an extended
poem composed of carefully arranged and thematically unified short lyric
sections. The sequence soon became the dominant structure for longer
Modernist poems, and it proved indispensable to writers as different as
Pound, Williams, Eliot, H. D., Wallace Stevens, Gertrude Stein, and Hart
Crane. (Only Robinson Jeffers among the major Modernists worked consistently in the narrative mode.)

Pound's *Cathay* can be read as a sequence, though it is composed of discrete translations from Chinese; his two Mauberley sequences, however, demonstrate the full possibilities of this new form. "Hugh Selwyn Mauberley"
(1920) describes an alter ego for Pound. Mauberley is a thirty-one-year-old
American author trying to write great poetry in literary London in the era
around World War I. In this poem and many others, Pound adopted a persona (literally "a mask"), an invented character whose voice allows him to
speak indirectly about his own life and time. The most ambitious example
of Pound's persona poems is "Homage to Sextus Propertius," a brilliant sequence of lyric and dramatic monologues supposedly spoken by the title

character, a Roman poet living under the Caesars, re-created in a way that reflected the American writer's own life in London during the twilight years of the British Empire.

In London, Pound also began what would become the central creative undertaking of his life, the *Cantos*. Begun in 1917, this Modernist epic occupied him for the remainder of his life (by 1926 he had more or less stopped writing all other poetry), but it was never finished to the author's satisfaction. The final version, *The Cantos of Ezra Pound* (1970), contained final versions, drafts, or fragments of 115 cantos, some of which existed only as short passages. (The book omitted two overtly pro-fascist cantos written in Italian, so the total number of sections in Pound's final version was 117.)

The *Cantos* has been controversial since its inception. Many critics offer it as conclusive evidence of the poet's genius—a modern epic, which Pound defined as "a poem including history," that addresses world culture, politics, economics, and mythology. Other critics see its nonlinear organization and densely allusive language (which contains numerous Latin, Greek, Italian, Chinese, Provençal, and French quotations in the original) as signs of Pound's decline into obscurantism and megalomania. The most reasonable reaction is probably a compromise between the two. The entire poem surely fails to deliver the author's grand intention of a powerfully poetic Modernist epic that summarizes and critiques the best of world culture. In his old age Pound himself declared the work a "botch." Yet few readers who study the richly textured and carefully sculpted poem can fail to recognize the lyric power of its best sections or the intellectual energy of certain themes—especially the figure and ideas of Confucius, whose philosophy and poetry exercised a decisive influence on Pound's views. Ultimately, the *Cantos* represents a test case for the Modernist method: How effectively can a literary work communicate when it abandons the traditional techniques like narrative or linear argumentation for lyric methods of indirection, allusion, and symbolism? Successful or failed, the *Cantos* stands at the center of Modernist literature, and its considerable influence has not been limited to English-language poets.

Had Pound died at forty in 1925, he would probably be universally venerated as the central genius of American Modernism whose innovative brilliance, critical acumen, and personal generosity had refashioned poetry. But he lived another forty-seven years. After leaving London in 1921, he stayed in Paris for four years, where he moved among the American émigrés now known as "The Lost Generation," who include Ernest Hemingway, Gertrude Stein, Archibald MacLeish, and E. E. Cummings. But finding it too expensive, he and his British wife, Dorothy Shakespear, moved to Rapallo, Italy, in 1924. By now Pound had become increasingly involved in politics and economics, and the intellectual isolation of the Italian seaside town aggravated his already idiosyncratic views of modern society. He became a devoted admirer of the fascist dictator, Benito Mussolini, and he used his unreliable economic theories to vent his growing anti-Semitism. When Britain declared war on Germany and Italy in 1939, Pound's book royalties stopped and his wife's English investments were frozen.

Pound contemplated returning to the United States but instead he took a job broadcasting for the Italian government's *American Hour* radio show.

Hired to talk about literary matters, Pound could not resist the opportunity to promulgate his political views. His broadcasts were self-indulgent and digressive to the point of incoherence, but there was no mistaking his devotion to fascism, his hatred of President Franklin Roosevelt, and his virulent anti-Semitism. (Pound's talks were so chaotic and bizarre that some Italian officials suspected that he was an American spy broadcasting in a secret code.) When America declared war on Italy in 1941, Pound did not cease broadcasting, nor change his citizenship, but continued praising Mussolini and eventually Hitler, while criticizing America in crude, racist terms. That same year Pound was indicted in absentia for treason, a capital offense. The fifty-nine-year-old poet was arrested by the U.S. Army in 1945.

After several months in a military prison near Pisa (partly confined in an open outdoor cage) during which time he wrote the "Pisan Cantos" (Nos. 74–84), Pound was flown to Washington, D.C., for trial. Through the efforts of his literary friends, he was declared unfit for trial by reason of insanity and confined to Washington's St. Elizabeths Hospital for the Criminally Insane, where he remained for the next thirteen years. During his confinement Pound received a steady stream of visitors, including Charles Olson, Elizabeth Bishop, and Marshall McLuhan. Due to the efforts of Frost, MacLeish, and Hemingway, Pound was finally discharged as "unimproved" in 1958. As soon as he was issued a passport, the seventy-two-year-old poet returned to Italy. His final years were marked by mental deterioration. He sat silently for days but occasionally broke out with normal conversation as when he reportedly told Allen Ginsberg who visited him in 1967, "The worst mistake I made was the stupid, suburban prejudice of anti-Semitism." Pound died in Venice in 1972. His body was taken by gondola to the tiny island cemetery of San Michele in the Venetian lagoon where he was buried.

Pound was, with T. S. Eliot, the generative critical intelligence of Modernism. He has been condemned—often with some justice—as an elitist, aesthete, obscurantist, fraud, egotist, racist, and totalitarian, but his central position in the renewal of English-language poetry in the early twentieth century remains indisputable. His intellectual impact on literary practice and critical thinking comes less from any coherent system of poetics than from the brilliance of individual insights, often expressed in vibrant, memorable, and even witty language. "Poetry must be as well written as prose." "The tradition is a beauty we preserve and not a set of fetters to bind us." "Great literature is simply language charged with meaning to the utmost degree possible." There are individual paragraphs and even single sentences in his *Literary Essays* or *ABC of Reading* that exercised a decisive influence on Modernist poetics. Likewise, Pound's insistence on the importance of certain principles—verse technique, poetic compression, creative translation, expansion of the literary canon, and the interdependence of national literatures—has helped shape contemporary attitudes. His best criticism was mostly written early in his career, before his obsessions with social economics and fascist politics overwhelmed his literary judgment. After the publication of *ABC of Reading* and *Make It New* (both in 1934), his already eccentric prose deteriorated noticeably, and his later criticism is an embarrassment to all but his most devout admirers. His pioneering early essays, however, remain required reading for any student of modern American literature.

A RETROSPECT[1]

There has been so much scribbling about a new fashion in poetry, that I may perhaps be pardoned this brief recapitulation and retrospect.

In the spring or early summer of 1912, "H. D.," Richard Aldington and myself decided that we were agreed upon the three principles following:

1. Direct treatment of the "thing" whether subjective or objective.
2. To use absolutely no word that does not contribute to the presentation.
3. As regarding rhythm: to compose in the sequence of the musical phrase, not in sequence of a metronome.

Upon many points of taste and of predilection we differed, but agreeing upon these three positions we thought we had as much right to a group name, at least as much right, as a number of French "schools" proclaimed by Mr Flint in the August number of Harold Monro's magazine for 1911.

This school has since been "joined" or "followed" by numerous people who, whatever their merits, do not show any signs of agreeing with the second specification. Indeed *vers libre* has become as prolix and as verbose as any of the flaccid varieties that preceded it. It has brought faults of its own. The actual language and phrasing is often as bad as that of our elders without even the excuse that the words are shovelled in to fill a metric pattern or to complete the noise of a rhyme-sound. Whether or no the phrases followed by the followers are musical must be left to the reader's decision. At times I can find a marked meter in "vers libres," as stale and hackneyed as any pseudo-Swinburnian, at times the writers seem to follow no musical structure whatever. But it is, on the whole, good that the field should be ploughed. Perhaps a few good poems have come from the new method, and if so it is justified.

Criticism is not a circumscription or a set of prohibitions. It provides fixed points of departure. It may startle a dull reader into alertness. That little of it which is good is mostly in stray phrases; or if it be an older artist helping a younger it is in great measure but rules of thumb, cautions gained by experience.

I set together a few phrases on practical working about the time the first remarks on imagism were published. The first use of the word "Imagist" was in my note to T. E. Hulme's five poems, printed at the end of my "Ripostes" in the autumn of 1912. I reprint my cautions from *Poetry* for March, 1913.

A FEW DON'TS

An "Image" is that which presents an intellectual and emotional complex in an instant of time. I use the term "complex" rather in the technical sense employed by the newer psychologists, such as Hart, though we might not agree absolutely in our application.

Originally published in *Pavannes and Divisions* (New York: Knopf, 1918). All numbered notes are Ezra Pound's; punctuation and spelling have been Americanized for this volume.

1. A group of early essays and notes which appeared under this title in *Pavannes and Divisions* (1918). "A Few Dont's" was first printed in *Poetry,* I, 6 (March, 1913).

It is the presentation of such a "complex" instantaneously which gives that sense of sudden liberation; that sense of freedom from time limits and space limits; that sense of sudden growth, which we experience in the presence of the greatest works of art.

It is better to present one Image in a lifetime than to produce voluminous works.

All this, however, some may consider open to debate. The immediate necessity is to tabulate A LIST OF DON'TS for those beginning to write verses. I can not put all of them into Mosaic negative.

To begin with, consider the three propositions (demanding direct treatment, economy of words, and the sequence of the musical phrase), not as dogma—never consider anything as dogma—but as the result of long contemplation, which, even if it is some one else's contemplation, may be worth consideration.

Pay no attention to the criticism of men who have never themselves written a notable work. Consider the discrepancies between the actual writing of the Greek poets and dramatists, and the theories of the Graeco-Roman grammarians, concocted to explain their meters.

LANGUAGE

Use no superfluous word, no adjective which does not reveal something.

Don't use such an expression as "dim lands of *peace*." It dulls the image. It mixes an abstraction with the concrete. It comes from the writer's not realizing that the natural object is always the *adequate* symbol.

Go in fear of abstractions. Do not retell in mediocre verse what has already been done in good prose. Don't think any intelligent person is going to be deceived when you try to shirk all the difficulties of the unspeakably difficult art of good prose by chopping your composition into line lengths.

What the expert is tired of today the public will be tired of tomorrow.

Don't imagine that the art of poetry is any simpler than the art of music, or that you can please the expert before you have spent at least as much effort on the art of verse as the average piano teacher spends on the art of music.

Be influenced by as many great artists as you can, but have the decency either to acknowledge the debt outright, or to try to conceal it.

Don't allow "influence" to mean merely that you mop up the particular decorative vocabulary of some one or two poets whom you happen to admire. A Turkish war correspondent was recently caught red-handed babbling in his despatches of "dove-grey" hills, or else it was "pearl-pale," I can not remember.

Use either no ornament or good ornament.

RHYTHM AND RHYME

Let the candidate fill his mind with the finest cadences he can discover, preferably in a foreign language,[2] so that the meaning of the words may be less likely to divert his attention from the movement; e.g. Saxon charms, Hebridean Folk Songs, the verse of Dante, and the lyrics of Shakespeare—if he can dissociate the vocabulary from the cadence. Let him dissect the lyrics of Goethe coldly into their component sound values, syllables long and short, stressed and unstressed, into vowels and consonants.

2. This is for rhythm, his vocabulary must of course be found in his native tongue.

It is not necessary that a poem should rely on its music, but if it does rely on its music that music must be such as will delight the expert.

Let the neophyte know assonance and alliteration, rhyme immediate and delayed, simple and polyphonic, as a musician would expect to know harmony and counterpoint and all the minutiae of his craft. No time is too great to give to these matters or to any one of them, even if the artist seldom have need of them.

Don't imagine that a thing will "go" in verse just because it's too dull to go in prose.

Don't be "viewy"—leave that to the writers of pretty little philosophic essays. Don't be descriptive; remember that the painter can describe a landscape much better than you can, and that he has to know a deal more about it.

When Shakespeare talks of the "Dawn in russet mantle clad" he presents something which the painter does not present. There is in this line of his nothing that one can call description; he presents.

Consider the way of the scientists rather than the way of an advertising agent for a new soap.

The scientist does not expect to be acclaimed as a great scientist until he has *discovered* something. He begins by learning what has been discovered already. He goes from that point onward. He does not bank on being a charming fellow personally. He does not expect his friends to applaud the results of his freshman class work. Freshmen in poetry are unfortunately not confined to a definite and recognizable class room. They are "all over the shop." Is it any wonder "the public is indifferent to poetry"?

Don't chop your stuff into separate *iambs*. Don't make each line stop dead at the end, and then begin every next line with a heave. Let the beginning of the next line catch the rise of the rhythm wave, unless you want a definite longish pause.

In short, behave as a musician, a good musician, when dealing with that phase of your art which has exact parallels in music. The same laws govern, and you are bound by no others.

Naturally, your rhythmic structure should not destroy the shape of your words, or their natural sound, or their meaning. It is improbable that, at the start, you will be able to get a rhythm-structure strong enough to affect them very much, though you may fall a victim to all sorts of false stopping due to line ends and cæsurae.

The Musician can rely on pitch and the volume of the orchestra. You can not. The term harmony is misapplied in poetry; it refers to simultaneous sounds of different pitch. There is, however, in the best verse a sort of residue of sound which remains in the ear of the hearer and acts more or less as an organ-base.

A rhyme must have in it some slight element of surprise if it is to give pleasure; it need not be bizarre or curious, but it must be well used if used at all.

Vide further Vildrac and Duhamel's notes on rhyme in *"Technique Poétiqué."*

That part of your poetry which strikes upon the imaginative *eye* of the reader will lose nothing by translation into a foreign tongue; that which appeals to the ear can reach only those who take it in the original.

Consider the definiteness of Dante's presentation, as compared with Milton's rhetoric. Read as much of Wordsworth as does not seem too unutterably dull.[3]

If you want the gist of the matter go to Sappho, Catullus, Villon, Heine when he is in the vein, Gautier when he is not too frigid; or, if you have not the tongues,

3. Vide infra.

seek out the leisurely Chaucer. Good prose will do you no harm, and there is good discipline to be had by trying to write it.

Translation is likewise good training, if you find that your original matter "wobbles" when you try to rewrite it. The meaning of the poem to be translated can not "wobble."

If you are using a symmetrical form, don't put in what you want to say and then fill up the remaining vacuums with slush.

Don't mess up the perception of one sense by trying to define it in terms of another. This is usually only the result of being too lazy to find the exact word. To this clause there are possibly exceptions.

The first three simple prescriptions will throw out nine-tenths of all the bad poetry now accepted as standard and classic; and will prevent you from many a crime of production.

". . . *Mais d'abord il faut être un poète*,*" as MM. Duhamel and Vildrac have said at the end of their little book, "*Notes sur la Technique Poétique.*"

Since March 1913, Ford Madox Hueffer has pointed out that Wordsworth was so intent on the ordinary or plain word that he never thought of hunting for *le mot juste.*

John Butler Yeats has handled or man-handled Wordsworth and the Victorians, and his criticism, contained in letters to his son, is now printed and available.

I do not like writing *about* art, my first, at least I think it was my first essay on the subject, was a protest against it.

PROLEGOMENA[4]

Time was when the poet lay in a green field with his head against a tree and played his diversion on a ha'penny whistle, and Caesar's predecessors conquered the earth, and the predecessors of golden Crassus embezzled, and fashions had their say, and let him alone. And presumably he was fairly content in this circumstance, for I have small doubt that the occasional passerby, being attracted by curiosity to know why any one should lie under a tree and blow diversion on a ha'penny whistle, came and conversed with him, and that among these passers-by there was on occasion a person of charm or a young lady who had not read *Man and Superman;* and looking back upon this naïve state of affairs we call it the age of gold.

Metastasio, and he should know if any one, assures us that this age endures—even though the modern poet is expected to holloa his verses down a speaking tube to the editors of cheap magazines—S. S. McClure, or some one of that sort—even though hordes of authors meet in dreariness and drink healths to the "Copyright Bill"; even though these things be, the age of gold pertains. Imperceivably, if you like, but pertains. You meet unkempt Amyclas in a Soho restaurant and chant together of dead and forgotten things—it is a manner of speech among poets to chant of dead, half-forgotten things, there seems no special harm in it; it has always been done—and it's rather better to be a clerk in the Post Office than to look after a lot of stinking, verminous sheep—and at another hour of the day one substitutes the drawing-room for the restaurant and tea is probably more palatable than mead and mare's milk, and little cakes than honey. And in this fashion one

---

**Mais d'abord il faut être un poète:* But first it was necessary to be a poet.
4. *Poetry and Drama* (then the *Poetry Review,* edited by Harold Monro), Feb. 1912.

survives the resignation of Mr Balfour, and the iniquities of the American customs-house, *e quel bufera infernal**, the periodical press. And then in the middle of it, there being apparently no other person at once capable and available one is stopped and asked to explain oneself.

I begin on the chord thus querulous, for I would much rather lie on what is left of Catullus' parlor floor and speculate the azure beneath it and the hills off to Salo and Riva with their forgotten gods moving unhindered amongst them, than discuss any processes and theories of art whatsoever. I would rather play tennis. I shall not argue.

CREDO

Rhythm.—I believe in an "absolute rhythm," a rhythm, that is, in poetry which corresponds exactly to the emotion or shade of emotion to be expressed. A man's rhythm must be interpretative, it will be, therefore, in the end, his own, uncounterfeiting, uncounterfeitable.

Symbols.—I believe that the proper and perfect symbol is the natural object, that if a man use "symbols" he must so use them that their symbolic function does not obtrude; so that *a* sense, and the poetic quality of the passage, is not lost to those who do not understand the symbol as such, to whom, for instance, a hawk is a hawk.

Technique.—I believe in technique as the test of a man's sincerity; in law when it is ascertainable; in the trampling down of every convention that impedes or obscures the determination of the law, or the precise rendering of the impulse.

Form.—I think there is a "fluid" as well as a "solid" content, that some poems may have form as a tree has form, some as water poured into a vase. That most symmetrical forms have certain uses. That a vast number of subjects cannot be precisely, and therefore not properly rendered in symmetrical forms.

"Thinking that alone worthy wherein the whole art is employed"[5] I think the artist should master all known forms and systems of metric, and I have with some persistence set about doing this, searching particularly into those periods wherein the systems came to birth or attained their maturity. It has been complained, with some justice, that I dump my note-books on the public. I think that only after a long struggle will poetry attain such a degree of development, or, if you will, modernity, that it will vitally concern people who are accustomed, in prose, to Henry James and Anatole France, in music to Debussy. I am constantly contending that it took two centuries of Provence and one of Tuscany to develop the media of Dante's masterwork, that it took the latinists of the Renaissance, and the Pleiade, and his own age of painted speech to prepare Shakespeare his tools. It is tremendously important that great poetry be written, it makes no jot of difference who writes it. The experimental demonstrations of one man may save the time of many—hence my furor over Arnaut Daniel—if a man's experiments try out one new rime or dispense conclusively with one iota of currently accepted nonsense, he is merely playing fair with his colleagues when he chalks up his result.

No man ever writes very much poetry that "matters." In bulk that is, no one produces much that is final, and when a man is not doing this highest thing, this saying the thing once for all and perfectly; when he is not matching Ποικιλόθρον',

---

*e quel bufera infernal: and what an infernal storm.
5. Dante, *De Vulgari Eloquentia.*

ἀθάνατ' Ἀφρόδιτα: eternal Aphrodite on your patterned throne. Or "Hist—said Kate the Queen," he had much better be making the sorts of experiment which may be of use to him in his later work, or to his successors.

"The lyf so short, the craft so long to lerne." It is a foolish thing for a man to begin his work on a too narrow foundation, it is a disgraceful thing for a man's work not to show steady growth and increasing fineness from first to last.

As for "adaptations"; one finds that all the old masters of painting recommend to their pupils that they begin by copying masterworks and proceed to their own composition.

As for "Every man his own poet," the more every man knows about poetry the better. I believe in every one writing poetry who wants to; most do. I believe in every man knowing enough of music to play "God bless our home" on the harmonium, but I do not believe in every man giving concerts and printing his sin.

The mastery of any art is the work of a lifetime. I should not discriminate between the "amateur" and the "professional." Or rather I should discriminate quite often in favour of the amateur, but should discriminate between the amateur and the expert. It is certain that the present chaos will endure until the Art of poetry has been preached down the amateur gullet, until there is such a general understanding of the fact that poetry is an art and not a pastime such a knowledge of technique; of technique of surface and technique of content, that the amateurs will cease to try to drown out the masters.

If a certain thing was said once for all in Atlantis or Arcadia in 450 Before Christ or in 1290 after, it is not for us moderns to go saying it over, or to go obscuring the memory of the dead by saying the same thing with less skill and less conviction.

My pawing over the ancients and semi-ancients has been one struggle to find out what has been done, once for all, better than it can ever be done again, and to find out what remains for us to do, and plenty does remain, for if we still feel the same emotions as those which launched the thousand ships, it is quite certain that we come on these feelings differently, through different nuances, by different intellectual gradations. Each age has its own abounding gifts yet only some ages transmute them into matter of duration. No good poetry is ever written in a manner twenty years old, for to write in such a manner shows conclusively that the writer thinks from books, convention and *cliché*, and not from life, yet a man feeling the divorce of life and his art may naturally try to resurrect a forgotten mode if he finds in that mode some leaven, or if he think he sees in it some element lacking in contemporary art which might unite that art again to its sustenance, life.

In the art of Daniel and Cavalcanti, I have seen that precision which I miss in the Victorians, that explicit rendering, be it of external nature, or of emotion. Their testimony is of the eyewitness, their symptoms are first hand.

As for the nineteenth century, with all respect to its achievements, I think we shall look back upon it as a rather blurry, messy sort of a period, a rather sentimentalistic, mannerish sort of a period. I say this without any self-righteousness, with no self-satisfaction.

As for there being a "movement" or my being of it, the conception of poetry as a "pure art" in the sense in which I use the term, revived with Swinburne. From the puritanical revolt to Swinburne, poetry had been merely the vehicle—yes, definitely, Arthur Symon's scruples and feelings about the word not withholding—the ox-cart and post-chaise for transmitting thoughts poetic or otherwise. And perhaps the "great Victorians," though it is doubtful, and assuredly the "nineties" continued the development of the art, confining their improvements, however, chiefly to sound and to refinements of manner.

Mr Yeats has once and for all stripped English poetry of its perdamnable rhetoric. He has boiled away all that is not poetic—and a good deal that is. He has become a classic in his own lifetime and *nel mezzo del cammin*. He has made our poetic idiom a thing pliable, a speech without inversions.

Robert Bridges, Maurice Hewlett and Frederic Manning are[6] in their different ways seriously concerned with overhauling the metric, in testing the language and its adaptability to certain modes. Ford Hueffer is making some sort of experiments in modernity. The Provost of Oriel continues his translation of the *Divina Commedia*.

As to Twentieth century poetry, and the poetry which I expect to see written during the next decade or so, it will, I think, move against poppy-cock, it will be harder and saner, it will be what Mr Hewlett calls "nearer the bone." It will be as much like granite as it can be, its force will lie in its truth, its interpretative power (of course, poetic force does always rest there); I mean it will not try to seem forcible by rhetorical din, and luxurious riot. We will have fewer painted adjectives impeding the shock and stroke of it. At least for myself, I want it so, austere, direct, free from emotional slither.

What is there now, in 1917, to be added?

RE VERS LIBRE

I think the desire for vers libre is due to the sense of quantity reasserting itself after years of starvation. But I doubt if we can take over, for English, the rules of quantity laid down for Greek and Latin, mostly by Latin grammarians.

I think one should write vers libre only when one "must," that is to say, only when the "thing" builds up a rhythm more beautiful than that of set meters, or more real, more a part of the emotion of the "thing," more germane, intimate, interpretative than the measure of regular accentual verse; a rhythm which discontents one with set iambic or set anapestic.

Eliot has said the thing very well when he said, "No *vers* is *libre* for the man who wants to do a good job."

As a matter of detail, there is vers libre with accent heavily marked as a drumbeat (as par example my "Dance Figure"), and on the other hand I think I have gone as far as can profitably be gone in the other direction (and perhaps too far). I mean I do not think one can use to any advantage rhythms much more tenuous and imperceptible than some I have used. I think progress lies rather in an attempt to approximate classical quantitative meters (NOT to copy them) than in a carelessness regarding such things.[7]

I agree with John Yeats on the relation of beauty to certitude. I prefer satire, which is due to emotion, to any sham of emotion.

I have had to write, or at least I have written a good deal about art, sculpture, painting and poetry. I have seen what seemed to me the best of contemporary work

6. (Dec. 1911)
7. Let me date this statement 20 Aug. 1917

reviled and obstructed. Can any one write prose of permanent or durable interest when he is merely saying for one year what nearly every one will say at the end of three or four years? I have been battistrada for a sculptor, a painter, a novelist, several poets. I wrote also of certain French writers in *The New Age* in nineteen twelve or eleven.

I would much rather that people would look at Brzeska's sculpture and Lewis's drawings, and that they would read Joyce, Jules Romains, Eliot, than that they should read what I have said of these men, or that I should be asked to republish argumentative essays and reviews.

All that the critic can do for the reader or audience or spectator is to focus his gaze or audition. Rightly or wrongly I think my blasts and essays have done their work, and that more people are now likely to go to the sources than are likely to read this book.

Jammes's "Existences" in "*La Triomphe de la Vie*" is available. So are his early poems. I think we need a convenient anthology rather than descriptive criticism. Carl Sanburg wrote me from Chicago, "It's hell when poets can't afford to buy each other's books." Half the people who care, only borrow. In America so few people know each other that the difficulty lies more than half in distribution. Perhaps one should make an anthology: Romains's "Un Etre en Marche" and "Prières," Vildrac's "Visite." Retrospectively the fine wrought work of Laforgue, the flashes of Rimbaud, the hard-bit lines of Tristan Corbière, Tailhade's sketches in "Poèmes Aristophanesques," the "Litanies" of De Gourmont.

It is difficult at all times to write of the fine arts, it is almost impossible unless one can accompany one's prose with many reproductions. Still I would seize this chance or any chance to reaffirm my belief in Wyndham Lewis's genius, both in his drawings and his writings. And I would name an out of the way prose book, the "*Scenes and Portraits*" of Frederic Manning, as well as James Joyce's short stories and novel, "Dubliners" and the now well known "Portrait of the Artist" as well as Lewis' "Tarr," if, that is, I may treat my strange reader as if he were a new friend come into the room, intent on ransacking my bookshelf.

ONLY EMOTION ENDURES

"ONLY emotion endures." Surely it is better for me to name over the few beautiful poems that still ring in my head than for me to search my flat for back numbers of periodicals and rearrange all that I have said about friendly and hostile writers.

The first twelve lines of Padraic Colum's "Drover"; his "O Woman shapely as a swan, on your account I shall not die"; Joyce's "I hear an army"; the lines of Yeats that ring in my head and in the heads of all young men of my time who care for poetry: Braseal and the Fisherman, "The fire that stirs about her when she stirs"; the later lines of "The Scholars," the faces of the Magi; William Carlos Williams's "Postlude," Aldington's version of "Atthis," and "H. D.'s" waves like pine tops, and her verse in "Des Imagistes" the first anthology; Hueffer's "How red your lips are" in his translation from Von der Vogelweide, his "Three Ten," the general effect of his "On Heaven"; his sense of the prose values or prose qualities in poetry; his ability to write poems that half-chant and are spoiled by a musician's additions; beyond these a poem by Alice Corbin, "One City Only," and another ending "But sliding water over a stone." These things have worn smooth in my head and I am not through with them, nor with Aldington's "In Via Sestina" nor his other poems in "Des Imagistes," though people have told me their flaws. It may be that their content is too much embedded in me for me to look back at the words.

I am almost a different person when I come to take up the argument for Eliot's poems.

1913–1918

━◦━━◀━━◦━

HOW TO READ

Part One: Introduction

Largely Autobiographical, Touching the Present, and More or Less Immediately Past, "State of Affairs".

Literary instruction in our "institutions of learning"[1] was, at the beginning of this century, cumbrous and inefficient. I dare say it still is. Certain more or less mildly exceptional professors were affected by the "beauties" of various authors (usually deceased), but the system, as a whole, lacked sense and co-ordination. I dare say it still does. When studying physics we are not asked to investigate the biographies of all the disciples of Newton who showed interest in science, but who failed to make any discovery. Neither are their unrewarded gropings, hopes, passions, laundry bills, or erotic experiences thrust on the hurried student or considered germane to the subject.

The general contempt of "scholarship," especially any part of it connected with subjects included in university "Arts" courses; the shrinking of people in general from any book supposed to be "good"; and, in another mode, the flamboyant advertisements telling "how to seem to know it when you don't," might long since have indicated to the sensitive that there is something defective in the contemporary methods of purveying letters.

As the general reader has but a vague idea of what these methods are at the "center," i.e. for the specialist who is expected to serve the general reader, I shall lapse or plunge into autobiography.

In my university I found various men interested (or uninterested) in their subjects, but, I think, no man with a view of literature as a whole, or with any idea whatsoever of the relation of the part he himself taught to any other part.

Those professors who regarded their "subject" as a drill manual rose most rapidly to positions of executive responsibility (one case is now a provost). Those professors who had some natural aptitude for comprehending their authors and for communicating a general sense of comfort in the presence of literary masterwork remained obscurely in their less exalted positions.

A professor of Romantics admitted that the *Chanson de Roland* was inferior to the *Odyssey,* but then the Middle Ages were expected to present themselves with apologies, and this was, if I remember rightly, an isolated exception. English novelists

From *How to Read* (London: Desmond Harmsworth, 1931).
1. Foot-note a few decades later: The proper definition would be "Institutions for the obstruction of learning."

were not compared with the French. "Sources" were discussed; forty versions of a Chaucerian anecdote were "compared," but not on points of respective literary merit. The whole field was full of redundance. I mean that what one had learned in one class, in the study of one literature, one was told again in some other.

One was asked to remember what some critic (deceased) had said, scarcely to consider whether his views were still valid, or ever had been very intelligent.

In defence of this dead and uncorrelated system, it may be urged that authors like Spengler, who attempt a synthesis, often do so before they have attained sufficient knowledge of detail: that they stuff expandable and compressible objects into rubber-bag categories, and that they limit their reference and interest by supposing that the pedagogic follies which they have themselves encountered, constitute an error universally distributed, and encountered by every one else. In extenuation of their miscalculations we may admit that any error or clumsiness of method that has sunk into, or been hammered into one man, over a period of years, probably continues as an error—not merely passively, but as an error still being propagated, consciously or unconsciously, by a number of educators, from laziness, from habits, or from natural cussedness.

"Comparative literature" sometimes figures in university curricula, but very few people know what they mean by the term, or approach it with a considered conscious method.

To tranquillize the low-brow reader, let me say at once that I do not wish to muddle him by making him read more books, but to allow him to read fewer with greater result. (I am willing to discuss this privately with the book trade.) I have been accused of wanting to make people read all the classics; which is not so. I have been accused of wishing to provide a "portable substitute for the British Museum," which I would do, like a shot, were it possible. It isn't.

American "taste" is less official than English taste, but more derivative. When I arrived in England (A.D. 1908), I found a greater darkness in the British "serious press" than had obtained on the banks of the Schuylkill. Already in my young and ignorant years they considered me "learned." It was impossible, at first, to see why and whence the current opinion of British weeklies. It was incredible that literate men—men literate enough, that is, to write the orderly paragraphs that they did write constantly in their papers—believed the stupidities that appeared there with such regularity. (Later, for two years, we ran fortnightly in the *Egoist,* the sort of fool-column that the French call a *sottisier,* needing nothing for it but quotations from the *Times Literary Supplement.* Two issues of the *Supplement* yielding, easily, one page of the *Egoist.*) For years I awaited enlightenment. One winter I had lodgings in Sussex. On the mantelpiece of the humble country cottage I found books of an earlier era, among them an anthology printed in 1830, and yet another dated 1795, and there, there by the sox of Jehosaphat was the British taste of this century, 1910, 1915, and even the present, A.D. 1931.

I had read Stendhal's remark that it takes eighty years for anything to reach the general public, and looking out on the waste heath, under the December drizzle, I believed him. But that is not all of the story. Embedded in that naïve innocence that does, to their credit, pervade our universities, I ascribed the delay to mere time. I still thought: With the attrition of decades, ah, yes, in another seventy, in another, perhaps, ninety years, they will admit that . . . etc.

I mean that I thought they wanted to, but were hindered.

Later it struck me that the best history of painting in London was the National Gallery, and that the best history of literature, more particularly of poetry, would be a twelve-volume anthology in which each poem was chosen not merely because it was a nice poem or a poem Aunt Hepsy liked, but because it contained an invention, a definite contribution to the art of verbal expression. With this in mind, I approached a respected agent. He was courteous, he was even openly amazed at the list of three hundred items which I offered as an indication of outline. No autochthonous Briton had ever, to his professed belief, displayed such familiarity with so vast a range, but he was too indolent to recast my introductory letter into a form suited to commerce. He, as they say, "repaired" to an equally august and long-established publishing house (which had already served his and my interest). In two days came a hasty summons: would I see him in person. I found him awed, as if one had killed a cat in the sacristy. Did I know what I had said in my letter? I did. Yes, but about Palgrave? I did. I had said: "It is time we had something to replace that doddard Palgrave." "But don't you know," came the awstruck tones, "that the whole fortune of X & Co. is founded on Palgrave's *Golden Treasury*"?

From that day onward no book of mine received a British imprimatur until the appearance of Eliot's castrated edition of my poems.

I perceived that there were thousands of pounds sterling invested in electroplate, and the least change in the public taste, let alone swift, catastrophic changes, would depreciate the value of those electros (of Hemans, let us say, or of Collins, Cowper, and of Churchill, who wrote the satiric verses, and of later less blatant cases, touched with a slighter flavor of mustiness).

I sought the banks of the Seine. Against ignorance one might struggle, and even against organic stupidity, but against a so vast vested interest the lone odds were too heavy.

Two years later a still more august academic press reopened the question. *They* had ventured to challenge Palgrave: they had been "interested"—would I send back my prospectus? I did. They found the plan "too ambitious." They said they might do "something," but that if they did it would be "more in the nature of gems."

FOR A METHOD

Nevertheless, the method I had proposed was simple, it is perhaps the only one that can give a man an orderly arrangement of his perception in the matter of letters. In opposition to it, there are the forces of superstition, of hang-over. People regard literature as something vastly more flabby and floating and complicated and indefinite than, let us say, mathematics. Its subject-matter, the human consciousness, is more complicated than are number and space. It is not, however, more complicated than biology, and no one ever supposed that it was. We apply a loose-leaf system to book-keeping so as to have the live items separated from the dead ones. In the study of physics we begin with simple mechanisms, wedge, lever and fulcrum, pulley and inclined plane, all of them still as useful as when they were first invented. We proceed by a study of discoveries. We are not asked to memorize a list of the parts of a side-wheeler engine.

And we could, presumably, apply to the study of literature a little of the common sense that we currently apply to physics or to biology. In poetry there are simple procedures, and there are known discoveries, clearly marked. As I have said in various places in my unorganized and fragmentary volumes: in each age one or two men of genius find something, and express it. It may be in only a line or in two lines, or in some quality of a cadence; and thereafter two dozen, or two hundred, or two or more thousand followers repeat and dilute and modify.

And if the instructor would select his specimens from works that contain these discoveries and solely on the basis of discovery—which may lie in the dimension of depth, not merely of some novelty on the surface—he would aid his student far more than by presenting his authors at random, and talking about them *in toto*.

Needless to say, this presentation would be entirely independent of consideration as to whether the given passages tended to make the student a better republican, monarchist, monist, dualist, rotarian, or other sectarian. To avoid confusion, one should state at once that such method has nothing to do with those allegedly scientific methods which approach literature as if it were something *not literature,* or with scientists' attempts to sub-divide the elements in literature according to some non-literary categoric division.

You do not divide physics or chemistry according to racial or religious categories. You do not put discoveries by Methodists and Germans into one category, and discoveries by Episcopalians or Americans or Italians into another.

DEFECTIVE RELATIVITIES

It is said that in America nothing is ever consciously related to anything else. I have cited as an exception the forty versions of the Chaucerian anecdote; they and the great edition of Horace with the careful list and parallel display of Greek sources for such line or such paragraph, show how the associative faculty can be side-tracked. Or at any rate they indicate the first gropings of association. Let us grant that some bits of literature have been, in special cases, displayed in relation to some other bits; usually some verbose gentleman writes a trilogy of essays, on three grandiose figures, comparing their "philosophy" or personal habits.

Let us by all means glance at "philology" and the "germanic system." Speaking as an historian, "we" may say that this system was designed to inhibit thought. After 1848 it was, in Germany, observed that some people thought. It was necessary to curtail this pernicious activity, the thinkists were given a china egg labelled scholarship, and were gradually unfitted for active life, or for any contact with life in general. Literature was permitted as a subject of study. And its study was so designed as to draw the mind of the student away from literature into inanity.

WHY BOOKS?

I

This simple first question was never asked.

The study of literature, or more probably of morphology, verb-roots, etc., was permitted the German professor in, let us say, 1880–1905, to keep his mind off life in general, and off public life in particular.

In America it was permitted from precedent; it was known to be permitted in Germany; Germany had a "great university tradition," which it behoved America to equal and perhaps to surpass.

This study, or some weaker variety of it, was also known to be permitted at Oxford, and supposed to have a refining influence on the student.

II

The practice of literary composition in private has been permitted since "age immemorial," like knitting, crocheting, etc. It occupies the practitioner, and, so long as he keeps it to himself, *ne nuit pas aux autres,* it does not transgress the definition of liberty which we find in the declaration of the *Droits de l'Homme:* Liberty is the right to do anything which harms not others. All of which is rather negative and unsatisfactory.

III

It appears to me quite tenable that the function of literature as a generated prize-worthy force is precisely that it does incite humanity to continue living; that it eases the mind of strain, and feeds it, I mean definitely as *nutrition of impulse.*

This idea may worry lovers of order. Just as good literature does often worry them. They regard it as dangerous, chaotic, subversive. They try every idiotic and degrading wheeze to tame it down. They try to make a bog, a marasmus, a great putridity in place of a sane and active ebullience. And they do this from sheer simian and pig-like stupidity, and from their failure to understand the function of letters.

IV

Has literature a function in the state, in the aggregation of humans, in the republic, in the *res publica,* which ought to mean the public convenience (despite the slime of bureaucracy, and the execrable taste of the populace in selecting its rulers)? It has.

And this function is *not* the coercing or emotionally persuading, or bullying or suppressing people into the acceptance of any one set or any six sets of opinions as opposed to any other one set or half-dozen sets of opinions.

It has to do with the clarity and vigour of "any and every" thought and opinion. It has to do with maintaining the very cleanliness of the tools, the health of the very matter of thought itself. Save in the rare and limited instances of invention in the plastic arts, or in mathematics, the individual cannot think and communicate his thought, the governor and legislator cannot act effectively or frame his laws, without words, and the solidity and validity of these words is in the care of the damned and despised *litterati.* When their work goes rotten—by that I do not mean when they express indecorous thoughts—but when their very medium, the very essence of their work, the application of word to thing goes rotten, i.e. becomes slushy and inexact, or excessive or bloated, the whole machinery of social and of individual thought and order goes to pot. This is a lesson of history, and a lesson not yet half learned.

The great writers need no debunking.

The pap is not in them, and doesn't need to be squeezed out. They do not lend themselves to imperial and sentimental exploitations. A civilization was founded on Homer, civilization not a mere bloated empire. The Macedonian domination rose and grew after the sophists. It also subsided.

It is not only a question of rhetoric, of loose expression, but also of the loose use of individual words. What the renaissance gained in direct examination of natural phenomena, it in part lost in losing the feel and desire for exact descriptive terms. I mean that the medieval mind had little but words to deal with, and it was more careful in its definitions and verbiage. It did not define a gun in terms that would just as well define an explosion, nor explosions in terms that would define triggers.

Misquoting Confucius, one might say: It does not matter whether the author desire the good of the race or acts merely from personal vanity. The thing is mechanical in action. In proportion as his work is exact, i.e., true to human consciouness and to the nature of man, as it is exact in formulation of desire, so is it durable and so is it "useful"; I mean it maintains the precision and clarity of thought, not merely for the benefit of a few dilettantes and "lovers of literature," but maintains the health of thought outside literary circles and in non-literary existence, in general individual and communal life.

Or "*dans ce genre on n'émeut que par la clarté.*" One "moves" the reader only by clarity. In depicting the motions of the "human heart" the durability of the writing depends on the exactitude. It is the thing that is true and stays true that keeps fresh for the new reader.

With this general view in mind, and subsequent to the events already set forth in this narrative, I proposed (from the left bank of the Seine, and to an American publishing house), not the twelve-volume anthology, but a short guide to the subject. That was after a few years of "pause and reflection." The subject was pleasantly received and considered with amity, but the house finally decided that it would pay neither them to print nor me to write the book, because we "weren't in the text-book ring." For the thing would have been a text-book, its circulation would have depended on educators, and educators have been defined as "men with no intellectual interests."

Hence, after a lapse of four years, this essay, dedicated to Mr Glenn Frank, and other starters of ideal universities, though not with any great hope that it will rouse them.

Part Two: Or what may be an introduction to method

It is as important for the purpose of thought to keep language efficient as it is in surgery to keep tetanus bacilli out of one's bandages.

In introducing a person to literature one would do well to have him examine works where language is efficiently used; to devise a system for getting directly and expeditiously at such works, despite the smokescreens erected by half-knowing and half-thinking critics. To get at them, despite the mass of dead matter that these people have heaped up and conserved round about them in the proportion: one barrel of sawdust to each half-bunch of grapes.

Great literature is simply language charged with meaning to the utmost possible degree.

When we set about examining it we find that this charging has been done by several clearly definable sorts of people, and by a periphery of less determinate sorts.

(*a*) *The inventors*, discoverers of a particular process or of more than one mode and process. Sometimes these people are known, or discoverable; for example, we know, with reasonable certitude, that Arnaut Daniel introduced certain methods of rhyming, and we know that certain finenesses of perception appeared first in such a troubadour or in G. Cavalcanti. We do not know, and are not likely to know, anything definite about the precursors of Homer.

(*b*) *The masters.* This is a very small class, and there are very few real ones. The term is properly applied to inventors who, apart from their own inventions, are able to assimilate and co-ordinate a large number of preceding inventions. I mean to say they either start with a core of their own and accumulate adjuncts, or they digest a vast mass of subject-matter, apply a number of known modes of expression, and succeed in pervading the whole with some special quality or some special character of their own, and bring the whole to a state of homogeneous fullness.

(*c*) *The diluters,* these who follow either the inventors or the "great writers," and who produce something of lower intensity, some flabbier variant, some diffuseness or tumidity in the wake of the valid.

(*d*) (And this class produces the great bulk of all writing.) The men who do more or less good work in the more or less good style of a period. Of these the delightful anthologies, the song books, are full, and choice among them is the matter of taste, for you prefer Wyatt to Donne, Donne to Herrick, Drummond of Hawthornden to Browne, in response to some purely personal sympathy, these people add but some slight personal flavor, some minor variant of a mode, without affecting the main course of the story.

At their faintest "*Ils n'existent pas, leur ambiance leur confert une existence.*" They do not exist: their ambience confers existence upon them. When they are most prolific they produce dubious cases like Virgil and Petrarch, who probably pass, among the less exigent, for colossi.

(*e*) *Belles Lettres.* Longus, Prévost, Benjamin Constant, who are not exactly "great masters," who can hardly be said to have originated a form, but who have nevertheless brought some mode to a very high development.

(*f*) And there is a supplementary or sixth class of writers, the starters of crazes, the Ossianic McPhersons, the Gongoras[2] whose wave of fashion flows over writing for a few centuries or a few decades, and then subsides, leaving things as they were.

It will be seen that the first two classes are the more sharply defined: that the difficulty of classification for particular lesser authors increases as one descends the list, save for the last class, which is again fairly clear.

The point is, that if a man knows the facts about the first two categories, he can evaluate almost any unfamiliar book at first sight. I mean he can form a just estimate of its worth, and see how and where it belongs in this schema.

As to crazes, the number of possible diseases in literature is perhaps not very great, the same afflictions crop up in widely separated countries without any previous communication. The good physician will recognize a known malady, even if the manifestation be superficially different.

The fact that six different critics will each have a different view concerning what author belongs in which of the categories here given, does not in the least invalidate the categories. When a man knows the facts about the first two categories, the reading of work in the other categories will not greatly change his opinion about those in the first two.

---

2. One should perhaps apologize, or express a doubt as to the origin of Gongorism, or redefine it or start blaming it on some other Spaniard.

LANGUAGE

Obviously this knowledge cannot be acquired without knowledge of various tongues. The same discoveries have served a number of races. If a man has not time to learn different languages he can at least, and with very little delay, be told what the discoveries were. If he wish to be a good critic he will have to look for himself.

Bad critics have prolonged the use of demoded terminology, usually a terminology originally invented to describe what had been done before 300 B.C., and to describe it in a rather exterior fashion. Writers of second order have often tried to produce works to fit some category or term not yet occupied in their own local literature. If we chuck out the classifications which apply to the outer shape of the work, or to its occasion, and if we look at what actually happens, in, let us say, poetry, we will find that the language is charged or energized in various manners.

That is to say, there are three "kinds of poetry":

MELOPŒIA, wherein the words are charged, over and above their plain meaning, with some musical property, which directs the bearing or trend of that meaning.

PHANOPŒIA, which is a casting of images upon the visual imagination.

LOGOPŒIA, "the dance of the intellect among words," that is to say, it employs words not only for their direct meaning, but it takes count in a special way of habits of usage, of the context we *expect* to find with the word, its usual concomitants, of its known acceptances, and of ironical play. It holds the aesthetic content which is peculiarly the domain of verbal manifestation, and cannot possibly be contained in plastic or in music. It is the latest come, and perhaps most tricky and undependable mode.

The *melopœia* can be appreciated by a foreigner with a sensitive ear, even though he be ignorant of the language in which the poem is written. It is practically impossible to transfer or translate it from one language to another, save perhaps by divine accident, and for half a line at a time.

Phanopœia can, on the other hand, be translated almost, or wholly, intact. When it is good enough, it is practically impossible for the translator to destroy it save by very crass bungling, and the neglect of perfectly well-known and formulative rules.

Logopœia does not translate; though the attitude of mind it expresses may pass through a paraphrase. Or one might say, you can *not* translate it "locally," but having determined the original author's state of mind, you may or may not be able to find a derivative or an equivalent.

PROSE

The language of prose is much less highly charged, that is perhaps the only availing distinction between prose and poesy. Prose permits greater factual presentation, explicitness, but a much greater amount of language is needed. During the last century or century and a half, prose has, perhaps for the first time, perhaps for the second or third time, arisen to challenge the poetic pre-eminence. That is to say, *Cœur Simple*, by Flaubert, is probably more important than Théophile Gautier's *Carmen*, etc.

The total charge in certain nineteenth-century prose works possibly surpasses the total charge found in individual poems of that period; but that merely indicates that the author has been able to get his effect cumulatively, by a greater heaping up of factual data; imagined fact, if you will, but nevertheless expressed in factual manner.

By using several hundred pages of prose, Flaubert, by force of architectonics, manages to attain an intensity comparable to that in Villon's *Heaulmière,* or his prayer for his mother. This does not invalidate my dissociation of the two terms: poetry, prose.

In *phanopœia* we find the greatest drive toward utter precision of word; this art exists almost exclusively by it.

In *melopœia* we find a contrary current, a force tending often to lull, or to distract the reader from the exact sense of the language. It is poetry on the borders of music and music is perhaps the bridge between consciousness and the unthinking sentient or even insentient universe.

All writing is built up of these three elements, plus "architectonics" or "the form of the whole," and to know anything about the relative efficiency of various works one must have some knowledge of the maximum already attained by various authors, irrespective of where and when.[3]

. . . I don't in the least admit or imply that any man in our time can think with only one language. He may be able to invent a new carburetor, or even work effectively in a biological laboratory, but he probably won't even try to do the latter without study of at least one foreign tongue. Modern science has always been multilingual. A good scientist simply would not be bothered to limit himself to one language and be held up for news of discoveries. The writer or reader who is content with such ignorance simply admits that his particular mind is of less importance than his kidneys or his automobile. The French who know no English are as fragmentary as the Americans who know no French. One simply leaves half of one's thought untouched in their company.

Different languages—I mean the actual vocabularies, the idioms—have worked out certain mechanisms of communication and registration. No one language is complete. A master may be continually expanding his own tongue, rendering it fit to bear some charge hitherto borne only by some other alien tongue, but the process does not stop with any one man. While Proust is learning Henry James, preparatory to breaking through certain French paste-board partitions, the whole American speech is churning and chugging, and every other tongue doing likewise.

To be "possible" in mentally active company the American has to learn French, the Frenchman has to learn English or American. The Italian has for some time learned French. The man who does not know the Italian of the duocento and trecento has in him a painful lacuna, not necessarily painful to himself, but there are simply certain things he don't know, and can't; it is as if he were blind to some part of the spectrum. Because of the determined attempt of the patriotic Latinists of Italy in the renaissance to "conquer" Greek by putting every Greek author effectively into Latin it is now possible to get a good deal of Greek through Latin cribs. The disuse of Latin cribs in Greek study, beginning, I suppose, about 1820, has caused no end of damage to the general distribution of "classic culture."

Another point miscomprehended by people who are clumsy at languages is that one does not need to learn a whole language in order to understand some one

3. Lacuna at this point to be corrected in criticism of Hindemith's "Schwanendreher". E.P. Sept. 1938.

or some dozen poems. It is often enough to understand thoroughly the poem, and every one of the few dozen or few hundred words that compose it.

This is what we start to do as small children when we memorize some lyric of Goethe or Heine. Incidentally, this process leaves us for life with a measuring rod (*a*) for a certain type of lyric, (*b*) for the German language, so that, however bored we may be by the *Grundriss von Groeber,* we never wholly forget the feel of the language.

VACCINE

Do I suggest a remedy? I do. I suggest several remedies. I suggest that we throw out all critics who use vague general terms. Not merely those who use vague terms because they are too ignorant to have a meaning; but the critics who use vague terms to *conceal* their meaning, and all critics who use terms so vaguely that the reader can think he agrees with them or assents to their statements when he doesn't.

The first credential we should demand of a critic is *his* ideograph of the good; of what he considers valid writing, and indeed of all his general terms. Then we know where he is. He cannot simply stay in London writing of French pictures that his readers have not seen. He must begin by stating that such and such *particular* works seem to him "good," "best," "indifferent," "valid," "non-valid." I suggest a definite curriculum in place of the present *émiettements,* of breaking the subject up into crumbs quickly dryable. A curriculum for instructors, for obstreperous students who wish to annoy dull instructors, for men who haven't had time for systematized college courses. Call it the minimum basis for a sound and liberal education in letters (with French and English "aids" in parenthesis).

CONFUCIUS—In full (there being no complete and intelligent English version, one would have either to learn Chinese or make use of the French version by Pauthier).

HOMER—in full (Latin cribs, Hugues Salel in French, no satisfactory English, though Chapman can be used as reference).

OVID—And the Latin "personal" poets, Catullus and Propertius. (Golding's *Metamorphoses,* Marlowe's *Amores.* There is no useful English version of Catullus.)

A PROVENÇAL SONG BOOK—With cross reference to Minnesingers, and to Bion, perhaps thirty poems in all.

DANTE—"And his circle"; that is to say Dante, and thirty poems by his contemporaries, mostly by Guido Cavalcanti.

VILLON—

PARENTHETICALLY—Some other medieval matter might be added, and some general outline of history of thought through the Renaissance.

VOLTAIRE—That is to say, some incursion into his critical writings, not into his attempts at fiction and drama, and some dip into his contemporaries (prose).

STENDHAL—(At least a book and half).

FLAUBERT (omitting *Salambô* and the *Tentation*)—And the Goncourts.

GAUTIER, CORBIÈRE, RIMBAUD.

This would not overburden the three- or four-year student. After this inoculation he could be "with safety exposed" to modernity or anything else in literature. I mean he wouldn't lose his head or ascribe ridiculous values to works of secondary intensity. He would have axes of reference and, would I think, find them dependable.

For the purposes of general education we could omit all study of monistic totemism and voodoo for at least fifty years and study of Shakespeare for thirty on the ground that acquaintance with these subjects is already very widely diffused, and that one absorbs quite enough knowledge of them from boring circumjacent conversation.

This list does not, obviously, contain the names of every author who has ever written a good poem or a good octave or sestet. It is the result of twenty-seven years' thought on the subject and a résumé of conclusions. That may be a reason for giving it some consideration. It is not a reason for accepting it as a finality. Swallowed whole it is useless. For practical class work the instructor should try, and incite his students to try, to pry out some element that I have included and to substitute for it something more valid. The intelligent lay reader will instinctively try to do this for himself.

I merely insist that *without* this minimum the critic has almost no chance of sound judgment. Judgment will gain one more chance of soundness if he can be persuaded to consider Fenollosa's essay or some other, and to me unknown but equally effective, elucidation of the Chinese written character.

Before I die I hope to see at least a few of the best Chinese works printed bilingually, in the form that Mori and Ariga prepared certain texts for Fenollosa, a "crib," the picture of each letter accompanied by a full explanation.

For practical contact with all past poetry that was actually *sung* in its own day I suggest that each dozen universities combine in employing a couple of singers who understand the meaning of words. Men like Yves Tinayre and Robert Maitland are available. A half-dozen hours spent in listening to the lyrics actually performed would give the student more knowledge of that sort of *melopœia* than a year's work in philology. The Kennedy-Frasers have dug up music that fits the *Beowulf*. It was being used for heroic song in the Hebrides. There is other available music, plenty of it, from at least the time of Faidit (A.D. 1190).

I cannot repeat too often or too forcibly my caution against so-called critics who talk "all around the matter," and who do not define their terms, and who won't say frankly that certain authors are demnition bores. Make a man tell you *first* and specially what writers he thinks are good writers, after that you can listen to his explanation.

Naturally, certain professors who have invested all their intellectual capital, i.e., spent a lot of time on some perfectly dead period, don't like to admit they've been sold, and they haven't often the courage to cut a loss. There is no use in following them into the shadows.

1931

─── •─◄ ROBINSON JEFFERS ►─• ───
(1887–1962)

John Robinson Jeffers, the great poet of the American West Coast, was born in the suburbs of Pittsburgh, Pennsylvania. His father, William Hamilton Jeffers, was a professor of Old Testament biblical theology and a Presbyterian minister. A strict disciplinarian and serious intellectual, the elder Jeffers was a middle-aged widower when he met and courted Annie Tuttle, who was twenty-two years his junior. Robin was the first of their two sons. His father determined that his older son should be properly educated and gave him rigorous private lessons in Greek, Latin, and religion. In 1898 the family journeyed overseas where the young Jeffers was enrolled first in a German school in Leipzig, then the following year in a French school in Switzerland. By the time he was twelve, Jeffers was fluent in French, German, Greek, Latin, and English, but awkward among other children. Not surprisingly, the boy developed complex feelings toward his deeply loving but authoritarian father, whose image haunts the many tragic patriarchs who figure in Jeffers's later narrative poems.

Jeffers entered the University of Pittsburgh at fifteen and was awarded sophomore standing. When his father retired the next year, the family moved to Los Angeles. Jeffers transferred to Occidental College, from which he graduated in 1905 at seventeen. Entering graduate school at the University of Southern California, the precocious teenager eventually did graduate work at several universities in literature, medicine, and forestry, but soon realized that poetry was his calling. At USC, Jeffers met Una Call Kuster, a beautiful woman who was not only three years older than he, but married to a wealthy local attorney. Robin and Una fell irrevocably in love. After seven years of guilt-ridden romance with many renunciations, separations, reconciliations, and eventually a public scandal (reported in the *Los Angeles Times*), Una obtained a divorce on August 1, 1913. The next day she and Jeffers married.

By now Jeffers had dedicated himself fully to poetry. His first collection, *Flagons and Apples,* had appeared in 1912, but the restless young writer had already improved beyond this early volume of rhymed love lyrics. He and Una traveled north on a horse-drawn mail coach to the wild Big Sur region of coastal California, where the road ended. They rented a small cabin in the village of Carmel, which they recognized as their "inevitable place." Jeffers later remembered, "For the first time in my life I could see people living—amid magnificent unspoiled scenery—as they did in the Idyls or the Sagas or in Homer's Ithaca. . . . Here was a contemporary life that was also permanent life."

The twenty-seven-year-old poet knew that he had not yet written anything of enduring value. The death of both his father and his own newborn daughter in 1914 heightened his sense of mortality. After issuing a second collection, *Californians* (1916), Jeffers published nothing for eight years. He divided his time between writing and building a stone house for his family, which now included twin sons, on a promontory overlooking the Pacific. He carefully reconsidered his poetic aims and underwent a slow but radical transformation. He rejected rhyme and traditional meter, which inhibited him from telling a story flexibly in verse. He also rejected the obscurity of Modernist poetry. "It became clear to me," he wrote, "that poetry—if it were to survive at all—must reclaim some of the power and reality that it has so hastily surrendered to prose." He determined to write a timeless and truthful poetry purged of ephemeral things.

In 1924 Jeffers published *Tamar and Other Poems* with a small vanity press in New York. This volume announced the mature Jeffers in style, form, subject, and theme. The book even took the characteristic shape of most of his subsequent volumes—a long narrative poem followed by a group of shorter lyric and meditative poems. *Tamar* attracted no initial notice, but a year later it was suddenly taken up by several influential critics. Jeffers produced an expanded trade edition containing what would be his most famous narrative poem, "Roan Stallion." Both public and critical opinion was extraordinary. *Roan Stallion, Tamar and Other Poems* (1925) went into multiple reprintings. Praising his narrative energy, stylistic originality, and thematic profundity, critics compared him to Sophocles and Shakespeare.

Jeffers ignored his sudden celebrity and focused on his work. Over the next ten years he wrote the most remarkable, ambitious, and odd series of narrative poems in American literature. Published in eight major collections—*The Women at Point Sur* (1927), *Cawdor* (1928), *Dear Judas* (1929), *Descent to the Dead* (1931), *Thurso's Landing* (1932), *Give Your Heart to the Hawks* (1933), *Solstice* (1935), and *Such Counsels You Gave to Me* (1937)—these books appeared at the rate of about one per year and add up to almost one thousand pages of verse in all. Nearly every volume centers on a long narrative, usually set in or around Big Sur. Violent, sexual, philosophical, and subversive, these verse novels are difficult to describe. Their tragic stories of family rivalry and primal emotion usually move with determined pace to a bloody finale. In sheer narrative energy and visual scope they resemble movies—not real ones but imaginary cinema where high and low art collide. The poems reveal Jeffers's obsessions, as the suffocating burden of the past (often in the form of religious dogmatism, patriotic hypocrisy, or social convention) bears down to destroy human freedom. Alternately magnificent and hyperbolic, powerful and excessive, dramatic and overblown, they are unlike anything else in Modernist American poetry.

Almost immediately Jeffers's long narrative poems divided audiences. His explicit sexuality, violent plots, and overt anti-Christianity alienated conservative readers. Leftists were dismayed by his distrust of all political programs for human improvement. Meanwhile the New Critics perceived Jeffers's commitment to poetry of direct statement, expansive treatment, and linear narrative as a rejection of the compressed, indirect, and lyric, high Modernist mode they had all championed. He rarely found a place in academic anthologies, and his critical reception increasingly tended to be hostile.

The controversy over Jeffers's narratives unfortunately overshadowed his shorter works tucked in the back pages of each new book. These lyric meditations generally written in long rhythmic free verse lines marked a new kind of nature poem that tried to understand the physical world not from a human perspective but on its own terms. Humanity existed, he asserted, as an integral part of nature, not as its master. "Not man apart," was his phrase, which became a famous rallying cry among environmentalists and conservationists, who consider him a seminal figure in the movement to protect natural habitat, wilderness, and coastal land. Jeffers's nature poetry is emotionally direct, magnificently musical, and philosophically profound. His language is strong, concise, and timeless. His ideas are boldly expressed in memorable images. The poems unfold as clearly as prose without the indirection common in the work of overtly Modernist poets like Pound, Eliot, and Moore, who were his contemporaries.

By World War II Jeffers's critical reputation had collapsed and would not rise again until after his death. The depression and the war had made his cosmic fatalism and distrust of all political systems less palatable to intellectuals caught up in international events. To the disgust of many Americans, he opposed America's entry into World War II, warning that the conflict would turn the United States into an imperial power. Jeffers still commanded a large group of serious readers, and his books sold well, but the literary establishment dominated by New Critics on the right and Marxists on the left had both rejected him.

The poet's complete isolation from public literary life aggravated the situation. Hating big cities, Jeffers hardly stirred from Carmel. He would not teach or lecture. He scarcely answered his mail. Remote from the centers of literary power in London and New York, he seemed indifferent to the slow decline of his reputation. In 1945, however, the noted actress, Judith Anderson, asked the poet to translate and adapt Euripides' classical tragedy for the modern stage. When Jeffers's *Medea* opened on Broadway in 1947, it stunned audiences and critics with its power and intensity. *New York Times* critic Brook Atkinson called it "a landmark in the theater." *Medea* played to sold-out houses, a national touring company was soon formed, and productions were staged across Europe. As its frequent revivals demonstrate, it is one of the finest adaptations of classical drama in English.

Medea's success relieved Jeffers's financial worries, but the happiest days of his life were now behind him. After Una's slow death from cancer in 1950, Jeffers sank into a prolonged depression aggravated by heavy drinking. His eyesight failed. He continued writing but with less energy and little savor. Jeffers published only one book during the last fourteen years of his life—*Hungerfield and Other Poems* (1954). The title poem is a violent and nightmarish narrative that ends unexpectedly with an authorial interruption, Jeffers's heartbreaking invocation to his dead wife. A few days after his seventy-fifth birthday he died in his sleep at Tor House, the home he had built.

As Scottish poet George MacBeth has observed, Jeffers "is one of the few American poets of the twentieth century who can be approached in terms of his ideas rather than technique." His poetic technique was both strong and original, but once he had developed his style in the mid-1920s, he never significantly altered it. Unlike his Modernist contemporaries Wallace Stevens, Marianne Moore, and T. S. Eliot, Jeffers was not interested in poetry as an exploration of language's ability to describe its own processes. "Language itself," as Robert Hass commented, "is simply not one of Jeffers's subjects."

Jeffers's philosophy has frequently been called pessimistic. That term seems vague and misleading since the poet shares almost nothing in common with major philosophical pessimists, like Arthur Schopenhauer who believed the sensory world was illusory and human existence was in bondage to the evils of irrational desire. Jeffers, by contrast, asserts the supreme—and joyfully beautiful—reality of the physical world. Trained in the sciences, Jeffers took a coldly rational view of humanity's small place in the cosmos. He called his new philosophical stance "Inhumanism," a term that has been much misunderstood. It does not endorse cruelty or inhumanity in the common sense of the word. Jeffers's Inhumanism is a simple but radical realignment of moral values, which he described as "a shifting of emphasis and significance from man to not-man." Humanity was not, he felt, the measure of all things. It was merely one species, albeit the triumphantly dominant one, but it neither understood its place nor responsibility to the world. Overpopulation, urbanization, pollution, and industrialization would have dire consequences on the planet, Jeffers warned in his prophetic poems.

What saves Jeffers's poetry from unrelieved bitterness and nihilism is its joyful awe and, indeed, religious devotion to the natural world. Living on the edge of the Pacific, he drew wisdom, strength, and perspective from observing the forces of nature around him. In "Rock and Hawk" he offers the image of a falcon perched on a tall coastal rock as a symbol of the proper human values: "bright power, dark peace; / Fierce consciousness joined with final / Disinterestedness, / Life with calm death." That unusual combination of sensual delight and stoical resolve underlies much of Jeffers's best work. Magnificent, troubling, idiosyncratic, and uneven, Jeffers remains the great prophetic voice of American Modernism.

Jeffers published little formal criticism, but when the occasion arose to explain his literary beliefs, he expressed himself with force, poise, and clarity. A deeply philosophic man, grounded in both the classics and science, he took the long view of poetic enterprise. "Poetry is less bound by time and circumstances than the other arts," he asserted, believing that poetry did not depend on materials as much as human imagination. Disdainful of contemporary literary fashion, Jeffers used his criticism to argue that "Permanent things or things forever renewed, like the grass or human passion," were the proper materials for poetry. He understood and often appreciated Modernist works against which he framed his arguments, but he considered them mostly examples of ephemeral artistic vogues. His criticism, therefore, stands in complete contrast to that of his most influential contemporaries, Pound and Eliot. Jeffers's motto was not "make it new" but rather "make it last." His dream was to write work that still could be read with understanding after a thousand years.

POETRY, GONGORISM AND A THOUSAND YEARS

It used to be argued, and I think it is still accepted by many people, that poetry is a flower of racial childhood and must wither away as civilization advances. For civilization is based on reason and restraint, poetry on imagination and passion; poetry (they say) is dreams, and civilization the daylight that disperses them. This would be an interesting theory if it were true, but there is no truth in it. The greatest Greek poetry, after Homer, was written at the clear and rational summit of Greek civilization, by the Athenian tragic poets in the fifth century B.C.; and then, as civilization declined, Greek poetry declined. It had its revivals, in Sicily, in Alexandria, and these coincided with revivals of civilization. Latin poetry also, though less typical, because the Romans were not originators but cultivators, has a similar history. It flowered at the peak of Roman civilization, in the late republic and early empire, and declined with it.

These are but two examples out of many that could be cited, but they are enough to scuttle the supposed rule. They do not reverse it, for actually there is no rule at all; or at least none is discernible. Poetry is less bound by time and circumstance than any other of the arts; it does not need tangible materials; good poetry comes almost directly from a man's mind and senses and bloodstream, and no one can predict the man. It does not need a school nor an immediate tradition; and it does not need, though Whitman said so, 'great audiences too.' How much of an audience did Keats have in his lifetime?

The present is a time of high civilization rapidly declining; it is not a propitious period for any of the arts; men's minds are a little discouraged, and are too much occupied with meeting each day's distractions or catastrophe. Yet there is no final reason why great poetry should not be written by someone, even today. Whether its greatness would be recognized is another question, for greatness is strange, unexpected and sometimes repellent, but probably it would, in time.

What seems to me certain is that this hypothetical great poet would break sharply away from the directions that are fashionable in contemporary poetic literature. He would understand that Rimbaud was a young man of startling genius but not to be imitated; and that "The Waste Land," though one of the finest poems of this century and surely the most influential, marks the close of a literary dynasty, not the beginning. He would think of Gerard Hopkins as a talented eccentric, whose verse is so overloaded with self-conscious ornament and improbable emotion that it is hardly readable, except by enthusiasts, and certainly not a model to found one's work on, but a shrill note of warning.

Aside from these instances, and to put the matter more fundamentally, I believe that our man would turn away from the self-consciousness and naive learnedness, the undergraduate irony, unnatural metaphors, hiatuses and labored obscurity that are too prevalent in contemporary verse. His poetry would be natural and direct. He would have something new and important to say, and just for that reason he

Originally published in *New York Times Magazine* 18 Jan. 1948. Collected in *Poetry, Gongorism and a Thousand Years* (Los Angeles: Ward Ritchie Press, 1949) 3–11.

would wish to say it clearly. He would be seeking to express the spirit of his time (as well as all times), but it is not necessary, because an epoch is confused, that its poet should share its confusions.

On the contrary, detachment is necessary to understanding. I do not think that Shakespeare mixed Hamlet or Lear into his life, as Byron did Childe Harold; the greater poet saw his creatures objectively, all the way through, but also all the way around; and thus our supposed poet, being distinctly separate from his time, would be able to see it and to see around it. And I do not think he would give much attention to its merely superficial aspects, the neon lights and toothpaste advertising of this urban civilization, and the momentary popular imbecilities; these things change out of recognition, but great poetry is pointed at the future. Its author, whether consciously or not, intends to be understood a thousand years from now; therefore he chooses the more permanent aspects of things, and subjects that will remain valid. And therefore he would distrust the fashionable poetic dialect of his time; but the more so if it is studiously quaint and difficult; for if a poem has to be explained and diagrammed even for contemporary readers, what will the future make of it?

There was a seventeenth-century Spanish poet named Góngora, a man of remarkable talents, but he invented a strange poetic idiom, a jargon of dislocated constructions and far-fetched metaphors, self-conscious singularity, studious obscurity. It is now only grotesque, but for its moment it was admired in the best circles, and it stimulated many imitators. Then fashion changed, Gongorism was named and ridiculed, and its poet is now remembered because his name was given to one of the diseases of literature.

Euphuism in England had a similar vogue and a similar catastrophe. It seems to me that the more extreme tendencies of modernist verse—and shall I say also of painting and sculpture?—are diseases of like nature, later forms of Gongorism; doctrinaire corruptions of instinct. It is not generally a failure of execution but a collapse of taste—of critical and creative instinct—that brings an art to eclipse. The error in the artist, which perhaps was only momentary and experimental, is echoed with approval by his admirers and a shoal of imitators, and gregariousness and snobbery complete the corruption. ("We understand this art, which the ordinary person can only gape at: we are distinguished people.") So the flock gathers sheep.

But poetry has never fallen so deep into this bog as painting and sculpture have, and I believe is now pulling out of it. Poetry must use language, which has a resistant vitality of its own; while sculpture (for instance) may sink to fiddling with bits of wire and tin trinkets.

On the other hand, let it be far from me to propose the average educated man as an arbiter of poetry or any other art. He has his own perversions of taste or complete nullity, duller than Gongorism. Usually he does not care for poetry—and no harm in that—but alas that he has a deep uneasy respect for it; he associates it vaguely with "ideals" and a better world, and may quote Longfellow on solemn occasions. This piety without instinct or judgment is a source of boredom, insincerity and false reputations; it is as bad as the delusions of the little groups; it is worse, because more constant.

I write verses myself, but I have no sympathy with the notion that the world owes a duty to poetry, or any other art. Poetry is not a civilizer, rather the reverse, for great poetry appeals to the most primitive instincts. It is not necessarily a moralizer;

it does not necessarily improve one's character; it does not even teach good manners. It is a beautiful work of nature, like an eagle or a high sunrise. You owe it no duty. If you like it, listen to it; if not, let it alone.

Lately I had occasion to read more attentively the *Medea* of Euripides, and considering the reverence that cultivated people feel toward Greek tragedy I was a little shocked by what I read. Tragedy has been regarded, ever since Aristotle, as a moral agent, a purifier of the mind and emotions. But the story of *Medea* is about a criminal adventurer and his gun-moll; it is no more moral than the story of Frankie and Johnny; only more ferocious. And so with the yet higher summits of Greek tragedy, the Agamemnon series and the *Oedipus Rex;* they all tell primitive horror-stories, and the conventional pious sentiments of the chorus are more than balanced by the bad temper and wickedness, or folly, of the principal characters. What makes them noble is the poetry; the poetry, and the beautiful shapes of the plays, and the extreme violence born of extreme passion.

That is to say, three times, the poetry—the poetry of words, the poetry of structure and the poetry of action. These are stories of disaster and death, and it is not in order to purge the mind of passions but because death and disaster are exciting. People love disaster, if it does not touch them too nearly—as we run to see a burning house or a motor crash—and also it gives occasion for passionate speech; it is a vehicle for the poetry.

To return now to the great poet whom we have imagined arising among us at this time. He would certainly avoid the specialists, the Góngorist groups, and he would hardly expect response from the average, the average educated person: then whom should he speak to? For poetry is not a monologue in a vacuum; it is written in solitude, but it needs to have some sort of audience in mind. Well: there has been a great poet in our time—must I say comparatively great?—an Irishman named Yeats, and he met this problem, but his luck solved it for him. The first half of his life belonged mostly to the specialists, the Celtic Twilight people, the Decadents, even the Góngorists; he was the best among them but not a great poet, and he resented it. He had will and ambition, while Dowson and the others dropped by the wayside.

Yeats went home to Ireland and sought in the theater his liberation from mediocrity; and he might possibly have found it there if he had been as good a playwright as he was a poet. For the theater—unless it is a very little one—cannot belong wholly to a group; it has to be filled if possible; and it does not inevitably belong to the average. When many people together see and hear the thing—if it is fierce enough, and the actors and author can make it beautiful—it cuts deep. It cuts through many layers. The average person may even forget his education and delight in it, though it is poetry.

But Yeats found in another way his immortality. He was not a first-rate playwright but he had an insuperable will; and when his Ireland changed he was ready. Suddenly, in that magic time when a country becomes a nation, it was Ireland's good fortune that there was a great poet in Ireland. Her unique need, and his will, had produced him.

But the great poet whom we have imagined would not expect all that luck. He might not have a fighting will, as Yeats did, to push on with time and abide its turnings; or his time might never come. If he should write a great poetic play he would probably never see it staged; for that is a matter of luck, and against the odds. And it is not likely that his country will ever feel the need of a great national poet, as Ireland did; or as Germany did in her stormy awakening, and produced Goethe. Yet our poet must feel (in his own mind I mean) the stimulation of some worthy audience. He will look, of course, to the future. "What do I care about the present?" Charles Lamb exclaimed, "I write for antiquity!"

But our man will reverse that. It may seem unlikely that he will have readers a thousand years from now, but it is not impossible, if he is really a great poet; and these are the audience whom he will habitually address. If the present time overhears him, and listens too—all the better. But let him not be distracted by the present; his business is with the future. This is not pleasantry; it is practical advice.

For thus his work will be sifted of what is transient and crumbling, the chaff of time and the stuff that requires footnotes. Permanent things, or things forever renewed, like the grass and human passions, are the material for poetry; and whoever speaks across the gap of a thousand years will understand that he has to speak of permanent things, and rather clearly too, or who would hear him?

"But," a young man cries, "what good will it do me to imagine myself remembered after death? If I am to have fame and an audience I want them now while I can feel them." It seems to me that the young man speaks in ignorance. To be peered at and interviewed, to be pursued by idlers and autograph hunters and inquiring admirers, would surely be a sad nuisance. And it is destructive too, if you take it seriously; it wastes your energy into self-consciousness; it destroys spontaneity and soils the springs of the mind. Whereas posthumous reputation could do you no harm at all, and is really the only kind worth considering.

1949

MARIANNE MOORE
(1887–1972)

Marianne Craig Moore was born in the Kirkwood, Missouri, home of her grandfather, John Riddle Warner, a Presbyterian minister, where her mother, Mary Warner Moore, retreated after her husband was institutionalized following a nervous breakdown. Moore and her older brother, Warner, never knew their father. After Mr. Moore was released from the sanitarium his wife never returned to him, preferring to raise the children on her own, despite the economic and social trials of such a choice. When Moore was seven, her grandfather died, and the family moved to a Pittsburgh suburb to reside with an uncle. Two years later they resettled in Carlisle, Pennsylvania, where Mrs. Moore taught English at the Metzger Institute, a preparatory school for girls that her daughter attended. These early hardships created a tight bond between the Moores that they solidified through their Presbyterian faith, an ethos of strict privacy, and a determination to bear difficulty with fortitude and equanimity. The family's fierce insularity and religious devotion provided Moore with the emotional and philosophical support that buttressed her career and motivated her ideas about art. Moore is a consummate Modernist, although her moral bent—such as her attacks on pretentious behavior and egotism, her advocacy of precision, endurance, and humility, and her insistence on hope in the face of despair—chafes against definitions of Modernism that consider experimental work incompatible with Christianity.

In 1905, Moore matriculated at Bryn Mawr College, where, denied admission to the English major, she majored in law, history, and politics and minored in biology. But Moore was undissuaded from pursuing her writing. She contributed poems to the college literary magazine, *Tipyn O'Bob,* and served on its editorial board. She also took a class in "Imitative Prose," in which students were required to model their own essays on the work of seventeenth-century prose stylists such as Thomas Browne and Francis Bacon. "I was really fond of all those sermons and the antique sentence structure," she later said. Her minor in biology also influenced her poetry. She later remarked that the habits of careful observation she had cultivated in her science courses helped foster the attentiveness to detail that characterizes her writing: "Precision, economy of statement, logic employed to ends that are disinterested, drawing and identifying, liberate—at least have some bearing on—the imagination."

After graduation in 1909 she returned to Carlisle, where she completed the business course at Carlisle Commercial College in 1910, taught stenography and typewriting at the Carlisle Indian School, and worked for women's suffrage. Meanwhile, she began to place poems in magazines such as the *Egoist, Poetry,* and *Others.* In 1916 she and her mother moved to Chatham, New Jersey. Moore made frequent trips into New York, solidifying her connections to avant-garde writers and artists. She also established friendships through correspondence, exchanging letters with H. D., whom she had known briefly at Bryn Mawr, and William Carlos Williams. In 1918 mother and daughter moved to New York, where Marianne worked half days at the Hudson Park Branch of the New York Public Library. Mrs. Moore staunchly supported her daughter's literary career, and in drafting her poems Moore found her mother's incisive criticism indispensable.

Moore's composition process was eclectic, for she often drew from the notebooks in which she meticulously recorded quotations from her diverse readings, letters she had received, lectures and sermons she had heard, and even conversations. In the poetry, Moore integrates her own words with material from the notebooks. From a paragraph-long quotation, she would lift a sentence or a phrase to splice into a poem, sometimes acknowledging her borrowings through quotation marks and citations, sometimes not. Moore stands, along with T. S. Eliot, Ezra Pound, and William Carlos Williams, as one of the poets who first developed the Modernist method of juxtaposing fragments from other sources against her own words to create a collage effect. As early as 1907—well before Eliot's quotation-laden poem, *The Waste Land,* appeared—Moore was weaving quotations into her poems. She also became notorious for her revisions, changing poems after she had published them, usually through cuts rather than additions.

In 1919 Moore began corresponding with Pound, and in 1921 with Eliot, both of whom contacted her about publishing her poems. Their initial inquiries led to supportive friendships that were sustained primarily through letters. But her first book was made possible by H. D. and her companion Bryher, who gathered many of the poems that Moore had contributed to journals in *Poems* (1921). The book's appearance came as a surprise to Moore, who felt that she was not yet ready for a collection.

In 1924 she released a longer book, *Observations,* whose chronological arrangement included fifty-two of the sixty-five poems she had published since 1915, some of them in revised versions. The book was distinctive not only because of the poetry—particularly the remarkable longer poems, "Marriage" and "An Octopus"—but also because of its extensive notes and index. Her choice to write about uncommon subjects, such as a steamroller or an elephant, and her eschewal of traditional forms in favor of free verse or the intricate patterns of syllabic verse, underscored her call, in "Poetry," for poets to be "'literalists of the imagination.'" Her work paid precise attention to literal details, but framed them in unexpected, highly subjective ways. The book won the prestigious Dial Award in 1924 and solidified Moore's reputation as a key Modernist poet.

The award also led to Moore's appointment as editor of the *Dial,* a leading arts and letters magazine. During her tenure, lasting from 1925 to 1929, she became a powerful literary arbiter. In addition to editing, Moore dedicated herself to writing prose for the magazine: book reviews and a total of forty-two editorial columns in which she reflected not only on art and literature, but on an idiosyncratic array of subjects. Moore developed a prose style that shared many attributes with her poetry: complex syntax, frequent quotations, and electric shifts of thought that seem to launch the argument in unrelated directions but whose relevance Moore establishes as the essay develops. She continued to write prose after the *Dial* folded in 1929, publishing her essays and reviews in both mainstream and literary journals.

Although her work for the *Dial* gave her considerable power in the literary world and a venue for her essays, it left her little energy to draft poems. From 1925 until 1932 she did not publish any poetry. In 1930 Moore and her mother moved from Manhattan to Brooklyn, where distance from the literary scene enabled her to write new poems, including such important works as "The Steeple-Jack," "The Jerboa," and "The Plumet Basilisk," many of which intensified her focus on animals as analogues for virtues, such as perseverance and discipline. She positioned the group of new poems at the end of *Selected Poems* (1935). More new work appeared in *The Pangolin and Other Verse* (1936) and *What Are Years* (1941).

Despite her self-imposed distance from the literary life of Manhattan, Moore visited the city often and kept up her relationships with other writers through extensive correspondence. She served as a mentor to younger women writers, particularly Elizabeth Bishop, whom she met in 1934.

The vast devastation of World War II challenged Moore to change some of her ideas about poetry, and her poems became less dense and more direct than they had been before. (After the death of her mother in 1947, Moore shifted her style, becoming even more pronounced.) Nevertheless, her *Collected Poems* (1951) won the Pulitzer Prize, the National Book Award, and the Bollingen Prize—the three most significant awards in American poetry—and Moore followed the book with four new volumes of poetry before she published *Complete Poems* (1967) on her eightieth birthday.

Moore's later poetry often featured accessible subjects such as baseball, and she became a minor celebrity, the subject of articles in popular magazines as diverse as *Life, Vogue,* and *Sports Illustrated.* She appeared as a guest on *The Tonight Show* and became friends with athletes such as Cassius Clay (Muhammad Ali). But the media tended to feature Moore as a grandmotherly eccentric rather than as a major poet, and her achievements as a Modernist innovator were ignored in favor of her interests in baseball, fashion, and zoos. Nevertheless, at the time of her death from a stroke in 1972, readers of poetry and especially other poets considered her work indispensable and counted her among the most important American poets of the twentieth century.

In her essay "Idiosyncrasy and Technique," Moore explores possibilities for affirmation in a jaded time. In this piece we can see not only Moore the poet and demanding reviewer, but also Moore the cultural critic. As always, her prose is refreshing for the aptness and openness of her observations.

-◦━━◀▶━◦-

IDIOSYNCRASY AND TECHNIQUE

I. TECHNIQUE

In his inaugural lecture as Professor of Poetry at Oxford,[1] Mr. Auden said, "There is only one thing that all poetry must do; it must praise all it can for being as for happening." He also said, "Every poem is rooted in imaginative awe." These statements answer, or imply an answer, to the question: Why does one write?

I was startled, indeed horrified, when a writing class in which I have an interest was asked, "Is it for money or for fame?" as though it must be one or the other—and writing were not for some a felicity, if not a species of intellectual self-preservation. Gorgeously remunerated as I am for being here, it would seem both hypocritical and inappropriate to feign that a love of letters renders money irrelevant. Still, may I say, and with emphasis, that I do not write for money or fame. To earn a living is needful, but it can be done in routine ways. One writes because one has a burning desire to objectify what it is indispensable to one's happiness to express; a statement which is not at variance with the fact that Sir Walter Scott, driven by a fanatically sensitive conscience, shortened his life writing to pay what was not a personal debt. And Anthony Trollope, while writing to earn a living, at the same time was writing what he very much loved to write.

Amplifying the impression which Bernard Shaw, as music critic, himself gives of his "veracity, catholicity, and pugnacity,"[2] Hesketh Pearson says of him as stage manager of his plays, "No author could be more modest than Shaw. He did not regard his text as sacrosanct. He laughed over his own lines as if they were jokes by somebody else and never could repeat them accurately. Once, when an actor apologized for misquoting a passage, he remarked, 'What you said is better than what I wrote. If you can always misquote so well, keep on misquoting—but remember to give the right cues!' "[3] Writing was resilience. Resilience was an adventure. Is it part of the adventure to revise what one wrote? Professor Ewing has suggested that something be said about this. My own revisions are usually the result of impatience with unkempt diction and lapses in logic; together with an awareness that for most defects, to delete is the instantaneous cure.

The rhythms of the King James Version of the Bible stand forever as writing, although certain emendations as to meaning seem obligatory. The King James Epistle of Paul to the Philippians, 3:20, reads: "For our conversation is in heaven"; the Revised Standard Version reads: "We are a heavenly body"; each a mistranslation, according to Dr. Alvin E. Magary, who feels that Dr. Moffat got it right: " 'We are a colony of heaven'—a Roman outpost as it were, in which people

---

Originally delivered as one of the inaugural lectures of the Ewing Lectures of the University of California, Los Angeles, October 3 and 5, 1956. Published as *Idiosyncrasy and Technique: Two Lectures* (Berkeley and Los Angeles: University of California Press, 1958). The notes are Miss Moore's.

1. *Making, Knowing and Judging: An Inaugural Lecture by W. H. Auden Delivered before the University of Oxford on 11 June 1956* (Oxford at the Clarendon Press).
2. Michael Tippett, "An Irish Basset-Horn," *The Listener*, July 26, 1956.
3. Hesketh Pearson, "Bernard Shaw as Producer," *The Listener*, August 16, 1956.

conformed their lives to the life of Rome—an interpretation which makes sense as applied to Christianity"; Dr. Magary also emphasizes that the beatitude, blessed are the meek, should have no connotation of subservience, since if rendered more strictly, the word would be, not the meek, but the "begging."

The revisions by Henry James of his novels, are evidently in part the result of an insistent desire to do justice to first intention. Reverting to pronouncements on Milton and Goethe made previously, T. S. Eliot seems to feel that after-judgment can not merely be taken for granted, and when accepting the Goethe Prize in 1954 he said, "As one's reading is extended [one begins] to develop that critical ability, that power of self-criticism without which the poet will do not more than repeat himself . . ."; then further on: "To understand what Wisdom is, is to be wise one-self: and I have only the degree of understanding that can be obtained by a man who knows that he is not wise, yet has some faith that he is wiser than he was twenty years ago. I say twenty years ago, because I am under the distressing neces-sity of quoting a sentence I printed in 1939. It is this:

> Of Goethe perhaps it is truer to say that he dabbled in both philosophy and poetry and made no great success at either; his true role was that of a man of the world and a sage, a la Rochefoucauld, a La Bruyère, a Vauvenargues."

Mr. Eliot says he ". . . never re-read the passage in which this sentence is buried [and had] discovered it not so long ago in Mr. Michael Hamburger's introduction to his edition and translation of the text of Holderlin's poems." He then goes on to say of Goethe, "It may be that there are areas of wisdom that he did not pene-trate: but I am more interested in trying to understand the wisdom he possessed than to define its limitations. When a man is a good deal wiser than oneself, one does not complain that he is no wiser than he is."[4]

Since writing is not only an art but a trade embodying principles attested by experience, we would do well not to forget that it is an expedient for making one's self understood and that what is said should at least have the air of having meant something to the person who wrote it—as is the case with Gertrude Stein and James Joyce. Stewart Sherman one time devised a piece of jargon which he offered as indistinguishable from work by Gertrude Stein, which gave itself away at once as lacking any private air of interest. If I may venture to say again what I have al-ready said when obscurity was deplored, one should be as clear as one's natural reticence allows one to be. Laurence Binyon, reflecting on the state of letters after completing his Dante, said: "How indulgent we are to infirmity of structure . . ."[5] and structural infirmity truly has, under surrealism, become a kind of horticul-tural verbal blight threatening firmness to the core; a situation met long ago in *The Classic Anthology Defined by Confucius:*

> Enjoy the good yet sink not in excess.
> True scholar stands by his steadfastness.[6]
> . . . .
> Lamb-skin for suavity, trimmed and ornate,
> But a good soldier who will get things straight.[7]

4. "Discourse in Praise of Wisdom," reentitled "Goethe as the Sage."
5. *The Dalhousie Review,* January 1943.
6. Translated by Ezra Pound (Cambridge: Harvard University Press, 1954), p. 55.
7. *Ibid.,* p. 80.

In attaining this noble firmness, one must have clarity, and clarity depends on precision; not that intentional ambiguity cannot be an art. Reinhold Niebuhr is not famed as easy reading, but is at times a study in precision as when he says, "The self does not realize itself most fully when self-realization is its conscious aim"; and of conscience says, "We will define it provisionally at least as capacity to view itself and judge obligation in contrast with inclination."[8] It is not "the purpose [but] the function of roots to absorb water," Dr. Edmund Sinnott notes in his book *The Biology of the Spirit,* in which he discusses the self-regulating properties of protoplasm—digressing, with a shade of outrage, to deplore untidiness in the use of terms. One is corrected when referring to certain African tribes for saying they worship the devil; they propitiate the devil; and if precise, one weeds text of adjective, adverbs, and unnecessary punctuation. As an instance of such concision, we have Mr. Francis Watson's account of Edward Arnold, "the traveler, linguist, and semi-mystic, with whom Matthew Arnold did not like to be confused."[9] Informing us that Edwin Arnold had been married three times and that two of his wives had died—a lack-luster kind of statement which few of us perhaps would avoid— Mr. Watson says, "after being twice bereaved, he found a third wife from Japan, a land whose culture he extolled in articles. . . ." Paramount as a rule for any kind of writing—scientific, commercial, informal, prose or verse—we dare not be dull. Finding Akira Kurosawa's film *The Magnificent Seven* too reiterative, Bosley Crowther says that "the director shows so many shots of horses' feet tromping in the mud that we wonder if those horses have heads."[1]

In his "Advice to a Young Critic" (Golding Bright),[2] Bernard Shaw says, "Never strike an attitude, national, moral, or critical"—an axiom he did not observe too fanatically if judged by the telegram he is said to have sent to an actress with a leading part in one of his plays: ". . . wonderful, marvelous, superb . . ." to which the actress replied, "Undeserving such praise"; and he: "I meant the play"; and she: "So did I."

I have a mania for straight writing—however circuitous I may be in what I myself say of plants, animals, or places; and although one may reverse the order of words for emphasis, it should not be to rescue a rhyme. There are exceptions, of course, as when Mr. Oliver Warner, speaking of Captain Cook, the explorer, in commending the remarkable drawings made by members of the Captain's staff, says: "None of Cook's artists worked to preconceived notions. They drew what they saw and wonderful it was."[3] To say "and it was wonderful" would have been very flat. We have literature, William Archer said, when we impart distinctiveness to ordinary talk and make it still seem ordinary.

Like dullness, implausibility obscures the point; so, familiar though we are with "Fenimore Cooper's Literary Offenses," by Mark Twain,[4] allow me to quote a line or two. "It is a rule of literary art in the domain of fiction," Mark Twain says, "that always the reader shall be able to tell the corpses from the others. But this detail often has been overlooked in the *Deerslayer* tale. [Cooper] bends 'a sapling' to the form of an arch over [a] narrow passage, and conceals six Indians

8. *The Self and the Dramas of History* (New York: Scribner, 1955).
9. "Edwin Arnold and 'The Light of Asia,'" *The Listener,* June 14, 1956.
1. *The New York Times,* November 20, 1957.
2. *The Listener,* June 14, 1956.
3. "In Honor of James Cook," *The Listener,* June 14, 1956.
4. *The Shock of Recognition,* edited by Edmund Wilson (New York: Doubleday, 1943).

in its foliage." Then, ". . . one of his acute Indian experts, Chingachgook (pronounced Chicago, I think) has lost the trail of a person he is tracking . . . turned a running stream out of its course, and there, in the slush of its old bed, were that person's moccasin-tracks. . . ." Even the laws of nature take a vacation when Cooper is practicing "the delicate art of the forest."

What has been said pertains to technique (*teknikos* from the Greek, akin to *tekto:* to produce or bring forth—as art, especially the useful arts). And, indeed if technique is of no interest to a writer, I doubt that the writer is an artist.

What do I mean by straight writing, I have been asked. I mean, in part, writing that is not mannered, overconscious, or at war with common sense, as when a reviewer of *The Evolution of Cambridge Publishing,* by S. C. Roberts, refers to "a demure account of Cambridge's flirtation with the *Encyclopaedia Britannica.*"[5] At the risk of seeming to find every virtue in certain authors and these authors in a certain few books or critiques, let me contrast with the unreal manner, W. D. Howells' *My Mark Twain* and a similar uninfected retrospect by the Duke of Windsor. "Of all the literary men I have known," Howells says of Mark Twain, "he was the most unliterary in his make and manner. . . . His style was what we know, for good or for bad, but his manner, if I may difference the two, was as entirely his own as if no one had ever written before. [He] despised the avoidance of repetitions out of fear of tautology. If a word served his turn better than a substitute, he would use it as many times on a page as he chose. . . . [There] never was a more biddable man in things you could show him a reason for. . . . If you wanted a thing changed, very good, he changed it; if you suggested that a word or a sentence or a paragraph had better be struck out, very good, he struck it out. His proof sheets came back each with a veritable 'mush of concession,' as Emerson says." "He was always reading some vital book . . . which gave him life at first hand," Howells continues. "It is in vain that I try to give a notion of the intensity with which he compassed the whole world. . . ."

The other instance of straight writing to which I referred is "My Garden," by the Duke of Windsor.[6] Prosperity and royalty are always under suspicion. "Of course they had help," people say. "Someone must have written it for them"; as they said of the shepherd made judge, in the fable of the shepherd and the King, ". . . *he* is given the credit; we did the work; he has amassed riches; we are poor."[7] So let me say, I have in the following narrative an impression of individuality, conviction, and verbal selectiveness.

"I think my deep enjoyment of gardening must be latent," the Duke begins. "At least it was not inherited. . . . The gardens at Sandringham and Windsor . . . made a fine show in summertime [a word with flavor, for me], but people did not really live with them. A garden is a mood, as Rousseau said, and my mood was one of intimacy, not splendor." Of his present gardening at The Mill, not far from Paris, he says, ". . . French gardens can be remarkably beautiful things. They look like continuations of the Savonnerie of Aubusson carpets in the great chateaus rolled outside the windows onto the lawns, perfectly patterned and mathematically precise. . . . I

5. Unsigned review in *The Times Literary Supplement,* London, March 2, 1956.
6. *Life,* July 16, 1956.
7. *The Fables of La Fontaine,* translated by Marianne Moore (New York: Viking, 1954), Book Ten, IX.

wanted an English type of garden, which means green grass and seemingly casual arrangement of flowers, and here I had the perfect framework." Commenting on one of the color photographs which supplement the account, he says, "The main entrance to the property has an old covered gateway with ancient oak doors and a cobbled drive which leads to the main building. There is a big sundial above the front door, put there when The Mill was restored about 1732. In the foreground is Trooper, one of our four Pugs." Technically an oversight, perhaps—the f-o-r-e ground and f-o-u-r pugs in close proximity—this clash lends authenticity, has the charm of not too conscious writing. Unmistakably all along, the article embodies a zeal for the subject, a deep affection for flowers as seen in the complaint, "The mildest stone-mason turns scourge when it comes to plant life." The piece smiles, whereas saturninity is a bad omen. "We do not praise God by dispraising man."[8]

II. IDIOSYNCRASY

In considering technique, I tried to say that writing can be affirmative and that we must, as Dr. Nathan Scott says, "reject the attitude of philosophic distrust." The writer should have "a sense of upthrusting vitality and self-discovery"[9] without thinking about the impression made, except as one needs to make oneself understood.

We are suffering from too much sarcasm, I feel. Any touch of unfeigned gusto in our smart press is accompanied by an arch word implying, "Now to me, of course, this is a bit asinine." Denigration, indeed, is to me so disaffecting that when I was asked to write something for the Columbia Chapter of Phi Beta Kappa Class Day exercises, I felt that I should not let my sense of incapacity as an orator hinder me from saying what I feel about the mildew of disrespect and leave appreciation to Mr. Auden, to salute "literary marines landing in little magazines." I then realized that what I was so urgent to emphasize is reduced in the First Psalm to a sentence: Blessed is the man who does not sit in the seat of the scoffer.

Odd as it may seem that a few words of overwhelming urgency should be a mosaic of quotations, why paraphrase what for maximum impact should be quoted verbatim? I borrowed, at all events, Ambassador Conant's title *The Citadel of Learning*, taken for his book from Stalin: "[Facing us] stands the citadel of learning. This citadel we must capture at any price. This citadel must be taken by our youth, if they wish to be the builders of a new life, if they wish, in fact, to take the place of the old guard."[1]

Blessed is the man

who does not sit in the seat of the scoffer—
    the man who does not denigrate, depreciate, denunciate;
      who is not "characteristically intemperate,"
who does not "excuse, retreat, equivocate; and will be heard."

---

8. Dr. Alvin E. Magary.
9. Maxwell Geismar, *The Nation*, April 14, 1956.
1. As "freely translated" by Charles Poore, reviewing James B. Conant, *The Citadel of Learning* (New Haven: Yale University Press, 1956), in the *New York Times*, April 7, 1956.

(Ah, Giorgione! there are those who mongrelize
    and those who heighten anything they touch; although it may well be
        that if Giorgione's self-portrait were not said to be he,
it might not take my fancy. Blessed the geniuses who know

that egomania is not a duty.)
    "Diversity, controversy; tolerance"—in that "citadel
        of learning" we have a fort that ought to armor us well.
Blessed is the man who "takes the risk of a decision"—asks

himself the question: "Would it solve the problem?
    Is it right as I see it? Is it in the best interests of all?"
        Alas. Ulysses' companions are now political—
living self-indulgently until the moral sense is drowned,

having lost all power of comparison,
    thinking license emancipates one, "slaves whom they themselves have bound."
        Brazen authors, downright soiled and downright spoiled as if sound
and exceptional, are the old quasi-modish counterfeit,

mitin-proofing conscience against character.
    Affronted by "private lives and public shame," blessed is the author
        who favors what the supercilious do not favor—
who will not comply. Blessed, the unaccommodating man.

Blessed the man whose faith is different
    from possessiveness—of a kind not framed by "things which do appear"—
        who will not visualize defeat, too intent to cower;
whose illumined eye has seen the shaft that gilds the sultan's tower.

    I had written these lines about denigration as treason, and was assembling advice for some students of verse, when I found that Rolfe Humphries, in his little treatise entitled "Writing the Lyric,"[2] has thrown light on the use of consonants. "Take the letter *s*," he says, "one of the most insidious sounds in the language, one which will creep in, in a sibilant reptilian fashion like the original serpent in the garden, and if you are not careful, not only drive you out of Paradise, but hiss you off the stage; . . . see if you can write a quatrain without using it at all." Pondering my "Blessed is the man who does not sit in the seat of the scoffer," I could only say that another's expertise might save one considerable awkwardness. Initiate John Barry came to my rescue by citing the *Aeneid* (II,8):

Et iam nox umida caelo
praecipitat suadentque cadentia sidera somnos.[3]

Convinced that denigration is baneful, one readily sanctions the attack prompted by affection. In fact nothing is more entertaining than the fraternal accolade in reverse; as when *The London News Chronicle* of November 16, 1954, published a cartoon, and lines entitled "Winniehaha,"[4] concerning Mr. Churchill—Prime Minister then—

---

2. In *Writers on Writing*, edited by Herschel Brickell (New York: Doubleday, 1949).
3. And now the night calls dew down from heaven
   And the falling stars urge us to sleep.
4. Anonymous. Reprinted in the *New York Times*, November 17, 1954.

after a cousin of his, Captain Lionel Leslie, had referred to the drop of Indian blood inherited by Sir Winston through his grandmother, Clara Jerome. The complimentary cast of the sally—a parody of Longfellow's *Hiawatha*—which was written before Mr. Churchill had been knighted, when the date of his retirement was a subject of speculation, is apparent from even a line or two:

> In the center of the village
> In the wigwam of the wise ones,
> Where the head men of the nation
> Come to talk in solemn council,
> Squats the old chief, Winniehaha,
> Also known as Sitting Bulldog; . . .
> Some there are with minds that wander
> From the purpose of the powwow;
> Minds that wonder will he give us
> Just an inkling, to be candid,
> Of the date of his retirement?
> Not that we would wish to rush him,
> Wish to rush old Winniehaha,
> Rush our splendid Sitting Bulldog
> From the headship of the head men
> In the center of the village,
> In the wigwam of the wise ones.
> Still, it's just a bit unsettling
> Not to know when Winniehaha
> Will give place to handsome Pinstripe.
> Will he tell us? Will he tell us?

In connection with personality, it is a curiosity of literature how often what one says of another seems descriptive of one's self. Would-be statesmen who spike their utterances with malice should bear this in mind and take fright as they drive home the moral of The Lion, The Wolf, and the Fox: "Slander flies home faster than rumor of good one has done."[5] In any case, Sir Winston Churchill's pronouncement on Alfred the Great does seem appropriate to himself—his own defeats, triumphs, and hardihood: "This sublime power to rise above the whole force of circumstances, to remain unbiased by the extremes of victory or defeat, to greet returning fortune with a cool eye, to have faith in men after repeated betrayals, raises Alfred far above the turmoil of barbaric wars to his pinnacle of deathless glory."[6]

Walter de la Mare found "prose worthy of the name of literature . . . tinged with that erratic and unique factor, the personal . . ." reminding one of the statement by Mr. F. O. Matthiessen, in his study of Sarah Orne Jewett, that "style means that the author has fused his material and his technique with the distinctive quality of his personality . . ." and of the word "idiolect" used by Professor Harry Levin as meaning "the language of a speaker or writer who has an inflection of his own." In saying there is no substitute for content, one is partly saying there is no substitute for individuality—that which is peculiar to the person (the Greek *idioma*). One also

---

5. *The Fables of La Fontaine*, Book Eight, III.
6. *A History of the English-Speaking Peoples*, Vol. I: *The Birth of Britain* (New York: Dodd, Mead, 1956).

recalls the remark by Henry James: "a thing's being one's own will double the use of it." Discoveries in art, certainly, are personal before they are general.

Goya—in *The Taste of Our Times* series,[7] reviewed by Pierre Gassier somewhat as follows—should afford us creative impetus. After surviving a lethal threat, severe illness at Cadiz in 1792, Goya was left with his right side paralyzed, with dizzy spells, a buzzing in his head, and partial blindness. He recovered, only to find himself irremediably deaf. On returning to Madrid, he began work at once, painted eleven pictures for the Academy of San Fernando, and sent them with a letter to the director, Don Berbardo Iriarte. "In order to occupy an imagination mortified by the contemplation of my sufferings," he said, "and recover, partially at all events, the expenses incurred by illness, I fell to painting a set of pictures in which I have given observation a place usually denied it in works made to order, in which little scope is left for fancy and invention." Fancy and invention—not made to order—perfectly describe the work; the *Burial of the Sardine,* say: a careening throng in which one can identify a bear's mask and paws, a black monster wearing a horned hood, a huge turquoise quadracorne, a goblin mouth on a sepia fish-tailed banner, and twin dancers in filmy gowns with pink satin bows in their hair. Pieter Bruegel, the Elder, an observer as careful and as populous as Goya, "crossed the Alps and traveled the length of Italy, returning in 1555 to paint as though Michaelangelo had never existed," so powerful was predilective intention.[8] In a television interview after receiving the National Book Award for *Ten North Frederick,* John O'Hara was asked if he might not have to find, as a background for fiction, something different from small-town life in Pennsylvania, to which he replied, "There is in one room in one day of one man's life, material for a lifetime." The artist does not—as we sometimes hear—"seek fresh sources of inspiration." A subject to which he is susceptible entices him to it; as we see in the epics of Marko Marulić (1450–1524), the fifth centenary of whose birth Yugoslavia has celebrated, in honor of his Latin epic *Judita* (1501), enhanced by woodcuts such as *The Muster at Dubrovnic:* trumpeters, men at arms in an elephant-castle; dog; king, queen, and attendants. The New York Yugoslav Information Center says, "What is important is that in following the classics, Marulić did not transplant . . . mechanically . . . but depended on his own poetic abilities," his novelty consisting in "comparisons taken from his own field of experience, in language abounding in speech forms of the people." An author, that is to say, is a fashioner of words, stamps them with his own personality, and wears the raiment he has made, in his own way.

Psychoanalysis can do some harm "taking things to pieces that it cannot put together again," as Mr. Whit Burnett said in a discourse entitled "Secrets of Creativeness." It has also been of true service, sharpening our faculties and combating complacence. Mr. Burnett drew attention to the biography of Dr. Freud by Ernest Jones, and to what is said there of genius as being not a quality but qualitative—a combination of attributes which differs with the person—three of which are honesty, a sense of the really significant, and the power of concentration.

Curiosity seems to me connected with this sense of significance. Thoreau, you may recall, demurred when commended for originality and said that it was curiosity: "I am curiosity from top to toe." I think I detect curiosity in the work of

7. "Essay on Prose," *The National and English Review* (in three sections, concluded in March 1955), quoted by *Arts* (New York).
8. Fritz Grossmann, *The Paintings of Bruegel* (New York: Phaidon Press, 1955).

Sybille Bedford—in her novel *A Legacy*—in the statement, ". . . no one in the house was supposed to handle *used* [banknotes]. Everybody was paid straight off the press. The problem of change was not envisaged"; sententiousness in the writing, being offset by the unstereotyped juxtaposing of a word or two such as querulous and placid. Grandma Merz, for instance, "was a short bundle of a woman swaddled in stuffs and folds . . . stuck with brooches of rather gray diamonds. Her face was a round, large, indeterminate expanse . . . with features that escaped attention and an expression that was at once querulous and placid."[9] In Marguerite Yourcenar's "Author's Note" to her *Memoirs of Hadrian*[1]—a study which does "border on the domain of fiction and sometimes of poetry," as has been said— one sees what concentration editorially can be. And Paul Delarue's "Sources and Commentary" appended to the *Borzoi Book of French Folk Tales*[2] are similarly impressive—besides affording an exciting knowledge of variants. In "The White Dove" (the story of Bluebeard, abridged by Perrault), the ninth victim's pretexts for delay become specific—in this early version—"to put on my petticoat, my wedding-gown, my cap, my bouquet." And we learn that "The Ass's Skin," enshrined for us by La Fontaine in "The Power of the Fable,"[3] is the "Story of Goldilocks," and of Madame d'Aulnoy's "Beauty and the Beast" (1698). The presentment here of obscure minutiae, demonstrating that tales of all nations have a common fabric, makes the most artful of detective stories seem tame.

Creative secrets, are they secrets? Impassioned interest in life, that burns its bridges behind it and will not contemplate defeat, is one, I would say. Discouragement is a form of temptation; but paranoia is not optimism. In an essay entitled "Solitude" (the theme chosen by the *Figaro* for an essay contest), Maxime Bennebon, a boy of seventeen, visualizes "Michelangelo's *Moses*, head in hands, the attitude of the child who prays with eyes closed; of the pianist—his back to the audience; they must be alone that they may offer what is most treasurable, themselves."

The master secret may be steadfastness, that of Nehemiah, Artaxerxes' cupbearer, as it was of the three youths in the fiery furnace, who would not bow down to the image which the king had set up. "Why is thy countenance sad, seeing that thou are not sick?" the King asked. Nehemiah requested that he be allowed to rebuild the wall of Jerusalem and the King granted his request; gave him leave of absence and a letter to the keeper of the forest that he might have timber for the gates of the palace—subject to sarcasm while building, such as Sanballet's, "If a fox go up, he shall break down their wall." Summoned four times to a colloquy, Nehemiah sent word: "I am doing a great work and I cannot come down." Then when warned that he would be slain, he said, "Should such a man as I flee?" "So the wall was finished."[4] A result which is sensational is implemented by what to the craftsman was private and unsensational. Tyrone Guthrie, in connection with the theater, made a statement which sums up what I have been trying to say about idiosyncrasy and technique: "It is one of the paradoxes of art that a work can only be universal if it is rooted in a part of its creator which is most privately and particularly himself."[5]

9. Sybille Bedford, *A Legacy* (New York: Simon and Schuster, 1957).
1. Translated from the French by Grace Frick (New York: Farrar, Straus and Young, 1954).
2. Translated by Austin E. Fife (New York: Knopf, 1956).
3. *The Fables of La Fontaine*, Book Eight, IV: "The moment The Ass's Skin commences, Away with appearances; I am enraptured, really am."
4. Nehemiah 2, 4, and 6.
5. *The New York Times Magazine*, November 27, 1955.

Thomas Mann, fending off eulogy, rendered a service when he said, "Praise will never subdue skepticism." We fail in some degree—and know that we do, if we are competent; but can prevail; and the following attributes, applied by a London journal to Victor Gollancz, the author and publisher, I adopt as a prescription: we can in the end prevail, if our attachment to art is sufficiently deep; "unpriggish, subtle, perceptive, and consuming."[6]

1958

---

6. *The Observer*, March 11, 1956.

T. S. ELIOT
(1888–1965)

Thomas Stearns Eliot was born the seventh child of Henry Ware Eliot and Charlotte Champe Stearns Eliot in St. Louis, Missouri, where his father was a prominent executive in the Hydraulic Press Brick Company. His grandfather, the Reverend William Greenleaf Eliot, had settled in St. Louis in 1834, eventually founding Washington University. A poet and biographer, Charlotte Eliot was highly influential in the development of her son's literary sensibilities. The family summered in Maine and Massachusetts, and at seventeen Eliot went east to Milton Academy. He entered Harvard in 1906, where his distant cousin, Charles William Eliot, was then president of the university. After taking his degree in 1909, Eliot began graduate studies in philosophy at Harvard. By then he had encountered his teacher Irving Babbitt's dislike of Romanticism, and also, in 1908, he read Arthur Symons's highly influential study of late nineteenth-century French poetry, *The Symbolist Movement in Literature*—a book that profoundly affected his own aesthetic. He had written poetry since childhood with his mother's approval, but now the work took new directions. He wrote his first masterpiece, "The Love Song of J. Alfred Prufrock," while still at Harvard in 1910.

That same year, having earned his master's degree, Eliot went to the Sorbonne in Paris. There he heard the lectures of philosopher Henri Bergson on personality. Upon returning to Harvard, Eliot began his dissertation on the philosopher F. H. Bradley, author of *Appearance and Reality*. He was also studying modern poetry and learning Sanskrit. Although Eliot's attitude toward religion was skeptical at this point, he objected to the way the Harvard Philosophy Department distanced itself from religious studies. Eliot was already a serious student of comparative religions. He was also taking dancing lessons to compensate for his intense shyness with women. After a year's assistantship at Harvard, Eliot obtained a fellowship to travel and study in Europe. He intended to go to Germany, but the outbreak of World War I forced him instead to take up studies at Oxford.

At the time, the London literary scene was full of vitality and ferment. Ford Madox Ford was editing and writing; Yeats held forth in his *salon,* where he was visited by young poets like Ezra Pound and Robert Frost. In September 1914, Eliot met Pound in London. Pound, who had already been at the forefront of the London poetry scene for several years, quickly saw that Eliot had "modernized himself *on his own.*" By early 1915, Eliot doubted that he wanted an academic career in philosophy. Work on his dissertation, *Knowledge and Experience in the Philosophy of F. H. Bradley,* had been completed, but increasingly Eliot thought of himself as a poet and man of letters. The dissertation concerned knowledge as a "relational" phenomenon, the difficulty of communication between people, the desire to comprehend an absolute and the problem of doing so in a context of skepticism. These ideas were foundational for his future poetry and criticism.

Everything in Eliot's life came to a climax in the spring of 1915: the war, which kept him in England and eventually killed his friend Jean Verdenal, his parents' desire that he pursue an academic career, the cauldron of literary London, and even his relations with women. Although he had been in love with a young American, Emily Hale, he suddenly married an Englishwoman, Vivien Haigh-Wood, whom he hardly knew. Eliot had decided against America and his parents' wishes, and his precipitous marriage seemed partly an effort to affirm his choice.

That same month, "The Love Song of J. Alfred Prufrock" appeared in *Poetry* in Chicago; it was easily the strongest and most indelible poem in the issue, but also the strangest. A kind of interior monologue, suggestive of dream journeys and multiple anxieties, its allusiveness, apparent disconnection, and defiance of easy interpretation were utterly new. The first issue of the journal *BLAST* contained Eliot's "Preludes" and "Rhapsody on a Windy Night." His poetic career was launched.

Vivien was a vivacious, talented woman, but already so beset with nervous disorders that friends would soon refer to her as an "invalid." To support her, Eliot tried teaching at various schools, then in 1917 took a job as a clerk in the Colonial and Foreign Department at Lloyds Bank. At the same time, he was working several hours a night on book reviews, essays, and poems. *Prufrock and Other Observations* appeared in 1917, *Poems* two years later. Both Eliot and Pound had begun to feel that contemporary *vers libre* was enervated and experimented with writing sharply ironic poems in rhymed quatrains. Again the work was densely allusive and violently disjunctive, requiring both real erudition and careful attention on the part of readers. In 1919 Eliot's father died without having seen his son since before the war, and Eliot now had to bear some responsibility for his mother as well, even while he kept up his productive literary life. He published his first book of criticism, *The Sacred Wood,* in 1920. Three essays stand out in that collection. In one, "The Perfect Critic," he concludes that "the critic and the creative artist should frequently be the same person." In another, "Hamlet and His Problems," Eliot coined the term "objective correlative":

The only way of expressing emotion in the form of art is by finding an "objective correlative"; in other words, a set of objects, a situation, a chain of events which shall be the formula of that *particular* emotion.

Finally, in "Tradition and the Individual Talent," he developed a theory of impersonal poetry not unlike Keats's image of the poet as chameleon. Eliot would later refine or disavow this doctrine of impersonality, but its influence on the next two generations of poets cannot be overstated, and to some degree it lies at the heart of what would come to be known as the New Criticism.

For Eliot, however, this literary self-denial may have arisen from his increasingly traumatic personal life. His marriage to Vivien was troubled by her poor health and his uncompromising fastidiousness. To meet expenses, he worked himself into a state of exhaustion. He spent six days a week at Lloyds while also reviewing books and composing in fragments his disturbing poem *The Waste Land*—a poem that expresses his vision of a complete breakdown in human communications and sexuality. Eliot suffered his own breakdown in 1921 and was advised to take a holiday, which he began at Margate and continued in Lausanne, Switzerland, with a course of psychiatric treatment. There he quickly wrote the final section of his poem and sought the opinion of Pound, who had moved to Paris after the war. Pound's editing of *The Waste Land* is legendary. As he wrote to Eliot in December, "The thing now runs from April . . . to shantih without break. That is 19 pages, and let us say the longest poem in the English langwidge. Don't try to bust all records by prolonging it three pages further." With typical humor Pound concluded, "Complimenti, you bitch. I am wracked by the seven jealousies. . . ."

The Waste Land was published in 1922, the same year as Joyce's *Ulysses*. Eliot's poem was notable not only for its difficulty and allusiveness (or "mythic method")—two qualities he had identified in Joyce—but also for its extraordinary compression. Critics differed on whether it was a collage of distinct voices or a kind of disturbed dramatic monologue. In either case, the poem eventually engendered as much critical commentary as any modern work of art. Eliot himself seemed almost embarrassed by the scholarly attention paid *The Waste Land* and is later reported to have said, "To me it was only the relief of a personal and wholly insignificant grouse against life; it is just a piece of rhythmical grumbling." In 1922 Eliot had also begun to edit the *Criterion*, an important journal, and in 1925 he left banking to join the publishing firm of Faber and Faber, where he worked for the rest of his life. Between his poetry, his criticism, and his editing he had become one of the most significant and powerful literary figures in the world.

During the 1920s, Eliot experienced a growing religious faith, and in 1927 he received baptism in the Anglican Church, although he kept his conversion private for a year. In 1927 he also became a British subject. One can trace these developments in poems such as "The Hollow Men" (1925), "Journey of the Magi" (1928), and "Ash-Wednesday" (1930), and also in his essays collected in *For Lancelot Andrewes* (1928), where he openly proclaimed himself "classical in literature, royalist in politics, and Anglo-Catholic in religion."

In 1932 Eliot separated from his wife, who was soon hospitalized for mental illness. The scrupulously religious Eliot never divorced her and remained celibate until after her death in 1947. He collected more essays in *The Use of Poetry and the Use of Criticism* (1933). In 1935 he saw his first major play, *Murder in the Cathedral,* produced. Eliot was a pioneer of modern poetic drama, and four other plays would follow, including *The Family Reunion* (1939) and *The Cocktail Party* (1950). During World War II Eliot wrote a series of religious meditations in a quasi-musical form based on the structure of the classical string quartet. Each of the four resulting poems, *East Coker* (1940), *Burnt Norton* (1941), *The Dry Salvages* (1941), and *Little Gidding* (1942), was named after a place with deep personal significance to the author. After being published as separate chapbooks, they were collected as *Four Quartets* (1944) and constitute Eliot's last major poetic work. In these probing Christian poems the author examines intersections of the secular and sacred worlds and meditates on the relation between time and eternity. He is also concerned with personal failures and whether art can or will prove redemptive in the context of sin. Eliot sees religious questing as "exploration" that will not end in the explorer's lifetime. There would be other books, but Eliot's major work was finished by the end of World War II. In 1948 he won the Nobel Prize, and thereafter he became more and more the literary eminence.

Eliot's prose from the mid-1930s was sometimes disturbing in its shift from literary criticism to conservative cultural criticism. The lectures he published in *After Strange Gods* (1934) contained several anti-Semitic remarks that created controversy among critics and readers. The controversy led Eliot to suppress the book, which has never been reprinted. Decades after his death, however, those passages along with several unflattering depictions of Jews in the early poetry led to a heated debate about the extent of Eliot's anti-Semitism. Some critics have also objected to the obsession with authority that characterizes *The Idea of a Christian Society* (1940) and *Notes Toward a Definition of Culture* (1949).

Eliot was long sustained by his work, but toward the end of his life he was granted some personal happiness. In 1957 he married his secretary, Valerie Fletcher, who would later publish a posthumous edition of *The Waste Land: A Facsimile and Transcript of the Original Drafts Including the Annotations of Ezra Pound* (1971), and Eliot's letters. She would also see the popular success that had eluded him when his collection of light verse, *Old Possum's Book of Practical Cats* (1939), provided the lyrics for what became the longest running musical in history, Andrew Lloyd Weber's *Cats*.

As a poet Eliot was famous for the difficulty of his poetry, a position that made him uneasy as time wore on. But Eliot had equal impact as a literary critic. Although his reputation has been seriously and repeatedly challenged in recent years, he remains the most influential American poet-critic of the twentieth century. He left behind certain phrases and formulations that have proved extremely helpful in critical discussion—about the impersonality of art, the nature of verse form, the uses of allusion, and the structure of verse drama. He helped formulate a canon of literature that would reign for two or more generations, including the metaphysical poets like Donne, but also Dante, Dryden, Yeats, Tennyson, and Kipling. Perhaps most importantly, his criticism was written in lucid prose that could be understood by anyone with an interest in literature.

Of the two essays collected below, "Reflections on *Vers Libre*" (1917) surveys what was already the dominant formal trend of twentieth-century poetry—the wholesale abandonment of metrical verse—and warns poets that free verse may not be so easy as it seems. Eliot defines free verse, or *vers libre* in the French, mostly by what it lacks, but he finds that a "ghost of meter" still pulses in some examples of it. Eliot's celebrated essay, "Tradition and the Individual Talent" from *The Sacred Wood* (1920), is frequently in-voked but often misunderstood. This short essay offers a radical revision of the concept of literary tradition, which Eliot presents not as a fixed collection of literary masterpieces but as a dynamic and unstable arrangement transformed by every major new work.

◆━━◆━━◆

REFLECTIONS ON VERS LIBRE

Ceux qui possèdent leur vers libre y tiennent:
on n'abandonne que le vers libre.
DUHAMEL ET VILDRAC

A lady, renowned in her small circle for the accuracy of her stop-press information of literature, complains to me of a growing pococurantism. "Since the Russians came in I can read nothing else. I have finished Dostoevski, and I do not know what to do." I suggested that the great Russian was an admirer of Dickens, and that she also might find that author readable. "But Dickens is a sentimentalist; Dostoevski is a realist." I reflected on the amours of Sonia and Rashkolnikov, but forbore to press the point, and I proposed *It Is Never too Late to Mend*. "But one cannot read the Victorians at all!" While I was extracting the virtues of the proposition that Dostoevski is a Christian, while Charles Reade is merely pious, she added that she could not longer read any verse but *vers libre*.

It is assumed that *vers libre* exists. It is assumed that *vers libre* is a school; that it consists of certain theories; that its group or groups of theorists will either revolutionize or demoralize poetry if their attack upon the iambic pentameter meets with any success. *Vers libre* does not exist, and it is time that this preposterous fiction followed the *élan vital** and the eighty thousand Russians into oblivion.

When a theory of art passes it is usually found that a groat's worth of art has been bought with a million of advertisement. The theory which sold the wares may be quite false, or it may be confused and incapable of elucidation, or it may never have existed. A mythical revolution will have taken place and produced a few works of art which perhaps would be even better if still less of the revolutionary theories clung to them. In modern society such revolutions are almost inevitable. An artist, happens upon a method, perhaps quite unreflectingly, which is new in the sense that it is essentially different from that of the second-rate people about him, and different in everything but essentials from that of any of his great predecessors. The novelty meets with neglect; neglect provokes attack; and attack demands a theory. In an ideal state of society one might imagine the good New growing naturally out of the good Old, without the need for polemic and theory; this would be a society with a living tradition. In a sluggish society, as actual societies are, tradition is ever lapsing into superstition, and the violent stimulus of novelty is required. This is bad for the artist and his school, who may become circumscribed by their theory and narrowed by their polemic; but the artist can always console himself for his errors in his old age by considering that if he had not fought nothing would have been accomplished.

Originally published in *New Statesman* 8 (3 Mar. 1917): 518–19. Collected in *Selected Prose* (London: Penguin, 1953).
**élan vital:* life force

Vers libre has not even the excuse of a polemic; it is a battle-cry of freedom, and there is no freedom in art. And as the so-called *vers libre* which is good is anything but "free", it can better be defended under some other label. Particular types of *vers libre* may be supported on the choice of content, or on the method of handling the content. I am aware that many writers of *vers libre* have introduced such innovations, and that the novelty of their choice and manipulation of material is confused—if not in their own minds, in the minds of many of their readers—with the novelty of the form. But I am not here concerned with imagism, which is a theory about the use of material; I am only concerned with the theory of the verse-form in which imagism is cast. If *vers libre* is a genuine verse-form it will have a positive definition. And I can define it only in negatives: (1) absence of pattern, (2) absence of rhyme, (3) absence of meter.

The third of these qualities is easily disposed of. What sort of a line that would be which would not scan at all I cannot say. Even in the popular American magazines, whose verse columns are now largely given over to *vers libre*, the lines are usually explicable in terms of prosody. Any line can be divided into feet and accents. The simpler meters are a repetition of one combination, perhaps a long and a short, or a short and a long syllable, five times repeated. There is, however, no reason why, within the single line, there should be any repetition; why there should not be lines (as there are) divisible only into feet of different types. How can the grammatical exercise of scansion make a line of this sort more intelligible? Only by isolating elements which occur in other lines, and the sole purpose of doing this is the production of a similar effect elsewhere. But repetition of effect is a question of pattern.

Scansion tells us very little. It is probable that there is not much to be gained by an elaborate system of prosody, but the erudite complexities of Swinburnian meter. With Swinburne, once the trick is perceived and the scholarship appreciated, the effect is somewhat diminished. When the unexpectedness, due to the unfamiliarity of the meters to English ears, wears off and is understood, one ceases to look for what one does not find in Swinburne; the inexplicable line with the music which can never be recaptured in other words. Swinburne mastered his technique, which is a great deal, but he did not master it to the extent of being able to take liberties with it, which is everything. If anything promising for English poetry is hidden in the meters of Swinburne, it probably lies far beyond the point to which Swinburne has developed them. But the most interesting verse which has yet been written in our language has been done either by taking a very simple form, like the iambic pentameter, and constantly withdrawing from it, or taking no form at all, and constantly approximating to a very simple one. It is this contrast between fixity and flux, this unperceived evasion of monotony, which is the very life of verse.

I have in mind two passages of contemporary verse[1] which would be called *vers libre*. Both of them I quote because of their beauty:

Once, in finesse of fiddles found I ecstasy,
In the flash of gold heels on the hard pavement.
Now see I
That warmth's the very stuff of poesy.
Oh, God, make small
The old star-eaten blanket of the sky,
That I may fold it round me and in comfort lie.

---

1. The first is "The Embankment," by T. E. Hulme. The second is a fragment from Pound's "Near Perigord."

This is a complete poem. The other is part of a much longer poem:

> There shut up in his castle, Tairiran's,
> She who had nor ears nor tongue save in her hands,
> Gone—ah, gone—untouched, unreachable—
> She who could never live save through one person,
> She who could never speak save to one person,
> And all the rest of her a shifting change,
> A broken bundle of mirrors . . .

It is obvious that the charm of these lines could not be, without the constant suggestion and the skillful evasion of iambic pentameter.

At the beginning of the seventeenth century, and especially in the verse of John Webster, who was in some ways a more cunning technician than Shakespeare, one finds the same constant evasion and recognition of regularity. Webster is much freer than Shakespeare, and that his fault is not negligence is evidenced by the fact that it is often at moments of the highest intensity that his verse acquires this freedom. That there is also carelessness I do not deny, but the irregularity of carelessness can be at once detected from the irregularity of deliberation. (In *The White Devil* Brachiano dying, and Cornelia mad, deliberately rupture the bonds of pentameter.)

> I recover, like a spent taper, for a flash
> and instantly go out.
>
> Cover her face; mine eyes dazzle; she died young.
>
> You have cause to love me, I did enter you in my heart
> Before you would vouchsafe to call for the keys.
>
> This is a vain poetry: but I pray you tell me
> If there were proposed me, wisdom, riches, and beauty,
> In three several young men, which should I choose?

These are not lines of carelessness. The irregularity is further enhanced by the use of short lines and the breaking up of lines in dialogue, which alters the quantities. And there are many lines in the drama of this time which are spoilt by regular accentuation.

> I loved this woman in spite of my heart. *(The Changeling)*
> I would have these herbs grow up in his grave. *(The White Devil)*
> Whether the spirit of greatness or of woman . . . *(The Duchess of Malfi)*

The general charge of decadence cannot be preferred. Tourneur and Shirley, who I think will be conceded to have touched nearly the bottom of the decline of tragedy, are much more regular than Webster or Middleton. Tourneur will polish off a fair line of iambics even at the cost of amputating a preposition from its substantive, and in the *Atheist's Tragedy* he has a final "of" in two lines out of five together.

We may therefore formulate as follows: the ghost of some simple meter should lurk behind the arras in even the "freest" verse; to advance menacingly as we doze, and withdraw as we rouse. Or, freedom is only truly freedom when it appears against the background of an artificial limitation.

Not to have perceived the simple truth that *some* artificial limitation is necessary except in moments of the first intensity is, I believe, a capital error of even so distinguished a talent as that of Mr. E. L. Masters. The *Spoon River Anthology* is not material of the first intensity; it is reflective, not immediate; its author is a moralist, rather than an observer. His material is so near to the material of Crabbe that one wonders why he should have used a different form. Crabbe is, on the whole, the more intense of the two; he is keen, direct, and unsparing. His material is prosaic, not in the sense that it would have been better done in prose, but in the sense of requiring a simple and rather rigid verse-form and this Crabbe has given it. Mr. Masters requires a more rigid verse-form than either of the two contemporary poets quoted above, and his epitaphs suffer from the lack of it.

So much for meter. There is no escape from meter; there is only mastery. But while there obviously is escape from rhyme, the *vers librists* are by no means the first out of the cave.

> The boughs of the trees
> Are twisted
> By many bafflings;
> Twisted are
> The small-leafed boughs.
> But the shadow of them
> Is not the shadow of the mast head
> Nor of the torn sails.

> When the white dawn first
> Through the rough fir-planks
> Of my hut, by the chestnuts,
> Up at the valley-head,
> Came breaking, Goddess,
> I sprang up, I threw round me
> My dappled fawn-skin . . .

Except for the more human touch in the second of these extracts a hasty observer would hardly realize that the first is by a contemporary,[2] and the second by Matthew Arnold.

I do not minimize the services of modern poets in exploiting the possibilities of rhymeless verse. They prove the strength of a Movement, the utility of a Theory. What neither Blake nor Arnold could do alone is being done in our time. "Blank verse" is the only accepted rhymeless verse in English—the inevitable iambic pentameter. The English ear is (or was) more sensitive to the music of the verse and less dependent upon the recurrence of identical sounds in this meter than in any other. There is no campaign against rhyme. But it is possible that excessive devotion to rhyme has thickened the modern ear. The rejection of rhyme is not a leap at facility; on the contrary, it imposes a much severer strain upon the language. When the comforting echo of rhyme is removed, success or failure in the choice of words, in the sentence structure, in the order, is at once more apparent. Rhyme removed, the poet is at once held up to the standards of prose. Rhyme removed, much ethereal music leaps up from the word, music which has hitherto chirped unnoticed in the expanse of prose. Any rhyme forbidden, many Shagpats were unwigged.

And this liberation from rhyme might be as well a liberation *of* rhyme. Freed from its exacting task of supporting lame verse, it could be applied with greater

2. From H.D.'s "Hermes of the Ways."

effect where it is most needed. There are often passages in an unrhymed poem where rhyme is wanted for some special effect, for a sudden tightening-up, for a cumulative insistence, or for an abrupt change of mood. But formal rhymed verse will certainly not lose its place. We only need the coming of a Satirist—no man of genius is rarer—to prove that the heroic couplet has lost none of its edge since Dryden and Pope laid it down. As for the sonnet I am not so sure. But the decay of intricate formal patterns has nothing to do with the advent of *vers libre*. It had set in long before. Only in a closely-knit and homogeneous society, where many men are at work on the same problems, such a society as those which produced the Greek chorus, the Elizabethan lyric, and the Troubadour canzone, will the development of such forms ever be carried to perfection. And as for *vers libre,* we conclude that it is not defined by absence of pattern or absence of rhyme, for other verse is without these; that it is not defined by non-existence of meter, since even the *worst* verse can be scanned; and we conclude that the division between Conservative Verse and *vers libre* does not exist, for there is only good verse, bad verse, and chaos.

1917

TRADITION AND THE INDIVIDUAL TALENT

In English writing we seldom speak of tradition, though we occasionally apply its name in deploring its absence. We cannot refer to "the tradition" or to "a tradition"; at most, we employ the adjective in saying that the poetry of So-and-so is "traditional" or even "too traditional." Seldom, perhaps, does the word appear except in a phrase of censure. If otherwise, it is vaguely approbative, with the implication, as to the work approved, of some pleasing archaeological reconstruction. You can hardly make the word agreeable to English ears without this comfortable reference to the reassuring science of archaeology.

Certainly the word is not likely to appear in our appreciations of living or dead writers. Every nation, every race, has not only its own creative, but its own critical turn of mind; and is even more oblivious of the shortcomings and limitations of its critical habits than of those of its creative genius. We know, or think we know, from the enormous mass of critical writing that has appeared in the French language the critical method or habit of the French; we only conclude (we are such unconscious people) that the French are "more critical" than we, and sometimes even plume ourselves a little with the fact, as if the French were the less spontaneous. Perhaps they are; but we might remind ourselves that criticism is as inevitable as breathing, and that we should be none the worse for articulating what passes in our minds when we read a book and feel an emotion about it, for criticizing our own minds in their work of criticism. One of the facts that might come to light in this process is our tendency to insist, when we praise a poet, upon those aspects of his work in which he least resembles any one else. In these aspects or parts of his work we pretend to find what is individual, what is the peculiar essence of the man. We dwell with satisfaction upon the poet's difference from his predecessors, especially his immediate

From *The Sacred Wood* (London: Methuen, 1920).

predecessors; we endeavour to find something that can be isolated in order to be enjoyed. Whereas if we approach a poet without this prejudice we shall often find that not only the best, but the most individual parts of his work may be those in which the dead poets, his ancestors, assert their immortality most vigorously. And I do not mean the impressionable period of adolescence, but the period of full maturity.

Yet if the only form of tradition, of handing down, consisted in following the ways of the immediate generation before us in a blind or timid adherence to its successes, "tradition" should positively be discouraged. We have seen many such simple currents soon lost in the sand; and novelty is better than repetition. Tradition is a matter of much wider significance. It cannot be inherited, and if you want it you must obtain it by great labor. It involves, in the first place, the historical sense, which we may call nearly indispensable to any one who would continue to be a poet beyond his twenty-fifth year; and the historical sense involves a perception, not only of the pastness of the past, but of its presence; the historical sense compels a man to write not merely with his own generation in his bones, but with a feeling that the whole of the literature of Europe from Homer and within it the whole of the literature of his own country has a simultaneous existence and composes a simultaneous order. This historical sense, which is a sense of the timeless as well as of the temporal and of the timeless and of the temporal together, is what makes a writer traditional. And it is at the same time what makes a writer most acutely conscious of his place in time, of his own contemporaneity.

No poet, no artist of any art, has his complete meaning alone. His significance, his appreciation is the appreciation of his relation to the dead poets and artists. You cannot value him alone; you must set him, for contrast and comparison, among the dead. I mean this as a principle of aesthetic, not merely historical, criticism. The necessity that he shall conform, that he shall cohere, is not onesided; what happens when a new work of art is created is something that happens simultaneously to all the works of art which preceded it. The existing monuments form an ideal order among themselves, which is modified by the introduction of the new (the really new) work of art among them. The existing order is complete before the new work arrives; for order to persist after the supervention of novelty, the *whole* existing order must be, if ever so slightly, altered; and so the relations, proportions, values of each work of art toward the whole are readjusted; and this is conformity between the old and the new. Whoever has approved this idea of order, of the form of European, of English literature will not find it preposterous that the past should be altered by the present as much as the present is directed by the past. And the poet who is aware of this will be aware of great difficulties and responsibilities.

In a peculiar sense he will be aware also that he must inevitably be judged by the standards of the past. I say judged, not amputated, by them; not judged to be as good as, or worse or better than, the dead; and certainly not judged by the canons of dead critics. It is a judgment, a comparison, in which two things are measured by each other. To conform merely would be for the new work not really to conform at all; it would not be new, and would therefore not be a work of art. And we do not quite say that the new is more valuable because it fits in; but its fitting in is a test of its value—a test, it is true, which can only be slowly and cautiously applied, for we are none of us infallible judges of conformity. We say: it appears to conform, and is perhaps individual, or it appears individual, and may conform; but we are hardly likely to find that it is one and not the other.

To proceed to a more intelligible exposition of the relation of the poet to the past: he can neither take the past as a lump, an indiscriminate bolus, nor can he form himself wholly on one or two private admirations, nor can he form himself wholly upon one preferred period. The first course is inadmissible, the second is an important experience of youth, and the third is a pleasant and highly desirable supplement. The poet must be very conscious of the main current, which does not at all flow invariably through the most distinguished reputations. He must be quite aware of the obvious fact that art never improves, but that the material of art is never quite the same. He must be aware that the mind of Europe—the mind of his own country—a mind which he learns in time to be much more important than his own private mind—is a mind which changes, and that this change is a development which abandons nothing *en route*, which does not superannuate either Shakespeare, or Homer, or the rock drawing of the Magdalenian draughtsmen. That this development, refinement perhaps, complication certainly, is not, from the point of view of the artist, any improvement. Perhaps not even an improvement from the point of view of the psychologist or not to the extent which we imagine; perhaps only in the end based upon a complication in economics and machinery. But the difference between the present and the past is that the conscious present is an awareness of the past in a way and to an extent which the past's awareness of itself cannot show.

Some one said: "The dead writers are remote from us because we *know* so much more than they did." Precisely, and they are that which we know.

I am alive to a usual objection to what is clearly part of my program for the *métier* of poetry. The objection is that the doctrine requires a ridiculous amount of erudition (pedantry), a claim which can be rejected by appeal to the lives of poets in any pantheon. It will even be affirmed that much learning deadens or perverts poetic sensibility. While, however, we persist in believing that a poet ought to know as much as will not encroach upon his necessary receptivity and necessary laziness, it is not desirable to confine knowledge to whatever can be put into a useful shape for examinations, drawing-rooms, or the still more pretentious modes of publicity. Some can absorb knowledge, the more tardy must sweat for it. Shakespeare acquired more essential history from Plutarch than most men could from the whole British Museum. What is to be insisted upon is that the poet must develop or procure the consciousness of the past and that he should continue to develop this consciousness throughout his career.

What happens is a continual surrender of himself as he is at the moment to something which is more valuable. The progress of an artist is a continual self-sacrifice, a continual extinction of personality.

There remains to define this process of depersonalization and its relation to the sense of tradition. It is in this depersonalization that art may be said to approach the condition of science. I, therefore, invite you to consider, as a suggestive analogy, the action which takes place when a bit of finely filiated platinum is introduced into a chamber containing oxygen and sulphur dioxide.

II

Honest criticism and sensitive appreciation are directed not upon the poet but upon the poetry. If we attend to the confused cries of the newspaper critics and the *susurrus* of popular repetition that follows, we shall hear the names of poets in great numbers; if we seek not Blue-book knowledge but the enjoyment of poetry, and ask for a poem, we shall seldom find it. I have tried to point out the importance of the relation of the poem to other poems by other authors, and suggested the conception of poetry as a living whole of all the poetry that has ever been written. The other aspect of this Impersonal theory of poetry is the relation of the poem to its author. And I hinted, by an analogy, that the mind of the mature poet differs from that of the immature one not precisely in any valuation of "personality," not being necessarily more interesting, or having "more to say," but rather by being a more finely perfected medium in which special, or very varied, feelings are at liberty to enter into new combinations.

The analogy was that of the catalyst. When the two gases previously mentioned are mixed in the presence of a filament of platinum, they form sulphurous acid. This combination takes place only if the platinum is present; nevertheless the newly formed acid contains no trace of platinum, and the platinum itself is apparently unaffected; has remained inert, neutral, and unchanged. The mind of the poet is the shred of platinum. It may partly or exclusively operate upon the experience of the man himself; but, the more perfect the artist, the more completely separate in him will be the man who suffers and the mind which creates; the more perfectly will the mind digest and transmute the passions which are its material.

The experience, you will notice, the elements which enter the presence of the transforming catalyst, are of two kinds: emotions and feelings. The effect of a work of art upon the person who enjoys it is an experience different in kind from any experience not of art. It may be formed out of one emotion, or may be a combination of several; and various feelings, inhering for the writer in particular words or phrases or images, may be added to compose the final result. Or great poetry may be made without the direct use of any emotion whatever: composed out of feelings solely. Canto XV of the *Inferno* (Brunetto Latini) is a working up of the emotion evident in the situation; but the effect, though single as that of any work of art, is obtained by considerable complexity of detail. The last quatrain gives an image, a feeling attaching to an image, which "came," which did not develop simply out of what precedes, but which was probably in suspension in the poet's mind until the proper combination arrived for it to add itself to. The poet's mind is in fact a receptacle for seizing and storing up numberless feelings, phrases, images, which remain there until all the particles which can unite to form a new compound are present together.

If you compare several representative passages of the greatest poetry you see how great is the variety of types of combination, and also how completely any semi-ethical criterion of "sublimity" misses the mark. For it is not the "greatness," the intensity, of the emotions, the components, but the intensity of the artistic process, the pressure, so to speak, under which the fusion takes place, that counts. The episode of Paolo and Francesca employs a definite emotion, but the intensity of the poetry is something quite different from whatever intensity in the supposed experience it may give the impression of. It is no more intense, furthermore, than Canto XXVI, the voyage of Ulysses, which has not the direct dependence upon an emotion. Great variety is possible in the process of transmutation of emotion: the murder of Agamemnon, or the agony of Othello, gives an artistic effect apparently closer to a possible original than the scenes from Dante. In the *Agamemnon,* the artistic emotion approximates to the emotion of an actual spectator; in *Othello* to the emotion of the protagonist himself. But the difference between art and the event is always absolute; the combination which is the murder of Agamemnon is probably as complex as that which is the voyage of Ulysses. In either case there has been a fusion of elements. The ode of Keats contains a number of feelings which have nothing particular to do with the nightingale, but which the nightingale, partly, perhaps, because of its attractive name, and partly because of its reputation, served to bring together.

The point of view which I am struggling to attack is perhaps related to the metaphysical theory of the substantial unity of the soul: for my meaning is, that the poet has, not a "personality" to express, but a particular medium, which is only a medium and not a personality, in which impressions and experiences combine in peculiar and unexpected ways. Impressions and experiences which are important for the man may take no place in the poetry, and those which become important in the poetry may play quite a negligible part in the man, the personality.

I will quote a passage which is unfamiliar enough to be regarded with fresh attention in the light—or darkness—of these observations:

> And now methinks I could e'en chide myself
> For doating on her beauty, though her death
> Shall be revenged after no common action.
> Does the silkworm expend her yellow labours
> For thee? For thee does she undo herself?
> Are lordships sold to maintain ladyships
> For the poor benefit of a bewildering minute?
> Why does yon fellow falsify highways,
> And put his life between the judge's lips,
> To refine such a thing—keeps horse and men
> To beat their valours for her? . . .

In this passage (as is evident if it is taken in its context) there is a combination of positive and negative emotions: an intensely strong attraction toward beauty and an equally intense fascination by the ugliness which is contrasted with it and which destroys it. This balance of contrasted emotion is in the dramatic situation to which the speech is pertinent, but that situation alone is inadequate to it. This is, so to speak, the structural emotion, provided by the drama. But the whole effect, the dominant tone, is due to the fact that a number of floating feelings, having an affinity to this emotion by no means superficially evident, have combined with it to give us a new art emotion.

It is not in his personal emotions, the emotions provoked by particular events in his life, that the poet is in any way remarkable or interesting. His particular emotions may be simple, or crude, or flat. The emotion in his poetry will be a very complex thing, but not with the complexity of the emotions of people who have very complex or unusual emotions in life. One error, in fact, of eccentricity in poetry is to seek for new human emotions to express; and in this search for novelty in the wrong place it discovers the perverse. The business of the poet is not to find new emotions, but to use the ordinary ones and, in working them up into poetry, to express feelings which are not in actual emotions at all. And emotions which he has never experienced will serve his turn as well as those familiar to him. Consequently, we must believe that "emotion recollected in tranquillity" is an inexact formula. For it is neither emotion, nor recollection, nor, without distortion of meaning, tranquillity. It is a concentration, and a new thing resulting from the concentration, of a very great number of experiences which to the practical and active person would not seem to be experiences at all; it is a concentration which does not happen consciously or of deliberation. These experiences are not "recollected," and they finally unite in an atmosphere which is "tranquil" only in that it is a passive attending upon the event. Of course this is not quite the whole story. There is a great deal, in the writing of poetry, which must be conscious and deliberate. In fact, the bad poet is usually unconscious where he ought to be conscious, and conscious where he ought to be unconscious. Both errors tend to make him "personal." Poetry is not a turning loose of emotion, but an escape from emotion; it is not the expression of personality, but an escape from personality. But, of course, only those who have personality and emotions know what it means to want to escape from these things.

III

ὁ δὲ νοῦς ἴσως θειότερόν τι χαὶ ἀπαθές ἐστν.[1]

This essay proposes to halt at the frontier of metaphysics or mysticism, and confine itself to such practical conclusions as can be applied by the responsible person interested in poetry. To divert interest from the poet to the poetry is a laudable aim: for it would conduce to a juster estimation of actual poetry, good and bad. There are many people who appreciate the expression of sincere emotion in verse, and there is a smaller number of people who can appreciate technical excellence. But very few know when there is an expression of *significant* emotion, emotion which has its life in the poem and not in the history of the poet. The emotion of art is impersonal. And the poet cannot reach this impersonality without surrendering himself wholly to the work to be done. And he is not likely to know what is to be done unless he lives in what is not merely the present, but the present moment of the past, unless he is conscious, not of what is dead, but of what is already living.

1920

---

1. Aristotle, "On the Soul": "Surely the mind is divine and not subject to outside impressions."

LOUISE BOGAN
(1897–1970)

Born in Livermore Falls, Maine, Louise Bogan (pronounced Bogán) grew up buffeted by the storms of her parents' troubled marriage. Her father, Daniel Bogan, served as a foreman of various New England mills, and the family moved frequently, living in hotels and boarding houses in Milton, New Hampshire, from 1901 to 1904, Ballardvalle, Massachusetts, from 1904 to 1909, and Roxbury, near Boston, after 1909. Her mother, May Shields Bogan, engaged in extramarital affairs, which led to several prolonged disappearances from the family. Considering the effects of these disruptions in the autobiographical writings collected in *Journey Around My Room* (1980), Bogan admitted that in childhood she became "the semblance of a girl, in which some desires and illusions had been early assassinated: shot dead." The skepticism about love and the preoccupation with romantic betrayal that characterize Bogan's poetry, as well as the severe depressions that afflicted her during adulthood, were likely engendered during these difficult years.

In her education, however, Bogan found a haven against disorder. She attended a convent school from 1906 to 1908 and then studied at the prestigious Girls' Latin School in Boston, where she received a superb classical education and began to write poetry. After a year at Boston University, she was offered a scholarship to Radcliffe, but chose instead to marry Curt Alexander, a German native who was a corporal in the U.S. army. When the United States declared war, Alexander was shipped to Panama in April 1917. Bogan, who was four months pregnant, joined him there in May and gave birth to a daughter in October. Miserable in Panama and disillusioned with her marriage, she returned to Massachusetts with the baby a year later. After a brief rapprochement with Alexander, she left him in 1919 and moved to Manhattan, entrusting her daughter to her parents. Her husband's death in 1920 from pneumonia made Bogan eligible for widow's benefits, which, along with work at Brentano's Bookstore and the New York Public Library, gave her the financial security to concentrate on poetry.

In New York, Bogan soon forged friendships with writers who helped her embark on a literary career. Her poems appeared in journals such as *Poetry, Others,* and the *Measure,* and in 1923 she published her first book, *Body of This Death.* The following year, at the urging of Edmund Wilson, she published her first book review. By the early 1930s, she had established herself as a formidable poet and critic, but reached a crisis in her personal life. In 1925 she married the poet Raymond Holden, and three years later they purchased a home in Hillsdale, New York, where they savored an idyllic country life that included Bogan's daughter. But on December 26, 1929, three months after the publication of her second book, *Dark Summer,* the house was destroyed in a fire. The couple returned to New York City, but the marriage deteriorated, and in 1931 Bogan was hit with depression severe enough that she required a three-month hospitalization.

After her release from the sanitarium, Bogan began to write poetry reviews for the *New Yorker,* and until 1969 she contributed biannual, omnibus reviews of new poetry, as well as incisive essays on a variety of authors, to the magazine. Along with the criticism she published in the *New Republic* and the *Nation,* Bogan's *New Yorker* reviews earned her a reputation as one of the most powerful literary arbiters in the country—her judgments were concise, high-minded, and never tainted by influence peddling. She was willing to criticize the work of her friends. Bogan also opposed the ideological poetry popular during the 1930s and insisted that "poetry has something to do with the imagination: I still think it ought to be well-written. I still think it is private feeling, not public speech." For Bogan "private feeling" was compromised by public enumeration, and her aversion to the self-pity that she heard in much of the confessional poetry of the 1960s reflected her disinclination toward overt autobiography in her own verse.

That landscape grew increasingly bleak for Bogan during the early 1930s. In the summer of 1933, returning early from a solo trip to Europe that she had funded through a Guggenheim Fellowship, she discovered that Holden had committed adultery, and the marriage blew apart. In November, suffering again from severe depression, she checked herself into New York Hospital's Westchester Division. After her release seven months later, she found the strength to pursue her work again and separate from Holden. Although she experienced financial difficulties, including eviction from her apartment, by the decade's close she had rebounded. In 1935 she was energized by a brief affair with the young Theodore Roethke, and in 1937, the year of her divorce from Holden, she published her third book, *The Sleeping Fury,* whose lyrics celebrate her new-found equilibrium yet do not flinch from contemplating the darkness she had weathered. But *The Sleeping Fury* was to be her last book made up entirely of new poems, for the three additional poetry books that she published before her death were compilations that included only slim selections of new work. Over the next three decades, Bogan poured most of her literary energy into prose, essays, reviews, translations, and a book-length study of modern American poetry. She served as Consultant in Poetry to the Library of Congress in 1945 and 1946, shared the 1955 Bollingen Prize with Léonie Adams, and was elected to the American Academy of Arts and Letters in 1968.

At the time of her death in 1970 from a coronary occlusion, she was best known as a critic. Yet many poets prized her lyrics, as W. H. Auden noted at her funeral, both for their technical excellence and for "her determination never to surrender to self-pity, but to wrest beauty and joy out of dark places." Bogan, who called the lyric "the most intense, the most compressed, the most purified form of language," developed a severe attitude toward her writing, for she not only pursued formal perfection, but favored subjects so psychically charged that she eschewed ordinary occasions—so much so that her collected poems, *The Blue Estuaries* (1968), contains only 107 poems. As Malcolm Cowley argued, Bogan "has done something that has been achieved by very few of her contemporaries: she has added a dozen or more to our small stock of memorable lyrics. She has added nothing whatever to our inexhaustible store of trash." In writing of women's experience, Bogan also set herself in the line of American female lyricists that begins with Anne Bradstreet and includes Bogan's contemporaries, Sara Teasdale, Elinor Wylie, and Edna St. Vincent Millay. Never denying the primacy of personal experience to poetry, Bogan aimed to distill internal experience rather than chronicle external events. As she wrote in 1961, "The poet represses the outright narrative of his life. He absorbs it, along with life itself. The repressed becomes the poem. Actually, I have written down my experiences in the closest detail. But the rough and vulgar facts are not there."

◄◦━━◖▶━◦►

THE SPRINGS OF POETRY

When he sets out to resolve, as rationally as he may, the tight irrational knot of his emotion, the poet hesitates for a moment. Unless the compulsion be absolute, as is rarely the case, the excitement of the resolution sets in only after this pause, filled with doubt and terror. He would choose anything, anything, rather than the desperate task before him: a book, music, or talk and laughter. Almost immediately the interruption is found, and the emotion diverted, or the poem is begun, and the desperation has its use.

The author of the *Poetica* recognized this necessary intensity when he wrote that distress and anger are most faithfully portrayed by one who is feeling them at the moment, that poetry demands a man with a special gift for it, or else one with a touch of madness in him. Few poems are written in that special authentic rage because even a poet has a great many uses for grief and anger, beyond putting them into a poem. The poem is always a last resort. In it the poet makes a world in little, and finds peace, even though, under complete focused emotion, the evocation be far more bitter than reality, or far more lovely.

Sometimes the poet does not entirely succeed in diverting his energies. He expresses himself, determined to take a holiday from any emotion at all, being certain that to hear, see, smell and touch, merely, is enough. His hand has become chilled, from being held too long against the ground to feel how it is cold; his mind flinches at cutting down once again into the dark with the knife of irony or analysis.

So he writes a poem at third, fourth, or fifth hand, bred out of some delicate fantastic ruse of the brain. Even at its best a poem cannot come straight out of the heart, but must break away in some oblique fashion from the body of sorrow or

Originally published in *New Republic* 5 Dec. 1923.

joy,—be the mask, not the incredible face,—yet the synthetic poem can never be more than a veil dropped before a void. It may sound, to change the images, in ears uninitiate to the festival, but never to those, who, having once heard, can recognize again the maenad cry.

It would seem best, in order that his temptation to second-rate work be kept negligible, that for long periods the poet himself be his only audience. He has no business with the shifting criteria with which each little year would charge him. He should have no thought of a descending scale of editors to whom his best and his worst may be fed.

One would wish for the poet a stern countryside that could claim him completely, identify him rigidly as its own under the color of every season. He should be blessed by the power to write behind clenched teeth, to subsidize his emotion by every trick and pretense so that it trickle out through other channels, if it be not essential to speech,—blessed too, by a spirit as loud as a houseful of alien voices, ever tortured and divided with itself. And most completely blessed by that reticence celebrated by the old prophetic voice: "I kept silent, even from good words . . . the fire kindled, and at the last I spoke with my tongue." Under the power of such reticence, in which passion is made to achieve its own form, definite and singular, those poems were written that keep an obscure name still alive, or live when the name of their author is forgotten. Speaking thus, as though the very mind had a tongue, Yeats achieves his later work: poems terribly beautiful, in which the hazy adverbial quality has no place, built of sentences reduced to the bones of noun, verb, and preposition.

This is the further, the test simplicity, in the phrase of Alice Meynell, sprung from the passion of which every poet will always be afraid, but to which he should vow himself forever.

1923

HART CRANE
(1899–1932)

Immensely gifted, Hart Crane pursued poetry with uncompromising dedication, yet his life was marred by the emotional imbalances that ultimately led
to debilitating alcoholism and suicide. Born in Garrettsville, Ohio, Harold
Hart Crane grew up as a pawn in marital battles waged between his mother,
Grace Hart Crane, an intelligent, high-strung woman, and his father, Clarence
("C. A.") Crane, an ambitious and successful businessman. The family lived
in Warren, Ohio, from 1903 until 1908, when domestic conflicts drove Grace
into a sanitarium and C. A. to Chicago. Harold was sent to live with his
mother's parents in Cleveland, where Grace returned in 1909, and C. A. later
rejoined her. The Cranes remained there until 1916, when Grace and C. A.
arranged to divorce, and their son, determined to become a poet, set off
for New York City without graduating from high school. But he was never
able to free himself from the family miasma; throughout his life he felt
obliged to ally himself either with one parent or the other. In 1917, he sided
with his mother so strongly that he chose to call himself "Hart," her maiden
name, because Grace encouraged his vocation as a poet while C. A. expected
him to learn the family business.

Between 1917 and 1919 Crane shuttled between Ohio and New York,
where he established connections with two literary magazines, the *Little
Review* and *Seven Arts*. He remained in Cleveland from 1920 to 1923, working first for his father and then in advertising. Whenever possible, he continued the precocious pattern of reading that he had begun in his high school
years; he also wrote many of the lyrics that appeared in his first book, *White
Buildings* (1926). By the time he returned to New York in 1923, he had
established a reputation as an important young poet, which enabled him to
forge friendships with artists and writers such as Alfred Stieglitz, Jean Toomer,
and Allen Tate. He soon left his job with the advertising firm of J. Walter
Thompson to devote himself entirely to writing. For the rest of his life, Crane
supported himself through short-term jobs, small stipends from his parents,
money borrowed from friends, and occasional grants from benefactors.

Crane saw poetry in extreme terms, as an all-consuming vocation that
demanded sacrifice and the utmost intensity. Consequently, his poetry places

extreme demands on the reader. He sought to push language to its limits in an effort to voice ideas and feelings that are inexpressible—an aim that was Romantic in its ends but Modernist in its means. In a 1926 letter to Harriet Monroe, he explained that "the nuances of feeling and observation in a poem may well call for certain liberties" that go beyond the strictures of rational logic. Metaphor allows for unexpected parallels between different realms of experience, and, serving as "something like short-hand as compared to usual description and dialectics," it leads both poet and reader "toward fresh concepts, more inclusive evaluations." Among those "more inclusive evaluations" was Crane's emphasis on seeking (though not necessarily finding) spiritual transcendence amidst the desperate conditions of modern life. Thus, he opposed the pessimism he saw in T. S. Eliot's work and countered with a poetry of visionary possibility.

For Crane, those moments of possibility were often inspired by homoerotic relationships, and "the new *word*" that he strove to enunciate through metaphor encompassed experiences that could not be proclaimed in public. But among his literary friends he made no secret of his homosexuality, nor of the sharp emotional swings that his affairs brought on. His most important relationship, although it lasted only a year, was intense enough that Crane described it in religious terms. Emil Opffer, who worked as a ship's writer, invited Crane to share his rooms near the Brooklyn Bridge shortly after they met in 1924, and, in April, Crane confessed to his friend and mentor, Waldo Frank: "I have seen the Word made flesh." For Crane, the relationship veered between agonized separations when Opffer was at sea to joyous reunions in which even a simple walk across the bridge became charged with illumination. Meditating on the view from the harbor, Crane told Frank: "I think the sea has thrown itself upon me and been answered, at least in part, and I believe I am a little changed—not essentially, but changed and transubstantiated as anyone is who has asked a question and been answered." The relationship with Opffer culminated in "Voyages," in which Crane developed complex analogies between love and the sea's overwhelming fluctuations, psychological dissolution and sensual ecstasy. Crane pursued both of these poles in his life as well as in his art. His high spirits brought him numerous friends, yet too many of his friendships soured due to the excesses of his drinking.

Although the alcoholism eventually compromised his writing, in 1926 he was at the height of his powers. Otto Kahn, a banker and patron of the arts, granted him funds to work on *The Bridge*, a sequence of poems that Crane hoped would "enunciate a new cultural synthesis" of America. In a burst of energy, he wrote the last poem, "Atlantis," first, and then worked on the beginning poems until quarrels with Allen Tate and his wife Caroline Gordon, with whom he was staying in upstate New York, forced him to relocate. From May to October, he lived on his grandparents' defunct Caribbean plantation on the Isle of Pines, off the coast of Cuba. After his return to New York, his mother's financial and emotional troubles drew his attention away from the poem; her letters often spurred his self-destructive drinking sprees. In November 1927 he lived in Pasadena as a paid companion to a wealthy invalid, but moved in the spring to Hollywood to help Grace, who was nursing her mother through a terminal illness. Eventually, the nervous collapses that afflicted his mother whenever he tried to go out at night drove him to leave for New York. After Crane's grandmother died in September, Grace tried to block his inheritance, and he feared that she would tell his father about his homosexuality.

When he obtained the money in December 1928, he set off for Europe, where in Paris he met Harry Crosby, owner of the Black Sun Press, whose enthusiastic agreement to publish *The Bridge* inspired Crane to finish the poem after he returned to New York. The Black Sun edition, including photographs by Walker Evans of the Brooklyn Bridge, appeared in January 1930, and an American edition followed in April. Although it received favorable reviews in several publications, the book was attacked by Yvor Winters and Allen Tate, friends to whom Crane had written often during the years he had worked on the poem, offering his thoughts on the work in progress. Both critics accused Crane of sentimentality and argued that the poem failed to cohere into a unified whole; they also complained that it lacked substance as an epic.

Crane's last years were overshadowed by alcoholism and diminished poetic production. The Great Depression made finding employment a hopeless task, and by the end of 1930 Crane returned to Cleveland, having reconciled with his father. For three months he helped out at the restaurant his father owned, until a Guggenheim fellowship enabled him to make more ambitious plans. In April he left for Mexico, where he intended to draft a verse drama about Cortés and Montezuma, but instead resumed his heavy drinking. The novelist Katherine Anne Porter, a fellow Guggenheim recipient with whom he first stayed in Mexico City, recalled his nightly returns from the bars, when he stood outside of her house and raged "with words so foul there is no question of repeating them, he cursed separately and by name the moon, and its light: the heliotrope, the heaven-tree, the sweet-by-night, the star jessamine, and their perfumes. He cursed the air we breathed together, the pool of water with its two small ducks huddled at the edge, and the vines on the wall and the house."

The emotional crisis that precipitated such incidents was exacerbated in July, when he learned of his father's death from a stroke. After a trip to Cleveland for the funeral, he returned to Mexico in September and was soon caught up in his first heterosexual love affair, with Peggy Baird Cowley, who was in Mexico seeking a divorce from her husband, the writer Malcolm Cowley. Although the energy of the relationship enabled Crane to finish one important poem, "The Broken Tower," it could not stanch his feelings of financial desperation—his father's estate had been claimed by creditors. Moreover, the affair with Peggy, which he had promised her would end in marriage, conflicted with his continuing attraction to men. Deciding to return to New York City, he and Peggy set sail from Veracruz in April 1932. During the early morning of April 27, Crane was badly beaten, perhaps by sailors whom he had solicited for sex. At noon, he returned to the stateroom that he shared with his lover, bade her good-bye, went up to the deck, and leapt into the sea.

When news of Crane's suicide reached New York, many writers felt that it symbolized the end of the previous decade's remarkable surge of literary energy. Other writers, particularly Winters, used it to cast moral aspersions on Crane's poetry. More recently, critics such as Thomas Yingling have faulted society's lack of tolerance for homosexuality. Regardless of Crane's troubled life, readers have continued to be drawn in by the intensity of his poetry, even as they acknowledge its difficulty. The poetry's complexity, and the indelible power of Crane's voice, confirm the early assessment of Allen Tate, in his review of *White Buildings,* who lauded Crane's work as "one of the finest achievements of this age."

Crane published almost no formal criticism, but he was a passionate correspondent with poets and editors. He sometimes took great pains to explain his creative assumptions and practices in his letters, several of which have been republished separately as poetic manifestos. "General Aims and Theories" is a set of "notes" that Crane wrote for playwright Eugene O'Neill who had agreed to write a preface to *White Buildings.* Liveright had accepted the manuscript for publication under the condition that the famous dramatist would endorse it. O'Neill never wrote the preface, although Allen Tate offered to ghostwrite it for him. The book eventually appeared with a foreword by Tate.

GENERAL AIMS AND THEORIES

When I started writing "Faustus & Helen" it was my intention to embody in modern terms (words, symbols, metaphors) a contemporary approximation to an ancient human culture or mythology that seems to have been obscured rather than illumined with the frequency of poetic allusions made to it during the last century. The name of Helen, for instance, has become an all-too-easily employed crutch for evocation whenever a poet felt a stitch in his side. The real evocation of this (to me) very real and absolute conception of beauty seemed to consist in a reconstruction in these modern terms of the basic emotional attitude toward beauty that the Greeks had. And in so doing I found that I was really building a bridge between so-called classic experience and many divergent realities of our seething, confused cosmos of today, which has no formulated mythology yet for classic poetic reference or for religious exploitation.

So I found "Helen" sitting in a street car; the Dionysian revels of her court and her seduction were transferred to a Metropolitan roof garden with a jazz orchestra; and the *katharsis* of the fall of Troy I saw approximated in the recent World War. The importance of this scaffolding may easily be exaggerated, but it gave me a series of correspondences between two widely separated worlds on which to sound some major themes of human speculation—love, beauty, death, renascence. It was a kind of grafting process that I shall doubtless not be interested in repeating, but which is consistent with subsequent theories of mine on the relation of tradition to the contemporary creating imagination.

It is a terrific problem that faces the poet today—a world that is so in transition from a decayed culture toward a reorganization of human evaluations that

First published in *The Complete Poems and Selected Letters and Prose,* ed. Brom Weber (Garden City: Doubleday, 1966) 217–223.

there are few common terms, general denominators of speech that are solid enough or that ring with any vibration or spiritual conviction. The great mythologies of the past (including the Church) are deprived of enough façade to even launch good raillery against. Yet much of their traditions are operative still—in millions of chance combinations of related and unrelated detail, psychological reference, figures of speech, precepts, etc. These are all a part of our common experience and the terms, at least partially, of that very experience when it defines or extends itself.

The deliberate program, then, of a "break" with the past or tradition seems to me to be a sentimental fallacy. . . . The poet has a right to draw on whatever practical resources he finds in books or otherwise about him. He must tax his sensibility and his touchstone of experience for the proper selections of these themes and details, however—and that is where he either stands, or falls into useless archeology.

I put no particular value on the simple objective of "modernity." The element of the temporal location of an artist's creation is of very secondary importance; it can be left to the impressionist or historian just as well. It seems to me that a poet will accidentally define his time well enough simply by reacting honestly and to the full extent of his sensibilities to the states of passion, experience and rumination that fate forces on him, first hand. He must, of course, have a sufficiently universal basis of experience to make his imagination selective and valuable. His picture of the "period," then, will simply be a by-product of his curiosity and the relation of his experience to a postulated "eternity."

I am concerned with the future of America, but not because I think that America has any so-called par value as a state or as a group of people. . . . It is only because I feel persuaded that here are destined to be discovered certain as yet undefined spiritual quantities, perhaps a new hierarchy of faith not to be developed so completely elsewhere. And in this process I like to feel myself as a potential factor; certainly I must speak in its terms and what discoveries I may make are situated in its experience.

But to fool one's self that definitions are being reached by merely referring frequently to skyscrapers, radio antennae, steam whistles, or other surface phenomena of our time is merely to paint a photograph. I think that what is interesting and significant will emerge only under the conditions of our submission to, and examination and assimilation of the organic effects on us of these and other fundamental factors of our experience. It can certainly not be an organic expression otherwise. And the expression of such values may often be as well accomplished with the vocabulary and blank verse of the Elizabethans as with the calligraphic tricks and slang used so brilliantly at times by an impressionist like Cummings.

It may not be possible to say that there is, strictly speaking, any "absolute" experience. But it seems evident that certain aesthetic experience (and this may for a time engross the total faculties of the spectator) can be called absolute, inasmuch as it approximates a formally convincing statement of a conception or apprehension of life that gains our unquestioning assent, and under the conditions of which our imagination is unable to suggest a further detail consistent with the design of the aesthetic whole.

I have been called an "absolutist" in poetry, and if I am to welcome such a label it should be under the terms of the above definition. It is really only a *modus operandi*, however, and as such has been used organically before by at least a dozen poets such as Donne, Blake, Baudelaire, Rimbaud, etc. I may succeed in defining it better by contrasting it with the impressionistic method. The impressionist is interesting as far as he goes—but his goal has been reached when he has succeeded in projecting certain selected factual details into his reader's consciousness. He is really not interested in the *causes* (metaphysical) of his materials, their emotional derivations or their utmost spiritual consequences. A kind of retinal registration is enough, along with a certain psychological stimulation. And this is also true of your realist (of the Zola type), and to a certain extent of the classicist, like Horace, Ovid, Pope, etc.

Blake meant these differences when he wrote:

We are led to believe in a lie
When we see *with* not *through* the eye.

The impressionist creates only with the eye and for the readiest surface of the consciousness, at least relatively so. If the effect has been harmonious or even stimulating, he can stop there, relinquishing entirely to his audience the problematic synthesis of the details into terms of their own personal consciousness.

It is my hope to go *through* the combined materials of the poem, using our "real" world somewhat as a spring-board, and to give the poem *as a whole* an orbit or predetermined direction of its own. I would like to establish it as free from my own personality as from any chance evaluation on the reader's part. (This is, of course, an impossibility, but it is a characteristic worth mentioning.) Such a poem is at least a stab at a truth, and to such an extent may be differentiated from other kinds of poetry and called "absolute." Its evocation will not be toward decoration or amusement, but rather toward a state of consciousness, an "innocence" (Blake) or absolute beauty. In this condition there may be discoverable under new forms certain spiritual illuminations, shining with a morality essentialized from experience directly, and not from previous precepts or preconceptions. It is as though a poem gave the reader as he left it a single, new *word*, never before spoken and impossible to actually enunciate, but self-evident as an active principle in the reader's consciousness henceforward.

As to technical considerations: the motivation of the poem must be derived from the implicit emotional dynamics of the materials used, and the terms of expression employed are often selected less for their logical (literal) significance than for their associational meanings. Via this and their metaphorical inter-relationships, the entire construction of the poem is raised on the organic principle of a "logic of metaphor," which antedates our so-called pure logic, and which is the genetic basis of all speech, hence consciousness and thought-extension.

These dynamics often result, I'm told, in certain initial difficulties in understanding my poems. But on the other hand I find them at times the only means possible for expressing certain concepts in any forceful or direct way whatever. To cite two examples:—when, in "Voyages" (II), I speak of "adagios of islands," the reference is to the motion of a boat through islands clustered thickly, the rhythm of the motion, etc. And it seems a much more direct and creative statement than any more logical employment of words such as "coasting slowly through the islands," besides ushering in a whole world of music. Similarly in "Faustus and Helen" (III), the speed and tense altitude of an aeroplane are much better suggested by the idea of "nimble blue plateaus"—*implying* the aeroplane and its speed against a contrast of stationary elevated earth. Although the statement is pseudo in relation to formal logic—it *is* completely logical in relation to the truth of the imagination, and there is expressed a concept of speed and space that could not be handled so well in other terms.

In manipulating the more imponderable phenomena of psychic motives, pure emotional crystallizations, etc. I have had to rely even more on these dynamics of inferential mention, and I am doubtless still very unconscious of having committed myself to what seems nothing but obscurities to some minds. A poem like "Possessions" really cannot be technically explained. It must rely (even to a large extent with myself) on its organic impact on the imagination to successfully imply its meaning. This seems to me to present an exceptionally difficult problem, however, considering the real clarity and consistent logic of many of the other poems.

I know that I run the risk of much criticism by defending such theories as I have, but as it is part of a poet's business to risk not only criticism—but folly—in the conquest of consciousness I can only say that I attach no intrinsic value to what means I use beyond their practical service in giving form to the living stuff of the imagination.

New conditions of life germinate new forms of spiritual articulation. And while I feel that my work includes a more consistent extension of traditional literary elements than many contemporary poets are capable of appraising, I realize that I am utilizing the gifts of the past as instruments principally; and that the voice of the present, if it is to be known, must be caught at the risk of speaking in idioms and circumlocutions sometimes shocking to the scholar and historians of logic. Language has built towers and bridges, but itself is inevitably as fluid as always.

[c. 1925] 1966

ALLEN TATE
(1899–1979)

John Orley Allen Tate was born the youngest of three sons to John Orley
Tate and Eleanor Varnell Tate in Winchester, Kentucky, "the heart of blue-
grass country." His mother's family hailed from Fairfax County, Virginia,
however; and when his parents became estranged due to his father's business
failures and erratic behavior, Tate was led to believe that he had been born
in her native state. His recollections of a largely Presbyterian childhood in
the South were infused with Southern aristocratic mythology, but also with
shame at the interracial violence he occasionally witnessed and at his own
family's declining fortunes. Although his formal schooling was sporadic,
he impressed his teachers early on with his facility for memorizing poems.
By the time Tate entered Vanderbilt University in 1918, both the institution
and the South were changing, but he resisted those new social and cultural
forces that, he believed, would rob the South of its old agrarian identity
and code of honor.

At Vanderbilt he and his roommate, Robert Penn Warren, joined forces
with the Fugitives, a group of poets including two young professors, John
Crowe Ransom and Donald Davidson. Deeply aware of their Southern heritage, these poet-critics, who would soon become immensely influential, fell
under the spell of Modernism. Tate was introduced to T. S. Eliot's work by
Hart Crane, who initiated a correspondence after reading some of his poems
in a New Orleans journal, the *Double-Dealer*. Tate conveyed his new enthusiasm for Eliot to the other Fugitives. At one point Warren even decorated
the walls of their room with painted images from *The Waste Land*. The
literary sophistication of Eliot's poetry appealed to these future priests
of the New Criticism.

Poor health, including an interlude in a tuberculosis sanatorium, and a
brief stint as a public schoolteacher, interrupted Tate's college education. In
1923, however, he finally took his degree. Soon he went to work for his
brother, Ben, a successful businessman. Ill-suited to such a career, Tate later
confessed, "In one day I lost the company $700 by shipping some coal to
Duluth that should have gone to Cleveland. . . ." Leaving business in 1924,
he married the future novelist, Caroline Gordon, and the couple moved to

New York, where Tate worked as a magazine editor and book reviewer. There he befriended writers like E. E. Cummings, Kenneth Burke, and Malcolm Cowley. When they tired of the city, Tate and Gordon rented a farmhouse in the country. For four months they shared their home with Hart Crane, but the latter's refusal to help with household chores led to a quarrel, after which they communicated with Crane by slipping notes under his door. Soon Crane moved out, but Tate remained one of his staunchest literary supporters. He had written a foreword to Crane's *White Buildings* (1926) and understood the deeper coherence of Crane's often obscure and difficult poems.

Tate's own poetry could also be difficult—baroque in its diction and densely allusive. Nevertheless, he aimed for what John Frederick Nims would call a "fidelity to the experience of this world, which is the only sign our senses have of any other." Tate said he wanted "to unify religion, morality, and art." But Nims's comment also illuminates Tate's exacting standards as a poet. He began to write his most famous poem, "Ode to the Confederate Dead," in 1925, and revised it for the next twelve years, even after its initial publication. Lacking the headlong romanticism of Crane's work, Tate's poems were cerebral and classically balanced. His classicism, however, often served as a necessary force to control the violence and horror of his material.

A Guggenheim Fellowship allowed Tate and Gordon to live in France for more than a year, and when they returned they moved into a Tennessee mansion purchased for them by Tate's brother, Ben. They affectionately called it "Benfolly" and hosted many of their literary friends within its walls. Tate's personal life was sometimes troubled. He and Gordon were married and divorced twice; the second divorce, occurring after his conversion to Catholicism, resulted in his excommunication. From 1959 to 1966 he was married to poet Isabelle Gardiner. One of his sons by his third wife, Helen Heinz, died in infancy.

Despite his personal troubles, Tate was steadily productive. *Poems: 1928–1931* appeared in 1932, *The Mediterranean and Other Poems* in 1936, and his one novel, *The Father,* two years later. It was also in the thirties that he began teaching at several small colleges, and from 1939 to 1942 he served as Princeton's poet-in-residence. He was an influential editor of the *Sewanee Review* (1944–1946) and in 1951 began teaching at the University of Minnesota, where his colleagues would include Warren, James Wright, and John Berryman. By the time he retired from the post in 1968, he was regarded as one of America's preeminent academic men of letters. He maintained friendships with well-established figures like Malcolm Cowley and T. S. Eliot and also with younger poets, including Randall Jarrell, John Berryman, and Robert Lowell.

Tate was also one of the most articulate and influential poetry critics of his era. His highly regarded critical essays helped to shape the New Criticism. Like the other New Critics, he believed in the formal integrity and coherence of the successful literary work—a perfect balance between the parts and whole that creates the necessary tension to convey a poem's imaginative energy. Tate resisted the notion that literary work should be analyzed and judged by the practical uses—social, political, or religious—to which it might be put. Instead he saw that poetry's human role was to provide a "special, unique, and complete knowledge" that was as valuable as scientific or philosophical discovery. Poetic knowledge combined thought, emotion, and sensory experience into an indivisible whole.

Tate was also a formidable practical critic. His incisive book reviews contributed to the reception of many modern poets, including Robinson, Pound, Eliot, MacLeish, Ransom, Millay, Cummings, Benét, Auden, Tolson, and Crane. If his literary criticism occasionally became abstract or impenetrable, his reviews displayed an uncanny skill at finding essential elements of a poet's work. Not counting such reviews, Tate published more than one hundred essays, many of them collected in books such as *Reason in Madness* (1941), *On the Limits of Poetry* (1948), and *The Man of Letters in the Modern World* (1955).

TENSION IN POETRY

Many poems that we ordinarily think of as good poetry—and some, besides, that we neglect—have certain common features that will allow us to invent, for their sharper apprehension, the name of a single quality. I shall call that quality tension. In abstract language, a poetic work has distinct quality as the ultimate effect of the whole, and that whole is the "result" of a configuration of meaning which it is the duty of the critic to examine and evaluate. In setting forth this duty as my present procedure I am trying to amplify a critical approach that I have used on other occasions, without wholly giving up the earlier method, which I should describe as the isolation of the general ideas implicit in the poetic work.

Towards the end of this essay I shall cite examples of "tension," but I shall not say that they exemplify tension only, or that other qualities must be ignored. There are all kinds of poetry, as many as there are good poets, as many even as there are good poems, for poets may be expected to write more than one kind of poetry; and no single critical insight may impute an exclusive validity to any one kind. In all ages there are schools demanding that one sort only be written—their sort: political poetry for the sake of the cause; picturesque poetry for the sake of the home town; didactic poetry for the sake of the parish; even a generalized personal poetry for the sake of the reassurance and safety of numbers. This last I suppose is the most common variety, the anonymous lyricism in which the common personality exhibits its commonness, its obscure yet standard eccentricity, in a language that seems always to be deteriorating; so that today many poets are driven to inventing private languages, or very narrow ones, because public speech has become heavily tainted with mass feeling.

Mass language is the medium of "communication," and its users are less interested in bringing to formal order what is sometimes called the "affective state" than in arousing that state.

Once you have said that everything is One it is obvious that literature is the same as propaganda; once you have said that no truth can be known apart

From *Reason in Madness* (New York: Putnam, 1941). All footnotes are Tate's except for translated lines.

from the immediate dialectical process of history it is obvious that all contemporary artists must prepare the same fashionplate. It is clear too that the One is limited in space as well as time, and the no less Hegelian Fascists are right in saying that all art is patriotic.

What Mr. William Empson calls patriotic poetry sings not merely in behalf of the State; you will find it equally in a lady-like lyric and in much of the political poetry of our time. It is the poetry of the mass language, very different from the "language of the people" which interested the late W. B. Yeats. For example:

> What from the splendid dead
> We have inherited—
> Furrows sweet to the grain, and the weed subdued—
> See now the slug and the mildew plunder.
> Evil does overwhelm
> The larkspur and the corn;
> We have seen them go under.

From this stanza by Miss Millay we infer that her splendid ancestors made the earth a good place that has somehow gone bad—and you get the reason from the title: "Justice Denied in Massachusetts." How Massachusetts could cause a general desiccation, why (as we are told in a footnote to the poem) the execution of Sacco and Vanzetti should have anything to do with the rotting of the crops, it is never made clear. These lines are mass language: they arouse an affective state in one set of terms, and suddenly an object quite unrelated to those terms gets the benefit of it; and this effect, which is usually achieved, as I think it is here, without conscious effort, is sentimentality. Miss Millay's poem was admired when it first appeared about ten years ago, and is no doubt still admired, by persons to whom it communicates certain feelings about social justice, by persons for whom the lines are the occasion of feelings shared by them and the poet. But if you do not share those feelings, as I happen not to share them in the images of desiccated nature, the lines and even the entire poem are impenetrably obscure.

I am attacking here the fallacy of communication in poetry. (I am not attacking social justice.) It is no less a fallacy in the writing of poetry than of critical theory. The critical doctrine fares ill the further back you apply it; I suppose one may say— if one wants a landmark—that it began to prosper after 1798; for on the whole nineteenth-century English verse is a poetry of communication. The poets were trying to use verse to convey ideas and feelings that they secretly thought could be better conveyed by science (consult Shelley's *Defense*), or by what today we call, in a significantly bad poetic phrase, the Social Sciences. Yet possibly because the poets believed the scientists to be tough, and the poets joined the scientists in thinking the poets tender, the poets stuck to verse. It may scarcely be said that we change this tradition of poetic futility by giving it a new name, Social Poetry. May a poet hope to deal more adequately with sociology than with physics? If he seizes upon either at the level of scientific procedure, has he not abdicated his position as poet?

At a level of lower historical awareness than that exhibited by Mr. Edmund Wilson's later heroes of the Symbolist school, we find the kind of verse that I have been quoting, verse long ago intimidated by the pseudo-rationalism of the Social Sciences. This sentimental intimidation has been so complete that, however easy the verse looked on the page, it gave up all claim to sense. (I assume here what I cannot now demonstrate, that Miss Millay's poem is obscure but that Donne's "Second Anniversarie" is not.) As another example of this brand of obscurity I have selected at random a nineteenth-century lyric, "The Vine," by James Thomson:

> The wine of love is music,
>   And the feast of love is song:
> When love sits down to banquet,
>   Love sits long:
>
> Sits long and rises drunken,
>   But not with the feast and the wine;
> He reeleth with his own heart,
>   That great rich Vine.

The language here appeals to an existing affective state; it has no coherent meaning either literally or in terms of ambiguity or implication; it may be wholly replaced by any of its several paraphrases, which are already latent in our minds. One of these is the confused image of a self-intoxicating man-about-town. Now good poetry can bear the closest literal examination of every phrase, and is its own safeguard against our irony. But the more closely we examine this lyric, the more obscure it becomes; the more we trace the implications of the imagery, the denser the confusion. The imagery adds nothing to the general idea that it tries to sustain; it even deprives that idea of the dignity it has won at the hands of a long succession of better poets going back, I suppose, to Guinizelli:

> Al cor gentil ripara sempre Amore
> Come alla selva augello in la verdura . . .*

What I want to make clear is the particular kind of failure, not the degree, in a certain kind of poetry. Were we interested in degrees we might give comfort to the nineteenth century by citing lines from John Cleveland or Abraham Cowley, bad lyric verse no better than "The Vine," written in an age that produced some of the greatest English poetry. Here are some lines from Cowley's "Hymn: to light," a hundred-line inventory of some of the offices performed by the subject in a universe that still seems to be on the whole Ptolemaic; I should not care to guess the length the poem might have reached under the Copernican system. Here is one of the interesting duties of light:

> Nor amidst all these Triumphs does thou scorn
>   The humble glow-worm to adorn,
>   And with those living spangles gild,
> (O Greatness without Pride!) the Bushes of the Field.

Again:

> The Violet, springs little Infant, stands,
>   Girt in thy purple Swadling-bands:
>   On the fair Tulip thou dost dote;
> Thou cloath'st it in a gay and party-colour'd Coat.

---

*Translated by Dante Gabriel Rossetti as follows: "Within the gentle heart Love shelters him / As birds within the green shade. . . ."

This, doubtless, is metaphysical poetry; however bad the lines may be—they are pretty bad—they have no qualities, bad or good, in common with "The Vine." Mr. Ransom has given us, in a remarkable essay, "Shakespeare at Sonnets"[1] (*The World's Body*, 1938), an excellent description of this kind of poetry: "The impulse to metaphysical poetry . . . consists in committing the feelings in the case . . . to their determination within the elected figure." That is to say, in metaphysical poetry the logical order is explicit; it must be coherent; the imagery by which it is sensuously embodied must have at least the appearance of logical determinism: perhaps the appearance only, because the varieties of ambiguity and contradiction possible beneath the logical surface are endless, as Mr. Empson has demonstrated in his elucidation of Marvel's "The Garden." Here it is enough to say that the development of imagery by extension, its logical determinants being an Ariadne's thread that the poet will not permit us to lose, is the leading feature of the poetry called metaphysical.

But to recognize it is not to evaluate it; and I take it that Mr. Ransom was giving us a true Aristotelian definition of a *genus,* in which the identification of a type does not compel us to discern the implied values. Logical extension of imagery is no doubt the key to the meaning of Donne's "Valediction: forbidding mourning"; it may equally initiate inquiry into the ludicrous failure of "Hymn: to light," to which I now return.

Although "The Vine" and "Hymn: to light" seem to me equally bad poetry, Cowley's failure is somewhat to be preferred; its negative superiority lies in a firmer use of the language. There is no appeal to an affective state; the leading statement can be made perfectly explicit: God is light, and light is life. The poem is an analytical proposition exhibiting the properties inherent in the major term; that is, exhibiting as much of the universe as Cowley could get around to before he wearied of logical extension. But I think it is possible to infer that good poetry could have been written in Cowley's language; and we know that it was. Every term, even the verbs converted into nouns, denotes an object, and in the hands of a good poet would be amenable to controlled distortions of literal representation. But here the distortions are uncontrolled. Everything is in this language that a poet needs except the poetry, or the imagination, or what I shall presently illustrate under the idea of tension.

I have called "Hymn: to light" an analytical proposition. That is the form in which the theme must have appeared to Cowley's mind; that is to say, simple analysis of the term *God* gave him, as it gave everybody else in Christendom, the proposition: God is light. (Perhaps, under neo-Platonic influence, the prime Christian symbol, as Professor Fletcher and others have shown in reducing to their sources the powers of the Three Blessed Ladies of *The Divine Comedy*.) But in order to write his poem Cowley had to develop the symbol by synthetic accretion, by adding to light properties not inherent in its simple analysis:

> The Violet, springs little Infant, stands,
>   Girt in thy purple Swadling-bands . . .

The image, such as it is, is an addition to the central figure of light, an assertion of a hitherto undetected relation among the objects, light, diapers, and violets—a

---

1. His rejection of Shakespeare's sonnets seems to be a result of deductive necessity in his premises, or of the courage of mere logic; but the essay contains valuable insights into the operation of the metaphysical "conceit."

miscellany that I recommend to the consideration of Mr. E. E. Cummings, who could get something out of it that Cowley did not intend us to get. If you will think again of "The Vine," you will observe that Thomson permits, in the opposite direction, an equal license with the objects *de*noted by his imagery, with the unhappy results that we have already seen.

"The Vine" is a failure in denotation. "Hymn: to light" is a failure in connotation. The language of "The Vine" lacks objective content. Take "music" and "song" in the first two lines; the context does not allow us to apprehend the terms in extension; that is, there is no reference to objects that we may distinguish as "music" and "song"; the wine of love could have as well been song, its feast music. In "Hymn: to light," a reduction to their connotations of the terms *violet, swadling-bands,* and *light* (the last being represented by the pronoun *thou*) yields a clutter of images that may be unified only if we forget the firm denotations of the terms. If we are going to receive as valid the infancy of the violet, we must ignore the metaphor that conveys it, for the metaphor renders the violet absurd; by ignoring the diaper, and the two terms associated with it, we cease to read the passage, and begin for ourselves the building up of acceptable denotations for the terms of the metaphor.

Absurd: but on what final ground I call these poems absurd I cannot state as a principle. I appeal to the reader's experience, and invite him to form a judgment of my own. It is easy enough to say, as I shall say in detail in a moment, that good poetry is a unity of all the meanings from the furthest extremes of intension and extension. Yet our recognition of the action of this unified meaning is the gift of experience, of culture, of, if you will, our humanism. Our powers of discrimination are not deductive powers, though they may be aided by them; they wait rather upon the cultivation of our total human powers, and they represent a special application of those powers to a single medium of experience—poetry.

I have referred to a certain kind of poetry as the embodiment of the fallacy of communication: it is a poetry that communicates the affective state, which (in terms of language) results from the irresponsible denotations of words. There is a vague grasp of the "real" world. The history of this fallacy, which is as old as poetry but which towards the end of the eighteenth century began to dominate not only poetry, but other arts as well—its history would probably show that the poets gave up the language of denotation to the scientists, and kept for themselves a continually thinning flux of peripheral connotations. The companion fallacy, to which I can give only the literal name, the fallacy of mere denotation, I have also illustrated from Cowley: this is the poetry which contradicts our most developed human insights in so far as it fails to use and direct the rich connotation with which language has been informed by experience.

II

We return to the inquiry set for this discussion: to find out whether there is not a more central achievement in poetry than that represented by either of the extreme examples that we have been considering. I proposed as descriptive of that achievement, the term *tension*. I am using the term not as a general metaphor, but as a special one, derived from lopping the prefixes off the logical terms *ex*tension and *in*tension. What I am saying, of course, is that the meaning of poetry is its "tension," the full organized body of all the extension and intension that we can find in it. The remotest figurative significance that we can derive does not invalidate the extensions of the literal statement. Or we may begin with the literal statement and by stages develop the complications of metaphor: at every stage we may pause to state the meaning so far apprehended, and at every stage the meaning will be coherent.

The meanings that we select at different points along the infinite line between extreme intension and extreme extension will vary with our personal "drive," or "interest," or "approach": the Platonist will tend to stay pretty close to the end of the line where extension, and simple abstraction of the object into a universal, is easiest, for he will be a fanatic in morals or some kind of works, and will insist upon the shortest way with what will ever appear to him the dissenting ambiguities at the intensive end of the scale. The Platonist (I do not say that his opponent is the Aristotelian) might decide that Marvel's "To His Coy Mistress" recommends immoral behavior to the young men, in whose behalf he would try to suppress the poem. That, of course, would be one "true" meaning of "To His Coy Mistress," but it is a meaning that the full tension of the poem will not allow us to entertain exclusively. For we are compelled, since it is there, to give equal weight to an intensive meaning so rich that, without contradicting the literal statement of the lover-mistress convention, it lifts that convention into an insight into one phase of the human predicament—the conflict of sensuality and asceticism.

I should like to quote now, not from Marvel, but a stanza from Donne that I hope will reinforce a little what I have just said and connect it with some earlier remarks.

> Our two soules therefore, which are one,
> > Though I must goe, endure not yet
> A breach, but an expansion,
> > Like gold to aiery thinnesse beate.

Here Donne brings together the developing imagery of twenty lines under the implicit proposition: the unity of two lovers' souls is a nonspatial entity, and is therefore indivisible. That, I believe, is what Mr. John Crowe Ransom would call the logic of the passage; it is the abstract form of its extensive meaning. Now the interesting feature here is the logical contradiction of embodying the unitary, non-spatial soul in a spatial image: the malleable gold is a plane whose surface can always be extended mathematically by one-half towards infinity; the souls are this infinity. The finite image of the gold, in extension, logically contradicts the intensive meaning (infinity) which it conveys; but it does not invalidate that meaning. We have seen that Cowley compelled us to ignore the denoted diaper in order that we might take seriously the violet which it pretended to swathe. But in Donne's "Valediction: forbidding mourning" the clear denotation of the gold contains, by intension, the full meaning of the passage. If we reject the gold, we reject the meaning, for the meaning is wholly absorbed into the image of the gold. Intension and extension are here one, and they enrich each other.

Before I leave this beautiful object, I should like to notice two incidental features in further proof of Donne's mastery. "Expansion"—a term denoting an abstract property common to many objects, perhaps here one property of a gas: it expands visibly the quality of the beaten gold.

> > > . . . endure not yet
> > a breach . . .

But if the lovers' souls are the formidable, inhuman entity that we have seen, are they not superior to the contingency of a breach? Yes and no: both answers are true answers; for by means of the sly "yet" Donne subtly guards himself against our irony, which would otherwise be quick to scrutinize the extreme metaphor. The lovers have not endured a breach, but they are simple, miserable human beings, and they may quarrel tomorrow.[2]

Now all this meaning and more, and it is all one meaning, is embedded in that stanza: I say more because I have not exhausted the small fraction of significance that my limited powers have permitted me to see. For example, I have not discussed the rhythm, which is of the essential meaning; I have violently isolated four lines from the meaning of the whole poem. Yet, fine as it is, I do not think the poem the greatest poetry; perhaps only very little of Donne makes that grade, or of anybody else. Donne offers many examples of tension in imagery, easier for the expositor than greater passages in Shakespeare.

But convenience of elucidation is not a canon of criticism. I wish now to introduce other kinds of instance, and to let them stand for us as a sort of Arnoldish touchstones to the perfection that poetic statement has occasionally reached. I do not know what bearing my comment has had, or my touchstones may have, upon the larger effects of poetry or upon long poems. The long poem is partly a different problem. I have of necessity confined both commentary and illustration to the slighter effects that seemed to me commensurate with certain immediate qualities of language. For, in the long run, whatever the poet's "philosophy," however wide may be the extension of his meaning—like Milton's Ptolemaic universe in which he didn't believe—by his language shall you know him; the quality of his language is the valid limit of what he has to say.

I have not searched out the quotations that follow: they at once form the documentation and imply the personal bias from which this inquiry has grown. Only a few of the lines will be identified with the metaphysical technique, or, in Mr. Ransom's fine phrase, the metaphysical strategy. Strategy would here indicate the point on the intensive-extensive scale at which the poet deploys his resources of meaning. The metaphysical poet as a rationalist begins at or near the extensive or denoting end of the line; the romantic or Symbolist poet at the other, intensive end; and each by a straining feat of the imagination tries to push his meanings as far as he can towards the opposite end, so as to occupy the entire scale. I have offered one good and one bad example of the metaphysical strategy, but only defective examples of the Symbolist, which I cited as fallacies of mass language: Thomson was using language at its mass level, unhappily ignorant of the need to embody his connotations in a rational order of thought. (I allude here also, and in a quite literal sense, to Thomson's personal unhappiness, as well as to the excessive pessimism and excessive optimism of other poets of his time.) The great Symbolist poets, from Rimbaud to Yeats, have heeded this necessity of reason. It would be a hard task to choose between the two strategies, the Symbolist and the metaphysical; both at their best are great, and both are incomplete.

2. Mr. F. O. Matthiessen informs me that my interpretation here, which detaches the "yet" from the developing figure, is not the usual one. Mr. Matthiessen refers the phrase to the gold, for which in his view it prepares the way.

These touchstones, I believe, are not poetry of the extremes, but poetry of the center: poetry of tension, in which the "strategy" is diffused into the unitary effect.

Ask me no more whither doth hast
The Nightingale when *May* is past:
For in your sweet dividing throat
She winters, and keeps warm her note.

* * *

O thou Steeled Cognizance whose leap commits
The agile precincts of the lark's return . . .

* * *

That time of year thou mayst in me behold
When yellow leaves, or none, or few do hang
Upon those boughs which shake against the cold,
Bare ruined choirs where late the sweet birds sang.

* * *

Beauty is but a flower
Which wrinkles will devour;
Brightness falls from the air,
Queens have died young and fair,
Dust hath closed Helen's eye.
I am sick, I must die.
    Lord, have mercy upon us!

* * *

And then may chance thee to repent
The time that thou hast lost and spent
    To cause thy lovers sigh and swoon;
Then shalt thou know beauty but lent,
    And wish and want as I have done.

* * *

We have lingered in the chambers of the sea
By seagirls wreathed with seaweed red and brown
Till human voices wake us and we drown.

* * *

I am of Ireland
And the Holy Land of Ireland
And time runs on, cried she.
Come out of charity
And dance with me in Ireland.

* * *

And my poor fool is hanged! No, no, no life!
Why should a dog, a horse, a rat, have life
And thou no breath at all? Thou'lt come no more,
Never, never, never, never, never!—
Pray you undo this button; thank you, sir.—
Do you see this? Look on her,—look,—her lips,—
Look there, look there!

* * *

'Tis madness to resist or blame
The force of angry heavens flame:
        And, if we would speak true,
        Much to the Man is due,
Who, from his private Gardens, where
He liv'd reserved and austere,
        As if his highest plot
        To plant the Bergamot,
Could by industrious Valour climbe
To ruin the great Work of Time,
        And cast the Kingdome old
        Into another Mold.

* * *

Cover her face; mine eyes dazzle; she died young.

III

There are three more lines that I wish to look at: a tercet from *The Divine Comedy*. I know little of either Dante or his language; yet I have chosen as my final instance of tension—the instance itself will relieve me of the responsibility of the term—not a great and difficult passage, but only a slight and perfect one. It is from a scene that has always been the delight of the amateur reader of Dante; we can know more about it with less knowledge than about any other, perhaps, in the poem. The damned of the Second Circle are equivocally damned: Paolo and Francesca were illicit lovers but their crime was incontinence, neither adultery nor pandering, the two crimes of sex for which Dante seems to find any real theological reprobation, for they are committed with the intent of injury.

You will remember that when Dante first sees the lovers they are whirling in a high wind, the symbol here of lust. When Francesca's conversation with the poet begins, the wind dies down, and she tells him where she was born, in these lines:

Siede la terra dove nata fui
    Sulla marina dove il Po discende
    Per aver pace co' seguaci sui.

Courtney Landon renders the tercet:

The town where I was born sits on the shore,
Whither the Po descends to be at peace
Together with the streams that follow him.

But it misses a good deal; it misses the force of *seguaci* by rendering it as a verb. Professor Grandgent translates the third line: "To have peace with its pursuers," and comments: "The tributaries are conceived as chasing the Po down to the sea." Precisely; for if the *seguaci* are merely followers, and not pursuers also, the wonderfully ordered density of this simple passage is sacrificed. For although Francesca has told Dante where she lives, in the most directly descriptive language possible, she has told him more than that. Without the least imposition of strain upon the firmly denoted natural setting, she fuses herself with the river Po near which she was born. By a subtle shift of focus we see the pursued river as Francesca in Hell: the pursuing tributaries are a new visual image for the pursuing winds of lust. A further glance yields even more: as the winds, so the tributaries at once pursue and become one with the pursued; that is to say, Francesca has completely absorbed the substance of her sin—she is the sin; as, I believe it is said, the damned of the *Inferno* are plenary incarnations of the sin that has put them there. The tributaries of the Po are not only the winds of lust by analogy of visual images; they become identified by means of sound:

> . . . discende
> Per aver pace co' seguaci sui.

The sibilants dominate the line; they are the hissing of the wind. But in the last line of the preceding tercet Francesca has been grateful that the wind has subsided so that she can be heard—

> Mentre che il vento, come fa, si tace.*

After the wind has abated, then, we hear in the silence, for the first time, its hiss, in the susurration to the descending Po. The river is thus both a visual and an auditory image, and since Francesca is her sin and her sin is embodied in this image, we are entitled to say that it is a sin that we can both hear and see.

1941

---

*While the wind is quiet, now, in this place.

──○◄ YVOR WINTERS ►○──
(1900–1968)

Arthur Yvor Winters was born in Chicago, the son of a successful stock- and grain broker. When he was still a child, his family moved to Eagle Rock, California, a small town near Pasadena, which his paternal grandfather and uncle had helped found. Now part of metropolitan Los Angeles, the area was then still rural. "I used to climb over the hills when I was about ten," he later told the writer Hisaye Yamamoto, "and wander around in La Cañada, which was uncontaminated live-oak forest, not a house in miles, and almost knee-deep in leaf mold." The California landscape would become a central presence in his poetry. By the time he was ready for college, however, his family had returned to Chicago. He entered the University of Chicago where he joined the Poetry Club, which included several significant future writers, including Glenway Wescott and Elizabeth Madox Roberts.

In late 1918, however, Winters contracted tuberculosis and had to leave college. He soon settled in the Sunmount sanitarium in Santa Fe, New Mexico. The only available treatment was immobility, and the young poet slowly recuperated for three years—afflicted by "a fatigue so heavy that it was an acute pain, pervasive and poisonous." During this time Winters wrote his first book of poems, *The Immobile Wind* (1921), and most of his second, *The Magpie's Shadow* (1922). Both volumes show his absorption of the Imagist aesthetic and the influence of Japanese haiku and American Indian poetry. Written mostly in free verse or syllabics, his early poems are mostly very short—sometimes only a single line of six syllables—usually focusing on one or two images that serve as an entryway into a mental state of heightened awareness. The young Winters was deeply committed to Modernist experiment, and his early work also revealed the influence of Ezra Pound, Wallace Stevens, H. D., and William Carlos Williams. By the time he left the sanitarium, Winters had quarreled with his parents and needed to support himself. He first became a schoolteacher in the mining town of Madrid, New Mexico. Isolated from intellectual life, he corresponded with Marianne Moore, then a librarian in New York City who lent him books, "very kindly," he later remarked, "but I am sure illegally."

Living in the West and reclusive by nature, Winters would conduct several important literary friendships by mail. He and Hart Crane met only once, but their letters had a decisive influence on both poets' lives. On a trip back to Chicago he met Janet Lewis. She, too, had contracted tuberculosis and went to the same sanitarium Winters had recently left. He reconciled with his parents and entered the University of Colorado, where he studied French, Latin, and Spanish and completed an M.A. in 1926. That year he and Lewis were married at Sunmount, where she was still a patient. Winters taught French and Spanish at the University of Idaho in Moscow. Then in 1927 he entered Stanford as a graduate student in English. (Significantly, Winters's formal literary education consisted mostly of Romance language and classical poetry—supplemented by his passionate private reading of contemporary verse; he did not study premodern English-language poetry until he arrived at Stanford.) He remained there for the rest of his life, eventually becoming a full professor. Once resettled in California, Winters rarely left the West and never traveled abroad. For better and worse, he cultivated a distance between himself and the Eastern centers of literary opinion. He became the only major New Critic to live in the West. Rather than attending literary conferences, he raised Airdales and tended a small orchard.

In 1928 Winters experienced a radical aesthetic shift. He abandoned free verse and returned to traditional meters. The shift was initially pragmatic and not ideological. Winters decided that he could not equal the poets he most admired—Baudelaire, Rimbaud, Valéry, Hardy, Bridges, and Stevens—by the Imagist methods he was using, so he decided to try other techniques. Gradually, however, he began to develop a new theory of poetry based on his experiments with meter and form. "My shift from the methods of these early poems," he later wrote, "was not a shift from formlessness to form; it was a shift from certain kinds of form to others."

Winters had written reviews since leaving New Mexico, but in the late 1920s he began focusing enormous energy on criticism. He published prominent early essays on Hart Crane, Louise Bogan, Wallace Stevens, Marianne Moore, and the Fugitives. He also wrote dissenting essays on Robert Frost, Robinson Jeffers, and Archibald MacLeish, which helped define and consolidate the New Critical rejection of populist Modernism. In 1929 Winters and Lewis created *Gyroscope,* an influential small literary magazine dedicated to correcting the excesses of Modernism. The journal, which was printed by mimeograph on their kitchen table, lasted only four issues, but it confirmed Winters's growing importance as a major poet-critic. In his essays and reviews Winters articulated his dissatisfaction with the subjectivity, irrationality, and vague mysticism of American poetry. In three cantankerously contrarian and brilliantly iconoclastic critical volumes, *Primitivism and Decadence* (1937), *Maule's Curse: Seven Studies in the History of American Obscurantism* (1938), and *The Anatomy of Nonsense* (1943), Winters chronicled and dissected the philosophical contradictions inherent in Romantic and Modernist poetry. Eventually collected as *In Defense of Reason* (1947), these studies defined Winters's new sense of poetry as a means of "comprehension on a moral plane" of human experience cast in language that fully conveyed the feeling of the given experiences.

Winters's later poetry employed a lucid and exact neoclassical style in tight formal meters. His imagery maintained the bright exactitude of his early experimental work, but now it operated in an ordered rational context. He created a style, which he called "post-Symbolist," in which complex associational poetry was written with "no sacrifice to rational intelligence." While Winters's brand of Modernism was conservative and classical, his personal politics were firmly leftist and progressive. He was a lifelong member of the ACLU and NAACP, and once contemplated joining the Communist Party. His example demonstrates that among Modernists there was little connection between aesthetic and political radicalism.

In 1946 Winters helped his Stanford colleague, Wallace Stegner, create one of the nation's first graduate programs in creative writing. Over the next two decades the demanding and opinionated professor became one of the most influential poetry writing teachers in the history of American letters. Some of his students accepted his aesthetics, others rejected it, but few left unchallenged or unchanged. A short list of Winters's students includes Donald Justice, Edgar Bowers, Philip Levine, Thom Gunn, Donald Hall, Robert Hass, N. Scott Momaday, Robert Pinsky, and Ann Stanford. Winters's outspoken contrarian views kept him from receiving most literary honors, but in 1960, just as he published his *Collected Poems,* he won the Bollingen Prize for lifetime contribution to American poetry. He died of cancer in 1968.

◦—◦━━◗━━◦—◦

FOREWORD TO THE TESTAMENT OF A STONE

Being Notes on the Mechanics of the Poetic Image

These notes presuppose a knowledge of Fenollosa's *The Chinese Written Character,* a large part of T. S. Eliot's *The Sacred Wood,* and scattered paragraphs from Pound, Lewis, Croce, and the Hindus.

I reserve the right to add to or alter these notes later in case of any second publication. It is possible that they are not complete (the last section is obviously incomplete, as my interest in it is temporarily secondary), but they are an attempt to incite the beginnings of a scientific criticism of poetry, which up to date we do not have, except in a few scattered fragments.

The poet himself will be more sensitive to, or more moved by, some material than other material, will perceive it more completely, and so will write his best poems when dealing with it. Speculation upon the sensitivity of the individual poet and its possible modification by his environment is of some psychological interest and perhaps more "human interest," but it has little to do with the art of poetry. The degree of fusion of the parts of a poem will depend upon the degree of fusion of the poet with his material, and that, to be sure, is the result of the nature of his sensitivity and his environment. But one is usually—and theoretically—forced by circumstances to approach the poet and his environment—if one so desires—through his poems, and not the other way round.

Originally published in Italy, *Secession* 8 (Apr. 1924): 1–21.

Supposing one to be possessed of some intelligence, it is possible, after a reasonable amount of study, to decide whether a poem represents a perfect fusion of perceptions or not, and supposing one to have some education, it is possible, after similar study, to decide whether the poem be original or merely a restatement of the perceptions of others. As different poets are moved equally by different types of material, finished poems, composed of different types of material, may be equally intense; thus indicating that the material is of no importance to the critic, who is dealing with poems; but only to the poet, who is dealing with material, and that is his own affair. The cause of a perfectly fused poem is the fusion of the poet's consciousness with an object or a group of objects of whatever nature. The means by which this fusion is achieved is the poet's "technique." In the mature poet, the technique is the medium of fusion; and the ratio of what the poet sees or feels to what he gets down is in direct proportion to the perfection of his technique. Why one poet is moved by this and another by that, it is impossible to say. It is possible only to remark the fact. But technique can be analysed, and analysed minutely; and this analysis may be of value to other poets in perfecting and extending the range of their perceptions, and it may be of value to critics, private and public, insofar as it may make them more acutely aware of their poets' achievements.

A poem is a state of perfection at which a poet has arrived by whatever means. It is a stasis in a world of flux and indecision, a permanent gateway to waking oblivion, which is the only infinity and the only rest. It has no responsibilities except to itself and its own perfection—neither to the man who may come to it with imperfect understanding nor to the mood from which it may originally have sprung. It is not a means to any end, but is in itself an end, and it, or one of the other embodments of beauty, is the only end possible to the man of intellect.

The artist whose deity is art, has a religion as valid and as capable of producing great art as any religion of the past or as the recently defined religion of money. As a conscious and intelligent being, no other religion will be possible for him, and he cannot, because of his religion, be called a decadent, a heretic.

Driven into a corner of which we are unaware, we pursue our ends. For in infinity, those who withdraw in terror are those who drive us off with bitterness, and at the same instant, in the same thought and gesture. Yet equanimity is all we seek.

A poem is the result of a poet moving in a milieu. A poet is born into a certain intellectual and physical milieu, and this milieu may, to some extent, form the poet. But the poet will also be born with certain peculiar and unchangeable qualities, and these will, in the course of time, modify the milieu with respect to the particular poet. If the poet be of a very plastic nature, he may be greatly changed by his milieu. If he be of a more or less immobile nature, he will absorb into his own mind, and, in the process of absorption, change as becomes necessary, such part of his milieu as is to some extent forced upon him.

A poet's technique is a portion of the milieu into which he is born (tradition) modified by his peculiar qualities to serve their needs.

The milieu of any place and time is a relatively constant factor. The peculiar qualities of individual poets are infinitely variable. The resulting milieu of the individual poet is therefore infinitely variable. So it is infantile to say that a poet "does not interpret his time," to demand that he write in any specified manner. It is infantile to say that he can do this or that only with this or that technique. The individual can only say truly, "I can do this or that only with this or that technique." And even then he cannot be too sure.

So that the poem can be judged, not in relation to any time or place, nor to any mode of thought, but to itself alone, and as a part of literature; for it is not a means, but an end. The mind that can judge a poem accurately is very rare—even more rare than the mind that can create a poem. For this act of weighing requires a mind infinitely balanced, infinitely sensitive, and infinitely familiar with all the technical phases of the medium. Such a mind is, with one exception in a thousand, the mind of the master poet.

The intellectual poet is often accused of obscurity, merely because his reader is unfamiliar with the milieu in which he moves. If we imagine a poet writing in our own language but on a remote planet, whose vegetation and population, whose entire physical aspect, are different from anything we know, and expressing himself largely in terms of the physical, we cannot imagine ourselves receiving from his poems more than a very blurred impression. So is the poet moving in a world that is largely composed of thought and otherwise greatly modified by thought, to the reader unacquainted with the philosophies.

The poet moving in a world that is largely thought, so long as he regard it curiously and as a world, perceives certain specific things, as a walker in a field perceives a grassblade. These specific things are the material of the image, of art. When he loses his sense of the infinite nature of his world and organizes it into a knowable and applicable principle, he loses sight of the particulars themselves and sees their relationships to each other and his newly-created whole; and so becomes a philosopher; for it is only in the finite that the particular can be detected as a complete and uncoordinated whole; but he may still have occasional perceptions, and at times revert to the poet. When he becomes more interested in the application of his principle, in its possible effects, than in the principle itself, he becomes a preacher in perceptions, but he attempts to save a humanity that he cannot possibly understand by fitting it into a mutilated fragment of an infinity whose nature he once felt, but could never understand, and has now forgotten.

The poet, in creating, must lose himself in his object. If he becomes more interested in himself observing than in his object, and still continues to write about his object rather than himself observing, he will create a mannerism but no image. It is from this weakness that the various familiar pretty and paternal mannerisms arise. Such a mannerism may be held down to the point of producing poetry of whatever degree of impurity, or it may not.

The poet who is preoccupied with his object desires a speech without idiom and a style without mannerism, that the clarity of his perception may not be clouded by inessentials. In any absolute sense, both are impossible, but both can be closely approximated.

Perhaps it is true that the poet, moving through his world, reaches, for chemical or other reasons, a point of spiritual intensity, and that those objects that fall under his eye or his mind's eye at this point are transformed into something simpler and greater than actuality, with or without his consciousness of any sequence save the actual sequence of their appearance; that the reproduction of this simplification in words will reproduce in the reader the original emotion or point of intensity. Perhaps it is true that the poet, moving through his world, becomes aware of beautiful existences, and being moved by them to a sufficient point of intensity, is able to reproduce them in words with sufficient accuracy to create in his reader the emotion which they created in him. Or perhaps, and this is probably nearer to the truth, he is sufficiently moved by certain beautiful existences, to be able to create other beautiful existences; and this approaches T. S. Eliot's analogy of the catalyst, and his "significant emotion," which is probably the only sound statement of the creative process that we have.

All functions of man save the creation of art and pure thought tend to complicate his physical life without simplifying his mental life. The sciences, as abstractions, might have the same value as art. Indiscriminately applied, they have wrecked the world.

1924

◦►◄ LANGSTON HUGHES ►◄◦
(1902–1967)

The man who would become one of the leading figures in the Harlem Renaissance, and later the major American poet of Civil Rights protest, was born
James Langston Hughes in Joplin, Missouri. His father, James Hughes, was a
mining company stenographer, his mother, Carrie Mercer Langston Hughes,
an amateur poet and actress. His parents' marriage was troubled, and soon
after the poet's birth his father left, first for Cuba and then Mexico. His
mother took her son back to her hometown of Lawrence, Kansas. Langston
Hughes's grandmother, with whom he lived for most of a dozen years, had
once been married to an abolitionist member of John Brown's band who was
killed at Harper's Ferry in 1859. Her second husband, Charles Langston, had
been an abolitionist, and after the Civil War, a Republican businessman. The
poet, conscious of his mixed blood and heritage, grew up with his grandmother's stories, which gave him a sense of American history. "Nobody ever
cried in my grandmother's stories," he once wrote. "They worked, schemed,
or fought. But no crying."

After his grandmother's death, Langston moved with his mother to
Lincoln, Illinois, where she remarried. The poet now had a stepfather and
stepbrother, but still felt drawn to his own father's powerful presence in
Mexico. His new family moved to Cleveland, Ohio, where his stepfather
worked in a steel mill. The summer before his senior year at Cleveland's
Central High School, Langston went to stay with his father. He was already
writing poems that displayed the influence of Walt Whitman and Carl
Sandburg, and when he finished high school he was named "class poet."

Hughes's first literary fame came in 1921 when the *Crisis*, the official
organ of the NAACP, published his poem "The Negro Speaks of Rivers."
He enrolled at Columbia University for a year at his father's expense. He
met W. E. B. DuBois, the founder and editor of *Crisis* as well as the young
Harlem poet Countee Cullen. Refusing his father's invitation to return to
Mexico, he stayed on in New York to be a writer, continuing to absorb
the cultural influences of the time, including jazz and the blues.

The twenties were for Hughes a time of travel and frenetic literary activity. After a period doing odd jobs, he began working on merchant ships,
sailing to Africa in 1923 and twice to Europe. In 1924 he lived in France

and Italy, then returned the following year to live with his mother in Washington, D.C., where again he held down various menial jobs. Another of his poems, "The Weary Blues," made him new literary friends. Carl Van Vechten arranged to have Knopf publish a book of his poetry. One day Vachel Lindsay, who was on a public reading tour, happened to dine at a hotel where Hughes was a busboy. Hughes shyly left some of his poems at Lindsay's table, and the older poet, attracted by their deliberate informality, performed some of them that night, earning Hughes minor celebrity. Hughes soon had a patroness as well, a wealthy widow named Charlotte Mason, who also supported the work of Zora Neale Hurston and others.

In 1929 he took a degree from Lincoln University in Pennsylvania. After a successful tour of Cuba, he worked on a play, *Mule Bone*, with Hurston; but a powerful disagreement caused them to break with each other, and Hughes also lost the support of their patroness. Nevertheless, he continued to travel—to Haiti, Russia, California—and write at a prolific rate. Increasingly Hughes involved himself in leftist causes. In 1937, as a reporter covering the Spanish Civil War, he spent three months in Madrid while it was under siege. In Spain he also began to translate poems by the recently murdered Federico García Lorca. (He later translated Lorca's verse drama, *Blood Wedding*.) Several of his plays having been performed in New York, Hughes soon found himself writing a screenplay for a motion picture, *Way Down South* (1939).

During World War II Hughes lived in New York, publishing a weekly column in the *Chicago Defender* newspaper. There he introduced his Harlem character, Jesse B. Semple (or "Simple"), perhaps his most popular creation. Over the years he published several collections of Semple sketches. When his musical, *Street Scene*, done in collaboration with German composer Kurt Weill, opened on Broadway in 1947, it was greeted with rave reviews and became a hit. In the next decade, however, his earlier pro-Soviet poetry and his past friendships with figures like former Communist agent Whittaker Chambers resulted in his being called before Senator Joseph McCarthy's subcommittee on anti-American activities. Hughes survived the ordeal in part by admitting that his past radicalism had been a mistake. His connections and social activism caused problems for the rest of his life.

Hughes's populist aesthetic caused him a different sort of problem with the next generation of African American writers. In 1959 his *Selected Poems* was dismissed in the *New York Times* by novelist James Baldwin for its apparent lack of literary sophistication. In fact, Hughes's work often met with disdain, particularly by academic critics who considered it simple-minded. Nevertheless, he was clearly the most famous and popular African American poet of his generation. In works like his long poem, *Ask Your Mama: 12 Moods for Jazz* (1961), also one of the most ambitious, Hughes created an original blend of folk tradition, jazz, and Midwestern Modernism in plain language that appealed to a broad readership and profoundly influenced later black writers. Hughes objected to the more militant black poets of the 1960s, such as LeRoi Jones (Amiri Baraka), and defended the nonviolent strategies of Martin Luther King, Jr.

Hughes died in 1967 of complications following prostate surgery. It was typical of his productive life that two more volumes appeared posthumously that same year. The speed and facility with which he wrote resulted in uneven output, but he was one of the most innovative poets of his time. Many of his poems have the lightness and transparency of song lyrics; indeed, Hughes often wrote poetry with the intention of having it set to music.

Hughes was a prolific writer of prose, but it was almost entirely autobiography, satiric fiction, and journalism. His few serious critical essays, however, are remarkably rich and provocative—most notably, "The Negro Artist and the Racial Mountain," which stands as one of the key documents of the Harlem Renaissance. The essay, which first appeared in the *Nation* in 1926 as a response to George Schuyler's dismissive article, "The Negro-Art Hokum," meditates upon race and class as defining factors for artists in the Harlem Renaissance.

◄●━━◄▷━━●►

THE NEGRO ARTIST AND THE RACIAL MOUNTAIN

One of the most promising of the young Negro poets said to me once, "I want to be a poet—not a Negro poet," meaning, I believe, "I want to write like a white poet"; meaning subconsciously, "I would like to be a white poet"; meaning behind that, "I would like to be white." And I was sorry the young man said that, for no great poet has ever been afraid of being himself. And I doubted then that, with his desire to run away spiritually from his race, this boy would ever be a great poet. But this is the mountain standing in the way of any true Negro art in America— this urge within the race toward whiteness, the desire to pour racial individuality into the mold of American standardization, and to be as little Negro and as much American as possible.

But let us look at the immediate background of this young poet. His family is of what I suppose one would call the Negro middle class: people who are by no means rich yet never uncomfortable nor hungry—smug, contented, respectable folk, members of the Baptist church. The father goes to work every morning. He is a chief steward at a large white club. The mother sometimes does fancy sewing or supervises parties for the rich families of the town. The children go to a mixed school. In the home they read white papers and magazines. And the mother often says "Don't be like niggers" when the children are bad. A frequent phrase from the father is, "Look how well a white man does things." And so the word white comes to be unconsciously a symbol of all virtues. It holds for the children beauty, morality, and money. The whisper of "I want to be white" runs silently through their minds. This young poet's home is, I believe, a fairly typical home of the colored middle class. One sees immediately how difficult it would be for an artist born in such a home to interest himself in interpreting the beauty of his own people. He is never taught to see that beauty. He is taught rather not to see it, or if he does, to be ashamed of it when it is not according to Caucasian patterns.

For racial culture the home of a self-styled "high-class" Negro has nothing better to offer. Instead there will perhaps be more aping of things white than in

Originally published in *Nation* (23 June 1926).

a less cultured or less wealthy home. The father is perhaps a doctor, lawyer, land-owner, or politician. The mother may be a social worker, or a teacher, or she may do nothing and have a maid. Father is often dark but he has usually married the lightest woman he could find. The family attend a fashionable church where few really colored faces are to be found. And they themselves draw a color line. In the North they go to white theaters and white movies. And in the South they have at least two cars and house "like white folks." Nordic manners, Nordic faces, Nordic hair, Nordic art (if any), and an Episcopal heaven. A very high mountain indeed for the would-be racial artist to climb in order to discover himself and his people.

But then there are the low-down folks, the so-called common element, and they are the majority—may the Lord be praised! The people who have their hip of gin on Saturday nights and are not too important to themselves or the community, or too well fed, or too learned to watch the lazy world go round. They live on Seventh Street in Washington or State Street in Chicago and they do not particularly care whether they are like white folks or anybody else. Their joy runs, bang! into ecstasy. Their religion soars to a shout. Work maybe a little today, rest a little tomorrow. Play awhile. Sing awhile. O, let's dance! These common people are not afraid of spirituals, as for a long time their more intellectual brethren were, and jazz is their child. They furnish a wealth of colorful, distinctive material for any artist because they still hold their own individuality in the face of American standardizations. And perhaps these common people will give to the world its truly great Negro artist, the one who is not afraid to be himself. Whereas the better-class Negro would tell the artist what to do, the people at least let him alone when he does appear. And they are not ashamed of him—if they know he exists at all. And they accept what beauty is their own without question.

Certainly there is, for the American Negro artist who can escape the restrictions the more advanced among his own group would put upon him, a great field of unused material ready for his art. Without going outside his race, and even among the better classes with their "white" culture and conscious American manners, but still Negro enough to be different, there is sufficient matter to furnish a black artist with a lifetime of creative work. And when he chooses to touch on the relations between Negroes and whites in this country with their innumerable overtones and undertones surely, and especially for literature and the drama, there is an inexhaustible supply of themes at hand. To these the Negro artist can give his racial individuality, his heritage of rhythm and warmth, and his incongruous humor that so often, as in the Blues, becomes ironic laughter mixed with tears. But let us look again at the mountain.

A prominent Negro clubwoman in Philadelphia paid eleven dollars to hear Raquel Meller sing Andalusian popular songs. But she told me a few weeks before she would not think of going to hear "that woman," Clara Smith, a great black artist, sing Negro folksongs. And many an upper-class Negro church, even now, would not dream of employing a spiritual in its services. The drab melodies in white folks' hymnbooks are much to be preferred. "We want to worship the Lord correctly and quietly. We don't believe in 'shouting.' Let's be dull like the Nordics," they say, in effect.

The road for the serious black artist, then, who would produce a racial art is most certainly rocky and the mountain is high. Until recently he received almost no encouragement for his work from either white or colored people. The fine novels of Chesnutt go out of print with neither race noticing their passing. The quaint charm and humor of Dunbar's dialect verse brought to him, in his day, largely the same kind of encouragement one would give a sideshow freak (A colored man writing poetry! How odd!) or a clown (How amusing!).

The present vogue in things Negro, although it may do as much harm as good for the budding colored artist, has at least done this: it has brought him forcibly to the attention of his own people among whom for so long, unless the other race had noticed him beforehand, he was a prophet with little honor. I understand that Charles Gilpin acted for years in Negro theaters without any special acclaim from his own, but when Broadway gave him eight curtain calls, Negroes, too, began to beat a tin pan in his honor. I know a young colored writer, a manual worker by day, who had been writing well for the colored magazines for some years, but it was not until he recently broke into the white publications and his first book was accepted by a prominent New York publisher that the "best" Negroes in his city took the trouble to discover that he lived there. Then almost immediately they decided to give a grand dinner for him. But the society ladies were careful to whisper to his mother that perhaps she'd better not come. They were not sure she would have an evening gown.

The Negro artist works against an undertow of sharp criticism and misunderstanding from his own group and unintentional bribes from the whites. "Oh, be respectable, write about nice people, show how good we are," say the Negroes. "Be stereotyped, don't go too far, don't shatter our illusions about you, don't amuse us too seriously. We will pay you," say the whites. Both would have told Jean Toomer not to write *Cane*. The colored people did not praise it. The white people did not buy it. Most of the colored people who did read *Cane* hate it. They are afraid of it. Although the critics gave it good reviews the public remained indifferent. Yet (excepting the work of Du Bois) *Cane* contains the finest prose written by a Negro in America. And like the singing of Robeson, it is truly racial.

But in spite of the Nordicized Negro intelligentsia and the desires of some white editors we have an honest American Negro literature already with us. Now I await the rise of the Negro theater. Our folk music, having achieved world-wide fame, offers itself to the genius of the great individual American composer who is to come. And within the next decade I expect to see the work of a growing school of colored artists who paint and model the beauty of dark faces and create with new technique the expressions of their own soul-world. And the Negro dancers who will dance like flame and the singers who will continue to carry our songs to all who listen—they will be with us in even greater numbers tomorrow.

Most of my own poems are racial in theme and treatment, derived from the life I know. In many of them I try to grasp and hold some of the meanings and rhythms of jazz. I am as sincere as I know how to be in these poems and yet after every reading I answer questions like these from my own people: Do you think Negroes should always write about Negroes? I wish you wouldn't read some of your poems to white folks. How do you find anything interesting in a place like a cabaret? Why do you write about black people? You aren't black. What makes you do so many jazz poems?

But jazz to me is one of the inherent expressions of Negro life in America; the eternal tom-tom beating in the Negro soul—the tom-tom of revolt against weariness in a white world, a world of subway trains, and work, work, work; the tom-

tom of joy and laughter, and pain swallowed in a smile. Yet the Philadelphia club-woman is ashamed to say that her race created it and she does not like me to write about it. The old subconscious "white is best" runs through her mind. Years of study under white teachers, a lifetime of white books, pictures, and papers, and white manners, morals, and Puritan standards made her dislike the spirituals. And now she turns up her nose at jazz and all its manifestations—likewise almost everything else distinctly racial. She doesn't care for the Winold Reiss portraits of Negroes because they are "too Negro." She does not want a true picture of herself from anybody. She wants the artist to flatter her, to make the white world believe that all Negroes are as smug and as near white in soul as she wants to be. But, to my mind, it is the duty of the younger Negro artist, if he accepts any duties at all from outsiders, to change through the force of his art that old whispering "I want to be white," hidden in the aspirations of his people, to "Why should I want to be white? I am a Negro—and beautiful"?

So I am ashamed for the black poet who says, "I want to be a poet, not a Negro poet," as though his own racial world were not as interesting as any other world. I am ashamed, too, for the colored artist who runs from the painting of Negro faces to the painting of sunsets after the manner of the academicians because he fears the strange un-whiteness of his own features. An artist must be free to choose what he does, certainly, but he must also never be afraid to do what he might choose.

Let the blare of Negro jazz bands and the bellowing voice of Bessie Smith singing Blues penetrate the closed ears of the colored near-intellectuals until they listen and perhaps understand. Let Paul Robeson singing "Water Boy," and Rudolph Fisher writing about the streets of Harlem, and Jean Toomer holding the heart of Georgia in his hands, and Aaron Douglas drawing strange black fantasies cause the smug Negro middle class to turn from their white, respectable, ordinary books and papers to catch a glimmer of their own beauty. We younger Negro artists who create now intend to express our individual dark-skinned selves without fear or shame. If white people are pleased we are glad. If they are not, it doesn't matter. We know we are beautiful. And ugly too. The tom-tom cries and the tom-tom laughs. If colored people are pleased we are glad. If they are not, their displeasure doesn't matter either. We build our temples for tomorrow, strong as we know how, and we stand on top of the mountain, free within ourselves.

1926

LOUIS ZUKOFSKY
(1904–1978)

The man whose work Robert Creeley would call a bridge between the Modernist poetry of the 1920s and the experimental poetry of the 1950s learned to bridge cultures from an early age. The son of Jewish immigrants from Lithuania, Louis Zukofsky was born on Manhattan's Lower East Side and initially spoke only Yiddish, learning English in elementary school. Although he soon rebelled against his parents' Orthodox faith, their work ethic and family devotion became central components of his poetry, both in his unstinting dedication to literature and as recurring themes. Despite the financial burden, his parents sent him to Columbia University, where he studied philosophy and English, graduating in 1924 with a master's degree in English. The poetry he wrote during his college years was accomplished enough to appear in *Poetry* magazine. At Columbia he also began reading the work of Karl Marx, and although Zukofsky never joined the Communist Party, Marx's ideas about class, economics, and materialism would deeply influence his poetry.

By 1926 Zukofsky had thoroughly schooled himself in Modernism, displaying his skills in his ambitious "Poem beginning 'The.'" Zukofsky not only built his poem on Modernist techniques such as fragmentation and collage, but styled it as both a parody of *The Waste Land* and an assertion (pitted against Eliot's anti-Semitism) of Jewish identity. In 1927 Zukofsky took the bold step of sending the poem to Ezra Pound, who published it in his journal, *Exile*. The correspondence that developed between Zukofsky and Pound, who was then living in Italy, grew into a lifelong friendship that was strained at times due to Pound's anti-Semitism but remained productive for both writers. Zukofsky apprenticed himself to Pound so studiously that some readers consider his work too derivative. But Zukofsky differentiated himself from his mentor by developing a Marxist, Jewish perspective and by taking Modernist quotation, rapid juxtaposition, and concern with language even further than Pound—using language abstractly as a system like music or mathematics, so that composition became a matter of arrangement (especially of quoted material) that highlighted the building blocks of the system, such as prepositions, articles, and sonic patterns.

Pound was so impressed with Zukofsky's skill and intelligence that he persuaded Harriet Monroe to allow the young poet to edit the February 1931 issue of *Poetry*. Zukofsky included his own verse, along with work by William Carlos Williams, George Oppen, Carl Rakosi, and Charles Reznikoff—the group who was thereafter loosely associated with the name Zukofsky gave to the issue: "Objectivist." At Monroe's request, Zukofsky also wrote an essay that indicated the poets' shared concerns, "Sincerity and Objectification: With Special Reference to the Work of Charles Reznikoff," which Zukofsky later revised, merging it with two other early essays, and retitled "An Objective." Opening the essay with a definition that links poetry with optical precision, Zukofsky stressed poetry's need to register the concrete particulars of a world embedded in history. He also drew attention to a poem's identity as an object: a thing made of words.

Although some critics have questioned Objectivism's provenance as a legitimate school of poetry (Zukofsky later claimed that he only created a movement at Monroe's request), there is no doubt that the essay articulated his own aims for poetry. His view of poetry—and even of language itself—as contingent upon history and as a material thing, an object that exists in and of itself, arose from his Marxist perspective. During the course of his career, he worked assiduously to develop the implications of these ideas in numerous volumes of verse, most notably his dense book-length poem "*A*," which he began in 1928 and completed in 1974; in experimental translations from Catullus; and in criticism. Much of Zukofsky's work is formalist in the strictest sense possible; for example, he bases a section of "*A*" on a careful count of "n" and "r" sounds, and his translations from Catullus aim for sonic accuracy, rather than accuracy of meaning. Yet he was also capable of moving lyricism, as in the 1945 elegy for his mother, "A Song for the Year's End."

Apart from teaching at the University of Wisconsin from 1930 to 1931, Zukofsky spent his life in New York City. From 1935 until 1942, he worked for the Federal Writers' Project of the Works Progress Administration (WPA), and in 1947 he began teaching English at the Polytechnic Institute of Brooklyn, where he remained until his retirement in 1966. After ending an affair with the Wisconsin poet Lorine Niedecker, with whom he remained close friends, in 1939 he married Celia Thaew, a musician and composer, whose work became increasingly important to his poetry. Zukofsky's *Autobiography* (1970) consists almost entirely of her musical settings of his short poems, and the last section of "*A*" features her settings of his poetry and prose to Handel's *Harpsichord Pieces*. Their only child, Paul Zukofsky, was a violin prodigy who debuted at Carnegie Hall in 1956, at the age of thirteen.

The son's fame stood in stark contrast to the father's obscurity, for as Zukofsky aged, he became increasingly reclusive and resentful of his lack of recognition, despite the homage he received from a diverse array of younger poets, including Creeley, Charles Olson, Denise Levertov, Allen Ginsberg, and Robert Duncan. After Zukofsky's death in 1978 his influence increased. Language Poets such as Ron Silliman and Lyn Hejinian acknowledge him as an important forerunner of their work. Although his poetry is not widely read, Zukofsky's ideas have exerted considerable influence on mid-century and contemporary American poetry.

AN OBJECTIVE

I

An Objective: (Optics)—The lens bringing the rays from an object to a focus. That which is aimed at. (Use extended to poetry)—Desire for what is objectively perfect, inextricably the direction of historic and contemporary particulars.

It is understood that historic and contemporary particulars may mean a thing or things as well as an event or a chain of events: i.e. an Egyptian pulled-glass bottle in the shape of a fish or oak leaves, as well as the performance of Bach's *Matthew Passion* in Leipzig, and the rise of metallurgical plants in Siberia.

Omission of names is prompted by the historical method of the Chinese sage who wrote, "Then for nine reigns there was no literary production."

None at all; because there was neither consciousness of the "objectively perfect" nor an interest in clear or vital "particulars." Nothing—neither a new object nor the stripping of an old to the light—was "aimed at." Strabismus may be a topic of interest between two strabismics; those who see straight look away.

II

In sincerity shapes appear concomitants of word combinations, precursors of (if there is continuance) completed sound or structure, melody or form. Writing occurs which is the detail, not mirage, of seeing, of thinking with the things as they exist, and of directing them along a line of melody. Shapes suggest themselves, and the mind senses and receives awareness. Parallels sought for in the other arts call up the perfect line of occasional drawing, the clear beginnings of sculpture not proceeded with.

Presented with sincerity, the mind even tends to supply, in further suggestion, which does not attain rested totality, the totality not always found in sincerity and necessary only for perfect rest, complete appreciation. This rested totality may be called objectification—the apprehension satisfied completely as to the appearance of the art form as an object. That is: distinct from print which records action and existence and incites the mind to further suggestion, there exists, though it may not be harbored as solidity in the crook of an elbow, writing (audibility in two-dimensional print) which is an object or affects the mind as such. The codifications of the rhetoric books may have something to do with an explanation of this attainment, but its character may be simply described as the arrangement, into one apprehended unit, of minor units of sincerity—in other words, the resolving of words and their ideation into structure. Granted that the word combination "minor unit of sincerity" is an ironic index of the degradation of the power of the individual word in a culture which seems hardly to know that each word in itself is an arrangement, it may be said that each word possesses objectification to a powerful degree; but that the facts carried by one word are, in view of the preponderance of facts

This essay originally appeared, in a different version, in *Poetry* Feb. 1931. Collected in *Prepositions: The Collected Critical Essays* (London: Rapp and Carroll, 1967) 12–18.

carried by combinations of words, not sufficiently explicit to warrant a realization of rested totality such as might be designated an art form. Yet the objectification which is a poem, or a unit of structural prose, may exist in a line or very few lines. The mind may conceivably prefer one object to another—the energy of the heat which is Aten to the benignness of the light which is Athena. But this is a matter of preference rather than the invalidation of the object not preferred. It is assumed that epistemological problems do not affect existence, that a personal structure of relations might be a definite object, or *vice versa*.

At any time, objectification in writing is rare. The poems or the prose structures of a generation are few. Properly no verse should be called a poem if it does not convey the totality of perfect rest.

It is questionable, however, whether the state of rest achieved by objectification is more pertinent to the mind than presentation in detail: the isolation of each noun so that in itself it is an image, the grouping of nouns so that they partake of the quality of things being together without violence to their individual intact natures, simple sensory adjectives as necessary as the nouns.

The disadvantage of strained metaphor is not that it is necessarily sentimental (the sentimental may at times have its positive personal qualities) but that it carries the mind to a diffuse everywhere and leaves it nowhere. One is brought back to the entirety of the single word which is in itself a relation, an implied metaphor, an arrangement, a harmony or a dissonance.

The economy of presentation in writing is a reassertion of faith that the combined letters—the words—are absolute symbols for objects, states, acts, interrelations, thoughts about them. If not, why use words—new or old?

III

The several definitions of *An Objective* and the use of this term extended to poetry are from the sixth movement of "A". The lines referred to read:

The melody, the rest are accessory—
. . . my one voice; my other . . .
An objective—rays of the object brought to a focus,
An objective—nature as creator—desire for what is objectively perfect,
Inextricably the direction of historic and contemporary particulars.

Assuming the intention of these lines to be poetry, the implications are that a critic began as a poet, and that as a poet he had implicitly to be a critic.

A poet finds the continuously present analysis of his work preferable to criticism so-called. Yet what other criticism exclusive of his poem seems permissible? In preference to the brands of circumlocution requisite to ponderous journals, a "prose" criticism whose analysis follows without undue length of misinterpretation the more concise analysis of a considered poem seems permissible, if the general good demands such a prose. The direction of this prose, though it will be definition, will also be poetry, arising from the same source or what to a third reader might seem the same source as the poetry—a poetically charged mentality. Though perhaps gratifying to the poet whose poem is under observation—this prose, with all its poetic direction and right impetus, should, to the critic himself with his merely poetically charged mentality, seem secondary even tertiary and less; i.e. compared with that act which is a poem.

The graceless error of writing down to those who consciously want something else from poetry—not poetry—as some stay for their own vanity; to "sometimes" think that minds elaborately equipped with specific information, like science, must always confuse it with other specific information, like poetry. That may be the case with unfortunates. The point, however, would be not to proffer solemnly or whiningly confusions to the confused, but to indicate by energetic mental behavior how certain information may be useful to other information, and when the divisions which signalize them are necessary.

Such a process does not need to be accurately painful; rather it should be painlessly complete—as certain people are complete and ready to go anywhere but to the doctor.

Certainly the more precise the writing, the purer the poetry—and going back to the critic, he should know what pure poetry is. Or we shall never know how to dispose of our sensations before we begin to read poetry, or how to raise them to honesty and intelligence—as well as—those of us who are precisely afflicted—to that precision of style, we should do well to cultivate.

A poem. A poem as object—And yet certainly it arose in the veins and capillaries, if only in the intelligence—Experienced—(every word can't be overdefined) experienced as an object—Perfect rest—Or nature as creator, existing perfect, experience perfecting activity of existence, making it—theologically, perhaps—like the Ineffable—

A poem. Also the materials which are outside the veins and capillaries—The context—The context necessarily dealing with a world outside of it—The desire for what is objectively perfect, inextricably the direction of historic and contemporary particulars—A desire to place everything—everything aptly, perfectly, belonging within, one with, a context—

A poem. The context based on a world—Idle metaphor—a lime base—a fibre—not merely a charged vacuum tube—an aerie of personation—The desire for inclusiveness—The desire for an inclusive object.

A poem. This object in process—The poem as a job—A classic—

Homer's *the wet waves* not our *the wet waves* but enough association in the three words to make a context capable of extension from its time into the present. Because, there is, though meanings change, a linguistic etiquette, a record possibly clear to us as the usage of a past context—The context as it first meant—or if this may not be believed—an arrived-at equilibrium—or at least the past not even guessed by us arrived at an equilibrium of meaning determined by new meanings of word against word contemporarily read.

A poem: a context associated with "musical" shape, musical with quotation marks since it is not of notes as music, but of words more variable than variables, and used outside as well as within the context with communicative reference.

Impossible to communicate anything but particulars—historic and contemporary—things, human beings as things their instrumentalities of capillaries and veins binding up and bound up with events and contingencies. The revolutionary word if it must revolve cannot escape having a reference. It is not infinite. Even the infinite is a term.

Only good poetry—good an unnecessary adjective—is contemporary or classical. A standard of taste can be characterized only by acceptance of particular communication and concerned, so to speak, whenever the intelligence is in danger of being cluttered, with exclusions—not with books but with poetic invention. The nothing, not pure nothing, left over is not a matter of "recencies," but a matter of *pasts,* maybe *pasties.*

It would be just as well then dealing with "recencies" to deal with Donne or Shakespeare, if one knew them as well as a linguistic usage not their own can know them. And yet contexts and inventions seem to have been derived from them.

One can go further, try to dissect capillaries or intelligent nerves—and speak of the image felt as duration or perhaps of the image as the existence of the shape and movement of the poetic object. The poet's image is not dissociable from the movement or the cadenced shape of the poem.

An idea—not an empty concept. An idea—its value including its meaning. The desk, i.e. as object including its value—The object unrelated to palpable or predatory intent—Also the meaning, or what should be the meaning of science in modern civilization as pointed out in Thorstein Veblen.

No predatory manifestation—Yet a manifestation making the mind more temperate because the poem exists and has perhaps recorded both state and individual.

The components of the poetic object continued: the sound and pitch emphasis of a word are never apart from its meaning.

In this sense each poem has its own laws, since no criticism can take care of all the differences which each new composition in words is. Yet criticism would hardly be different if musical notations or signs were used instead of words. Example: any piece of original music and the special criticism it produces.

The components of the poetic object continued:

Typography—certainly—if print and the arrangement of it will help tell how the voice should sound. It is questionable on the other hand whether the letters of the alphabet can be felt as the Chinese feel their written characters. Yet most western poets of consequence seem constantly to communicate the letters of their alphabets as graphic representations of thought—no doubt the thought of the word influences the letters but the letters are there and seem to exude thought.

Add—the core that covers the work of poets who see with their ears, hear with their eyes, move with their noses and speak and breathe with their feet. And yet lunatics are sometimes profitably observed: the core that is covered, the valuable skeptic knows, may in itself be the intense vision of a fact.

Intention must, however, be distinguished from accomplishment which resolves the complexity of detail into a single object. Emphasize detail 130 times over—or there will be no poetic object.

Or put the job of explanation up to cabinet-making: certain joints show the carpentry not to advantage, certain joints are a fine evidence; some are with necessary craftsmanship in the object. The first type—showing the carpentry not to advantage—is always present in a great deal of unnecessary writing; the second and third are rare; the second—which is a fine evidence—is rare to this time; the third— which with necessary craftsmanship is hid in the object—is, whenever craftsmanship is present, characteristic of this time.

"Recencies?" No more modern than a Shakespearean conceit which manages to carry at least two ideas at a time. Or Dante's literal, anagogical and theological threefold meaning referred to in a letter to Can Grande.

In contemporary poetry three types of complexity are discernible: 1—the swift concatenation of multiple references usually lyrical in movement—almost any poem by Donne, for example; 2—the conceit—Shakespeare's "when to the sessions," his working out of love as book-keeping, or Donne's "Valediction," his "two twin compasses"; 3—the complexity of the epic—Byron's *Don Juan,* or most of it.

The word *complexity* is perhaps misleading. Ultimately, the matter of poetic object and its simple entirety must not be forgotten.

I.e. order and the facts as order. The order of all poetry is to approach a state of music wherein the ideas present themselves sensuously and intelligently and are of no predatory intention. A hard job, as poets have found reconciling contrasting principles of facts. In poetry the poet is continually encountering the facts which in the making seem to want to disturb the music and yet the music or the movement cannot exist without the facts, without its facts. The base matter, to speak hurriedly, which must receive the signet of the form. Poems are only acts upon particulars. Only through such activity do they become particulars themselves—i.e. poems.

The mind may construct its world—this is hardly philosophy—if the mind does construct its world there is always that world immanent or imminently outside which at least as a term has become an entity. Linguistic usage has somehow preserved these acts which were poems in other times and have transferred structures now. The good poems of today are not far from the good poems of yesterday.

1931

KENNETH REXROTH
(1905–1982)

Poet, critic, translator, anarchist, and cultural impresario, Kenneth Rexroth, who would occupy the intellectual center of the San Francisco Renaissance, was born in South Bend, Indiana. The only child of affluent, bohemian parents, Rexroth had a nourishing but unconventional childhood in a progressive Christian Socialist household. When he was four, his family relocated to Elkhart—the first of many moves his increasingly erratic parents made as their fortunes rose and fell. Eventually the couple separated, but briefly reunited before his mother's untimely death in 1916. In her final illness she refused to let her ten-year-old son attend school, but instead read to him from her sickbed, urging him to be a writer. Three years later his alcoholic father died suddenly. The orphaned adolescent went to Chicago to live with an aunt, but he quickly rebelled against the conventional new setting. Dropping out of high school at sixteen, Rexroth frequented bohemian Chicago, supporting himself through odd jobs and journalism. Soon he began hitchhiking across the country and later worked his way to Europe and Latin America aboard ships.

In 1927 Rexroth married Andrée Schafer, a painter, and the newlyweds soon moved to San Francisco, the city with which the poet would ever afterwards be associated. "It is the only city in the United States," he observed, "which was not settled overland by the westward-spreading puritan tradition." Deciding to "stay and grow up in the town," Rexroth wrote, painted, and worked in radical politics—usually just scraping by. He briefly joined the Communist Party but left because his own principles were pacifist and anarchist. His marriage also broke up—he would eventually marry four times. In 1932 his poems appeared in Louis Zukofsky's *An "Objectivists" Anthology*, and his first book, *In What Hour* (1940), was published to largely hostile reviews by Northeastern critics who either decried his political defection from the organized Left or considered his West Coast subject matter trivial. Despite his growing reputation and readership, Rexroth would never be read sympathetically by Eastern critics, and he never won a major establishment award.

A conscientious objector and pacifist, Rexroth engaged in antiwar activity during the early days of World War II, especially by helping Japanese

Americans resist internment, which made him the subject of a FBI investigation. He was eventually granted an exemption from the draft and escaped incarceration, although the strain of the situation contributed to the breakup of his second marriage. In 1944 he published a long poem, *The Phoenix and the Tortoise,* with New Directions, which was the start of a lifelong partnership between Rexroth and poet James Laughlin, the greatest American publisher of Modernist letters.

Now at the height of his powers, Rexroth published a steady stream of poetry, prose, translations, and drama. His most notable collections of poetry include *The Signature of All Things* (1950), *The Dragon and the Unicorn* (1952), *In Defense of the Earth* (1956), *Natural Numbers* (1963), and *The Heart's Garden, the Garden's Heart* (1967). Rexroth also began translating Asian poetry in an influential series of books, most notably *One Hundred Poems from the Japanese* (1955) and *One Hundred Poems from the Chinese* (1956).

By 1950 Rexroth had established himself—through hard work and sheer ambition—at the center of San Francisco literary life. He not only published in national journals but also conducted a weekly book review show on Berkeley's newly established KPFA, the nation's first listener-sponsored radio station. A public spokesman for Modernist literature, political dissent, and alternate lifestyles, Rexroth became the elder statesman of the new Beat movement emerging in San Francisco, which generated huge amounts of media coverage that turned several younger writers he had championed—most notably Allen Ginsberg, Lawrence Ferlinghetti, and Jack Kerouac—into international celebrities. Such fame never came to Rexroth himself; he was too mature, well-read, and intellectual to fit the media's definition of the Beat identity. (Instead, *Time* magazine dubbed him "the Daddy of the Beat Generation," not a particularly cool title.) The media craze did allow Rexroth to develop with the other Beats a new form of poetry reading—not the academic lecture style still prevalent today, but a performance spoken to the accompaniment of live jazz.

Rexroth's later years were secure and comfortable. In 1968 he took a teaching position at the University of California at Santa Barbara, which he held until his retirement in 1974. Also in 1974, Rexroth married his longtime companion, Carol Tinker, his fourth and final spouse. He wrote a popular literary column, "Classics Revisited," for *Saturday Review* and a twice weekly column in the *San Francisco Examiner* in which he was free to discuss any topic from avant-garde art to world politics. Rexroth died at seventy-six in Santa Barbara where, after a Catholic and Buddhist ceremony, he was buried facing the Pacific Ocean.

Rexroth worked to establish a West Coast identity for American poetry, one that would reflect the unique geographical, historical, cultural, and ethnic qualities of the region. "I am NOT Ivy League," he once asserted, as if anyone could have ever confused his self-educated libertarian anarchism with Ivy League elitism or New Critical detachment. He was both a populist and an intellectual—a potent combination of cultural values in the right circumstances. Rexroth also understood that regional literary identity need not—indeed must not—be provincial. His international sense of literary enterprise led him to translate from Chinese, Japanese, French, Spanish, and Greek, all as relevant sources for a California literary identity.

Rexroth's place in the American literary canon—like that of many Californian poets such as Robinson Jeffers, William Everson, Josephine Miles, Robert Duncan, and Jack Spicer—remains open to debate. Consistently ignored by the Eastern literary establishment, these poets continue to exercise an active influence on West Coast writers, and they continue to be read. Rexroth left a small but enduring body of original poems, elegant translations, and still potent essays out of the huge body of work he created. It remains impossible to discuss the changes in mid-twentieth-century American poetry responsibly without mentioning him.

A prolific prose writer, Rexroth published six critical collections in his lifetime: *Bird in the Bush* (1959), *Assays* (1961), *The Classics Revisited* (1968), *The Alternative Society* (1970), *With Eye and Ear* (1970), and *The Elastic Retort* (1973), as well as two full-length studies, *American Poetry in the Twentieth Century* (1971) and *Communalism* (1974). (There was also a posthumous collection, *More Classics Revisited,* published in 1989.) He wrote many uncollected reviews, essays, articles, and introductions. In his criticism Rexroth refused to separate literature from other human enterprises, especially politics, economics, philosophy, and religion—a stance in open opposition to the New Critics, who believed the poem should stand alone and be judged mostly on its internal merits. Rexroth also addressed his prose to the general reader rather than the academic critic. He once declared that his prose was "not criticism but journalism." If so, it was literary journalism of the highest order, since so much of it remains lively half a century after its composition—"news that stays news"—as in this engaged account of the Beat movement excerpted from *The Alternative Society*.

<hr />

DISENGAGEMENT: THE ART OF THE BEAT GENERATION

Literature generally, but literary criticism in particular, has always been an area in which social forces assume symbolic guise, and work out—or at least exemplify—conflicts taking place in the contemporary, or rather, usually the just past, wider arena of society. Recognition of this does not imply the acceptance of any general theory of social or economic determinism. It is a simple, empirical fact. Because of the pervasiveness of consent in American society generally, that democratic leveling up or down so often bewailed since de Tocqueville, American literature, especially literary criticism, has usually been ruled by a "line." The fact that it was spontaneously evolved and enforced only by widespread consent has never detracted from its rigor—but rather the opposite. It is only human to kick against the prodding of a Leopold Auerbach or an Andrey Zhdanov. An invisible, all-enveloping compulsion is not likely to be recognized, let alone protested against.

After World War I there was an official line for general consumption: "Back to Normalcy." Day by day in every way, we are getting better and better. This produced a literature which tirelessly pointed out that there was nothing whatsoever normal about us. The measure of decay in thirty years is the degree of acceptance of the official myth today—from the most obscure hack on a provincial newspaper to

Originally published in *New World Writing* 11 (1957). Collected in *The Alternative Society: Essays from the Other World* (New York: Herder and Herder, 1970).

the loftiest metaphysicians of the literary quarterlies. The line goes: "The generation of experimentation and revolt is over." This is an etherealized corollary of the general line: "The bull market will never end."

I do not wish to argue about the bull market, but in the arts nothing could be less true. The youngest generation is in a state of revolt so absolute that its elders cannot even recognize it. The disaffiliation, alienation, and rejection of the young has, as far as their elders are concerned, moved out of the visible spectrum altogether. Critically invisible, modern revolt, like X-rays and radioactivity, is perceived only by its effects at more materialistic social levels, where it is called delinquency.

"Disaffiliation," by the way, is the term used by the critic and poet, Lawrence Lipton, who has written several articles on this subject, the first of which, in the *Nation,* quoted as epigraph, "We disaffiliate . . ."—John L. Lewis.

Like the pillars of Hercules, like two ruined Titans guarding the entrance to one of Dante's circles, stand two great dead juvenile delinquents—the heroes of the post-war generation: the saxophonist, Charlie Parker, and Dylan Thomas. If the word "deliberate" means anything, both of them certainly deliberately destroyed themselves.

Both of them were overcome by the horror of the world in which they found themselves, because at last they could no longer overcome that world with the weapon of a purely lyrical art. Both of them were my friends. Living in San Francisco I saw them seldom enough to see them with a perspective which was not distorted by exasperation or fatigue. So as the years passed, I saw them each time in the light of an accelerated personal conflagration.

The last time I saw Bird, at Jimbo's Bob City, he was so gone—so blind to the world—that he literally sat down on me before he realized I was there. "What happened, man?" I said, referring to the pretentious "Jazz Concert." "Evil, man, evil," he said, and that's all he said for the rest of the night. About dawn he got up to blow. The rowdy crowd chilled into stillness and the fluent melody spiraled through it.

The last time I saw Dylan, his self-destruction had not just passed the limits of rationality. It had assumed the terrifying inertia of inanimate matter. Being with him was like being swept away by a torrent of falling stones.

Now Dylan Thomas and Charlie Parker have a great deal more in common than the same disastrous end. As artists, they were very similar. They were both very fluent. But this fluent, enchanting utterance had, compared with important artists of the past, relatively little content. Neither of them got very far beyond a sort of entranced rapture at his own creativity. The principal theme of Thomas's poetry was the ambivalence of birth and death—the pain of blood-stained creation. Music, of course, is not so explicit an art, but anybody who knew Charlie Parker knows that he felt much the same way about his own gift. Both of them did communicate one central theme: Against the ruin of the world, there is only one defense—the creative act. This, of course, is the theme of much art—perhaps most poetry. It is the theme of Horace, who certainly otherwise bears little resemblance to Parker or Thomas. The difference is that Horace accepted his theme with a kind of silken assurance. To Dylan and Bird it was an agony and terror. I do not believe that this is due to anything especially frightful about their relationship to their own creativity. I believe rather that it is due to the catastrophic world in which that creativity seemed to be the sole value. Horace's column of imperishable verse shines quietly enough in the lucid air of Augustan Rome. Art may have been for him the most enduring, orderly, and noble activity of man. But the other activities of his life partook of these values. They did not actively negate them. Dylan Thomas's verse had to find endurance in a world of burning cities and burning Jews. He was able to find meaning in his art as long as it was the answer to air raids and gas ovens. As the world began to take on the guise of an immense air raid or gas oven, I believe his art became meaningless to him. I think all this could apply to Parker just as well, although, because of the nature of music, it is not demonstrable—at least not conclusively.

Thomas and Parker have more in common than theme, attitude, life pattern. In the practice of their art, there is an obvious technical resemblance. Contrary to popular belief, they were not great technical innovators. Their effects are only superficially startling. Thomas is a regression from the technical originality and ingenuity of writers like Pierre Reverdy or Apollinaire. Similarly, the innovations of bop, and of Parker particularly, have been vastly overrated by people unfamiliar with music, especially by that ignoramus, the intellectual jitterbug, the jazz aficionado. The tonal novelties consist in the introduction of a few chords used in classical music for centuries. And there is less rhythmic difference between progressive jazz, no matter how progressive, and Dixieland, than there is between two movements of many conventional symphonies.

What Parker and his contemporaries—Gillespie, Davis, Monk, Roach (Tristano is an anomaly), etc.—did was to absorb the musical ornamentation of older jazz into the basic structure, of which it then became an integral part, and with which it then developed. This is true of the melodic line which could be put together from selected passages of almost anybody—Benny Carter, Johnny Hodges. It is true of the rhythmic pattern in which the beat shifts continuously, or at least is continuously sprung, so that it becomes ambiguous enough to allow the pattern to be dominated by the long pulsations of the phrase or strophe. This is exactly what happened in the transition from baroque to rococo music. It is the difference between Bach and Mozart.

It is not a farfetched analogy to say that this is what Thomas did to poetry. The special syntactical effects of a Rimbaud or an Edith Sitwell—actually ornaments—become the main concern. The metaphysical conceits, which fascinate the Reactionary Generation still dominant in backwater American colleges, were embroideries. Thomas's ellipses and ambiguities are ends in themselves. The immediate theme, if it exists, is incidental, and his main theme—the terror of birth—is simply reiterated.

This is one difference between Bird and Dylan which should be pointed out. Again, contrary to popular belief, there is nothing crazy or frantic about Parker either musically or emotionally. His sinuous melody is a sort of naïve transcendence of all experience. Emotionally, it does not resemble Berlioz or Wagner; it resembles Mozart. This is true also of a painter like Jackson Pollock. He may have been eccentric in his behavior, but his paintings are as impassive as Persian tiles. Partly this difference is due to the nature of verbal communication. The insistent talk-aboutiveness of the general environment obtrudes into even the most idyllic poetry. It is much more a personal difference. Thomas certainly wanted to tell people about the ruin and disorder of the world. Parker and Pollock wanted to substitute a work of art for the world.

Technique pure and simple, rendition, is not of major importance, but it is interesting that Parker, following Lester Young, was one of the leaders of the so-called saxophone revolution. In modern jazz, the saxophone is treated as a woodwind and played with conventional embouchure. Metrically, Thomas's verse was extremely conventional, as was, incidentally, the verse of that other tragic enragé, Hart Crane.

I want to make clear what I consider the one technical development in the first wave of significant post-war arts. Ornament is confabulation in the interstices of structure. A poem by Dylan Thomas, a saxophone solo by Charles Parker, a painting by Jackson Pollock—these are pure confabulations as ends in themselves. Confabulation has come to determine structure. Uninhibited lyricism should be distinguished from its exact opposite—the sterile, extraneous invention of the corn-belt metaphysicals, our present blight of poetic professors.

Just as Hart Crane had little influence on anyone except very reactionary writers—like Allen Tate, for instance, to whom Valéry was the last word in modern poetry and the felicities of an Apollinaire, let alone a Paul Éluard, were nonsense—so Dylan Thomas's influence has been slight indeed. In fact, his only disciple—the only person to imitate his style—was W. S. Graham, who seems to have imitated him without much understanding, and who has since moved on to other methods. Thomas's principal influence lay in the communication of an attitude—that of the now extinct British romantic school of the New Apocalypse—Henry Treece, J. F. Hendry, and others—all of whom were quite conventional poets.

Parker certainly had much more of an influence. At one time it was the ambition of every saxophone player in every high school band in America to blow like Bird. Even before his death this influence had begun to ebb. In fact, the whole generation of the founding fathers of bop—Gillespie, Monk, Davis, Blakey, and the rest—are just now at a considerable discount. The main line of development today goes back to Lester Young and bypasses them.

The point is that many of the most impressive developments in the arts nowadays are aberrant, idiosyncratic. There is no longer any sense of continuing development of the sort that can be traced from Baudelaire to Éluard, or for that matter from Hawthorne through Henry James to Gertrude Stein. The cubist generation before World War I, and, on a lower level, the surrealists of the period between the wars, both assumed an accepted universe of discourse, in which, to quote André Breton, it was possible to make definite advances, exactly as in the sciences. I doubt if anyone holds such ideas today. Continuity exists, but like the neo-swing music developed from Lester Young, it is a continuity sustained by popular demand.

In the plastic arts, a very similar situation exists. Surrealists like Hans Arp and Max Ernst might talk of creation by hazard—of composing pictures by walking on them with painted soles, or by tossing bits of paper up in the air. But it is obvious that they were self-deluded. Nothing looks anything like an Ernst or an Arp but another Ernst or Arp. Nothing looks less like their work than the happenings of random occasion. Many of the post-World War II abstract expressionists, apostles of the discipline of spontaneity and hazard, look alike, and do look like accidents. The aesthetic appeal of pure paint laid on at random may exist, but it is a very impoverished appeal. Once again what has happened is an all-consuming confabulation of the incidentals, the accidents of painting. It is curious that at its best, the work of this school of painting—Mark Rothko, Jackson Pollock, Clyfford Still, Robert Motherwell, William deKooning, and the rest—resembles nothing so much as the passage painting of quite unimpressive painters: the mother-of-pearl shimmer in the background of a Henry McFee, itself a formula derived from Renoir; the splashes of light and black which fake drapery in the fashionable imitators of Hals and Sargent. Often work of this sort is presented as calligraphy—the pure utterance of the brush stroke seeking only absolute painteresque values. You have only to compare such painting with the work of, say, Sesshu, to realize that someone is using words and brushes carelessly.

At its best the abstract expressionists achieve a simple rococo decorative surface. Its poverty shows up immediately when compared with Tiepolo, where the rococo rises to painting of extraordinary profundity and power. A Tiepolo painting, however confabulated, is a universe of tensions in vast depths. A Pollock is an object of art—bijouterie—disguised only by its great size. In fact, once the size is big enough to cover a whole wall, it turns into nothing more than extremely expensive wallpaper. Now there is nothing wrong with complicated wallpaper. There is just more to Tiepolo. The great Ashikaga brush painters painted wallpapers, too—at least portable ones, screens.

A process of elimination which leaves the artist with nothing but the play of his materials themselves cannot sustain interest in either artist or public for very long. So in recent years abstract expressionism has tended towards romantic suggestion—indications of landscape or living figures. This approaches the work of the Northwest school—Clayton Price, Mark Tobey, Kenneth Callahan, Morris Graves—who have of all recent painters come nearest to conquering a territory which painting could occupy with some degree of security. The Northwest school, of course, admittedly is influenced by the ink painters of the Far East, and by Tintoretto and Tiepolo. The dominant school of post-World War II American painting has really been a long detour into plastic nihilism. I should add that painters like Ernie Briggs seem to be opening up new areas of considerable scope within the main traditional abstract expressionism—but with remarkable convergence to Tobey or Tintoretto, as you prefer.

Today American painting is just beginning to emerge with a transvaluation of values. From the mid-nineteenth century on, all ruling standards in the plastic arts were subject to continual attack. They were attacked because each on-coming generation had new standards of its own to put in their place. Unfortunately, after one hundred years of this, there grew up a generation ignorant of the reasons for the revolt of their elders, and without any standards whatever. It has been necessary to create standards anew out of chaos. This is what modern education purports to do with finger painting in nursery schools. This is why the Northwest school has enjoyed such an advantage over the abstract expressionists. Learning by doing, by trial and error, is learning by the hardest way. If you want to overthrow the cubist tradition of architectural painting, it is much easier to seek out its opposites in the history of culture and study them carefully. At least it saves a great deal of time.

One thing can be said of painting in recent years—its revolt, its rejection of the classic modernism of the first half of the century, has been more absolute than in any other art. The only ancestor of abstract expressionism is the early Kandinsky—a style rejected even by Kandinsky himself. The only painter in a hundred years who bears the slightest resemblance to Tobey or Graves is Odilon Redon (perhaps Gustave Moreau a little), whose stock was certainly not very high with painters raised in the cubist tradition.

The ready market for prose fiction has had a decisive influence on its development. Sidemen with Kenton or Herman may make a good if somewhat hectic living, but any novelist who can write home to mother, or even spell his own name, has a chance to become another Brubeck. The deliberately and painfully intellectual fiction which appears in the literary quarterlies is a byproduct of certain class-rooms. The only significant fiction in America is popular fiction. Nobody realizes this better than the French. To them our late-born imitators of Henry James and E. M. Forster are just *chiens qui fument,** and arithmetical horses and bicycling seals. And there is no more perishable commodity than the middle-brow novel. No one today reads Ethel L. Voynich or Joseph Hergesheimer, just as no one in the future will read the writers' workshop pupils and teachers who fill the literary quarterlies. Very few people, except themselves, read them now.

On the other hand, the connection between the genuine highbrow writer and the genuinely popular is very close. Hemingway had hardly started to write before his style had been reduced to a formula in *Black Mask*, the first hard-boiled detective magazine. In no time at all he had produced two first-class popular writers, Raymond Chandler and Dashiell Hammett. Van Vechten, their middle-brow contemporary, is forgotten. It is from Chandler and Hammett and Hemingway that the best modern fiction derives; although most of it comes out in hard covers, it is always thought of as written for a typical pocketbook audience. Once it gets into pocketbooks it is sometimes difficult to draw the line between it and its most ephemeral imitators. Even the most *précieux* French critics, a few years ago, considered Horace McCoy America's greatest contemporary novelist. There is not only something to be said for their point of view; the only thing to be said against it is that they don't read English.

Much of the best popular fiction deals with the world of the utterly disaffiliated. Burlesque and carnival people, hipsters, handicappers and hop heads, wanted men on the lam, an expendable squad of soldiers being expended, anyone who by definition is divorced from society and cannot afford to believe even an iota of the social lie—these are the favorite characters of modern postwar fiction, from Norman Mailer to the latest ephemerid called *Caught,* or *Hung Up,* or *The Needle,* its bright cover winking invitingly in the drugstore. The first, and still the greatest, novelist of total disengagement is not a young man at all, but an elderly former I.W.W. of Germany ancestry, B. Traven, the author of *The Death Ship* and *The Treasure of Sierra Madre.*

It is impossible for an artist to remain true to himself as a man, let alone an artist, and work within the context of this society. Contemporary mimics of Jane Austen or Anthony Trollope are not only beneath contempt. They are literally unreadable. It is impossible to keep your eyes focused on the page. Writers as far apart as J. F. Powers and Nelson Algren agree in one thing—their diagnosis of an absolute corruption.

This refusal to accept the mythology of press and pulpit as a medium for artistic creation, or even enjoyable reading matter, is one explanation for the popularity of escapist literature. Westerns, detective stories, and science fiction are all situated beyond the pale of normal living. The slick magazines are only too well aware of this, and in these three fields especially exert steady pressure on their authors to accentuate the up-beat. The most shocking example of this forced perversion is the homey science-fiction story, usually written by a woman, in which a one-to-one correlation has been made for the commodity-ridden tale of domestic whimsey, the stand-by of magazines given away in the chain groceries. In writers

*chiens qui fument: dogs that smoke.

like Judith Merrill the space pilot and his bride bat the badinage back and forth while the robot maid makes breakfast in the jet-propelled lucite orange squeezer and the electronic bacon rotobroiler, dropping pearls of dry assembly plant wisdom (like plantation wisdom but drier), the whilst. Still, few yield to these pressures, for the obvious reason that fiction indistinguishable from the advertising columns on either side of the page defeats its own purpose, which is to get the reader to turn over the pages when he is told "continued on p. 47."

Simenon is still an incomparably better artist and psychologist than the psychological Jean Stafford. Ward Moore is a better artist than Eudora Welty, and Ernest Haycox than William Faulkner, just as, long ago, H. G. Wells was a better artist, as artist, than E. M. Forster, as well as being a lot more interesting. At its best, popular literature of this sort, coming up, meets high-brow literature coming down. It has been apparent novel by novel that Nelson Algren is rising qualitatively in this way. In *A Walk on the Wild Side*, thoroughly popular in its materials, he meets and absorbs influences coming down from the top, from the small handful of bona fide high-brow writers working today—Céline, Jean Genêt, Samuel Beckett, Henry Miller. In Algren's case this has been a slow growth, and he has carried his audience with him. Whatever the merits of his subject matter or his thesis—"It is better to be out than in. It is better to be on the lam than on the cover of *Time* Magazine"—his style started out as a distressing mixture of James Farrell and Kenneth Fearing. Only later did he achieve an idiom of his own.

There is only one thing wrong with this picture, and that is that the high-brow stimulus still has to be imported. Algren, who is coming to write more and more like Céline, has no difficulty selling his fiction. On the other hand, an author like Jack Kerouac, who is in his small way the peer of Céline, Destouches, or Beckett, is the most famous "unpublished" author in America. Every publisher's reader and adviser of any moment has read him and was enthusiastic about him. In other words, anybody emerging from the popular field has every advantage. It is still extremely difficult to enter American fiction from the top down.

The important point about modern fiction is that it is salable, and therefore negotiable in our society, and therefore successful in the best sense of the word. When a novelist has something to say, he knows people will listen. Only the jazz musician, but to a much lesser degree, shares this confidence in his audience. It is of the greatest social significance that the novelists who say, "I am proud to be delinquent" are sold in editions of hundreds of thousands.

Nobody much buys poetry. I know. I am one of the country's most successful poets. My books actually sell out—in editions of two thousand. Many a poet, the prestige ornament of a publisher's list, has more charges against his royalty account than credits for books sold. The problem of poetry is the problem of communication itself. All art is a symbolic criticism of values, but poetry is specifically and almost exclusively that. A painting decorates the wall. A novel is a story. Music . . . soothes a savage breast. But poetry you have to take straight. In addition, the entire educational system is in a conspiracy to make poetry as unpalatable as possible. From the seventh-grade teacher who rolls her eyes and chants H. D. to the seven types of ambiguity factories, grinding out little Donnes and Hopkinses with hayseeds in their hair, everybody is out to de-poetize forever the youth of the land. Again, bad and spurious painting, music, and fiction are not really well-organized, except on obvious commercial levels, where they can be avoided. But in poetry Gresham's Law is supported by the full weight of the powers that be. From about 1930 on, a conspiracy of bad poetry has been as carefully organized as the Communist Party, and today controls most channels of publication except the littlest of the little magazines. In all other departments of American culture, English influence has been at a steadily declining minimum since the middle of the nineteenth century. In 1929, this was still true of American poetry. Amy Lowell, Sandburg, H. D., Pound, Marianne Moore, William Carlos Williams, Wallace Stevens—all of the major poets of the first quarter of the century owed far more to Apollinaire or Francis Jammes than they did to the whole body of the English tradition. In fact, the new poetry was essentially an anti-English, pro-French movement—a provincial but clear echo of the French revolt against the symbolists. On the other hand, Jules Laforgue and his English disciples, Ernest Dowson and Arthur Symons, were the major influence on T. S. Eliot. Unfortunately Mr. Eliot's poetic practice and his thoroughly snobbish critical essays which owed their great cogency to their assumption, usually correct, that his readers had never heard of the authors he discussed—Webster, Crashaw, or Lancelot Andrewes—lent themselves all too easily to the construction of an academy and the production of an infinite number of provincial academicians—policemen entrusted with the enforcement of Gresham's Law.

Behind the façade of this literary Potemkin village, the mainstream of American poetry, with its sources in Baudelaire, Lautréamont, Rimbaud, Apollinaire, Jammes, Reverdy, Salmon, and later Breton and Éluard, has flowed on unperturbed, though visible only at rare intervals between the interstices of the academic hoax. Today the class magazines and the quarterlies are filled with poets as alike as two bad pennies. It is my opinion that these people do not really exist. Most of them are androids designed by Ransom, Tate, and Co., and animated by Randall Jarrell. They are not just counterfeit; they are not even real counterfeits, but counterfeits of counterfeits. On these blurred and clumsy coins the lineaments of Mr. Eliot and I. A. Richards dimly can be discerned, like the barbarized Greek letters which nobody could read on Scythian money.

This is the world in which over every door is written the slogan: "The generation of experiment and revolt is over. Bohemia died in the Twenties. There are no more little magazines." Actually there have never been so many little magazines. In spite of the fantastic costs of printing, more people than ever are bringing out little sheets of free verse and making up the losses out of their own pockets. This world has its own major writers, its own discoveries, its own old masters, its own tradition and continuity. Its sources are practically exclusively French, and they are all post-symbolist, even anti-symbolist. It is the Reactionary Generation who are influenced by Laforgue, the symbolists, and Valéry. Nothing is more impressive than the strength, or at least the cohesion, of this underground movement. Poets whom the quarterlies pretend never existed, like Louis Zukovsky and Jack Wheelwright, are still searched out in large libraries or obscure bookshops and copied into notebooks by young writers. I myself have a complete typewritten collection of the pre-reactionary verse of Yvor Winters. And I know several similar collections of "forgotten modernists" in the libraries of my younger friends. People are always turning up who say something like, "I just discovered a second-hand copy of Parker Tyler's *The Granite Butterfly* in a Village bookshop. It's great, man." On the other hand, I seriously doubt whether *The Hudson Review* would ever consider for a moment publishing a line of Parker Tyler's verse. And he is certainly not held up as an example in the Iowa Writers' Workshop. There are others who have disappeared entirely—Charles Snider, Sherry Mangan, R. E. F. Larsson, the early Winters, the last poems of Ford Madox Ford. They get back into circulation, as far as I know, only when I read them to somebody at home or on the air, and then I am always asked for a copy. Some of the old avant-garde seem to have written themselves out, for instance, Mina Loy. There are a few established old masters, outstanding of whom are, of course, Ezra Pound and William Carlos Williams. I am not a passionate devotee of Pound myself. In fact, I think his influence is largely pernicious. But no one could deny its extent and power amongst young people today. As for Williams, more and more people, even some of the Reactionary Generation, have come to think of him as our greatest living poet. Even Randall Jarrell and R. P. Blackmur have good words to say for him.

Then there is a middle generation which includes Kenneth Patchen, Jean Garrigue, myself, and a few others—notably Richard Eberhart, who looks superficially as if he belonged with the Tates and Blackmurs but who is redeemed by his directness, simplicity, and honesty; and Robert Fitzgerald and Dudley Fitts. Curiously enough, in the taste of the young, Kenneth Fearing is not included in this group, possibly because his verse is too easy. It does include the major work, for example, *Ajanta,* of Muriel Rukeyser.

I should say that the most influential poets of the youngest established generation of the avant-garde are Denise Levertov, Robert Creeley, Charles Olson, Robert Duncan, and Philip Lamantia. The most influential avant-garde editor is perhaps Cid Corman, with his magazine *Origin.* Richard Emerson's *Golden Goose* and Robert Creeley's *Black Mountain Review* seem to have suspended publication temporarily. Jonathan Williams, himself a fine poet, publishes the Jargon Press.

All of this youngest group have a good deal in common. They are all more or less influenced by French poetry, and by Céline, Beckett, Artaud, Genêt, to varying degrees. They are also influenced by William Carlos Williams, D. H. Lawrence, Whitman, Pound. They are all interested in Far Eastern art and religion; some even call themselves Buddhists. Politically they are all strong disbelievers in the State, war, and the values of commercial civilization. Most of them would no longer call themselves anarchists, but just because adopting such a label would imply adherence to a "movement." Anything in the way of an explicit ideology is suspect. Contrary to gossip of a few years back, I have never met anybody in this circle who was a devotée of the dubious notions of the psychologist Wilhelm Reich; in fact, few of them have ever read him, and those who have consider him a charlatan.

Although there is wide diversity—Olson is very like Pound; Creeley resembles Mallarmé; Denise Levertov in England was a leading New Romantic, in America she came under the influence of William Carlos Williams; Robert Duncan has assimilated ancestors as unlike as Gertrude Stein and Éluard, and so on—although this diversity is very marked, there is a strong bond of esthetic unity too. No avant-garde American poet accepts the I. A. Richards-Valéry thesis that a poem is an end in itself, an anonymous machine for providing esthetic experiences. All believe in poetry as communication, statement from one person to another. So they all avoid the studied ambiguities and metaphysical word play of the Reactionary Generation and seek clarity of image and simplicity of language.

In the years since the war, it would seem as though more and more of what is left of the avant-garde has migrated to Northern California. John Berryman once referred to the Lawrence cult of "mindless California," and Henry Miller and I have received other unfavorable publicity which has served only to attract people to this area. Mr. Karl Shapiro, for instance, once referred to San Francisco as "the last refuge of the bohemian remnant"—a description he thought of as invidious. Nevertheless it is true that San Francisco is today the seat of an intense literary activity not unlike Chicago of the first quarter of the century. A whole school of poets has grown up—almost all of them migrated here from somewhere else. Some of them have national reputations, at least in limited circles. For example, Philip Lamantia among the surrealists; William Everson (Brother Antoninus, O.P.)—perhaps the best Catholic poet. Others have come up, like Lawrence Ferlinghetti, Allen Ginsberg, Gary Snyder, Philip Whalen, David Meltzer, Michael McClure, still have largely local reputations. But the strength of these reputations should not be underestimated. The Poetry Center of San Francisco State College, directed by Ruth Witt-Diamant, gives a reading to a large audience at least twice a month. And there are other readings equally well attended every week in various galleries and private homes.

This means that poetry has become an actual social force—something which has always sounded hitherto like a Utopian dream of the William Morris sort. It is a very thrilling experience to hear an audience of more than three hundred people stand and cheer and clap, as they invariably do at a reading by Allen Ginsberg, certainly a poet of revolt if there ever was one.

There is no question but that the San Francisco renaissance is radically different from what is going on elsewhere. There are hand presses, poetry readings, young writers elsewhere—but nowhere else is there a whole younger generation culture pattern characterized by total rejection of the official high-brow culture—where critics like John Crowe Ransom or Lionel Trilling, magazines like the *Kenyon, Hudson* and *Partisan* reviews, are looked on as "The Enemy"—the other side of the barricades.

There is only one trouble about the renaissance in San Francisco. It is too far away from the literary market place. That, of course, is the reason why the bohemian remnant, the avant-garde have migrated here. It is possible to hear the story about what so-and-so said to someone else at a cocktail party twenty years ago just one too many times. You grab a plane or get on your thumb and hitchhike to the other side of the continent for good and all. Each generation, the great Latin poets came from farther and farther from Rome. Eventually, they ceased even to go there except to see the sights.

Distance from New York City does, however, make it harder to get things, if not published, at least nationally circulated. I recently formed a collection for one of the foundations of avant-garde poetry printed in San Francisco. There were a great many items. The poetry was all at least readable, and the hand printing and binding were in most cases very fine indeed. None of these books was available in bookstores elsewhere in the country, and only a few of them had been reviewed in newspapers or magazines with national circulation.

Anyway, as an old war horse of the revolution of the word, things have never looked better from where I sit. The avant-garde has not only not ceased to exist. It's jumping all over the place. Something's happening, man.

The disengagement of the creator, who, as creator, is necessarily judge, is one thing, but the utter nihilism of the emptied-out hipster is another. What is going to come of an attitude like this? It is impossible to go on indefinitely saying: "I am proud to be a delinquent," without destroying all civilized values. Between such persons no true enduring interpersonal relationships can be built, and of course, nothing resembling a true "culture"—an at-homeness of men with each other, their work, their loves, their environment. The end result must be the desperation of shipwreck—the despair, the orgies, ultimately the cannibalism of a lost lifeboat. I believe that most of an entire generation will go to ruin—the ruin of Céline, Artaud, Rimbaud, voluntarily, even enthusiastically. What will happen afterwards I don't know, but for the next couple of decades we are going to have to cope with the youth that we, my generation, put through the atom smasher. Social disengagement, artistic integrity, voluntary poverty—these are powerful virtues and may pull them through, but they are not the virtues we tried to inculcate—rather they are the exact opposite.

[1957] 1970

◄ CHARLES OLSON ►
(1910–1970)

A poet, theorist, and educator with broad influence, Charles Olson was
born in Worcester, Massachusetts. His father, a Swedish immigrant, worked
as a postman. His Irish American mother, a devout Catholic, was protective
of her only son, and Olson grew up in a supportive and indulgent household. As a senior at the Classical High School, he won third prize in
a national oratorical contest. His award was a ten-week trip to Europe,
which gave the young Olson the opportunity to meet the Irish poet William
Butler Yeats. In 1928 he matriculated at Wesleyan University, where he received his B.A. in 1932 and his M.A. in 1933. After two years teaching at
Clark University in Worcester, Olson began graduate studies at Harvard.
At 6'8" he cut an impressive figure, and he was described as both scholarly
and absentminded. Although he never completed his doctorate in American
studies, the dissertation he had researched on Herman Melville would
eventually become his first prose book—*Call Me Ishmael* (1947), a critique
of American culture.

In 1941 Olson joined the American Civil Liberties Union in New York
and became increasingly active in Democratic Party politics. He eventually went to work for the Roosevelt administration as Assistant Chief of
the Foreign Language Division of the Federal Office of War Information.
He held that post until 1944, when he quit in a dispute over censorship
of his press releases. Discouraged by government protocol and determined
to make his mark as a poet, Olson moved to Florida and continued his
work on Melville and other projects. In 1948 he joined the faculty of Black
Mountain College in rural North Carolina, an experimental school that
was becoming well known for its arts curriculum. Other faculty members
included the choreographer Merce Cunningham, painters Franz Kline and
Josef Albers, and at various times the poets Robert Duncan and Robert
Creeley. The latter two were invited to teach during Olson's tenure as
rector of the college, from 1951 until its close in 1956. Creeley founded
the *Black Mountain Review,* and a school of poetry emerged, the Black
Mountain Poets, including Olson, Creeley, Duncan, Edward Dorn,
and Joel Oppenheimer.

In his 1949 poem, "The Kingfishers," Olson declared, "What does not change / is the will to change," and much of his teaching was a reaction against a perceived status quo in American letters. This was the time in which the academic school of New Criticism was at its height. Olson and other Black Mountain Poets reacted against the stringent advocacy of traditional or "closed" forms in poetry. Olson's famous essay "Projective Verse," published as a pamphlet in 1950, became a manifesto for the movement. It began as an attempt to explain his own poetic practice in "The Kingfishers," in which he had made use of Aztec religious motifs in opposition to European literary inheritance. Olson, who would eventually call rhyme "the dross of verse," sought a reconception of poetry's formal principles. In "Projective Verse" he argued that "the line comes (I swear it) from the breath." These breath units were new measures placed on the "open field" of the page. While stressing oral presentation and breath, Olson saved particular praise for the typewriter as a tool of composition: "It can, for a poet, indicate exactly the breath, the pauses, the suspensions even of syllables, the juxtapositions even of parts of phrases, which he intends." Olson's prosodic method was conceived as a new musical form of composition, not to be confused with free verse, although this distinction is admittedly hard to see. He also rejected narrative as a way of organizing verse. *The Mayan Letters* (1953), a collection of his correspondence edited by Creeley, further explores Olson's fascination with cultural alternatives.

Olson's common-law marriage to Constance Wilcock lasted from 1941 to 1956. In 1957, with his new common-law partner, Betty Kaiser, Olson moved to Gloucester, Massachusetts, to devote himself to his poetry. From 1963 to 1965 he taught literature at the State University of New York at Buffalo, and during that time Kaiser was killed in an automobile accident. The trauma of this event contributed to Olson's continued difficulties with alcohol. In late 1969 he was diagnosed with liver cancer, and he died after a brief illness.

As a poet Olson is best known for *The Maximus Poems,* a sequence he began in the 1940s which was finally published in near-complete form only after his death. Loosely modeled on Pound's *Cantos,* though some critics call them a deliberate alternative to Pound, *The Maximus Poems* was conceived as "a poem of a person and a place," spoken by an ancient Phoenician wanderer and writer whose perceptions parallel Olson's own. Discursive, didactic, full of historical, mythological, and scientific references, the sequence accrued in separate volumes in 1953, 1968, and 1974. The entire work, edited by George F. Butterick, appeared in 1983 and won the author a posthumous Los Angeles Times Book Award. *The Collected Poems of Charles Olson* appeared in 1987. A number of poets have built upon Olson's literary legacy, including Denise Levertov, Robert Duncan, Robert Creeley, and Jack Foley.

Olson's most famous essay, his manifesto of "Projectivist" or "Open Field" poetry, has continued to challenge traditional notions of poetic form since its first publication as a pamphlet in 1950. "FORM IS NEVER MORE THAN AN EXTENSION OF CONTENT," Olson asserted, borrowing a key concept from Creeley. The "problem" he attempted to solve concerned what choices could be made by "the poet who departs from closed form." William Carlos Williams thought highly of the essay and related it to his own ideas about relative measure or the "variable foot" as something other than free verse. Few statements of modern poetics have proved so influential or controversial as Olson's theory of open form.

◄◦►━━━◖ ◗━━━◄◦►

PROJECTIVE VERSE

(projectile   (percussive   (prospective
vs.
The NON-Projective

(or what a French critic calls "closed" verse, that verse which print bred and which is pretty much what we have had, in English & American, and have still got, despite the work of Pound & Williams:

it led Keats, already a hundred years ago, to see it (Wordsworth's, Milton's) in the light of "the Egotistical Sublime"; and it persists, at this latter day, as what you might call the private-soul-at-any-public-wall)

Verse now, 1950, if it is to go ahead, if it is to be of *essential* use, must, I take it, catch up and put into itself certain laws and possibilities of the breath, of the breathing of the man who writes as well as of his listenings. (The revolution of the ear, 1910, the trochee's heave, asks it of the younger poets.)

I want to do two things: first, try to show what projective or OPEN verse is, what it involves, in its act of composition, how, in distinction from the non-projective, it is accomplished; and II, suggest a few ideas about what stance toward reality brings such verse into being, what that stance does, both to the poet and to his reader. (The stance involves, for example, a change beyond, and larger than, the technical, and may, the way things look, lead to new poetics and to new concepts from which some sort of drama, say, or of epic, perhaps, may emerge.)

I

First, some simplicities that a man learns, if he works in OPEN, or what can also be called COMPOSITION BY FIELD, as opposed to inherited line, stanza, over-all form, what is the "old" base of the non-projective.

(1) the *kinetics* of the thing. A poem is energy transferred from where the poet got it (he will have some several causations), by way of the poem itself to, all the way over to, the reader. Okay. Then the poem itself must, at all points, be a high energy-construct and, at all points, an energy-discharge. So: how is the poet to accomplish same energy, how is he, what is the process by which a poet gets in, at

Originally published in pamphlet, *Poetry New York* (New York, 1950). Collected in *Selected Writings*, ed. Robert Creeley (New York: New Directions, 1966).

all points energy at least the equivalent of the energy which propelled him in the first place, yet an energy which is peculiar to verse alone and which will be, obviously, also different from the energy which the reader, because he is a third term, will take away?

This is the problem which any poet who departs from closed form is specially confronted by. And it involves a whole series of new recognitions. From the moment he ventures into FIELD COMPOSITION—puts himself in the open—he can go by no track other than the one the poem under hand declares, for itself. Thus he has to behave, and be, instant by instant, aware of some several forces just now beginning to be examined. (It is much more, for example, this push, than simply such a one as Pound put, so wisely, to get us started: "the musical phrase," go by it, boys, rather than by, the metronome.)

(2) is the *principle*, the law which presides conspicuously over such composition, and, when obeyed, is the reason why a projective poem can come into being. It is this: FORM IS NEVER MORE THAN AN EXTENSION OF CONTENT. (Or so it got phrased by one, R. Creeley, and it makes absolute sense to me, with this possible corollary, that right form, in any given poem, is the only and exclusively possible extension of content under hand.) There it is, brothers, sitting there, for USE.

Now (3) the *process* of the thing, how the principle can be made so to shape the energies that the form is accomplished. And I think it can be boiled down to one statement (first pounded into my head by Edward Dahlberg): ONE PERCEPTION MUST IMMEDIATELY AND DIRECTLY LEAD TO A FURTHER PERCEPTION. It means exactly what it says, is a matter of, at *all* points (even, I should say, of our management of daily reality as of the daily work) get on with it, keep moving, keep in, speed, the nerves, their speed, the perceptions, theirs, the acts, the split second acts, the whole business, keep it moving as fast as you can, citizen. And if you also set up as a poet, USE USE USE the process at all points, in any given poem always, always one perception must must must MOVE, INSTANTER, ON ANOTHER!

So there we are, fast, there's the dogma. And its excuse, its usableness, in practice. Which gets us, it ought to get us, inside the machinery, now, 1950, of how projective verse is made.

If I hammer, if I recall in, and keep calling in, the breath, the breathing as distinguished from the hearing, it is for cause, it is to insist upon a part that breath plays in verse which has not (due, I think, to the smothering of the power of the line by too set a concept of foot) has not been sufficiently observed or practiced, but which has to be if verse is to advance to its proper force and place in the day, now, and ahead. I take it that PROJECTIVE VERSE teaches, is, this lesson, that that verse will only do in which a poet manages to register both the acquisitions of his ear *and* the pressures of his breath.

Let's start from the smallest particle of all, the syllable. It is the king and pin of versification, what rules and holds together the lines, the larger forms, of a poem. I would suggest that verse here and in England dropped this secret from the late Elizabethans to Ezra Pound, lost it, in the sweetness of meter and rime, in a honey-head. (The syllable is one way to distinguish the original success of blank verse, and its falling off, with Milton.)

It is by their syllables that words juxtapose in beauty, by these particles of sound as clearly as by the sense of the words which they compose. In any given instance, because there is a choice of words, the choice, if a man is in there, will be, spontaneously, the obedience of his ear to the syllables. The fineness, and the practice, lie here, at the minimum and source of speech.

O western wynd, when wilt thou blow
And the small rain down shall rain
O Christ that my love were in my arms
And I in my bed again

It would do no harm, as an act of correction to both prose and verse as now written, if both rime and meter, and, in the quantity words, both sense and sound, were less in the forefront of the mind than the syllable, if the syllable, that fine creature, were more allowed to lead the harmony on. With this warning, to those who would try: to step back here to this place of the elements and minims of language, is to engage speech where it is least careless—and least logical. Listening for the syllables must be so constant and so scrupulous, the exaction must be so complete, that the assurance of the ear is purchased at the highest—40 hours a day—price. For from the root out, from all over the place, the syllable comes, the figures of, the dance:

"Is" comes from the Aryan root, *as*, to breathe. The English "not" equals the Sanscrit *na*, which may come from the root *na*, to be lost, to perish. "Be" is from *bhu*, to grow.

I say the syllable, king, and that it is spontaneous, this way: the ear, the ear which has collected, which has listened, the ear, which is so close to the mind that it is the mind's, that it has the mind's speed . . .

it is close, another way: the mind is brother to this sister and is, because it is so close, is the drying force, the incest, the sharpener . . .

it is from the union of the mind and the ear that the syllable is born.

But the syllable is only the first child of the incest of verse (always, that Egyptian thing, it produces twins!). The other child is the LINE. And together, these two, the syllable *and* the line, they make a poem, they make that thing, the—what shall we call it, the Boss of all, the "Single Intelligence." And the line comes (I swear it) from the breath, from the breathing of the man who writes, at the moment that he writes, and thus is, it is here that, the daily work, the WORK, gets in, for only he, the man who writes, can declare, at every moment, the line its metric and its ending—where its breathing, shall come to, termination.

The trouble with most work, to my taking, since the breaking away from traditional lines and stanzas, and from such wholes as, say, Chaucer's *Troilus* or S's *Lear*, is: contemporary workers go lazy RIGHT HERE WHERE THE LINE IS BORN.

Let me put it baldly. The two halves are:

the HEAD, by way of the EAR, to the SYLLABLE
the HEART, by way of the BREATH, to the LINE

And the joker? that it is in the 1st half of the proposition that, in composing, one lets-it-rip; and that it is in the 2nd half, surprise, it is the LINE that's the baby that gets, as the poem is getting made, the attention, the control, that it is right here, in the line, that the shaping takes place, each moment of the going.

I am dogmatic, that the head shows in the syllable. The dance of the intellect is there, among them, prose or verse. Consider the best minds you know in this here business: where does the head show, is it not, precise, here, in the swift currents of the syllable? Can't you tell a brain when you see what it does, just there? It is true, what the master says he picked up from Confusion: all the thots men are capable of can be entered on the back of a postage stamp. So, is it not the PLAY of a mind we are after, is not that that shows whether a mind is there at all?

And the threshing floor for the dance? Is it anything but the LINE? And when the line has, is, a deadness, it is not a heart which has gone lazy, is it not, suddenly, slow things, similes, say, adjectives, or such, that we are bored by?

For there is a whole flock of rhetorical devices which have now to be brought under a new bead, now that we sight with the line. Simile is only one bird who comes down, too easily. The descriptive functions generally have to be watched, every second, in projective verse, because of their easiness, and thus their drain on the energy which composition by field allows into a poem. *Any* slackness takes off attention, that crucial thing, from the job in hand, from the *push* of the line under hand at the moment, under the reader's eye, in his moment. Observation of any kind is, like argument in prose, properly previous to the act of the poem, and, if allowed in, must be so juxtaposed, apposed, set in, that it does not, for an instant, sap the going energy of the content toward its form.

It comes to this, this whole aspect of the newer problems. (We now enter, actually, the large area of the whole poem, into the FIELD, if you like, where all the syllables and all the lines must be managed in their relations to each other.) It is a matter, finally, of OBJECTS, what they are, what they are inside a poem, how they got there, and, once there, how they are to be used. This is something I want to get to in another way in Part II, but, for the moment, let me indicate this, that every element in an open poem (the syllable, the line, as well as the image, the sound, the sense) must be taken up as participants in the kinetic of the poem just as solidly as we are accustomed to take what we call the objects of reality; and that these elements are to be seen as creating the tensions of a poem just as totally as do those other objects create what we know as the world.

The objects which occur at every given moment of composition (of recognition, we can call it) are, can be, must be treated exactly as they do occur therein and not by any ideas or preconceptions from outside the poem, must be handled as a series of objects in field in such a way that a series of tensions (which they also are) are made to *hold*, and to hold exactly inside the content and the context of the poem which has forced itself, through the poet and them, into being.

Because breath allows *all* the speech-force of language back in (speech is the "solid" of verse, is the secret of a poem's energy), because, now, a poem has, by speech, solidity, everything in it can now be treated as solids, objects, things; and, though insisting upon the absolute difference of the reality of verse from that other dispersed and distributed thing, yet each of these elements of a poem can be allowed to have the play of their separate energies and can be allowed, once the poem is well composed, to keep, as those other objects do, their proper confusions.

Which brings us up, immediately, bang, against tenses, in fact against syntax, in fact against grammar generally, that is, as we have inherited it. Do not tenses, must they not also be kicked around anew, in order that time, that other governing absolute may be kept, as must the space-tensions of a poem, immediate, contemporary to the acting-on-you of the poem? I would argue that here, too, the LAW OF THE LINE, which projective verse creates, must be hewn to, obeyed, and that the conventions which logic has forced on syntax must be broken open as quietly as must the too set feet of the old line. But an analysis of how far a new poet can stretch the very conventions on which communication by language rests, is too big for these notes, which are meant, I hope it is obvious, merely to get things started.

Let me just throw in this. It is my impression that *all* parts of speech suddenly, in composition by field, are fresh for both sound and percussive use, spring up like unknown, unnamed vegetables in the patch, when you work it, come spring. Now take Hart Crane. What strikes me in him is the singleness of the push to the nominative, his push along that one arc of freshness, the attempt to get back to word as handle. (If logos is word as thought, what is word as noun, as, pass me that, as Newman Shea used to ask, at the galley table, put a jib on the blood, will ya.) But there is a loss in Crane of what Fenollosa is so right about, in syntax, the sentence as first act of nature, as lightning, as passage of force from subject to object, quick, in the case, from Hart to me, in every case, from me to you, the VERB, between two nouns. Does not Hart miss the advantages, by such an isolated push, miss the point of the whole front of syllable, line, field, and what happened to all language, and to the poem, as a result?

I return you now to London, to beginnings, to the syllable, for the pleasures of it, to intermit;

> If music be the food of love, play on,
> give me excess of it, that, surfeiting,
> the appetite may sicken, and so die.
> That strain again. It had a dying fall,
> o, it came over my ear like the sweet sound
> that breathes upon a bank of violets,
> stealing and giving odour.

What we have suffered from, is manuscript, press, the removal of verse from its producer and its reproducer, the voice, a removal by one, by two removes from its place of origin *and* its destination. For the breath has a double meaning which latin had not yet lost.

The irony is, from the machine has come one gain not yet sufficiently observed or used, but which leads directly on toward projective verse and its consequences. It is the advantage of the typewriter that, due to its rigidity and its space precisions, it can, for a poet, indicate exactly the breath, the pauses, the suspensions even of syllables, the juxtapositions even of parts of phrases, which he intends. For the first time the poet has the stave and the bar a musician has had. For the first time he can, without the convention of rime and meter, record the listening he has done to his own speech and by that one act indicate how he would want any reader, silently or otherwise, to voice his work.

It is time we picked the fruits of the experiments of Cummings, Pound, Williams, each of whom has, after his way, already used the machine as a scoring to his composing, as a script to its vocalization. It is now only a matter of the recognition of the conventions of composition by field for us to bring into being an open verse as formal as the closed, with all its traditional advantages.

If a contemporary poet leaves a space as long as the phrase before it, he means that space to be held, by the breath, an equal length of time. If he suspends a word or syllable at the end of a line (this was most Cummings' addition) he means that time to pass that it takes the eye—that hair of time suspended—to pick up the next line. If he wishes a pause so light it hardly separates the words, yet does not want a comma—which is an interruption of the meaning rather than the sounding of the line—follow him when he uses a symbol the typewriter has ready to hand:

What does not change / is the will to change

Observe him, when he takes advantage of the machine's multiple margins, to juxtapose:

Sd he:
    to dream takes no effort
      to think is easy
        to act is more difficult
        but for a man to act after he has taken thought, this!
is the most difficult thing of all

Each of these lines is a progressing of both the meaning and the breathing forward, and then a backing up, without a progress or any kind of movement outside the unit of time local to the idea.

There is more to be said in order that this convention be recognized, especially in order that the revolution out of which it came may be so forwarded that work will get published to offset the reaction now afoot to return verse to inherited forms of cadence and rime. But what I want to emphasize here, by this emphasis on the typewriter as the personal and instantaneous recorder of the poets' work, is the already projective nature of verse as the sons of Pound and Williams are practicing it. Already they are composing as though verse was to have the reading its writing involved, as though not the eye but the ear was to be its measurer, as though the intervals of its composition could be so carefully put down as to be precisely the intervals of its registration. For the ear, which once had the burden of memory to quicken it (rime & regular cadence were its aids and have merely lived on in print after the oral necessities were ended) can now again, that the poet has his means, be the threshold of projective verse.

II

Which gets us to what I promised, the degree to which the projective involves a stance toward reality outside a poem as well as a new stance towards the reality of a poem itself. It is a matter of content, the content of Homer or of Euripides or of Seami as distinct from that which I might call the more "literary" masters. From the moment the projective purpose of the act of verse is recognized, the content does—it will—change. If the beginning and the end is breath, voice in its largest sense, then the material of verse shifts. It has to. It starts with the composer. The dimension of his line itself changes, not to speak of the change in his conceiving, of the matter he will turn to, of the scale in which he imagines that matter's use. I myself would pose the difference by a physical image. It is no accident that Pound and Williams both were involved variously in a movement which got called "objectivism." But that word was then used in some sort of a necessary quarrel, I take it, with "subjectivism." It is now too late to be bothered with the latter. It has excellently done itself to death, even though we are all caught in its dying. What seems to me a more valid formulation for present use is "objectism," a word to be taken to stand for the kind of relation of man to experience which a poet might state as the necessity of a line or a work to be as wood is, to be as clean as wood is as it issues from the hand of nature, to be as shaped as wood can be when a man has had his hand to it. Objectism is the getting rid of the lyrical interference of the individual as ego, of the "subject" and his soul, that peculiar presumption by which western man has interposed himself between what he is as a creature of nature (with certain instructions to carry out) and those other creations of nature which we may, with no derogation, call objects. For a man is himself an object, whatever he may take to be his advantages, the more likely to recognize himself as such the greater his advantages, particularly at that moment tha he achieves an humilitas sufficient to make him of use.

It comes to this: the use of a man, by himself and thus by others, lies in how he conceives his relation to nature, that force to which he owes his somewhat small existence. If he sprawl, he shall find little to sing but himself, and shall sing, nature has such paradoxical ways, by way of artificial forms outside himself. But if he stays inside himself, if he is contained within his nature as he is participant in the larger force, he will be able to listen, and his hearing through himself will give him secrets objects share. And by an inverse law his shapes will make their own way. It is in this sense that the projective act, which is the artist's act in the larger field of objects, leads to dimensions larger than the man. For a man's problem, the moment he takes s h up in all its fullness, is to give his work his seriousness, a seriousness sufficie   to cause the thing he makes to try to take its place alongside the things of natur   his is not easy. Nature works from reverence, even in her destructions (specie go down with a crash). But breath is man's special qualification as animal. Sound is a dimension he has extended. Language is one of his proudest acts. And when a poet rests in these as they are in himself (in his physiology, if you like, but the life in him, for all that) then he, if he chooses to speak from these roots, works in that area where nature has given him size, projective size.

It is projective size that the play, *The Trojan Women*, possesses, for it is able to stand, is it not, as its people do, beside the Aegean—and neither Andromache or the sea suffer diminution. In a less "heroic" but equally "natural" dimension Seami causes the Fisherman and the Angel to stand clear in *Hagoromo*. And Homer, who is such an unexamined cliché that I do not think I need to press home in what scale Nausicaa's girls wash their clothes.

Such works, I should argue—and I use them simply because their equivalents are yet to be done—could not issue from men who conceived verse without the full relevance of human voice, without reference to where lines come from, in the individual who writes. Nor do I think it accident that, at this end point of the argument, I should use, for examples, two dramatists and an epic poet. For I would hazard the guess that, if projective verse is practiced long enough, is driven ahead hard enough along the course I think it dictates, verse again can carry much larger material than it has carried in our language since the Elizabethans. But it can't be jumped. We are only at its beginnings, and if I think that the *Cantos* make more "dramatic" sense than do the plays of Mr. Eliot, it is not because I think they have solved the problem but because the methodology of the verse in them points a way by which, one day, the problem of larger content and of larger forms may be solved. Eliot is, in fact, a proof of a present danger, of "too easy" a going on the practice of verse as it has been, rather than as it must be, practiced. There is no question, for example, that Eliot's line, from "Prufrock" on down, has speech-force, is "dramatic," is, in fact, one of the most notable lines since Dryden. I suppose it stemmed immediately to him from Browning, as did so many of Pound's early things. In any case Eliot's line has obvious relations backward to the Elizabethans, especially to the soliloquy. Yet O. M. Eliot is *not* projective. It could even be argued (and I say this carefully, as I have said all things about the non-projective, having considered how each of us must save himself after his own fashion and how much, for that matter, each of us owes to the non-projective, and will continue to owe, as both go alongside each other) but it could be argued that it is because Eliot has stayed inside the non-projective that he fails as a dramatist—that his root is the mind alone, and a scholastic mind at that (no high *intelletto* despite his apparent clarities)—and that, in his listenings he has stayed there where the ear and the mind are, has only gone from his fine ear outward rather than, as I say a projective poet will, down through the workings of his own throat to that place where breath comes from, where breath has its beginnings, where drama has to come from, where, the coincidence is, all act springs.

1950

J. V. CUNNINGHAM
(1911–1985)

James Vincent Cunningham was born in Cumberland, Maryland, one of
four children of a working-class Irish Catholic family. In his early teens his
father, a steam-shovel operator, moved the family to Billings, Montana.
Cunningham there attended St. Vincent's Parochial School, spending summers on a nearby ranch. When he was twelve, his family moved to Denver,
where he completed the eighth grade and the following year entered a
rigorous Jesuit high school which required four years of Latin and Greek.
When Cunningham was fifteen, his father died in an industrial accident,
leaving the family in difficult straits. After graduating high school at sixteen,
Cunningham worked for various Denver newspapers and as a delivery
boy for a local brokerage house. His literary consciousness was formed not
only by the discipline of Catholic schools, but also by the austere emptiness
of Montana, the family troubles in Denver, and the deprivations of the
Great Depression.

Cunningham spent the first few years of the Depression wandering
through the Southwest, looking for work. Meanwhile he satisfied his hunger
for education by constant reading. His early grounding in the classics had
been strong, but on his own he discovered Eliot and Pound, as well as the
satires of Jonathan Swift. With the help of the poet Yvor Winters, Cunningham
eventually entered Stanford University. (The impoverished student initially
lived in a tiny study shed in Winters's backyard.) Cunningham took his B.A.
in 1934 and a Ph.D. eleven years later. Eventually, he taught at a number of
universities, including Harvard and the University of Virginia, Charlottesville,
before settling at Brandeis in 1953 (where one of his best students was poet
Timothy Steele). Cunningham was never a prolific writer. The first of his slim
poetry collections, *The Helmsman*, appeared in a small handprinted edition
in 1942, and five more small books were published before *The Collected
Poems and Epigrams of J. V. Cunningham* in 1971.

The influence of Winters upon Cunningham's life and work may have
been overstated by some critics. Certainly Cunningham was grateful for the
older poet's help, and the two shared a commitment to formal verse. Yet
Cunningham took his own path and is considered the consummate outsider
of modern American poetry. His work seems—at least initially—to stand at

a complete remove from the general trends of his era. He eschewed free verse, rejected stylistic fragmentation, rarely relied on imagery as a structural device, and unabashedly reveled in abstract ideas. And yet in his own idiosyncratic way Cunningham is a thoroughly modern poet. The characteristic compression of his poems and elliptical use of imagery reflect the influence of Pound, Stevens, and the Imagists. His antiromanticism and cultural pessimism show the presence of Eliot. His savage wit and genius for memorable concision, however, are entirely his own. Cunningham is indisputably the finest epigrammatist in American literature, and his best short lyrics are remarkable in their evocative force, especially his masterful 1964 cycle of love poems, *To What Strangers, What Welcome*. In his prose Cunningham writes of "a chastity of diction and a crispness of technique," adding to his values a "sinuous exacting speech."

As a critic, Cunningham's interests ranged from Renaissance scholarship to theoretical poetics. His scholarly collections included *Woe or Wonder: The Emotional Effect of Shakespearean Tragedy* (1951) and *Tradition and Poetic Structure* (1960). He also published a study of Emily Dickinson, *Dickinson, Lyric and Legend* (1980).

Cunningham was also fascinated with theories of poetics. Much of his best writing is frankly speculative. In *The Quest of the Opal* (1950) he examined the motives and methods of his first book of verse by creating prose equivalents for a dozen of his poems. In *The Journal of John Cardan* (1964) he spoke through a thinly disguised persona to discuss the life of art and intellect. A witty and concise critic, he began the Introduction of *The Collected Essays of J. V. Cunningham* (1976) by saying, "there is less to be said about literature than has been said, and this book adds a little more." His provocative essay, "The Problem of Form," displays Cunningham's ability to propound a complex theoretic argument clearly, cogently, and succinctly.

◀◼━━◼━━◼▶

THE PROBLEM OF FORM

I shall stipulate that there is a problem of form in the poetry of our day, but I shall treat *form*, for the moment, as an undefined term, and I shall not until later specify the nature of some of the problems. I am, at the outset, interested in pointing to certain generalities, and to certain broad, simpleminded, pervasive attitudes and dualisms, of which the problem in poetry is to a large extent only a localization. These will give in outline the larger context of the problem.

To begin with, it is apparent that in our society we have too many choices. When we ask the young what they are going to do when they grow up, we should not be surprised or amused that the answers are whimsical and bewildered. The young poet today has a large and not too discriminated anthology of forms to realize: only illiterate ignorance or having made the pilgrimage to Gambier or to Los Altos will reduce the scope of options to manageable size—and even then there will be a

Originally read at the Library of Congress in October 1962. First printed in *Shenandoah* 14.2 (1963): 3–6. First collected in *The Journal of John Cardan: Together with the Quest of the Opal and the Problem of Form* (Denver: Swallow Press, 1964).

hankering for further options. On the other hand, the young poet 250 years ago had it easy in this respect. He wrote octosyllabic or decasyllabic couplets, and the rhetoric and areas of experience of each were fairly delimited. For recreation he wrote a song in quatrains, and once or twice in a lifetime a Pindaric ode.

We come now to those attitudes and dualisms that make the problem of particular forms peculiarly our problem. We are a democratic society and give a positive value to informality, though some of the ladies still like to dress up. We will have nothing to do with the formal language and figured rhetoric of the *Arcadia*, for that is the language and rhetoric of a hierarchical and authoritarian society in which ceremony and formality were demanded by and accorded to the governing class. Instead, we praise, especially in poetry, what we call the accents of real speech—that is, of uncalculated and casual utterance, and sometimes even of vulgar impropriety. Now, if this attitude is a concomitant of the Democratic Revolution, the value we give to antiformality, to the deliberate violation of form and decorum, is a concomitant of its sibling, the Romantic Revolution. The measured, or formal, the contrived, the artificial are, we feel, insincere; they are perversions of the central value of our life, genuineness of feeling. "At least I was honest," we say with moral benediction as we leave wife and child for the sentimental empyrean.

If informality and antiformality are positive values, then the problem of form is how to get rid of it. But to get rid of it we must keep it; we must have something to get rid of. To do this we need a method, and we have found it in our dualisms of science and art, of intellectual and emotional, of regularity and irregularity, of norm and variation. We have been convinced, without inquiry or indeed adequate knowledge, that the regularities of ancient scientific law, of Newton's laws of motion, are regularities of matter, not of spirit, and hence are inimical to human significance. And so we embrace the broad, pervasive, simpleminded, and scarcely scrutinized proposition that regularity is meaningless and irregularity is meaningful—to the subversion of Form. For one needs only so much regularity as will validate irregularity. But Form is regularity.

So we come to definition. The customary distinctions of form and matter, or form and content, are in the discussion of writing at least only usable on the most rudimentary level. For it is apparent to any poet who sets out to write a sonnet that the form of the sonnet is the content, and its content the form. This is not a profundity, but the end of the discussion. I shall define form, then, without a contrasting term. It is that which remains the same when everything else is changed. This is not at all, I may say, a Platonic position. It is rather a mathematical and, as it should be, linguistic notion: $a^2 - b^2 = (a + b)(a - b)$ through all the potentialities of a and b. The form of the simple declarative sentence in English is in each of its realizations.

It follows, then, that form is discoverable by the act of substitution. It is what has alternative realizations. And the generality or particularity of a form lies in the range or restriction of alternatives. It follows, also, that the form precedes its realization, even in the first instance, and that unique form, or organic form in the sense of unique form, is a contradiction in terms. For it is the essence of form to be repetitive, and the repetitive is form. It follows, further, that there may be in a given utterance simultaneously a number of forms, so that the common literary question, What is the form of this work? can only be answered by a tacit disregard of all the forms other than the one we are momently concerned with.

It is time for illustration. Donne has a little epigram on Hero and Leander:

Both robbed of air, we both lie in one ground,
Both whom one fire had burnt, one water drowned.

What are the forms of this poem? First, both lines are decasyllabic in normal iambic pattern. Second, they rhyme. Third, it is phrased in units of four and six syllables in chiasmic order. Fourth, there are three "both's" and three "one's" in overlapping order. Fifth, the whole story of the lovers is apprehended, summarized, and enclosed in the simple scheme or form of the four elements. Finally, it is recognizably an epigram. Now Sir Philip Sidney, a few years earlier, in one of the *Arcadia* poems has the following lines:

Man oft is plagued with air, is burnt with fire,
In water drowned, in earth his burial is.

The lines are decasyllabic in normal iambic pattern. The adjacent lines do not rhyme, for the form of the poem is terza rima, an alternative form. It is phrased in units of six and four in chiasmic order. The first line repeats "with," the second "in." Man, not Hero and Leander, is apprehended in the scheme of the four elements, and in both cases the order of the elements is not formally predetermined. Finally, it is not an epigram, but part of an eclogue.

I have illustrated in these examples and in this analysis something of the variety of what may be distinguished as form: literary kind, conceptual distinctions, and all the rhetorical figures of like ending, equal members, chiasmus, and the various modes of verbal repetition. That some of the forms of Sidney's lines are repeated in Donne's, with the substitution of Hero and Leander for man, shows they have alternate realizations, and that so many operate simultaneously shows, not that a literary work has form, but that it is a convergence of forms, and forms of disparate orders. It is the coincidence of forms that locks in the poem.

Indeed, it is the inherent coincidence of forms in poetry, in metrical writing, that gives it its place and its power—a claim for poetry perhaps more accurate and certainly more modest than is customary. For this is the poet's *Poetics:* prose is written in sentences; poetry in sentences and lines. It is encoded not only in grammar, but also simultaneously in meter, for meter is the principle or set of principles, whatever they may be, that determines the line. And as we perceive of each sentence that it is grammatical or not, so the repetitive perception that this line is metrical or that it is not, that it exemplifies the rules or that it does not, is the metrical experience. It is the ground bass of all poetry.

And here in naked reduction is the problem of form in the poetry of our day. It is before all a problem of meter. We have lost the repetitive harmony of the old tradition, and we have not established a new. We have written to vary or violate the old line, for regularity we feel is meaningless and irregularity meaningful. But a generation of poets, acting on the principles and practice of significant variation, have at last nothing to vary from. The last variation is regularity.

1964

━◦►◄ ROBERT HAYDEN ►◄◦━
(1913–1980)

Robert Hayden was born Asa Bundy Sheffey, son of Asa and Ruth Sheffey, in Detroit, Michigan. While still an infant, he was given up by his impoverished mother to William and Sue Ellen Hayden. His new parents renamed him Robert, and the poet did not discover until he was forty years old that they had never officially adopted him. Hayden's childhood contained some stability. As a teenager, he knew his natural mother, who took an interest in his education. His adoptive parents tried their best to encourage his interests, but the family was riven by domestic strife and violence. Sue Ellen Hayden was a storyteller who had experienced firsthand the great migration of blacks after the Civil War. But his foster mother's troubled past, suggested in "The Ballad of Sue Ellen Westerfield," had left her with a burden of disappointment which she carried to her new life in the North. In a 1972 interview Hayden said:

> My family were uneducated, poor. But worse, much worse, than being poor—there were anyway periods when we lived fairly well—worse than the poverty were the conflicts, the quarreling, the tensions that kept us most of the time on the edge of some shrill domestic calamity. This is what the line "the chronic angers of that house" in my poem "Those Winter Sundays" refers to. We had a terrible love-hate relationship with one another, and dreadful things happened I can never forget.

Another difficulty the young Hayden faced was his extreme nearsightedness. Forced to wear thick glasses, he fell victim to the cruelty of other children. In an effort to protect his weak eyes, teachers limited his reading, so books seemed especially precious to him. Music, books, and theater became the consolations he sought for a painful life. By the time he entered high school, he was already familiar with a variety of poets, including Edna St. Vincent Millay, Carl Sandburg, and Langston Hughes. The critic Arnold Rampersad has written, "He was especially taken with the example of Countee Cullen, whose emotional and lyrical blending of race consciousness with traditional poetics left an immediate mark on Hayden's youthful writing."

Hayden grew up in a racially mixed, poor Detroit neighborhood ironically nicknamed Paradise Valley. But race consciousness was not at first a large part of his pain. In an unfinished autobiography he remembered, "I never thought of the people I knew as anything but human." As a student at Detroit City College during the Depression, however, Hayden became radicalized and wrote protest poetry. After college, he joined the Federal Writers' Project, a Depression-era government program to employ out-of-work journalists, editors, and imaginative writers. In addition to reinforcing his leftist politics, the project helped make Hayden an important poet of history by encouraging his research on antislavery activity.

His first collection of poems, *Heart-Shape in the Dust,* was published in 1940. In the same year, he married Erma Inez Morris. Their marriage produced a daughter, Maia, born in 1942. Although brought up a Baptist, Hayden eventually turned to the Baha'i faith, which became a major influence on both his life and writing. The Baha'i believe that all religions are one, that the sexes are equal, and that simplicity of lifestyle is a virtue. Already inclined to ecumenism, the poet became a man whom his fellow poet William Meredith would call "as gifted in humanity as he was in poetry."

Hayden moved to his first full-time teaching position in 1946 at Fisk University, a historically black college in Nashville, Tennessee. He remained there until he was offered a professorship at the University of Michigan in 1969—the post he held until his death in 1980.

Hayden never won any of the major American literary awards such as the Pulitzer, National Book Award, or Bollingen. His poetic path was too independent, and he never actively sought the public limelight. His most significant award was Grand Prize in Poetry at the First World Festival of Negro Arts in Dakar, Senegal. He did earn one signal honor in his native land—in 1976 Hayden became the first African American to serve as Consultant in Poetry to the Library of Congress.

Although Hayden wrote constantly of the African American experience, his poetic models were various. An important factor in Hayden's literary development was his friendship with W. H. Auden, with whom he had studied at the University of Michigan in the 1940s. Auden inspired Hayden by his impeccable craftsmanship and deep humanity. From Yeats he learned that a poet could be steeped in his own culture and speak of his own people while remaining an individual. When Hayden began to publish his best work in the 1960s—just as the Black Power and Black Arts movements were voicing angry condemnation of the white world—his polite, professorial manner and seemingly traditional verse made him an outsider. In "How It Strikes a Contemporary," his final address at the Library of Congress, he had this to say on the subject of race and poetry:

As a poet I am trying to come to grips with reality, as I perceive it. Isn't that what every poet worthy of the name is attempting to do? Why does a particular racial identity make me any less aware of life, life as human beings live it? What is a poet but a human being speaking to other human beings about things that matter to all of us?

Despite his universalist beliefs, Hayden's first mature collection, *A Ballad of Remembrance* (1962), is nonetheless saturated with African American history—from the personal past in "The Ballad of Sue Ellen Westerfield" and "Those Winter Sundays" to more public matters in "Middle Passage" and "Frederick Douglass." Yet one also can see the influence of Eliot and Auden in "Middle Passage," not only in the Eliotic collage of voices in Parts 1 and 2, but also in the ironic juxtapositions of religious faith and murderous hypocrisy.

In 1966 Hayden published his *Selected Poems,* and he followed it with four important collections in the next twelve years: *Words for the Mourning Time* (1970), *The Night-Blooming Cereus* (1972), *Angle of Ascent* (1975), and *American Journal* (1978). All of these books contain poems characterized by Hayden's social conscience and lyrical grace.

Hayden's later volumes reflect growing commitment to nonviolence as the only moral means of social change. Although the later poems still deal with historical and individual acts of violence, the author, influenced by his Baha'i faith, now articulates the futility of such action to improve the world. Ultimately, Hayden must be seen as an important American poet, one of the more accomplished and distinctive voices of his generation. He was a writer who understood anger and injustice, but would not allow his art to be consumed by them. His *Collected Prose,* edited by Frederick Glaysher, was published in 1984. His *Collected Poems,* also edited by Glaysher, was published in 1985. The following piece by Hayden served as the introduction to his anthology, *Kaleidoscope: Poems by American Negro Poets* (1967).

◄◦►━━◄┣━◄◦►

INTRODUCTION TO KALEIDOSCOPE:

Poems by American Negro Poets

The question whether we can speak with any real justification of "Negro poetry" arises often today. Some object to the term because it has been used disparagingly to indicate a kind of pseudo-poetry concerned with the race problem to the exclusion of almost everything else. Others hold that Negro poetry *per se* could only be produced in black Africa. Seen from this point of view, the poetry of the American Negro, its "specialized" content notwithstanding, is obviously not to be thought of as existing apart from the rest of our literature, but as having been shaped over some three centuries by social, moral, and literary forces essentially American.

Those who presently avow themselves "poets of the Negro revolution" argue that they do indeed constitute a separate group or school, since the purpose of their writing is to give Negroes a sense of human dignity and provide them with ideological weapons. A belligerent race pride moves these celebrants of Black Power to declare themselves not simply "poets," but "Negro poets." However, Countee Cullen, the brilliant lyricist of the Harlem Renaissance in the 1920's, insisted that he be

Introduction to *Kaleidoscope: Poems by American Negro Poets* (New York: Harcourt, Brace & World, 1967) xix–xxiv.

considered a "poet," not a "Negro poet," for he did not want to be restricted to racial themes nor have his poetry judged solely on the basis of its relevance to the Negro struggle.

Cullen was aware of a peculiar risk Negro poets have had to face. The tendency of American critics has been to label the established Negro writer a "spokesman for his race." There are, as we have seen, poets who think of themselves in that role. But the effect of such labeling is to place any Negro author in a kind of literary ghetto where the standards applied to other writers are not likely to be applied to him, since he, being a "spokesman for his race," is not considered primarily a writer but a species of race-relations man, the leader of a cause, the voice of protest.

Protest has been a recurring element in the writing of American Negroes, a fact hardly to be wondered at, given the social conditions under which they have been forced to live. And the Negro poet's devotion to the cause of freedom is not in any way reprehensible, for throughout history poets have often been champions of human liberty. But bad poetry is another matter, and there is no denying that a great deal of "race poetry" is poor, because its content seems ready-made and art is displaced by argument.

Phillis Wheatley (c. 1750–1784), the first poet of African descent to win some measure of recognition, had almost nothing to say about the plight of her people. And if she resented her own ambiguous position in society, she did not express her resentment. One reason for her silence is that, although brought to Boston as a slave, she never lived as one. Another is that as a neoclassical poet she would scarcely have thought it proper to reveal much of herself in her poetry, although we do get brief glimpses of her in the poem addressed to the Earl of Dartmouth and in "On Being Brought from Africa to America." Neoclassicism emphasized reason rather than emotion and favored elegance and formality. The English poet, Alexander Pope, was the acknowledged master of this style, and in submitting to his influence Phillis Wheatley produced poetry that was as good as that of her American contemporaries. She actually wrote better than some of them.

But the poetry of Phillis Wheatley and her fellow poet, Jupiter Hammon, has historical and not literary interest for us now. The same can be said of much of eighteenth-century American poetry in general. Not until the nineteenth century did the United States begin to have literature of unqualified merit and originality. There were no Negro poets of stature in the period before the Civil War, but there were several with talent, among them George Moses Horton (1797–c. 1883) and Frances E. W. Harper (1825–1911). Didactic and sentimental, they wrote with competence and moral fervor in the manner of their times. Their poetry is remembered chiefly because it contributed to the antislavery struggle, and because it testifies to the creative efforts of Negroes under disheartening conditions.

During the Reconstruction era, writers of "local color" turned for material to the history, the customs, and the dialect that made each section of the country different from the others. James Whitcomb Riley published poems in the Hoosier dialect of Indiana. White southern authors wrote nostalgically of The Old South and through their idealization of ante-bellum plantation life created the "plantation tradition" in literature. Thomas Nelson Page, for example, wrote Negro dialect verse that was an apology for slavery, picturing the Negro as docile and happy in servitude. Both Riley and Page had some influence on Paul Laurence Dunbar (1872–1906), the most important Negro poet to emerge in the latter part of the century.

Some of Dunbar's dialect verse is in the plantation tradition, but it is essentially different from the kind written by the southern apologists, his portrayals of Negro life being more sympathetic and more authentic. Dunbar became famous for his work in this medium, and other Negro poets imitated him. But he himself put less value on his dialect verse than he did on his poems in standard English.

In the twentieth century Negro poets have abandoned dialect for an idiom truer to folk speech. The change has been due not only to differences in social outlook on their part but also to revolutionary developments in American poetry. The New Poetry movement, which began before the First World War and reached its definitive point in the 1920's, represented a break with the past. Free verse, diction close to everyday speech, a realistic approach to life, and the use of material once considered unpoetic—these were the goals of the movement. The Negro poet-critic, William Stanley Braithwaite, encouraged the "new" poetry through his articles in the *Boston Evening Transcript* and his yearly anthologies of magazine verse.

The New Negro movement or Negro Renaissance, resulting from the social, political, and artistic awakening of Negroes in the twenties, brought into prominence poets whose work showed the influence of the poetic revolution. Protest became more defiant, racial bitterness and racial pride more outspoken than ever before. Negro history and folklore were explored as new sources of inspiration. Spirituals, blues, and jazz suggested themes and verse patterns to young poets like Jean Toomer and Langston Hughes. Certain conventions, notably what has been called "literary Garveyism," grew out of a fervent Negro nationalism. Marcus Garvey, leader of the United Negro Improvement Association, advocated a "return" to Africa, the lost homeland, and nearly all the Renaissance poets wrote poems about their spiritual ties to Africa, about the dormant fires of African paganism in the Negro soul that the white man's civilization could never extinguish. Countee Cullen's "Heritage" is one of the best of these poems, even though the Africa it presents is artificial, romanticized, and it reiterates exotic clichés in vogue during the period when it was written.

Harlem was the center of the Negro Renaissance, which for that reason is also referred to as the Harlem Renaissance. Two magazines, *The Crisis* and *Opportunity,* gave aid and encouragement to Negro writers by publishing their work and by awarding literary prizes.

In the decades since the New Negro movement, which ended with the twenties, protest and race consciousness have continued to find expression in the poetry of the American Negro. But other motivating forces are also in evidence. There are Negro poets who believe that any poet's most clearly defined task is to create with honesty and sincerity poems that will illuminate human experience—not exclusively "Negro experience." They reject the idea of poetry as racial propaganda, of poetry that functions as a kind of sociology. Their attitude is not wholly new, of course, being substantially that of Dunbar and Cullen. In counterpoise to it is the "Beat" or "nonacademic" view held by poets who are not only in rebellion against middle-class ideals and the older poetic traditions but who also advocate a militant racism in a definitely "Negro" poetry.

It has come to be expected of Negro poets that they will address themselves to the race question—and that they will all say nearly the same things about it. Such "group unity" is more apparent than real. Differences in vision and emphasis, fundamental differences in approach to the art of poetry itself, modify and give diversity to the writing of these poets, even when they employ similar themes. And certainly there is no agreement among them as to what the much debated role of the Negro poet should be.

This anthology is not intended as a comprehensive survey, but, rather, as a guide that will help students gain some notion of the salient features of a particular area of the American literary landscape. Not all the selections will be read with the same degree of interest, but it is hoped that the majority of them will afford enjoyment and deepen the appreciation of poetry.

Perhaps it would not be amiss to say in conclusion that neither the editor nor his publisher should be understood as necessarily endorsing the long-established custom of segregating the work of Negro poets within the covers of a separate anthology. Yet where, except in a collection such as the present one, is the student to gather any impression of the nature and scope of the Negro's contribution to American poetry?

1967

MURIEL RUKEYSER
(1913–1980)

Born to wealthy Jewish parents in New York City, Muriel Rukeyser led a privileged childhood that included elite schools, summer homes, and country clubs. She joked that, "I was expected to grow up and become a golfer." Instead, she broke from her parents to pursue poetry, political activism, journalism, and biography. She attended Vassar College for two years but left in 1932, already sure of her dedication to writing. Along with other intellectuals of her generation, she joined the Communist Party, and during the Depression years of the 1930s she worked as a journalist for leftist publications such as *New Masses*. Her assignments took her to Decatur, Alabama, in 1933, where she witnessed the trial of the Scottsboro boys, and in 1936 to Gauley Bridge, West Virginia, to help expose the life-threatening working conditions countenanced by a silica mining conglomerate. She also traveled to Spain, where her assignment to cover the antifascist Olympics coincided with the start of the Spanish Civil War. By the end of the decade she had left the Party, in part because she refused to conform to its expectations that she write narrow, propagandistic poetry. For the rest of her life, however, she remained committed to political activism and leftist ideals.

By the time she was thirty, she had published extensively journalism, reviews, poetry, and an ambitious biography. *Theory of Flight* (1935), which won the Yale Younger Poets' Prize, was inspired in part by her experiences as an amateur pilot and is notable for presenting socially concerned poetry with a Whitmanesque expansiveness and Modernist techniques derived from Hart Crane. Her next book, *U. S. 1* (1938), continues these juxtapositions; her long poem, "Book of the Dead," blends documentary realism with Modernist collage through her portraits of workers and their families and her quotations from sources such as congressional subcommittee testimony on the corporate cover-up of the miners' deaths from silicosis. "Book of the Dead" caused controversy because Rukeyser refused to limit herself to only one perspective on poetry. Critics on the right attacked her for being overly political, while critics on the left complained that her Modernist techniques were obscurantist. Rukeyser continued her independent path in *A Turning Wind* (1939) and *Wake Island* (1942). She never wavered from what she saw as the democratic inclusiveness of her poetry and her goal of crossing boundaries—whether between disciplines or between types of poetry. In a series of lectures that she eventually published as *The Life of Poetry* (1949), she argued against divisions—between human beings, disciplines, modes of poetry, even between poets and readers. Writing out of her own individual consciousness as a woman and a Jew, Rukeyser aimed to expand outward to reach readers everywhere, even though she recognized the obstacles that often impede such exchanges.

An openness to change characterized not only Rukeyser's poetry, but her life as well. By the end of the 1940s she had published four more books of poetry, including *Beast in View* (1944), with a long poem that contained the sonnet, "To Be a Jew in the Twentieth Century." This sonnet would eventually be made part of the Reform Liturgy. In 1945 she moved to California, taught at the California Labor School, and married a painter. But the marriage lasted only two months, and in 1947 she gave birth to a son by another man, whose identity she never made public. Single mother-hood sapped some of her writing energy, and her publication rate slowed during the years that she raised her son and worked to support him by teaching at Sarah Lawrence College in New York, where she had returned in 1954. Nevertheless, she was able to complete two books of poetry, *Body of Waking* (1958) and *Waterlily Fire: Poems 1935–1962* (1962).

In the late 1960s she returned full force to poetry writing and political activism, buoyed by the renewed climate for socially responsive poetry and the burgeoning feminist movement. She participated in demonstrations against the Vietnam War, and in 1972 traveled to South Vietnam to lobby for peace. Her books included *The Speed of Darkness* (1968), *Breaking Open* (1973), *The Gates* (1976), *The Collected Poems of Muriel Rukeyser* (1979), as well as an experimental novel, *The Orgy* (1966).

Although Rukeyser had always emphasized the female perspective, her later work became more explicitly feminist, and women poets found inspi-ration in both her writing and her uncompromising life. Because of her stubborn independence from the various schools that dominated American poetry, her strong political content, and her identity as "a she-poet," Rukeyser was often omitted from anthologies and critical surveys. After her death in 1980 her books fell out of print. But the publication of *Out of Silence: Selected Poems* (1992) and *A Muriel Rukeyser Reader* (1994) with an introduction by Adrienne Rich, eventually helped to reestablish her reputation as a twentieth-century innovator.

In the following excerpt from *The Life of Poetry*, Rukeyser condemns the "static mechanics" of the New Critics and advocates a poetry based on a notion of a relationship that shatters boundaries between disciplines, such as literature and science, and also between individuals, especially the poet and the reader. Arguing that "the poem is a process," she defines readers as "witnesses," whose active experience of the poem may spur a change in consciousness.

◄○►━━◄ ○ ►━━◄○►

FROM THE LIFE OF POETRY

FORM, TIME, TENSION

The form of a poem is much more organic, closer to other organic form, than has been supposed. D'Arcy Wentworth Thompson, whose book *On Growth and Form* is a source and a monument, says that organic form is, mathematically, a function of time. There is, in the growth of a tree, the story of those years which saw the rings being made: between those wooden rippled rings, we can read the wetness or dryness of the years before the charts were kept. But the tree is in itself an image of adjustment to its surroundings. There are many kinds of growth: the inorganic shell or horn presents its past and present in the spiral; the crocus grows through minute pulsations, each at an interval of twenty seconds or so, each followed by a partial recoil.

A poem moves through its sounds set in motion, and the reaction to these sounds, their rhymes and repetitions and contrast, has a demonstrable physical basis which can be traced as the wavelength of the sounds themselves can be traced. The wavelength is measurable; the reaction, if you wish such measurements, could be traced through heartbeat and breath, although I myself do not place much value on such measurement.

The impact of the images, and the tension and attraction between meanings, these are the clues to the flow of contemporary poetry. Baudelaire, Lawrence, Eliot have been masters here, and well have known the effects and the essences they offered. But to go on, to recognize the energies that are transferred between people when a poem is given and taken, to know the relationships in modern life that can make the next step, to see the tendencies in science which can indicate it, that is for the new poets.

In the exchange, the human energy that is transferred is to be considered.

THE EXCHANGE

Exchange is creation; and the human energy involved is consciousness, the capacity to produce change from the existing conditions.

Into the present is flung naked life. Life is flung into the present language. The new forms emerge, with their intensive properties, or potentials—their words and images; and their extensive properties, existing in time: sound, forms, subjects, content, and that last includes all the relations between the words and images of the poem.

When the poem arrives with the impact of crucial experience, when it becomes one of the turnings which we living may at any moment approach and enter, then we become more of our age and more primitive. Not primitive as the aesthetes have used the term, but complicated, fresh, full of dark meaning, insisting on discovery, as the experience of a woman giving birth to a child is primitive.

From *The Life of Poetry* (New York: Current Books, 1949).

I cannot say what poetry is; I know that our sufferings and our concentrated joy, our states of plunging far and dark and turning to come back to the world—so that the moment of intense turning seems still and universal—all are here, in a music like the music of our time, like the hero and like the anonymous forgotten; and there is an exchange here in which our lives are met, and created.

A LIGHTNING FLASH

Exchange is creation.

In poetry, the exchange is one of energy. Human energy is transferred, and from the poem it reaches the reader. Human energy, which is consciousness, the capacity to produce change in existing conditions.

But the manner of exchange, the gift that is offered and received—these must be seen according to their own nature.

Fenollosa, writing of the Chinese written character as a medium for poetry, says this: "All truth is the transference of power. The type of sentence in nature is a flash of lightning. It passes between two terms, a cloud and the earth."

This is the threshold, now the symbols are themselves in motion. Now we have the charge, flaming along the path from its reservoir to the receptive target. Even that is not enough to describe the movement of reaching a work of art.

One of our difficulties is that, accepting a science that was static and seeing the world about us according to the vision it afforded, we have tried to freeze everything, including living functions, and the motions of the imaginative arts.

We have used the term "mind" and allowed ourselves to be trapped into believing there was such a *thing*, such a *place*, such a locus of forces. We have used the word "poem" and now the people who live by division quarrel about "the poem as object." They pull it away from their own lives, from the life of the poet, and they attempt to pull it away from its meaning, from itself; finally, in a trance of shattering, they deny qualities and forms and all significance. Then, cut off from its life, they see the dead Beauty: they know what remorse is, they begin to look for some single cause of their self-hatred and contempt. There is, of course, no single cause. We are not so mechanical as that. But there was a symptom: these specialists in dying, they were prepared to believe there was such a thing as Still Life. For all things change in time; some are made of change itself, and the poem is of these. It is not an object; the poem is a process.

POET, POEM, AND WITNESS

Charles Peirce takes Fenollosa's lightning flash, sets it away from the giving. Peirce writes: "All dynamical action, or action of brute force, physical or psychical, either takes place between two subjects . . . or at any rate is a resultant of such actions between pairs." It is important here to understand what Peirce means by *semiosis*. "By semiosis I mean, on the contrary, an action, or influence, which is, or involves, a cooperation of *three* subjects, such as a sign, its object, and its interpretant; this tri-relative influence not being in any way resolvable into actions between pairs. . . ."

The giving and taking of a poem is, then, a triadic relation. It can never be reduced to a pair: we are always confronted by the poet, the poem, and the audience.

The poet, at the moment of his life at which he finished the poem.

The poem, as it is available, heard once, or in a book always at hand.

The audience, the individual reader or listener, with all his life, and whatever capacity he has to summon up his life appropriately to receive more life. At this point, I should like to use another word: "audience" or "reader" or "listener" seems inadequate. I suggest the old word "witness," which includes the act of seeing or knowing by personal experience, as well as the act of giving evidence. The overtone of responsibility in this word is not present in the others; and the tension of the law makes a climate here which is that climate of excitement and revelation giving air to the work of art, announcing with the poem that we are about to change, that work is being done on the self.

These three terms of relationship—poet, poem, and witness—are none of them static. We are changing, living beings, experiencing the inner change of poetry.

The relationships are the meanings, and we have very few of the words for them. Even our tests, the personality tests of which we presently are so proud, present the static forms of Rohrschach blotches. Any change must be seen as specifically in the examinee. Tests are to be made for the perception of change. We need tests in time, moving images on film, moving sounds and syllables on records; or both on sound film. Then we could begin to see how changing beings react to changing signs—how the witness receives the poem.

In a test of recognition, hardly a person knew his own hands, or his face in profile, or his body from behind. It was only when the group was shown films in which they could see themselves walking—face blanked out—that empathy arrived, and with it, recognition.

We know our own rhythms. Our rhythms are more recognizably our selves than any of our forms. Sometimes in nature, form and rhythm are very close: the shape of a tree, for example, is the diagram of its relation to every force which has acted on it and in it; the "shape" of our consciousness—but you see to what folly use of models may lead.

The laws of exchange of consciousness are only suspected. Einstein says, "Now I believe that events in nature are controlled by a much stricter and more closely binding law than we recognize today, when we speak of one event being the *cause* of another. We are like a child who judges a poem by the rhymes and knows nothing of the rhythmic pattern. Or we are like a juvenile learner at the piano, *just* relating one note to that which immediately precedes or follows. To an extent this may be very well when one is dealing with very simple and primitive compositions; but it will not do for an interpretation of a Bach fugue."

I believe that one suggestion of such law is to be found in the process of poetry.

It is the process and the arrangement that give us our clues. Here the links between the scientist and the poet are strong and apparent.

The links between poetry and science are a different matter. For, in recent poetry, there is to be seen a repetition of old fallacies. The by-products, the half-understood findings of science have been taken over, with the results of tragedy.

You may see these results in fashionable poetry: in the poetry of the sense of annihilation, of the smallness of things, of aversion, guilt, and the compulsion toward forgiveness. This is strong magic here: if they want smallness, they will have their smallness; if they want it, they will at last have their forgiveness. But these artists go blaming, blaming. Let us look at what has happened. With the exploration of time and the newer notions of the universe, we have a generation who half-read the findings as they are popularized, and who emerge with little but self-pity. A characteristic title is The World Has Shrunk in the Wash.

ADAM WHO DARES

What has really happened? What does this "smallness" mean to us?

It means that in ourselves we go on from the world of primitive man, a "small" world surrounded by the unknown—whether that unknown be the jungle or curved infinity. Again, the "large" things are human capacities and the beliefs they live among. Our relation to each other and to ourselves are the only things with survival value, once again. We can go on from a source in ourselves which we had almost lost. We can go on with almost forgotten strengths which are—according to your bias—profoundly religious, profoundly human. We can understand the primitive—not as the clumsy, groping naif of a corrupted definition, or even the unskilled "unsophisticate" of modern aesthetic usage—for what he was and what we have to be: the newborn of an age, the pioneer, Adam who dares.

The century has only half-prepared us to be primitives. The time requires our full consciousness, humble, audacious, clear; but we have nightmares of contradiction. For all its symptoms of liberation, its revolutionary stirrings in persons and peoples, the Victorian period was also one of swollen dreams. Behind us overhang the projections of giantism, the inflated powers over all things, according to which nature became some colony of imperial and scientific man, and Fact and Logic his throne and sceptre. He forgot that that sceptre and that throne were signs. Fact is a symbol, Logic is a symbol: they are symbols of the real.

THE COMPLETION OF EXPERIENCE

And reality may be seen as the completion of experience.

Experience itself cannot be seen as a point in time, a fact. The experience with which we deal, in speaking of art and human growth, is not only the event, but the event *and the entire past of the individual.* There is a series in any event, and the definition of the event is the last unit of the series. You read the poem: the poem you now have, the poem that exists in your imagination, is the poem and all the past to which you refer it.

The poet, by the same token, is the man (is the woman) with all the poet's past life, at the moment the poem is finished; that is, at the moment of reaching a conclusion, of understanding further what it means to feel these relationships.

THE POEM SEEN AS SYSTEM

The role of memory is not explored. We know the memory of the unfinished act, or story, or joke, is stronger than that of the finished. These symbols are never finished; they continue to grow; perhaps that is their power. We know that the poetic strategy, if one may call it that, consists in leading the memory of an unknown witness, by means of rhythm and meaning and image and coursing sound and always-unfinished symbol, until in a blaze of discovery and love, the poem is taken. This is the music of the images of relationship, its memory, and its information.

Functions of information and memory have been related in Norbert Wiener's book of many sides and many excitements, *Cybernetics.* Here, among a hundred suggestions, we hear the "philosophical echoes" of "the transition from a New-tonian, reversible time to a Gibbsian, irreversible time." We are shown the necessity to be dynamically minded, and the line of one philosopher is traced, from Leibniz' continuum of monads to the post-Gibbsian dynamic interpretations. We meet again that hero of our century, Clerk Maxwell's demon, and, confronted as he is with his problems of entropy and equilibrium, we see something about the information which the sorting demon may receive from particles approaching the gate he guards in his container. We see that information here represents negative entropy.

Now a poem, like anything separable and existing in time, may be considered as a system, and the changes taking place in the system may be investigated. The notion of feedback, as it is used in calculating machines and such linked structures as the locks of the Panama Canal, is set forth. The relations of information and feedback in computing machines and the nervous system, as stated here, raise other problems. What are imaginative information and imaginative feedback in poetry? What are the emotional equivalents for these relationships? How far do these truths of control and communication apply to art?

The questions are raised, even with the older questions, like Proust's madeleine, still setting challenges to the sciences.

We know that the relationships in poetry are clearer when we think in terms of a dynamic system, whose tendencies toward equilibrium, and even toward entropy, are the same as other systems'. (Even Orpheus approached maximum entropy be-fore he became a god.)

We know that poetry is not isolated here, any more than any phenomena can be isolated. Now again we see that all is unbegun.

The only danger is in not going far enough. The usable truth here deals with change. But we are speaking of the human spirit. If we go deep enough, we reach the common life, the shared experience of man, the world of possibility.

If we do not go deep, if we live and write half-way, there are obscurity, vul-garity, the slang of fashion, and several kinds of death.

All we can be sure of is that our art has life in time, it serves human meaning, it blazes on the night of the spirit; all we can be sure of is that at our most subjective we are universal; all we can be sure of is the profound flow of our living tides of meaning, the river meeting the sea in eternal relationship, in a dance of power, in a dance of love.

For this is the world of light and change: the real world; and the reality of the artist is the reality of the witnesses.

1949

RANDALL JARRELL

(1914–1965)

In a letter to a college sweetheart, Randall Jarrell once wrote, "I've lived all over, and always been separated from at least half of a very small family, and been alone as children ever are." Childhood and loneliness would become two of his most important subjects. He was born in Nashville, Tennessee, to Owen and Anna Jarrell. When his parents separated, he was shuttled back and forth between his mother in Nashville and his father and grandparents in Southern California. He would remember his grandparents' home in Hollywood as a childhood Eden lost to him through forces beyond his control. As a boy in Nashville, he was befriended by sculptors Belle Kinney and Leopold Scholz, who nearly adopted him. They had been at work on the concrete replica of the Parthenon in Centennial Park, and Jarrell posed for the figure of Ganymede, cupbearer to the gods.

While at Vanderbilt University (B.A. 1936, M.A. 1939), Jarrell was quickly recognized as a brilliant and somewhat overbearing student. His teachers included men who were then becoming powerful literary figures—John Crowe Ransom and Robert Penn Warren, the Southern Agrarian poets who had helped edit the *Fugitive,* an influential Modernist journal published in Nashville from 1922 to 1925. Ransom and Warren were also key figures in New Criticism, a revisionist movement only beginning to exert what would soon become a decisive influence on the academic study of literature. Although Jarrell's politics were left of center (and his contemporary favorite poet was the Marx- and Freud-inspired early Auden), he was influenced by the *Fugitive* poets who were mostly very conservative in their political views. His literary connections helped him secure early and prestigious publication. Allen Tate, an early mentor, took five of Jarrell's undergraduate poems for a supplement to the *American Review,* and when Warren established the *Southern Review* at Louisiana State University, Jarrell appeared in the premiere issue. He was invited to review books for the magazine and immediately displayed a prodigious talent for succinctness and wit.

When Ransom moved to Kenyon College, founding the *Kenyon Review* and establishing his "school" of New Critical writers, Jarrell followed him there as instructor and tennis coach. At Kenyon he befriended Robert Lowell

and the fiction writer Peter Taylor. From 1939 to 1942, Jarrell taught at
the University of Texas at Austin. He was also writing brilliant reviews for
Edmund Wilson and Malcolm Cowley at the *New Republic* and was beginning to publish poems in prominent magazines. In Texas he began to write
poems in what would become his mature style, like "90 North," an uncanny
blending of images from polar expeditions and ordinary life. In 1940 he
published a selection of poems with an important prose preface, "A Note
on Poetry," in the New Directions Anthology *Five Young American Poets*.
His ideas in that statement would be extended in his famous essay "The
End of the Line" in which he argued that Modernism was not a response to
Romanticism but, in fact, Romanticism's last gasp. That same year he married
one of his colleagues, Mackie Langham.

In 1942 Jarrell enlisted in the Army Air Corps, just as he published his
first collection of poems, *Blood for a Stranger*. That book was followed in his
lifetime by nine more collections of poetry, two books of critical prose, several translations, various editions of other writers' work, and four children's
books. While in the air corps (he eventually became a celestial navigation
tower operator), Jarrell wrote some of his best-known poems, including
"Eighth Air Force" and "The Death of the Ball Turret Gunner," frequently
imagining combat conditions that he never saw firsthand. After the war there
were brief teaching stints at Sarah Lawrence College, which eventually served
as the setting for his satirical novel *Pictures from an Institution* (1954), and
Princeton University before Jarrell joined the faculty of the Women's College
of the University of North Carolina at Greensboro, where he taught for most
of his remaining years. His first marriage ended in divorce; in 1952 he married Mary Eloise von Schrader, a divorcee with two daughters. While acting
as Consultant in Poetry to the Library of Congress, Jarrell began to experience
episodes of manic depression. Eventually these events required hospitalization, and it was during one of these hospital stays that Jarrell, out walking
along a country highway in the evening, was struck by a car and killed. The
coroner ruled Jarrell's death an accident, though several friends assumed it
was a suicide.

By the time of his death, Jarrell had worn out some of his prodigious
energy as a critic and had begun to discover himself anew as a poet. His final
collection, *The Lost World* (1965), showed him at the height of his powers.
He had also established himself as a children's writer of unusual lyrical
sweep tinged with wonder and melancholy, with books such as *The Bat-Poet*
(1964) and *The Animal Family* (1965), which appeared a few weeks after
his death. His poetry was sometimes faulted for sentimentality—and it
is often drenched in nostalgia, sadness, or regret—but at its best it achieves
surprising and memorable moments of deep sympathy. He once wrote to
Allen Tate, "I think all in all I've got a poetic and semifeminine mind," and
critics noticed his ability to write dramatic monologues from a woman's
point of view.

When Jarrell's posthumous *Collected Poems* (1968) appeared, Helen
Vendler quipped that he had "put his genius into his criticism and his talent
into his poetry." On the whole, that assessment has held. No book of his
poetry can equal the extraordinary energy and élan of his first book of essays,
Poetry and the Age (1953), one of the glories of modern American literature.

Jarrell's criticism is unusual in that he was not particularly interested in broad theoretical issues or general critical ideas. He adhered to no critical system, claimed never to have had "any certainties, religious or metaphysical," but responded to each work he read as an individual defining his own tastes. When he discovered the dark power of Robert Frost's poetry, he composed two remarkable, revisionist essays that changed critical notions of that master poet's work. Jarrell also went against the proprieties of the New Critics by publishing a persuasive appreciation of Walt Whitman. (These essays all appeared in *Poetry and the Age*.) He was famous for his ability to cut a mediocre poet to ribbons with a single memorable sentence. Here is a characteristic lead sentence from a Jarrell review: "Oscar Williams's new book is pleasanter and a little quieter than his old, which gave the impression of having been written on a typewriter by a typewriter." Yet Jarrell could also praise with equal force and accuracy, and his passionate advocacy helped establish the careers of Robert Lowell and Elizabeth Bishop as well as reinvigorate the critical reputations of Robert Frost and William Carlos Williams. Among his major essays there were also important overviews of the situation of poetry, including "The Obscurity of the Poet," a lecture he had delivered to approving howls of laughter at Harvard. Although occasionally mean-spirited and inaccurate, Jarrell was almost always penetrating and fresh, and he composed some of the liveliest prose any American writer has ever written.

THE OBSCURITY OF THE POET

When I was asked to talk about the Obscurity of the Modern Poet I was delighted, for I have suffered from this obscurity all my life. But then I realized that I was being asked to talk not about the fact that people don't read poetry, but about the fact that most of them wouldn't understand it if they did: about the difficulty, not the neglect, of contemporary poetry. And yet it is not just modern poetry, but poetry, that is today obscure. *Paradise Lost* is what it was; but the ordinary reader no longer makes the mistake of trying to read it—instead he glances at it, weighs it in his hand, shudders, and suddenly, his eyes shining, puts it on his list of the ten dullest books he has ever read, along with *Moby Dick, War and Peace, Faust,* and Boswell's *Life of Johnson*. But I am doing this ordinary reader an injustice: it was not the Public, nodding over its lunchpail, but the educated reader, the reader the universities have trained, who a few weeks ago, to the Public's sympathetic delight, put together this list of the world's dullest books.

Since most people know about the modern poet only that he is *obscure—i.e.,* that he is *difficult, i.e.,* that he is *neglected*—they naturally make a causal connection between the two meanings of the word, and decide that he is unread because he is difficult. Some of the time this is true; some of the time the reverse is true: the poet seems difficult *because* he is not read, *because* the reader is not accustomed to reading his or any other poetry. But most of the time neither is a cause—both are no more than effects of that long-continued, world-overturning cultural and

From *Poetry and the Age* (New York: Knopf, 1953).

social revolution (seen at its most advanced stage here in the United States) which has made the poet difficult and the public unused to any poetry exactly as it has made poet and public divorce their wives, stay away from church, dislike bull-baiting, free the slaves, get insulin shots for diabetes, or do a hundred thousand other things, some bad, some good, and some indifferent. It is superficial to extract two parts from this world-high whole, and to say of them: "This one, here, is the cause of that one, there; and that's all there is to it."

If we were in the habit of reading poets their obscurity would not matter; and, once we are out of the habit, their clarity does not help. Matthew Arnold said, with plaintive respect, that there was hardly a sentence in *Lear* that he hadn't needed to read two or three times; and three other appreciable Victorian minds, Beetle, Stalky, and McTurk, were even harder on it. They are in their study; Stalky reads:

> Never any.
> It pleased the king his master, very late,
> To strike at me, upon his misconstruction,
> When he, conjunct, and flattering in his displeasure,
> Tripped me behind: being down, insulted, railed,
> And put upon him such a deal of man
> That worthy'd him, got praises of the King
> For him attempting who was self-subdued;
> And, in the fleshment of this dread exploit,
> Drew me on here.

Stalky says: "Now, then, my impassioned bard, *construez!* That's Shakespeare"; and Beetle answers, "at the end of a blank half minute": "Give it up! He's drunk." If schoolboys were forced to read "The Phoenix and the Turtle," what *would* Beetle have said of these two stanzas?

> Property was thus appalled
> That the self was not the same;
> Single nature's double name
> Neither two nor one was called,
>
> Reason, in itself confounded,
> Saw division grow together;
> To themselves yet either-neither,
> Simple were so well compounded. . . .

You and I can afford to look at Stalky and Company, at Arnold, with dignified superiority: we know what those passages mean; we know that Shakespeare is never *obscure,* as if he were some modernist poet gleefully pasting puzzles together in his garret. Yet when we look at a variorum Shakespeare—with its line or two of text at the top of the page, its forty or fifty lines of wild surmise and quarrelsome conjecture at the bottom—we are troubled. When the Alexandrian poet Lycophron refers—and he is rarely so simple—to the *centipede, fair-faced, stork-hued daughters of Phalacra,* and they turn out to be boats, one ascribes this to Alexandrian decadence; but then one remembers that Welsh and Irish and Norse poets, the poets of a hundred barbarous cultures, loved nothing so much as referring to the very dishes on the table by elaborate descriptive epithets—periphrases, kennings—which their hearers had to be specially educated to understand. (Loved nothing so much, that is, except riddles.) And just consider the amount of classical allusions that those polite readers, our ancestors, were expected to recognize—and did recognize. If I recite to you, *The brotherless Heliades/Melt in such amber tears as these,* many of you will think, *Beautiful;* a good many will think, *Marvell;* but how many of you will know to whom Marvell is referring?

Yet the people of the past were not repelled by this obscurity (seemed, often, foolishly to treasure it); nor are those peoples of the present who are not so far removed from the past as we: who have preserved, along with the castles, the injustice, and the social discrimination of the past, a remnant of its passion for reading poetry. It is hard to be much more difficult than Mallarmé; yet when I went from bookstore to bookstore in Paris, hunting for one copy of Corbière, I began to feel a sort of mocking frustration at the poems by Mallarmé, letters by Mallarmé, letters to Mallarmé, biographies of, essays on, and homage to Mallarmé with which the shelves of those bookstores tantalized me. For how long now the French poet has been writing as if the French public did not exist—as if it were, at best, a swineherd dreaming of that faraway princess the poet; yet it looks at him with traditional awe, and reads in dozens of literary newspapers, scores of literary magazines, the details of his life, opinions, temperament, and appearance. And in the Germanic countries people still glance at one with attentive respect, as if they thought that one might at any moment be about to write a poem; I shall never forget hearing a German say, in an objective considering tone, as if I were an illustration in a book called *Silver Poets of the Americas:* "You know, he looks a little like Rilke." In several South American countries poetry has kept most of the popularity and respect it formerly enjoyed; in one country, I believe Venezuela, the president, the ambassador whom he is sending to Paris, and the waiter who serves their coffee will four out of five times be poets. "What sort of poetry do *these* poets write?" is a question of frightening moment for us poor Northern poets; if the answer is, "Nice simple stuff," we shall need to question half our ways. But these poets, these truly popular poets, seem to have taken as models for their verse neither the poems of Homer, of Shakespeare, nor of Racine, but those of Pablo Picasso: they are all surrealists.

Is Clarity the handmaiden of Popularity, as everybody automatically assumes? how much does it help to be immediately plain? In England today few poets are as popular as Dylan Thomas—his magical poems have corrupted a whole generation of English poets; yet he is surely one of the most obscure poets who ever lived. Or to take an opposite example: the poems of the students of Yvor Winters are quite as easy to understand as those which Longfellow used to read during the Children's Hour; yet they are about as popular as those other poems (of their own composition) which *grave Alice, and laughing Allegra, and Edith with golden hair* used to read to Longfellow during the Poet's Hour. If Dylan Thomas is obscurely famous, such poets as these are clearly unknown.

When someone says to me something I am not accustomed to hearing, or do not wish to hear, I say to him: *I do not understand you;* and we respond in just this way to poets. When critics first read Wordsworth's poetry they felt that it was silly, but many of them *said,* with Byron, that "he who understands it would be able/To add a story to the Tower of Babel." A few years before, a great critic praising the work of that plainest of poets, John Dryden, had remarked that he "delighted to tread on the brink where sense and nonsense mingle." Dryden himself had found Shakespeare's phrases "scarcely intelligible; and of those which we understand some are ungrammatical, others coarse; and his whole style is so pestered with figurative expressions that it is as affected as it is coarse." The reviewers of "The Love Song of J. Alfred Prufrock," even those who admired it most, found it almost impossible to understand; that it was hopelessly obscure seemed to them self-evident. Today, when college girls find it exactly as easy, exactly as hard, as "The Bishop Orders his Tomb at St. Praxed's," one is able to understand these critics' despairing or denunciatory misunderstanding only by remembering that the first generation of critics spoke of Browning's poem in just the terms that were later applied to Eliot's. How long it takes the world to catch up! Yet it really never "catches up," but is simply replaced by another world that does not need to catch up; so that when the old say to us, "What shall I do to understand Auden (or Dylan Thomas, or whoever the latest poet is)?" we can only reply: "You must be born again." An old gentleman at a party, talking to me about a poem we both admired, the *Rubaiyat,* was delighted to find that our tastes agreed so well, and asked me what modern poet I like best. Rather cutting my coat to his cloth, I answered: "Robert Frost." He looked at me with surprise, and said with gentle but undisguised finality: "I'm afraid he is a little after my time." This happened in 1950; yet surely in 1850 some old gentleman, fond of Gray and Cowper and Crabbe, must have uttered to the young Matthew Arnold the same words, but this time with reference to the poetry of William Wordsworth.

We cannot even be sure what people will find obscure; when I taught at Salzburg I found that my European students did not find "The Waste Land" half as hard as Frost's poetry, since one went with, and the other against, all their own cultural presuppositions; I had not simply to explain "Home-Burial" to them, I had to persuade them that it was a poem. And another example occurs to me: that of Robert Hillyer. In a review of *The Death of Captain Nemo* that I read, the reviewer's first complaint was that the poem is obscure. I felt as if I had seen Senator McCarthy denounced as an agent of the Kremlin; for how could Mr. Hillyer be obscure?

That the poet, the modern poet, is, understandably enough, for all sorts of good reasons, more obscure than even he has any imaginable right to be—this is one of those great elementary (or, as people say nowadays, *elemental*) attitudes about which it is hard to write anything that is not sensible and gloomily commonplace; one might as well talk on faith and works, on heredity and environment, or on that old question: why give the poor bath-tubs when they only use them to put coal in? Anyone knows enough to reply to this question: "They don't; and, even if they did, *that's* not the reason you don't want to help pay for the tubs." Similarly, when someone says, "I don't read modern poetry because it's all stuff that nobody on earth can understand," I know enough to be able to answer, though not aloud: "It isn't; and, even if it were, *that's* not the reason you don't read it." Any American poet under a certain age, a fairly advanced age—the age, one is tempted to say, of Bernard Shaw—has inherited a situation in which no one looks at him and in which, consequently, everyone complains that he is invisible: for that corner into which no one looks is always dark. And people who have inherited the custom of not reading poets justify it by referring to the obscurity of the poems they have never read—since most people decide that poets are obscure very much as legislators decide that books are pornographic: by glancing at a few fragments someone has strung together to disgust them. When a person says accusingly that he can't understand Eliot, his tone implies that most of his happiest hours are spent at the fireside among worn copies of the *Agamemnon, Phèdre,* and the Symbolic Books of William Blake; and it is melancholy to find, as one commonly will, that for months at a time he can be found pushing eagerly through the pages of *Gone with the Wind* or *Forever Amber,* where *with head, hands, wings, or feet* this poor fiend *pursues his way, and swims, or sinks, or wades, or creeps, or flies;* that all his happiest memories of Shakespeare seem to come from a high school production of *As You Like It* in which he played the wrestler Charles; and that he has, by some obscure process of free association, combined James Russell, Amy, and Robert Lowell into one majestic whole: a bearded cigar-smoking ambassador to the Vatican who, after accompanying Theodore Roosevelt on his first African expedition, came home to dictate on his deathbed the "Concord Hymn." Many a man, because Ezra Pound is too obscure for him, has shut forever the pages of *Paradise Lost;* or so one would gather, from the theory and practice such people combine.

The general public [in this lecture I hardly speak of the happy few, who grow fewer and unhappier day by day] has set up a criterion of its own, one by which every form of contemporary art is condemned. This criterion is, in the case of music, melody; in the case of painting, representation; in the case of poetry, clarity. In each case one simple aspect is made the test of a complicated whole, becomes a sort of loyalty oath for the work of art. Although judging by this method is almost as irrelevant as having the artist pronounce *shibboleth,* or swear that he is not a Know-Nothing, a Locofocoist, or a Bull Moose, it is as attractive, in exactly the same way, to the public that judges: instead of having to perceive, to enter, and to interpret those new worlds which new works of art are, the public can notice at a glance whether or not these pay lip-service to its own "principles," and can then praise or blame them accordingly. Most of the music of earlier centuries, of other continents, has nothing the public can consider a satisfactory melody; the tourist looking through the galleries of Europe very soon discovers that most of the Old Masters were not, representationally speaking, half so good as the painters who illustrate *Collier's Magazine;* how difficult and dull the inexperienced reader would find most of the great poetry of the past, if he could ever be induced to read it! Yet it is always in the name of the easy past that he condemns the difficult present.

Anyone who has spent much time finding out what people do when they read a poem, what poems actually mean for them, will have discovered that a surprising part of the difficulty they have comes from their almost systematic unreceptiveness, their queer unwillingness to pay attention even to the reference of pronouns, the meaning of the punctuation, which subject goes with which verb, and so on; "after all," they seem to feel, "I'm not reading *prose.*" You need to read good poetry with an attitude that is a mixture of sharp intelligence and of willing emotional empathy, at once penetrating and generous: as if you were listening to *The Marriage of Figaro,* not as if you were listening to *Tristan* or to Samuel Butler's Handelian oratorios; to read poetry—as so many readers do—like Mortimer Snerd pretending to be Dr. Johnson, or like Uncle Tom recollecting Eva, is hardly to read poetry at all. When you begin to read a poem you are entering a foreign country whose laws and language and life are a kind of translation of your own; but to accept it because its stews taste exactly like your old mother's hash, or to reject it because the owl-headed goddess of wisdom in its temple is fatter than the Statue of Liberty, is an equal mark of that want of imagination, that inaccessibility to experience, of which each of us who dies a natural death will die.

That the poetry of the first half of this century often *was* too difficult—just as the poetry of the eighteenth century *was* full of antitheses, that of the metaphysicals full of conceits, that of the Elizabethan dramatists full of rant and quibbles—is a truism that it would be absurd to deny. How our poetry got this way—how romanticism was purified and exaggerated and "corrected" into modernism; how poets carried all possible tendencies to their limits, with more than scientific zeal;

how the dramatic monologue, which once had depended for its effect upon being a departure from the norm of poetry, now became in one form or another the norm; how poet and public stared at each other with righteous indignation, till the poet said, "Since you won't read me, I'll make sure you can't"—is one of the most complicated and interesting of stories. But Modernism was not "that lion's den from which no tracks return," but only a sort of canvas whale from which Jonah after Jonah, throughout the late '20's and early '30's, made a penitent return, back to rhyme and metre and plain broad Statement; how many young poets today are, if nothing else, plain! Yet how little posterity—if I may speak of that imaginary point where the poet and the public intersect—will care about all the tendencies of our age, all those good or bad intentions with which ordinary books are paved; and how much it will care for those few poems which, regardless of intention, manage at once to sum up, to repudiate, and to transcend both the age they appear in and the minds they are produced by. One judges an age, just as one judges a poet, by its best poems—after all, most of the others have disappeared; when posterity hears that our poems are obscure, it will smile indifferently—just as we do when we are told that the Victorians were sentimental, the Romantics extravagant, the Augustans conventional, the metaphysicals conceited, and the Elizabethans bombastic—and go back to its (and our) reading: to Hardy's "During Wind and Rain," to Wordsworth's story of the woman Margaret, to Pope's "Epistle to Dr. Arbuthnot," to Marvell's "Horatian Ode," to Shakespeare's *Antony and Cleopatra,* to Eliot's *Four Quartets,* and to all the rest of those ageless products of an age.

In this age, certainly, poetry persists under many disadvantages. Just as it has been cut off from most of the people who in another age would have read it, so it has been cut off from most of the people who in another age would have written it. Today poems, good poems, are written almost exclusively by "born poets." We have lost for good the poems that would have been written by the modern equivalents of Henry VIII or Bishop King or Samuel Johnson; born novelists, born theologians, born princes; minds with less of an innate interest in words and more of one in the world which produces words. We are accustomed to think of the poet, when we think of him at all, as someone Apart; yet was there—as so many poets and readers of poetry seem to think—*was* there in the Garden of Eden, along with Adam and Eve and the animals, a Poet, the ultimate ancestor of Robert P. Tristram Coffin? . . . When I last read poems in New York City, a lady who, except for bangs, a magenta jersey blouse, and the expression of Palamède de Charlus, was indistinguishable from any other New Yorker, exclaimed to me about a poet whom the years have fattened for the slaughter: "He read like a young god." I felt that the next poet was going to be told that I read like the young Joaquin Miller; for this lady was less interested in those wonderful things poems than in those other things, poets—not realizing that it is their subordination to the poems they write that makes them admirable. She seemed to me someone who, because he has inherited a pearl necklace, can never again look at an oyster without a shudder of awe. And this reminds one that, today, many of the readers a poet would value most have hardly learned to read any poetry; and many of those who regularly read his poems have values so different from his that he is troubled by their praise, and vexed but reassured by their blame.

Tomorrow morning some poet may, like Byron, wake up to find himself famous—for having written a novel, for having killed his wife; it will not be for having written a poem. That is still logically, but no longer socially, possible. Let me illustrate with a story. I once met on a boat, travelling to Europe with his wife and daughter, a man with whom I played ping-pong. Having learned from a friend that I wrote poetry, he asked one day with uninterested politeness, "Who are the American poets you like best?" I said, "Oh, T. S. Eliot, Robert Frost." Then this man—this father who every night danced with his daughter with the well-taught, dated, decorous attractiveness of the hero of an old *Saturday Evening Post* serial by E. Phillips Oppenheim; who had had the best professional in Los Angeles teach his wife and daughter the tennis strokes he himself talked of with wearying authority; who never in his life had gone through a doorway before anyone over the age of seven—this well-dressed, well-mannered, travelled, urbane, educated gentleman said placidly: "I don't believe I've heard of them." For so far as literature, the arts, philosophy, and science were concerned, he might better have been the policeman on the corner. But he was perfectly correct in thinking—not that he had ever thought about it—that a knowledge of these things is not an essential requirement of the society of which he is a part. We belong to a culture whose old hierarchy of values—which demanded that a girl read Pope just as it demanded that she go to church and play the pianoforte—has virtually disappeared; a culture in which the great artist or scientist, in the relatively infrequent cases in which he has become widely known, has the status of Betty Grable or of the columnist who writes that, the night before, he met both these "celebrities" at the Stork Club.

When, a hundred and fifty years ago, a man had made his fortune, he found it necessary to provide himself with lace, carriages, servants, a wife of good family, a ballerina, a fencing master, a dancing master, a chaplain, a teacher of French, a string quartet perhaps, the editions of Pope and Steele and Addison through which he worked a laborious way on unoccupied evenings: there was so much for him to learn to *do,* there in his new station in life, that he must often have thought with nostalgia of the days in which all that he had to do was make his fortune. We have changed most of that: in our day the rich are expected not to do but to be; and those ties, tenuous, ambiguous, and immemorial, which bound to the Power of a state its Wisdom and its Grace, have at last been severed.

When Mill and Marx looked at a handful of workingmen making their slow firm way through the pages of Shelley or Herbert Spencer or *The Origin of Species,* they thought with confident longing, just as Jefferson and Lincoln had, of the days when every man would be literate, when an actual democracy would make its choices with as much wisdom as any imaginary state where the philosopher is king; and no gleam of prophetic insight came to show them those workingmen, two million strong, making their easy and pleasant way through the pages of the New York *Daily News.* The very speeches in which Jefferson and Lincoln spoke of their hope for the future are incomprehensible to most of the voters of that future, since the vocabulary and syntax of the speeches are more difficult—more obscure—than anything the voters have read or heard. For when you defeat me in an election simply because you were, as I was not, born and bred in a log cabin, it is only a question of time until you are beaten by someone whom the pigs brought up out in the yard. The truth that all men are politically equal, the recognition of the injustice of fictitious differences, becomes a belief in the fictitiousness of differences, a conviction that it is reaction or snobbishness or Fascism to believe that any individual differences of real importance can exist. We dislike having to believe in what Goethe called inborn or innate merits; yet—as a later writer more or less says—many waiters are born with the taste of duchesses, and most duchesses are born (and die) with the tastes of waiters: we can escape from the level of society, but not from the level of intelligence, to which we were born.

One of our universities recently made a survey of the reading habits of the American public; it decided that forty-eight percent of all Americans read, during a year, no book at all. I picture to myself that reader—non-reader, rather; one man out of every two—and I reflect, with shame: "Our poems are too hard for him." But so, too, are *Treasure Island, Peter Rabbit,* pornographic novels—any book whatsoever. The authors of the world have been engaged in a sort of conspiracy to drive this American away from books; have, in 77 million out of 160 million cases, succeeded. A sort of dream-situation often occurs to me in which I call to this imaginary figure, "Why don't you read books?"—and he always answers, after looking at me steadily for a long time: "Huh?"

If my tone is mocking, the tone of someone accustomed to helplessness, this is natural: the poet is a condemned man for whom the State will not even buy breakfast—and as someone said, "If you're going to hang me, you mustn't expect to be able to intimidate me into sparing your feelings during the execution." The poet lives in a world whose newspapers and magazines and books and motion pictures and radio stations and television stations have destroyed, in a great many people, even the capacity for understanding real poetry, real art of any kind. The man who monthly reads, with vacant relish, the carefully predigested sentences which the *Reader's Digest* feeds to him as a mother pigeon feeds her squabs—this man *cannot* read the *Divine Comedy,* even if it should ever occur to him to try: it is too obscure. Yet one sort of clearness shows a complete contempt for the reader, just as one sort of obscurity shows a complete respect. Which patronizes and degrades the reader, the *Divine Comedy* with its four levels of meaning, or the *Reader's Digest* with its one level so low that it seems not a level but an abyss into which the reader consents to sink? The writer's real dishonesty is to give an easy paraphrase of the hard truth. Yet the average article in our magazines gives any subject whatsoever the same coat of easy, automatic, "human" interest; every year *Harper's Magazine* sounds more like *Life* and the *Saturday Evening Post.* Goethe said, "The author whom a lexicon can keep up with is worth nothing"; Somerset Maugham says that the finest compliment he ever received was a letter in which one of his readers said: "I read your novel without having to look up a single word in the dictionary." These writers, plainly, lived in different worlds.

Since the animal organism thinks, truly reasons, only when it is required to, thoughtfulness is gradually disappearing among readers; and popular writing has left nothing to the imagination for so long now that imagination too has begun to atrophy. Almost all the works of the past are beginning to seem to the ordinary reader flat and dull, because they do not supply the reader's response along with that to which he responds. Boys who have read only a few books in their lives, but a great many comic books, will tell one, so vividly that it is easy to sympathize: "I don't like books because they don't really show you things; they're too slow; you have to do all the work yourself." When, in a few years, one talks to boys who have read only a few comic books, but have looked at a great many television programs—what will *they* say?

On this subject of the obscurity of the poet, of the new world that is taking the place of the old, I have written you a poem—an obscure one. I once encountered, in a book, a house that had a formal garden, an English garden, a kitchen garden, and a cutting garden; through these gardens gentlemen walked in silk stockings, their calves padded like those of Mephistopheles; and I made that cutting garden, those padded calves, my symbols for the past. For the present and the future I had so many symbols I didn't know what to do: they came into the poem without knocking, judged it, and did not leave when they had judged; but the one that summed them all up—that had, for me, the sound of the Last Morning of Judgment—was a slogan from a wine-advertisement, one that I used to see every day in the New York subways. My poem is called "The Times Worsen":

If sixteen shadows flapping on the line
All sleek with bluing—a Last Morning's wash—
Whistle, "Now that was thoughty, Mrs. Bean,"
I tell myself, I try: *A dream, a dream.*
But my plaid spectacles are matt as gouache;
When, Sundays, I have finished all the funnies,
I have not finished all the funnies. Men
Walk in all day (to try me) without knocking—
My jurors: these just, vulgar, friendly shades.
The cutting garden of my grandmama,
My great-great-great-grandfather's padded calves
(Greeted, at cockcrow, with the soft small smile
Of Lilith, his first morganatic wife)
Are only a tale from E. T. W. Hoffmann.
When Art goes, what remains is Life.
The World of the Future does not work by halves:
Life is that "wine like Mother used to make—
So rich you can almost cut it with a knife."

The World of the Future! That world where vegetables are either frozen, canned, or growing in the fields; where little children, as they gaze into the television viewplate at the Babes dead under the heaped-up leaves of the Wood, ask pleadingly: "But where was their electric blanket?"; where old books, hollowed-out to hold fudge, grace every coffee-table; where cavemen in grammar school pageants, clad in pelts of raw cotton, are watched by families dressed entirely—except for the Neolite of their shoe-soles—in rayon, cellulose, and spun nylon; where, among the related radiances of a kitchen's white-enamelled electric stove, electric dishwasher, electric refrigerator, electric washing-machine, electric dryer, electric ironer, disposal unit, air conditioner, and Waring Blendor, the home-maker sits in the trim coveralls of her profession; where, above the concrete cavern that holds a General Staff, the rockets are invisible in the sky . . . Of this world I often think.

I do not know whether, at this point, any of my hearers will feel like saying to me, "But all this is Negative. What do you want us to *do* about all this?" If I have sounded certain about "all this," let me apologize: these are conclusions which I have come to slowly and reluctantly, as the world forced them on me. Would that I were one of those happy reactionaries, born with a Greek vocabulary as other children are born with birthmarks or incomes, who at the age of four refuse indignantly to waste on that "humanitarian phantasy of a sentimental liberalism, the Kindergarten," the hours they instead devote to memorizing their catechism! But I had a scientific education and a radical youth; am old-fashioned enough to believe, like Goethe, in Progress—the progress I see and the progress I wish for and do not see. So I say what I have said about the poet, the public, and their world angrily and unwillingly. If my hearers say, "But what should we do?" what else can I answer but "Nothing"? There is nothing to do different from what we already do: if poets write poems and readers read them, each as best they can—if they try to live not as soldiers or voters or intellectuals or economic men, but as human beings—they are doing all that can be done. But to expect them (by, say, reciting one-syllable poems over the radio) to bring back that Yesterday in which people stood on chairs to look at Lord Tennyson, is to believe that General Motors can bring back "the tradition of craftsmanship" by giving, as it does, prizes to Boy Scouts for their scale-models of Napoleonic coaches; to believe that the manners of the past can be restored by encouraging country-people to say *Grüss Gott* or *Howdy, stranger* to the tourists they meet along summer lanes.

Art matters not merely because it is the most magnificent ornament and the most nearly unfailing occupation of our lives, but because it is life itself. From Christ to Freud we have believed that, if we know the truth, the truth will set us free: art is indispensable because so much of this truth can be learned through works of art and through works of art alone—for which of us could have learned for himself what Proust and Chekhov, Hardy and Yeats and Rilke, Shakespeare and Homer learned for us? and in what other way could they have made us see the truths which they themselves saw, those differing and contradictory truths which seem nevertheless, to the mind which contains them, in some sense a single truth? And all these things, by their very nature, demand to be shared; if we are satisfied to know these things ourselves, and to look with superiority or indifference at those who do not have that knowledge, we have made a refusal that corrupts us as surely as anything can. If while most of our people (the descendants of those who, ordinarily, listened to Grimm's Tales and the ballads and the Bible; who, exceptionally, listened to Aeschylus and Shakespeare) listen not to simple or naive art, but to an elaborate and sophisticated substitute for art, an immediate and infallible synthetic as effective and terrifying as advertisements or the speeches of Hitler—if, knowing all this, we say: *Art has always been a matter of a few,* we are using a truism to hide a disaster. One of the oldest, deepest, and most nearly conclusive attractions of democracy is manifested in our feeling that through it not only material but also spiritual goods can be shared: that in a democracy bread and justice, education and art, will be accessible to everybody. If a democracy should offer its citizens a show of education, a sham art, a literacy more dangerous than their old illiteracy, then we should have to say that it is not a democracy at all, but one more variant of those "People's Democracies" which share with any true democracy little more than the name. Goethe said: The only way in which we can come to terms with the great superiority of another person is love. But we can also come to terms with superiority, with true Excellence, by denying that such a thing as Excellence can exist; and, in doing so, we help to destroy it and ourselves.

I was sorry to see this conference given its (quite traditional) name of The Defense of Poetry. Poetry does not need to be defended, any more than air or food needs to be defended; poetry—using the word in its widest sense, the only sense in which it is important—has been an indispensable part of any culture we know anything about. Human life without some form of poetry is not human life but animal existence. Our world today is not an impossible one for poets and poetry: poets can endure its disadvantages, and good poetry is still being written—Yeats, for instance, thought the first half of this century the greatest age of lyric poetry since the Elizabethan. But what will happen to the public—to that portion of it divorced from any real art even of the simplest kind—I do not know. Yet an analogy occurs to me.

One sees, in the shops of certain mountainous regions of Austria, bands of silver links, clasped like necklaces, which have at the front jeweled or enameled silver plates, sometimes quite large ones. These pieces of jewelry are called *goiterbands*: they are ornaments which in the past were used to adorn a woman's diseased, enormously swollen neck. If the women who wore them could have been told that they had been made hideous by the lack of an infinitesimal proportion of iodine in the water of the mountain valley in which they lived, they would have laughed at the notion. They would have laughed even more heartily at the notion that their necks *were* hideous—and their lovers would have asked, as they looked greedily at the round flesh under the flaxen pigtails, how anyone could bear to caress the poor, thin, scrawny, chickenish necks of those other women they now and then saw, foreigners from that flatland which travellers call the world.

I have talked about the poet and his public; but who is his public, really? In a story by E. M. Forster called *The Machine Stops*, there is a conversation between a mother and her son. They are separated by half the circumference of the earth; they sit under the surface of the earth in rooms supplied with air, with food, and with warmth as automatically as everything else is supplied to these people of the far future. "Imagine," as Forster says, "a swaddled lump of flesh—a woman, about five feet high, with a face as white as a fungus." She has just refused to go to visit her son; she has no time. Her son replies:

"The air-ship barely takes two days to fly between me and you."
"I dislike air-ships."
"Why?"
"I dislike seeing the horrible brown earth, and the sea, and the stars when it is dark. I get no ideas in an air-ship."
"I do not get them anywhere else."
"What kind of ideas can the air give you?"
He paused for an instant.
"Do you not know four big stars that form an oblong, and three stars close together in the middle of the oblong, and hanging from these stars, three other stars?"
"No, I do not. I dislike the stars. But did they give you an idea? How interesting; tell me."
"I had an idea that they were like a man."
"I do not understand."
"The four big stars are the man's shoulders and his knees. The three stars in the middle are like the belts that men wore once, and the three stars hanging are like a sword."
"A sword?"
"Men carried swords about with them, to kill animals and other men."
"It does not strike me as a very good idea, but it is certainly original."

As long as these stars remain in this shape; as long as there is a man left to look at them and to discover that they are the being Orion: for at least this long the poet will have his public. And when this man too is gone, and neither the poems, the poet, nor the public exist any longer—and this possibility can no longer seem to us as strange as it would once have seemed—there is surely some order of the world, some level of being, at which they still subsist: an order in which the lost plays of Aeschylus are no different from those that have been preserved, an order in which the past, the present, and the future have in some sense the same reality. Or so—whether we think so or not—so we all feel. People always ask: *For whom does the poet write?* He needs only to answer, *For whom do you do good? Are you kind to your daughter because in the end someone will pay you for being? . . .* The poet writes his poem for its own sake, for the sake of that order of things in which the poem takes the place that has awaited it.

But this has been said, better than it is ever again likely to be said, by the greatest of the writers of this century, Marcel Proust; and I should like to finish this lecture by quoting his sentences:

"All that we can say is that everything is arranged in this life as though we entered it carrying the burden of obligations contracted in a former life; there is no reason inherent in the conditions of life on this earth that can make us consider ourselves obliged to do good, to be fastidious, to be polite even, nor make the talented artist consider himself obliged to begin over again a score of times a piece of work the admiration aroused by which will matter little to his body devoured by worms, like the patch of yellow wall painted with so much knowledge and skill by an artist who must for ever remain unknown and is barely identified under the name Vermeer. All these obligations which have not their sanction in our present life seem to belong to a different world, founded upon kindness, scrupulosity, self-sacrifice, a world entirely different from this, which we leave in order to be born into this world, before perhaps returning to the other to live once again beneath the sway of those unknown laws which we have obeyed because we bore their precepts in our hearts, knowing not whose hand had traced them there—those laws to which every profound work of the intellect brings us nearer and which are invisible only— and still!—to fools."

1953

WILLIAM STAFFORD
(1914–1993)

Born in Hutchinson, Kansas, to parents who loved books but struggled to survive during the Great Depression, William Edgar Stafford learned early on to value literature, hard work, and independence of mind. As his family moved from town to town during the 1930s looking for work, Stafford took jobs delivering newspapers, raising vegetables to sell from door to door, and serving as an electrician's assistant in an oil refinery. After graduating from high school and spending two years at El Dorado junior college, Stafford enrolled at the University of Kansas, waiting tables to pay his way.

He received his B.A. in 1937 and hoped to become a writer, but his ambition was tested during World War II when he registered as a conscientious objector. Stafford served in C.O. camps in Arkansas, Illinois, and California— an experience he documented in his novel, *Down in My Heart* (1947). Despite the forced isolation and constant labor, Stafford did not put his life on hold; he continued writing and even married in 1944. Because physical exhaustion allowed no time to write at night, Stafford devised a strategy he maintained for the rest of his life: rising at four A.M. "Since those days" he noted, "I have had the habit of writing in the early morning. That dawn time is precious: the world is quiet; no one will interrupt; you are rested and ready."

The habit was especially useful after his release from the camps. He completed his master's degree at the University of Kansas, fathered four children, taught high school in California, and then worked for a relief agency. In 1948, he was hired to teach English at Lewis and Clark College in Portland, Oregon, a job he held until his retirement in 1980. From 1950 to 1952, the college granted him a leave to study creative writing at the University of Iowa, where he earned a Ph.D. in 1954. Although he enjoyed having daily exchanges with other writers there, he felt that the competitive climate of the Iowa workshops was antithetical to his goal of making writing a process of discovery rather than dictated by a group's definition of good poetry. After Stafford returned to teaching, this nonconformist attitude shaped his own approach to the classroom, for he tried not to praise or criticize students, but instead to help them discover their own directions. Stafford's faith in the creative process also clarified his own writing—especially his practice of letting poems develop almost by chance, as a means of exploration.

Despite his immense productivity, book publication came late for Stafford. His first collection, *West of Your City* (1960), did not appear until he was forty-six. But he went on to publish twelve volumes of poetry with mainstream presses, as well as numerous broadsides, chapbooks, and full-length collections with small presses. After his second book, *Traveling Through the Dark* (1962), won the National Book Award, he continued to receive honors for his poetry: the Shelley Memorial Award (1964), a Guggenheim Fellowship (1966), an appointment to serve as Consultant in Poetry to the Library of Congress (1970), the Award in Literature from the American Academy and Institute of Arts and Letters (1981), and—a year before his death—the Western States Book Award for Lifetime Achievement in Poetry (1992). Although academic critics have rarely found Stafford's direct and heartfelt style compelling, his fellow poets admired him greatly. When *Writer's Digest* polled U.S. poets in 1986 to determine their nominations for "the ten major living American poets," Stafford ranked first in votes.

Stafford's belief in the power of "the inner life" to shape his work linked him with the Deep Image poets, for whom poetry was a way of mining the unconscious. His best poems take disquieting turns and offer unsentimental meditations on human limitations and nature's inscrutability. His pared down language and spare syntax are supple enough to echo the forbidding landscapes of the great plains and the American West that he often contemplates and also to balance between seriousness and lightness so that his poems develop complex perspectives on ordinary experience.

In the following essay, Stafford advises poets to be led by language, rather than by preconceived ideas about what constitutes "good diction" in a poem. In his opening, Stafford compares some assumptions about poetry to Gresham's Law, an Elizabethan formula in which bad money drives out good. He sees writing not as an act that helps a poet describe or understand experience, but as something to be experienced, so that the poet can be led into new territory through the opportunities afforded by a language's unexpected distortions.

SOME ARGUMENTS AGAINST GOOD DICTION

. . . it is with words mainly that we delineate the conceivable and if we never allow words to be a little eccentric, never allow ourselves to apply a word to any state of affairs actual or conceivable, to which it would not customarily be applied, we are without means to refer to any state of affairs for which there is not a word, any possibility undreamt of in our philosophy.

—John Wisdom, Paradox and Discovery (Oxford: Basil Blackwell, 1965), p. 132.

First published in *New York Quarterly* 5 (1971). Collected in *Writing the Australian Crawl* (Ann Arbor: University of Michigan Press, 1978).

Ordinary statements about diction and literature and the process of writing often have such convenience and such easy links to what we say about other activities, that we are tempted to accept the superficial formula. This tendency—a kind of Gresham's law of art discussion we have to guard against. Whatever is distinctive in some intricate activity is *felt* by the practitioners, but in talking about the activity with others (and even in conceiving it to themselves), people accept quick formulations that *generally* help. But the cumulative effect of the assumptions thus woven into art discussion becomes misleading. To avoid such misunderstandings, we try restating, but we have to use the language, again full of distortions; so we do something like taking off a rubber glove with one hand, and it is a glove that *wants to stay on.*

One such topic confounded by Gresham's law is that of diction. Apparently for many people the writer is conceived as a person sitting at a big desk with cubbyholes containing all the words there are—or all the words the writer knows. The person writes his story or essay, or anything, by carefully reaching with long tweezers into the cubbyholes to get the right words (proper words in proper places—everyone knows that poems are made with words). *Le mot juste* is the slogan of excellence in writing.

Following the implied advice of such a picture and of those apparently helpful phrasings, a novice learns an adequate vocabulary, sits down at his desk with all the cubbyholes, and is a writer. But somehow he does not write *War and Peace.* That picture and those words have misled the would-be writer, and they can even menace the accomplished writer who lives perilously surrounded by such pleasant, simple concepts and sayings that superficially delineate his art.

The process of writing that I experience has little connection with the formulations I most often hear. Where words come from, into consciousness, baffles me. Speaking or writing, the words bounce instantaneously into their context, and I am victimized by them, rather than controlling them. They do not wait for my selection; they volunteer. True, I can reject them, but my whole way of writing induces easy acceptance—at first—of any eager volunteer. I want to talk about these volunteers, but first want to consider another reason for trying carefully to set the record straight, about attitudes toward language. The point concerns how a writer feels about language, in general. Many opine that a writer, and particularly a poet, for some reason, must love language; often there is even a worshipful attitude assumed. I have noticed this assumption with particular attention because it happens that insofar as I can assess my own attitudes in relation to others' I have an unusually intense distrust of language. What people say or write comes to me attenuated or thinned by my realization that talk merely puts into the air an audio counterpart of mysterious, untrustworthy, confused events in the creature making the sounds. "Truth," or "wonder," or any kind of imaginative counterpart of "absolute realities"—these I certainly do not expect in human communication.

An illustration of this distrust—an illustration that brings in contrary attitudes held by very imposing people, and hence is highly dangerous for my own case—came when I saw inscribed in gold on a pillar in the Library of Congress this saying: "The inquiry, knowledge and belief of truth is the sovereign good of human nature." To me, such a saying is hollow; I see it as demonstrating man's pathetic infatuation with an apparent power that is essentially just a redundancy. The highest we know is high for us, but its communication is an interior, not an absolute, phenomenon. And I cringe to realize that my own saying of my kind of truth is hazardous at best. Language—others' and my own—is very thin.

But back to diction. When we talk or write we venture into an immediate engagement with the language we happen to have. This accumulation of sounds and assumptions and automatic, unconscious logicings provides us with a progressing experience we feel as meaningful. If we find ourselves in a state of emergency when applying our natural language to the emerging opportunities, we can slog through words and make some kind of communication without necessarily feeling that the language is being helpful in any local way—we speak or write in a workaday fashion, and our language may not have any lift or "poetic" feeling. That is one way to use the language.

Another way is to let the language itself begin to shape the event taking place by its means. If it happens that at this time in history and at this place in our own experience we happen on a word with a syllable that reverberates with many other syllables in contexts that reinforce what the immediate word is doing, we have "powerful language." The internal reinforcements of the historically opportune language we happen to own come into something like focus or harmony. We speak or write poetry. Even if what we write is prose, we may speak of it as "poetical." This kind of link with poetry I take to mean that some kind of dynamism in the language itself—syllables, cadences, local or larger surges in sound or imagery—is carrying the *now*-conditioned reader or hearer into his own blissful redundancy inside his own experience. Like the philosophers who admire the scope of thought, the artists are exhilarated by the "power of art."

Let me try for a direct statement of what is disquieting about what ordinarily surfaces when we talk about "good diction." For a writer, it is not the past or present of words that counts, but their futures, and those futures are approaching by means of influences too various for rules or derivations to control or predict. When the poet says, "The fog comes pussyfooting along," or something like that, it isn't that the isolated words have been drafted, but that some kind of yearning connection among experiences has taken over. Reluctantly, the writer enters language and fearfully entrusts that limited and treacherous medium to keep from absolutely violating the feeling he has entrusted to it. In the ensuing transaction, language accomplishes several things at once.

1. It begins to distort, by congealing parts of the total experience into successive, partially relevant signals (just as this sentence is doing now).

2. It begins to entice the reader or hearer away into his own version or variation on the speaker's or writer's relations to the words.

3. But—and an important but—the transaction also begins to enhance the experience because of a weird quality in language: the successive distortions of language have their own kind of cumulative potential, and under certain conditions the distortions of language can reverberate into new experiences more various, more powerful, and more revealing than the experiences that set off language in the first place.

It is that cumulative potential in language that writers find themselves relying on again and again as they fearfully advance, leaving behind some of the purposes and aims they started with and accepting the wondrous bonuses that chance and the *realizing* elements of the future's approach allows them. *Le mot juste* does not exist. For people, the truth does not exist. But language offers a continuous encounter with our own laminated, enriched, experiences; and sometimes those encounters lead to further satisfactions derived from the cumulative influences in language as it spins out. That kind of language experience we grope for and identify with various tags. One of them is just a word—poetry.

1978

GWENDOLYN BROOKS
(1917–2000)

Gwendolyn Brooks was born in Topeka, Kansas, but grew up on the South Side of Chicago, where her parents created a sustaining home life despite economic hardship and fostered her love of poetry. Brooks published her first poem at age thirteen, and by the time she was seventeen had contributed over seventy-five poems to the *Chicago Defender,* an African American newspaper. Before graduating from Englewood High School in 1934, she had corresponded with Langston Hughes, who encouraged her to listen to the blues, and James Weldon Johnson, who led her to the work of Modernists such as T. S. Eliot and Ezra Pound.

Brooks graduated from Warren Wilson Junior College in 1936 and joined the NAACP youth council, where she met Henry Blakey II, whom she married in 1939. After the birth of their first child, in 1941 Brooks became a member of a poetry workshop run by Inez Cunningham Stark, a wealthy white woman who, Brooks recalls, "flew in the face of her society tradition, coming among blacks. . . . She gave us an education in modern poetry." Equally important to Brooks's poetry was her experience living in Chicago's South Side ghetto. After her marriage she moved from her parents' home to a small kitchenette apartment in a crowded building, and the vibrant, complex life of the South Side (christened "Bronzeville" by the *Chicago Defender*) became the primary subject of her work.

Brooks's poetry is notable for its technical ingenuity, emotional vitality, and nuanced explorations of African American city life. During the early 1940s, the literary world was dominated by "The New Criticism," whose practitioners wrote poetry characterized by complex forms, dense verbal textures, wit, irony, and allusion. Brooks not only mastered this style, but took it to new lengths, for the poetry of her first three books depends on wordplay, heavy alliteration and assonance, and ease with a variety of forms, both traditional and invented. Whereas much New Critical poetry suffers from overemphasis on wit and technique so that it becomes a form of intellectual gamesmanship, Brooks's work is invigorated by her passionate portrayals of ordinary African American women and men and by her arguments against prejudice. And because Brooks deploys irony to attack racial and social inequalities, she implicitly challenges the New Critics' view that poetry should be disengaged from politics. Yet Brooks also continues the traditions of African American folk forms, especially in her ballads and character portraits.

Brooks soon received national recognition. After she won the Midwestern Writers' Conference Poetry Award in 1943, Harper published her first book, *A Street in Bronzeville* (1945), which garnered her the American Academy of Letters Award (1946) and two Guggenheim Fellowships (1946 and 1947). With the publication of *Annie Allen* (1949), Brooks became the first African American to win the Pulitzer Prize. The focus on black women's experience that she developed in *Annie Allen* continued in her lyrical novella, *Maud Martha* (1953). As the 1960s came to a close, African American protests for civil rights intensified, and Brooks's third book of poetry, *The Bean Eaters* (1960), became more openly political than her earlier books, although she still favored traditional forms.

During the first half of the 1960s, Brooks was honored by President John F. Kennedy, who invited her to read at the Library of Congress, and by Columbia College in Chicago (where she began teaching in 1963), which gave her the first of the fifty-one honorary degrees she was to receive from American universities over the next thirty years. But Brooks's most momentous experience of the decade was her participation in the 1967 Second Black Writers' Conference at Fisk University in Nashville, Tennessee. There, she met proponents of the Black Arts Movement, including Amiri Baraka and Don L. Lee (Haki R. Madhubuti), who espoused black nationalism and argued that African American poets should write strictly for a black audience, view poetry as a vehicle for community building and social change, and use only forms such as the blues or a free verse based on African American speech rhythms. Their ideas reflected her own growing convictions—so much so that, with the publication of *In the Mecca* (1968), she changed her style to make it more easily accessible to an African American audience. Describing her new work, Brooks stressed that, "my aim . . . is to write poems that will somehow successfully 'call' all black people: black people in taverns, black people in alleys, black people in gutters, schools, offices, factories, prisons, the consulate; I wish to reach black people in pulpits, black people in mines, on farms, on thrones; *not* always to 'teach'—I shall wish often to entertain, to illumine."

In the spirit of community building, after 1969 she broke with Harper and Row and began publishing with African American presses, where she released many small chapbooks of new poems, as well as her autobiography, *Report from Part One* (1972) and *Report from Part Two* (1995), and *Blacks* (1987), a retrospective poetry collection spanning her whole career. Brooks also continued her dedicated involvement in her own community through the workshops and contests for young writers that she sponsored as Poet Laureate of Illinois, a position she held from 1968 to her death in 2000, and through the Gwendolyn Brooks Center for Black Literature and Creative Writing, founded in 1993 by Chicago State University, where she was Distinguished Professor of English. Brooks's many national honors— including being the first black woman elected to the National Institute of Arts and Letters and also the first black woman appointed as Consultant in Poetry to the Library of Congress—attest to the broad appeal of her work. When asked in a 1967 interview, "What is your Poet's Premise?" she responded: "'Vivify the contemporary fact,' said Whitman. I like to vivify the *universal* fact, when it occurs to me. But the universal wears contemporary clothing very well."

◄•══◄►══•►

THE NEW BLACK

The Field of the Fever. The Time of the Tall-Walkers.

Everybody has to go to the bathroom.
That's good.
That's a great thing.

If by some quirk of fate blacks had to go to the bathroom and whites didn't I shudder to think of the genocidal horrors that would be visited on the blacks of the whole world. Here is what my little green *Webster's New World* has to say about a world-shaking word:

black (blak), adj. (A S *blaec*) 1. opposite to white: see color. 2. dark-complexioned. 3. Negro. 4. without light; dark. 5. dirty. 6. evil; wicked. 7. sad; dismal. 8. sullen. n.1. black pigment; opposite of white. 2. dark clothing, as for mourning. 3. a Negro. v.t.&v.i., to blacken.—black-out, to lose consciousness.—blackly, adv:—blackness, n.

Interestingly enough, we do not find that "white" is "opposite of black." That would "lift" black to the importance-level of white.

white (hwit), adj. (A S hwit). 1. having the color of pure snow or milk. 2. of a light or pale color. 3. pale; wan. 4. pure; innocent. 5. having a light-colored skin. n. 1. the color of pure snow or milk. 2. a white or light-colored thing, as the albumen of an egg, the white part of the eyeball, etc. 3. a person with a light-colored skin; Caucasian.—whiteness, n.

Until 1967 my own blackness did not confront me with a shrill spelling of itself. I knew that I was what most people were calling "a Negro;" I called myself that, although always the word fell awkwardly on a poet's ear; I had never liked the sound of it (Caucasian has an ugly sound, too, while the name Indian is beautiful to look at and to hear.) *And* I knew that people of my coloration and distinctive history had been bolted to trees and sliced or burned or shredded; knocked to the back of the line; provided with separate toilets, schools, neighborhoods; denied, when possible, voting rights; hounded, hooted at, or shunned, or patronizingly patted (often the patting-hand was, I knew, surreptitiously wiped after the Kindness, so that unspeakable contamination might be avoided.) America's social

From *Report from Part One* (Detroit: Broadside Press, 1972) 82–86.

climate, it seemed, was trying to tell me something. It was trying to tell me something Websterian. Yet, although almost secretly, I had always felt that to be black was good. Sometimes, there would be an approximate whisper around me: *others* felt, it seemed, that to be black was good. The translation would have been something like "Hey—being black is *fun.*" Or something like "Hey—our folks have got stuff to be proud of!" Or something like "Hey—since we are so good why aren't we treated like the other 'Americans?'"

Suddenly there was New Black to meet. In the spring of 1967 I met some of it at the Fisk University Writers' Conference in Nashville. Coming from white white white South Dakota State College I arrived in Nashville, Tennessee, to give one more "reading." But blood-boiling surprise was in store for me. First, I was aware of a general energy, an electricity, in look, walk, speech, *gesture* of the young blackness I saw all about me. I had been "loved" at South Dakota State College. Here, I was coldly Respected. Here, the heroes included the novelist-director, John Killens, editors David Llorens and Hoyt Fuller, playwright Ron Milner, historians John Henrik Clarke and Lerone Bennett (and even poor Lerone was taken to task, by irate members of a no-nonsense young audience, for affiliating himself with *Ebony Magazine,* considered at that time a traitor for allowing skin-bleach advertisements in its pages, and for over-featuring light-skinned women). Imamu Amiri Baraka, then "LeRoi Jones", was expected. He arrived in the middle of my own offering, and when I called attention to his presence there was jubilee in Jubilee Hall.

All that day and night, Margaret Danner Cunningham—another Old Girl, another coldly Respected old Has-been—and an almost hysterical Gwendolyn B. walked about in amazement, listening, looking, learning. *What was going on!*

In my cartoon basket I keep a cartoon of a stout, dowager-hatted, dowager-furred Helen Hokinson woman. She is on parade in the world. She is a sign-carrier in the wild world. Her sign says "Will someone please tell me what is going on?" Well, although I cannot give a full-blooded answer to that potent question, I have been supplied—the sources are plural—with helpful materials: hints, friendly *and* inimical clues, approximations, statistics, "proofs" of one kind and another; from these I am trying to weave the coat that I shall wear. In 1967's Nashville, however, the somewhat dotty expression in the eyes of the cartoon-woman, the *agapeness,* were certainly mine. I was in some inscrutable and uncomfortable wonderland. I didn't know what to make of what surrounded me, of what with hot sureness began almost immediately to invade me. *I* had never been, before, in the general presence of such insouciance, such live firmness, such confident vigor, such determination to mold or carve something DEFINITE.

Up against the wall, white man! was the substance of the Baraka shout, at the evening reading he shared with fierce Ron Milner among intoxicating drum-beats, heady incense and organic underhumming. Up against the wall! And a pensive (until that moment) white man of thirty or thirty three abruptly shot himself into the heavy air, screaming "Yeah! *Yeah!* Up against the wall, Brother! KILL 'EM ALL! KILL 'EM *ALL!*"

I thought that was interesting.

There is indeed a new black today. He is different from any the world has known. He's a tall-walker. Almost firm. By many of his own *brothers* he is not understood. And he is understood by *no* white. Not the wise white; not the Schooled white; not the Kind white. Your *least* pre-requisite toward an understanding of the new black is an exceptional Doctorate which can be conferred only upon those with the proper properties of bitter birth and intrinsic sorrow. I know this is infuriating, especially to those professional Negro-understanders, some of them so *very* kind, with special portfolio, special savvy. But I cannot say anything other, because nothing other is the truth.

I—who have "gone the gamut" from an almost angry rejection of my dark skin by some of my brainwashed brothers and sisters to a surprised queenhood in the new black sun—am qualified to enter at least the kindergarten of new consciousness now. New consciousness and trudge-toward-progress.

I have hopes for myself.

1972

ROBERT DUNCAN
(1919–1988)

Robert Duncan's lifelong fascination with myth, signs, wonders, and hidden meanings that exist as "felt presences" and can be revealed through poetry originated in his childhood, which was far from ordinary. Born Edward Howard Duncan in Oakland, California, in 1919, the poet was put up for adoption at the age of six months. His mother died shortly after he was born, and his father, a day laborer already supporting a large family, could not care for the baby. His new parents, who were theosophists, believers in occult mysteries, chose the baby because they found his astrological chart auspicious. He grew up as Robert Edward Symmes but changed his name back to "Duncan" in 1941. Throughout his childhood, he was surrounded by family members steeped in the wisdom literature of many cultures and who saw cosmic significance in everything. In "The Truth and Life of Myth," Duncan recalls that, for his family, "the truth of things was esoteric (locked inside) or occult (masked by) the apparent, and one needed a 'lost key' in order to piece out the cryptogram of . . . who created the universe and what his real message was." His awareness of inner dimensions, truths that cannot be apprehended through ordinary means, was also heightened by an unfortunate accident. At the age of three, Duncan injured an eye in a fall. For the rest of his life he was cross-eyed and experienced double vision.

By the time Duncan had graduated from Kern High School in Bakersfield, he had already decided to devote his life to poetry, even though he knew that such a decision went against his family's expectations. In another essay, "Man's Fulfillment in Order and Strife," he emphasizes the need for "creative strife" and recalls the family conflict that his vocation caused: "Poetry was not in the order of things. One could not earn a living at poetry. Writing poems was not such a bad thing, but to give one's life over to poetry, to become a *poet,* was to evidence a serious social disorder." Also "not in the order of things" was his sexual orientation, and he came to link his feelings of outsiderhood as a poet with those he experienced as a homosexual. "The structure of my life, like the structure of my work," he later remarked, "was to emerge in a series of trials, a problematic identity."

Those trials were pronounced during the next ten years of his life. Although he had entered the University of California at Berkeley in 1936, he left after two years to follow a lover to New York City. There he became part of a bohemian group of writers led by the novelist and diarist Anaïs Nin. In 1941 he was drafted into the army. Refusing to hide his homosexuality, he was soon discharged on psychiatric grounds. He returned to San Francisco in 1942, and then went back to New York in 1943, where he was married for a few months to a painter, Marjorie McKee. Meanwhile he wrote and published poems in journals and helped edit a little magazine, the *Experimental Review.*

In 1944 he was on the verge of breaking into the literary mainstream when John Crowe Ransom accepted a poem of his for the *Kenyon Review.* In the same year, however, Duncan published "The Homosexual in Society" in the journal *Politics.* The essay was important for its bold discussion of homosexuality in terms of individual rights and its equally frank consideration of how sexuality inflects the work of gay writers such as Herman Melville and Hart Crane. Duncan showed his independence not only by identifying homosexuals as a persecuted minority group, but also by criticizing the exclusionary attitudes he observed among them. He also bravely declared his own sexuality in the piece. When Ransom read the essay, he wrote Duncan to say that he had decided not to publish his poem. At least partially because of his sexual candor—aggravated by his West Coast location—Duncan was never fully accepted by mainstream literary culture during his lifetime.

Such exclusion, however, had its benefits, for Duncan was free to make his sexuality one of his major themes. His work explores the variety of gay experience, from the "creative strife" of desire to the rewards of long-term partnership. But his failure to achieve a mainstream audience was also due to the difficulty of his work. Even learned readers are challenged by his eclectic combination of mystical lore, world mythology, and wide-ranging literary allusions. Yet his poetry also offers clear and moving expressions of feeling, which freshen even his difficult poems.

Duncan became an influential figure in the alternative poetry movements of the mid-century. After his return to Berkeley in 1945, he joined with other poets such as Jack Spicer and Kenneth Rexroth to create a poetry "renaissance" in the Bay Area long before most of the Beat poets moved west. Duncan's first book, *Heavenly City Earthly City* (1947), reflects the studies of medieval history and literature he was pursuing at Berkeley. It also contains his first experiments in process-oriented writing, in which, as he notes in *The Years as Catches,* "The poems are not ends in themselves but forms arising from the final intention of the whole in which they have their form and in turn giving rise anew to that intention." In 1951 he fell in love with a painter and collagist, Jess Collins (known professionally as "Jess"), and the two men soon established a household together in San Francisco. Their partnership lasted until Duncan's death in 1988, and Duncan benefited from the stability of their commitment and from contemplating Jess's collage techniques.

Duncan's fascination with the creative process, interactive patterns of meaning, and energetic motion in poetry was also fostered by Charles Olson, whose concept of "Projective Verse" coalesced with Duncan's own ideas. In 1956 Duncan taught for several months at Black Mountain College, where Olson was rector, and Duncan's second full-length book, *The Opening of the Field* (1960), explores the possibilities of Olson's vision of the poem as "a field of action." As Duncan argues in the introduction to his fourth collection, *Bending the Bow* (1968), "The artist, after Dante's poetics, works with all parts of the poem as *polysemous*, taking each thing of the composition as generative of meaning, a response to and a contribution to the building form." Duncan now conceived of his poetry as an ongoing sequence, a "building form," that weaves together all elements of his life, including his reading life, dream life, domestic life, and, increasingly, his alarm over the life of the nation.

Many readers of Duncan find his deployment of Projective Verse more successful than Olson's experiments, for Duncan succeeds in creating poetry that is supple and energetic in its form, learned in its remarkable breadth of references, yet invigorated by deep feeling and great clarity of description. Moreover, though sometimes long-winded, Duncan convincingly assumes a visionary, prophetic voice, supported by his passionate conviction and his deep knowledge of mysticism. In *Bending the Bow,* his condemnations of U.S. involvement in Vietnam take on an apocalyptic fervor. Unlike many poets who attacked the war, Duncan, who saw connections between all things, argued that all Americans, including himself, were implicated in the violence. In 1972 his linkage of personal and political strife and his commitment to developing an ongoing sequence of poems led him to announce that he would not publish another book for fifteen years—a decision that surely did not help foster more mainstream attention. His last two books, *Ground Work: Before the War* (1984) and *Ground Work II: In the Dark* (1987), offer sequences that aim for the inclusiveness of Whitman's and Pound's work, and Duncan strikes a balance between his visionary themes and contemplation of the nature of love and war. Although his poetry attracted a small but devoted following during his lifetime, since his death in 1988 many readers have begun to recognize the scope of his accomplishments.

The version of "The Homosexual in Society" reprinted below includes not only the original 1944 essay, but Duncan's own commentary from 1959, in the form of footnotes and a postscript, as well as his 1985 introduction. These layers of commentary, each from a different era, interact with one another, offering a window into the times during which they were written and also into the evolution of Duncan's ideas about sexuality and creativity.

◄●━━━━◆━━━━●►

THE HOMOSEXUAL IN SOCIETY

INTRODUCTION

Seymour Krim has urged me to reprint this early essay as "a pioneering piece," assuring me "that it stands and will stand on its own feet." At the time it was printed (*Politics,* August 1944) it had at least the pioneering gesture, as far as I know, of being the first discussion of homosexuality which included the frank avowal that

Originally published in *Politics* Aug. 1944. Collected in *A Selected Prose,* ed. Robert J. Bertholf (New York: New Directions, 1995) 38–50. All notes are Robert Duncan's.

the author was himself involved; but my view was that minority associations and identifications were an evil wherever they supersede allegiance to and share in the creation of a human community good—the recognition of fellow-manhood.

Blind lifeliness—what Darwin illuminates as evolution—has its creative design, and in that process a man's sexuality is a natural factor in a biological economy larger and deeper than his own human will. What we create as human beings is a picture of the meaning and relation of life; we create perspectives of space and time or a universe; and we create ideas of "man" and of "person," of gods and attendant powers—a drama wherein what and who we are are manifest. And this creation governs our knowledge of good and evil.

For some, there are only the tribe and its covenant that are good, and all of mankind outside and their ways are evil; for many in America today good is progressive, their professional status determines their idea of "man" and to be genuinely respectable their highest concept of a good "person"—all other men are primitive, immature, or uneducated. Neither of these perspectives was acceptable to me. I had been encouraged by my parents, by certain teachers in high school, by friends, through Socialist and Anarchist associations, and through the evidence of all those artists, philosophers and mystics who have sought to give the truth of their feeling and thought to mankind, to believe that there was an entity in the imagination "mankind," and that there was a community of thoughtful men and women concerned with the good of that totality to whom I was responsible. The magazine *Politics* represented for me during the Second World War an arena where intellectuals of that community were concerned, and I came to question myself in the light of the good they served.

It was not an easy essay to write. As a form an essay is a field in which we try ideas. In this piece I try to bring forward ideas of "homosexual," "society," "human" and, disguised but evident, my own guilt; and their lack of definition is involved with my own troubled information. Our sense of terms is built up from a constant renewed definition through shared information, and one of the urgencies of my essay was just that there was so little help here where other writers had concealed their own experience and avoided discussion.

Then too, the writing of the essay was a personal agony. Where we bear public testimony we face not only the community of thoughtful men and women who are concerned with the good, but facing the open forum we face mean and stupid men too. The involved disturbed syntax that collects conditional clauses and often fails to arrive at a full statement suggests that I felt in writing the essay that I must gather forces and weight to override some adversary; I have to push certain words from adverse meanings which as a social creature I share with the public to new meanings which might allow for an enlarged good. In the polemics of the essay it is not always possible to find the ground of accusation unless we recognize that I was trying to rid myself of one persona in order to give birth to another, and at the same time to communicate the process and relate it to what I called "society," a public responsibility. I was likely to find as little intellectual approval for the declaration of an idealistic morality as I was to find for the avowal of my homosexuality. The work often has value as evidence in itself of the conflict concerned and of the difficulty of statement then just where it is questionable as argument. I had a likeness to the public and shared its conflicts of attitude—an apprehension which shapes the course of the essay.

I feel today as I felt then that there is a service to the good in bringing even painful and garbled truth of the nature of our thought and feeling to the light of print, for what I only feel as an urgency and many men may condemn me for as an aberration, some man reading may render as an understanding and bring into the wholeness of human experience. Reading this essay some fifteen years later, I need courage to expose the unhappiness of my writing at that time, for I am not today without conflicting feelings and have the tendency still to play the adversary where I had meant only to explore ideas. In preparing the text then I have eliminated certain references that were topical at the time but would be obscure now and have cut where economy was possible without losing the character of the original; but I have not sought to rewrite or to remedy the effect.

[Robert Duncan's footnotes for the 1944 publication of this essay have been indicated by asterisks and set in a typeface different from the rest of the text. Duncan also added footnotes when he made revisions to the text in 1959. These notes have been indicated by numbers.]

THE TEXT

I propose to discuss a group whose only salvation is in the struggle of all humanity for freedom and individual integrity; who have suffered in modern society persecution, excommunication; and whose intellectuals, whose most articulate members, have been willing to desert that primary struggle, to beg, to gain at the price if need be of any sort of prostitution, privilege for themselves, however ephemeral; who have been willing rather than to struggle toward self-recognition, to sell their product, to convert their deepest feelings into marketable oddities and sentimentalities.

Although in private conversation, at every table, at every editorial board, one *knows* that a great body of modern art is cheated out by what amounts to a homosexual cult; although hostile critics have at times opened fire in attack as rabid as the attack of Southern senators upon "niggers"; critics who might possibly view the homosexual with a more humane eye seem agreed that it is better that nothing be said.[1] Pressed to the point, they may either, as in the case of such an undeniable homosexual as Hart Crane, contend that he was great despite his "perversion"*— much as my mother used to say how much better a poet Poe would have been had he not taken dope; or where it is possible they have attempted to deny the role of the homosexual in modern art, defending the good repute of modern art against any evil repute of homosexuality.

1. 1959. At a round table on Modern Art held in San Francisco in 1949 a discussion emerged between Frank Lloyd Wright and Marcel Duchamp where both showed the courage of forthright statement, bringing the issue publicly forward, which I lamented the lack of in 1944. *Wright* (who had been challenged on his reference to modern art as "degenerate"): "Would you say homosexuality was degenerate?" *Duchamp:* "No, it is not degenerate." *Wright:* "You would say that this movement which we call modern art and painting has been greatly or is greatly in debt to homosexualism?" *Duchamp:* "I admit it, but not in your terms . . . I believe that the homosexual public has shown more interest or curiosity for modern art than the heterosexual—so it happened, but it does not involve modern art itself."

What makes comment complicated here is that, while I would like to answer as Duchamp does because I believe with him that art itself is an expression of vitality, in part I recognize the justice of Wright's distaste, for there is a homosexual clique which patronizes certain kinds of modern art and even creates because, like Wright, they believe both homosexuality and the art they patronize and create to be decadent and even fashionably degenerate.

*Critics of Crane, for instance, consider that his homosexuality is the cause of his inability to adjust to society. Another school feels that inability to adjust to society causes homosexuality. What seems fairly obvious is that Crane's effort to communicate his inner feelings, his duty as a poet, brought him into conflict with social opinion. He might well have adjusted his homosexual desires within society as many have done by "living a lie" and avoiding any unambiguous reference in his work.

But one cannot, in face of the approach taken to their own problem by homosexuals, place any weight of criticism upon the liberal body of critics for avoiding the issue. For there are Negroes who have joined openly in the struggle for human freedom, made articulate that their struggle against racial prejudice is part of the struggle for all; there are Jews who have sought no special privilege or recognition for themselves as Jews but have fought for *human* rights, but there is in the modern American scene no homosexual who has been willing to take in his own persecution a battlefront toward human freedom. Almost coincident with the first declarations for homosexual rights was the growth of a cult of homosexual superiority to heterosexual values; the cultivation of a secret language, the *camp,* a tone and a vocabulary that are loaded with contempt for the uninitiated.

Outside the ghetto the word "goy" disappears, wavers, and dwindles in the Jew's vocabulary as he becomes a member of the larger community. But in what one would believe the most radical, the most enlightened "queer" circles, the word "jam" remains, designating all who are not wise to homosexual ways, filled with an unwavering hostility and fear, gathering an incredible force of exclusion and blindness. It is hard (for all the sympathy which I can bring to bear) to say that this cult plays any other than an evil role in society.[2]

But names cannot be named.[3] There are critics whose cynical, backbiting joke upon their audience is no other than this secret special reference; there are poets

---

2. 1959. The alienation has not decreased but increased when the "Beat" cult projects its picture of themselves as saintly—junkies evoking an apocalyptic crisis in which behind the mask of liberal tolerance is revealed the face of the hated "square." Their intuition is true, that tolerance is no substitute for concern; but their belief that intolerance is more true, dramatizes their own share in the disorder. "Goy," "jam," and "square" are all terms of a minority adherence where the imagination has denied fellow-feeling with the rest of mankind. Where the community of human experience is not kept alive, the burden of meaning falls back upon individual abilities. But the imagination depends upon an increment of associations.

Where being "queer" or a "junkie" means being a pariah (as it does in beat mythology), behavior may arise not from desire but from fear or even hatred of desire; dope-addiction may not be a search for an artificial paradise, an illusion of magical life, but an attack upon life, a poisoning of response; and sexual acts between men may not mean responses of love but violations of inner nature. Ginsberg (who believes the self is subject to society), Lamantia (who believes the self has authority from God), and McClure (who believes the self is an independent entity) have in common their paroxysms of self-loathing in which the measure of human failure and sickness is thought so true that the measure of human achievement and life is thought false.

But this attitude had already appeared in the work of urban sophisticates like Edmund Wilson and Mary McCarthy where there was an observable meanness of feeling. Robert Lowell's "Tamed by Miltown, we lie on Mother's bed" expresses in the *realism* of neurotic inhibition what Allen Ginsberg's "Creation glistening backwards to the same grave, size of universe" expresses in the *surrealism* of psychotic exuberance. "Mother your master-bedroom/looked away from the ocean" and "O Mother . . . with your nose of bad lay with your nose of the smell of the pickles of Newark" dramatizes with the difference of class the common belief in oedipal grievance.

3. 1959. That even serious socio-sexual studies are curbed is shown by the following letter written by an eminent poet when I wrote in 1945 asking if I could attempt an essay on his work in the light of my concept that his language had been diverted to conceal the nature of his sexual life and that because he could never write directly he had failed to come to grips with immediacies of feeling:

"... I am very sorry but I must ask you not to publish the essay you propose. I'm sure you will realize that the better the essay you write, the more it will be reviewed and talked about, and the more likelihood there would be of it being brought publicly to my attention in a way where to ignore it would be taken as an admission of guilt."

"As you may know, I earn a good part of my livelihood by teaching, and in that profession one is particularly vulnerable. Further, both as a writer and as a human being, the occasion may always arise, particularly in these times, when it becomes one's duty to take a stand on the unpopular side of some issue. Should that ever occur, your essay would be a very convenient red-herring for one's opponents. (Think of what happened to Bertrand Russell in New York.)"

"I hope you will believe me when I say that for myself personally I wish I could let you publish it, and that anyway I hope the other essays will be as good as you would like them to be."

whose nostalgic picture of special worth in suffering, sensitivity, and magical quality is no other than this intermediate "sixth sense"; there are new cult leaders whose special divinity, whose supernatural and visionary claim is no other than this mystery of sex.[4] The law has declared homosexuality secret, inhuman, unnatural (and why not then supernatural?). The law itself sees in it a crime—not in the sense that murder, thievery, seduction of children, or rape are seen as *human* crimes—but as a crime against the way of nature.* It has been lit up and given an awful and lurid attraction such as witchcraft was given in the 17th century. Like early witches, the homosexuals, far from seeking to undermine the popular superstition, have accepted and even anticipated the charge of demonism. Sensing the fear in society that is generated in ignorance of their nature, they have sought not understanding but to live in terms of that ignorance, to become witch doctors in the modern chaos.

To go about this they have had to cover with mystery, to obscure the work of all those who have viewed homosexuality as but one of the many ways which human love may take and who have had primarily in mind as they wrote (as Melville, Proust, or Crane had) mankind and its liberation. For these great early

My own conviction is that no public issue is more pressing than the one that would make a man guilty and endanger his livelihood for the open knowledge of his sexual nature; for the good of humanity lies in a common quest through shared experience toward the possibility of sexual love. Where we attend as best we can the volitions and fulfillments of the beloved in sexual acts we depend upon all those who in arts have portrayed openly the nature of love; and as we return ourselves through our writing to that commune of spirit we come close to the sharing in desire that underlies the dream of universal brotherhood. Undeclared desires and private sexuality feed the possibility of sexual lust which has many betrayals, empty cravings, violations, and wants to void the original desire.

That this eminent poet was not wrong in speaking of his professional vulnerability were his sexual nature openly avowed can be verified by the following passage from a letter of an eminent editor after reading "The Homosexual In Society" concerning my poem "Toward An African Elegy" which he had previously admired and accepted for publication:

". . . I feel very sure we do not wish to print the poem, and I regret very much to decline it after an original acceptance. I must say for the record that the only right I feel in this action is that belatedly, and with your permission, I read the poem as an advertisement or a notice of overt homosexuality, and we are not in the market for literature of this type.

"I cannot agree with you that we should publish it nevertheless in the name of freedom of speech; because I cannot agree with your position that homosexuality is not abnormal. It is biologically abnormal in the most obvious sense. I am not sure whether or not state and federal law regard it so, but I think they do; I should not take the initiative in the matter, but if there are laws to this effect I concur in them entirely. There are certainly laws prohibiting incest and polygamy, with which I concur, though they are only abnormal conventionally and are not so damaging to a society biologically."

Both these men are leaders in just that community of thoughtful men and women I imagined; both have had and deserved highest honors as literary figures; and, while I believe one to be mistaken in his belief that sexual forthrightness is not a primary issue for the social good; and the other to be as misled by the unhappy conventions of his thought as by the atmosphere of guilty confession that he gathered from my essay; both, like I, are concerned not with the minority in question but rightly with what they consider the public good, an intimation of the human good. Much understanding yet is needed before men of good intentions can stand together.

4. 1959. I find myself in this passage accusing certain "critics," "poets," and "new cult leaders" of what I might be suspected of in my poetry myself. "Suffering, sensitivity, and magical quality" are constants of mood; divinities and cults, supernatural and visionary claims, and sexual mystery are all elements in subject matter that give rise to poetic inspiration for me. In recent years I have had an increased affinity with imaginative reaches of religious thought, searching gnostic and cabalistic speculation for a more diverse order.

The Demon of Moral Virtue exacts his dues wherever he is evoked. Where we seek the Good he urges us to substitute what will be men's good opinion of us. I may have felt then that I might redeem my sexuality as righteous in the sight of certain critics, if I disavowed my heterodoxy in religious imagination as wicked or deluded.

*"Just as certain judges assume and are more inclined to pardon murder in inverts and treason in Jews for reasons derived from original sin and racial predestination." Sodom and Gomorrah, Proust.

artists their humanity was the source, the sole source, of their work. Thus in *Remembrance of Things Past,* Charlus is not seen as the special disintegration of a homosexual but as a human being in disintegration, and the forces that lead to that disintegration, the forces of pride, self-humiliation in love, jealousy, are not special forces but common to all men and women. Thus in Melville, though in *Billy Budd* it is clear that the conflict is homosexual, the forces that make for that conflict, the guilt in passion, the hostility rising from subconscious sources, and the sudden recognition of these forces as it comes to Vere in that story—these are forces which are universal, which rise in other contexts, which in Melville's work have risen in other contexts.

It is, however, the body of Crane that has been most ravaged by these modern ghouls and, once ravaged, stuck up cult-wise in the mystic light of their special cemetery literature. The live body of Crane is there, inviolate in the work; but in the window display of modern poetry, in so many special critics' and devotees' interest, is a painted mummy, deep sea green. One may tiptoe by, as the visitors to Lenin's tomb tiptoe by, and, once outside, find themselves in a world in his name that has celebrated the defeat of all that he was devoted to. One need only point out in all the homosexual imagery of Crane, in the longing and vision of love, the absence of the private sensibility that colors so much of modern writing. Where the Zionists of homosexuality have laid claim to a Palestine of their own—asserting in their miseries their nationality; Crane's suffering, his rebellion and his love are sources of poetry for him, not because they are what makes him different from his fellow-men, but because he saw in them his link with mankind; he saw in them his share in universal human experience.[5]

What can one do in the face of this, both those critics and artists, not homosexual, who are, however, primarily concerned with dispelling all inhumanities, all forces of convention and law that impose a tyranny over man's nature, and those critics and artists who, as homosexuals, must face in their own lives both the hostility of society in that they are "queer" and the hostility of the homosexual élite in that they are merely human?

For the first group the starting point is clear, that they must recognize homosexuals as equals, and, as equals, allow them neither more nor less than can be allowed any human being. There are no special rights. For the second group the starting point is more difficult, the problem more treacherous.

5. 1959. The principal point is that the creative genius of a writer lies in his communication of personal experience as a communal experience. He brings us to realize our own inner being in a new light through the sense of human being he creates, or he creates in us as we read a new sense of our being. And in Melville, Crane, and Proust I saw their genius awaken a common share in homosexual desire and love, in its suffering and hope, that worked to transform the communal image of man.

Professors of literature do not always have minds of the same inspiration as the minds of writers whose work they interpret and evaluate for consumption; and an age of criticism has grown up to keep great spirits cut down to size so as to be of use in the self-esteem of sophisticated pusillanimous men in a continual self-improvement course. Thus Freud's courageous analysis of his motives and psychic dis-ease has furnished material for popular analysts like Fromm to be struck by how normal their psyches are compared to Freud's, how much more capable of mature love they are.

Homosexuality affords a ready point at which a respectable reader disassociates himself from the work of genius and seeks to avoid any sense of realizing his own inner being there. Some years after my essay, Leslie Fiedler, whom I take to be heterosexual, was able to gain some notoriety by writing about homosexual undercurrents in American literature, playing, not without a sense of his advantage, upon the cultural ambivalence between the appreciation of literature as a commodity of education and the depreciation of genius as it involves a new sense of being, and upon the sexual ambivalence in which the urbane American male can entertain the idea of homosexuality providing he is not responsible, providing he preserves his contempt for or his disavowal of sexual love between males.

In the face of the hostility of society which I risk in making even the acknowledgment explicit in this statement, in the face of the "crime" of my own feelings, in the past I publicized those feelings as private and made no stand for their recognition but tried to sell them as disguised, for instance, as conflicts arising from mystical sources.[6] I colored and perverted simple and direct emotions and realizations into a mysterious realm, a mysterious relation to society. Faced by the inhumanities of society I did not seek a solution in humanity but turned to a second outcast society as inhumane as the first. I joined those who, while they allowed for my sexual nature, allowed for so little of the moral, the sensible, and creative direction which all of living should reflect. They offered a family, outrageous as it was, a community in which one was not condemned for one's homosexuality, but it was necessary there for one to desert one's humanity, for which one would be suspect, "out of key." In drawing rooms and in little magazines I celebrated the cult with a sense of sanctuary such as a medieval Jew must have found in the ghetto; my voice taking on the modulations which tell of the capitulation to snobbery and the removal from the "common sort"; my poetry exhibiting the objects made divine and tyrannical as the Catholic church has made bones of saints, and bread and wine tyrannical.[7]

6. 1959. But there is no "explicit" statement here! What emerges is a "confession" (analyzed further below) instead of what was needed and what I was unable to say out. While I had found a certain acceptance in special circles of homosexuals and opportunities for what Kinsey calls "contacts," this was a travesty of what the heart longed for. I could not say "I am homosexual," because exactly this statement of minority identity was the lie. Our deepest sexuality is free and awakens toward both men and women where they are somehow akin to us. Perhaps the dawning realization that we are all exiles from paradise, and that somehow goods have their reality in that impossible dream where all men have come into their full nature, gave rise to and a thread of truth to the feeling of guilt that prompts this voice.

7. 1959. I am reminded in the foregoing passage of those confessions of duplicity, malice, and high treason made before the courts of Inquisition or the Moscow trials. "Society" appears as the merciless "hostile" judge; what I meant to avow—the profound good and even joyful life that might be realized in sexual love between men—becoming a confession that I had "disguised," "colored," "perverted," "celebrated the cult" and even in my work exhibited objects of alienation from the common law. Some remnant of Protestant adherence suggests there was Holy Roman wickedness, "divine and tyrannical as the Catholic Church has made."

Might there be a type of social reaction to which "confession" of "witches," "Trotskyites," and my confession as a "homosexual," conform? In the prototype there is first the volunteered list of crimes one has committed that anticipates the condemnation of church or party or society. Then there is the fact that what one confesses as a social "crime" has been held somewhere as a hope and an ideal, contrary to convention. The heretic is guilty in his love or his righteousness because he has both the conventional common mind and the imagination of a new common mind; he holds in his own heart the adversary that he sees in the actual prosecutor. Often there was torture to bring on the confession, but it enacted the inner torture of divided mind. "Names cannot be named" I exclaim in this essay, and perhaps akin to that felt necessity is the third phase in which "witches" and "Trotskyites" eventually named their accomplices in heresy, throwing up their last allegiance to their complicity in hope.

The Jungian revival of alchemy with its doctrine of the *nigredo* and the related surrealist cult of black humor or bile has complicated the contemporary sense of a belief that in some phase the psyche must descend against its nature into its adversary. It is an exciting idea just as a great destruction of the world by war is an exciting idea. Part of the force which "Beat" poets have is the authority which we give after Freud and Jung to the potency of crime.

"Being a junkie in America today," Ginsberg writes, "is like being a Jew in Nazi Germany." This leads to humorous comment, like the parody of Marx, that "Marijuana is the opium of the people," or that "Opium is the religion of the people." But the revelation of Ginsberg's formula is that in taking to junk he is trying to become like a Jew in Germany. He cannot realize in his Jewishness a sufficient extreme of persecution (even he cannot quite believe in racial guilt—the American idea of the melting pot as virtue is too strong). The "fuzz" cannot live up to the projection of wrath that might externalize inhibition as rank and unjust punishment and satisfy his guilt without calling his need to account. So he takes up "the angry fix." "Holy Burroughs" and heroin addiction will surely test the frustrating tolerance of a liberal state and reveal beneath the "Moloch whose breast is a cannibal dynamo."

After an evening at one of those salons where the whole atmosphere was one of suggestion and celebration, I returned recently experiencing again the aftershock, the desolate feeling of wrongness, remembering in my own voice and gestures the rehearsal of unfeeling. Alone, not only I, but, I felt, the others who had appeared as I did so mocking, so superior in feeling, had known, knew still, those troubled emotions, the deep and integral longings that we as human beings feel, holding us from archaic actions by the powerful sense of humanity that is their source, longings that lead us to love, to envision a creative life. "Towards something far," as Hart Crane wrote, "now farther away than ever."

Among those who should understand those emotions which society condemned, one found that the group language did not allow for any feeling at all other than this self-ridicule, this "gaiety" (it is significant that the homosexual's word for his own kind is "gay"), a wave surging forward, breaking into laughter and then receding, leaving a wake of disillusionment, a disbelief that extends to oneself, to life itself. What then, disowning this career, can one turn to?

What I think can be asserted as a starting point is that only one devotion can be held by a human being seeking a creative life and expression, and that is a devotion to human freedom, toward the liberation of human love, human conflicts, human aspirations. To do this one must disown *all* the special groups (nations, churches, sexes, races) that would claim allegiance. To hold this devotion every written word, every spoken word, every action, every purpose must be examined and considered. The old fears, the old specialties will be there, mocking and tempting; the old protective associations will be there, offering for a surrender of one's humanity congratulation upon one's special nature and value. It must be always recognized that the others, those who have surrendered their humanity, are not less than oneself. It must be always remembered that one's own honesty, one's battle against the inhumanity of his own group (be it against patriotism, against bigotry, against—in this special case—the homosexual cult) is a battle that cannot be won in the immediate scene. The forces of inhumanity are overwhelming, but only one's continued opposition can make any other order possible, will give an added strength for all those who desire freedom and equality to break at last those fetters that seem now so unbreakable.

REFLECTIONS 1959

In the fifteen years since the writing of "The Homosexual in Society," my circumstances have much changed. Life and my work have brought me new friends, where the community of values is more openly defined, and even, in recent years, a companion who shares my concern for a creative life. Distressed where I have been distressed and happy where I have been happy, their sympathy has rendered absurd whatever apprehension I had concerning the high moral resolve and radical reformation of character needed before I would secure recognition and understanding. It is a kinship of concern and a sharing of experience that draws us together.

The phantasmic idea of a "society" that was somehow hostile, the sinister affiliation offered by groups with whom I had no common ground other than the specialized sexuality, the anxiety concerning the good opinion of the community—all this sense of danger remains, for I am not a person of reserved nature; and conventional morality, having its roots in Judaic tribal law and not in philosophy, holds homosexual relations to be a crime. Love, art, and thought are all social goods for me; and often I must come, where I would begin a friendship, to odd moments of trial and doubts when I must deliver account of my sexual nature that there be no mistake in our trust.

But the inspiration of the essay was toward something else, a public trust, larger and more demanding than the respect of friends. To be respected as a member of the political community for what one knew in one's heart to be respectable! To insist, not upon tolerance for a divergent sexual practice, but upon concern for the virtues of a homosexual relationship! I was, I think, at the threshold of a critical concept: sexual love wherever it was taught and practiced was a single adventure, that troubadours sang in romance, that poets have kept as a traditional adherence, and that novelists have given scope. Love is dishonored where sexual love between those of the same sex is despised; and where love is dishonored there is no public trust.

It is my sense that the fulfillment of man's nature lies in the creation of that trust; and where the distrusting imagination sets up an image of "self" against the desire for unity and mutual sympathy, the state called "Hell" is created. There we find the visceral agonies, sexual aversions and possessions, excitations and depressions, the omnipresent "I" that bears true witness to its condition in "Howl" or "Kaddish," in McClure's *Hymns to St. Geryon* or the depressive "realism" of Lowell's *Life Studies.* "We are come to the place," Virgil tells Dante as they enter Hell, "where I told thee thou shouldst see the wretched people, who have lost the good of the intellect." In Hell, the homosexuals go, as Dante rightly saw them, as they still go often in the streets of our cities, looking "as in the evening men are wont to look at one another under a new moon," running beneath the hail of a sharp torment, having wounds, recent and old, where the flames of experience have burned their bodies.

It is just here, when he sees his beloved teacher, Brunetto Latini, among the sodomites, that Dante has an inspired intuition that goes beyond the law of his church and reaches toward a higher ethic: "Were my desire all fulfilled," he says to Brunetto, "you had not yet been banished from human nature: for in my memory is fixed . . . the dear and kind, paternal image of you, when in the world, hour by hour, you taught me how man makes himself eternal. . . ."

"Were my desire all fulfilled . . ." springs from the natural heart in the confidence of its feelings that has often been more generous than conventions and institutions. I picture that fulfillment of desire as a human state of mutual volition and aid, a shared life.

Not only in sexual love, but in work and in play, we suffer from the dominant competitive ethos which gives rise to the struggle of interests to gain recognition or control, and discourages the recognition of the needs and interests which we all know we have in common. Working for money (and then, why not stealing or cheating for money?) is the "realistic" norm, and working for the common good is the "idealistic" exception. "I have always earned my living at manual labor," an old friend writes. And his voice breaks through, like a shaft of sunlight through an industrial smog, the oppressive voices of junkies and pushers, petty thieves and remittance men of social security with their need and misery set adrift of itself. Oppressive, because these are sensitive young men and women I am thinking of, some of them the artists and poets of a new generation.

The sense of this essay rests then upon the concept that sexual love between those of the same sex is one with sexual love between men and women; and that this love is one of the conditions of the fulfillment of the heart's desire and the restoration of man's free nature. Creative work for the common good is one of the conditions of that nature. And our hope lies still in the creative imagination wherever it unifies what had been thought divided, wherever it transforms the personal experience into a communal good, "that Brunetto Latini had not been banished from human nature."

1944/1959/1985

DENISE LEVERTOV
(1923–1997)

Denise Levertov's ancestry and upbringing set her apart from most American poets of her generation: She was born in Ilford, England, the daughter of Paul Philip Levertoff, a Russian Jew who had become an Anglican minister, and Beatrice Adelaide Spooner-Jones; her most famous ancestors were, on her mother's side, the Welsh tailor and mystic, Angel Jones of Mold and, on her father's side, the Russian rabbi Schneour Zaimon, who was reputed to know the language of birds. Both Denise and her older sister, Olga, were largely educated at home. "As a child," she remembered, "I 'did lessons' at home under the tutelage of my mother and listened to the BBC Schools Programs." She also had a year of nursing school and worked in several London hospitals during World War II.

Denise came early to poetry and at age twelve had the temerity to send some of her poems to T. S. Eliot, who responded with encouragement and advice—unfortunately his letter was lost. In 1946 she published her first book of poems, *The Double Image,* and quickly found that she had several other champions. One of them, the American poet Kenneth Rexroth, would call Levertov "the baby of the new Romanticism."

While still in England, Levertov met and married an American writer, Mitchell Goodman, in 1947. The couple emigrated to the United States the following year, and Levertov became a naturalized citizen in 1955. They had one child, a son.

In America, Levertov set about remaking her poetic voice. She retained a degree of her early Romanticism, but almost immediately felt the influence of Wallace Stevens and Williams Carlos Williams. Her first significant American publications were in magazines associated with the Black Mountain poets, *Origin* and the *Black Mountain Review.* The Black Mountain poets, including Charles Olson, Robert Creeley, and Robert Duncan, advocated theories of "open" and "organic" forms for poetry, often modeled on the work of Pound and Williams but also indebted to the examples of D. H. Lawrence and Walt Whitman. Although Levertov was never associated with Black Mountain College, she knew several of the poets in Olson's circle and regarded them (especially Duncan) highly.

But Williams, with whom she corresponded from 1951 until 1962, was her primary American mentor. When asked in a 1967 interview to sum up Williams's influence on her work, she replied:

> Williams's interest in the ordinary, in the present, in local history as microcosm, in the lives and speech of ordinary people; and his unsentimental compassion, which illumined the marvelous in the apparently banal, so deeply affected my "sense of living, of being alive" (which effect is, according to Wallace Stevens [in Adagia], one of the main functions of poetry) that it is impossible for me to measure.

Although Williams's example helped Levertov develop her own strongly enjambed free verse, she preferred to emphasize correspondences between style of writing and attitude toward living as the moral foundation of poetry. Beginning with *Here and Now* (1957) and culminating in *The Jacob's Ladder* (1961) and *O Taste and See* (1964), she developed a poetry focused on epiphanies discovered in ordinary moments and grounded on the sensuous perception of concrete particulars. Her poems often arose from domestic situations like marriage or motherhood, but were increasingly characterized by a spare lucidity. In one poem she wrote, "The best work is made / from hard, strong materials, / obstinately precise. . . ."

As one of only four women poets included in Donald Allen's influential anthology *The New American Poetry* (1960), Levertov gained notice as a leading proponent of the Black Mountain style, even as her ideas about poetry began to diverge from those of Olson, Creeley, and Duncan. Whereas Creeley and Olson argued that "form is never more than the extension of content," Levertov stressed in her 1965 essay "Some Notes on Organic Form" that "form is never more than a *revelation* of content." The religious language here suggests that for Levertov, poetry is a form of spiritual discipline whose practice can lead the poet (and reader) to a visionary apprehension of ordinary experience.

As the decade of the 1960s progressed, Levertov and her husband became deeply involved in the antiwar movement, not only protesting American policy in Vietnam but letting their anger and political commitment become a main focus of their writing. With Muriel Rukeyser and others, Levertov founded Writers and Artists Protest against the War in Vietnam. In books such as *The Sorrow Dance* (1967), *Relearning the Alphabet* (1970), *To Stay Alive* (1971), and *Footprints* (1972), she sometimes questioned her poetics of perception even as she used her skills of evoking the concrete to write poems of protest and outrage. Critics had mixed responses to the political turn her career took. But Levertov saw her political orientation as a natural outgrowth of her engagement with the world. In a 1975 essay, "On the Edge of Darkness: What Is Political Poetry?" she argued for a poetic melding of the personal and the political.

Her subsequent books reach for this goal, fusing her individual experience and perceptions with her consciousness of speaking as a public poet. In *The Freeing of the Dust* (1975) and *Life in the Forest* (1978), she meditates on death, change, the rhythms of nature, and the return of love following her 1972 divorce from Goodman. Her books of the 1980s and

1990s display an increasing concern for environmental problems in the United States and a renewed spiritual dimension, born of her own late conversion to Christianity. By the time of her 1997 death from lymphoma in Seattle, she had won numerous awards for her work and published more than fifty books, including a late collection of autobiographical essays, *Tesserae: Memories and Suppositions* (1995).

◄•━━◖━━•►

SOME NOTES ON ORGANIC FORM

For me, back of the idea of organic form is the concept that there is a form in all things (and in our experience) which the poet can discover and reveal. There are no doubt temperamental differences between poets who use prescribed forms and those who look for new ones—people who need a tight schedule to get anything done, and people who have to have a free hand—but the difference in their conception of "content" or "reality" is functionally more important. On the one hand is the idea that content, reality, experience, is essentially fluid and must be given form; on the other, this sense of seeking out inherent, though not immediately apparent, form. Gerard Manley Hopkins invented the word *inscape* to denote intrinsic form, the pattern of essential characteristics both in single objects and (what is more interesting) in objects in a state of relation to each other; and the word *instress* to denote the experiencing of the perception of inscape, the *apperception* of inscape. In thinking of the process of poetry as I know it, I extend the use of these words, which he seems to have used mainly in reference to sensory phenomena, to include intellectual and emotional experience as well; I would speak of *the inscape of an experience* (which might be composed of any and all of these elements, including the sensory) or of the inscape of a sequence or constellation of experiences.

A partial definition, then, of organic poetry might be that it is a *method of apperception*, i.e., of recognizing what we perceive, and is based on an intuition of an order, a form beyond forms, in which forms partake, and of which man's creative works are analogies, resemblances, natural allegories. Such a poetry is exploratory.

How does one go about such a poetry? I think it's like this: First there must be an experience, a sequence or constellation of perceptions of sufficient interest, felt by the poet intensely enough to demand of him their equivalence in words: he is *brought to speech*. Suppose there's the sight of the sky through a dusty window, birds and clouds and bits of paper flying through the sky, the sound of music from his radio, feelings of anger and love and amusement roused by a letter just received, the memory of some long ago thought or event associated with what's seen or heard or felt, and an idea, a concept, he has been pondering, each qualifying the other; together with what he knows about history; and what he has been dreaming—whether or not he remembers it—working in him. This is only a rough outline of a possible moment in a life. But the condition of being a poet is that periodically such a cross-section, or constellation, of experiences (in which one or another element may predominate) demands, or wakes in him this demand, *the poem*. The beginning of the

Originally published in *Poetry* (1965). First collected in *New Directions in Prose and Poetry #20*, ed. James Laughlin (New York: New Directions, 1968).

fulfillment of this demand is to contemplate, to meditate; words which connote a state in which the heat of feeling warms the intellect. To contemplate comes from "templum, temple, a place, a space for observation, marked out by the augur." It means, not simply to observe, to regard, but to do these things in the presence of a god. And to meditate is "to keep the mind in a state of contemplation"; its synonym is "to muse," and to muse comes from a word meaning "to stand with open mouth"—not so comical if we think of "inspiration"—to breathe in.

So—as the poet stands open-mouthed in the temple of life, contemplating his experience, there come to him the first words of the poem: the words which are to be his *way in* to the poem, if there is to be a poem. The pressure of demand and the meditation on its elements culminate in a moment of vision, of crystallization, in which some inkling of the correspondence between those elements occurs; *and it occurs as words*. If he forces a beginning before this point, it won't work. These words sometimes remain the first, sometimes in the completed poem their eventual place may be elsewhere, or they may turn out to have been only forerunners, which fulfilled their function in bringing him to the words which are the actual beginning of the poem. It is faithful attention to the experience from the first moment of crystallization that allows those first or those forerunning words to rise to the surface: and with that same fidelity of attention the poet, from that moment of being *let in* to the possibility of the poem, must *follow through*, letting the experience lead him through the world of the poem, its unique inscape revealing itself as he goes.

During the writing of a poem the various elements of the poet's being are in communion with each other, and heightened. Ear and eye, intellect and passion, interrelate more subtly than at other times; and the "checking for accuracy," for precision of language, that must take place throughout the writing is not a matter of one element supervising the others but of intuitive interaction between all the elements involved.

In the same way, content and form are in a state of dynamic interaction; the understanding of whether an experience is a linear sequence or a constellation raying out from and in to a central focus or axis, for instance, is discoverable only *in the work,* not before it.

Rhyme, chime, echo, repetition: they not only serve to knit the elements of an experience but often are the very means, the sole means, by which the density of texture and the returning or circling of perception can be transmuted into language, apperceived. *A* may lead to *E* directly through *B, C,* and *D:* but if then there is the sharp remembrance or revisioning of *A,* this return must find its metric counterpart. It could do so by actual repetition of the words that spoke of *A* the first time (and if this return occurs more than once, one finds oneself with a refrain—not put there because one decided to write something with a refrain at the end of each stanza but directly because of the demand of the content). Or it may be that since the return to *A* is now conditioned by the journey through *B, C,* and *D,* its words will not be a simple repetition but a variation. . . . Again, if *B* and *D* are of a complementary nature, then their thought- or feeling-rhyme may find its corresponding word-rhyme. Corresponding images are a kind of non-aural rhyme. It usually happens that within the whole, that is between the point of crystallization that marks the beginning or onset of a poem and the point at which the intensity of contemplation has ceased, there are distinct units of awareness; and it is—for me anyway—these that indicate the duration of stanzas. Sometimes these units are of such equal duration that one gets a whole poem of, say, three-line stanzas, a regularity of pattern that looks like, but is not, predetermined.

When my son was eight or nine I watched him make a crayon drawing of a tournament. He was not interested in the forms as such but was grappling with the need to speak in graphic terms, to say, "And a great crowd of people were watching the jousting knights." There was a need to show the tiers of seats, all those people sitting in them. And out of the need arose a formal design that was beautiful—composed of the rows of shoulders and heads. It is in very much the same way that there can arise, out of fidelity to instress, a design that is the form of the poem—both its total form, its length and pace and tone, and the form of its parts (e.g., the rhythmic relationships of syllables within the line, and of line to line; the sonic relationships of vowels and consonants; the recurrence of images, the play of associations, etc.). "Form follows function" (Frank Lloyd Wright).

Frank Lloyd Wright also wrote that the idea of organic architecture is that "the reality of the building lies in the space within it, to be lived in." And he quotes Coleridge: "Such as the life is, such is the form." (Emerson says, "Ask the fact for the form.") The Oxford Dictionary quotes Huxley (Thomas, presumably) as stating that he used the word *organic* "almost as an equivalent for the word 'living.'"

In organic poetry the metric movement, the measure, is the direct expression of the movement of perception. And the sounds, acting together with the measure, are a kind of *extended onomatopoeia*—i.e., they imitate, not the sounds of an experience (which may well be soundless, or to which sounds contribute only incidentally)—but the feeling of an experience, its emotional tone, its texture. The varying speed and gait of different strands of perception within an experience (I think of strands of seaweed moving within a wave) result in counterpointed measures.

Thinking about how organic poetry differs from free verse, I wrote that "most free verse is failed organic poetry, that is, organic poetry from which the attention of the writer had been switched off too soon, before the intrinsic form of the experience had been revealed." But Robert Duncan pointed out to me that there is a "free verse" of which this is not true, because it is written not with any desire to seek a form, indeed perhaps with the longing to *avoid* form (if that were possible) and to express inchoate emotion as purely as possible. There is a contradiction here, however, because if, as I suppose, there is an inscape of emotion, of feeling, it is impossible to avoid presenting something of it if the rhythm or tone of the feeling is given voice in the poem. But perhaps the difference is this: that free verse isolates the "rightness" of each line or cadence—if it seems expressive, O.K., never mind the relation of it to the next; while in organic poetry the peculiar rhythms of the parts are in some degree modified, if necessary, in order to discover the rhythm of the whole.

But doesn't the character of the whole depend on, arise out of, the character of the parts? It does; but it is like painting from nature: suppose you absolutely imitate, on the palette, the separate colors of the various objects you are going to paint; yet when they are closely juxtaposed in the actual painting, you may have to lighten, darken, cloud, or sharpen each color in order to produce an effect equivalent to what you see in nature. Air, light, dust, shadow, and distance have to be taken into account.

Or one could put it this way: in organic poetry the *form sense*, the *tragic sense*, as Stefan Wolpe speaks of it, is ever present *along with* (yes, paradoxically) fidelity to the revelations of meditation. The form sense is a sort of Stanislavsky of the imagination: putting a chair two feet downstage there, thickening a knot of bystanders upstage left, getting this actor to raise his voice a little and that actress to enter more slowly; *all in the interest of a total form he intuits.* Or it is a sort of helicopter scout flying over the field of the poem, taking aerial photos and reporting on the state of the forest and its creatures—or over the sea to watch for the schools of herring and direct the fishing fleet towards them.

A manifestation of form sense is the sense the poet's ear has of some rhythmic norm peculiar to a particular poem, from which the individual lines depart and to which they return. I heard Henry Cowell tell that the drone in Indian music is known as the *horizon note*. Al Kresch, the painter, sent me a quotation from Emerson: "The health of the eye demands a horizon." This sense of the beat or pulse underlying the whole I think of as the horizon note of the poem. It interacts with the nuances or forces of feeling which determine emphasis on one word or another, and decides to a great extent what belongs to a given line. It relates the needs of that feeling-force which dominates the cadence to the needs of the surrounding parts and so to the whole.

Duncan also pointed to what is perhaps a variety of organic poetry: the poetry of linguistic impulse. It seems to me that the absorption in language itself, the awareness of the world of multiple meaning revealed in sound, word, syntax, and the entering into this world in the poem, is as much an experience or constellation of perceptions as the instress of non-verbal sensuous and psychic events. What might make the poet of linguistic impetus appear to be on another tack entirely is that the demands of his realization may seem in opposition to truth as we think of it; that is, in terms of sensual logic. But the apparent distortion of experience in such a poem for the sake of verbal effects is actually a precise adherence to truth since the experience itself was a verbal one.

Form is never more than a *revelation* of content.

"The law—one perception must immediately and directly lead to a further perception." I've always taken this to mean, no *loading of the rifts with ore*, because there are to be no rifts. Yet, alongside of this truth is another truth (that I've learned from Duncan more than from anyone else)—that there must be a place in the poem for rifts too—(never to be stuffed with imported ore). Great gaps between perception and perception which must be leapt across if they are to be crossed at all. The X factor, the magic, is when we come to those rifts and make those leaps. A religious devotion to the truth, to the splendor of the authentic, involves the writer in a process rewarding in itself; but when that devotion brings us to undreamed abysses and we find ourselves sailing slowly over them and landing on the other side—that's ecstasy.

1965

⊶◄ LOUIS SIMPSON ►⊷
(B. 1923)

Louis Simpson's life and work are marked by frequent changes. Like many other poets of his generation, he began as a formalist, often using rhyme and meter, but in midcareer he underwent a radical aesthetic transformation. For awhile associated with "deep image" poets like James Wright and Robert Bly, he has in recent decades emerged as a poet of free verse suburban narratives, frequently told with a Chekhovian obliqueness and humor. As such, he has produced his most distinctive and original work—understated, even prosaic, conveying aspects of contemporary American life most poets rarely touch upon.

Yet Simpson had the upbringing of an English colonial schoolboy. Born in Jamaica, he was the second son of Aston Simpson, a prosperous lawyer, and Rosalind Marantz Simpson, a Russian Jewish immigrant who had been a dancer and aspiring opera singer. (His mother later called herself De Marantz to give an aristocratic air to her business ventures.) His privileged childhood did not impede his awareness of racial and class differences on the island, and his mother's stories of Russia were fraught with poverty and suffering. When Simpson was seven, his parents divorced. "No one explained it to me—one day I had a mother, the next she was gone." She moved away to Toronto and New York. In addition to this trauma, Louis and his brother did not get along with their stepmother and her children. They were soon alienated from their own home. At age nine he began to attend Munro College, a boarding school a hundred miles away. In various memoirs he described the strict, traditional curriculum and his budding love of literature.

While publishing poems as a teenager, Simpson thought of joining his mother in New York. When his father died suddenly of complications from diabetes, Louis and his brother learned that they had been left out of the family estate. At age seventeen, Louis left Jamaica for New York and a new life. At Columbia University he studied with Lionel Trilling and Mark Van Doren. When America entered World War II, Simpson decided to ignore his foreign birthright, registered for the draft, and in 1943 was inducted into the U.S. Army. For the next three years he served in the 101st Airborne Division, seeing combat in Normandy, Holland, Belgium, and Germany. He was awarded both the Purple Heart and the Bronze Star with Oak Leaf for valor, and he left the army a sergeant. The shock of war was not easy to shrug off, however. While back at Columbia to finish his degree, Simpson suffered a nervous breakdown that required hospitalization.

A disability pension and the G.I. bill allowed him to travel to France, where he briefly studied at the Sorbonne. There he began to recall the war in dreams and poems, starting with the ballad "Carentan O Carentan." His first collection, *The Arrivistes* (French for "go-getters"), was privately printed in 1949. He acquired a New York distributor for the book, and it was favorably reviewed by Randall Jarrell. Yet six difficult years would pass before Simpson published his second collection, *Good News of Death and Other Poems,* in a Scribner's series called *Poets of Today.* During this time he continued his studies toward a Ph.D. at Columbia and worked as a book editor at Bobbs-Merrill in New York (1950–1955). His third collection of poems, *A Dream of Governors,* appeared in 1959. That same year he began to teach at the University of California, Berkeley, where he remained until 1967. His one novel, the highly autobiographical *Riverside Drive,* appeared in 1962.

By this time, critics had begun to notice changes in Simpson's verse style. "At the end of the 1950s," he recalled, "I felt the need to express my thoughts more intimately, and began writing in free forms and a conversational style." Simpson had been reading Whitman, and he combined the earlier poet's vision with his own experience in a searching reexamination of his adoptive country. His new collection, *At the End of the Open Road* (1963), won the Pulitzer Prize. A *Selected Poems* appeared two years later. In 1967 Simpson began to teach on Long Island at SUNY Stony Brook. He remained there until his retirement from teaching in 1993. Among his many poetry collections since winning the Pulitzer, the most significant were *Searching for the Ox* (1976) and *Collected Poems* (1988).

Throughout his career, Simpson has been a prolific editor and literary critic. With Donald Hall and Robert Pack, he edited one of the key anthologies of postwar poetry, *The New Poets of England and America* (1957). There have also been two full-length critical volumes on modern poetry: *Three on the Tower: The Lives and Works of Ezra Pound, T. S. Eliot and William Carlos Williams* (1975) and *A Revolution in Taste: Studies of Dylan Thomas, Allen Ginsberg, Sylvia Plath and Robert Lowell* (1978). In these books and three other collections of essays and reviews, Simpson proves an informed, entertaining, and occasionally curmudgeonly critic whose strong opinions are not held back.

REFLECTIONS ON NARRATIVE POETRY

Why tell stories in lines of verse? Isn't prose a more suitable medium?

It would be, if poets only had ideas and wished to convey them. But feeling is more urgent, and their feelings are expressed by the movement of lines. In poetry the form, more than the idea, creates the emotion we feel when we read the poem.

From *A Company of Poets* (Ann Arbor: University of Michigan Press, 1981) 346–355.

In everything else poets share the concerns of the writer of prose, and may indeed learn more about writing narrative poems from the novelist than from other poets, for in the past two hundred years it has been the novelist whose labor it was to imitate life, while the poet prided himself on his originality, his remoteness from the everyday. "Life" was the business of the middle class and the novelists who entertained it.

As a result, poetry has been impoverished. In the theory of poetry held by Poe and his French translators, poetry is lyrical and intense, the reflection of an unearthly beauty. Many people believe that poetry is a language we do not speak, and that the best poetry is that which we are least able to understand.

I wish to discuss another kind of poetry, that which undertakes to be an imitation of life. The aim of the narrative poet is the same as for the writer of prose fiction: to interpret experience, with the difference I have mentioned: his writing will move in measure. And this measure evokes a harmony that seems apart from life. I say "seems" because it would be impossible to prove that it exists. Readers of poetry, however, feel it. This harmony is what poetry is, as distinct from prose.

Let us learn from the novelist, however, how to deal with the world, for it is his specialty. We may learn from Chekhov, and Conrad, and Joyce . . . and a hundred other writers of fiction. I see no reason that a poet should not take notes, as prose writers do, or write out his story first in prose. I believe that Yeats sometimes worked in this way.

I once read an interview with a poet in which she spoke contemptuously of "subject-seeking" poets. It was Charles Olson's teaching, I believe, that the poet should not have a subject but should put himself into a dynamic relationship with the environment, and poetry would rise out of this. But when I read the books of the poet who was so down on subject-seekers, I found that her own poems always had a subject. In fact, she could be all too explicit, writing about her family or writing poems with a political message. Either she was deceived about the nature of her writing or felt that she could dispense with the rule she had made for others.

There are kinds of poetry that seem visionary, having little resemblance to life. But even these rely on images, and the images, however farfetched, have points of contact with our experience. The room envisioned by Rimbaud at the bottom of a lake is still a room. But I shall not insist on the point. Let us admit that there are kinds of poetry that are not representations of life. This does not concern us: we are speaking of narrative poetry. This has to do with actions and scenes. The action may be subtle, the scene barely sketched, but the aim is to move the reader, and to increase understanding, by touching the springs of nature.

But it is not enough to hold a mirror up to nature. As Henry James says in the preface to *The Spoils of Poynton*, "Life has no direct sense whatever for the subject and is capable, luckily for us, of nothing but splendid waste. Hence the opportunity for the sublime economy of art."

So you take what you need and rearrange it, and you invent. Invention is supposed to be the sine qua non of the so-called creative arts. It is what people usually mean when they use the word "imagination." The poet, says Longinus, thinks that he sees what he describes, and so is able to place it before the eyes of the reader.

Yes, of course. But I wonder how useful this description is to the man who does the job? It may actually do more harm than good, by urging the writer to strain his powers of invention. Rather than try to work himself up to a pitch of imagination, the poet would do well to discover what is there, in the subject. Let him immerse himself in the scene and wait for something to happen . . . the right, true thing.

"There can be," says James, "evidently, only one logic for these things; there can be for [the writer] only one truth and one direction—the quarter in which his subject most completely expresses itself."

So you choose the direction that has most to offer. Some writers, however, are unwilling to go so far. It is instructive to take up a book of poems and see, with every poem, which direction the poet has chosen to take. Some poets take the easiest direction, an ending that will please most people. The sad thing about these poets is that they don't please anyone very much: for all their attempts to be good-natured the public will desert them for some poet whose writing is obscure and who seems to despise them. The mob does not admire those who flatter it—at any rate, not for long. They know they are only a mob and reserve their admiration for those who tell them so.

One day you were stopped on a street corner by an old panhandler. While the lights were changing and people hurrying by, he told you his story.

He served in Mexico with "Black Jack" Pershing, over forty years ago. He had a wife who was unfaithful. One day he followed her and confronted her with it. "Baby," he said, "I'm wise to you and the lieutenant."

A few days later you wrote a poem about it, trying to describe a Mexican landscape and evoke the atmosphere. But something was missing.

It was not until you asked yourself why you were interested that the story began to move. The account of his following touched upon some unease in your soul. The rest was merely scaffolding: you were not interested in the landscape or the history of the time. But the tale of jealousy affected you . . . you could imagine yourself in his shoes.

But though poetry rises out of feeling, the poem is not just personal. You could put yourself in the old man's shoes . . . you saw yourself following the woman through a lane in the dust and heat. But, and this is my point, you *saw* . . . you were a character in the story. Your feelings had been separated from yourself. You were therefore able to make them move in one direction or another. You were writing a poem to be read by others, not just getting a feeling out of your system.

Storytelling is an impersonal kind of art, even when the story appears to be about oneself. The "I" who appears in the poem is a dramatic character. "Je est un *autre*."*

In recent years there was talk of "confessional poetry." Robert Lowell and Sylvia Plath, among others, were said to be confessional poets—that is, to be writing directly about their lives. But when we read the poems in *Life Studies* and *Ariel* we find that the incidents they relate have been shaped so as to make a point. The protagonist is seen as on a stage. In confessional poetry, on the other hand, there is no drama. The drama is not in the poem but outside it, in a life we cannot share.

I would advise the poet to be as objective about himself as possible. In this way you will not be locked into the treadmill of your own personal history, treading the same stairs again and again.

For twenty years there has been an outpouring of subjective art. There was a generation that believed that poetry should be nothing more than an expression of the poet's feelings. "Why talk about art? Be sincere and tell it like it is."

*Je est un *autre*: "I is an *other*." An allusion to Arthur Rimbaud.

That was an unhappy generation. They could never advance beyond themselves. It is ironic that, at the same time that they were abolishing art, they complained of a lack of understanding. For art is a key to understanding.

Everyone has feelings—indeed it is impossible not to feel. But we need to understand one another. Scripture tells us that all the ways of a man are right in his own eyes but the Lord pondereth the hearts. The ways of the poet James Merrill must surely be right in his own eyes, and I cannot explain my aversion to his style except as an aversion to the personality it presents. The style is the man.

> Tap on the door and in strolls Robert Morse,
> Closest of summer friends in Stonington.
> (The others are his Isabel, of course,
>
> And Grace and Eleanor—to think what fun
> We've had throughout the years on Water Street . . .)
> He, if no more the youthful fifty-one
>
> Of that first season, is no less the complete
> Amateur. Fugue by fugue Bach's honeycomb
> Drips from his wrist—then, whoops! the Dolly Suite.

What else can one possibly say on this subject? There is one thing: one can say, as an absolute rule, that poets must not use words loosely.

When I was a young man I wrote a poem in which I said that poetry had made me "nearly poor." I showed this to a friend, himself a writer, and he advised me to change "nearly poor" to "poor"—it would be more striking. I kept the line as it was, and never again did I pay attention to anything this critic had to say. A man who does not know the difference between being nearly poor and being poor, or who is willing to disregard it in order to make a better-sounding line, is not to be trusted. A man like that would say anything.

Since we have moved away from standard forms, the movement of the line, also, depends on the movement of the poet's soul, how he feels, and thinks, and breathes. As late as the 1950s American poets were expected to write in meter and rhyme. And a few years ago there was talk of songwriters' bringing about a renaissance of rhyme. But there has been no talk of this lately. Most American poets write free verse. This may fall into groups of lines that make a repeating pattern, but the pattern is still irregular. I do not know of any poet who writes in regular forms—meter, stanza, and rhyme—with the assurance of Robert Lowell and Richard Wilbur thirty years ago.

I believe that we shall continue to write free verse of one kind and another, and that it is possible to write a sustained narrative in free verse just as effectively as though it were written in hexameters or the meters used by Walter Scott. The long narrative poem by Patrick Kavanagh titled "The Great Hunger" is a case in point. It moves just as well as writing in rhyme and meter, and, moreover, echoes the speech of a modern world, which meter and rhyme cannot.

I can see no reason for writing in the old forms of verse. Finding the form for the poem as one writes is half the joy of poetry.

Poets try to think of new images. But it does not matter whether the image be new or old—what matters is that it be true. Poets who think that by producing far-fetched images they are changing our consciousness are doing nothing of the kind. One comes to expect the unexpected.

As the painter Magritte points out, everyone is familiar with the bird in a cage. Anyone can visualize a fish in a cage, or a shoe. But these images, though they are curious, are, unfortunately, arbitrary and accidental. If you wish to surprise, alarm, and alert the reader on the deeper levels of consciousness, visualize a large egg in the cage.

"There exists a secret affinity between certain images; it holds equally for the objects represented by these images."

One writes, refusing temptations, sailing past the siren voices. Are the lines about morphology really necessary? What worked for another may not work for you. All sorts of ideas come into a writer's head, but only some are in keeping with his nature, his way of saying a thing.

Imagine that you are reading your poem aloud, and that two or three people whose intelligence you respect are sitting in the audience. If you say something banal, or try to conceal a poverty of thought in a cloud of verbiage, you will see them yawn, their eyes beginning to close.

If you visualize an audience you won't go in for merely descriptive writing. It was description that killed the narrative poem in the nineteenth century. Think of the long poems of Tennyson or Swinburne. What was it the Victorians found in all that scenery? Perhaps it had something to do with sex. The shopkeepers who ruled Western Europe and, later, the United States, couldn't tolerate talk of sex in their houses. But the woods were loaded with naked bums and flying feet.

Since movies were invented we have had no time for descriptions of scenery and for long drawn-out transitions. Nor for the working-out of an obvious plot. And still this kind of poetry continues to be written. The history of the conquistadors and wagon trains are favorite subjects. Sometimes these volumes are handsomely bound—American publishers are incurable optimists, they hope for another *John Brown's Body*, but what they are more likely to get is the equivalent of the Thanksgiving play, with scenes of the Pilgrim Fathers—the parts being taken by members of the town council—Red Indians, the minister and the minister's wife, and the farmhand and his girl. It ends with bringing on a cow and baskets heaped with corn and pumpkins. Perhaps this is what people have in mind when they warn us of the danger of having a subject.

I have been reading an article on prose fiction in which the writer says that, without anyone's noticing, we have entered upon a new period of realism. I believe this to be true, and true of poetry as well.

"Most artists and critics," said Susan Sontag, writing in the sixties, "have discarded the theory of art as representation of an outer reality in favor of art as subjective expression."

Critics define movements in art just as they come to an end. For twenty years we have been reading poetry that expressed the personal feelings and opinions of the poet. The movement is exhausted—this is apparent in the visual arts as well as poetry and fiction. People long for understanding and a community of some kind.

The word "realism" can be misleading. I do not mean reporting, but writing that penetrates beneath the surface to currents of feeling and thought. Not Champfleury but Flaubert.

I do not know a better way to explain my ideas than by showing how I have applied them. I shall therefore end with a poem.

The images have the affinities Magritte speaks of, though I do not think I should point them out—to do so would take away the pleasure of reading, for myself as well as the reader. I may point out, however, that realism allows for fantastic images and ideas . . . but they have a reason for being. The landscape that suddenly appears in the poem . . . the old man sitting with his back to the wall, the woman who appears in a doorway . . . are in the mind of one of the characters.

1981

━•►◄ DONALD JUSTICE ►◄•━
(B. 1925)

One of the most distinctive and accomplished poets of his generation, Donald Justice is also a painter and composer, and those two arts have exerted profound influences upon his writing. His quiet, carefully wrought poems seem composed with a musician's touch for tonality and a painter's deliberate eye. A Southerner, he evokes nostalgia for the lost world of childhood, but he manages to summon powerful emotions without sentimentality. Often impersonal and avoiding overt autobiography, Justice's poems nonetheless convey their highly personal emotions as musical compositions do, working on our nerves in ways we might not fully comprehend. His poems are often haunted by a rueful sense of lost possibility and passing time.

Justice was born in Miami, Florida, where his father worked as a carpenter. While attending public schools, he took piano lessons and developed a serious interest in music. At the University of Miami, where he received his B.A. in 1945, he studied with the Modernist composer Carl Ruggles, but poetry gradually became his primary interest. He was especially attracted to the works of Charles Baudelaire, Wallace Stevens, and W. H. Auden, and he ultimately decided to continue his studies in English, although he never abandoned his interest in musical composition.

Justice earned an M.A. at the University of North Carolina in 1947, and that same summer married Jean Catherine Ross, a writer, with whom he had one son. The following academic year, Justice studied with Yvor Winters at Stanford, then moved on to what is now the University of Iowa in Iowa City, earning a Ph.D. in English in 1954. Iowa had the first major program in creative writing, and in 1957 Justice returned there to teach. Except for sabbaticals or visiting professorships at other institutions, Justice remained primarily at the Iowa Writers' Workshop for a quarter-century, becoming perhaps the most influential poetry teacher of the postwar era. His students would include Mark Strand, Charles Wright, Jorie Graham, William Logan, and Mark Jarman. In 1982 he returned to his native Florida, finishing his teaching career at the University of Florida, Gainesville. After retiring in 1992, he returned to Iowa City where he writes, paints, and composes.

Justice's first collection of poems, *The Summer Anniversaries* (1960), won the Lamont Award from the Academy of American Poets. Although he would later appear to criticize his early poems in a line of verse—"How fashionably sad those early poems are!"—several of them are among his best works, such as "On the Death of Friends in Childhood" and "Counting the Mad." *The Summer Anniversaries* was notable not only for its formal range, but also for the restless experimentation that always characterizes Justice's work. Few poets of equal distinction have ever shown such a strong disinclination to repeat themselves. Another characteristic that arose early was Justice's delight in borrowing from other poets—demonstrating T. S. Eliot's dictum, "Immature poets imitate; mature poets steal: bad poets deface what they take, and good poets make it into something better or at least different."

Never a prolific poet, always as demanding of himself as he was of his students, Justice waited seven years to publish another collection, although these gaps between full-length books were punctuated by the publication of important chapbooks in limited editions. *Night Light* (1967) contained poems of darker moods and freer range, and *Departures* (1973) provided further extensions of both form and content. Written almost entirely in free verse, it contained poems in the surrealist mode as well as others composed by aleatory, or chance, procedures. Critics who objected to rhyme and meter were happy to see Justice writing in seemingly open forms, but many failed to understand that he always regarded any formal technique as a viable means to achieve a memorable utterance. In an interview he said, "Probably more than other poets I know I play games in my poems (as I do in my life), and one of the unwritten rules of the game for me, as I like it played, is that you can risk this much personality or that much confession if the voice is promised to be that of someone else to start with." Thus, in his "Variations on a Text by Vallejo," Justice used a literary borrowing to compel new music that was at some level personal.

When Justice won the Pulitzer Prize for his *Selected Poems* (1979), the award seemed an acknowledgment that he had become one of the country's indispensable poets, a master of what Emily Grosholz would call "illusionless wit." His next collection, *The Sunset Maker* (1987), concluded with two prose pieces building on his themes of music and memory. *A Donald Justice Reader: Selected Poetry and Prose*, appeared in 1991, the same year in which he won the Bollingen Prize. His *New and Selected Poems* (1995) led to a Lannan Literary Award in 1996. The fifteen new poems collected in that volume convey again Justice's strong sense of the ephemeral, but also his faith in what endures. The book begins with the ironic epigram "On a Picture by Burchfield": "Writhe no more, little flowers. Art keeps long hours. / Already your agony has outlasted ours."

Those who know Justice often recount his love of high-stakes poker as well as music and painting, and perhaps there is something of the card-player's skill in his poems—the ability to mask himself, revealing only what is necessary for a given effect. It should also be remarked that he has always been a generous supporter of good poetry where he finds it and has championed several poets in danger of neglect. He was the first to champion the posthumous reputation of the important poet, Weldon Kees, by editing and introducing Kees's *Collected Poems* (1960)—a service Justice has performed for several other dead writers. With Robert Mezey he edited *The Collected Poems of Henri Coulette* (1990), and with others *The Comma after Love: Selected Poems of Raeburn Miller* (1994). He also collected *The Last Nostalgia* (1999), poems of Joe Bolton, a former student who committed suicide. To have rescued these poets from oblivion is by itself no small contribution.

That so discerning a reader and writer has published little of his own criticism is cause for regret, as Justice himself has acknowledged. He began his short preface to *Platonic Scripts* (1984), a volume made up half of interviews, with the elegiac admission, "Of all the poets of my generation who did not get much into the habit of criticism—and that would include the great majority of us—I may be the only one with any regrets at having kept my thoughts more or less to myself." Although Justice's critical *oeuvre* is modest in size, his two overlapping prose collections, *Platonic Scripts* and *Oblivion* (1998), contain some of the best essays on poetics any American poet has written. Compact, informed, and original, his criticism argues its points with vivid clarity. In the following selection he discusses the interrelatedness of memory and a poet's formal choices, suggesting that "some psychological compulsion" underlies meters—"magic to keep an unpredictable world under control."

METERS AND MEMORY

The mnemonic value of meters seems always to have been recognized. There are, to begin with, the weather saws, counting spells, and the like, which one does more or less get by heart in childhood. But any ornament, however trivial and even meaningless, probably assists the recollection to some degree, if by ornament we mean a device of sound or structure not required by the plain sense of passage. Repetition obviously functions in this way—anaphora, refrains, even the sort of repetition which involves nothing more than an approximate equivalence of length, as in Pound's Sapphic fragment:

        Spring. . . . .
        Too long. . . . .
        Gongula. . . . .

Likewise with such structural features as parallel parts or syllogistic order, whether in verse or prose. For that matter, fine and exact phrasing alone enables the memory to take hold about as well as anything. A friend of mine, at parties, preferred to recite prose rather than verse, usually, as I recall, the opening paragraph of *A Farewell to Arms.*

The purely mnemonic character of a passage, however, appears to contribute little to its esthetic power. Often enough rhymes are more effective mnemonically than meters, and occasionally other devices may prove to be. But the meters, where employed at all, are likely to be the groundwork underlying other figurations, hence

From *Platonic Scripts* (Ann Arbor: University of Michigan Press, 1984). All footnotes are Donald Justice's.

basic, if not always dominant. Consider a couplet like "Red sky at morning, / Sailor take warning." Here the meters cooperate with the rhymes to fit the lines to one another, not only as lines of verse but as linked parts of a perception. It is no more than a slight exaggeration to claim that the couplet becomes fixed in memory by reason of this sense of fittedness. But few devices of sound are enough in themselves to ensure recall. If, for example, the sky of the couplet should be changed from red to blue, although neither rhyme nor meter would be affected, I cannot believe the couplet would survive. Survival in this case has something to do with aptness of observation, with use, that is, as well as cleverness or beauty. The kernel of lore provides a reason for keeping the jingle: the jingle preserves the lore in stable form.

Now all this is to consider memory, as is customary, from the viewpoint of an audience, as if a significant purpose of poetry were simply to put itself in the way of being memorized. For my part, when I am at work on a poem, the memory of an audience concerns me less than my own. While the meters and other assorted devices may ultimately make the lines easier for an audience to remember, they are offering meanwhile, like the stone of the sculptor, a certain resistance to the writer's efforts to call up his subject, which seems always to be involved, one way or another, with memory. (Hobbes somewhere calls imagination the same thing as memory.) In any case, memory is going to keep whatever it chooses to keep not just because it has been made easy and agreeable to remember but because it comes to be recognized as worth the trouble of keeping, and first of all by the poet. The audience will find it possible to commit to memory only what the poet first recalls for himself. Anything can be memorized, including numbers, but numbers that refer to something beyond themselves, as to the combination of a safe, are for that reason easier to keep in mind. Something other than themselves may likewise be hidden in the meters, and an aptness to be committed to memory might almost be taken as a sign of this other presence. Pattern is not enough. The trivial and insignificant pass beyond recall, no matter how patterned, discounting perhaps a double handful of songs and nonsense pieces,[1] where the pattern itself has somehow become a part of what is memorable. But such a result is exceptional. What happens in the more serious and ordinary case is that some recollection of a person, of an incident or a landscape, whatever we are willing to designate as subject, comes to seem worth preserving. The question for the poet is how to preserve it.

One motive for much if not all art (music is probably an exception) is to accomplish this—to keep memorable what deserves to be remembered. So much seems true at least from the perspective of the one who makes it. Nor should any resemblance to the more mechanical functions of camera and tape recorder prove embarrassing: like a literary text in the making, film and tape also permit editing, room enough for the artist. Let emotion be recollected, in tranquillity or turmoil, as luck and temperament would have it. And then what? Art lies still in the future. The emotion needs to be fixed, so that whatever has been temporarily recovered may become as nearly permanent as possible, allowing it to be called back again and again at pleasure. It is at this point that the various aids to memory, and meter most persistently, begin to serve memory beyond mnemonics. Such artifices are, let us say, the fixatives. Like the chemicals in the darkroom, they are useful in developing the negative. The audience is enabled to call back the poem, or pieces of it, the poet to call back the thing itself, the subject, all that was to become the poem.

---

1. Nonsense may be the condition, in any case, to which devices of sound in themselves aspire.

The transcriptions of experience represented by the meters ought not to be confused with the experience itself. At best the meters can perform no more than a reenactment, as on some stage of the mind. This being so, to object to the meters as unnatural because unrealistic is to miss the point. Like the odd mustaches and baggy pants of the old comedians, they put us on notice that we are at a certain distance from the normal rules and expectations of life. The effect has been variously called a distancing or a framing. Wordsworth described it as serving "to divest language in a certain degree of its reality, and thus to throw a sort of half consciousness of unsubstantial existence over the whole composition." The meters signify this much at least, that we are at that remove from life which traditionally we have called art.

Their very presence seems to testify to some degree of plan, purpose, and meaning. The meters seem always faintly teleological by implication, even in company with an anti-teleological argument, as the case may be. They are proof of the hand and ear of a maker (uncapitalized), even in a poetry which otherwise effaces the self. They seem to propose that an emotion, however uncontrollable it may have appeared originally, was not, in fact, unmanageable. "I don't know why I am crying" becomes "Tears, idle tears, I know not what they mean." The difference seems important to me. The poetic line comes to constitute a sort of paraphrase of the raw feeling, which will only get broken back down close to its original state in some future critic's reparaphrase. The writer in meters, I insist, may feel as deeply as the nonmetrical writer, and the choice whether or not to use meters is as likely to be dictated by literary fashion as by depth of feeling or sincerity. Nevertheless, they have become a conventional sign for at least the desire for some outward control; though their use cannot be interpreted as any guarantee of inner control, the very act of writing at all does usually imply an attempt to master the subject well enough to understand it, and the meters reinforce the impression that such an attempt is being made and perhaps succeeding. Even so, the technology of verse does not of itself affirm a philosophy, despite arguments to the contrary. Certain recent critics have argued that even syntax is now "bogus," since the modern world contains no such order as that implied in an ordinary sentence, much less a metrical one. But the imitation theory underlying this argument seems naive and unhistorical to me, for it was never the obligation of words or of word-order to imitate conditions so reflexively. Syntax deals, after all, primarily with word-order, not world-order, and even the meters, or so it seems to me, can imitate only by convention.

Let me take a simple case. Yvor Winters once offered his line, "The slow cry of a bird," as an example of metrical imitation, not strictly of a birdcall itself but of "the slowness of the cry." The convention would seem to be that two or more strong syllables in succession carry associations of slowness and heaviness, while two or more weak syllables in succession carry contrary associations of rapidity and lightness: melancholy on the one hand, playfulness on the other. But the displacement of a stress from *of* to *cry* in the Winters line, bringing two stresses together, fails to slow the line down, as I hear it. Substitute for this "The *quick* cry of a bird," and the two weak syllables following *cry* can be said to do as much to speed the line up, or as little. But whether the cry is to sound quick or slow, the metrical situation itself remains, practically speaking, identical. If any question of interpretation arises from the reversed foot, the meaning of the reversal must depend on the denotation of the adjective rather than on the particular arrangement of syllables and stresses, for denotation overrides any implication of the meters apart from it. Though apparently agreed on by generations of poets, the minor convention on which Winters was depending is hardly observed any longer except in criticism or occasionally the classroom. Nor was it, for that matter, observed by Milton in his great melancholy-playful pair, "Il Penseroso" and "L'Allegro," or if observed, then only to be consciously played against. Composers of music for the movies learned early that direct imitation of a visual image through sound was best restricted to comic effects (pizzicati, trombone glissandi, staccato bassoons). Pushed far enough, and that is not very far at all, the results of metrical imitations can seem similarly cartoon-like:

> I sank to the pillow, and Joris, and he;
> I slumbered, Dirck slumbered, we slumbered all three.[2]

In any case, simple imitation by means of rhythm would seem to be more plausible in free verse, with its greater flexibility, and most workable in prose, which is allowed any and every arrangement of syllables. The point seems obvious and incontrovertible to me, though never brought up in quite this way, I think. Wordsworth ascribes to the meters a different and greater power, finding in them a "great efficacy in tempering and restraining the passion by an intertexture of ordinary feeling," and, he goes on to add, "of feeling not strictly and necessarily connected with the passion." The meters move along in their own domain, scarcely intersecting the domain of meaning, except in some illusory fashion or by virtue of conventions nearly private. The responsibility they bear to the sense, comic writing aside, is mostly not to interfere. By so effacing themselves they will have accomplished all that they must accomplish in relation to the sense. Speech they can and do imitate, from a little distance, but rarely by quoting, that is to say, by attempting to become speech. Song they perhaps are or can become, their natural inclination: no question in that of imitating anything outside their own nature.

Whether their nature really embodies an imitation of natural processes may be arguable. But I do not think the meters can be, in any such sense, organic. A recognition of this, conscious or not, has been reason enough for their rejection by contemporary organicists, poets and critics both. The meters seem more to resemble the hammer-work of carpenters putting together a building, say, than waves coming to shore or the parade of seasons. We do inhale and exhale more or less rhythmically, as long as we stay healthy; our hearts do beat without much skipping, for years on end. Breath and heart are the least remote of these similitudes, but any connection between them and the more or less regular alternation of weak and strong syllables in verse seems doubtful to me and, valid or not, need carry no particular prestige. In urban life, far from the Lake Country of 1800, are to be found analogies as appropriate as any from nature, if no more convincing. Signals timed to regulate the flow of traffic not only seem analogous but at times remarkably beautiful, as on a nearly deserted stretch of Ninth Avenue in New York City at three a.m., especially in a mild drizzle. If the meters do represent or imitate anything in general, it may be nothing more (or less) than some psychological compulsion, a sort of counting on the fingers or stepping on cracks, magic to keep an unpredictable world under control.

Where the meters are supposed to possess anything of an imitative character, the implicit purpose must be to bring the poetic text closer to its source in reality or nature by making it more "like" the thing it imitates. Such an illusion may be enhanced if the poet's conviction is strong enough to persuade an audience to

---

2. Cf. Browning: I sprang to the stirrup, and Joris, and he;
      I galloped, Dirck galloped, we galloped all three.

share his faith, but such conversions are more likely to be accomplished through criticism than through poetry. The twin illusions of control and understanding seem more valuable to me than this illusion of the real, since it is through them, I suspect, that the meters are more firmly connected to memory. To remember an event is almost to begin to control it, as well as to approach an understanding of it; incapable of recurring now, it is only to be contemplated rather than acted on or reacted to. Any sacrifice of immediate reality is compensated for by these new perspectives. The terror or beauty or, for that matter, the plain ordinariness of the original event, being transformed, is fixed and thereby made more tolerable. That the event can recur only in its new context, the context of art, shears it of some risks, the chief of which may anyhow have been its transitory character.

If for an audience the meters function in part to call back the words of the poem, so for the poet they may help to call the words forth, at the same time casting over them the illusion of a necessary or at least not inappropriate fitness and order. There is a kind of accrediting in the process, a warrant that things are being remembered right and set down right, so long as the meters go on working. In this way the meters serve as a neutral and impersonal check on self-indulgence and whimsy; a subjective event gets made over into something more like an object. It becomes accessible to memory, repeatedly accessible, because it exists finally in a form that can be perused at leisure, like a snapshot in an album. Memory itself tends to act not without craft, but selectively, adding here to restore a gap, omitting the incongruous there, rearranging and shifting the emphasis, striving, consciously or not, to make some sense and point out of what in experience may have seemed to lack either. That other presence of which I spoke earlier—the charge of feeling, let us say, which attaches perhaps inexplicably to the subject, what the psychologist might call its *affect*—is not much subject to vicissitudes and manipulations of this sort, except for a natural enough diminution. It remains, but more than likely beneath the surface.

The meters are worth speculating about because they are so specific to the medium, if not altogether essential. Without them nothing may, on occasion, be lost; with them, on occasion, something may be gained, though whatever that is probably has little or nothing to do with sense or ostensible subject. This, in fact, appears to be the sticking point, that in themselves the meters signify so little. It seems a mistake for a rationalist defender of the meters to insist on too much meaningfulness. Let us concede that the effects of the meters are mysterious, from moment to moment imprecise, often enough uncertain or ambiguous. Like Coleridge's incense or wine, however, their presence may "act powerfully, though themselves unnoticed." To which he adds an interesting comparison to yeast—"worthless," as he says, "or disagreeable by itself, but giving vivacity and spirit to the liquor" in right combination. Meters do accompany the sense, like a kind of percussion only, mostly noise. Over and above syntax, they bind the individual words together, and the larger structural parts as well, over and above whatever appearance of logic survives in the argument; as a result, the words and parts seem to cohere, more perhaps than in plain fact may be the case. How they assist the recollection is by fixing it in permanent, or would-be permanent, form. This, for the poet, may be the large and rather sentimental purpose which gives force to all their various combining and intersecting functions.

JACK SPICER
(1925–1965)

Jack Spicer was born in Los Angeles in 1925, the elder of two sons of Midwestern parents. His father, a former radical labor unionist, managed hotels and apartment buildings, and the family lived comfortably even during the Great Depression. A bookish and unattractive child with poor eyesight who was teased by other boys, Spicer sought refuge in local libraries where he read escapist detective novels and thrillers. Declared physically unfit to serve in the military during World War II, Spicer attended the University of Redlands for two years before transferring in 1945 to the University of California at Berkeley where he majored in philosophy and literature. In the thriving nonconformist Berkeley community, the young Spicer gradually reinvented himself as a poet, a bohemian, a radical, and—very slowly and timidly—a gay man. His first English teacher at Berkeley was the poet Josephine Miles who generously encouraged his literary ambitions. Spicer also became interested in radical politics and joined San Francisco's Libertarian Circle, a group of "philosophical anarchists" led by Kenneth Rexroth.

The decisive encounter for Spicer, however, came in 1946 when he met Robert Duncan, whose flamboyant and self-assured public persona as poet and homosexual so dazzled the younger writer that he declared afterwards that 1946 was the true year of his birth. The two young poets soon announced—only half-seriously at first—"The Berkeley Renaissance," which essentially meant the group of their literary friends gathered around bookstore owner George Leite who published the international arts magazine, *Circle*.

Amid this bohemian ferment, Spicer continued his academic studies. After earning an M.A. in linguistics at Berkeley in 1950, he entered a doctoral program in Anglo-Saxon and Old Norse, although he never finished his dissertation. For the rest of his short life Spicer eked out a living as a "research linguist," working on scholarly projects. He taught at the University of Minnesota for two years but returned to California in 1952. While he moved briefly to New York and then Boston, he returned to San Francisco in late 1956 and never left the West again. He also taught a "Poetry as Magic" workshop at the San Francisco Public Library while working part time as a researcher in Berkeley.

During the next few years Spicer finally came into his own as a poet. The key to his artistic development was his concept of the "serial poem." Unhappy with his earlier work, Spicer decided that it had failed because he had tried to write poems that stood alone. "There is no single poem," he now realized. "Poems should echo and reecho against each other. . . . They should create resonances." Spicer now began to conceive of his work in terms of individual books or booklets of interrelated poems. A serial poem, he explained in a lecture, uses the book as its unit of composition. Unlike traditional poetic sequences, however, these books were not necessarily conceived as progressive sequences of individual poems; rather, they existed as a competitive community of synchronous alternatives.

The first of Spicer's "serial" books was *After Lorca* (1957), an ingenious and moving compilation of genuine translations, fake translations, and prose letters to the dead Spanish poet, Federico García Lorca, who also supposedly provided an introduction from beyond the grave. *After Lorca* was published by the newly created White Rabbit Press, which printed the stapled chapbook on a mimeograph press on a Saturday night at the San Francisco Greyhound Bus offices—a representative genesis for books in bohemian North Beach of the era. Other "books" quickly followed, many of which were published only after Spicer's death. *A Book of Music* was finished in 1958, for example, but not published until 1969. *Billy the Kid* (1959) appeared with drawings by Jess, the Bay Area artist who was Robert Duncan's lover. *The Heads of the Town Up to the Aether* (1962), his longest book, was followed by *The Holy Grail* (1964) and *Language* (1965), as well as half a dozen other "books" that appeared posthumously.

Unreviewed and hardly noticed at the time of their creation, these playful and profoundly inventive collections today provide the most exuberant and accessible entry into the experimental West Coast poetry of the era. Spicer never fell into the common fallacy that experimental art need not be interesting. His poems eagerly charm, cajole, argue, and amuse the reader, and they gleefully adopt every available technique to accomplish their task. Depending on what works one cites, the dexterously diverse Spicer can with equal justice be classified as a Beat or Surrealist, a late Modernist or early Postmodernist, a proto-Language Poet or premature New Formalist.

Until the posthumous publication of *The Collected Books of Jack Spicer* (1975), edited by his friend Robin Blaser, the poet's reputation was confined to San Francisco and Berkeley. This situation was mostly Spicer's doing. He printed his books in tiny editions and did not allow them to be sold outside San Francisco—often giving them away free at readings. He also broke bitterly with Duncan after his mentor joined with the Black Mountain School, which Spicer found abstract and humorless. He was happiest in his small "magic circle" of friends talking drunkenly late into the night at North Beach bars.

As the national media touted the "San Francisco Renaissance" and catapulted many friends and former friends into international fame as Beat poets in the late 1950s, Spicer knew he had become a marginal figure. After being injured in an automobile crash sometime in the winter of 1962–63, the poet increased his already heavy drinking, which eventually led to his being fired from his research job. In July 1965 Spicer collapsed and fell into a coma. Waking only intermittently, he died three weeks later in the alcoholic ward of the public hospital.

Spicer's criticism consists mostly of four lectures delivered and taped in 1965 and a series of short fugitive pieces published in small journals. "On Spoken Poetry" is reprinted from a 1949 *Occident* symposium on "the most interesting problems in writing poetry." Spicer's commentary provides perhaps the earliest identification of the massive shift in literary sensibility just then underway—the shift from the printed page to the public reading as the primary means of presenting new poetry. Prophetically, Spicer speculates on how the role of poet as public performer or even entertainer would soon become central to American literary culture.

❦

ON SPOKEN POETRY

Here we are, holding a ghostly symposium—five poets holding forth on their peculiar problems. One will say magic; one will say God; one will say form. When my turn comes I can only ask an embarrassing question—"Why is nobody here? Who is listening to us?"

Most of us are rather good poets. If we were actors or singers or cartoonists of the same relative talent, a sizable percentage of the students of this University would recognize our names and be familiar with our work. As it now stands, I doubt if there is a reader of this magazine (including the editorial staff and the poets themselves) who is familiar with the work of all five poets. Yet, I repeat, there is not one of us that has not been recognized as a good poet by critics, magazines, or publishers.

The usual answer to this complaint, given, to use a home-grown example, in the letter column of the *Daily Californian* every time a new issue of *Occident* comes out, is so much hog-wash: "Modern poetry does not make sense," the letter-writer will passionately exclaim, "Nobody reads it because nobody understands it."

That is just not true. If a lack of intelligibility makes a work unpopular with the public, why is it that there is always at least one song with nonsense lyrics near the top of the Hit Parade? "Chickery Chick" was far less capable of prose analysis than *Finnegans Wake* and no one can claim that its bare, monotonous tune was responsible for its popular favor.

As a matter of fact recently some of the same people that condemn modern poetry as unintelligible express (weirdly enough) admiration for Edith Sitwell and Gertrude Stein. The phonograph records of "Façade" and "Four Saints In Three Acts" have made two writers (who are hardly paragons of intelligibility) perfectly acceptable to a large audience. What this audience has found is not the intelligibility that it had modestly asked for, but that greater boon that it did not dare to ask—entertainment.

The truth is that pure poetry bores everybody. It is even a bore to the poet. The only real contribution of the New Critics is that they have demonstrated this so well.

Originally published in *Occident* Fall 1949. Collected in *The House that Jack Built: Collected Lectures of Jack Spicer,* ed. Peter Gizzi (Hanover, New Hampshire: Wesleyan University Press, 1998) 229–230.

They have taken poetry (already removed from its main source of interest—the human voice) and have completed the job of denuding it of any remaining connection with person, place and time. What is left is proudly exhibited in their essays—the dull horror of naked, pure poetry.

Live poetry is a kind of singing. It differs from prose, as song does, in its complexity of stress and intonation. Poetry demands a human voice to sing it and demands an audience to hear it. Without these it is naked, pure, and incomplete—a bore.

If plays were only printed and never acted, who would read them? If songs were only printed on song sheets, who would read them? It would be like playing a football game on paper. Do you wonder where the audience is?

It affects the nature of the poetry too. There was a time in the middle ages when music was mainly written and not sung. It was a time when crab canons were composed, complicated puzzles made of notes that no ear would think of hearing. Poetry, when it is removed from a living audience, loses its living form, becomes puzzling. It becomes blind like the salamanders that live in dark caves. It atrophies.

Orpheus was a singer. The proudest boast made about Orpheus was not that his poems were beautiful in and of themselves. There were no New Critics then. The proudest boast was that he, the singer with the songs, moved impossible audiences—trees, wild animals, the king of hell himself.

Today we are not singers. We would rather publish poetry in a little magazine than read it in a large hall. If we do read in a hall, we do not take the most elementary steps to make our poetry vivid and entertaining. We are not singers. We do not use our bodies. We *recite* from a printed page.

Thirty years ago Vachel Lindsay saw that poetry must connect itself to vaudeville if it was to regain its voice. (Shakespeare, Webster, and Marlowe had discovered this three centuries before him.) Our problem today is to make this connection, to regain our voices.

We must become singers, become entertainers. We must stop sitting on the pot of culture. There is more of Orpheus in Sophie Tucker than in R. P. Blackmur; we have more to learn from George M. Cohan than from John Crowe Ransom.

1949

►◄ ROBERT BLY ►◄◄
(B. 1926)

Although he became a media celebrity for his best-selling study of male identity, *Iron John: A Book about Men,* Robert Bly had already long exerted influence upon the culture of contemporary American poetry. Through his poetry, translations, criticism, editing, and public appearances, Bly not only inspired many poets of his own generation but built a large following among general readers. Often criticized for his prophetic posturing, literary dogmatism, and occasionally slapdash writing, Bly nonetheless played an indispensable role in the significant change of sensibility in American poetry during the 1960s, and he remained a pivotal figure in the literary world during the last three decades of the twentieth century.

Robert Elwood Bly was born into a Norwegian Lutheran farming family in Madison, Minnesota, close to the Lac Qui Parle River and the lake of the same name. He would later speak and write about the emotional isolation he felt in his early years, partly due to his father's alcoholism, partly to the family's Nordic stoicism. He and his older brother attended a small one-room country schoolhouse where they were sometimes the only students. Graduating from high school during World War II, Bly postponed college and enlisted in the U.S. Navy. He served from 1944 to 1946, but never left the United States or saw combat. After the war he attended St. Olaf College for a year before transferring to Harvard, where his fellow students included the poets Donald Hall, Adrienne Rich, John Ashbery, Kenneth Koch, L. E. Sissman, and Frank O'Hara. His lifelong friend Hall has described meeting Bly in 1948, "He was skinny, never smiled, and wore three-piece suits with narrow striped ties; he was very intelligent."

The severity and isolation of Bly's early experience would to some degree be reinforced by years spent far from cultural centers. After graduating from Harvard magna cum laude, he spent time in New York City and his ancestral Norway. He also earned a master's degree from the University of Iowa in 1956. But Bly's determined independence was most exemplified by his return to the family farm, where he has lived on his own parcel of land most of his adult life. In 1955 he married Carolyn McLean (now well known as the writer Carol Bly). Although they would divorce twenty-four years later, they were for the duration of their marriage an influential literary couple, often entertaining writers and artists at the farm.

Bly named his farmhouse Odin House, and soon created what would prove to be one of the most innovative, influential, and openly combative small magazines of the postwar era, the *Fifties*. (Named for the decades in which it was published, the journal was regularly rechristened the *Sixties*, the *Seventies*, the *Eighties*, and the *Nineties*.) The journal, subtitled "A Magazine of Poetry and Opinion," declared open warfare on the New Critical orthodoxy then dominant in academic English departments. Often writing under a pseudonym, "Crunk," Bly promoted his own poetic agenda, attacked American provincialism, and mercilessly ridiculed his opponents— sometimes awarding them the "Order of the Blue Toad," a mock literary prize for stupidity, crassness, and commercialism. Through this journal Bly gradually became well known on a national level.

Although Bly had begun as a traditional poet, writing in rhyme and meter, and continued to admire masters of form like W. B. Yeats and Rainer Maria Rilke, he increasingly associated poetic meter and form with literary rationalism and stale academicism. Decrying the ignorance of monolingual American literati, he championed and translated modern Latin American and European poetry including the work of Antonio Machado, Juan Ramón Jiménez, Federico García Lorca, and Tomas Tranströmer. Among the poets who came to see him on his farm were Donald Hall, Louis Simpson, and James Wright. Under Bly's influence, Wright changed his style and became a predominantly free verse poet with a visionary bent. The two men became associated with what was called "Deep Image" poetry.

Once Bly had abandoned meter in his own poems, having shown little talent for it in the first place, he fashioned a quiet, direct voice of his own, effectively displayed in his first important book, *Silence in the Snowy Fields* (1962). This volume announced a flat, imagistic, and minimalist style that would exercise enormous influence on American poetry for the next twenty years. Bly's main objection to the academic poetry of the fifties had been that its rationality became a formal and psychological straitjacket. Strongly influenced by Jung's method of associating archetypes, Bly developed poetry intended to speak from a source deep in the unconscious. "Inward poetry deepens all life around it," he declared, and his essays began to use such terms as "inwardness," "association," "leaping," and "revolutionary feeling." Although it differed from the more exuberant and expansive Beat poetry, Bly's quiet and introspective work moved on a parallel countercultural path.

Bly's activism against the Vietnam War provided another career high point. When his second full-length collection, *The Light around the Body* (1967), won the National Book Award in 1968, the poet used the ceremony to publicly donate the award money to an antiwar organization. Such bold acts contributed to Bly's image as a courageous and generous public figure. He published his best antiwar poems in *The Teeth Mother Naked at Last* (1971). Many volumes of translations followed, including a version of the Norwegian Knut Hamsun's classic novel, *Hunger* (1967), and the Persian ecstatic poet Kabir. He also edited a series of short polemical anthologies like *The Sea and the Honeycomb* (1971) and *Leaping Poetry* (1975) to proselytize his new aesthetic. Many of his essays were collected in *American Poetry: Wildness and Domesticity* (1990). Increasingly, Bly was reaching beyond the poetry audience to a broader readership of people experimenting with New Age mysticism and alternative lifestyles. For these readers, Bly has become less a poet than a secular priest or shaman, whose ideas about male grief, the loss of wildness, and the power of myths have been guiding principles.

Bly's best-selling books of prose—*Iron John* (1990) and *The Sibling Society* (1996)—and his many appearances on public television, have made him wealthy and famous, but they have also obscured his earlier contributions as an editor and critic. In the piece that follows, Bly decries the flatness and rationality he sees in certain American poets, setting himself in opposition to many of them. He stands outside the colleges and universities, pointing out what he perceives as the weaknesses of poets who work inside them.

It is possible to quarrel with particular positions or assertions by Bly, but there is no denying his enormous influence on contemporary letters both inside the poetry subculture and with general readers. His early impact on American poetry during the 1960s and 1970s is now part of the historical record, but his later accomplishments are still much debated. In broad cultural terms the great contribution of his later career has been to insist on the spiritual and psychological importance of literature at a time when those values had been called into question. As academic discourse on literature became obsessed with theoretical concerns almost unintelligible to nonspecialists, including postmodern approaches like deconstruction that explicitly denied the notion of literature as a medium of truth or spiritual value, Bly compellingly argued for the abiding importance of poetry and myth as irreplaceable media for passing on complex truths of human existence. Composed in equal parts of brilliant insight, powerful metaphor, and sheer bravado, Bly's criticism reached a huge audience and exerted a significant influence on literary culture. If he failed in his quest to be the visionary prophet of contemporary poetry, no one in his generation came half so close in articulating the spiritual vocation of the poet in modern society.

◄●►━━◄ ◗ ►━━◄●►

A WRONG TURNING IN AMERICAN POETRY

I

American poetry resembles a group of huge spiral arms whirling about in space. Eliot and Pound are moving away at tremendous speeds. Marianne Moore and Jeffers are driving into space also. This island universe is rushing away from its own center.

Let me contrast this picture with another. Spanish poetry of this century is moving inward, concentrating. Antonio Machado stands at the center of Spanish poetry, standing at the center of himself as well. His poems are strange without

Originally published in *Choice* 3 (1963): 33–47. Collected in *American Poetry: Wildness and Domesticity* (New York: Harper, 1991) 7–35.

being neurotic. His thought is abundant and clear, near the center of life. The younger Spanish poets can judge where they are from where he is. They can look in and see him standing there.

In American poetry, on the other hand, a young poet cannot take Pound, Eliot, or Moore for a master without severe distortion of his own personality. They whirled about so far out that anyone who follows them will freeze to death. If American poetry has a center it would seem to be William Carlos Williams. His poetry however shows a fundamental absence of spiritual intensity. He is in fact as much caught up in destructive expansion as the others.

II

Eliot, Pound, Moore, and Williams, all born within five years of each other, form a poetic generation we might call the generation of 1917. They support certain ideas with great assurance. Eliot's support of the idea of the "objective correlative" is an example. His phrasing of the idea is as follows: "The only way of expressing emotion in the form of art is by finding an 'objective correlative'; in other words, a set of objects, a situation, a chain of events which shall be the formula of that *particular* emotion." The tone is authoritative, but the statement is not true. With "objective" here, we stumble onto a word we will find over and over again in the work of the 1917 generation. These men have more trust in the objective, outer world than in the inner world. As poets, they want to concern themselves with objects. The word "formula" above suggests the desire to be scientific, to study things. Eliot says in essence that *objects* are essential in a poem. He wants to arrange them in a formula, as a scientist would, so that the controlled experiment can be repeated any number of times.

As a program, the search for the objective correlative merely obstructs poetry. What does the search for this formula result in? The impulse for the poem does not flow forward into the language. Instead the impulse is stopped: the poet searches about for the proper formula in the public world. This means working up the poem as an idea—for example, in terms of the lower classes ("Sweeney Erect") or in terms of Greek myth ("Sweeney Agonistes"). Greek myths and the lower classes are thought to be very objective. However, the impulse to the poem is broken. True freshness and surprise are impossible. The poet's eyes are not on the impulse but are constantly looking over the public world for reliable sets of objects. Finally, the poet's own mind becomes objective: he becomes the public.

Modern Spanish poetry—to continue our contrast—denies Eliot's thesis of the relevance of the objectivizing process. Ricardo Gullon, for example, has said that the purpose of poetry "is to transfer an intuition." How is an intuition to be transferred? Guillaume de Torre, the greatest contemporary Spanish critic, holds up the personal, even the intimate poem. Intuition is embodied in experiences private to the poet (which the reader can nonetheless share) "and not in common experiences from the public domain masquerading as unique and vital. T. S. Eliot's 'objective correlative' and other vulgarities dressed up in cryptic terms are nothing but so many frauds."

Lorca has a poem describing his emotions while walking on the streets of New York, feeling that he is aging, being rapidly killed by the sky. He does not talk of Circe or the clothes of bums sleeping on the sidewalk. He says,

Among the forms which are moving toward the serpent,
And the forms which are searching for the crystal,
I'll grow long hair.

With the tree of amputated limbs which does not sing,
And the boy child with the white face of the egg.

With all the tiny animals who have gone insane,
And the ragged water which walks on its dry feet.

Lorca conveys his emotion not by any "formula" but by means that do not occur to Eliot—by passionate spontaneity. The phrase "objective correlative" is astoundingly passionless. For Lorca there is no time to think of a cunning set of circumstances that would carry the emotion in a dehydrated form to which the reader need only add water.

Pound said in 1911, "I believe that the proper and perfect symbol is the natural object." Pound considers poetry to be fundamentally a repository of wisdom. He wishes to put into the *Cantos* as many important thoughts and conversations and fragments of the classics as he can, so that should a man be able to own only one book he could own the *Cantos* and thereby possess the truth about economics and government as well as culture. The poem is thus defined with no reference to the unconscious. Instead of the unconscious there is economics. Relations between parts of the outer world take the place of inner relations and of the inner world. The book takes what it needs by force. As a poem, the *Cantos* annexes other people's ideas, facts, other languages. The poem is like an infinitely expanding metropolis, eating up more and more of the outer world, with less and less life at the center. The personality of the poet is driven out of the poem. The expanding poem, like the expanding city, has no personality. The idea of the poem as the essence of the author's personality—Yeats believed this is what a poem was—is entirely lost. How can the personality be present if the unconscious is pushed out?

Marianne Moore's poetry also represents a treasure-house—a feminine one. The objects in the poem are fragments, annexed, and the poem is a parlor full of knick-knacks carefully arranged. Melville leaves such a room and goes to sea: there he sees whales moving about in the sea their whole lives, winds thrashing freely, primitive forces that act out their own inward strength. Returning to land he becomes a revolutionary because in society he sees such elementary forces curtailed; he asks why they must be checked and lamed. The purpose of Marianne Moore's art is exactly opposite: it is to reconcile us to living with hampered forces. She brings in animals and fish, but only fragments of them—beaks of birds, single wings of dragonflies, the dorsal fin of a whale, the teeth of snakes, the forepaw of an otter—all adopted to domestic life. Everything is reduced in size, reduced to human dimensions, as in old New England parlors, where there was "a shark's backbone made into a walking stick." The poem becomes a temporary excursion into the dangerous world of nature, with an immediate and safe return already envisioned—a kind of picnic. The fragments of animals that appear are separated from their inner force, their wildness, and turned from living things into objects. A poem is conceived as an exercise in propriety.

William Carlos Williams's work reflects a similar attachment to objects. "No ideas but in things!" he said. His poems show great emotional life mingled with the drive of the intelligence to deal with outward things—but no inward life, if by inward life we mean an interest in spiritual as well as psychological intensity. Williams was a noble man, of all the poets in his generation the warmest and most human. Still, his ideas contained something destructive: there is in them a drive toward the extinction of personality. Williams's "No ideas but in things!" is a crippling program. Besides the ideas in things there are ideas in images and in feelings. True, bits of broken glass are preferable for poetry to fuzzy generalities such as virtue or patriotism. But images like Lorca's "black horses and dark people are riding over the deep roads of the guitar" also contain ideas and give birth to ideas. Williams asked poetry to confine itself to wheelbarrows, bottle caps, weeds—with the artist "limited to the range of his contact with the objective world." Keeping close to the surface becomes an obsession. The effect of Williams's thought, therefore, was to narrow the language of poetry—to narrow it to general remarks mixed with bits of glass and paper bags, with what Pound called "natural objects." Williams says, "The good poetry is where the vividness comes up true like in prose but better. That's poetry."

BETWEEN WALLS

The back wings
of the

hospital where
nothing

will grow lie
cinders

in which shine
the broken

pieces of a green
bottle

In that Williams poem, the personality and the imagination are merely two among many guests. The imagination has to exist as best it can in a poem crowded with objects. In the bare poems of some of Williams's followers the personality of the poet is diffused among lampposts and match folders, and vanishes. The poet appears in the poem only as a disembodied anger or an immovable eye.

The point in contrasting Lorca's language with Williams's is not that Lorca's poems are richer but that Lorca approaches his poetry with entirely different artistic principles—among them the absolute essentiality of the image. These ideas bear fruit in the poems. Lorca's poems have many things in them sharply observed ("black doves puttering the putrid waters"), but they also have images, also passion, wild leaps, huge arsenic lobsters falling out of the sky.

Charles Olson, about fifty, is generally considered the main transmitter of the ideas of Williams and Pound to the present generation. In Olson's prose, their outward direction is set down even more programmatically, as in "Projective Verse"—an essay that echoes T. E. Hulme—in which Olson says,

Objectism is the getting rid of the lyrical interference of the individual as ego, of the "subject" and his soul, that peculiar presumption by which western man has interposed himself between what he is as creature of nature (with certain instructions to carry out) and those other creations of nature which we may, with no derogation, call objects.

In demanding that the poet get rid of himself as a subjective person Olson is simply restating Eliot's belief in the desirability of "extinguishing the personality." To Olson the poet's inwardness is "lyrical interference." Some Zen teachers use language like this, but their meaning is exactly the opposite. The aim of Zen, as of a poet like Rilke, is to make men more and more inward until they stop admiring objects, at which point they will be able to see them clearly, if they wish to.

The ideas of the 1917 generation are quite consistent. Eliot and Pound conceive maturity as a growth of outwardness. Eliot's later plays are naturally more outward than his earlier plays, the *Cantos* more outward than *Lustra*. The opposite is true of Yeats and Rilke. Rilke was more inward at thirty than at twenty; more inward at fifty than at thirty.

In this country we have a great reluctance to admit that directions can be incompatible. We want to follow both the Pound-Olson direction and the Rilke direction. Yet in *Letters to a Young Poet* Rilke writes, "Give up all that. You are looking outward, and that above all you should not do now. There is only one single way. Go into yourself." And he tells Kappus that poetry will come "from this turning inward, from this sinking into your private world." Rilke believes that the poet actually experiences the soul, does not share the mass's preoccupation with objects.

If we are to develop clear principles in our poetry we must honestly say that we cannot reconcile the inward direction of Rilke with the outward direction of the Williams-Pound-Olson movement. This is why Pound talks of Rilke so little. A man cannot turn his face at the same moment toward the inward world and the outer world: he cannot face both south and north at the same moment.

III

I have tried to point out that the 1917 generation had a rather unified set of ideas centered on objectivism—shared by all the major poets of that generation despite their other differences. All later poetry has been written, necessarily, under the influence of these ideas. Now how can we describe our poetry since the twenties in a way that will include Winters as well as Lowell, Eberhart as well as Ciardi?

It is first of all a poetry without spiritual life. The beginning of spiritual life is a horror of emptiness that our people feel every day, but it is Rilke who has described such a state, not one of us.

> Already the ripening barberries are red,
> And in their bed the aged asters hardly breathe.
> Whoever now is not rich inside, at the end of summer,
> Will wait and wait, and never be himself.
>
> Whoever now is unable to close his eyes
> Absolutely certain that a crowd of faces
> Is only waiting till the night comes
> In order to stand up around him in the darkness—
> That man is worn out, like an old man.
>
> Nothing more will happen to him, no day will arrive,
> And everything that does happen will cheat him.
> Even you, my God. And you are like a stone
> Which draws him daily deeper into the depths.

Our recent poetry is also a poetry in which the poem is considered to be a construction independent of the poet. It is imagined that when the poet says "I" in a poem he does not mean himself, but rather some other person—"the poet"—a dramatic hero. The poem is conceived as a clock that one sets going. This idea encourages the poet to construct automated and flawless machines. Such poems have thousands of intricately moving parts, dozens of iambic belts and pulleys, precision trippers that rhyme at the right moment, lights flashing alternately red and green, steam valves that whistle like birds. This is the admired poem. Richard Wilbur, for all his ability, fell a victim to this narrow conception of the poem. His earlier "Water Walker," written before this oppressive concept of the poem penetrated him, remains his most personal and freshest poem. Robert Lowell in *Lord Weary's Castle* constructed machines of such magnitude that he found it impossible to stop them. Like the automated, chain-reacting tool of the sorcerer's apprentice, the poems will not obey. The references to Mary or Jesus that end several of them are last-minute expedients, artistically dishonest and resembling a pile of cloths thrown into a machine to stop it.

The great poets of this century have written their poems in exactly the opposite way. In the poems of Neruda, Vallejo, Jiménez, Machado, and Rilke, the poem is an extension of the substance of the man, no different from his skin or his hands. The substance of the man who wrote the poem reaches far out into the darkness and the poem is his whole body, seeing with his ears and his fingers and his hair.

Here is a poem of Machado's, written before the death of his wife; here the "I" *is* the poet.

> From the doorsill of a dream they called my name . . .
> It was the good voice, the voice I loved so much.
>
> —Listen. Will you go with me to visit the soul?
> A soft stroke reached up to my heart.
>
> —With you always . . . And in my dream I walked
> Down a long and solitary corridor,
> Aware of the touching of the pure robe,
> And the soft beating of blood in the hand that loved me.

Next, the poetry we have had in this country is a poetry without even a trace of revolutionary feeling—in either language or politics.

It is startling to realize that in the last twenty years there have been almost no poems touching on political subjects, although such concerns have been present daily. The *Kenyon Review*, under Ransom, and the *Southern Review*, under Tate, have been effective forces here. The guiding impulse in both Ransom's and Tate's minds is fear of revolution. As Southerners they act to exaggerate the fear felt by even Northerners. This kind of Southerner thinks of himself as a disinherited aristocrat. Their holding position in poetry has more resemblance to the attitude of Governor Ross Barnett of Mississippi than most people would be willing to admit. Laforgue says, "The only remedy is to break everything." Ransom says, in effect, that the only remedy is to keep everything. This is why there is so much talk of Donne and New Criticism in the *Kenyon Review*—such concerns tend to damp down any tendencies toward revolution. Ransom remarked that he never published poems by Dylan Thomas because Thomas didn't know how to behave in a drawing room. Neruda and Brecht were not welcome in the *Kenyon Review* either.

If revolutionary thought is put down, revolution in language also dies. The absence of any interest in fresh language in literary magazines shows up in the thirties and forties. Compared with that of Hart Crane or Cummings, the language of Nemerov or Ciardi or Jarrell is inexpressibly dull. Jarrell, for example, opens a poem:

One looks from the train
Almost as one looked as a child. In the sunlight
What I see still seems to me plain.

There is almost no contrast inside the line. A poet who has higher standards in language can put together inside a line words that have different natures—like strange animals together in a wood. Mallarmé uses this kind of contrast as a foundation for his poems. Awareness of the different kinds of fur that words have is instantly apparent in Lorca's poems:

One day
The horses will live in the saloons
And the outraged ants
Will throw themselves on the yellow skies that
    have taken refuge in the eyes of cows.

Compare this with a typical stanza of ours:

Youth comes to jingle nickels and crack wise;
The baseball scores are his, the magazines
Devoted to lust, the jazz, the Coca-Cola,
    The lending library of love's latest.
                    —Karl Shapiro, "The Drug Store"

In Shapiro's stanza the words are all one color: gray.

The poetry of the thirties and forties moves backward. Art Buchwald once described the scene he imagined could take place as a Fly Now–Pay Later plan collides with a failure to make a payment on time. A man from the travel agency comes to your house with a curious electric machine. You sit down in it, the current is turned on, and the machine removes all your memories of Europe. In the poetry of the thirties and forties we are supposed to forget that there were even any ideas of a different language for poetry—forget that the German expressionist poets ever lived, forget the experiments in language represented by French poets and later by Alberti and Lorca. Poetry is forgotten, if by poetry we mean exploration into the unknown, and not entertainment; an intellectual adventure of the greatest importance, not an attempt to teach manners, an attempt to face the deep inwardness of the twentieth century, not attempts to preserve the virtues of moderation. The forties generation succeeds in forgetting both the revolution in language and any revolutionary feeling toward society.

Our postwar poets defend the status quo. Nemerov, Ransom, and Ciardi, for instance, by their examples, urge poets not to make too much trouble in the universities. Ransom urges us to have a "civilized attitude." Most of these men are merely accepting the ideas of T. S. Eliot, who supports the Establishment. Hölderlin wrote a short poem on this subject, which has great common sense.

Deep down I despise the herd of leaders and ministers,
But I despise even more the genius who takes their side.

The poetry we have now is a poetry without the image. The only movement in American poetry that concentrates on the image was imagism, in 1911–1913. But "imagism" was largely "picturism." An image and a picture differ in that the image, being the natural speech of the imagination, cannot be drawn from or inserted back into the real world. It is an animal native to the imagination. Like Bonnefoy's "interior sea lighted by turning eagles," it cannot be seen in real life. A picture, on the other hand, is drawn from the objective "real" world. "Petals on a wet black bough" can actually be seen.

We have merely to glance at a typical American stanza of the last years to see that the image is destroyed before birth by pressure of the direct statement or the picture. John Ciardi writes,

Now mist takes the hemlocks and nothing
stirs. This is a gray-green and a
glassy thing and nothing stirs. A plane
to or from Newark burrs down idling on
its flaps or grinds full-rich up its
airy grade, and I hear it.

But if there is no image how is the unconscious going to make its way into the poem? Let us consider the typical "formal poem." Suppose there is no image: then such a statement in a poem as "I must perfect my will" is composed by the conscious mind, rhymes searched for and found by the conscious mind. The efficient workaday conscious mind creates the entire poem. The important thing about an image, on the other hand, is that it is made by both the conscious and the unconscious mind. This is true of Yeats's image of the beast of the "Second Coming" and of Lorca's "the glasses of the dawn are broken."

Finally, then, our poetry has been a poetry essentially without the unconscious. This is not surprising. Two of our strongest traditions have been puritanism (our so-called religious tradition) and business (our secular tradition). The mind of the puritan shows fear of the unconscious—a belief that only ugly and horrible images and ideas come from it. All animal life and sexual life are met with fear and disdain. These are the impulses behind the poetry of Eliot and Pound and that of the neoclassic school as well. The impulses do not describe the poetry of Hart Crane and Theodore Roethke, exceptions of almost all the points I have been making.

Max Weber showed that the apparent asceticism of the puritan had a secret purpose: to adapt the man to an efficient life in business. Working in business "ascetically" fifteen hours a day is the mark of a man who has resisted Satan; success in outward things becomes a proof of religious virtue. The drive toward outward things in the 1917 generation and in recent poets is essentially obedience to business traditions.

These two strains—puritan fear of the unconscious and the business drive toward dealing in outer things—meet in our poetry to push out the unconscious. The 1917 poets tried to adapt poetry to business and science. They looked for "formulas." They tried to deal efficiently with natural objects. They studied to develop "technical skill"—like engineers.

Then, brandishing their technical skill, the poets of the thirties and forties evict the unconscious. And poetry sinks—plunges, sometimes—into the outer world. Titles of books indicate this in an interesting way. Richard Wilbur's third book is called *Things of This World*. Shapiro titled his first book *Person, Place, and Thing,* and his new one *The Bourgeois Poet.*

IV

Ortega y Gasset in *Man and Crisis* suggests that the intellectual history of a nation hinges on the difference between generations. Members of the younger generation, when they get to be about thirty years old, find that the ideas of the older men do not seem to describe the world accurately. As the young man "meditates on the world in force" (the world of the men who in his time are mature) he finds "his problems, his doubts, are very different from those which the mature men felt in their own youth." The ideas of mature men seem false or at least no longer adequate. The men of the younger generation therefore advance their own ideas and attack the ideas of the older generation. In this debate—in which all can take part— the old ideas are examined, ideas themselves are made real, new ideas hammered out. A nation's intellectual life depends on this struggle between generations.

I have discussed briefly the generation of 1917. (Frost and Stevens, considerably older men, belong to an earlier group.) After the 1917 generation a group of this country's poets appeared who might be called the metaphysical generation. Not only were these poets of the twenties and thirties profoundly influenced by the English metaphysical poets, but their basic attitude was detached, doctrinaire, "philosophical." Eberhart's poetry is destroyed, in most poems, by philosophical terms used with fanaticism. Poetry becomes abstract. The poet takes a step back and brings doctrines between himself and his experience. The presence of doctrines, metaphysical or political, marks both the puritan metaphysicals and the left-wing radicals—Eberhart and Tate as well as the *New Masses* poets. The interest in doctrine is all taken from the 1917 poets. Tate, for example, is a disciple of Eliot, a man nearly a decade older.

The next clearly defined generation is that of 1947—the war generation, including Karl Shapiro, Robert Lowell, John Berryman, Delmore Schwartz, Randall Jarrell, and Howard Nemerov. Their convictions about poetry are so impersonal and changeable that it would be truer to say they have no convictions at all. Ortega remarks, "Imagine a person who, when in the country, completely loses his sense of direction. He will take a few steps in one direction, then a few more in another, perhaps the exact opposite." We are reminded of Shapiro, who in his first book has a vicious attack on D. H. Lawrence; this is followed by wholehearted praise of Lawrence; his worship of New Criticism is followed by pointed disgust for it; he pursues the academic style in his own poetry, and then discards it for the Ginsberg style. Both styles are for him equally bankrupt.

The generation of 1947 might very well be called the hysterical generation. Its response to the question of literary style or content is hysterical. In fact, hysteria itself is often a subject matter of these men's poetry, as in Berryman's *Homage to Mistress Bradstreet.* The history of Lowell's style shows the same pattern as Shapiro's. Accepting Tate's ideas, Lowell adopts a fanatically formal verse only to abandon it abruptly for the prose style of *Life Studies.* The sad fact is that he is not really fitted for either of these styles, and his own style remains undiscovered.

The progress of the generations since 1917 might then be described as the progress from the objectivist generation to the metaphysical generation to the hysterical—three clearly marked psychic steps. They are not steps toward irrationality but toward dullness and lack of conviction. They are states that succeed one another in a process of disintegration of personality. After the initial step away from inwardness, and toward the world of things, this country's poets increasingly lose touch with their own inward reality and become less and less sure of themselves. They no longer stand firmly inside their own convictions.

The outstanding characteristic of the generation of 1947 is its reluctance to criticize ideas handed to them. That new generation did not create an idea of its own. Randall Jarrell's criticism is occupied with praise of Marianne Moore and others, without any serious discussions of ideas. If Richard Wilbur has any criticism of the ideas or poetry of men older than himself, he doesn't mention it. Robert Lowell reviewed Yvor Winters's collected poems for *Poetry* and reported that the reason Winters had been left out of so many anthologies was that he is "so original and radical," an "immortal poet." In the *Hudson Review* Lowell later gave a similar blanket endorsement of William Carlos Williams. There is something intellectually shameful about his accepting the standards of both of these men, because their standards are not only different but contradictory. Such acceptance of the ideas of older men by younger men is unnatural as well as unhealthy.

What is the result of this strange lack of intellectual struggle between the generations? Ortega remarks,

> Entire generations falsify themselves to themselves; that is to say, they wrap themselves up in artistic styles, in doctrines, in political movements which are insincere and which fill the lack of genuine convictions. When they get to be about forty years old, these generations become null and void, because at that age one can no longer live in fictions.

v

I have been putting forward general ideas about poetry. Let us see if these ideas hold up when poems are in front of us.

Here is an entire poem by Juan Ramón Jiménez, which has an inner intensity.

> Music—
> Naked woman
> Running mad through the pure night!

And here are lines in which the intensity is all on the surface:

> Would you perhaps consent to be
> The very rack and crucifix of winter, winter's wild
> Knife-edged, continuing and unreleasing,
> Intent and stripping, ice-caressing wind?
>   (Delmore Schwartz, "Will You Perhaps")

This is the opening of a poem by Rafael Alberti, translated by Anthony Kerrigan:

> By the side of the sea and a river in my early days
> I wanted to be a horse.
> The reed shores were made of wind and mares.
> I wanted to be a horse.

And here are lines from a recent American anthology:

The old man accepts a Lucky Strike.
He was a friend of my grandfather.
We talk of the decline of the population
and of codfish and herring
while he waits for a herring boat to come in
          (Elizabeth Bishop, "At the Fishhouses")

In the Bishop poem we can feel the outer world driving in, invading the poem. The facts of the outer world push out the imagination and occupy the poem themselves. The lines become inflexible. The poem becomes heavy and stolid, like a toad that has eaten ball bearings.

Here are lines from *Life Studies:*

Father and Mother moved to Beverly Farms
to be a two-minute walk from the station,
half an hour by train from the Boston doctors.
      (Robert Lowell, "Terminal Days at Beverly Farms")

And from Jarrell:

"In a minute the doctor will find out what is wrong
and cure me," the patients think as they wait.
They are patient as their name, and look childishly
And religiously at the circumstances of their hope,
The nurse, the diplomas, the old magazines.
        (Randall Jarrell, "A Utopian Journey")

In this country's poems the facts are put in because they happened, regardless of how much they lame the poem. *Life Studies* is a very important book on the development of the outward poem, because it shows that the outward poem moves inevitably toward sociology. Here is a poem by Juan Ramón Jiménez, which makes an interesting contrast with the American sociological poem:

I am not I.
           I am this one
Walking beside me whom I do not see,
Whom at times I manage to visit,
And at other times I forget.
The one who remains silent when I talk,
The one who forgives, sweet, when I hate,
The one who takes a walk when I am indoors,
The one who will remain standing when I die.

And one of ours:

whenever he left a job,
he bought a smarter car.
Father's last employer
was Scudder, Stevens, and Clark, Investment Advisors,
himself his only client.
While Mother dragged to bed alone,
read Menninger . . .
          ("Commander Lowell")

This is seriously reviewed as poetry, because U.S. critics demand very little from our poets. And the poets demand very little from themselves.

Apollinaire insisted on the presence of poetry, even in four lines. His poem "Flies":

Our flies know all the tunes
Which they learned from the flies in Norway—
Those giant flies that are
The divinities of the snow.

The poem devoid of any revolutionary feeling, in politics or language, has no choice but to become descriptive prose, sociological prose—or worse, light verse. Often in recent American poetry the poet adopts a genial, joshing tone, indicating that what he is saying doesn't seem to be of any importance, even to him. To point up the difference between real poetry and what passes among us for poetry, let me quote a stanza by the Peruvian poet Vallejo, followed by a stanza in the joshing tone.

The anger that breaks a man down into small boys,
That breaks the small boy down into equal birds,
And the birds, then, into tiny eggs;
The anger of the poor
Owns one smooth oil against two vinegars.

And this is the opening of a poem by Howard Nemerov in *Fifteen Modern American Poets:*

Her laughter was infectious; so, some found,
Her love. Several young men reasonably
Regret inciting her to gratitude
And learning of her ardent facility.

Poetry without inwardness or revolutionary feeling has no choice but to end in a kind of fabricated grossness. Poetry on this level of imagination must become more and more coarse to achieve sensation. Poets like Karl Shapiro are convinced that if they can only make a poem gross or outrageous enough it will be a great poem. A poem, then, becomes defined as something more prosy than prose.

New York, killer of poets, do you remember the day
you passed me through your lower intestine? The troop
train paused under Grand Central. That line of women
in mink coats handed us doughnuts through the smutty
windows. They were all crying. For that I forgave New
York. (We smuggled a postcard off at New Haven.)

In this Shapiro passage the senses are completely dead. In fact, there has been a steady deadening of the senses in our poetry since 1918. There were fewer odors and colors in new poems in 1958 than there were in 1918. The absence of the senses in our poems at times is astonishing.

Here is a medieval Arabic poem called "Storm":

Each flower in the dark air opens its mouth,
Feeling about for the breasts of the abundant rain.
Meanwhile armies of the black-skinned clouds, loaded with water, march by
Majestically, bristling with the golden swords of lightening.

Here are some lines by Stanley Kunitz that are typical of our time:

The compass of the ego is designed
To circumscribe intact a lesser mind
With definition . . .
                    ("Lovers Relentlessly")

Abstraction is merely another form of the flight from inwardness; the objectivist takes flight into the outward world, and the rationalist into the efficient intellect. Rationalists try to convince us that the atrophying of the senses is a good thing,
and they describe it as the development of abstract language in poetry.

In this country intellectual statement about passion is thought to be superior
to passion—or at least equal to it. Yvor Winters urges us to be sure our rational
mind is present when we write a poem:

A poem is good in so far as it makes a defensible rational statement about a
given human experience (the experience need not be real but must in some
sense be possible) and at the same time communicates the emotion which
ought to be motivated by that rational understanding of the experience.
          ("In Defense of Reason")

Passion cannot be trusted unless taken apart and put together again by the reason.
The mind will tell us what we *ought* to feel. Rilke has an entirely different vision
of poetry:

O Lord, give each person his own personal death.
A dying that moves out of the same life he lived.
In which he had love, and intelligence, and trouble.

Here are Winters's lines:

This passion is the scholar's heritage.
The imposition of a busy age.
The passion to condense from book to book
Unbroken wisdom in a single look.

The program is quite mad. If all senses died, all images die, all association with
the unconscious dies, all revolutionary feeling dies, then, it is believed, we are near
poetry. Let me quote as a final contrast a medieval Arabic poem—a true poem—
followed by some lines of Louise Bogan.

Never have I seen or heard of anything like this:
A pearl that changes out of modesty into a red jewel.

Her face is so white that when you look at its beauty,
You see your own face under its clear water.

and Bogan:

I burned my life that I might find
A passion wholly of the mind,
Thought divorced from eye and bone,
Ecstasy come to breath alone.

Under the influence of objectivism and abstraction, not only does our poetry become mediocre but our criticism also. When the senses die, the sense within us that delights in poetry dies also. And it is this sense of delight that tells us whether a given group of words contains genuine poetry or not. A great poet and a great critic are like the mule who can smell fresh water ten miles away. There is a sense that tells us where the water of poetry is, abroad or at home, West or East, even under the earth.

When this sense is dead, critics have to decide whether certain books are poetry by the presence of forms, or of "important statements," or of wit, or even of length. The longer a poem is the more poetry it is thought to contain. The American lines I have quoted are often very bad and I chose them partially with that in mind. Yet in each case they show the direction of the quoted poet's work as a whole. Moreover, the very fact that the poet wrote them, printed them in a book, and allowed them to stand is evidence of the atrophying of the sense of poetry. It is possible that the American lines I have quoted are bad poetry, but another possibility is that they aren't poetry at all.

A human body, just dead, is very like a living body except that it no longer contains something that was invisible anyway. In a poem, as in a human body, what is invisible makes all the difference. The presence of poetry in words is extremely mysterious. As we know from the Japanese experience of the haiku, as well as from the experience of many brief poems in the Western tradition, poetry can be present in fifteen words, or in ten words. Length or meter or rhyme have nothing to do with it. Ungaretti has a poem of four words ("m'illumino / d'immenso") which is unquestionably a poem.

> Everyone stands alone on the midpoint of the earth
> pierced by a ray of sunlight;
> and suddenly it's evening.

This poem of Quasimodo's manages to slip suddenly inward.

A poem is something that penetrates for an instant into the unconscious. If it can penetrate in this way, freshly, several times, then it is a poem of several lines. But if it does not do this it is not a poem at all—no matter how long it is.

The outward poem is like a pine tree made half of tin and half of wood. The poem of things conceives itself to be describing the world correctly because there are pieces of the world in it. This poetry cannot sustain the poet or itself because the imagination has no privacy in which to grow. In the last thirty years in America the intelligence of the poet runs back and forth hurriedly between the world inside his head and the world outside. The imagination meanwhile is thinking in its chamber. The intelligence knocks at the door, demanding some imagination to put between a flat statement and a piece of glass, and rushes out with the gift. Then it hurries back to get a little more imagination to prevent two subway cars from rubbing together. The imagination is continually disturbed, torn away bit by bit, consumed like a bin or corn eaten gradually by mice.

The imagination does not want to hear these constant knockings on the door. It prefers to remain in its chamber, undisturbed, until it can create the poem all of one substance—itself. The imagination out of its own resources creates a poem as strong as the world that it faces. Rilke speaks of "*die Befreiung der dichterischen Figur,*" which may be translated as "the liberation of the poetic image," "the releasing of the image from jail." The poet is thinking of a poem in which the image is released from imprisonment among objects. The domination of the imagination is established over the entire poem. When this happens the poem enters the unconscious naturally.

Our poetry took a wrong turning years ago. Some centuries have a profound spiritual movement: poetry, when vigorous, always is a part of it. We know ours is a century of technical obsession, of business mentality, of human effort dissipated among objects, of expansion, of a destructive motion outward. Yet there is also a movement in the opposite direction that is even more powerful. The best thought in this century moves inward. This movement has been sustained by Freud, by great poetry of Europe and South America, by painting, by the most intelligent men. This is the important movement. The weakness of our poetry is that it does not share in this movement.

Most of our poetry so far has nothing to give us because, like its audience, it drifts aimlessly in the world. A country's poetry can drift outward, like the lives of most of its people, or it can plunge inward, trying for great intensity. Inward poetry deepens all life around it. Other poets have given their countries this gift. If we fail in this, of what use is our life? As Lorca says, life is not a dream.

1963

━━━━●━◄ ROBERT CREELEY ►━●━━━━
(B. 1926)

Robert Creeley was born in Arlington, Massachusetts, but his family soon relocated to a farm in West Acton, where at the age of two Creeley suffered a laceration of his left eye so severe that he lost sight in it three years later. After his father died in 1930, his mother supported the family by resuming her nursing career. Of his New England upbringing, Creeley has said—playfully quoting Longfellow—that "life was real and life was earnest, and one had best get on with it," and he attributes the laconic style of his poetry in part to the New England tradition of pithy speech. He attended high school at a New Hampshire boarding school and then enrolled at Harvard in 1943 but left in 1944 to drive an ambulance in India and Burma for the American Field Service. He returned to Harvard in the fall of 1945 and soon after married Ann McKinnon, with whom he would have three children. Afflicted by the anomie experienced by many men returning from the war, Creeley dropped out of college in the last semester of his senior year, and he and his wife bought a farm in New Hampshire with the help of money from her trust fund.

Unable to sustain the farm, the Creeleys left for France in 1951, but not before he had initiated correspondence with Charles Olson of Black Mountain College in North Carolina. His exchanges with Olson were fruitful, for Olson's influential essay "Projective Verse" was grounded in part on Creeley's declaration that "form is never more than an extension of content." Both men became vocal proponents of "open form," process-oriented free verse that countered what Creeley called the "closed system, . . . poems patterned on exterior and traditionally accepted models."

After the Creeleys relocated to Majorca in 1952, Olson invited Creeley to edit the *Black Mountain Review,* an influential little magazine that featured core poets of the Projectivist group, such as Olson, Robert Duncan, Denise Levertov, and Creeley himself. On his own small printing press, Creeley also began issuing books by Projectivist poets. In 1954, Olson asked him to teach at the alternative college, whose faculty included not only poets, but dancers, musicians, and painters, all seeking alternatives to convention and exploring working methods that centered on motion and process rather than representation. Creeley felt a particular affinity for the

Abstract Expressionist painters there and later admitted that "the attraction the artist had for people like myself . . . was that lovely, uncluttered directness of perception and act we found in so many of them," qualities he sought in his own poetry.

After divorcing Ann McKinnon in 1955, Creeley grew increasingly restless. Early the next year he resigned from Black Mountain and headed for San Francisco where for three months he imbibed Beat poetics from Allen Ginsberg, Gary Snyder, Jack Kerouac, and others. Moving to Albuquerque, New Mexico, he began teaching at a boys' school, his credentials boosted by Olson's gift of a B.A. from Black Mountain. In January 1957, he met Bobbie Louise Hall and married her within two weeks.

With the security provided by his new marriage and job, and the insights into emotional expansiveness that he gained from his sojourn with the Beats, Creeley achieved a new level of intimacy and directness in his poetry. In 1960, he won the Levinson Prize for ten poems published in *Poetry*, and his work was included in Donald Allen's *The New American Poetry: 1945–1960*, a book that introduced the alternative poets of the 1950s to a wide audience. In 1962, Scribners released *For Love*, which included selections from the myriad small press books that Creeley had published in the 1950s. Nominated for the National Book Award and selling over 47,000 copies, *For Love*, with its blend of halting self-examination, restless isolation, and qualified articulations of love, appealed to a generation wrestling with similar misgivings during the sexual revolution.

Finishing an M.A. at the University of New Mexico in 1960, Creeley began an academic career, holding visiting posts at many universities but keeping permanent ties with the State University of New York at Buffalo, where he began teaching in 1966. In 1976 he divorced Bobbie and in 1977 married Penelope Highton, whom he met on a reading tour of New Zealand. Since the 1960s his reputation has been solidified by the many reading tours he has embarked upon and the prizes he has garnered, including two Guggenheim Fellowships, the Shelley Memorial Award (1981), the Poetry Society of America's Frost Medal (1987), and election to the National Academy of Arts and Letters.

In keeping with his emphasis on process and improvisation, Creeley has generated a constant stream of writing throughout his career, producing not only poems, but stories, novels, an autobiography, essays on poetry, and a voluminous correspondence. Like William Carlos Williams, Creeley sees writing as a means of discovery. Taking Williams's work as his model, Creeley aims to create tension through balancing terse lines against often heavily qualified sentences to create the illusion of immediacy. Creeley's poems tend to include spontaneous revisions and consider whether writing aids or inhibits communication with others or even understanding of one's self. For Creeley, love never involves escape from the self but the opportunity for the self to confirm its subjective existence.

After *For Love*, his books became increasingly experimental; *Words* (1967) and *Pieces* (1968) fragmented language and challenged its sufficiency. Although they were faulted by many reviewers for a lack of coherence, *Words* and *Pieces* have been hailed by other critics as harbingers of

Language Poetry. Nevertheless, since the late 1970s Creeley has returned to exploring the boundaries of the self and varied registers of feeling. He emphasizes in the introduction to his *Selected Poems* (1991) that the materials of poetry are "constant, simple, elusive, specific." Poetry, he adds, "costs so little and so much. It preoccupies a life, yet can only find one in living. It is a music, a playful construct of feeling, a last word and communion."

TO DEFINE

The process of definition is the intent of the poem, or is to that sense—"Peace comes of communication." Poetry stands in no need of any sympathy, or even goodwill. One acts from bottom, the root is the purpose quite beyond any kindness.

A poetry can act on this: "A poem is energy transferred from where the poet got it (he will have some several causations), by way of the poem itself to, all the way over to, the reader." One breaks the line of aesthetics, or that outcrop of a general division of knowledge. A sense of the KINETIC impells recognition of force. Force is, and therefore stays.

The means of poetry are, perhaps, related to Pound's sense of the *increment of association;* usage coheres value. Tradition is an aspect of what anyone is now thinking—not what someone once thought. We make with what we have, and in this way anything is worth looking at. A tradition becomes inept when it blocks the necessary conclusion; it says we have felt nothing, it implies others have felt more.

A poetry denies its end in any *descriptive* act, I mean any act which leaves the attention outside the poem. Our anger cannot exist usefully without its objects, but a description of them is also a perpetuation. There is that confusion—one wants the thing to act on, and yet hates it. *Description* does nothing, it includes the object—it neither hates nor loves.

If one can junk these things, of the content which relates only to denial, the negative, the impact of dissolution—act otherwise, on other things. There is no country. Speech is an assertion of one man, by one man. "Therefore each speech having its own character the poetry it engenders will be peculiar to that speech also in its own intrinsic form."

1953

POEMS ARE A COMPLEX

Poems are a complex, and exist by virtue of many things. First, they are a structure of sounds and rhythms which cohere to inform the reader (whether he listen aloud

"To Define" first published in *Nine American Poets* (Liverpool, United Kingdom: Heron Press, 1953). Collected in Creeley's *Was That a Real Poem and Other Essays,* ed. Donald Allen (Bolinas, California: Four Seasons Foundation, 1979) 72–75.

"Poems Are a Complex" first published as "A Note," *A Nosegay in Black* 1.1 (Autumn 1966). Collected in Creeley's *Was That a Real Poem and Other Essays,* ed. Donald Allen (Bolinas, California: Four Seasons Foundation, 1979) 76–77.

or in silence) with a recognition of their order. In this respect, I much agree with Louis Zukofsky's note of his own poetics, which, as he says, comprise a function having as lower limit speech, and upper limit music. Pound's note, that "Prosody is the articulation of the total sound of a poem," has equal relevance.

Since words are the material, and words have meanings in other senses, that fact also has pertinence. But I do not feel that *thing* in the language we call a poem has to do with a literal issue of semantic meaning. Yet that aspect of meaning is a material also, and clearly enters into the issue of image, or statement—or all such effects of something said.

I think for myself the primary term is that words can move in the measure of song, although I do not wish to confuse poetry with music. But in a poem I tend to hear whatever can be called its melody long before I have reached an understanding of all that it might mean.

Finally, I use several measures though never with much literal consciousness. Two further statements of Pound's long ago attracted me: "Only emotion endures . . ." and "Nothing counts save the quality of the emotion. . . ." I have used that sense with respect to all instances of writing, but I would feel, as he, that poetry is that one most fully charged with meaning. To that I would now add a recent emphasis of Olson's: "That which exists through itself is what is called meaning."

In other words, poems are not referential, or at least not importantly so. They have "meaning" in that they do "exist through themselves." I have no very clear sense of where they may come from, but I have felt them most evident when least assumed. Lorca's "Theory and Function of the *Duende*" is interesting to me, although I would not so simply discredit either the Angel or the Muse to gain the "dark sounds" only. But I do feel poems to involve an occasion to which a man pays obedience, and which intentions alone never yield.

There are many ways indeed to say any of this, and I can't feel any one to be sufficient. I think I first felt a poem to be what might exist in words as primarily the fact of its own activity. Later, of course, I did see that poems might comment on many things, and reveal many attitudes and qualifications. Still, it was never what they said *about* things that interested me. I wanted the poem itself to exist and that could never be possible as long as some subject significantly elsewhere was involved. There had to be an independence derived from the very fact that words are *things* too. Poems gave me access to this fact more than any other possibility in language.

1966

FRANK O'HARA
(1926–1966)

Frank O'Hara was so attached to the variety and hectic pace of New York City life that he once claimed, "I can't even enjoy a blade of grass, unless I know there's a subway handy, or a record store or some other sign that people do not totally *regret* life." Yet this exuberantly urban poet grew up in rural Grafton, in central Massachusetts, where his father oversaw three farms and a dealership for farm machinery. Art became the young O'Hara's refuge. In "Autobiographical Fragments," O'Hara recalls that "I was sent against my will to Catholic schools, but fortunately I also began at the age of seven to study music. A lot of my aversions to Catholicism dumped themselves into my musical enthusiasms." Although he still hoped to pursue a career as a concert pianist, O'Hara joined the Navy immediately after his 1944 graduation from St. John's High School in Worcester. During the next two years, he worked as a shore patrolman in San Francisco, where he kept up his studies in piano and attended symphony concerts, and served on the destroyer USS *Nicholas*, which was stationed in the South Pacific. In the long months at sea, the young O'Hara turned to literature and music for solace, and he began to write poetry.

After his military service ended in 1946, O'Hara enrolled at Harvard University where he initially majored in music but soon changed to English. He read French and German poetry as well and published poems and stories in the *Harvard Advocate*. Although John Ashbery, whose work is often linked to O'Hara's, also attended Harvard at the same time, the two poets did not meet until their senior year, when at a party Ashbery overheard O'Hara rank the twentieth-century French composer Francis Poulenc's eighteen-minute cantata, *Les Sécheresses*, over Richard Wagner's four-hour opera, *Tristan und Isolde*. In a 1978 essay paying tribute to O'Hara, Ashbery remarked that "Frank didn't really believe that *Les Sécheresses* was greater than *Tristan* . . . but at the same time he felt . . . that art is already serious enough; there is no point in making it seem even more serious by taking it too seriously."

After graduation from Harvard in 1950, O'Hara spent a year at the University of Michigan, where he earned a master's in comparative literature, winning in spring 1951 a university-sponsored Hopwood Award for a manuscript of poems and a play. In 1951 he settled permanently in New York City. Until his premature death fifteen years later, he thrived on the city's energy and liberality, for in New York he was free to live an openly homosexual life and to become part of the avant garde art scene. Both the rhythms of city life and the details of his social life became subjects of his poems. O'Hara was gregarious and maintained an extensive network of friendships, especially with painters. He made his living as an editorial assistant for *ArtNews*, to which he contributed reviews, and later at the Museum of Modern Art, where he began in 1951 by selling tickets and postcards at the information desk, rising to the rank of curator by 1960. His friendships with painters gave him an understanding of new trends in art. This knowledge, combined with his energy and enthusiasm, led to his achievements as a curator, for he helped organize traveling exhibitions that introduced Abstract Expressionism to Europe.

As a poet, O'Hara achieved fluency, generosity, and expansiveness through a lack of premeditation that is the result of knowledge and constant practice, rather than mere accident. O'Hara wanted to embrace all dimensions of experience in his poetry, whether momentous or banal. He included allusions to high culture alongside references to popular culture, particularly movies and advertising. Although his poems often chronicled his feelings and experiences, O'Hara is not considered a "confessional poet," for rather than focus on "the self" as his main subject, he gave equal value to the self and to the world and imbued his work with wry humor. His humility led not only to his habit of writing quickly, but to a casual attitude toward publication. Ashbery recalls, "Dashing the poems off at odd moments—in his office at the Museum of Modern Art, in the street at lunchtime or even in a room full of people—he would then put them away in drawers and cartons and half forget them."

For O'Hara, the process of writing mattered more than the pursuit of literary fame. His poems often appeared in limited editions that were sometimes printed by art galleries and included artwork by his friends. Only two short collections of poems, *Second Avenue* (1960) and *Lunch Poems* (1964), received wide distribution during his lifetime. After his sudden death in 1966 from injuries sustained when he was hit by a dune buggy on Fire Island, his friends began gathering his poems. *The Collected Poems of Frank O'Hara* appeared in 1971, and was followed by additional volumes of poetry, plays, and art criticism, most notably *Art Chronicles: 1954–1966* (1975). Today, O'Hara remains one of the most influential mid-twentieth-century poets. His work is much imitated, especially by young poets, but his idiosyncratic combination of attentive spontaneity, disjunctive wit, and openness to all levels of experience is seldom matched.

Inspired by a lunchtime conversation with LeRoi Jones (Amiri Baraka) on August 27, 1959, in which the two jokingly decided to dream up a movement, O'Hara wrote "Personism" very quickly one week later as a contribution to Donald Allen's *The New American Poetry*. Like much of O'Hara's poetry, "Personism" walks the line between mockery and seriousness, for he satirizes the ubiquitousness of poetry movements, and the need felt by mid-century poets to create and promote them, yet also reveals a great deal about his own attitude toward writing.

PERSONISM: A MANIFESTO

Everything is in the poems, but at the risk of sounding like the poor wealthy man's Allen Ginsberg I will write to you because I just heard that one of my fellow poets thinks that a poem of mine that can't be got at one reading is because I was confused too. Now, come on. I don't believe in god, so I don't have to make elaborately sounded structures. I hate Vachel Lindsay, always have, I don't even like rhythm, assonance, all that stuff. You just go on your nerve. If someone's chasing you down the street with a knife you just run, you don't turn around and shout, "Give it up! I was a track star for Mineola Prep."

That's for the writing poems part. As for their reception, suppose you're in love and someone's mistreating (*mal aimé*) you, you don't say, "Hey, you can't hurt me this way, I *care!*" you just let all the different bodies fall where they may, and they always do may after a few months. But that's not why you fell in love in the first place, just to hang onto life, so you have to take your chances and try to avoid being logical. Pain always produces logic, which is very bad for you.

I'm not saying that I don't have practically the most lofty ideas of anyone writing today, but what difference does that make? they're just ideas. The only good thing about it is that when I get lofty enough I've stopped thinking and that's when refreshment arrives.

But how can you really care if anybody gets it, or gets what it means, or if it improves them. Improves them for what? for death? Why hurry them along? Too many poets act like a middle-aged mother trying to get her kids to eat too much cooked meat, and potatoes with drippings (tears). I don't give a damn whether they eat or not. Forced feeding leads to excessive thinness (effete). Nobody should experience anything they don't need to, if they don't need poetry bully for them, I like the movies too. And after all, only Whitman and Crane and Williams, of the American poets, are better than the movies. As for measure and other technical apparatus, that's just common sense: if you're going to buy a pair of pants you want them to be tight enough so everyone will want to go to bed with you. There's nothing metaphysical about it. Unless, of course, you flatter yourself into thinking that what you're experiencing is "yearning."

Abstraction in poetry, which Allen recently commented on in *It is,* is intriguing. I think it appears mostly in the minute particulars where decision is necessary. Abstraction (in poetry, not in painting) involves personal removal by the poet. For instance, the decision involved in the choice between "the nostalgia of the infinite" and "the nostalgia *for* the infinite" defines an attitude towards degree of abstraction. The nostalgia *of* the infinite representing the greater degree of abstraction, removal, and negative capability (as in Keats and Mallarmé). Personism, a movement which I recently founded and which nobody yet knows about, interests me a great deal, being so totally opposed to this kind of abstract removal that it is verging on a true abstraction for the first time, really, in the history of poetry. Personism is to Wallace Stevens what *la poésie pure* was to Béranger. Personism has nothing to do

Originally written as a letter to Donald Allen dated September 3, 1959. First published in *The New American Poetry: 1945–1960,* ed. Donald Allen (New York, Grove Press, 1960).

with philosophy, it's all art. It does not have to do with personality or intimacy, far from it! But to give you a vague idea, one of its minimal aspects is to address itself to one person (other than the poet himself), thus evoking overtones of love without destroying love's life-giving vulgarity, and sustaining the poet's feelings towards the poem while preventing love from distracting him into feeling about the person. That's part of personism. It was founded by me after lunch with LeRoi Jones on August 27, 1959, a day in which I was in love with someone (not Roi, by the way, a blond). I went back to work and wrote a poem for this person. While I was writing it I was realizing that if I wanted to I could use the telephone instead of writing the poem, and so Personism was born. It's a very exciting movement which will undoubtedly have lots of adherents. It puts the poem squarely between the poet and the person, Lucky Pierre style, and the poem is correspondingly gratified. The poem is at last between two persons instead of two pages. In all modesty, I confess that it may be the death of literature as we know it. While I have certain regrets, I am still glad I got there before Alain Robbe-Grillet did. Poetry being quicker and surer than prose, it is only just that poetry finish literature off. For a time people thought that Artaud was going to accomplish this, but actually, for all its magnificence, his polemical writings are not more outside literature than Bear Mountain is outside New York State. His relation is no more astounding than Dubuffet's to painting.

What can we expect of Personism? (This is getting good, isn't it?) Everything, but we won't get it. It is too new, too vital a movement to promise anything. But it, like Africa, is on the way. The recent propagandists for technique on the one hand, and for content on the other, had better watch out.

1959

JOHN ASHBERY
(B. 1927)

Born in Rochester, New York, John Ashbery grew up in Sodus, a small town in upstate New York on the shores of Lake Ontario. While his father was a fruit farmer and his mother a former high school biology teacher, both fostered Ashbery's interest in painting and literature, as did his maternal grandfather, a professor of physics at the University of Rochester. When Ashbery was thirteen, his younger brother died of leukemia. After Ashbery graduated from Deerfield Academy in 1945, he entered Harvard University, where he majored in English and wrote an honors thesis on W. H. Auden, whose urbane wit deeply influenced his own poetry.

After graduation in 1949, Ashbery moved to New York City, to pursue a master's degree in literature at Columbia University, which he received in 1951. Along with his Harvard friends, the poets Kenneth Koch and Frank O'Hara, he kept company with painters, and the world of avant garde art inspired him to take new risks in his poetry. In an essay on the work of his friend, the painter Jane Frielicher, he recalls:

> I hadn't realized it, but my arrival in New York coincided with the cresting of the "heroic" period of Abstract Expressionism, as it was later to be known, and somehow we all seemed to benefit from this strong movement even if we paid little attention to it and seemed to be going our separate ways.

Interested in capturing in words the energetic disjunctions and emphasis on artistic process that he witnessed in nonrepresentational painting, as well as in the music, and theater scenes of mid-century Manhattan, Ashbery became increasingly experimental in his poetry. In the same essay, he notes that, in response to a 1950 exhibit of the Lithuanian painter, Chaim Soutine, he, like many of the Abstract Expressionist painters, saw Soutine's work as "full of possibilities. . . . The fact that the sky could come crashing joyously into the grass, that trees could dance upside down and houses roll over like cats eager to have their tummies scratched was something I hadn't realized before, and I began pushing my poems around and standing words on end."

The "possibilities" that he absorbed from his immersion in the art world and from modern poets such as Auden, Wallace Stevens, Marianne Moore, and Gertrude Stein nurtured his imagination. In 1955, Ashbery submitted the manuscript of his first book to the prestigious Yale Series of Younger Poets contest, only to have it rejected in the initial screening process. But W. H. Auden, who was then judge of the series, disliked the work of the twelve finalists. Against the advice of the press personnel, Auden asked two young poets he knew whose work had been rejected—Ashbery and Frank O'Hara—to resubmit their manuscripts. A few days later he chose Ashbery's book as the winner. For the collection, retitled *Some Trees* (1956), Auden wrote a foreword praising Ashbery's linguistic virtuosity and elegant lyrics, but warned the young poet against his tendencies toward surrealism.

Although Ashbery was influenced by surrealist writers and painters, and in his next book, *The Tennis Court Oath* (1962), his poems grew increasingly experimental, he was never a disciple of surrealism. He came to believe, as he argues in an essay on the poet David Schubert, that "surrealism, in abandoning itself to the unconscious, can never accurately reflect experience in which both the conscious and the unconscious play a role." Instead, in his poetry Ashbery tries to chart the interplay between the unconscious and conscious minds to show how the mind, in the process of thinking, responds both to its own fluctuations and to the often random occurrences of everyday life. "My poetry is disjunct," he remarked in an interview, "but then so is life."

Aware that disjunction alone can easily descend into mannerism, throughout his career Ashbery sought new forms in which to explore the patterns of consciousness. Thus, in many of the seventeen new books of poetry that followed *Some Trees,* Ashbery tries out different forms. In *The Tennis Court Oath,* for example, he includes a long collage poem, "Europe," intercut with quotations from *Beryl of the Bi-plane,* a 1917 British detective novel. *Three Poems* (1972) consists entirely of prose poems. Written on two sides of a notebook, the sixty-page poem "Litany," from *As We Know* (1979), appears in two columns, which Ashbery describes as "simultaneous but independent monologues." But his books, regardless of their forms, all explore the poetic process, extending almost to their limits the Modernist practice of writing poems about poetry and the shifts of perspective that he adapted from his study of experimental poets and painters.

His engagement with the fine arts, in fact, has continued to nourish his poetry over the years. From 1959 to 1957 he lived in France, as a Fulbright scholar. After spending a year at New York University pursuing graduate studies in French, he returned to France to research his dissertation on Raymond Roussel, whose elusive writing Ashbery later described as being full of puzzles and word games that "continually frustrate and sidetrack the reader." He remained in France for the next eight years, earning his living by writing art criticism for the European edition of the *New York Herald Tribune* and contributing articles on European exhibitions to *ARTnews* and *Art International.* After the death of his father in 1965, he returned to the United States and became the executive editor of *ARTnews.* Even after he began teaching in the creative writing program at Brooklyn College in 1972, he continued to contribute art criticism to various magazines, including *New York* and *Newsweek.*

After Ashbery won the Pulitzer Prize, the National Book Award, and the National Book Critics Circle Award in 1976 for *Self Portrait in a Convex Mirror* (1975), critics have acknowledged him as one of the most important and influential poets writing in the United States, and he has continued to receive other important awards, including the Bollingen Prize (1985) and a MacArthur Fellowship (1985–1990). Whether in book-length poems or short lyrics, Ashbery's poetry depends on techniques that make it both difficult and strangely compelling. The poems often contain abrupt shifts of tense, pronouns, and levels of diction, so that within the space of a few lines Ashbery will coast from gorgeous, "poetic" language and allusions to high culture into slang, clichés, and references to popular culture, such as movies and cartoons. In a 1993 interview he claims that, "My idea is to democratize all forms of expression, an idea which comes to me from afar, perhaps from Whitman's *Democratic Vistas*—the idea that both the most demotic and the most elegant forms of expression deserve equally to be taken into account. It seems to me that there is something of this in post-modernism." Ashbery's dislocated grammar and syntax, his shifting allusions, and his habit of addressing an unspecified "you" have angered some critics of his work while inspiring legions of younger poets to imitate him. All of these techniques create a poetry that is open to interpretation from multiple perspectives. Although Ashbery did not make his homosexuality an overt theme, as Frank O'Hara did, some of his poetry can be interpreted as homoerotic. Over-all, his techniques draw attention to the process of writing and create poems that seem always on the verge of disclosing a meaning, but that also seem to withhold and frustrate meaning.

When asked to explain his poems, Ashbery usually demurs. In the introduction to *Other Traditions* (2000), his book of essays based on his series of Charles Eliot Norton lectures at Harvard, he admits that:

> Unfortunately, I'm not very good at "explaining" my work. I once tried to do this in a question-and-answer period with some students of my friend [the poet] Richard Howard, after which he told me: "They want the key to your poetry, but you presented them with a new set of locks." That sums up for me my feelings on the subject of "unlocking" my poetry. I am unable to do so because I feel that my poetry is the explanation. The explanation of what? Of my thought, whatever that is.

In 1989 his best pieces of art criticism were collected in *Reported Sightings: Art Chronicles 1957–1987*. Lucid and wide-ranging, his essays on art reveal much about his attitudes toward poetry, for even while detailing the accomplishments of individual artists and weighing the strengths and weakness of various nineteenth- and twentieth-century movements in art, Ashbery meditates on factors common to both painting and poetry, as in his important essay "The Invisible Avant-Garde," originally a lecture given at the Yale Art School in 1968.

THE INVISIBLE AVANT-GARDE

The fact that I, a poet, was invited by the Yale Art School to talk about the avant-garde, in one of a series of lectures under this general heading, is in itself such an eloquent characterization of the avant-garde today that no further comment seems necessary. It would appear then that this force in art which would be the very antithesis of tradition if it were to allow itself even so much of a relationship with tradition as an antithesis implies, is, on the contrary, a tradition of sorts. At any rate it can be discussed, attacked, praised, taught in seminars, just as a tradition can be. There may be a fine distinction to be made between "a" tradition and "the" tradition, but the point is that there is no longer any doubt in anyone's mind that the vanguard *is*—it's there, before you, solid, tangible, "alive and well," as the buttons say.

Things were very different twenty years ago when I was a student and was beginning to experiment with poetry. At that time it was the art and literature of the Establishment that were traditional. There was in fact almost no experimental poetry being written in this country, unless you counted the rather pale attempts of a handful of poets who were trying to imitate some of the effects of the French Surrealists. The situation was a little different in the other arts. Painters like Jackson Pollock had not yet been discovered by the mass magazines—this was to come a little later, though in fact *Life* did in 1949 print an article on Pollock, showing some of his large drip paintings and satirically asking whether he was the greatest living painter in America. This was still a long way from the decorous enthusiasm with which *Time* and *Life* today greet every new kink. But the situation was a bit better for the painters then, since there were a lot of them doing very important work and this fact was known to themselves and a few critics. Poetry could boast of no such good luck. As for music, the situation also was bleak but at least there *was* experimental music and a few people knew about it. It is hard to believe, however, that as late as 1945 such an acceptably experimental and posthumously successful composer as Bartók could die in total poverty, and that until a very few years ago such a respectable composer as Schönberg was considered a madman. I remember that in the spring of 1949 there was a symposium on the arts at Harvard during which a number of new works were performed including Schönberg's Trio for Strings. My friend the poet Frank O'Hara, who was majoring in music at Harvard, went to hear it and was violently attacked for doing so by one of the young instructors in the music department, who maintained that Schönberg was literally insane. Today the same instructor would no doubt attack O'Hara for going to hear anything so academic. To paraphrase Bernard Shaw, it is the fate of some artists, and perhaps the best ones, to pass from unacceptability to acceptance without an intervening period of appreciation.

At that time I found the avant-garde very exciting, just as the young do today, but the difference was that in 1950 there was no sure proof of the existence of the avant-garde. To experiment was to have the feeling that one was poised on some

Originally delivered as a lecture at Yale Art School, May 1968, and published in *ARTnews Annual* in the same year. Collected in *Reported Sightings: Art Chronicles 1957–1987* (New York: Knopf, 1989) 389–394.

outermost brink. In other words if one wanted to depart, even moderately, from the norm, one was taking one's life—one's life as an artist—into one's hands. A painter like Pollock for instance was gambling everything on the fact that he *was* the greatest painter in America, for if he wasn't, he was nothing, and the drips would turn out to be random splashes from the brush of a careless housepainter. It must often have occurred to Pollock that there was just a possibility that he wasn't an artist at all, that he had spent his life "toiling up the wrong road to art" as Flaubert said of Zola. But this very real possibility is paradoxically just what makes the tremendous excitement in his work. It is a gamble against terrific odds. Most reckless things are beautiful in some way, and recklessness is what makes experimental art beautiful, just as religions are beautiful because of the strong possibility that they are founded on nothing. We would all believe in God if we knew He existed, but would this be much fun?

The doubt element in Pollock—and I am using him as a convenient symbol for the avant-garde artist of the previous school—is what keeps his work alive for us. Even though he has been accepted now by practically everybody from *Life* on down, or on up, his work remains unresolved. It has not congealed into masterpieces. In spite of public acceptance the doubt is there—maybe the acceptance is there because of the doubt, the vulnerability which makes it possible to love the work.

It might be argued that traditional art is even riskier than experimental art; that it can offer no very real assurances to its acolytes, and since traditions are always going out of fashion it is more dangerous and therefore more worthwhile than experimental art. This could be true, and in fact certain great artists of our time have felt it necessary to renounce the experiments of their youth just in order to save them. The poet Ron Padgett has pointed out that the catalogue of the recent Museum of Modern Art exhibition of Dada and Surrealism praises Picabia's early work but ruefully assumes that with his later work he had "passed out of serious consideration as a painter." Padgett goes on to say:

> A parallel example is provided by de Chirico, who many feel betrayed his own best interests as a painter. Possibly so. But in Picabia's case, the curiosity that compelled him to go on to become a less "attractive" painter is the same that carried his adventure into Dada in the first place, and it is this spirit, as much as the paintings themselves, which is significant.

I think one could expand this argument to cover de Chirico and Duchamp as well. The former passed from being one of the greatest painters of this century to a crotchety fabricator of bad pictures who refuses to hear any good said of his early period, but he did so with such a vengeance that his act almost becomes exemplary. And Duchamp's silence *is* exemplary without question for a whole generation of young artists.

Therefore it is a question of distinguishing bad traditional art and bad avant-garde art from good traditional art and good avant-garde art. But after one has done this, one still has a problem with good traditional art. One can assume that good avant-garde art will go on living because the mere fact of its having been able to struggle into life at all will keep it alive. The doubt remains. But good traditional art may disappear at any moment when the tradition founders. It is a perilous business. I would class de Chirico's late paintings as good traditional art, though as bad art, because they embrace a tradition which everything in the artist's career seemed to point away from, and which he therefore accepted because, no doubt, he felt as an avant-garde artist that only the unacceptable is acceptable. On the other hand a painter like Thomas Hart Benton, who was Pollock's teacher, was at his best a better painter than de Chirico is now, but is a worse artist because he accepted the acceptable. *Life* used to have an article on Benton almost every month, showing his murals for some new post office or library. The fact that *Life* switched its affections from Benton to Pollock does not make either of them any worse, but it does illustrate that Benton's is the kind of art that cannot go on living without acceptance, while Pollock's is of the kind which cannot be destroyed by acceptance, since it is basically unacceptable.

What has happened since Pollock? The usual explanation is that "media" have multiplied to such an extent that it is no longer possible for secrets to remain secret very long, and that this has had the effect of turning the avant-garde from a small contingent of foolhardy warriors into a vast and well-equipped regiment. In fact the avant-garde has absorbed most of the army, or vice versa—in any case the result is that the avant-garde can now barely exist because of the immense amounts of attention and money that are focused on it, and that the only artists who have any privacy are the handful of decrepit stragglers behind the big booming avant-garde juggernaut. This does seem to be what has happened. I was amazed the other night while watching the news on television when the announcer took up a new book by the young experimental poet Aram Saroyan and read it aloud to the audience from beginning to end. It is true that this took only a couple of minutes and that it was done for purposes of a put-down—nevertheless we know that the way of the mass media is to pass from put-down to panegyric without going through a transitional phase of straight reportage, and it may be only a matter of weeks before Aram Saroyan has joined Andy Warhol and Viva and the rest of the avant-garde on *The Tonight Show*.

Looking back only as far as the beginning of this century we see that the period of neglect for an avant-garde artist has shrunk for each generation. Picasso was painting mature masterpieces for at least ten years before he became known even to a handful of collectors. Pollock's incubation period was a little shorter. But since then the period has grown shorter each year so that it now seems to be something like a minute. It is no longer possible, or it seems no longer possible, for an important avant-garde artist to go unrecognized. And, sadly enough, his creative life expectancy has dwindled correspondingly, since artists are no fun once they have been discovered. Dylan Thomas summed it up when he wrote that he had once been happy and unknown and that he was now miserable and acclaimed.

I am not convinced that it is "media" that are responsible for all this—there have always been mediums of one sort or another and they have taken up the cause of the avant-garde only recently. I am at a loss to say what it is, unless that it is that events during the first decades of this century eventually ended up proving that the avant-garde artist is a kind of hero, and that a hero is, of course, what everybody wants to be. We all have to be first, and it is now certain—as it was not, I think, before—that the experimenting artist does something first, even though it may be discarded later on. So that, paradoxically, it is safest to experiment. Only a few artists like de Chirico have realized the fallacy of this argument, and since his course was to reject his own genius and produce execrable art it is unlikely that many artists will follow him.

What then must the avant-garde artist do to remain avant-garde? For it has by now become a question of survival both of the artist and of the individual. In both art and life today we are in danger of substituting one conformity for another, or, to use a French expression, of trading one's one-eyed horse for a blind one. Protests against the mediocre values of our society such as the hippie movement seem to imply that one's only way out is to join a parallel society whose stereotyped manners, language, speech and dress are only reverse images of the one it is trying to reject. We feel in America that we have to join something, that our lives are directionless unless we are part of a group, a clan—an idea very different from the European one, where even friendships are considered not very important and life centers around oneself and one's partner, an extension of oneself. Is there nothing then between the extremes of Levittown and Haight-Ashbury, between an avant-garde which has become a tradition and a tradition which is no longer one? In other words, has tradition finally managed to absorb the individual talent?

On the other hand, perhaps these are the most exciting times for young artists, who must fight even harder to preserve their identity. Before they were fighting against general neglect, even hostility, but this seemed like a natural thing and therefore the fight could be carried on in good faith. Today one must fight acceptance which is much harder because it seems that one is fighting oneself.

If people like what I do, am I to assume that what I do is bad, since public opinion has always begun by rejecting what is original and new?

Perhaps the answer is not to reject what one has done, nor to be forced into a retrograde position, but merely to take into account that if one's work automatically finds acceptance, there may be a possibility that it could be improved. The Midas-like position into which our present acceptance-world forces the avant-garde is actually a disguised blessing which previous artists have not been able to enjoy, because it points the way out of the predicament it sets up—that is, toward an attitude which neither accepts nor rejects acceptance but is independent of it. Previously, vanguard artists never had to face the problems of integration into the art of their time because this usually happened at the end of a long career when the direction their art would take had long been fixed. When it took place earlier it could be dealt with by an explosion of bad temper, as in the possibly apocryphal story about Schönberg: when someone finally learned to play his violin concerto he stormed out of the concert hall, vowing to write another one that *nobody* would be able to play.

Today the avant-garde has come full circle—the artist who wants to experiment is again faced with what seems like a dead end, except that instead of creating in a vacuum he is now at the center of a cheering mob. Neither climate is exactly ideal for discovery, yet both are conducive to it because they force him to take steps that he hadn't envisaged. And today's young artist has the additional advantage of a fuller awareness of the hazards that lie in wait for him. He must now bear in mind that *he,* not *it,* is the avant-garde.

A few remarks by Busoni in his book *The Essence of Music* seem to apply to all the arts and also to the situation of the experimental artist today. Busoni's music has the unique quality of being excellent and of sounding like nobody else's: it has not even been successfully imitated. The essays that make up the book were written about the time of World War I when a crisis had developed in German music, involving on the one hand Expressionists like Schönberg, of whom he disapproved, and of conservative Neoclassicists like Reger, of whom he equally disapproved—a crisis which, without going into details, rather parallels that in the arts today. Somehow Busoni alone managed to avoid these extremes by taking what was valid in each and forging a totality.

He wrote:

I am a worshipper of Form—I have remained sufficiently a Latin for that. But I demand—no! the organism of art demands—that every idea fashion its own form for itself; the organism—not I—revolts against having one single form for all ideas; today especially and how much more in the coming centuries.

The creator really only strives for perfection. And as he brings this into harmony with his individuality a new law arises unintentionally.

The "new" is included in the idea of "Creation"—for in that way creation is distinguished from imitation.

One follows a great example most faithfully if one does not follow it, for it was through turning away from its predecessor that the example became great.

And finally, in an article addressed to his pupils he wrote, "Build up! But do not content yourself any longer with self-complacent experiments and the glory of the success of the season: but turn toward the perfection of the work seriously and joyfully. Only he who looks toward the future looks cheerfully."

1968

W. S. MERWIN
(B. 1927)

Author of more than fifty books of poetry and translations, W. S. Merwin
is one of the most prolific poets of his generation. Given the multiple forms in
which his poems have been written, he is also one of the most protean and
difficult poets to pin down. Three primary obsessions in his work are translation, narrative, and, as subject matter, the environment, or the place of
the human in the natural setting. What links these matters is a mind aware
of lost or neglected connections and a belief that nothing exists entirely
in isolation.

He was born William Stanley Merwin, the son of a Presbyterian minister in New York City, and grew up in New Jersey and Pennsylvania. "I
started writing hymns for my father almost as soon as I could write at all,
illustrating them. But the first writers that held me were not the poets:
Conrad first, and then Tolstoy, and it was not until I had received a scholarship and gone away to the university that I began to read poetry steadily and
try incessantly, and with abiding desperation, to write it." He was a precocious if unruly student and took his B.A. from Princeton at the age of twenty,
followed by an additional year of graduate study in modern languages.
R. P. Blackmur and John Berryman were two particularly important teachers
for him at Princeton. While a student, Merwin also corresponded with Ezra
Pound, who was in St. Elizabeth's hospital in Washington, D.C. During
an Easter recess, the young poet traveled to Washington and visited Pound
"a couple of times." It was Pound who advised Merwin to read the seeds,
not the twigs, of poetry.

Pound's twin examples of erudition and independence were models for
Merwin's subsequent career. Unlike so many postwar American poets, he
never had an academic career, despite sporadic teaching, but instead made a
living by translating, by writing for the BBC in the fifties, and by giving
readings and workshops in many different places. He has had a colorful life.
Living in France and Portugal in 1949, he worked as a tutor; the following
year he tutored Robert Graves's son in Majorca. From 1951 to 1954 he
lived in London, and he has often been to France, having bought a house
there with a small family inheritance. He has also spent time living in

Boston and New York; but since the late seventies, Merwin has made his home in Hawaii. One is tempted to see in his life a movement from West to East, Europe to Hawaii, and also notice a movement from West to East in the works he has chosen to translate over his long career. Important early translations include *The Poem of the Cid* (1959), *Spanish Ballads* (1961), and *The Song of Roland* (1963), while more recently he published *East Window: The Asian Translations* (1998). Between these collections there were translations of Pablo Neruda, Jean Follain, Osip Mandelstam, and many other writers.

Merwin's own poetic career got off to a strong start when W. H. Auden selected his first book, *A Mask for Janus* (1952), for the Yale Series of Younger Poets. The book showed a traditional formality common to poets of the time. It was followed by *The Dancing Bears* (1954), *Green with Beasts* (1956), and *The Drunk in the Furnace* (1960), which many regard as the best of his early collections. Merwin's grounding in medieval poetry and ancient mythology was clear in all of these books, although he also made use of North American landscapes. But he had already decided he wanted to change his style, and the title of his next collection, *The Moving Target* (1963), suggests this formal restlessness. He was beginning to make his poetry out of archetypal correspondences and to remove embroideries. He even went so far as to remove punctuation for reasons he gave in his prose statement "On Open Form" included here. These formal concerns, coupled with a growing environmentalism and pessimism, resulted in what may be his most powerful book, *The Lice* (1967). Here his verse technique was so reduced, so deliberately simplified, that many critics were reminded of Samuel Beckett. There was humor in the work of this period, but *The Lice* was a dark enough book that Merwin claimed it nearly made him consider not writing again.

The Carrier of Ladders (1970) won Merwin the Pulitzer Prize and contained a sequence of poems meditating on American expansion. In the same year Merwin published *The Miner's Pale Children*, his collection of short fiction. By 1979, when he won the Bollingen Prize for his work, he had published another important book of prose, *Houses and Travellers;* a collection of poems, *The Compass Flower;* and several more volumes of translations. His move to Hawaii was reflected in the poems of *Finding the Islands* (1982), *Opening the Hand* (1983), and *The Rain in the Trees* (1988). By the latter volume, Merwin was working his way out of the minimalism that had characterized some of his poetry from *The Moving Target* on. *The River Sound* (1999) contains narrative poems, and in 1998 Merwin published *The Folding Cliffs,* a book-length narrative about Hawaii. Yet another indication of Merwin's renewed interest in narrative was his translation of Dante's *Purgatorio* (2000).

Although he has published critical essays on Milton and other subjects, Merwin has generally not involved himself with literary criticism or literary politics. *Regions of Memory,* a selection of his essays edited by Cary Nelson and Ed Folsom, was published in 1987. "On Open Form" first appeared in *Naked Poetry* (1969), an influential anthology edited by Stephen Berg and Robert Mezey. In this provocative short essay Merwin speculates on the deeper reasons behind the shift to open forms then underway in American poetry.

--◦▬▬◗▬▬◦--

ON OPEN FORM

What is called its form may be simply that part of the poem that had directly to do with time: the time of the poem, the time in which it was written, and the sense of recurrence in which the unique moment of vision is set.

Perhaps this is why in much of the poetry of the high Middle Ages the form seems transparent. Both the role of time in the poem and the role of the poem in time doubtless seemed clear and simple to the Arcipreste de Hita, Dante, Guillaume de Lorris and Chaucer. We can be sure of neither, and we cannot even be certain whether the pretense to such certainty that characterizes some later periods of society (in particular certain phases of neoclassicism) is one of the absurd disguises that can help an art to survive, or merely one of the shrouds that are hardly more than wasted efforts to lend decency to its burial.

The invention of a new form of stanza was a matter of genuine poetic importance to the troubadours. To us it would probably seem scarcely a matter for much curiosity. For the troubadours the abstract form (which certainly they did not hear as an abstract thing) was unquestionably related to that part of the poem that was poetic. For us it is hard to remain convinced that the form, insofar as it is abstract, is not merely part of what in the poem is inescapably technical. For us, for whom everything is in question, the making keeps leading us back into the patterns of a world of artifice so intricate, so insidious, and so impressive, that often it seems indistinguishable from the whole of time.

In a world of technique *motions* tend to become methods. But the undependable life that appears on occasion as poetry would rather die, or so it seems, than follow this tendency, and when a poet himself follows it farther than the source of his gift warrants, his gains of technical facility are likely to render him the helpless master of mere confection.

And yet neither technique nor abstract form can be abandoned, finally. And no doubt neither is dangerous in itself as long as each is recognized as no more than a means, and is not made into an idol and loved for itself. (But it seems to be characteristic of a technological age that means come to dwarf and eclipse or destroy their ends.)

And certainly neither of them automatically excludes or implies the other.

* * *

In an age when time and technique encroach hourly, or appear to, on the source itself of poetry, it seems as though what is needed for any particular nebulous unwritten hope that may become a poem is not a manipulable, more or less predictably recurring pattern, but an unduplicatable resonance, something that would be like an echo except that it is repeating no sound. Something that always belonged to it: its sense and its conformation before it entered words.

* * *

At the same time I realize that I am a formalist, in the most strict and orthodox sense. For years I have had a recurring dream of finding, as it were in an attic,

From *Naked Poetry: Recent American Poetry in Open Forms*, ed. Stephen Berg and Robert Mezey (Indianapolis: Bobbs-Merrill, 1969) 270–271.

poems of my own that were as lyrically formal, but as limpid and essentially unliterary as those of Villon.

* * *

Much of what appears, or appeared, as great constructive energy in the poetic revolutions of the first half of this century must have been in part energy made available by the decomposition of a vast and finally anti-poetic poetic organism that had become a nuisance even to itself. The original iconoclasts have reared up other anti-poetic poetic monsters that have achieved senility far more quickly since their shapes were less definite and their substance more questionable from the start.

* * *

A poetic form: the setting down of a way of hearing how poetry happens in words. The words themselves do not make it. At the same time it is testimony of a way of hearing how life happens in time. But time does not make it.

* * *

To recur in its purest forms (whether they are strict, as in Waller's "Go, Lovely Rose," or apparently untrammelled, as in The Book of Isaiah in the King James Version) poetry seems to have to keep reverting to its naked condition, where it touches on all that is unrealized.

Our age pesters us with the illusion that we have realized a great deal. The agitation serves chiefly to obscure what we have forgotten, into whose limbo poetry herself at times seems about to pass.

* * *

What are here called open forms are in some concerns the strictest. Here only the poem itself can be seen as its form. In a peculiar sense if you criticize how it happens you criticize what it is.

* * *

Obviously it is the poem that is or is not the only possible justification for any form, however theory runs. The poem is or it is not the answer to 'why that form?' The consideration of the evolution of forms, strict or open, belongs largely to history and to method. The visitation that is going to be a poem finds the form it needs in spite of both.

* * *

The "freedom" that precedes strict forms and the "freedom" that follows them are not necessarily much alike. Then there is the "freedom" that accompanies poetry at a distance and occasionally joins it, often without being recognized, as in some proverbs. ("God comes to see without a bell." "He that lives on hope dances without music.")

[1967] 1969

◦—◄ DONALD HALL ►—◦
(B. 1928)

Author or editor of more than eighty books, Donald Hall is one of the pre-eminent American men of letters of the last fifty years. He appears to have known everyone and written about them with compassion, accuracy, and wit. His textbooks and anthologies have been among the most important of his generation, his memoirs are classics of American prose, his essays are judiciously outspoken and wide ranging, and the best of his poems give significant voice to concerns of family, history, and creativity.

Hall was born in New Haven, Connecticut, to a middle-class family. His father was a businessman, often frustrated with his career. Hall reports that his father once vowed that his son would never have to endure such humiliations. Perhaps because of this, Hall was encouraged by his parents when, at the age of twelve, he showed an interest in writing. At sixteen, he attended the prestigious Bread Loaf Writers' Conference, where he met Robert Frost for the first time. It was a precocious start for a memoirist. Among his classmates at Harvard were Robert Bly, John Ashbery, and Kenneth Koch. He won prizes for poetry at Harvard, where he also edited the undergraduate literary magazine, the *Advocate,* and studied under Archibald MacLeish. After graduating in 1951, Hall went on to Oxford, learning a great deal about the British literary establishment and winning the Newdigate Prize for his poem "Exile." From 1953 to 1961 he served as poetry editor for the *Paris Review,* and in that capacity he conducted important interviews with T. S. Eliot, Ezra Pound, and Marianne Moore. He also attended Stanford University in 1953–54, studying with Yvor Winters. In short, Hall seems to have set out to become a poet in part by developing a personal relationship with almost every significant poet and critic of his time.

His first full-length collection of poems, *Exiles and Marriages,* won the Lamont Poetry Prize from the Academy of American Poets and was published by Viking in 1955. The book was precocious, but only a few of its poems now seem to transcend the conventions of the period. Hall's subsequent early collections often suggest that he felt pressured to publish too quickly. Their poems sometimes seem to drift in search of a style or subject he could call his own. For awhile, work of various kinds interfered with his full self-realization as a poet. Married, a father, he joined the faculty of the University of Michigan, Ann Arbor, where he taught from 1957 to 1975. By almost any measure Hall enjoyed immense literary success, with six full-length collections of poems to his name by 1971, a highly regarded book of memoirs called *String Too Short to be Saved* (1979), books on sculptor Henry Moore and poet Marianne Moore, and several influential anthologies. One of these, *New Poets of England and America* (1957), co–edited with Robert Pack and Louis Simpson, with a preface by Robert Frost, was a landmark of the fifties, often contrasted to Donald Allen's *The New American Poetry* (1960). Hall also edited the influential *Contemporary American Poetry* for Penguin (1962).

Despite these public successes and the approbation of older writers, Hall felt that something essential was lacking from his own poetry. He also underwent the trauma of a divorce from his first wife in 1969 and married the poet Jane Kenyon in 1972. In 1975, frustrated by the compromises of academic life, Hall decided to change his life. He purchased his grandparents' farm in New Hampshire, a place he remembered fondly from childhood summers, left his teaching position, and, with Kenyon, set out to live by his wits. This liberating gesture was made possible only because of his prodigious industry. "In the culture I was born to," he once wrote, "'work' is a golden syllable." Hall made a habit of rising early, devoting his first and best hours to poems, then turning to prose, much of it done for hire.

The move proved decisive for his poetry, which developed and deepened in his new life. Among the important collections he published were *Kicking the Leaves* (1978), *The Happy Man* (1986), *The One Day* (1988), and *Old and New Poems* (1990). *The Museum of Clear Ideas* (1993) celebrated his favorite sport, baseball, just as he had done in his popular book of essays, *Fathers Playing Catch with Sons* (1985). Early in the nineties, however, Hall was diagnosed with cancer, and in the course of treatment lost two-thirds of his colon to surgery. It was widely reported in literary circles that he was dying. Ironically, Hall lived on while the younger Kenyon succumbed rapidly to leukemia in 1995. Hall's 1996 collection, *The Old Life*, comprised poems based upon old memoirs. Then in 1998 he published *Without*, his poems dealing with grief over the loss of his wife. A prolific writer of children's books, Hall has also written plays and has won numerous awards, including the National Book Critics Circle Award, the *Los Angeles Times* Book Prize, and the Robert Frost Silver Medal from the Poetry Society of America. He continues to live and write on his family's farm.

Hall's critical prose is notable for its lively intelligence, candor, and unpedantic scholarship. While his essay collections often comprise reviews written for newspapers and magazines, they are usually anchored by important essays meditating on topics like "The Psychic Origins of Poetry" or the nature of literary careers. Hall is also a master of that literary genre he calls "literary gossip, reminiscences by friends and acquaintances of authors." Among his important prose collections are *Goatfoot Milktongue Twinbird* (1978), *The Weather for Poetry* (1982), *Poetry and Ambition* (1988), and *The Principal Products of Portugal* (1995). His classic book of memoirs, *Remembering Poets* (1978), was revised and expanded as *Their Ancient, Glittering Eyes* (1992). It was followed by his highly regarded meditation on mortality and vocation, *Life Work* (1993).

POETRY AND AMBITION

1. I see no reason to spend your life writing poems unless your goal is to write great poems.

An ambitious project—but sensible, I think. And it seems to me that contemporary American poetry is afflicted by modesty of ambition—a modesty, alas, genuine . . . if sometimes accompanied by vast pretense. Of course the great majority of contemporary poems, in any era, will always be bad or mediocre. (Our time may well be characterized by more mediocrity and less badness.) But if failure is constant the types of failure vary, and the qualities and habits of our society specify the manners and the methods of our failure. I think that we fail in part because we lack serious ambition.

2. If I recommend ambition, I do not mean to suggest that it is easy or pleasurable. "I would sooner fail," said Keats at twenty-two, "than not be among the greatest." When he died three years later he believed in his despair that he had done nothing, the poet of "Ode to a Nightingale" convinced that his name was "writ in water." But he was mistaken, he was mistaken. . . . If I praise the ambition that drove Keats, I do not mean to suggest that it will ever be rewarded. We never know the value of our own work, and everything reasonable leads us to doubt it: for we can be certain that few contemporaries will be read in a hundred years. To desire to write poems that endure—we undertake such a goal certain of two things: that in all likelihood we will fail, and that if we succeed we will never know it.

Every now and then I meet someone certain of personal greatness. I want to pat this person on the shoulder and mutter comforting words: "Things will get better! You won't always feel so depressed! Cheer up!"

But I just called high ambition sensible. If our goal in life is to remain content, *no* ambition is sensible. . . . If our goal is to write poetry, the only way we are likely to be *any* good is to try to be as great as the best.

3. But for some people it seems ambitious merely to set up as a poet, merely to write and to publish. Publication stands in for achievement—as everyone knows, universities and grant-givers take publication as achievement—but to accept such a substitution is modest indeed, for publication is cheap and easy. In this country we publish more poems (in books and magazines) and more poets read more poems aloud at more poetry readings than ever before; the increase in thirty years has been tenfold.

So what? Many of these poems are often *readable*, charming, funny, touching, sometimes even intelligent. But they are usually brief, they resemble each other, they are anecdotal, they do not extend themselves, they make no great claims, they connect small things to other small things. Ambitious poems usually require a certain length for magnitude; one need not mention monuments like *The*

Originally delivered as a lecture at a meeting of the Associated Writing Programs and, with material added, at New England College; it was originally published in *Kenyon Review* 5 (1983). Collected in *Poetry and Ambition: Essays 1982–88* (Ann Arbor: University of Michigan Press, 1988) 1–19.

Canterbury Tales, The Faerie Queen, Paradise Lost, or *The Prelude.* "Epithala-
mion," "Lycidas," and "Ode: Intimations of Immortality" are sufficiently extended, not to mention "The Garden" or "Out of the Cradle." Not to mention
the poet like Yeats whose briefer works make great connections.

I do not complain that we find ourselves incapable of such achievement; I
complain that we seem not even to entertain the desire.

4. Where Shakespeare used "ambitious" of Macbeth we would say "over-
ambitious"; Milton used "ambition" for the unscrupulous overreaching of Satan;
the word describes a deadly sin like "pride." Now when I call Milton "ambitious"
I use the modern word, mellowed and washed of its darkness. This amelioration
reflects capitalism's investment in social mobility. In more hierarchal times pursuit
of honor might require revolutionary social change, or murder; but Protestantism
and capitalism celebrate the desire to rise.

Milton and Shakespeare, like Homer, acknowledge the desire to make words
that live forever: ambitious enough, and fit to the O.E.D.'s first definition of "ambition" as "eager desire of honor"—which will do for poets and warriors,
courtiers and architects, diplomats, Members of Parliament, and Kings. Desire
need not imply drudgery. Hard work enters the definition at least with Milton,
who is ready "To scorn delights, and live laborious days," to discover fame, "the
spur, that last infirmity of noble minds." We note the infirmity who note that fame
results only from laborious days' attendance upon a task of some magnitude: when
Milton invoked the Heavenly Muse's "aid to my adventurous song," he wanted
merely to "justify the ways of God to men."

If the word "ambitious" has mellowed, "fame" has deteriorated enough to require a moment's thought. For us, fame tends to mean Johnny Carson and *People*
magazine. For Keats as for Milton, for Hector as for Gilgamesh, it meant something like universal and enduring love for the deed done or the song sung. The idea
is more classic than Christian, and the poet not only seeks it but confers it. Who
knows Achilles' valor but for Homer's tongue? But in the 1980s—after centuries of
cheap printing, after the spread of mere literacy and the decline of qualified literacy, after the loss of history and the historical sense, after television has become
mother of us all—we have seen the decline of fame until we use it now as Andy
Warhol uses it, as the mere quantitative distribution of images. . . . We have a culture crowded with people who are famous for being famous.

5. True ambition in a poet seeks fame in the old sense, to make words that live forever. If even to entertain such ambition reveals monstrous egotism, let me argue that
the common alternative is petty egotism that spends itself in small competitiveness,
that measures its success by quantity of publication, by blurbs on jackets, by small
achievement: to be the best poet in the workshop, to be published by Knopf, to win
the Pulitzer or the Nobel. . . . The grander goal is to be as good as Dante.

Let me hypothesize the developmental stages of the poet.

At twelve, say, the American poet-to-be is afflicted with generalized ambition.
(Robert Frost wanted to be a baseball pitcher and a United States senator: Oliver
Wendell Holmes said that *nothing* was so commonplace as the desire to appear remarkable; the desire may be common but it is at least essential.) At sixteen the
poet reads Whitman and Homer and wants to be immortal. Alas, at twenty-four
the same poet wants to be in the *New Yorker.* . . .

There is an early stage when the poem becomes more important than the poet; one can see it as a transition from the lesser egotism to the greater. At the stage of lesser egotism, the poet keeps a bad line or an inferior word or image because *that's the way it was: that's what really happened.* At this stage the frail ego of the author takes precedence over art. The poet must develop, past this silliness, to the stage where the poem is altered for its own sake, to make it better art, not for the sake of its maker's feelings but because decent art is the goal. Then the poem lives at some distance from its creator's little daily emotions; it can take on its own character in the mysterious place of satisfying shapes and shapely utterance. The poem freed from its precarious utility as ego's appendage may possibly fly into the sky and become a star permanent in the night air.

Yet, alas, when the poet tastes a little fame, a little praise. . . . Sometimes the poet who has passed this developmental stage will forget duty to the art of poetry and again serve the petty egotism of the self. . . .

Nothing is learned once that does not need learning again. The poet whose ambition is unlimited at sixteen and petty at twenty-four may turn unlimited at thirty-five and regress at fifty. But if everyone suffers from interest, everyone may pursue disinterest.

Then there is a possible further stage: when the poet becomes an instrument or agency of art, the poem freed from the poet's ego may entertain the possibility of grandeur. And this grandeur, by a familiar paradox, may turn itself an apparent 180 degrees to tell the truth. Only when the poem turns wholly away from the petty ego, only when its internal structure fully serves art's delicious purposes, may it serve to reveal and envision. "Man can *embody* truth"—said Yeats; I add the italic—"he cannot *know* it." Embodiment is art and artfulness.

When Yeats was just south of fifty he wrote that he "sought an image not a book." Many aging poets leave the book behind to search for the diagram, and write no more poetry than Michael Robartes who drew geometrical shapes in the sand. The turn toward wisdom—toward gathering the whole world into a book—often leaves poetry behind as a frivolity. And though these prophets may delight in abstract revelation, we cannot follow them into knowing, who followed their earlier embodiments. . . . Yeats's soul knew an appetite for invisibility—the temptation of many—but the man remained composite, and although he sought and found a vision he continued to write a book.

6. We find our models of ambition mostly from reading.

We develop the notion of art from our reading. When we call the poem more important than ourselves, it is not that we have confidence in *our* ability to write it; we believe in *poetry*. We look daily at the great monuments of old accomplishment and we desire to add to their number, to make poems in homage to poems. Old poems that we continue to read and love become the standard we try to live up to. These poems, internalized, criticize our own work. These old poems become our Muse, our encouragement to song and our discouragement of comparison.

Therefore it is essential for poets, all the time, to read and reread the great ones. Some lucky poets make their living by publicly reacquainting themselves in the classroom with the great poems of the language. Alas, many poets now teach nothing but creative writing, read nothing but the words of children . . . (I will return to this subject).

It is also true that many would-be poets lack respect for learning. How strange that the old ones read books. . . . Keats stopped school when he was fifteen or so; but he translated the *Aeneid* in order to study it and worked over Dante in Italian and daily sat at the feet of Spenser, Shakespeare, and Milton. ("Keats studied the old poets every day / Instead of picking up his M.F.A.") Ben Jonson was learned and in his cups looked down at Shakespeare's relative ignorance of ancient languages—but Shakespeare learned more language and literature at his Stratford grammar school than we acquire in twenty years of schooling. Whitman read and educated himself with vigor; Eliot and Pound continued their studies after stints of graduate school.

On the other hand, we play records all night and write unambitious poems. Even talented young poets—saturated in S'ung, suffused in Sufi—know nothing of Bishop King's "Exequy." The syntax and sounds of one's own tongue, and that tongue's four-hundred-year-old ancestors, give us more than all the classics of all the world in translation.

But to struggle to read the great poems of another language—*in* the language—that is another thing. We are the first generation of poets not to study Latin; not to read Dante in Italian. Thus the puniness of our unambitious syntax and limited vocabulary.

When we have read the great poems we can study as well the lives of the poets. It is useful, in the pursuit of models, to read the lives and letters of the poets whose work we love. Keats's letters, heaven knows.

7. In all societies there is a template to which its institutions conform, whether or not the institutions instigate products or activities that suit such a pattern. In the Middle Ages the Church provided the model, and guilds and secret societies erected their colleges of cardinals. Today the American industrial corporation provides the template, and the university models itself on General Motors. Corporations exist to create or discover consumers' desires and fulfill them with something that satisfies briefly and needs frequent repetition. CBS provides television as Gillette supplies disposable razors—and, alas, the universities turn out degree-holders equally disposable; and the major publishers of New York City (most of them less profitable annexes of conglomerates peddling soap, beer, and paper towels) provide disposable masterpieces.

The United States invented mass quick-consumption and we are very good at it. We are not famous for making Ferraris and Rolls Royces; we are famous for the people's car, the Model T, the Model A—"transportation," as we call it: the particular abstracted into the utilitarian generality—and two in every garage. Quality is all very well but it is *not* democratic; if we insist on hand-building Rolls Royces most of us will walk to work. Democracy demands the interchangeable part and the worker on the production line; Thomas Jefferson may have had other notions but de Tocqueville was our prophet. Or take American cuisine: it has never added a sauce to the world's palate, but our fast-food industry overruns the planet.

Thus: Our poems, in their charming and interchangeable quantity, do not presume to the status of "Lycidas"—for that would be elitist and un-American. We write and publish the McPoem—*ten billion served*—which becomes our contribution to the history of literature as the Model T is our contribution to a history which runs from bare feet past elephant and rickshaw to the vehicles of space. Pull in any time day or night, park by the busload, and the McPoem waits on the steam shelf for us, wrapped and protected, indistinguishable, undistinguished, and reliable—the good old McPoem identical from coast to coast and in all the little towns between, subject to the quality control of the least common denominator.

And every year, Ronald McDonald takes the Pulitzer.

To produce the McPoem, institutions must enforce patterns, institutions within institutions, all subject to the same glorious dominance of unconscious economic determinism, template and formula of consumerism.

The McPoem is the product of the workshops of Hamburger University.

8. But before we look into the workshop, with its training program for junior poets, let us take a look at models provided by poetic heroes of the American present. The university does not invent the stereotypes; it provides technology for mass reproduction of a model created elsewhere.

Question: If you manufacture Pac-Man, or a car called Mustang, and everyone suddenly wants to buy what you make, how do you respond? Answer: You add shifts, pay overtime, and expand the plant in order to saturate the market with your product. . . . You make your product as quickly as you can manufacture it; notions of quality control do not disturb your dreams.

When Robert Lowell was young he wrote slowly and painfully and very well. On his wonderful Library of Congress LP, before he recites his early poem about "Falling Asleep over the Aeneid," he tells how the poem began when he tried translating Virgil but produced only eighty lines in six months, which he found disheartening. Five years elapsed between his Pulitzer book *Lord Weary's Castle,* which was the announcement of his genius, and its underrated successor *The Mills of the Kavanaughs.* Then there were eight more years before the abrupt innovation of *Life Studies. For the Union Dead* was spotty, *Near the Ocean* spottier, and then the rot set in.

Now, no man should be hanged for losing his gift, most especially a man who suffered as Lowell did. But one can, I think, feel annoyed when quality plunges as quantity multiplies: Lowell published six bad books of poems in those disastrous last eight years of his life.

(I say "bad books" and would go to the stake over the judgment, but let me hasten to acknowledge that each of these dreadful collections—dead metaphor, flat rhythm, narcissistic self-exploitation—was celebrated by leading critics on the front page of the *Times* and the *New York Review of Books* as the greatest yet of uniformly great emanations of great poetical greatness, greatly achieved. . . . But one wastes one's time in indignation. Taste is always a fool.)

John Berryman wrote with difficult concentration his difficult, concentrated *Mistress Bradstreet;* then he eked out *77 Dream Songs.* Alas, after the success of this product he mass-produced *His Toy His Dream His Rest,* 308 further dream songs—quick improvisations of self-imitation, which is the true identity of the famous "voice" accorded late Berryman-Lowell. Now Robert Penn Warren, our current grand old man, accumulates another long book of poems every year or so, repeating himself instead of rewriting the same poem until it is right—hurry, hurry, hurry—and the publishing tribe celebrates these sentimental, crude, trite products of our industrial culture.

Not all poets overproduce in a response to eminence: Elizabeth Bishop never went on overtime; T. S. Eliot wrote bad plays at the end of his life, but never watered the soup of his poems; nor did Williams nor Stevens nor Pound. Of course everyone writes some inferior work—but these poets did not gush out bad poems late in their lives when they were famous and the market required more products for selling.

Mind you, the workshops of Hamburger University turned out cheap, ersatz Bishop, Eliot, Williams, Stevens, and Pound. All you want. . . .

9. Horace, when he wrote the *Ars Poetica,* recommended that poets keep their poems home for ten years; don't let them go, don't publish them until you have kept them around for ten years: by that time, they ought to stop moving on you; by that time, you ought to have them right. Sensible advice, I think—but difficult to follow. When Pope wrote "An Essay on Criticism" seventeen hundred years after Horace, he cut the waiting time in half, suggesting that poets keep their poems for five years before publication. Henry Adams said something about acceleration, mounting his complaint in 1912; some would say that acceleration has accelerated in the seventy years since. By this time, I would be grateful—and published poetry would be better—if people kept their poems home for eighteen months.

Poems have become as instant as coffee or onion soup mix. One of our eminent critics compared Lowell's last book to the work of Horace, although some of its poems were dated the year of publication. Anyone editing a magazine receives poems dated the day of the postmark. When a poet types and submits a poem just composed (or even shows it to spouse or friend) the poet cuts off from the poem the possibility of growth and change; I suspect that the poet *wishes* to forestall the possibilities of growth and change, though of course without acknowledging the wish.

If Robert Lowell, John Berryman, and Robert Penn Warren publish without allowing for revision or self-criticism, how can we expect a twenty-four-year-old in Manhattan to wait five years—or eighteen months? With these famous men as models, how should we blame the young poet who boasts in a brochure of over four hundred poems published in the last five years? Or the publisher, advertising a book, who brags that his poet has published twelve books in ten years? Or the workshop teacher who meets a colleague on a crosswalk and buffs the backs of his fingernails against his tweed as he proclaims that, over the last two years, he has averaged "placing" two poems a week?

10. Abolish the M.F.A.! What a ringing slogan for a new Cato: *Iowa delenda est!**

The workshop schools us to produce the McPoem, which is "a mold in plaster, / Made with no loss of time," with no waste of effort, with no strenuous questioning as to merit. If we attend a workshop we must bring something to class or we do not contribute. What kind of workshop could Horace have contributed to, if he kept his poems to himself for ten years? No, we will not admit Horace and Pope to our workshops, for they will just sit there, holding back their own work, claiming it is not ready, acting superior, a bunch of *elitists.* . . .

When we use a metaphor, it is useful to make inquiries of it. I have already compared the workshop to a fast-food franchise, to a Ford assembly line. . . . Or should we compare Creative Writing 401 to a sweatshop where women sew shirts at an illegally low wage? Probably the metaphor refers to none of the above, because the workshop is rarely a place for starting and finishing poems; it is a place for repairing them. The poetry workshop resembles a garage to which we bring incomplete

---

*The Roman orator Cato had said, "*Delenda est Carthago*" or "Carthage must be destroyed." Hall's joke refers to the Iowa Writers Workshop.

or malfunctioning homemade machines for diagnosis and repair. Here is the home-made airplane for which the crazed inventor forgot to provide wings; here is the in-ternal combustion engine all finished except that it lacks a carburetor; here is the rowboat without oarlocks, the ladder without rungs, the motorcycle without wheels. We advance our nonfunctional machine into a circle of other apprentice in-ventors and one or two senior Edisons. "Very good," they say; "it *almost* flies. . . . How about, uh . . . how about *wings?*" Or, "Let me just show you how to build a carburetor. . . ."

Whatever we bring to this place, we bring it too soon. The weekly meetings of the workshop serve the haste of our culture. When we bring a new poem to the workshop, anxious for praise, others' voices enter the poem's metabolism before it is mature, distorting its possible growth and change. "It's only when you get far enough away from your work to begin to be critical of it yourself"—Robert Frost said—"that anyone else's criticism can be tolerable. . . ." Bring to class only, he said, "old and cold things. . . ." Nothing is old and cold until it has gone through months of drafts. Therefore workshopping is intrinsically impossible.

It is from workshops that American poets learn to enjoy the embarrassment of publication—too soon, too soon—because *making public* is a condition of workshopping. This publication exposes oneself to one's fellow-poets only—a condition of which poets are perpetually accused and frequently guilty. We learn to write poems that will please not the Muse but our contemporaries, thus poems that resemble our contemporaries' poems—thus the recipe for the McPoem. . . . If we learn one thing else, we learn to publish promiscuously; these premature ejacu-lations count on number and frequency to counterbalance ineptitude.

Poets who stay outside the circle of peers—like Whitman, who did not go to Harvard; like Dickinson for whom there was no tradition; like Robert Frost, who dropped out of two colleges to make his own way—these poets take Homer for their peer. To quote Frost again: "The thing is to write better and better poems. Setting our heart when we're too young on getting our poems appreciated lands us in the politics of poetry which is death." Agreeing with these words from Frost's dour middle-age, we need to add: and "setting our heart" when we are old "on getting our poems appreciated" lands us in the same place.

11. At the same time, it's a big country. . . .

Most poets need the conversation of other poets. They do not need mentors; they need friends, critics, people to argue with. It is no accident that Wordsworth, Coleridge, and Southey were friends when they were young; if Pound, H.D., and William Carlos Williams had not known each other when young, would they have become William Carlos Williams, H.D., and Pound? There have been some lone wolves but not many. The history of poetry is a history of friendships and rival-ries, not only with the dead great ones but with the living young. My four years at Harvard overlapped with the undergraduates Frank O'Hara, Adrienne Rich, John Ashbery, Robert Bly, Peter Davison, L. E. Sissman, and Kenneth Koch. (At the same time Galway Kinnell and W. S. Merwin attended Princeton.) I do not assert that we resembled a sewing circle, that we often helped each other overtly, or even that we *liked* each other. I do assert that we were lucky to have each other around for purposes of conversation.

We were not in workshops; we were merely attending college. Where else in this country would we have met each other? In France there is an answer to this question and it is Paris. Europe goes in for capital cities. Although England is less centralized than France or Romania, London is more capital than New York, San Francisco, or Washington. While the French poet can discover the intellectual life of his times at a café, the American requires a degree program. The workshop is the institutionalized café.

The American problem of geographical isolation is real. Any remote place may be the site of poetry—imagined, remembered, or lived in—but for almost every poet it is necessary to live in exile before returning home—an exile rich in conflict and confirmation. Central New Hampshire or the Olympic Peninsula or Cincinnati or the soybean plains of western Minnesota or the lower East Side may shine at the center of our work and our lives; but if we never leave these places we are not likely to grow up enough to do the work. There is a terrible poignancy in the talented artist who fears to leave home—defined as a place *first* to leave and *then* to return to.

So the workshop answers the need for a café. But I called it the *institutionalized* café, and it differs from the Parisian version by instituting requirements and by hiring and paying mentors. Workshop mentors even make assignments: "Write a persona poem in the voice of a dead ancestor." "Make a poem containing these ten words in this order with as many other words as you wish." "Write a poem without adjectives, or without prepositions, or without content. . . ." These formulas, everyone says, are a whole lot of fun. . . . They also reduce poetry to a parlor game; they trivialize and make safe-seeming the real terrors of real art. This reduction-by-formula is not accidental. We play these games *in order* to reduce poetry to a parlor game. Games serve to democratize, to soften, and to standardize; they are repellent. Although in theory workshops serve a useful purpose in gathering young artists together, workshop practices enforce the McPoem.

This is your contrary assignment: Be as good a poet as George Herbert. Take as long as you wish.

12. I mentioned earlier the disastrous separation, in many universities, of creative writing and literature. There are people writing poetry—teaching poetry, studying poetry—who find reading *academic*. Such a sentence sounds like a satiric invention; alas, it is objective reporting.

Our culture rewards specialization. It is absurd that we erect a barrier between one who reads and one who writes, but it is an absurdity with a history. It is absurd because in our writing our standards derive from what we have read, and its history reaches back to the ancient war between the poets and the philosophers, exemplified in Plato's "Ion" as the philosopher condescends to the rhapsode. In the thirties poets like Ransom, Tate, and Winters entered the academy under sufferance, condescended to. Tate and Winters especially made themselves academically rigorous. They secured the beachheads; the army of their grandchildren occupies the country: often grandsons and daughters who write books but do not read them.

The separation of the literature department from the writing department is a disaster; for poet, for scholar, and for student. The poet may prolong adolescence into retirement by dealing only with the products of infant brains. (If the poet, as in some schools, teaches literature, but only to writing students, the effect is better but not much better. The temptation exists then to teach literature as craft or trade; Americans don't need anyone teaching them trade.) The scholars of the department, institutionally separated from the contemporary, are encouraged to ignore it. In the ideal relationship, writers play gadfly to scholars, and scholars help writers connect to the body of past literature. Students lose the writer's special contribution to the study of literature. Everybody loses.

13. It is commonplace that, in the English and American tradition, critic and poet are the same person—from Campion to Pound, from Sidney to Eliot. This tradition started with controversies between poets over the propriety of rhyme and English meter, and with poets' defense of poetry against Puritan attack. It flourished, serving many purposes, through Dryden, Johnson, Coleridge, Wordsworth, Keats in his letters, Shelley, Arnold. . . . Although certain poets have left no criticism, there are *no* first-rate critics in the English tradition who are not also poets—except for Hazlitt. The poet and the critic have been almost continuous, as if writing poetry and thinking about it were not discrete activities.

When Roman Jakobson—great linguist, Harvard professor—was approached some years ago with the suggestion that Vladimir Nabokov might be appointed professor of Slavic, Jakobson was skeptical; he had nothing against elephants, he said, but he would not appoint one professor of zoology.

Oh, dear.

The analogy compares the elegant and stylish Nabokov—novelist in various languages, lepidopterist, lecturer, and critic—to the great, gray, hulking pachyderm, intellectually noted *only* for memory. . . . By jokes and analogies we reveal ourselves. Jakobson condescends to Nabokov—just as Plato patted little Ion on his head, just as Sartre makes charitable exception for poets in *What Is Literature?*, just as men have traditionally condescended to women and imperialists to natives. The points are clear: (1) "Artists are closer to nature than thinkers; they are more instinctive, more emotional; they are childlike." (2) "Artists like bright colors; artists have a natural sense of rhythm; artists screw all the time." (3) "Don't misunderstand. We *like* artists . . . in their place, which is in the zoo, or at any rate outside the Republic, or at any rate outside tenured ranks."

(One must admit, I suppose, that poets often find themselves in tenured ranks these days. But increasingly they enter by the zoo entrance, which in our universities is the department of creative writing.)

Formalism, with its dream of finite measurement, is a beautiful arrogance, a fantasy of materialism. When we find what's to measure and measure it, we should understand style-as-fingerprint, quantifying characteristic phonemic sequence . . . or whatever. But it seems likely that we will continue to intuit qualities, like degrees of intensity, for which objective measure is impossible. Then hard-noses will claim that only the measurable exists—which is why hard-nose usually means soft-head.

Once I audited a course of Jakobson's, for which I am grateful; the old formalist discoursed on comparative prosody, witty and energetic and learned, giving verbatim examples from Urdu and fifty other languages, exemplifying the multiplicity of countable noise. The journey was marvelous, the marvel diminished only a little by its terminus. The last lecture, pointed to for some weeks, turned out to be a demonstration, from an objective and untraditional approach, of how to scan (and the scansion was fine, and it was the way one scanned the poem when one was sixteen) of Edgar Poe's "The Raven."

14. A product of the creative writing industry is the writerly newsletter which concerns itself with publications, grants, and jobs—and with nothing serious. If poets meeting each other in 1941 discussed how much they were paid a line, now they

trade information about grants; left wing and right united; to be Establishment is to have received an N.E.A. grant; to be anti-Establishment is to denounce the N.E.A. as a conspiracy. . . . Like Republicans and Democrats, all belong to the same capitalist party.

Poets and Writers publishes *Coda* (now *Poets and Writers*), with chatty articles about self-publication, with lists of contests and awards. It resembles not so much a trade journal as a hobbyist's bulletin, unrelievedly cheerful, relentlessly trivial. The same organization issues the telephone-book, *A Directory of American Poets,* "Names and addresses of 1,500 poets. . . ." The same organization offers T-shirts and bookbags labeled "Poets and Writers."

Associated Writing Programs publishes *A.W.P. Newsletter,* which includes one article each issue—often a talk addressed to an A.W.P. meeting—and adds helpful business aids: The December, 1982, issue includes advice on "The 'Well Written' Letter of Application," lists of magazines requesting material ("The editors state they are looking for 'straightforward but not inartistic work'"), lists of grants and awards ("The annual HARRY SMITH BOOK AWARD is given by COSMEP to . . ."), and notices of A.W.P. competitions and conventions. . . .

Really, these newsletters provide illusion; for jobs and grants go to the eminent people. As we all know, eminence is arithmetical: it derives from the number of units published times the prestige of the places of publication. People hiring or granting do not judge quality—it's so subjective!—but anyone can multiply units by the prestige index and come off with the *product.* Eminence also brings readings. Can we go uncorrupted by such knowledge? I am asked to introduce a young poet's volume; the publisher will pay the going rate; but I did not know that there was a going rate. . . . Even blurbs on jackets are commodities. They are exchanged for pamphlets, for readings; reciprocal blurbs are only the most obvious exchanges. . . .

15. Sigh.

If it seems hopeless, one has only to look up in perfect silence at the stars . . . and it *does* help to remember that poems are the stars, not poets. Of most help is to remember that it is possible for people to take hold of themselves and become better by thinking. It is also necessary, alas, to *continue* to take hold of ourselves—if we are to pursue the true ambition of poetry. Our disinterest must discover that last week's nobility was really covert rottenness, etcetera. One is never free and clear; one must work continually to sustain, to recover. . . .

When Keats in his letters praised disinterestedness—his favorite moral idea, destroyed when it is misused as a synonym for lethargy (on the same day I found it misused in the *New York Times, Inside Sports,* and the *American Poetry Review*)—he lectured himself because he feared that he would lose it. (Lectures loud with moral advice are always self-addressed.) No one is guiltless of temptation, but it is possible to resist temptation. When Keats worried over his reputation, over insults from Haydon or the *Quarterly,* over Shelley's condescension or Wordsworth's neglect, he reminded himself to cultivate disinterest; to avoid distraction and to keep his eye on the true goal, which was to become one of the English Poets.

Yeats is responsible for a number of the stars in the sky, and when we read his letters we find that the young man was an extraordinary trimmer—soliciting reviews from Oscar Wilde and flattering Katherine Tynan, older and more established on the Celtic turf. One of the O.E.D.'s definitions of ambition, after "eager desire of honor," is "personal solicitation of honor." When he wrote, "I seek an image not a book," he acknowledged that as a young man he had sought a book indeed. None of us, beseeching Doubleday or Pittsburgh, has ever sought with greater fervor.

And Whitman reviewed himself, and Roethke campaigned for praise like a legislator at the state fair, and Frost buttered Untermeyer on both sides. . . . (Therefore let us abjure the old saw that self-promotion and empire-building mean bad poetry. Most entrepreneurs are bad poets—but then, so are most poets.) Self-promotion remains a side issue of poetry and ambition. It *can* reflect a greed or covetousness which displaces the grand ambition—the kind of covetousness which looks on the life lived only as a source of poems; "I got a poem out of it." Or it can show only the trivial side of someone who, on other occasions, makes great art. At any rate, we should spend our time worrying not about other people's bad characters, but our own.

Finally, of course, I speak of nothing except the modest topic: How shall we lead our lives? I think of a man I admire as much as anyone, the English sculptor Henry Moore, eighty-four as I write these notes, eighty when I spoke with him last. "Now that you are eighty," I asked him, "would you tell me the secret of life?" Being a confident and eloquent Yorkshireman, Moore would not deny my request. He told me:

"The greatest good luck in life, for *anybody,* is to have something that means *everything* to you . . . to do what you want to do, and to find that people will pay you for doing it . . . *if* it's unattainable. It's no good having an objective that's attainable! That's the big thing: you have an ideal, an objective, and that objective is unreachable. . . ."

16. There is no audit we can perform on ourselves, to assure that we work with proper ambition. Obviously it helps to be careful; to revise, to take time, to put the poem away; to pursue distance in the hope of objective measure. We know that the poem, to satisfy ambition's goals, must not express mere personal feeling or opinion—as the moment's McPoem does. It must by its language make art's new object. We must try to hold ourselves to the mark; we must not write to publish or to prevail. Repeated scrutiny is the only method general enough for recommending. . . .

And of course repeated scrutiny is not foolproof; and we will fool ourselves. Nor can the hours we work provide an index of ambition or seriousness. Although Henry Moore laughs at artists who work only an hour or two a day, he acknowledges that sculptors can carve sixteen hours at a stretch for years on end—tap-tap-tap on stone—and remain lazy. We can revise our poems five hundred times; we can lock poems in their rooms for ten years—and remain modest in our endeavor. On the other hand, anyone casting a glance over biography or literary history must acknowledge: Some great poems have come without noticeable labor.

But as I speak I confuse realms. Ambition is not a quality of the poem but of the poet. Failure and achievement belong to the poet, and if our goal remains unattainable, then failure must be standard. To pursue the unattainable for eighty-five years, like Henry Moore, may imply a certain temperament. . . . If there is no method of work that we can rely on, maybe at least we can encourage in ourselves a temperament that is not easily satisfied. Sometime when we are discouraged with our own work, we may notice that even the great poems, the sources and the standards, seem inadequate: "Ode to a Nightingale" feels too limited in scope, "Out of the Cradle" too sloppy, "To His Coy Mistress" too neat, and "Among School-children" padded. . . .

Maybe ambition is appropriately unattainable when we acknowledge: *No poem is so great as we demand that poetry be.*

[1983] 1988

ADRIENNE RICH
(B. 1929)

One of the most influential American writers of the past half-century, Adrienne Rich has consciously evolved over the course of her career, revising both her style and her ideas in response to changing times. Her searching changes arise from her determination to chart new territory opened by feminist perspectives. In her essay, "Blood, Bread, and Poetry" (1984), she described her goal and its consequences: "To write directly and overtly as a woman, out of a woman's experience, to take women's existence seriously as theme and source for art, was something I had been hungering to do, needing to do, all my writing life. It placed me nakedly face to face with both terror and anger; it did indeed *imply the breakdown of the world as I had always known it. . . .*" Writing "directly and overtly as a woman" has been a process of discovery for Rich that necessitated risks, both artistic and political, and those risks have involved not only the intellectual and spiritual evolution that fueled her poetry and prose, but life changes as well.

Adrienne Cecile Rich was born in Baltimore to Arnold Rice Rich, a doctor and professor of pathology at Johns Hopkins University, and Helen Jones Rich, who gave up her dream of a career as a concert pianist to devote all of her attention to her family. In "Split at the Root: An Essay on Jewish Identity" (1982), Rich describes household frictions resulting from her father's Judaism and her mother's Southern Protestantism and traces her own intimations of a Jewish identity that surfaced despite her family's efforts to live a life of assimilation. Her father encouraged her love of literature, directing her reading and offering serious criticism of the poems she wrote.

By the time she graduated from Radcliffe College, Rich had already won the Yale Series of Younger Poets Prize for her first book, *A Change of World* (1951). The prize helped her earn a Guggenheim Fellowship the next year to travel in Europe. After her return in 1953, she married Alfred Conrad, a young professor of economics at Harvard University. Her second book, *The Diamond Cutters,* appeared in 1955, but, due to the demands of caring for her three young sons, she did not publish her next collection, *Snapshots of a Daughter-in-Law,* until 1963. In *Of Woman Born: Motherhood as Experience and Institution* (1976), a substantial prose study of motherhood, Rich recalled the difficulties she had in raising three small children while trying to sustain her writing life. She concluded that, during these years, "I knew I was fighting for my life through, against, and with the lives of my children. . . . I had been trying to give birth to myself."

That second birth resulted in crucial changes both to her poetry and her worldview. In "Blood, Bread, and Poetry," she acknowledged her indebtedness to the work of Mary Wollestonecraft, Simone de Beauvoir, and James Baldwin:

> Each of them helped me to realize that what had seemed simply "the way things are" could actually be a social construct, advantageous to some people and detrimental to others, and that these constructs could be criticized and changed. The myths and obsessions of gender, the myths and obsessions of race, the violent exercise of power in these relationships could be identified, their territories mapped. They were not simply part of my private turmoil, a secret misery, an individual failure.

Beginning with *Snapshots of a Daughter-in-Law,* Rich set out to map those territories. The title poem's challenges to traditional literary views of women and its portrayal of a dissatisfied wife and mother drew criticism from reviewers, who expected Rich to exhibit the polish and emotional poise of her first two books. In 1966, she moved to New York City with her husband so that he could work at City College, and they both became active in social justice movements. Her opposition to the war in Vietnam, her commitment to the women's movement, and her job teaching remedial English to minority students taught her lessons that were vital to her poetry. "As a poet," she remarked, "I had learned much about both the value and the constraints of convention: the reassurances of traditional structures and the necessity to break from them in recognition of new experience. I felt more and more urgently the dynamic between poetry as language and poetry as a kind of action, probing, burning, stripping, placing itself in dialogue with others out beyond the individual self."

Her vision of poetry as action, a means of bringing about both individual and social change, governed the books following *Necessities of Life* (1966). In *Leaflets* (1969), *The Will to Change* (1971), and *Diving into the Wreck* (1973), Rich revised her views of herself and the world. The need to reimagine her identity was given added impetus by the difficult events in her life. Her father died in 1968, and by 1969 Rich had also become estranged from her husband, who committed suicide the following year. As she noted in her influential essay, "When We Dead Awaken: Writing as Re-Vision" (1971), *re-vision* means "re-seeing": "Re-vision—the act of looking back, of seeing with fresh eyes, of entering an old text from a new critical direction—is for women more than a chapter in cultural history: it is a form of survival." For Rich, feminist survival entailed not simply attacking male dominance, as some critics have accused her of doing, but tracing how women internalize and therefore perpetuate negative ideas about themselves, and her poems combined social criticism with unflinching explorations of her own consciousness. "Re-vision" also meant celebration of women's achievements and reclaiming women's history. Her essays went well beyond the literary concerns most poets address in their prose. Considering subjects as diverse as women's education, the psychology of antifeminist women, and (after 1976 when she came out as a lesbian) the varieties of women's love for other women, Rich's essays helped shape the course of the women's movement in the United States.

With *The Dream of a Common Language* (1978), which included a series of lesbian love poems, "Twenty-One Love Poems," her earlier emphasis on anger and fragmentation shifted to a search for human connection, especially through relationships with women. In her later poetry, Rich continued to emphasize women's experience, while opening out her inquiry to include race relations, class conflict, and radical economics, especially the inequalities fostered by corporate domination of American politics. Above all, she balances a public voice, witnessing to injustice and envisioning change, against her own private experience and considers how that experience is inseparable from her public concerns. Her own achievement of these goals has been honored through many awards, including the National Book Award in 1974, the Robert Frost Silver Medal for Lifetime Achievement in Poetry (1992), and a MacArthur Foundation Fellowship (1994). But her strongest measure of achievement is her large, devoted readership and her enduring influence in the cultural debates of her era.

◄●══━━◆━━══●►

"WHEN WE DEAD AWAKEN": WRITING AS RE-VISION

Ibsen's *When We Dead Awaken* is a play about the use that the male artist and thinker—in the process of creating culture as we know it—has made of women, in his life and in his work; and about a woman's slow, struggling awakening to the use to which her life has been put. Bernard Shaw wrote in 1900 of this play:

> [Ibsen] shows us that no degradation ever devized or permitted is as disastrous as this degradation; that through it women can die into luxuries for men and yet can kill them; that men and women are becoming conscious of this; and that what remains to be seen as perhaps the most interesting of all imminent social developments is what will happen "when we dead awaken."

It's exhilarating to be alive in a time of awakening consciousness; it can also be confusing, disorienting, and painful. This awakening of dead or sleeping consciousness has already affected the lives of millions of women, even those who don't know it yet. It is also affecting the lives of men, even those who deny its claims upon them. The argument will go on whether an oppressive economic class system is responsible for the oppressive nature of male/female relations, or whether, in fact, patriarchy—the domination of males—is the original model of oppression on which all

Originally presented at the December 1971 Modern Language Association meeting for the Commission on the Status of Women in the Profession. First published in *College English* 34.1 (Oct. 1972). Collected in *On Lies, Secrets, and Silence* (New York: Norton, 1979).

others are based. But in the last few years the women's movement has drawn in-escapable and illuminating connections between our sexual lives and our political institutions. The sleepwalkers are coming awake, and for the first time this awaken-ing has a collective reality; it is no longer such a lonely thing to open one's eyes.

Re-vision—the act of looking back, of seeing with fresh eyes, of entering an old text from a new critical direction—is for women more than a chapter in cul-tural history: it is an act of survival. Until we can understand the assumptions in which we are drenched we cannot know ourselves. And this drive to self-knowledge, for women, is more than a search for identity: it is part of our refusal of the self-destructiveness of male-dominated society. A radical critique of litera-ture, feminist in its impulse, would take the work first of all as a clue to how we live, how we have been living, how we have been led to imagine ourselves, how our language has trapped as well as liberated us, how the very act of naming has been till now a male prerogative, and how we can begin to see and name—and therefore live—afresh. A change in the concept of sexual identity is essential if we are not going to see the old political order reassert itself in every new revolution. We need to know the writing of the past, and know it differently than we have ever known it; not to pass on a tradition but to break its hold over us.

For writers, and at this moment for women writers in particular, there is the challenge and promise of a whole new psychic geography to be explored. But there is also a difficult and dangerous walking on the ice, as we try to find language and images for a consciousness we are just coming into, and with little in the past to support us. I want to talk about some aspects of this difficulty and this danger.

Jane Harrison, the great classical anthropologist, wrote in 1914 in a letter to her friend Gilbert Murray:

> By the by, about "Women," it has bothered me often—why do women never want to write poetry about Man as a sex—why is Woman a dream and a terror to man and not the other way around? . . . Is it mere convention and propriety, or something deeper?

I think Jane Harrison's question cuts deep into the myth-making tradition, the romantic tradition; deep into what women and men have been to each other; and deep into the psyche of the woman writer. Thinking about that question, I began thinking of the work of two twentieth-century women poets, Sylvia Plath and Diane Wakoski. It strikes me that in the work of both Man appears as, if not a dream, a fascination and a terror; and that the source of the fascination and the terror is, sim-ply, Man's power—to dominate, tyrannize, choose, or reject the woman. The charisma of Man seems to come purely from his power over her and his control of the world by force, not from anything fertile or life-giving in him. And, in the work of both these poets, it is finally the woman's sense of *herself*—embattled, possessed—that gives the poetry its dynamic charge, its rhythms of struggle, need, will, and fe-male energy. Until recently this female anger and this furious awareness of the Man's power over her were not available materials to the female poet, who tended to write of Love as the source of her suffering, and to view that victimization by Love as an almost inevitable fate. Or, like Marianne Moore and Elizabeth Bishop, she kept sex-uality at a measured and chiseled distance in her poems.

One answer to Jane Harrison's question has to be that historically men and women have played very different parts in each others' lives. Where woman has been a luxury for man, and has served as the painter's model and the poet's muse, but also as comforter, nurse, cook, bearer of his seed, secretarial assistant, and copyist of manuscripts, man has played a quite different role for the female artist. Henry James repeats an incident which the writer Prosper Mérimée described, of how, while he was living with George Sand,

> he once opened his eyes, in the raw winter dawn, to see his companion, in a dressing-gown, on her knees before the domestic hearth, a candlestick beside her and a red *madras* round her head, making bravely, with her own hands the fire that was to enable her to sit down betimes to urgent pen and paper. The story represents him as having felt that the spectacle chilled his ardor and tried his taste; her appearance was unfortunate, her occupation an inconsequence, and her industry a reproof—the result of all which was a lively irritation and an early rupture.

The specter of this kind of male judgment, along with the misnaming and thwarting of her needs by a culture controlled by males, has created problems for the woman writer: problems of contact with herself, problems of language and style, problems of energy and survival.

In rereading Virginia Woolf's *A Room of One's Own* (1929) for the first time in some years, I was astonished at the sense of effort, of pains taken, of dogged tentativeness, in the tone of that essay. And I recognized that tone. I had heard it often enough, in myself and in other women. It is the tone of a woman determined not to appear angry, who is *willing* herself to be calm, detached, and even charming in a roomful of men where things have been said which are attacks on her very integrity. Virginia Woolf is addressing an audience of women, but she is acutely conscious—as she always was—of being overheard by men: by Morgan and Lytton and Maynard Keynes and for that matter by her father, Leslie Stephen. She drew the language out into an exacerbated thread in her determination to have her own sensibility yet protect it from those masculine presences. Only at rare moments in that essay do you hear the passion in her voice; she was trying to sound as cool as Jane Austen, as Olympian as Shakespeare, because that is the way the men of the culture thought a writer should sound.

No male writer has written primarily or even largely for women, or with the sense of women's criticism as a consideration when he chooses his materials, his theme, his language. But to a lesser or greater extent, every woman writer has written for men even when, like Virginia Woolf, she was supposed to be addressing women. If we have come to the point when this balance might begin to change, when women can stop being haunted, not only by "convention and propriety" but by internalized fears of being and saying themselves, then it is an extraordinary moment for the woman writer—and reader.

I have hesitated to do what I am going to do now, which is to use myself as an illustration. For one thing, it's a lot easier and less dangerous to talk about other women writers. But there is something else. Like Virginia Woolf, I am aware of the women who are not with us here because they are washing the dishes and looking after the children. Nearly fifty years after she spoke, that fact remains largely unchanged. And I am thinking also of women whom she left out of the picture altogether—women who are washing other people's dishes and caring for other people's children, not to mention women who went on the streets last night in order to feed their children. We seem to be special women here, we have liked to think of ourselves as special, and we have known that men would tolerate, even romanticize us as special, as long as our words and actions didn't threaten their privilege of tolerating or rejecting us and our work according to *their* ideas of what a special woman ought to be. An important insight of the radical women's movement has been how divisive and how ultimately destructive is this myth of the special woman, who is also the token woman. Every one of us here in this room has had great luck—we are teachers, writers, academicians; our own gifts could not have been enough, for we all know women whose gifts are buried or aborted. Our struggles can have meaning and our privileges—however precarious under patriarchy—can be justified only if they can help to change the lives of women whose gifts—and whose very being—continue to be thwarted and silenced.

My own luck was being born white and middle-class into a house full of books, with a father who encouraged me to read and write. So for about twenty years I wrote for a particular man, who criticized and praised me and made me feel I was indeed "special." The obverse of this, of course, was that I tried for a long time to please him, or rather, not to displease him. And then of course there were other men—writers, teachers—the Man, who was not a terror or a dream but a literary master and a master in other ways less easy to acknowledge. And there were all those poems about women, written by men: it seemed to be a given that men wrote poems and women frequently inhabited them. These women were almost always beautiful, but threatened with the loss of beauty, the loss of youth—the fate worse than death. Or, they were beautiful and died young, like Lucy and Lenore. Or, the woman was like Maud Gonne, cruel and disastrously mistaken, and the poem reproached her because she had refused to become a luxury for the poet.

A lot is being said today about the influence that the myths and images of women have on all of us who are products of culture. I think it has been a peculiar confusion to the girl or woman who tries to write because she is peculiarly susceptible to language. She goes to poetry or fiction looking for *her* way of being in the world, since she too has been putting words and images together; she is looking eagerly for guides, maps, possibilities; and over and over in the "words' masculine persuasive force" of literature she comes up against something that negates everything she is about: she meets the image of Woman in books written by men. She finds a terror and a dream, she finds a beautiful pale face, she finds La Belle Dame Sans Merci, she finds Juliet or Tess or Salomé, but precisely what she does not find is that absorbed, drudging, puzzled, sometimes inspired creature, herself, who sits at a desk trying to put words together.

So what does she do? What did I do? I read the older women poets with their peculiar keenness and ambivalence: Sappho, Christina Rossetti, Emily Dickinson, Elinor Wylie, Edna Millay, H. D. I discovered that the woman poet most admired at the time (by men) was Marianne Moore, who was maidenly, elegant, intellectual, discreet. But even in reading these women I was looking in them for the same things I had found in the poetry of men, because I wanted women poets to be the equals of men, and to be equal was still confused with sounding the same.

I know that my style was formed first by male poets: by the men I was reading as an undergraduate—Frost, Dylan Thomas, Donne, Auden, MacNiece, Stevens, Yeats. What I chiefly learned from them was craft. But poems are like dreams: in them you put what you don't know you know. Looking back at poems I wrote before I was twenty-one, I'm startled because beneath the conscious craft are glimpses of the split I even then experienced between the girl who wrote poems, who defined herself in writing poems, and the girl who was to define herself by her relationships with men. "Aunt Jennifer's Tigers" (1951), written while I was a student, looks with deliberate detachment at this split.

Aunt Jennifer's tigers stride across a screen,
Bright topaz denizens of a world of green.
They do not fear the men beneath the tree;
They pace in sleek chivalric certainty.

Aunt Jennifer's fingers fluttering through her wool
Find even the ivory needle hard to pull.
The massive weight of Uncle's wedding band
Sits heavily upon Aunt Jennifer's hand.

When Aunt is dead, her terrified hands will lie
Still ringed with ordeals she was mastered by.
The tigers in the panel that she made
Will go on striding, proud and unafraid.

In writing this poem, composed and apparently cool as it is, I thought I was creating a portrait of an imaginary woman. But this woman suffers from the opposition of her imagination, worked out in tapestry, and her life-style, "ringed with ordeals she was mastered by." It was important to me that Aunt Jennifer was a person as distinct from myself as possible—distanced by the formalism of the poem, by its objective, observant tone—even by putting the woman in a different generation.

In those years formalism was part of the strategy—like asbestos gloves, it allowed me to handle materials I couldn't pick up bare-handed. A later strategy was to use the persona of a man, as I did in "The Loser" (1958):

A man thinks of the woman he once loved: first, after
her wedding, and then nearly a decade later.

I
I kissed you, bride and lost, and went
home from that bourgeois sacrament,
your cheek still tasting cold upon
my lips that gave you benison
with all the swagger that they knew—
as losers somehow learn to do.

Your wedding made my eyes ache; soon
the world would be worse off for one
more golden apple dropped to ground
without the least protesting sound,
and you would windfall lie, and we
forget your shimmer on the tree.

Beauty is always wasted: if
not Mignon's song sung to the deaf,
at all events to the unmoved.
A face like yours cannot be loved
long or seriously enough.
Almost, we seem to hold it off.

II
Well, you are tougher than I thought.
Now when the wash with ice hangs taut
this morning of St. Valentine,
I see you strip the squeaking line,
your body weighed against the load,
and all my groans can do no good.

Because you are still beautiful,
though squared and stiffened by the pull
of what nine windy years have done.
You have three daughters, lost a son.
I see all your intelligence
flung into that unwearied stance.

My envy is of no avail.
I turn my head and wish him well
who chafed your beauty into use
and lives forever in a house
lit by the friction of your mind.
You stagger in against the wind.

I finished college, published my first book by a fluke, it seemed to me, and broke off a love affair. I took a job, lived alone, went on writing, fell in love. I was young, full of energy, and the book seemed to mean that others agreed I was a poet. Because I was also determined to prove that as a woman poet I could also have what was then defined as a "full" woman's life, I plunged in my early twenties into marriage and had three children before I was thirty. There was nothing overt in the environment to warn me: these were the fifties, and in reaction to the earlier wave of feminism, middle-class women were making careers of domestic perfection, working to send their husbands through professional schools, then retiring to raise large families. People were moving out to the suburbs, technology was going to be the answer to everything, even sex; the family was in its glory. Life was extremely private; women were isolated from each other by the loyalties of marriage. I have a sense that women didn't talk to each other much in the fifties—not about their secret emptinesses, their frustrations. I went on trying to write; my second book and first child appeared in the same month. But by the time that book came out I was already dissatisfied with those poems, which seemed to me mere exercises for poems I hadn't written. The book was praised, however, for its "gracefulness"; I had a marriage and a child. If there were doubts, if there were periods of null depression or active despairing, these could only mean that I was ungrateful, insatiable, perhaps a monster.

About the time my third child was born, I felt that I had either to consider myself a failed woman and a failed poet, or to try to find some synthesis by which to understand what was happening to me. What frightened me most was the sense of drift, of being pulled along on a current which called itself my destiny, but in which I seemed to be losing touch with whoever I had been, with the girl who had experienced her own will and energy almost ecstatically at times, walking around a city or riding a train at night or typing in a student room. In a poem about my grandmother I wrote (of myself): "A young girl, thought sleeping, is certified dead" ("Halfway"). I was writing very little, partly from fatigue, that female fatigue of suppressed anger and loss of contact with my own being; partly from the discontinuity of female life with its attention to small chores, errands, work that others constantly undo, small children's constant needs. What I did write was unconvincing to me; my anger and frustration were hard to acknowledge in or out of poems because in fact I cared a great deal about my husband and my children. Trying to look back and understand that time I have tried to analyze the real nature of the conflict. Most, if not all, human lives are full of fantasy—passive day-dreaming which need not be acted on. But to write poetry or fiction, or even to think well, is not to fantasize, or to put fantasies on paper. For a poem to coalesce, for a character or an action to take shape, there has to be an imaginative transformation of reality which is in no way passive. And a certain freedom of the mind is needed—freedom to press on, to enter the currents of your thought like a glider pilot, knowing that your motion can be sustained, that the buoyancy of your attention will not be suddenly snatched away. Moreover, if the imagination is to transcend and transform experience it has to question, to challenge, to conceive of alternatives, perhaps to the very life you are living at that moment. You have to be free to play around with the notion that day might be night, love might be hate; nothing can be too sacred for the imagination to turn into its opposite or to call experimentally by another name. For writing is re-naming. Now, to be maternally with small children all day in the old way, to be with a man in the old way of marriage, requires a holding-back, a putting-aside of that imaginative activity, and demands instead a kind of conservatism. I want to make it clear that I am *not* saying that in order to write well, or think well, it is necessary to become unavailable to others, or to become a devouring ego. This has been the myth of the masculine artist and thinker; and I do not accept it. But to be a female human being trying to fulfill traditional female functions in a traditional way *is* in direct conflict with the subversive function of the imagination. The word *traditional* is important here. There must be ways, and we will be finding out more and more about them, in which the energy of creation and the energy of relation can be united. But in those years I always felt the conflict as a failure of love in myself. I had thought I was choosing a full life: the life available to most men, in which sexuality, work, and parenthood could coexist. But I felt, at twenty-nine, guilt toward the people closest to me, and guilty toward my own being.

I wanted, then, more than anything, the one thing of which there was never enough: time to think, time to write. The fifties and early sixties were years of rapid revelations: the sit-ins and marches in the South, the Bay of Pigs, the early antiwar movement, raised large questions—questions for which the masculine world of the academy around me seemed to have expert and fluent answers. But I needed to think for myself—about pacifism and dissent and violence, about poetry and society, and about my own relationship to all these things. For about ten years I was reading in fierce snatches, scribbling in notebooks, writing poetry in fragments; I was looking desperately for clues, because if there were no clues then I thought I might be insane. I wrote in a notebook about this time:

> Paralyzed by the sense that there exists a mesh of relationships—e.g., between my anger at the children, my sensual life, pacifism, sex (I mean sex in its broadest significance, not merely sexual desire)—an interconnectedness which, if I could see it, make it valid, would give me back myself, make it possible to function lucidly and passionately. Yet I grope in and out among these dark webs.

I think I began at this point to feel that politics was not something "out there" but something "in here" and of the essence of my condition.

In the late fifties I was able to write, for the first time, directly about experiencing myself as a woman. The poem was jotted in fragments during children's naps, brief hours in a library, or at 3:00 A.M. after rising with a wakeful child. I despaired of doing any continuous work at this time. Yet I began to feel that my fragments and scraps had a common consciousness and a common theme, one that I would have been very unwilling to put on paper at an earlier time because I had been taught that poetry should be "universal," which meant, of course, nonfemale. Until then I had tried very much *not* to identify myself as a female poet. Over two years I wrote a ten-part poem called "Snapshots of a Daughter-in-Law" (1958–1960), in a longer looser mode than I'd ever trusted myself with before. It was an extraordinary relief to write that poem. It strikes me now as too literary, too dependent on allusion; I hadn't found the courage yet to do without authorities, or even to use the pronoun "I"—the woman in the poem is always "she." One section of it, No. 2, concerns a woman who thinks she is going mad; she is haunted by voices telling her to resist and rebel, voices that she can hear but not obey.

> Banging the coffee-pot into the sink
> she hears the angels chiding, and looks out
> past the raked gardens to the sloppy sky.
> Only a week since They said: *Have no patience.*
>
> The next time it was: *Be insatiable.*
> Then: *Save yourself; others you cannot save.*
> Sometimes she's let the tapstream scald her arm,
> a match burn to her thumbnail,
>
> or held her hand above the kettle's snout
> right in the woolly steam. They are probably angels,
> since nothing hurts her anymore, except
> each morning's grit blowing into her eyes.

The poem "Orion," written five years later, is a poem of re-connection with a part of myself I had felt I was losing—the active principle, the energetic imagination, the "half-brother" whom I projected, as I had for many years, into the constellation Orion. It's no accident that the words "cold and egotistical" appear in this poem, and are applied to myself.

> Far back when I went zig-zagging
> through tamarack pastures
> you were my genius, you
> my cast-iron Viking, my helmed
> lion-heart king in prison.
> Years later now you're young
>
> my fierce half-brother, staring
> down from that simplified west
> your breast open, your belt dragged down
> by an oldfashioned thing, a sword
> the last bravado you won't give over
> though it weighs you down as you stride

and the stars in it are dim
and maybe have stopped burning.
But you burn, and I know it;
as I throw back my head to take you in
an old transfusion happens again:
divine astronomy is nothing to it.

Indoors I bruise and blunder,
break faith, leave ill enough
alone, a dead child born in the dark.
Night cracks up over the chimney,
pieces of time, frozen geodes
come showering down in the grate.

A man reaches behind my eyes
and finds them empty
a woman's head turns away
from my head in the mirror
children are dying my death
and eating crumbs of my life.

Pity is not your forte.
Calmly you ache up there
pinned aloft in your crow's nest,
my speechless pirate!
You take it all for granted
and when I look you back

it's with a starlike eye
shooting its cold and egotistical spear
where it can do least damage.
Breathe deep! No hurt, no pardon
out here in the cold with you
you with your back to the wall.

The choice still seemed to be between "love"—womanly, maternal love, altruistic love—a love defined and ruled by the weight of an entire culture; and egotism—a force directed by men into creation, achievement, ambition, often at the expense of others, but justifiably so. For weren't they men, and wasn't that their destiny as womanly, selfless love was ours? We know now that the alternatives are false ones—that the word "love" is itself in need of re-vision.

There is a companion poem to "Orion," written three years later, in which at last the woman in the poem and the woman writing the poem become the same person. It is called "Planetarium," and it was written after a visit to a real planetarium, where I read an account of the work of Caroline Herschel, the astronomer, who worked with her brother William, but whose name remained obscure, as his did not.

Thinking of Caroline Herschel, 1750–1848, astronomer, sister of William; and others

A woman in the shape of a monster
a monster in the shape of a woman
the skies are full of them

a woman   "in the snow
among the Clocks and instruments
or measuring the ground with poles"

in her 98 years to discover
8 comets

she whom the moon ruled
like us
levitating into the night sky
riding the polished lenses

Galaxies of women, there
doing penance for impetuousness
ribs chilled
in those spaces   of the mind

An eye,
          "virile, precise and absolutely certain"
          from the mad webs of Uranusborg
                              encountering the NOVA

every impulse of light exploding
from the core
as life flies out of us

          Tycho whispering at last
          "Let me not seem to have lived in vain"

What we see, we see
and seeing is changing

the light that shrivels a mountain
and leaves a man alive

Heartbeat of the pulsar
heart sweating through my body

The radio impulse
pouring in from Taurus

          I am bombarded yet   I stand

I have been standing all my life in the
direct path of a battery of signals
the most accurately transmitted most
untranslatable language in the universe
I am a galactic cloud so deep   so invo-
luted that a light wave could take 15
years to travel through me   And has
taken   I am an instrument in the shape
of a woman trying to translate pulsations
into images   for the relief of the body
and the reconstruction of the mind.

In closing I want to tell you about a dream I had last summer. I dreamed I was asked to read my poetry at a mass women's meeting, but when I began to read, what came out were the lyrics of a blues song. I share this dream with you because it seemed to me to say something about the problems and the future of the woman writer, and probably of women in general. The awakening of consciousness is not like the crossing of a frontier—one step and you are in another country. Much of women's poetry has been of the nature of the blues song: a cry of pain, of victimization, or a lyric of seduction. And today, much poetry by women—and prose for that matter—is charged with anger. I think we need to go through that anger, and we will betray our own reality if we try, as Virginia Woolf was trying, for an objectivity, a detachment, that would make us sound more like Jane Austen or Shakespeare. We know more than Jane Austen or Shakespeare knew: more than Jane Austen because our lives are more complex, more than Shakespeare because we know more about the lives of women—Jane Austen and Virginia Woolf included.

Both the victimization and the anger experienced by women are real, and have real sources, everywhere in the environment, built into society, language, the structures of thought. They will go on being tapped and explored by poets, among others. We can neither deny them, nor will we rest there. A new generation of women poets is already working out of the psychic energy released when women begin to move out towards what the feminist philosopher Mary Daly has described as the "new space" on the "boundaries of patriarchy." Women are speaking to and of women in these poems, out of a newly released courage to name, to love each other, to share risk and grief and celebration.

To the eye of a feminist, the work of Western male poets writing in the 1970s reveals a deep, fatalistic pessimism as to the possibilities of change, whether societal or personal, along with a familiar and threadbare use of women (and nature) as redemptive on the one hand, threatening on the other; and a new tide of phallocentric sadism and overt woman-hating that matches the sexual brutality of recent films. "Political" poetry by men remains stranded amid the struggles for power among male groups; in condemning U.S. imperialism or the Chilean junta the poet can claim to speak for the oppressed while remaining, as male, part of a system of sexual oppression. The enemy is always outside the self, the struggle somewhere else. The mood of isolation, self-pity, and self-imitation that pervades "nonpolitical" poetry suggests that a profound change in masculine consciousness will have to precede any new male poetic—or other—inspiration. The creative energy of patriarchy is fast running out; what remains is its self-generating energy for destruction. As women, we have our work cut out for us.

1971

RHINA ESPAILLAT
(B. 1932)

Rhina Espaillat was born in 1932 in the Dominican Republic, which was then ruled by the dictator, Rafael Trujillo. When her father, who was part of the Dominican diplomatic mission in Washington, D.C., was exiled for opposing the Trujillo regime, the family emigrated to the United States. In 1939 they came to New York where the young Espaillat was suddenly immersed in a new language and culture. She attended New York City public schools as she has remarked, "from grade to graduate school." After finishing her B.A. at Hunter College in 1953, she taught English for a year in the city's high school system. In 1952 she married Alfred Moskowitz, an industrial arts teacher, and had three sons. Once the children were older, she earned a Master's Degree in 1964 from Queen's College and taught English for fifteen years at Jamaica High School in Queens, New York. In 1990, she and her husband moved to Newburyport, Massachusetts, to be near two of their sons.

After retiring, Espaillat had the opportunity to work more assiduously on poetry, which she had written all her life—first in Spanish, then in English. Having published in a major journal as a high school junior in 1943, she had been invited to join the Poetry Society of America, the youngest member ever accepted into the organization. Her first volume *Lapsing to Grace* appeared in 1992. Shortly thereafter she won both the Howard Nemerov and the *Sparrow* sonnet awards. A second collection, *Where Horizons Go* (1998), appeared after having won the T. S. Eliot award. As X. J. Kennedy, the judge for the prize noted, "I'm won over by the way the poet writes of the most commonplace experience—she's a warm affirmer of life. Keen intelligence, keen feeling."

Espaillat's essay, "Bilingual / Bilingüe," began as a talk at the 1997 West Chester University Poetry Conference addressing the topic "Finding Something in Translation." A shorter version of the talk—reprinted here—served as the afterword to *Where Horizons Go*. In the essay Espaillat discusses the linguistic confusion and abundance encountered by bilingual poets.

BILINGUAL/BILINGÜE

Recent interest in the phenomenon known as "Spanglish" has led me to reexamine my own experience as a writer who works chiefly in her second language, and especially to recall my father's inflexible rule against the mixing of languages. In fact, no English was allowed in that midtown Manhattan apartment that became home after my arrival in New York in 1939. My father read the daily paper in English, taught himself to follow disturbing events in Europe through the medium of English-language radio, and even taught me to read the daily comic strips, in an effort to speed my learning of the language he knew I would need. But that necessary language was banished from family conversation: it was the medium of the outer world, beyond the door; inside, among ourselves, only Spanish was permitted, and it had to be pure, grammatical, unadulterated Spanish.

At the age of seven, however, nothing seems more important than communicating with classmates and neighborhood children. For my mother, too, the new language was a way out of isolation, a means to deal with the larger world and with those American women for whom she sewed. But my father, a political exile waiting for changes in our native country, had different priorities: he lived in the hope of return, and believed that the new home, the new speech, were temporary. His theory was simple: if it could be said at all, it could be said best in the language of those authors whose words were the core of his education. But his insistence on pure Spanish made it difficult, sometimes impossible, to bring home and share the jokes of friends, puns, pop lyrics, and other staples of seven-year-old conversation. Table talk sometimes ended with tears or sullen silence.

And yet, despite the friction it caused from time to time, my native language was also a source of comfort—the reading that I loved, intimacy within the family, and a peculiar auditory delight best described as echoes in the mind. I learned early to relish words as counters in a game that could turn suddenly serious without losing the quality of play, and to value their sound as a meaning behind their meaning.

Nostalgia, a confusion of identity, the fear that if the native language is lost the self will somehow be altered forever: all are part of the subtle flavor of immigrant life, as well as the awareness that one owes gratitude to strangers for acts of communication that used to be simple and once imposed no such debt.

Memory, folklore, and food all become part of the receding landscape that language sets out to preserve. Guilt, too, adds to the mix, the suspicion that to love the second language too much is to betray those ancestors who spoke the first and could not communicate with us in the vocabulary of our education, our new thoughts. And finally, a sense of grievance and loss may spur hostility toward the new language and those who speak it, as if the common speech of the perceived majority could weld together a disparate population into a huge, monolithic, and threatening Other. That Other is then assigned traits and habits that preclude sympathy and mold "Us" into a unity whose cohesiveness gives comfort.

Originally delivered as a lecture at the West Chester University Poetry Conference in June 1997 in an expanded form. Published as afterword to *Where Horizons Go* (Kirksville, Missouri: New Odyssey Press, 1998) 67–70.

Luckily, there is another side to bilingualism: curiosity about the Other may be as natural and pervasive as group loyalty. If it weren't, travel, foreign residence, and intermarriage would be less common than they are. For some bilingual writers, the Other—and the language he speaks—are appealing. Some acknowledge and celebrate the tendency of languages to borrow from each other and produce something different in the process. That is, in part, the tendency that has given rise to "Spanglish."

It's dangerous, however, to accept the inevitable melding of languages over time as a justification for speaking, in the short run, a mix that impoverishes both languages by allowing words in one to drive out perfectly good equivalent words in the other. The habitual speaker of such a mix ends by speaking not two, or even one complete language, but fragments of two that are no longer capable of standing alone or serving the speaker well with any larger audience. As a literary device with limited appeal and durability, "Spanglish," like other such blends, is expressive and fresh. But as a substitute for genuine bilinguality—the cultivation and preservation of two languages—I suspect it represents a danger to the advancement of foreign speakers, and a loss to both cultures. My father sensed as much in 1939, and stubbornly preserved my native language for me, through his insistence that I be truly bilingual rather than a traveler across boundaries that "Spanglish" has made all too permeable.

My father, who never learned to think in English, was persuaded that the words of his own language were the "true" names for things in the world. But for me that link between fact and word was broken, as it is for many who grow up bilingual. Having been taught to love words and take them seriously as reflections of reality, I felt it a loss to learn that, in fact, words are arbitrary, man-made, no more permanent than clothing: somewhere under all of them reality is naked.

Disconcerting as it is, however, to lose the security of words that are perceived as single keys to what they unlock, it is also exhilarating to see oneself as the maker of those words, even if they are now impermanent, provisional artifacts that have value for us only because they're ours. Anybody who has ever gone hunting for that one right and elusive word knows what bilingualism feels like, even if he's never left his native country or learned a word in any language but his own. There is a sense in which every poet is bilingual, and those of us who are more overtly so are only living metaphors for the condition that applies to us all. We use a language that seems deceptively like the language of the people around us, but isn't quite. The words are the same, but the weight we give them, the connections we find among them, the criteria we use to choose this one rather than that one, are our own.

At a recent poetry reading I closed with a poem in Spanish, and a member of the English-speaking audience approached me afterward to remark how moved she had been by that poem, and how she wished I had read others.

"Where did you learn Spanish?" I asked.

"I don't speak any Spanish," she replied. "What I understood was the music of what you read."

It occurred to me, during our subsequent conversation, that poetry may be precisely what is almost lost, not in translation, but in the wording, the transit from experience to paper. If we succeed in salvaging anything, maybe it is most often in the music, the formal elements of poetry that do travel from language to language, as the formal music of classic Spanish poetry my father loved followed me into English and draws me, to this day, to poems that are patterned and rich and playful.

It's occurred to me since that conversation that a poem in Spanish may have more in common with a poem in English—or any other language—than with a grocery list, say, or a piece of technical writing that happens to use Spanish words. There is something in poetry that transcends specific language, that makes it possible for transplanted people like me to recognize the songs of the Other as his own even before he understands them fully. Poetry may be used to draw very small circles around itself, identifying its speaker as a member of a narrowly delineated group and looking at "outsiders" with eyes that discern less and less detail as distance increases. But it may also be used to draw very large circles, circles that will draw in rather than exclude, as in Edwin Markham's apt four-line metaphor titled "Outwitted":

He drew a circle that shut me out—
Heretic, rebel, a thing to flout.
But Love and I had the wit to win:
We drew a circle that shut him in.

1998

ANNE STEVENSON
(B. 1933)

Although an American citizen, Anne Stevenson has lived much of her life in Britain. "This has meant a measure of flexibility," she once wrote, "and a constant state of flux." She was born in Cambridge, England, where her father, the American philosopher Charles Leslie Stevenson, was studying with G. E. Moore and Ludwig Wittgenstein. Stevenson grew up in a cultivated household. Her father, a prominent professor at the University of Michigan in Ann Arbor, was also an accomplished musician who played both piano and cello—instruments that Anne, too, would take up.

After graduating from University High School in Ann Arbor in 1950, Stevenson entered the University of Michigan. While an undergraduate, she won the prestigious Hopwood Literary Award three times. She earned her B.A. from Michigan in 1954, and that same year moved to England and married Robin Hitchcock, with whom she would have a daughter. The marriage lasted just a few years. Returning to Michigan, she earned her master's degree in 1962 and married Mark Elvin, with whom she would have two sons. By that time she was back in England composing the poems she would collect in *Living in America* (1965) and doing research for the first full-length study of Elizabeth Bishop. Her correspondence with Bishop has proved an irreplaceable archive for scholars.

A second collection, *Reversals* (1969), offered both light and troubling views of domesticity and sex spoken fearlessly from a woman's point of view. By this time it was clear that Stevenson was a relentlessly honest poet; like Sylvia Plath she was frank even about her negative emotions. In 1974 Stevenson published *Correspondences: A Family History in Letters,* which would later be the basis of a radio play for the BBC. This long ambitious work, which uses both verse and prose, is a sprawling family saga which moves from early nineteenth-century America to the present. Although *Correspondences* is fictional, its sense of family psychology is personal, and its conclusion displays some of the transatlantic complexity of her work: "It is a poem I can't continue. / It is America I can't contain."

Stevenson's poetic stance—fiercely intelligent, formally rigorous but not hidebound, negotiating personal and public subjects—characterizes the poetry she has published in more than a dozen collections. In her preface to the *Collected Poems* (1996) she wrote, "It may be possible to descry in these peregrinations stages in 'the growth of the poet's mind'; on the other hand, I myself regard most of these poems as experiments in words and sound." Yet the poems are often philosophical and always intellectually lucid, whether in free verse or meter. Her most recent collection, *Granny Scarecrow* (2000), is among her strongest, and it continues to develop Stevenson's sense of the world outside herself—a Darwinian vision she has adapted partly from Elizabeth Bishop. Now regarded in England as one of poetry's senior eminences, Stevenson currently divides her time between two houses—one in northern England, the other in Wales—with her fourth husband, historian Peter Lucas.

Her first critical study, *Elizabeth Bishop,* was published in 1966, her second, *Five Looks at Elizabeth Bishop,* in 1998. Yet Stevenson is best known for her brilliant and controversial biography of Sylvia Plath, *Bitter Fame* (1989). She has written with deep admiration, even love, about Plath's poetry, but refused to sentimentalize the poet's turbulent life or devastating mental illness. Indeed, as an American woman of Plath's generation living in England and participating in the same British literary milieu, Stevenson was ideally situated to understand her subject's life. Some critics reacted as if Stevenson had capitulated to Plath's widower, Ted Hughes, and his sister Olwyn, who acted as literary agent for the Plath estate, as if she had ma-liciously diminished Plath as a feminist icon. But Stevenson's revisionist por-trait is uncompromisingly truthful and vivid, a landmark in literary biography of the period.

Above all, Stevenson is a defender of "poetry's weird tyranny and un-governable need to exist." In her criticism she can be very tough-minded, but her essays and reviews are never merely clever. She has one of the most flu-ent prose styles of any American critic and a commanding range of intel-lectual allusion. An active literary critic, Stevenson has collected only one book of her shorter prose pieces, *Between the Iceberg and the Ship: Selected Essays* (1998), which was published by the University of Michigan Press. Its ironic title provides a metaphor that is indicative of Stevenson's critical mind—and perhaps the mind of her poetry as well. Neither the cold and inanimate destroyer in the world outside us nor the unsuspecting victim-to-be, the poet-critic measures the space between the iceberg and the ship, her bulletins frequent, lively, and accurate in the extreme.

WRITING AS A WOMAN

Suppose we begin by calling to mind some scenes from Sylvia Plath's *The Bell Jar.* Esther Greenwood, a heroine who more obviously than most is a version of the author, has returned from a disillusioning experience as a student editor of a ladies' magazine in New York. The glamorous world of fashion writing and famous

Originally published in *Women Writing and Women Writing about Women,* ed. Mary Jacobus (New York: Barnes and Noble Books, 1979). Collected in *Between the Iceberg and the Ship: Selected Essays* (Ann Arbor: University of Michigan Press, 1998) 3–21.

authors has proved to be a fraud. Her fellow students have been frivolous, the parties tedious; the men, vain or sadistic, have failed to seduce or even interest her. At the climactic dinner, crabmeat and avocado salad, roasted in photographer's lights, have laid the whole company flat with ptomaine poisoning. Finally, at the end of her stay, Esther stands on the parapet of her hotel feeding piece after piece of her fashionable wardrobe to the night winds—a gesture of anger and defiance so total that she is forced to barter her dressing gown for clothes to travel in the next day.

When Esther returns to her mother in suburban Westchester, the first thing she hears is that her application for a writers' course in Cambridge has been turned down. She has already seen through the shallow hypocrisy of her medical-student boyfriend, Buddy Willard, and his "clean-living" family. The summer has been a disaster in its first month, and Esther Greenwood, for the first time in the course of a stunningly successful adolescence, is forced to face up to what she is. What she is turns out to be a girl—a middle-class American girl, talented and ambitious, yes, but of whom things are expected that have nothing to do with her talents and ambitions. Poor Esther. Poor Sylvia.

Now, I want to disregard, temporarily, Sylvia Plath's own psychological troubles (they have been too much discussed in any case) and look instead at the predicament of Esther Greenwood. What are we to say of this account in *The Bell Jar* of a talented woman's first brush with—we must call it for lack of a better term—"the real world"?

If we are truly bigoted we can dismiss Esther's suffering as the neurosis of an "overachievement-oriented schoolgirl." But none of us would want to do that. More to the point, we can regard *The Bell Jar* as an honest, often brilliant, account of a woman's confrontation with a society many of whose values are an insult to her integrity. However, there is more to *The Bell Jar* than this. For as a writer, Esther Greenwood, like Sylvia Plath, has a vested interest *in* her society. She craves its approval and she needs it for material. She also has instinctive "womanly" feelings, and quite naturally she is curious about sex, babies, marriage, and what her future as a woman will be.

The trouble in *The Bell Jar* seems to be this: throughout most of her life Esther has pulled herself to the top of her society—at school, at college—by native intelligence and stupendous willpower. Now, suddenly, she finds that she is a victim of forces beyond her control . . . forces that are also desires. She wants to be a complete woman, but in most womanly roles she can't excel. Why can she not cook, take shorthand, dance, play the piano, translate languages, do all the things in the world women are expected to do to help men? And why, on the other hand, do the things she *can* do (write, win academic prizes, win scholarships) seem not to matter to other people, particularly men—or, if they do matter, lead to disillusionment? The editing job was a fiasco; the writing course wouldn't accept her.

These two streams of (seemingly) personal failure undermine and finally paralyze her will. After a series of imaginary flights to other, quite impossible selves (she should marry a prison guard on Deer Island and have a parcel of kids; she should become a Catholic and confess to a priest; she should study shorthand, become a typist, be a waitress)—after these flights away from her own personality have come to nothing, Esther turns to the only refuge from her torment she can think of and attempts to kill herself in a corner under the house.

It is not my purpose to undertake an analysis of *The Bell Jar*, though I might point out that, as a piece of writing, the tough, amused bitterness of the first third of the book dissolves into jerky passages of confession and crude resentment once the breakdown has occurred. What is of interest to us, however, is that Sylvia Plath implies all the way through that the roles of "writer" and "woman" are in some way incompatible. Yet, like so many of us, she was damned if she herself was going to forgo one to become the other. The tension between the two roles—the woman and the writer—is a source of energy in her poems, but it is also, I think, a source of their self-destructiveness. What seems most self-destructive in Plath's work is a haunting fear of failure. The emotional power she summons from her subconscious is a mixture of a fear of inadequacy and a knowledge of her superiority. She establishes her astringently defiant tone in a language of inventive complaint and embattled anger.

I hasten to add that this mixture of inadequacy and superiority is common in American writing. It is to be found all through Berryman and Lowell, and even in Whitman. Since we are talking of women, it is of interest to note that Emily Dickinson's letters—when she was exercising her ferocious wit—make use of the same defiant tone that Sylvia Plath perfected in parts of *The Bell Jar*. Let's compare two passages. Here is Emily Dickinson describing her family to Colonel Higginson.

> I have Brother & a Sister—My Mother does not care for thought—and Father, too busy with his Briefs—to notice what we do. He buys me many Books—but begs me not to read them—because he fears they joggle the Mind. They are all religious—except-me and address an Eclipse, every morning,—whom they call their "Father."

Can you think of a more devastating attack on the male-dominated family than that? And yet, the wit is suspect. We know that Emily Dickinson adored her father, rather pitied as well as despised her mother, relied on her sister to make her way in the world possible. So her *real* attitude is defensive of the system she is attacking. What is wrong with her world is exactly what gives her advantages in it, as a woman and as a writer. She is superior in intelligence to everyone she knows, but inferior in ability to meet the world on *its* terms. She decides, therefore, quite early in her life that it will suit her better not to try. In her letters she makes fun of a state of affairs she could never have borne to change.

Sylvia Plath was, of course, temperamentally a different creature altogether. She wanted to be a good writer, but she also wanted to be an exceptionally efficient wife, mother, and housekeeper; we know that from the recently published *Letters Home* (1975). Her attack on Dodo Conway, as Dodo pushes her creaking pram under Esther's window in the suburbs, is partly an attack on the general slovenlinesss of human beings when they allow themselves to go nature's way without the puritan constraints of self-control.

> A woman not five feet tall, with a grotesque protruding stomach, was wheeling an old black baby carriage down the street. Two or three small children of various sizes, all pale, with smudgy faces and bare smudgy knees, wobbled along in the shadow of her skirts.
>   A serene, almost religious smile lit up the woman's face. Her head tilted happily back, like a sparrow egg perched on a duck egg, she smiled into the sun.

But like Emily Dickinson, Sylvia Plath is not showing her full hand. For (as Plath herself sees) Dodo Conway is a *happy* woman. She is far happier, with her babies and her protruding stomach, than Esther is, or Esther's mother, whose efforts to bring up two children to be clean-living, responsible citizens are in some ways more threatening to Esther's creativeness than Dodo's untidy brood. Dodo presents Esther with an alternative that a part of her wants to accept.

Having no father, Sylvia Plath cannot fondly make fun of him, as Emily Dickinson could of hers. You remember how in *The Bell Jar*, Plath has Esther make a pilgrimage to her father's grave, not to honor him but to blame him. She can never forgive him for dying and leaving her to the mercies of her mother. The language of this passage is too double-edged to be accidental, and it is in some ways a key to the book: "I had a great yearning, lately, to *pay my father back* for all the years of neglect, and start tending his grave" (my italics). Literally, "to pay back" means to pay back what she owes, to pay her debt to her father. But "to pay back" also means to take revenge. Esther is revenging herself for *his* neglect of *her* at the same time as she is apologizing for *her* neglect of *him*. Still, the relationship between daughter and dead father is more interesting and creative than that between daughter and living mother. The mother is presented in every instance as a despicable object; her goodness and devotion only annoy. There are moments when Esther wants to kill her.

> The room blued into view, and I wondered where the night had gone. My mother turned from a foggy log into a slumbering, middle-aged woman, her mouth slightly open and a snore ravelling from her throat. The piggish noise irritated me, and for a while it seemed to me that the only way to stop it would be to take the column of skin and sinew from which it rose and twist it to silence between my hands.

We will go back to the question of fathers and mothers later, though we must take care not to fall into the swamp of amateur psychoanalysis. Halfway through *The Bell Jar*, nevertheless, we begin to form an idea of what this bell jar is of which Plath writes so frighteningly. It seems it is a kind of vacuum, a vacuum composed of self-canceling values. Some of these values are social and shared with most middle-class Americans; some are domestic and relate to women in society; some are personal and attributable to Esther's ambitions as a writer and her high expectations of herself. Others, of course, have to do with her relationship with her mother and her dead father. But up to the moment of breakdown, all these values have been held together by a bullying will to succeed. When her will weakens, Esther's conflicting self-images collapse in upon each other, leaving a vacuum in which her mind is incapable of breathing. It is because her mind is stifling that she attempts to kill the body that sustains it.

Now, I'd be willing to bet anything that nothing like this ever happened to Emily Dickinson. Miss Dickinson's tortures were religious and personal. She was, to an extreme degree, passionate and shy. Personal relationships were too highly charged for intercourse, so she had to confine her social life to letters. But she accepted the crushing provincial society in which she lived because, as we have seen, it suited the peculiar nature of her genius. Had she been a man she would have had to find a way of life that gave her equal privacy—not easy in nineteenth-century New England, where, if you went into the church, you had to preach to huge congregations, and if you went into literature you were meant to write for the *Atlantic Monthly*. Emerson and Whitman, at periods in their lives, had to work for their bread. Emily Dickinson was spared that indignity. It was no disgrace to be the family spinster. It was luck, and secretly Emily Dickinson knew it. That room with closed doors in the spacious house in Amherst saw terrible anguish, but it was not the cause of that anguish. It was a refuge from it. This was the principal difference between the bedroom in Amherst and the bedroom in Wellesley.

Other women have known their luck. It is surprising how many spinster writers there have been: Jane Austen, Emily Brontë, Stevie Smith, Charlotte Mew, Marianne Moore, Elizabeth Bishop. These women may have suffered, but they suffered as women who attempted neither to fight male domination nor compromise themselves to suit it. Theirs was a narrow independence, even a selfish one, but it was real. It was bought at the price of what used to be called "womanliness"—sex, marriage, children, and the socially acceptable position of wife.

Sometimes I think a woman writer has to pay that price. In my own case, however, I've not been willing, any more than Sylvia Plath was willing, to sacrifice my life as a woman in order to have a life as a writer. Surely, in the twentieth century, when society allows so much, it ought to be possible to be a fulfilled woman and an independent writer without guilt—or without creating a bell jar vacuum in which it is impossible to breathe. As I look back over my own experience, I see, however, that I have only *just* managed to survive. Writing poetry is not like most jobs; it can't be rushed or done well between household chores—at least not by me. The mood of efficiency, of checking things off the list as you tear through a day's shopping, washing, cleaning, mending, and so forth is totally destructive of the slightly bored melancholy that nurtures imagination. Even friends distract, though I often make them an excuse not to write. It is possible that marriage, children, social obligations have always been ways for me of avoiding the hard work of making poems. But even if this were so, I can't now reverse my decision to have a family. I have to be a writer with a handicap.

One way out of the dilemma of the woman/writer is to write poems about the dilemma itself. Though I have never considered myself to be a specifically feminist poet, many of my poems are about being trapped in domestic surroundings. I dread, and have always dreaded, that marriage, a home, and family would sap my creative energies, that they would devour my time and my personality, that they would, in a venomous way I can't easily explain, use me up. When I look at my early poems I am surprised that so many of them express what seems to me this particularly feminine dread.

The first poem I published in a magazine—when I was about twenty-three—was called "The Women." It was written in Yorkshire in 1956 when, although I didn't know it, I was going through a bell jar experience of my own. I was married to a young Englishman whom I assumed I adored. He was an athlete, a businessman who spent part of his time in the Territorial Army. Obviously his activities in these respects were not ones I could share. He and his friends, mostly just out of Cambridge, were the first men I had met who made me feel that being a girl made any difference to the way you were treated. In my coeducational American university women were, if anything, rather more in control of things than men. My poem, "The Women," however, referred not to the au pair girls and debutantes our life in London perplexed me by including but to the wives of the officers in my husband's regiment.

We were "billeted," I remember, with the colonel and his wife. During the day the men went out on maneuvers; if it was a weekend, they went shooting on the moors. The women stayed at home by the fire, surrounded by vases gorged with dahlias, gossiping, sighing, waiting for the men to come back so we could all broach the drinks cupboard. I spent the greater part of the mornings roaming the blustery streets of Halifax in hopes of bumping into the public library, but after lunch I was condemned to interminable cups of tea. One such afternoon I withdrew to my bedroom and wrote this poem.

Women, waiting for their husbands,
sit among dahlias all the afternoons,
while quiet processional seasons
drift and subside at the doors like dunes,
and echoes of ocean curl from the flowered wall.

The room is a murmuring shell of nothing at all.
As the fire dies under the dahlias, shifting embers
flake from the silence, thundering when they fall,
and wives who are faithful waken bathed in slumber;
the loud tide breaks and turns to bring them breath.

At five o'clock it flows about their death,
and then the dahlias, whirling
suddenly to catherine wheels of surf,
spin on their stems until the shallows sing,
and flower pools gleam like lamps on the lifeless tables.

Flung phosphorescence of dahlias tells
the women time. They wait to be,
prepared for the moment of inevitable
good evening when, back from the deep, from the mystery,
the tritons return and the women whirl in their sea.

After the experience of "The Women" I less frequently indulged my childhood fantasy of becoming a heroine out of Jane Austen, and began to wonder what I really wanted to do. Back in London I tried to write a novel, but like Esther Greenwood, I found I had nothing to say. My poems were better, but when I sent them to English magazines they were turned down. I offered myself to the PEN club in Chelsea as a typist, and they let me type some poems for them. But soon they discovered that I was too poor a typist even for their unpaid standards, and they let me go. I began to feel I hadn't got it in me to be a writer. The terrible parlors of "The Women" yawned before me.

When I had a baby, things got not better but worse. I was determined not to let such a natural event disturb my reading program (I was putting myself through James, Hardy, and Proust), but of course it did, even though I invented a way of breast-feeding and reading at the same time, propping my book up on a music stand. The baby was unimpressed. She howled every evening at dinner time, and since my husband disapproved of babies at our candlelit dinners, meals were served to an accompaniment of sobs—my own and the baby's in about equal proportion. I found, after a while, that I couldn't eat without vomiting, and soon I lost so much weight I had to go to hospital.

Shortly after I was released (no doctor could diagnose my ailment) we began moving, first to a village near Norwich, then to Grimsby, then to Belfast, then to New York, then to a Faulkner-like town called Corinth, Mississippi, and finally to Atlanta, Georgia, where we were divorced. All through this period—1957 to 1959—I was in a state of appalling numbness. My husband was puzzled, since he was having a difficult time establishing himself in his own business and wanted my support. In return he was prepared to provide me with a house, a maid, and time. Why was I not writing the novels and poems I had promised? When I grew more depressed and spent days and nights weeping, he decided he'd had enough. The terms of divorce taxed us both, since there was no third party except my bell jar. We had to concoct a separation on the grounds of mental cruelty—not mine to him, as so often had been the case, but his to me—which seemed, even to my foggy mind, unfair.

I mention these facts not because they are unique but because they are not. Thousands of educated women with small babies who have followed in the wake of an enterprising husband have undergone the same depressions, the same sense of failure, the same collapse into breakdown, if not divorce. Perhaps Emily Dickinson's father knew what he was talking about when he suggested that too many books joggle the mind. But I still wonder how much my depression had to do with my discontent with a woman's role in marriage and how much it had to do with my inability to write in uncongenial circumstances. The questions were distinct, though linked. Any writer has to keep his or her imagination alive, and that means he or she can't happily live a lie or write well in an alien role. On the other hand, it seems to me now that I blamed too much on the marriage and my role as a woman in it. I should have written in spite of everything that seemed against me. I should not have excused myself.

Luckily we are living in the middle of a century that, for all its drawbacks, allows people who have made a mistake in marriage to go back and try again. I returned to the University of Michigan with my daughter, wrote a book of poems, began a critical book and took an M.A. in English. Curiously, though, I have been unable to use the memory of those unhappy years directly in my poems. The reason for this may be the natural desire of human beings to suppress what is unpleasant. But I think there's a more important reason that has to do with the nature of writing itself. Unless you are setting out to write an autobiographical novel, like *The Bell Jar*, or a novel calculated to shock the public with its frankness, like *Fear of Flying*, it is better art to let your memory knit itself into your subconscious and twine around your imagination until you have found a way of transforming experience into fiction. "Facts," wrote Virginia Woolf, "are a very inferior form of fiction."

The facts of my experience, as I have said, were not interesting in themselves. They were familiar. It is because they were so familiar that they gave me an idea for a long poem that later became *Correspondences*. If I had suffered, in my ignorance of myself, from a sense of ignominy and numbness in marriage, other women must have suffered too. I began to think with troubled resentment of my mother. All through my childhood I'd seen her sacrifice herself and her interests for the sake of my father, myself, and my sisters. She had wanted to be a novelist, and we all encouraged her. But, as in my own case, encouragement only made her feel guilty when she was not doing her "duty" toward us. And when she did her "duty"— and sighed afterward—then *we* felt guilty for taking so much of her time. The process of "wifeing" and "mothering" was steeped in guilt. By modeling myself on my mother, I had plunged unwittingly into the same guilt; but in my slow way, like swimming to the surface of water I was drowning in, I began to realize that guilt could also be an *excuse*. If I had really wanted to write I would have done so. So would my mother. Writing for us was, or could be, wishful thinking. There is always time. No amount of housework or baby-tending takes time from writing if you really want to write. Sylvia Plath wrote her great last poems in the early morning before her babies were awake. Wilfred Owen wrote his best poems in the trenches. Sweet are the uses of adversity.

In a burst of self-knowledge that was unsettling at first, I knew I had rigged that divorce—and all the unhappiness that preceded it—in order not to repeat the experience of my mother. After my mother's death from cancer in the early 1960s (when I married again) I was still unable to rid myself of her image—her ghost. Yet I was inexpressibly upset by her death. I felt I had to tell her something, that she had cheated herself and me by dying just as I was about to speak. It was this urgency to resurrect her and at the same time to kill her spirit (remember Virginia Woolf's struggles with the Angel in the House) that made it impossible for me not to write *Correspondences*. It was a book I couldn't avoid.

The first poem I wrote on this theme—the theme of mothers—was called "Generations." Probably it was the seed from which *Correspondences* grew. It was written when I was living in Glasgow with my second husband and two babies, four years after my mother's death. The bell jar threatened again, but this time I was determined to smash it. Even if I had to be cruel to my family; even if I had to leave them.

"Generations" is a bitter poem where "The Women" is distanced and polite. The women in each stanza represent my grandmother, my mother, and myself in that order . . . three degrees of self-sacrifice.

Know this mother by her three smiles.
A grey one drawn over her mouth by frail hooks.
One hurt smile under each eye.

Know this mother by the frames she makes.
By the silence in which she suffers each child
to scratch out the aquatints in her mind.

Know this mother by the way she says
"darling" with her teeth clenched.
By the fabulous lies she cooks.

With that poem I felt I had made a breakthrough. Shortly afterward, in 1970, we left Glasgow and lived for six months in Cambridge, Massachusetts, where my husband and I both had scholarships. Mine was at the Radcliffe Institute for Independent Women, and I found myself surrounded there by discontented contemporaries. America itself was in a profound state of discontent. The puritan values of honesty, loyalty, piety, and self-sacrifice I'd been taught to respect in my childhood were everywhere being dismissed. Hippies, drug takers, dropouts, and failed intellectuals lined up for food and psychiatric treatment in the streets of Cambridge. Our flat in a racially mixed area was robbed five times; our four-year-old son was attacked by a gang of black children. All that time I was at Radcliffe writing *Correspondences* I was aware of living through a period of acute crisis. Excitement, despair, challenge, unhappiness, and anger infected the New England air. I began to understand why Sylvia Plath and Anne Sexton had gone mad.

And yet I was determined not to. It would have been too easy. All around me the world seemed mad. Lowell and Plath had set a fashion, and for a poet, madness (with blame on society and capitalist materialism) was all but obligatory. Two things saved me. In the first place, I had found an archive of letters from well-known American families in the Schlesinger Library, and reading them, I decided I could use them in a poem. The only way to fight the madness of the present was to gain some understanding of the past. I discovered a trunk of family letters in my sister's basement in New York, and these, too, profoundly moved me. In the second place, we had a weekly escape route from Harvard to Vermont. We drove up to my family's house in Wilmington nearly every weekend, and it was there I decided to set my poem in a mythical Clearfield, and make Vermont and the peace it stood for a symbol of the more solid America that had disappeared from the demented cities. I don't know when it occurred to me that my poem should take the form of letters. I think the family letters themselves suggested it; their language was already poetry, Victorian, distant. Why had no one thought of writing an epistolary poem before?

The central character in *Correspondences* is a woman like my mother—liberal, generous, self-sacrificing, devoted to good causes and prone to idealizing her family. I called her Ruth after Ruth in the Bible, the daughter of Naomi, who, you may remember, calls herself "Mara," meaning bitter. I turned Mara into the woman's name, Maura, and created both Maura and Ruth in the image of the self-sacrificing mother. Maura sacrifices her independent life as a writer to marry an idealistic but impractical reformer. Ruth sacrifices a lover to devote herself to her kindly but unexciting husband. In both cases I suspect these women took the *happiest* course open to them. That is to say, I doubt that Maura in 1900 would ever have become more than a mediocre writer; and Ruth, in 1940, was certainly better off with her unpretentious American. Nonetheless, neither one of these women was willing to take risks, and their happiness was bordered with wistfulness, with a longing for knowledge beyond their experience.

It is Ruth's children who are given the opportunity of risk, and two of them take it. Kay marries a fashionable psychiatrist in New York, has a baby, becomes very unhappy, and leaves her husband after a nervous breakdown. Nick, her younger brother, leaves New England after his mother's funeral and heads west, deserting his career at college. Only Eden, Kay's younger sister, stays at home in Vermont, trying to preserve the family's values.

The title, *Correspondences*, refers partly to the letters of the two sisters, Eden and Kay, each of whom confronts a disintegrating world that, after their mother's death, is impossible to hold together. Eden, in Vermont, discovers a box of family letters, dating from the 1830s, and in part 1 these letters make up the *Correspondences* within the correspondence of the sisters. Part 2 is entitled "Women in Marriage" and concerns three generations of women, Maura, Ruth, and Kay—the grandmother, mother, and daughter of "Generations." Each of these women makes a different compromise in her marriage. Part 3 is composed of journals written by Ruth's husband, Neil Arbeiter, and her son Nick. The entire poem ends with a letter from Kay to her father in which she explains her reasons for not being able to return to New England from London, to which she has made a partially satisfactory escape.

"In the floodtides of *Civitas Mundi*
New England is dissolving like a green chemical.
Old England bleeds out to meet it in mid-ocean.
        Nowhere is safe."

It is a poem I can't continue.
It is America I can't contain.

Dear Father, I love but can't know you.
        I've given you all that I can.

Can these pages make amends for what was not said?
Do justice to the living, to the dead?

You can see, even from the little I've said, that *Correspondences* is about more than women's predicament in American history. It was intended to be a study of puritan values in New England—of their strengths, their weaknesses, their corruption by ambition and greed, and their final overthrow in the world of Vietnam and Watergate. Yet, as I wrote I could not help but be aware of the amount of my own experience that was going into it. In each generation there is misunderstanding between the women and the men. In 1830, for instance, Elizabeth Boyd is all but crushed by her Calvinist father for not accepting the judgment of God when her husband is drowned. In 1840, Marianne Chandler, who loves parties but hates sex, suffers from the sexual blundering of her puritanical husband. Later he divorces her with contemptuous blame.

> Of the causes of strife between us—
> your selfishness, your vanity, your whims, wife,
> your insistent and querulous disobedience,
> no more.
> It is enough for you to live with your naked conscience
> upon which must lie the death of our infant daughter
> as her innocent body lies, unfulfilled in its grave.
> Farewell.
> Find peace if you can with your sister,
> her friends and fashions.
> Frivolity is an armor of lace
> against the mind's inner vengeance and poisons.

In later generations of Chandlers, pompous Jacob tells his daughter off for wasting her time "scribbling" in college when she should be taking care of her mother at home.

> Maura! Maura! Those kisses were never gifts.
> Bestowed as they were with the charity of Our Lord Himself,
> those kisses were loans! Loans upon interest these many
> long years! Now it is time to repay them graciously,
> selflessly, with little acts of kindness and understanding.

In 1900, Maura, chastened at last, determines to give up her dream of becoming a writer and vows to devote her life to her impractical, idealist husband, Ethan Boyd.

> What does Nature
> ask of Woman?
> Give to him that needeth.
> Employ the hour that passeth.
> Be resolute in submission.
> Love thy husband.
> Bear children.

Ruth, Maura's daughter, tries to follow in her mother's footsteps, but falls in love with an English novelist—a plummy, selfish fellow whose pseudosophistication impresses her. She lives a secret, divided life with her husband until she dies of cancer, publicly virtuous but privately horrified and undermined by a devouring sense of guilt. In a letter to her lover in 1945, she writes of this guilt.

And what are these terrible things
they are taking for granted? Air and grass,
houses and beds, laundry and things to eat—
so little clarity, so little space between them;
a crowd of distractions to be
bought and done and arranged for,
drugs for the surely incurable pain of
living misunderstood among many who love you.

Finally, for Kay, Ruth's daughter, the fiber of a repressive society breaks down just as she herself does. In 1954 she finds she can no longer tolerate her life in Westchester County and runs away to New York. But in an asylum she discovers there is no escape in madness either. Having rejected her mother, Kay at last turns to her for help. And yet she knows there is no way back to her mother's beliefs; any compromise with a former life will be forced. The hysteria at the end of this poem is one many of us felt in the 1950s and 1960s; Sylvia Plath was spokeswoman for a whole generation of Kays.

Come when you can, or when
the whitecoats let you.
But they may not let you, of course.
They think you're to blame.
Good God, mother, I'm not insane!
How can I get out of here?
Can't you get me out of here?

I'll try, I'll try, really,
I'll try again. The marriage.
The baby. The house. The whole damn bore!
Because for me, what the hell else is there?
Mother, what more? What more?

Naturally, when I was writing that poem I realized Kay was a version of myself. All that I had suffered in my first marriage, all that I had felt about my child, my husband, my mother, came together in it. It was a poem I found painful to write. And yet, Kay is not me, either. She is a sort of Esther Greenwood. I have never had a breakdown in a museum or lived in Westchester County or been married to a fashionable psychiatrist. Kay's *feelings,* her mixed love and hatred for her child, her sense of imprisonment in her house, her impulse to fly, to escape to drink or to an anonymous city—these feelings *have* been mine. They can be found in other poems . . . in one called "In the House," for instance, which I wrote long before any of the poems of *Correspondences.*

Whatever it is, it's clear it has claims on me.
Its surface establishes itself
outside and around me,
drawing me through or into
what I take to be my proper dominion.

These keys are my keys, this door my door.
The interior is entirely familiar . . .

Again, these interminable stairs, bristling with children.
"Mother, mother," they wail. They bleat with desire.
They quarrel and hold up their wounds to be kissed.
And yet when I bend to them
It's like kissing a photograph.
I taste chemicals.
My lips meet unexpectedly a flatness.

But in Kay's poem from *Correspondences* I learned how to put experience into poetry without "confessing" it. I should add, too, that the "facts" pertaining to the Chandler family in my poem differ from those pertaining to my own family history. The nearer I came to my time and to people I knew, the more imperative it seemed to me to get feelings right but to invent "facts." Apart from the embarrassment of taking family skeletons out of cupboards before the flesh is off, so to speak, fiction has to be more obvious than life. A reader has to see reasons for feelings in behavior.

But I see I have left the subject of women and women writers and got on to a theory of literature. I still haven't answered the question I asked at the beginning of this essay. Is it possible for a woman to be an adult, married, sexual person and a poet as well?

In one sense, poems like those I have quoted answer the question by writing about it. If—as women—our theme is woman's survival and self-discovery, then we have found a subject that meets the requirements of experience both as women and as writers. In the 1970s, too, we can say what we please. We no longer need to be embarrassed by social taboos. The problem, however, does not really concern itself with sexual explicitness. For a woman it goes deeper. I encountered it when I had finished *Correspondences,* for I realized then that I had written a woman's book—that is to say, the experiences of my characters were experiences I understood through having lived my life as a woman. The two world wars are scarcely mentioned. The Civil War is recognized only as it divides the family into allegiances North and South. Now, there are many people these days who would say that women's books are just what women should be writing. The American poet, Adrienne Rich, for example, believes that women are awakening into a shared, powerful consciousness of what it means to be female. The "drive to self-knowledge," she says, "is more than a search for identity; it is part of her refusal of the self-destructiveness of male-dominated society." We must find, she thinks, a language of our own to express "a whole new psychic geography" of female emotion.

For my part, despite *Correspondences,* I am inclined to disagree with Adrienne Rich. I am not convinced that women need a specifically female language to describe female experience. The question of language is in any case an especially thorny one. For even if we agree that women have a less aggressive, more instinctive, more "creative" nature than men (and I'm not sure that's true) language is difficult to divide into sexes. A good writer's imagination should be bisexual or transsexual. The only society I know of in which men and women traditionally have spoken different languages—and accepted roles accordingly—developed in Japan. At the risk of digression, let me remind you that in tenth-century Japan women wrote poetry and fiction in the vernacular (the language of society, love, grace, beauty), while men did business, politics and went about extending their territorial rights in Classical Chinese. The result of this sexual differentiation in language was a vast and marvelous literature created almost exclusively by women (high-class, aristocratic women, mind you) of which Lady Murasaki's *Tale of Genji* is perhaps the most famous example.

A flight of fancy prompts me to imagine a woman's language that appoints itself guardian of the traditional beauties of English as opposed to the speed-read efficiencies of American. Imagine a woman's language that preserves the dignity of the *King James Bible* and the *Prayer Book,* which forbids the use of technological jargon in any work of literature not intended for the laboratory or classroom. But such a dream is, of course, impossible. In our democratic society, such an exclusive language would be hooted down as "irrelevant"—not least by women who ask for equality at the same time as asking for an independent consciousness and a language of their own in which to express it.

For better or worse, women and men writers in the West, in the later twentieth century, share a common consciousness. Their language is a reflection, or even a definition, of that consciousness. If anything we want *more* communication, *more* understanding between the sexes. We are beginning to see that though our physical functions differ (necessarily) our psychic needs are alike. If there is to be a new creative consciousness—one that is not based on phallic values of conquest, power, ambition, greed, murder, and so forth—then this consciousness must have room for both male and female; a consciousness the greatest literature has, in fact, been defining for a long time.

What has all this to do with *Correspondences* and the writing of women's books? Well, now that *Correspondences* has been written, I'm proud of it. Through it I crossed a bridge—or rather built a bridge—into the twentieth century. All the anger, the confusion, the misery, and the doubt I experienced during the 1950s and 1960s went into it, and because they were a woman's angers and miseries, they exposed part of the general consciousness of the age—a part that in the past had been suppressed.

But now I want to stand on the shoulders of *Correspondences,* as it were, and look at a wider world. For both sexes it is important that we understand each other and the world we have to share. There must be no suppression and no play-acting either. For me it is as fraudulent to adopt the role of a "new" woman as that of an "old" one; being a writer proscribes role-playing. In both cases the role that is offered substitutes a public stance for particular perceptions. And a writer must leave herself free for particular perceptions.

Of course, choosing what often feels like a selfish independence means that one pays a price—a high price—in human terms. I don't think you can write truthfully and be entirely comfortable. Tension is a mainspring of the imagination. And something has to be sacrificed—the satisfaction of a role, the satisfaction of a cause, the satisfaction, even, of a sense of guilt. This is why I should like to conclude with a poem I wrote last year called "The Price." What I hoped to imply in this poem is that a price is asked for every engagement with the truth—but it need not be a price that destroys affection. It is also the price *of* affection, since what is most valuable in human understanding is so often what is least definable as politics or even as right or wrong.

The fear of loneliness, the wish
to be alone;
love grown rank as seeding grass
in every room,
and anger at it, raging at it
storming it down.

Also that four-walled chrysalis
and impediment, home;
that lamp and hearth, that easy fit
of bed to bone;
those children, too, sharp witnesses
of all I've done.

My dear, the ropes that bind us
are safe to hold;
the walls that crush us keep us
from the cold.
I know the price and still I pay it, pay it—
words, their furtive kiss,
illicit gold.

1979

►◄ CHARLES SIMIC ►◄
(B. 1938)

Charles Simic was born in Belgrade, Yugoslavia, and his early years were spent in that city as it endured World War II and the beginnings of the Tito regime. Much of his poetry is colored by the fear, violence, and hunger he experienced at that time. This dark perspective even shades his recent work, like his brief 1996 poem "Slaughterhouse Flies," which begins: "Evenings, they ran their bloody feet / Over the pages of my schoolbooks." And yet humor also plays an important role in his work. In one of his notebooks, Simic observes: "I grew up among some very witty people, I now realize. They knew how to tell stories and how to laugh, and that has made all the difference." The echo of Robert Frost in Simic's last phrase here may be indicative of his poetry's bridge between Europe and America.

Simic was a poor student and troubled youth who often had difficulty with authority. When he was fifteen, his family was allowed to travel to Paris and in 1954 they joined his father, living in Chicago. Simic had studied English while in France, and his high school experience in America seems to have been positive, awakening his interest in literature. Later, Simic worked as an office boy for the *Chicago Sun Times* and took night classes toward a college degree. But his college career was interrupted by service in the U.S. Army from 1961 to 1963. He earned his B.A. from New York University in 1966 and became a naturalized citizen in 1971. He currently teaches at the University of New Hampshire.

Simic published his first volume of poems, *What the Grass Says,* in 1967, and a second, *Somewhere among Us a Stone Is Taking Notes,* two years later—both published by Kayak, a small San Francisco press. These early books already show the mixture of humor and violence that would characterize much of his work. The early work also displays Simic's allegiances to surrealism and an absurdist sense of humor that seems particularly European. Surrealism has its own roots in Europe, started between the two world wars partly as a reaction against both bourgeois complacency and state terror. In America, Simic's brand of surrealism became popular during the political upheavals of the Vietnam era. The fact that he has never entirely abandoned such tendencies is one aspect of his distinctiveness as an American poet. "To be an exception to the rule is my sole ambition," he has written. At least one critic, Vernon Young, has argued that Simic's poetic stance may be due as much to the memory of European folklore as to a mature artist's theories. It is true that Simic's poems often prove to be fables or parables and are consistently brief. As he wrote in his notebooks, "Little said, much meant, is what poetry is all about."

Among the collections for which he is best known are *Classic Ballroom Dances* (1980), *Selected Poems 1963–1983* (1985), *Unending Blues* (1986), *The World Doesn't End* (1989), which won the Pulitzer Prize, *The Book of Gods and Devils* (1990), *Hotel Insomnia* (1992), *Walking the Black Cat* (1996), and *Jackstraws* (2000). His prose books include *Dime-Store Alchemy: The Art of Joseph Cornell* (1992) and *The Unemployed Fortune-Teller: Essays and Memoirs* (1994). Simic has translated many Yugoslavian poets, including Tomaz Salamun and Nicola Tadic, and has also championed jazz, the great art of his adoptive country. He also marks out his own literary territory in opposition to contemporary American trends: "Lately in the United States we have been caught between critics who do not believe in literature and writers who believe only in naïve realism. Imagination continues to be what everybody pretends does not exist."

◄•———◄ ▶———•►

NEGATIVE CAPABILITY AND ITS CHILDREN

. . . that is, when a man is capable of being in uncertainties, mysteries, doubts, without any irritable reaching after fact and reason.

—John Keats

Today what Keats said could be made even more specific. In place of "uncertainties," "mysteries" and "doubts," we could substitute a long list of intellectual and aesthetic events which question, revise and contradict one another on all fundamental issues. We could also bring in recent political history: all the wars, all the concentration camps and other assorted modern sufferings, and then return to Keats and ask how, in this context, are we capable of being in anything *but* uncertainties? Or, since we are thinking about poetry, ask how do we render this now overwhelming consciousness of uncertainty, mystery and doubt in our poems?

To be "capable of being in uncertainties" is to be literally in the midst. The poet is in the midst. The poem, too, is in the midst, a kind of magnet for complex historical, literary and psychological forces, as well as a way of maintaining oneself in the face of that multiplicity.

There are serious consequences to being in the midst. For instance, one is subject to influences. One experiences crises of identity. One suffers from self-consciousness. One longs for self-knowledge while realizing at the same time that under the circumstances self-knowledge can never be complete. When it comes to poetry, one has to confront the difficult question: Who or what vouches for the

First published in *Antaeus* 38 (1978). Collected in *The Uncertain Certainty: Interviews, Essays, and Notes on Poetry* (Ann Arbor: University of Michigan Press, 1985) 83–91.

authenticity of the act? After more than a century of increasing and finally all-embracing suspicions regarding traditional descriptions of reality and self, the question of authenticity ceases to be merely an intellectual problem and becomes a practical one which confronts the poet daily as he or she sits down to write a poem. What words can I trust? How can *I know* that I trust them?

There are a number of replies, as we'll see, but in an age of uncertainties there has to be a particular kind of answer. It includes, for example, the notion of experiment, that concept borrowed from science and which already appears in Wordsworth's *Advertisement to Lyrical Ballads* (1798) and implies a test, a trial, any action or process undertaken to demonstrate something not yet known, or (and this is important) to demonstrate something known and forgotten. I was simply quoting Webster's definition and he reminded me that "experimental" means based on experience rather than on theory or authority. Empiricism, yes, but with a difference. In experimental poetry it will have to be an empiricism of imagination and consciousness.

Back to the notion of being in the midst. "Given the imperfect correspondence between mind and objective reality" (Hegel), given the fact that this "imperfect correspondence" is the product of a critique of language which since the Romantics has undermined the old unity of word and object, of concept and image, then modern poetics is nothing more than the dramatization of the epistemological consequences of that disruption. Certainly, to call it "dramatic" is to suggest contending voices. My purpose here is to identify some of them and establish, as it were, their order of appearance.

We can proceed with our "translation" of Keats. We can speak of Chance in place of his "uncertainty." Is it with Keats that Chance, that major preoccupation of modern experimental poetics, enters aesthetics?

One aspect of that history is clear. Dada and then surrealism made Chance famous, made it ontological. They turned it into a weapon. Cause and effect as the archenemies. Nietzsche had already claimed that "the alleged instinct for causality is nothing more than the fear of the unusual." Fear, of course, and its offspring, habit, which is there, presumably, to minimize that fear. But isn't poetry too a habit, a convention with specific expectations of content and form which have their own causal relationship? Certainly—and this I believe was understood by these poets. So the project became one of using Chance to break the spell of our habitual literary expectations and to approach the condition of what has been called "free imagination."

There's more to it, however. There's a story, almost a parable, of how Marcel Duchamp suspended a book of Euclidian geometry by a string outside his window for several months and in all kinds of weather, and then presented the result to his sister as a birthday present, and of course as an art object. A lovely idea. Almost a philosophical gesture, a kind of ironic critique of Euclid by the elements. Even more, this example and others like it offer a fundamental revision of what we mean by creativity. In that view, the poet is not a *maker*, but someone able to detect the presence of poetry in the accidental.

This is a curious discovery, that there should be poetry at all in the accidental, that there should even be lyricism. The implications are troubling. If we say "lyricism," we imply an assertion of a human presence and will, but how do we locate even a hint of human presence in operations that have no conscious intent and are left to Chance? Is it because there's a kind of significance (meaning) which is not the function of causality? In any case, you don't achieve anonymity when you submit yourself to the law of accident. "Chance," as Antonin Artaud said, "is my-self." This is a magnificent insight. It humanizes the abstraction (Chance) and shifts the problem into an entirely different area.

Pound, Olson, and that whole other tradition we are heirs to, with its theory of "Energy," perhaps provides the next step. That theory, it seems to me, accounts for this astonishing discovery that the text is always here, that the content precedes us, that the labor of the poet is to become an instrument of discovery of what has al-ways been with us, inconspicuous in its familiarity.

Olson says "a poem is energy transferred from where the poet got it . . . by the way of the poem itself to, all the way over to, the reader." Pound called it "Vortex." Both of them were pointing to the experience of one's own existence and its dynam-ics as the original condition which the poet aims to repossess. And for Olson, "there's only one thing you can do about kinetic, re-enact it."

That's the key term: re-enactment. Their definitions are concerned with locating the agent that fuels the poetic act. Their hope, above all, is to give us a taste of that original preconscious complexity and unselected-ness. The problem next is how to accomplish it? And the question remains: What does Chance re-enact? Suppose what we call Chance is simply a submission to a message from the unconscious. The ran-dom then becomes a matter of obedience to inwardness and calls for an appropriate technique. The surrealists, as we know, took it over from professional mediums and renamed it "automatic writing." In any case, it's still an interior dictation they are after, a trance, an altered state of consciousness. Breton gives the prescription: "A monologue that flows as rapidly as possible, on which critical spirit of the subject brings no judgement to bear, which is therefore unmarred by any reticence, and which will reproduce as exactly as possible spoken thought."

Now anyone can cut up words from a newspaper and arrange them at ran-dom, while only a few have a gift of speaking in tongues, so the technique of auto-matic writing is problematic and in practice obviously less "automatic" than one would like. The hope that runs through Breton's writings is visionary. He was after the angelic orders. In his pronouncements there's an element of faith which in turn simplifies the actual experience.

On the surface of it, what the other modern tradition proposes has some simi-larity. Creeley, for example, quotes William Burroughs to describe his own tech-nique: "There is only one thing a writer can write about: *What is in front of his senses in the moment of writing*." Olson is even more categorical: "The objects which occur at every given moment of composition (of recognition, we can call it) are, can be, must be treated exactly as they occur therein, and not by any ideas or preconceptions from outside the poem." There's a difference, of course. The fac-ulty implied and cultivated here, and conspicuously missing from automatic writ-ing, is attention. Consequently, the emphasis in this kind of poetry is on clarity, precision, conciseness, although still without any attempt at interpretation. The object of attention is set down without a further comment. The aim is that "precise instant when a thing outward and objective transforms itself, or darts into the in-ward, the subjective." The cutting edge.

In both cases, however, the emphasis is on immediacy, and the purpose is an exchange of a particular kind of energy. In both instances, the ambition is identical: to discover an authentic ground where poetry has its being and on that spot build a new ontology.

Unfortunately, there's always the problem of language, the problem of conveying experience. It's in their respective views of language and what it does, that surrealism and imagism part company.

Surrealism suspects language and its representational powers. In its view, there's no intimacy between language and the world; the old equation, word equals object, is simply a function of habit. In addition, there's the problem of simultaneity of experience versus the linear requirements of grammar. Grammar moves in time. Only figurative language can hope to grasp the simultaneity of experience. Therefore, it's the connotative and not the denotative aspect of language that is of interest, the spark that sets off the figurative chain reaction and transcends the tyranny of the particular.

But Pound, Williams, Olson, and Creeley are in turn suspicious of figures of speech. The figurative drains attention. It tends to take us elsewhere, to absent us from what is at hand. Furthermore, there's a strong commitment in their poetry to living speech. "Nothing," as Ford Madox Ford advised Pound, "that you couldn't in some circumstances, in the stress of some emotion *actually* say." As for grammar, we have their related ideas of prosody, form, and poetic line, which are nothing more than attempts to create a grammar of poetic utterance which would pay heed to the simultaneity of experience.

I think what emerges out of these apposite views is a new definition of content. The content of the poem is determined by the attitude we have toward language. Both the attentive act and the figurative act are profoundly prejudiced by the poet's subjectivity. (Heisenberg's discovery that observation alters the phenomena observed applies here.) The content is that *prejudice,* at the expense of the full range of language. This is a constant in modern poetics regardless of whether we conceive of language as the expression of a moment of attention or, as in the case of surrealism, as the imaginative flight out of that privileged moment.

Nevertheless, we find both traditions speaking of *the image,* and insisting on its importance. And yet, the contexts are very different and carry incompatible views of the nature of our common reality.

For surrealism, the characteristic of a strong image is that it derives from the spontaneous association of two very distinct realities whose relationship is grasped solely by the mind. Breton says, "the most effective image is the one that has the highest degree of arbitrariness." For the imagists, an image is "an intellectual and emotional complex in an instant of time," but a complex (we might add) derived from a perception of an existing thing. Imagism names what is there. Surrealism, on the other hand, endlessly renames what is there, as if by renaming it it could get closer to the thing itself. The goal in surrealism as in symbolism is a texture of greatest possible suggestiveness, a profusion of images whose meaning is unknown and unparaphrasable through a prior system of signification. The surrealist poet offers the imaginary as the new definition of reality, or more accurately, he equates the imaginary with a truth of a psychological order. Here, the separation between intuition and what is real is abolished. Everything is arbitrary except metaphor, which detects the essential kinship of all things.

For imagism, that "necessary angel" of Stevens's, that reality out there with its pressures and complexities is unavoidable. Imagism accepts our usual description of that reality. The image for Pound is a moment of lucidity when the world and its presence is re-enacted by consciousness in language. He calls for sincerity, care for detail, wonder, faith to the actual. Zukofsky compared what was attempted to a photo lens "free or independent of personal feelings, opinions . . . detached, unbiased." In this context, attention and imagination mean almost the same thing, a power which brings the world into focus.

The surprising outcome of many surrealist operations is that they uncover the archetypal—those great images that have mythical resonance. Perhaps we can say that the imagination (surrealist) could be best described as "mythical," providing we understand what that implies. The characteristic of that mode is that it doesn't admit dualism. It is decidedly anthropomorphic. It intuits a link between the freedom of the imagination and the world. Owen Barfield has observed that already "the Romantic image was an idol-smashing weapon meant to return men to their original participation in the phenomena." Rimbaud, too, as we know, wanted to bridge that gap. However, the vision of the romantics and symbolists was essentially tragic, while that of the surrealists is comic. The surrealist mythmaker is a comic persona in a world which is the product of a language-act, and an age in which these language-acts have proliferated.

When Arp writes of a "bladeless knife from which a handle is missing," when Norge speaks of a "time when the onion used to make people laugh," we have images, configurations, which employ archetypal elements but are not properly speaking archetypes. Instead, we have the emergence of entities which only by the force of utterance and the upheaval they cause in the imagination and thought acquire existence and even reality. These "useless objects" have a strange authority. Even as visionary acts, they consist of particulars and thus curiously provide us with a semblance of an actual experience.

For as the imagists would say, "knowledge is in particulars." Nothing is in the intellect that was not before in the senses, or Williams's well-known "no ideas but in things." At issue here is an attempt to re-create experience which preceded thought and to uncover its phenomenological ground. To allow phenomena to speak for itself. "To let that which shows itself be seen from itself in the very way in which it shows itself from itself" (Heidegger). There's a kind of responsibility here, care toward the actual, the sheer wonder of dailiness, the manner of our *being* in the world. Authenticity in imagism is primarily this confrontation with the sensuous for the sake of recreating its intensities.

The great ambition in each case is *thought*. How to think without recourse to abstractions, logic and categorical postulates? How to sensitize thought and involve it with the ambiguity of existence? Poems, in the words of the Russian formalistic critic Potebnia, are a "method of simplifying the thinking process." The surrealist Benjamin Péret goes further. He says simply that "thought is one and indivisible." Eluard says somewhere that "images think for him." Breton, as we have seen, defines psychic automatism as "the actual functioning of thought." Not far is Pound with his poetry as "inspired mathematics," or Duncan's saying that a poem is "the drama of truth." These are outrageous claims, but only so if we equate thought with "reason" and its prerogatives. To say that Chance thinks wouldn't make much sense, but to admit that Chance causes thought would be closer to what these statements intend. Again Olson raises an interesting question: "The degree to which projective (that is, the kind of poem I've been calling here imagist) involves a stance toward reality outside a poem as well as a new stance towards the reality of the poem itself." This is the whole point. Obviously, the rigorous phenomenological analysis of imagination and perception that surrealists and imagists have done has opened a whole new range of unknowns which address themselves to thought, and in the process alter the premises of the poems being written and the way in which they conceive of meaning.

Current criticism has unfortunately tended to simplify that historical predicament. It has seen the developments in recent poetry only within one or another literary movement, even when the strategies of these poetries have partaken of multiple sources. One can say with some confidence that the poet writing today can no longer be bound to any one standpoint, that he no longer has the option of being a surrealist or an imagist fifty years after and to the exclusion of everything else that has been understood since. Their questioning has involved us with large and fundamental issues. Their poetics have to do with the nature of perception, with being, with psyche, with time and consciousness. Not to subject oneself to their dialectics and uncertainties is truly not to experience the age we have inherited.

The aim of every new poetics is to evolve its own concept of meaning, its own idea of what is authentic. In our case, it is the principle of uncertainty. Uncertainty is the description of that gap which consciousness proclaims: actuality versus contingency. A new and unofficial view of our human condition. The best poetry being written today is the utterance and record of that condition and its contradictions.

1978

►◄ JACK FOLEY ►◄
(B. 1940)

In the year 2000, Pantograph Press simultaneously published two large-format collections of critical prose by Bay Area writer and radio personality Jack Foley. Accompanied by a performance CD, these distinctive volumes— *O Powerful Western Star* and *Foley's Books*—consolidated Foley's reputation as one of the most vital literary intelligences on the West Coast. This impression was confirmed when the books received glowing reviews in the *Los Angeles Times,* the *San Francisco Chronicle,* and other periodicals. Here was a poet-critic who refused to accept the usual poetic camps and could write about any kind of poetry with grace, insight, and sympathy.

Born in Neptune, New Jersey, John Wayne "Jack" Foley was the son of John Foley, an Irish American vaudeville singer, dancer, and songwriter who, after a theatrical career, managed a Western Union office. Foley's mother, Joanna Teriolo, was Italian American, and this mixed heritage, plus his Catholic upbringing in Port Chester, New York, provided some of his complex identity. "My pattern," he would later write, "in more ways than one, has been that of the shape-shifter. . . ." He fell in love with poetry at an early age, and his father's theatrical background ensured that he would always understand both its performative aspect and its potential relationship to song.

Foley attended Cornell University on a scholarship from Western Union. While a student, he met and married Adelle Abramowitz, also a poet. In 1963 they moved to Berkeley, California, where he had a Woodrow Wilson Fellowship for graduate study at the university, and she found a job with the Federal Reserve Bank. Over the next decade, Foley's dissatisfaction with academic life increased, as he became more aware of the still thriving bohemian literary culture in the Bay Area. So when his son, Sean Ezra, was born in 1974, his wife kept working at the bank, and Foley stayed at home as a house-husband.

While making one last effort to research a Ph.D. dissertation on Shakespeare's *Cymbeline,* he came across Charles Olson's *The Maximus Poems,* which redirected his own efforts to write poems and convinced him to drop out of academic life. Immersing himself in the Bay Area poetry scene, Foley got to know most of the major figures of the San Francisco Renaissance, including Allen Ginsberg, Robert Duncan, Lawrence Ferlinghetti, and Michael McClure. His own poetry grew out of their experimental procedures, but it increasingly emphasized the spoken medium as well as the printed page.

Foley's performance-based aesthetic, which often uses multiple voices, made conventional publication of his work problematic—eventually he would include cassette tapes or CDs with his books. "Performance poetry," he has written, "is an insistence that absence, silence and whiteness—the page—are not the only conditions in which poetry can be 'heard.' " In 1988 he took charge of poetry programming on Berkeley's listener-sponsored radio station, KPFA-FM, where he currently hosts a weekly literary show, *Cover to Cover.* Among his books and cassettes of poetry are *Letters/Lights—Words for Adelle* (1987), *Gershwin* (1991), *Adrift* (1993), and *Exiles* (1996). He has also edited *The "Fallen Western Star" Wars: A Debate about Literary California* (2001). Foley served as editor of *Poetry USA,* the periodical of the National Poetry Association, from 1990 to 1995 and has been a contributing editor to *Poetry Flash,* the Bay Area calendar and review. He contributes a regular book column, "Foley's Books," to an online magazine, the *Alsop Review.* Posting a substantial essay-review nearly every week, "Foley's Books" is the most ambitious and comprehensive critical coverage of West Coast poetry currently underway.

Foley's criticism is sharply written, boldly theoretical, and historically informed. One of his most interesting enterprises has been to examine the impact of technology on literary culture. In the following essay Foley argues that print culture, which has long dominated the art of poetry, now faces a serious challenge from a new kind of orality fostered by the electronic media. This cultural shift, he suggests, has enormous implications for literature.

◄◦━◄ ► ◦►

"WHAT ABOUT ALL THIS . . ."
SPECULATIONS ON POETRY
AND MY RELATIONSHIP TO IT

Poetry needs to be liberated from literary criticism.
—Dana Gioia, *Can Poetry Matter?*

What about all this writing?" asked William Carlos Williams in the midst of his masterful *Spring and All.* James Breslin's *W. C. Williams: An American Artist* tells us that "an obscure expatriate press in France" published *Spring and All* in 1923—the year Williams turned 40.

Deliberately echoing Williams fifty-nine years later, Ron Silliman began his 1982 *Ironwood* anthology of "L=A=N=G=U=A=G=E" writing with the same question. At *this* point (January, 1998), one might ask: "What about all this *performance?*"—not that performance doesn't also involve "writing."

From *O Powerful Western Star: Poetry and Art in California* (Oakland, California: Pantograph Press, 2000) 14–28.

It is no new question. In 1885 Gerard Manley Hopkins made the following comment about performance to Robert Bridges. Hopkins is referring to his poem, "Spelt from Sibyl's Leaves," which he calls "the longest sonnet ever made":

> Of this long sonnet above all remember what applies to all my verse, that it is, as living art should be, made for performance and that its performance is not reading with the eye but loud, leisurely, poetical (not rhetorical) recitation, with long rests, long dwells on the rhyme and other marked syllables, and so on. This sonnet shd. be almost sung: it is most carefully timed in tempo rubato.

In the same year Hopkins wrote:

> O the mind, mind has mountains; cliffs of fall
> Frightful, sheer, no-man-fathomed. Hold them cheap
> May who ne'er hung there. . . .
> ("No Worst There Is None")

Those magnificent, musical lines are about as far from what Williams called "the American idiom" as one can get. It is hardly surprising to discover that Walter Pater was one of Hopkins' tutors at Oxford. Thinking of Pater and his famous assertion that "all art constantly aspires toward the condition of music," Williams wrote in *Spring and All:* "I do not believe that writing is music. I do not believe writing would gain in quality or force by seeking to attain to the conditions of music." *Spring and All* is dedicated to the *painter,* Charles Demuth.

Hopkins, however, is a musician as well as a poet, and part of the point of music is that it is *performed*. At a poetry reading Williams gave about 1950, he—sounds—like Hopkins. He asserts that "the modern poem . . . should be *heard*. It's very difficult sometimes to get it off the page. But once you hear it, then you should be able to appraise it."

Williams is here advocating the oral, but the idea of poetry as some kind of "painting" is never far from this poet's mind. (One thinks of his lifelong interest in painting and of his many painter friends.) At the same reading he also says that poems are "made of words, *pigments*, put on, here, there, made, actually" (my italics).

Is poetry like painting? Is it a silent art, an art of the eyes, an art of seeing? Or is it like music—an art of hearing? Is the page nothing but a *score* (as Stéphane Mallarmé was the first to assert in 1897), and is poetry made real, realized only when one *speaks* it—with perhaps, as Hopkins writes, "loud, leisurely, poetical (not rhetorical) recitation"? What is the opinion of our poets on this subject?

They are profoundly DIVIDED. Charles Olson, who regarded himself as a disciple of Williams', was extremely enthusiastic when folksinger Woody Guthrie told him that he wrote "by ear." Olson went on to quote that remark prominently in the *Maximus* poems. Nevertheless, Olson insisted in those same poems on the primacy of *seeing* in *his* work: "polis / is eyes . . . there are only / eyes in all heads / to be looked out of."

Why should such questions arise? What are their parameters?

Clearly, poetry *begins* as an oral art: Homer's "blindness" is an indication that he could *not* have been a writer. (No Braille in Homer's day.) Yet he was a poet. Yet most of us have *encountered* poetry as writing, and writing is, profoundly, a visual art. Poetry is thus an oral/aural art which is "preserved," made "permanent" by a visual art, and this fact has caused a kind of division at its center. In its involvement with sound—and poets continue to refer to their work as "song"—poetry tends to be rather atavistic in our writing culture. The Modernist hostility to rhyme ("the dross of verse," Olson called it, finding it in Pound's translations) arises partially out of an attempt to rid poetry of at least *that* aspect of its past, to make it "sound" less embarrassingly like not-prose. Poetry, unlike song, is devalued in our culture because it is understood as irrelevant, out of date, old-fashioned, something prose (the novel, for instance) had to *transcend* in order to arrive at a form of real value and relevance.

And yet . . .

"When he was reading," wrote St. Augustine of St. Ambrose in the sixth book of *The Confessions,* "his eye glided over the pages, and his heart searched out the sense, but his voice and tongue were at rest." Augustine was aware that a momentous change had come upon the world. The new consciousness was Christian, inward, and silent before the page. The privacy of the reading figure who does not pronounce his words to anyone, who does not *perform,* is of enormous importance here. "Who durst intrude on one so intent?" asks Augustine. In the introduction to his 1986 anthology of language poetry, *In the American Tree,* Ron Silliman writes of his movement's involvement with "a poetics not centered on speech." Leaving aside the question of whether any writing can be "not centered on speech," one would have to add—since performance involves speech—not centered on performance as well. Was St. Ambrose the first language poet? Is that figure "our" figure?

Writing, linked as it is with "Christianity," "inwardness," and "privacy," clearly became a defining issue of our culture. In a culture which so values silent reading—reading with the eyes alone—what is the status of an art whose primary symbol is a blind man? How could the oral aspects of poetry, which insist that our "tongues" be anything but "at rest," survive?

The answer is that poetry survived as an *atavism* in a culture essentially given over to writing and silent reading. Yet, at this point in the history of "communications," writing itself is beginning to look rather atavistic! For the very first time, writing finds itself in *competition* with other means of preserving speech. Is there a "Great Books" record or cassette or CD-ROM in which someone is reading aloud the passage about St. Ambrose's silence? Possibly. How would St. Ambrose deal with the "communications revolution"? What connection (if any) would he have to the TV evangelist? Or, more interestingly: What relationship does the eloquent silence of Ambrose have to our modern ability to communicate sound?

Within the realm of poetry itself, the "New Formalism" has made it clear how much American verse has been and continues to be written in "the dross of verse," rhyme and meter. Though Williams wrote very few formal poems, his friend and fellow Modernist, Ezra Pound, wrote a great many. Pound famously insisted that poetry "must be *as well written as prose*" (*Letters,* # 60, 1915).

"Poetry," Pound declared (quoting and translating Stendhal), "with its obligatory comparisons, the mythology the poet don't believe in, his so-called dignity of style, *à la Louis XIV,* and all that trail of what they call poetic ornament, is vastly inferior to prose if you are trying to give a clear and exact idea of the '*mouvements du coeur*'; if you are trying to show what a man feels . . ." (*ABC of Reading,* 1934).

Seen in this context, *vers libre* was in part an attempt to liberate poetry from some of its more obvious distinguishing characteristics: it was *an assertion of the partial separation of "poetry" from "verse,"* and, as I suggested earlier, it was undertaken partly in the hope that poetry, couched in a medium closer to prose and with some of the strengths of prose, would be able to regain an ascendency it seemed to have lost to (among other things) the novel. In this attempt Pound and the others were for the most part unsuccessful, though a few poets such as the now ignored Carl Sandburg were able to capitalize on at least one mode of free verse and find a fairly substantial readership. Whatever the success of such poets, the free verse of *The Cantos* was not read widely; *Paterson* never made it to the best-seller list—and both Williams and Pound complained bitterly about their lack of readers. In 1949 Pound groused: "We will be about as popular as Mr. John Adams / and less widely perused" (Canto LXXXIV).

There is, however, a deep division in American culture between books which sell well in the marketplace and books which university students are told are important and significant. Partly through the influence of T. S. Eliot, *The Cantos* (and, later, *Paterson*)—kept in print by the redoutable James Laughlin of New Directions—had considerable success in the academies. Books like *The Cantos* and *Ulysses* are nothing if not *teachable*, and, by a complicated trickle-down effect which we can only barely trace here, a *kind* of "free verse" became, as Dana Gioia puts it, the "ruling orthodoxy" of poetic composition (*Can Poetry Matter?*). In his 1972 book, *Mockingbird Wish Me Luck*, the widely-read poet Charles Bukowski dismisses certain poems simply by calling them "rhymers"—poems that rhyme; his audience, he feels, will understand exactly what he means and, furthermore, will understand that that single word is enough to condemn the poems.

What Gioia and other New Formalists insist upon is the fact that formal verse—"rhymers"—continued to be written throughout the "free verse revolution" and in fact is being written today. Bukowski aside, it is something of a revelation for a Modernist (or "Postmodernist") writer to realize that the wide-ranging audience of which poetry can only dream has never fully accepted free verse. This audience tends—and from the Modernist point of view this is still another "atavism"—precisely to *associate* "poetry" with "verse."

As early as 1918, Pound himself complained about the low quality of much of the free verse he read: "*vers libre* has become as prolix and as verbose as any of the flaccid varieties that preceded it" ("A Retrospect," *Literary Essays of Ezra Pound*). Gioia would agree, but his argument goes even further: he points out that the *teaching* of poetry-as-verse traditionally involved memorization and recitation—which is to say, *performance:* "Performance was," he writes, "the teaching technique that kept poetry vital for centuries" (*Can Poetry Matter?*).

Rhyme and meter are—or were initially—*oral* devices. In choosing to move against them, poetry necessarily moves (to some extent) against its own past. Much "New Formalist" verse is fine writing, but it tends to be nearly as "literary" (or "page-bound" or "visual") as the equivalent poem produced by a language poet attempting "a poetics not centered on speech." Here Gioia himself is a considerable exception. Not only is he continually performing his work (on the radio as well as in poetry "venues"); he has recently undertaken, in collaboration with composer Alva Henderson, the creation of an opera, *Nosferatu* (based on F. W. Murnau's 1922 film). For Gioia, the writing of a libretto is an extension of his activities as a poet, not something apart from them. A libretto is simply another *form:*

Opera began as a kind of poetic drama. The Renaissance Florentines who invented it were trying to recreate the ideal balance between poetry and music found in classical Greek drama. That balance between words and music should remain the artistic goal. I consider the libretto a significant poetic form whose literary potential has barely been realized in English.

(Dana Gioia Interview by Lequita Vance-Watkins)

The questions raised by "performance" are no doubt enormously complex. Yet there is no more "relevant" place to raise them than in the realm of poetry. Poetry, with its atavistic, oral past, has *always* had a problematical relationship to writing, and this problematical relationship has centered on the question of sound. "A poetics of speech" has resurfaced in the many performances of poetry one finds all over the country. Admittedly, many of these performances are not of high quality. (A poet may be somebody who has *failed* to learn to sing and play the guitar!) Yet many of them are of considerable quality, and one cannot deny the passion of even the most inept.

"Formalist" poets such as William Butler Yeats (like Hopkins a disciple of Pater) and Dylan Thomas took to the airwaves and to the podium to deliver their message. Like Gioia, these poets pushed poetry towards theater. (Pound was of course notorious for taking to the airwaves!) "Beat" poets, modeling themselves on bebop soloists, understood the raw power of public recitation. Allen Ginsberg performed thousands of readings, and Lawrence Ferlinghetti pointed out that a poem may be "published"—made "public"—not by being printed but by being recited in a *public* place. The questions raised by performance cut across issues of "schools": Modernist, Beat, Language Poetry, New Formalism. They do not arise out of any particular kind or style of poetry but out of the divided heart of poetry itself. They suggest the existence of a powerful, *public* aspect of consciousness which is not satisfied with what Gustaf Sobin calls "breaths' burials."

Behind these questions are not only issues of "communication" but the whole complicated history of the art.

Is poetry an oral or a visual art? Most poets would answer that it's "both," but for the most part that answer is nothing more than a way of privileging writing: most of these same poets would also insist that a poem which succeeds only in performance and not "on the page" is not a poem. (And I have not even mentioned "visual" poetry, which is of considerable importance here and which challenges writing in its own way.) But let's leave aside the idea of "essence"—poetry "is" this or that. Rather, let's say that, because of its history, poetry *may be* either oral or visual. It doesn't *have to be both* in all instances. What happens then?

2000

ROBERT PINSKY
(B. 1940)

As a critic, teacher, and one of the most active poet laureates of the United States, Robert Pinsky has had an enormous impact on the contemporary poetry scene. He is a writer who honors the past but enlivens the present with American idioms. In its ambitious range of subjects, his poetry presents a dialectic of private moments and public voices.

Born the son of an optician in Long Branch, New Jersey, Pinsky grew up in "this half-dead but still gaudy and once glorious setting," a town of "beachfront hotels and penny arcades." While a student at Rutgers University, where one of his professors was the critic and historian Paul Fussell, Pinsky discovered his vocation as a poet. It was also there that he met and married Ellen Jane Bailey, who would become a psychologist and with whom he would have three daughters. He went on to the doctoral program in English at Stanford, where he was given a one-on-one tutorial in Yvor Winters's "History of the Lyric" course. Later he recalled that "most of my graduate education consisted of reading English and American poetry with Winters as a series of these Directed Readings." Among his fellow graduate students at Stanford was the poet Robert Hass, who became a close friend and occasional collaborator.

After earning his Ph.D. in 1966, Pinsky took teaching jobs, first at the University of Chicago, then at Wellesley College, where colleague, poet, and translator David Ferry introduced him to Frank Bidart. Through his friendship with Bidart, Pinsky met Robert Lowell and Elizabeth Bishop, the latter of whom he credits as an important influence on his own work. By the time he left Wellesley for a position at Berkeley in 1980, he had published two collections of poems, *Sadness and Happiness* (1975) and *An Explanation of America* (1979). He taught at Berkeley until 1988, then moved to his present position at Boston University, a tenure interrupted in 1997 when he served as poet laureate for an unprecedented three terms.

Always an advocate of a public stance for poets, Pinsky has also displayed a more private range in such books as *History of My Heart* (1984), *The Want Bone* (1990), *The Figured Wheel: New and Collected Poems* (1996), and *Jersey Rain* (2000). As a translator, he is particularly well

known for his collaborations with Robert Hass on translations of Nobel
Prize winner Czeslaw Milosz in *The Separate Notebooks* (1984) and for his
version of Dante's *Inferno* (1994).

Pinsky's books of critical essays, *The Situation of Poetry* (1976) and
Poetry and the World (1988), mediate the personal and public stances of the
poet, advocating both American diction and a broad sense of tradition as
well as a social sense of poetry's purposes. He has also published a brief
primer on poetic form, *The Sounds of Poetry* (1998). In the following essay,
Pinsky examines the social, political, and moral accountability of the contemporary poet.

◄•❯━━❯━•►

RESPONSIBILITIES OF THE POET

Certain general ideas come up repeatedly, in various guises, when contemporary
poetry is discussed. One of these might be described as the question of what, if
anything, is our social responsibility as poets.

That is, there are things a poet may owe the art of poetry—work, perhaps.
And in a sense there are things writers owe themselves—emotional truthfulness:
attention toward one's own feelings. But what, if anything, can a poet be said to
owe other people in general, considered as a community? For what is the poet answerable? This is a more immediate—though more limited—way of putting the
question than such familiar terms as "political poetry."

Another recurring topic is what might be called Poetry Gloom. I mean the sour-
ness and kvetching that sometimes come into our feelings about our art: the mysterious disaffections, the querulous doubts, the dispirited mood in which we ask ourselves, has contemporary poetry gone downhill, does anyone at all read it, has poetry
become a mere hobby, do only one's friends do it well, and so forth. This matter often
comes up in the form of questions about the "popularity" or "audience" of poetry.

Possibly the appetite for poetry really was greater in the good old days, in other
societies. After the total disaster at Syracuse, when the Athenians, their great impe-
rialist adventure failed, were being massacred, or branded as slaves with the image
of a horse burned into the forehead, a few were saved for the sake of Euripides,
whose work, it seems, was well thought of by the Syracusans. "Many of the cap-
tives who got safe back to Athens," writes Plutarch,

> are said, after they reached home, to have gone and made their acknowledg-
> ments to Euripides, relating how some of them had been released from their
> slavery by teaching what they could remember of his poems and others, when
> straggling after the fight, had been relieved with meat and drink for repeating
> some of his lyrics.

This is enviable; but I think that at some vital level our answer must be, *so what?*
Jarrell wrote about those people who say they "just can't read modern poetry" in

Originally delivered as a craft lecture at the Napa Valley Writers' Conference in August 1984. Collected in *Poetry and the World* (New York: Ecco Press, 1988) 83–98. All footnotes are Robert Pinsky's.

a tone that implies their happiest hours are spent in front of the fireplace with a volume of Blake or Racine. To court such readers, or to envy Euripides, would be understandable, but futile, impulses.

And I think they are even frivolous impulses, beside the point. Of course every artist is in competition with the movies, in the sense that art tries to be as interesting as it can. But tailoring one's work to an audience any less hungry for one's art than oneself probably makes for bad movies and bad poems. And whether that is true or not, most poets would be bad at such tailoring anyway. Daydreams aside, more urgent questions are: what is our job? And: what are the roots of good and bad morale about it?

The second question is strange, if I am right in supposing that poetry is the very art of being interesting. The two most interesting things in the world, for our species, are ideas and the individual human body, two elements that poetry uniquely joins together. It is the nature of poetry to emphasize constantly that the physical sounds of words come from a particular body, one at a time, in a certain order. By memorizing lines of Euripides, the Athenian soldiers had incorporated certain precise shades of conception. This dual concern, bodily and conceptual, is what Pound means by saying that poetry is a centaur: prose hits the target with its arrow; poetry does the same from horseback. If you are too stupid, or too cerebral, you may miss half of it.

Here I arrive at the relation between the two questions, morale and responsibility. In the root sense of the glamourless word "responsibility," people crave not only answers but also answerability. Involving a promise or engagement, the word is related to "sponsor" and "spouse." We want our answers to be craved as in the testing and reassuring of any animal parent and child, or the mutual nudge and call of two liturgical voices. The corporeal, memorizable quality of verse carries with it a sense of social exchange. The visible image of the horse burned into the living human body says one thing; the memorized cadence of words, without exactly contradicting that statement, answers it with another.

An artist needs not so much an audience, as to feel a need to answer, a promise to respond. The response may be a contradiction, it may be unwanted, it may go unheeded, it may be embraced but twisted (William Blake the most quoted author in the modern House of Commons!)—but it is owed, and the sense that it is owed is a basic requirement for the poet's good feeling about the art. This need to answer, as firm as a borrowed object or a cash debt, is the ground where the centaur walks.

A critic, a passionate writer on poetry, culture and politics, once said to me, "When I ask American poets if they are concerned about United States foreign policy in Latin America, they all say yes, they are. But practically none of them write about it: why not?"

My response to this question was not dazzling. "I don't know," I said. And then, thinking about it for another moment: "It certainly isn't that they don't want to." The desire to make a good work, or the desire to deal with a given subject—in theory, the desire to deal with every subject—isn't automatically fulfilled.

The desire to see, and the desire to feel obliged to answer, are valuable, perhaps indispensable parts of the poet's feelings about the art. But in themselves they are not enough. In some way, before an artist can see a subject—foreign policy, or any other subject—the artist must transform it: answer the received cultural imagination of the subject with something utterly different. This need to answer by transforming is primary; it comes before everything else.

Something of the kind may explain the interesting phenomenon of bad work by good artists. Even a gifted, hard-working writer with a large and appreciative audience may write badly, I think, if this sense of an obligation to answer—a promised pushing-back or responding—is lacking. Irresponsibility subtly deadens the work. Conversely, a dutiful editorializing work, devoid of the kind of transformation I mean, may also be dead.

To put it differently, the idea of social responsibility seems to raise a powerful contradiction, in the light of another intuited principle, freedom. The poet needs to feel utterly free, yet answerable. This paradox underlies and confounds much discussion of our art; poetry is so bodily and yet so explicit, so capable of subjects and yet so subtly transforming of them, that it seems recurrently to be quite like the rest of life, and yet different.

One anecdotal example: I have a friend who drives a car impatiently, sometimes with a vivid running commentary on other drivers. One day while I sat next to him the car in front of us behaved in a notably indecisive, unpredictable, petulant, dog-in-the-manger manner. But my friend was calm, he did not gesture and he certainly did not honk. I asked him why, and his explanation was, "I never hassle anybody who is taking care of small children."

This self-conscious respect for child care seems to me more than simply sweet. It exemplifies a basic form of social responsibility, an element of communal life more basic even than the boss-and-henchmen *comitatus* celebrated in *Beowulf*. People in a bus or restaurant where there is a small child like to think, I believe, that in an emergency they would protect the child, despite gulfs of social class or race or mere difference that might intervene.

The feeling is not goodness, exactly, but rather the desire to think well of ourselves—the first civic virtue, the fission of subject and object emitting the bubble reputation. That desire is part of our nature as social animals whose hairless, pudgy offspring pass through a long period of learning and vulnerability. We live together, rather than separately like Cyclopes, or otherwise perish in a generation. We living in our majority need to mediate between the dead, who took care of us, and not only the young, but the unborn.

And as poets, too, one of our responsibilities is to mediate between the dead and the unborn: we must feel ready to answer, as if asked by the dead if we have handed on what they gave us, or asked by the unborn what we have for them. This is one answer, the great conservative answer, to the question of what responsibility the poet bears to society. By practicing an art learned partly from the dead, one keeps it alive for the unborn.

Arts do, after all, die. In a way it is their survival that is surprising. When I was in primary school, they showed us films provided by the paper industry or the glass industry depicting, with diagrams and footage of incredibly elaborate machines, the steps in making the innumerable kinds of paper, or glass jars and lenses and fiberglass curtains and fuselages. I remember thinking with some panic that it would soon all decay and fall apart: that the kids I knew in my own generation would be unable to learn those complex processes in time. When the adults died, we would botch the machines; I knew this with certainty, because I knew my peers and myself.

This fear still makes sense to me, and yet some of us went on not only to master those arcane processes and elaborate machines, but to improve them. Some people who were grubby, bored ten-year-olds in 1950 are now experts in fiber-optic controls in the manufacturing of semi-vitreous components, or in the editing of Provençal manuscripts.

So one great task we have to answer for is the keeping of an art that we did not invent, but were given, so that others who come after us can have it if they want it, as free to choose it and change it as we have been. A second task has been defined by Carolyn Forché, in a remarkable essay,[1] as "a poetry of witness": we must use the art to behold the actual evidence before us. We must answer for what we see.

Witness may or may not involve advocacy, and the line between the two will be drawn differently by each of us; but the strange truth about witness is that though it may include both advocacy and judgment, it includes more than them, as well. If political or moral advocacy were all we had to answer for, that would be almost easy. Witness goes further, I think, because it involves the challenge of not flinching from the evidence. It proceeds from judgment to testimony.

In the most uncompromising sense, this means that whatever important experience seems least poetic to me is likely to be my job. Forché, for example, writes:

> In those days I kept my work as a poet and journalist separate, of two distinct *mentalités*, but I could not keep El Salvador from my poems because it had become so much a part of my life. I was cautioned to avoid mixing art and politics, that one damages the other, and it was some time before I realized that "political poetry" often means the poetry of protest, accused of polemical didacticism, and not the poetry which implicitly celebrates politically acceptable values.[2]

That is, the poet realized that what had seemed "unpoetic" or fit only for journalism, because it was supposedly contaminated with particular political implications, was her task. The "contamination" or "politics" was her responsibility, what she had to answer for as if she had promised something about it when she undertook the art of poetry. A corollary realization is that "all poetry is political": what is politically acceptable to some particular observer may seem "unpolitical" to that observer.

Where does the debilitating falseness come from, that tempts us to look away from evidence, or fit it into some allegedly "poetic" pattern, with the inevitable result of Poetry Gloom? Forché continues, a few sentences later:

> From our tradition we inherit a poetic, a sense of appropriate subjects, styles, forms and levels of diction; that poetic might insist that we be attuned to the individual in isolation, to particular sensitivity in the face of "nature," to special ingenuity in inventing metaphor.[3]

The need to notice, to include the evidence as a true and reliable witness, can be confused and blunted by the other, conserving responsibility of mediation between the dead and the unborn. And just as society can vaguely, quietly diffuse an invisible, apparently "apolitical" political ideology, culture can efficiently assimilate and enforce an invisible idea of what is poetic. In a dim view of the dialectic, it seems that society's tribute to poetry is to incorporate each new, at first resisted sense of the poetic, and so to spread it—and blunt it—for each new generation. Even while seeming not to taste each new poetic, the world swallows it.

---

1. Carolyn Forché, "El Salvador: An Aide Memoire," *American Poetry Review,* July/August 1981, vol. 10, no. 4, pp. 3–7.
2. *Ibid.,* p. 6.
3. *Ibid.*

Two nearly paradoxical formulations emerge from this conflict. First, only the challenge of what may seem unpoetic, that which has not already been made poetic by the tradition, can keep the art truly pure and alive. Put to no new use, the art rots. Second, the habits and visions of the art itself, which we are responsible for keeping alive, can seem to conspire against that act of use or witness. The material or rhetoric that seems already, on the face of it, proper to poetry may have been made poetic already by Baudelaire, or Wordsworth, or Rilke, or Neruda.

To put it simply, and only a little fancifully, we have in our care and for our use and pleasure a valuable gift, and we must answer both for preserving it, and for changing it. And the second we fail to make good answer on either score, the gift stops giving pleasure, and makes us feel bad, instead.

Since there is no way to say what evidence will seem pressing but difficult to a given artist—Central America, the human body, the nature of art, taking care of one's paraplegic sister, theology, farming, American electoral politics, the ideological meaning of free verse, the art of domestic design—no subject ever is forbidden. Society depends on the poet to witness something, and yet the poet can discover that thing only by looking away from what society has learned to see poetically.

Thus, there is a dialectic between the poet and culture: the culture presents us with poetry, and with implicit definitions of what materials and means are poetic. The answer we must promise to give is "no." Real works revise the received idea of what poetry is; by mysterious cultural means the revisions are assimilated and then presented as the next definition to be resisted, violated and renewed. What poets must answer for is the unpoetic. And before we can identify it, or witness it, an act of judgment is necessary. This act of judgment can only be exemplified.

Here is one of the most valued poems in our language. In quoting the poem, I particularly want to point out the insistently repeated absolutes, especially the words "*every*" and "*most*":

LONDON

I wander thro' each charter'd street,
Near where the charter'd Thames does flow,
And mark in every face I meet
Marks of weakness, marks of woe.

In every cry of every Man,
In every Infant's cry of fear,
In every voice, in every ban,
The mind-forg'd manacles I hear:

How the Chimney-sweeper's cry
Every blackening Church appalls,
And the hapless Soldier's sigh
Runs in blood down Palace walls.

But most thro' midnight streets I hear
How the youthful Harlot's curse
Blasts the new-born Infant's tear
And blights with plagues the Marriage hearse.

The word "every" throbs through all of the stanzas except the final one, repeated five times in the drumlike second stanza. This insistent chain of "every's" leads to the capping, climactic movement of the conclusion, with its contrary, superlative

"*But most*": the immense force of the ending comes partly from the way "But most" piles its weight onto the already doubled and redoubled momentum of "every" and "every" and "every."

One thing that "every" and "every" brings into the poem is the sense of a social whole: it is all of us, we are part of it, no utter exception is possible, it is like a family, and a family that bears a "mark." And though my brother and not I may have poured your blood or blighted your tear, it would be stupid of me to think that your response to me—or mine to you—could go uncolored by what you know of my family. The poem witnesses the legal entity of a city in a way that transforms it into this social whole.

Blake's "most" is reserved for the blighting of future generations—the extension of social corruption forward, into the future, through the infection of those still *in utero*. This continuation forward in time of the omnipresent blight and pain, under the climactic "but most," suggests both of the broad kinds of answerability: it is literally conservative, and it reminds us that we are witnesses for the future. Those who want to know about London in Blake's time read this poem. They may read the contemporary journalism, as well, but for an inward understanding of such evidence, they will again read Blake. If someone in the future wants to understand *Newsweek* and *Time*, or the *CBS Evening News*, our poems must answer to the purpose. We are supposed to mark the evidence, as well as continuing the art.

In "London," all this is accomplished by the violently wholesale quality of what is "marked" in both senses, witnessed and scarred. The "unpoetic" part of the poem is the rhetoric that invents or enacts the vision of society as a kind of nightmarish, total family rather than an orderly contractual, chartered arrangement. In a sense, Blake had to transform the city imaginatively, put the mark of his judgment upon it, in order to portray it in the mock-hymn of "London."

If all poems were like "London," the question might seem relatively simple. But not all poems invite a social understanding of themselves nearly as strongly as this. And few of us were attracted to poetry to start with by the idea of being a good witness, still less the idea of mediating between the dead and the unborn. Most of us were attracted to poetry because of language that gave us enormous, unmistakable pleasure: not only the physical pleasure of beaded bubbles winking at the brim, but also the intellectual pleasure of thinking of the thin men of Haddam who rode over Connecticut in a glass coach, how they are both creatures of fantasy and suburban commuters on the train.

Such transformation seems to precede witness, in the working of poetry and in the history of our need for poetry. Its relation to witness is like that suggested by a passage in Ben Jonson's great poem "To Heaven":

As thou art all, so be thou all to me,
First, midst, and last, converted one, and three;
My faith, my hope, my love: and in this state
My judge, my witness, and my advocate.

Faith in the absolute fairness of a judge like the Father is parallel to hope regarding a witness (the Holy Ghost) and love for an advocate, whose Christian mercy extends beyond justice. In keeping with the biblical and religious models, the transforming certainty of judgment precedes the processes of witness and advocacy. Jonson's intellectually elegant revision of the courtroom sequence (evidence, argument, judgment) reflects the way that poetry seems to depend upon a prior and tremendously confident process of transformation.

Transformation, too, is a social role of poetry: its oldest, clearest form must be epideictic, the praising of heroes, celebrating one whose physical or moral gifts have brought gain or glory to the tribe: the woman in Robinson's "Eros Turannos," whose catastrophic love affair makes "all the town and harbor side / Vibrate with her seclusion" is a peculiar, American provincial version of such a figure. She makes the town more heroic, and the gossiping townfolk make her story more heroic:

> She fears him, and will always ask
> What fated her to choose him;
> She meets in his engaging mask
> All reasons to refuse him;
> But what she meets and what she fears
> Are less than are the downward years
> Drawn slowly to the foamless weirs
> Of age, were she to lose him.
>
> Between a blurred sagacity
> That once had power to sound him,
> And Love, that will not let him be
> The Judas that she found him,
> Her pride assuages her almost,
> As if it were alone the cost.—
> He sees that he will not be lost,
> And waits and looks around him.
>
> A sense of ocean and old trees
> Envelops and allures him;
> Tradition, touching all he sees,
> Beguiles and reassures him;
> And all her doubts of what he says
> Are dimmed with what she knows of days—
> Till even prejudice delays,
> And fades, and she secures him.
>
> The falling leaf inaugurates
> The reign of her confusion;
> The pounding wave reverberates
> The dirge of her illusion;
> And home, where passion lived and died,
> Becomes a place where she can hide,
> While all the town and harbor side
> Vibrate with her seclusion.
>
> We tell you, tapping on our brows,
> The story as it should be,—
> As if the story of a house
> Were told, or ever could be;
> We'll have no kindly veil between
> Her visions and those we have seen,—
> As if we guessed what hers have been,
> Or what they are or would be.

Meanwhile we do no harm; for they
    That with a god have striven,
Not hearing much of what we say,
    Take what the god has given;
Though like waves breaking it may be,
Or like a changed familiar tree,
Or like a stairway to the sea
    Where down the blind are driven.

The mean-minded little town, the superior, desperate woman, the vulgar man, even perhaps the complacent, spavined literary culture whose editors had no use for Robinson's work, all are resisted and transformed by a rhetoric that includes the coming together of the poem's peculiar form, its powerful narrative, and the heroic symbol of the ocean.

Formally, the resistant or "unpoetic" element in "Eros Turannos" is a kind of hypertrophy. As if in response to an insufficiently communal or folkloric relation between artist and audience, or heroine and community—even between the seemingly omniscient narrator of the beginning and the "we" speaking the ending—the poem exaggerates the formal, communal elements of the poem. With its feminine rhymes and triple rhymes and extension of ballad structure the poem is almost a parody ballad. The hypertrophy of traditional folk or ritualistic formal means resists an idea of poetic language, and of poetry in relation to social reality, by exaggeration. In its own terms this virtuoso exaggeration is as violent as the sweeping terms of Blake's "London," with its angry formal remaking of the hymn.

Based on a mighty, prior act of transforming judgment, "London" takes the rhetorical mode of witnessing ("I mark"); what is on trial is a transformed London, and the poet's eye roams through it like the Holy Ghost, seeing more than any literal social reality could make possible. His repeated "every" is in part a mark of ubiquity. Robinson's poem of tragic celebration, full of mercy and advocacy in relation to its heroine, evokes images and rhetoric of judgment; and judgment is formally emphasized almost to the point of parody by the quality of incantation. Yet the perspective in "Eros Turannos," too, is preternatural. Certainly, the viewpoint is more than socially located. It is the multiple perspective of the ubiquitous witness:

Meanwhile we do no harm; for they
    That with a god have striven,
Not hearing much of what we say,
    Take what the god has given;
Though like waves breaking it may be
Or like a changed familiar tree,
Or like a stairway to the sea
    Where down the blind are driven.

What "we" see or say; what is known of "her" fears and questions; what "they" hear or take; what the god gives; what "it" may be like—all of these narrated materials gain their authority from the underlying, invisible certainty of transformation. That certainty appears in the "changed familiar tree," and its invisible, generative power leads to the stairway "Where down the blind are driven." The poet's own voice changes from impersonal omniscience at the outset to a communal first-person plural by the close.

These examples suggest to me that society forms an idea of the poetic, an idea which has its implications about social reality, and that the poet needs to respond by answering with a rebuttal or transformation of terms. But what about a poem that is deliberately irresponsible, that is anarchic or unacceptable in its social attitude? What, for example, about Frank O'Hara's poem "Ave Maria"?

Mothers of America
                    let your kids go to the movies!
get them out of the house so they won't know what you're up to
it's true fresh air is good for the body
                              but what about the soul
that grows in darkness, embossed by silvery images
and when you grow old as grow old you must
                                        they won't hate you
they won't criticize you they won't know
                              they'll be in some glamorous country
they first saw on a Saturday afternoon or playing hookey

they may even be grateful to you
                         for their first sexual experience
which only cost you a quarter
                         and didn't upset the peaceful home
they will know where candy bars come from
                              and gratuitous bags of popcorn
as gratuitous as leaving the movie before it's over
with a pleasant stranger whose apartment is in the Heaven on Earth Bldg
near the Williamsburg Bridge
                              oh mothers you will have made the little tykes
so happy because if nobody does pick them up in the movies
they won't know the difference
                         and if somebody does it'll be sheer gravy
and they'll have been truly entertained either way
instead of hanging around the yard
                         or up in their room
                                   hating you
prematurely since you won't have done anything horribly mean yet
except keeping them from the darker joys
                              it's unforgivable the latter
so don't blame me if you won't take this advice
                              and the family breaks up
and your children grow old and blind in front of a TV set
                                   seeing
movies you wouldn't let them see when they were young

The language of this poem dodges and charges so brilliantly on its way, with energy that is so happily demotic, that a reader is likely to want to keep up, to want to show that one can keep up. Among other things, the poem expresses love for the flawed, for imperfection—especially American imperfection—and the dark. O'Hara sprints happily through this terrain, leaping between such oppositions as "silvery images" versus "the peaceful home," to find the genuinely friendly, intimate and

democratic note of "sheer gravy" and "so don't blame me if you won't take this advice." It is a contest between glamour and decency, apparently settled by an appeal
to American idiom. His understanding of such speech, and by implication of the
movies, is so clear and vivid that we want to share it, to assure ourselves that we,
too, understand the dark, stained charm of Heaven on Earth as it appears in an actual New York. The language streaks forward impatiently and we want to go along.

One thing we are invited to go along with is the idea that children young
enough to need permission to go to the movies may benefit from sexual use by
adult strangers; that they may be grateful for it. Considered as advocacy, this is
unacceptable: criminal, and worse. It is as if O'Hara chose the most repulsive
proposition he could think of, to embed in the middle of his poem.

Various matters of rhetoric may soften or deflect the issue of unacceptability:
since the group "Mothers of America" will for the most part not hear, and surely
not heed, this oration, it can be looked on as not literal advocacy but mock-
advocacy. And more legalistically, the seduction is conjectural: they "*may*" even
be grateful. So the advocacy is hemmed by irony and disclaimer, with the outrageous jokes of "only cost you a quarter" and "sheer gravy" signaling how very
much in the realm of rhetoric we are—an exuberant homosexual *schpritzing*.

But just the same, there is an element of the unacceptable in the poem, a violation of social boundaries. And far from seeming a regrettable, separable blemish,
this repugnant element seems essential. It is what makes us believe the "darker
joys," asking in effect if pleasure in the poem has a component of inexpensive, vi-
carious sexual naughtiness. Ultimately, I think it asks us to entertain the possibility
of some one unusual eleven-year-old (should we imagine the lines as actual or fan-
tasized autobiography?) who might conceivably feel grateful to his mother for the
opportunity described.

In other words, the poem breaks or bends ideas about poetic method and content. And this resistant act seems prior to the poem, part of a preceding judgment that
underlies what is seen and argued. Perhaps one thing I like in the poem is the daring
with which it plays—and so clearly plays—at the definitive terms of judgment:

> keeping them from the darker joys
> 　　　　　　　　　　　　it's unforgivable the latter

or the ratiocinative terms of advocacy:

> 　　　　because if nobody does pick them up in the movies
> they won't know the difference
> 　　　　　　　　　　　and if somebody does it'll be sheer gravy

The democratic, almost conspirational note of "sheer gravy," and "horribly
mean," deftly contrasted with language like "prematurely" and "the latter," invites an alliance in imperfection. The poem happily witnesses a great communal
imperfection ("what you're up to," "horribly mean") and excitement in American
life, all the grotesque, glorious fantasy life associated with the movies. The bite of
the poem comes from its comic perspectives: the imagination of a scene where the
poet addresses the Mothers, the imagination of the future at the end of the poem,
the imagination of an idyllic sexual initiation for "tykes."

He is willing to share his sense of the movies, and of our culture, with us, and
his willingness is rooted in his will to transform our idea of what is acceptable, in

poetry or in the imagined oration itself. Other works of those late Eisenhower years get higher marks in the category "does not advocate awful crimes," but we do not read them with the pleasure and recognition this one gives, with its stern standard of being "truly entertained." In one way, the poem is a daring, ebullient prank; in another, it embodies the way a poet's vision and language spring from a need to resist and challenge what the culture has given.

"All poetry is political." The act of judgment prior to the vision of any poem is a social judgment. It always embodies, I believe, a resistance or transformation of communal values: Blake's indictment of totally visible, monolithic London; Robinson's dry rage that an aristocracy of grace and moral insight has no worldly force; O'Hara's celebration of what is cheerfully lawless in American life. Even when Emily Dickinson defines the ultimate privacy of the soul, she does it in terms that originate in social judgment:

The soul selects her own Society—
Then—shuts the Door.

As one of the best-known lines in contemporary poetry indicates, the unpredictable effect upon a community of what one writes may be less to the point than discharging the responsibility:

America I'm putting my queer shoulder to the wheel.

The poet's first social responsibility, to continue the art, can be filled only through the second, opposed responsibility to change the terms of the art as given—and it is given socially, which is to say politically. What that will mean in the next poem anyone writes is by definition unknowable, with all the possibility of art.

1984

►◄ LYN HEJINIAN ►◄
(B. 1941)

One of the founding members of the Language Poetry movement, Hejinian was born Lyn Hall in San Francisco and raised in Alameda, California. She graduated from Harvard University in 1963, the year she began publishing poems in literary magazines. Her 1961 marriage to John Hejinian, with whom she had two children, lasted until 1972. Five years later she married a Bay Area jazz musician, Larry Ochs, a member of the ROVA Saxophone Quartet. During the seventies, she gave increased attention to her writing and founded Tuumba Press in 1976, with which she published several chapbooks, *A Thought Is the Bride of What Thinking* (1976), *Gesualdo* (1978), and *The Guard* (1978), as well as books by other Bay Area Language writers. Her first full collection, *Writing Is an Aid to Memory* (1978), explores the disjunctions of memory through correspondingly disjunctive lines and syntax. Her prose poem, *My Life* (1980), continues these explorations through its open-ended approach to autobiography. Hejinian gives many possible versions of her childhood self, stresses the instability of adult recollections of childhood, and, by omitting transitions between most of her sentences, invites the reader to participate in her narrative. In 1987 she made *My Life* even more open-ended by publishing a significantly revised and expanded edition, which effectively gave critics two versions to consider. Since *My Life* Hejinian has continued to focus on "a flow of contexts," the "transitions, transmutations, the endless radiating of denotation into relation" that she defines as the essential properties of language in the introduction to her book of essays, *The Language of Inquiry* (2000).

Although her early poetry was political in calling "the self" into question, her many visits to Russia in the 1980s increased her concern with poetry's social and political dimensions, and her subsequent books have raised even more explicit questions about identity. In particular, Hejinian challenges national identities and gender identities while continuing to highlight language's fluidity in *Oxota: A Short Russian Novel* (1991), *The Cell* (1992), and *A Border Comedy* (1999).

In the following essay, delivered as a talk in 1983, Hejinian advocates an "open text" whose form encourages multiple readings. Introducing "The Rejection of Closure" in *The Language of Inquiry,* she suggests that texts

367

should be open because perception itself lacks closure. For Hejinian, the incompletion and ambiguity of individual experience, the social world, and language itself present infinite opportunities for both writers and readers.

◄—◄()►—►

THE REJECTION OF CLOSURE

Two dangers never cease threatening
the world: order and disorder.
     Paul Valéry, *Analects*

Writing's initial situation, its point of origin, is often characterized and always complicated by opposing impulses in the writer and by a seeming dilemma that language creates and then cannot resolve. The writer experiences a conflict between a desire to satisfy a demand for boundedness, for containment and coherence, and a simultaneous desire for free, unhampered access to the world prompting a correspondingly open response to it. Curiously, the term *inclusivity* is applicable to both, though the connotative emphasis is different for each. The impulse to boundedness demands circumscription and that in turn requires that a distinction be made between inside and outside, between the relevant and the (for the particular writing at hand) confusing and irrelevant—the meaningless. The desire for unhampered access and response to the world (an encyclopedic impulse), on the other hand, hates to leave anything out. The essential question here concerns the writer's subject position.

The impasse, meanwhile, that is both language's creative condition and its problem can be described as the disjuncture between words and meaning, but at a particularly material level, one at which the writer is faced with the necessity of making formal decisions—devising an appropriate structure for the work, anticipating the constraints it will put into play, etc.—in the context of the ever-regenerating plenitude of language's resources, in their infinite combinations. Writing's forms are not merely shapes but forces; formal questions are about dynamics—they ask how, where, and why the writing moves, what are the types, directions, number, and velocities of a work's motion. The material aporia objectifies the poem in the context of ideas and of language itself.

These areas of conflict are not neatly parallel. Form does not necessarily achieve closure, nor does raw materiality provide openness. Indeed, the conjunction of *form* with radical *openness* may be what can offer a version of the "paradise" for which writing often yearns—a flowering focus on a distinct infinity.

For the sake of clarity, I will offer a tentative characterization of the terms *open* and *closed*. We can say that a "closed text" is one in which all the elements of the work are directed toward a single reading of it. Each element confirms that reading and delivers the text from any lurking ambiguity. In the "open text," meanwhile, all the elements of the work are maximally excited; here it is because ideas and things exceed (without deserting) argument that they have taken into the dimension of the work.

Though they may be different in different texts, depending on other elements in the work and by all means on the intention of the writer, it is not hard to discover

First given as a talk in San Francisco on April 17, 1983, at a panel discussion entitled "Who Is Speaking?" First published in *Poetics Journal*: "*Women and Language*" 4 (May 1984). First collected by Hejinian in *The Language of Inquiry* (Berkeley: University of California Press, 2000) 41–58. All notes are Lyn Hejinian's.

devices—structural devices—that may serve to "open" a poetic text. One set of such devices has to do with arrangement and, particularly, with rearrangement within a work. The "open text," by definition, is open to the world and particularly to the reader. It invites participation, rejects the authority of the writer over the reader and thus, by analogy, the authority implicit in other (social, economic, cultural) hierarchies. It speaks for writing that is generative rather than directive. The writer relinquishes total control and challenges authority as a principle and control as a motive. The "open text" often emphasizes or foregrounds process, either the process of the original composition or of subsequent compositions by readers, and thus resists the cultural tendencies that seek to identify and fix material and turn it into a product; that is, it resists reduction and commodification. As Luce Irigaray says, positing this tendency within a feminine sphere of discourse, "It is really a question of another economy which diverts the linearity of a project, undermines the target-object of a desire, explodes the polarization of desire on only one pleasure, and disconcerts fidelity to only one discourse."[1]

"Field work," where words and lines are distributed irregularly on the page, such as Robert Grenier's poster/map entitled *Cambridge M'ass* and Bruce Andrews's "Love Song 41" (also originally published as a poster), are obvious examples of works in which the order of the reading is not imposed in advance.[2] Any reading of these works is an improvisation; one moves through the work not in straight lines but in curves, swirls, and across intersections, to words that catch the eye or attract attention repeatedly.

Repetition, conventionally used to unify a text or harmonize its parts, as if returning melody to the tonic, instead, in these works, and somewhat differently in a work like my *My Life,* challenges our inclination to isolate, identify, and limit the burden of meaning given to an event (the sentence or line). Here, where certain phrases recur in the work, recontextualized and with new emphasis, repetition disrupts the initial apparent meaning scheme. The initial reading is adjusted; meaning is set in motion, emended and extended, and the rewriting that repetition becomes postpones completion of the thought indefinitely.

But there are more complex forms of juxtaposition. My intention (I don't mean to suggest that I succeeded) in a subsequent work, "Resistance," was to write a lyric poem in a long form—that is, to achieve maximum vertical intensity (the single moment into which the idea rushes) and maximum horizontal extensivity (ideas cross the landscape and become the horizon and weather).[3] To myself I proposed the paragraph as a unit representing a single moment of time, a single moment in the mind, its content all the thoughts, thought particles, impressions, impulses—all the diverse, particular, and contradictory elements—that are included in an active and emotional mind at any given instant. For the moment, for the writer, the poem *is* a mind.

To prevent the work from disintegrating into its separate parts—scattering sentence-rubble haphazardly on the waste heap—I used various syntactic devices to foreground or create the conjunction between ideas. Statements become interconnected

1. Luce Irigaray, "This sex which is not one," tr. Claudia Reeder, in *New French Feminisms,* ed. Elaine Marks and Isabelle de Courtivron (Amherst: University of Massachusetts Press, 1980), 104.
2. Robert Grenier, *Cambridge M'ass* (Berkeley: Tuumba Press, 1979); Bruce Andrews, *Love Songs* (Baltimore: Pod Books, 1982).
3. At the time this essay was written, "Resistance" existed only in manuscript form. A large portion of it was eventually incorporated into "The Green" and published in *The Cold of Poetry* (Los Angeles: Sun & Moon Press, 1994).

by being grammatically congruent; unlike things, made alike grammatically, become meaningful in common and jointly. "Resistance" began:

> Patience is laid out on my papers. Its visuals are gainful and equably square. Two dozen jets take off into the night. Outdoors a car goes uphill in a genial low gear. The flow of thoughts—impossible! These are the defamiliarization techniques with which we are so familiar.

There are six sentences here, three of which, beginning with the first, are constructed similarly: subject—verb—prepositional phrase. The three prepositions are *on*, *into*, and *in*, which in isolation seem similar but used here have very different meanings. *On* is locational: "on my papers." *Into* is metaphorical and atmospheric: "into the night." *In* is atmospheric and qualitative: "in a genial low gear." There are a pair of inversions in effect here: the unlike are made similar (syntactically) and the like are sundered (semantically). Patience, which might be a quality of a virtuous character attendant to work ("it is laid out on my papers"), might also be solitaire, a card game played by an idler who is avoiding attention to work. Two dozen jets can only take off together in formation; they are "laid out" on the night sky. A car goes uphill; its movement upward parallels that of the jets, but whereas their formation is martial, the single car is somewhat domestic, genial and innocuous. The image in the first pair of sentences is horizontal. The upward movement of the next two sentences describes a vertical plane, upended on or intersecting the horizontal one. The "flow of thoughts" runs down the vertical and comes to rest—"impossible!"

The work shifts between horizontal and vertical landscapes, and the corresponding sentences—the details of each composed on its particular plane—form distinct semantic fields. (In fact, I would like each individual sentence to be as nearly a complete poem as possible.)

One of the results of this compositional technique, building a work out of discrete fields, is the creation of sizable gaps between the units. To negotiate this disrupted terrain, the reader (and I can say also the writer) must overleap the end stop, the period, and cover the distance to the next sentence. Meanwhile, what stays in the gaps remains crucial and informative. Part of the reading occurs as the recovery of that information (looking behind) and the discovery of newly structured ideas (stepping forward).

In both *My Life* and "Resistance," the structural unit (grossly, the paragraph) was meant to be mimetic of both a space and a time of thinking. In a somewhat different respect, time predetermines the form of Bernadette Mayer's *Midwinter Day*. The work begins when the clock is set running (at dawn on December 22, 1978) and ends when the time allotted to the work runs out (late night of the same day). "It's true," Mayer has said: "I have always loved projects of all sorts, including say sorting leaves or whatever projects turn out to be, and in poetry I most especially love having time be the structure which always seems to me to save structure or form from itself because then nothing really has to begin or end."[4]

Whether the form is dictated by temporal constraints or by other exoskeletal formal elements—by a prior decision, for example, that the work will contain, say, *x* number of sentences, paragraphs, stanzas, stresses, or lines, etc.—the work gives the impression that it begins and ends arbitrarily and not because there is a necessary

4. Bernadette Mayer to Lyn Hejinian, letter (1981?).

point of origin or terminus, a first or last moment. The implication (correct) is that the words and the ideas (thoughts, perceptions, etc.—the materials) continue beyond the work. One has simply stopped because one has run out of units or minutes, and not because a conclusion has been reached nor "everything" said.

The relationship of form, or the "constructive principle," to the materials of the work (to its themes, the conceptual mass, but also to the words themselves) is the initial problem for the "open text," one that faces each writing anew. Can form make the primary chaos (the raw material, the unorganized impulse and information, the uncertainty, incompleteness, vastness) articulate without depriving it of its capacious vitality, its generative power? Can form go even further than that and actually generate that potency, opening uncertainty to curiosity, incompleteness to speculation, and turning vastness into plenitude? In my opinion, the answer is yes; that is, in fact, the function of form in art. Form is not a fixture but an activity.

In an essay titled "Rhythm as the Constructive Factor of Verse," the Russian Formalist writer Yurii Tynianov writes:

> We have only recently outgrown the well-known analogy: form is to content as a glass is to wine. . . . I would venture to say that in nine out of ten instances the word "composition" covertly implies a treatment of form as a static item. The concept of "poetic line" or "stanza" is imperceptibly removed from the dynamic category. Repetition ceases to be considered as a fact of varying strength in various situations of frequency and quantity. The dangerous concept of the "symmetry of compositional facts" arises, dangerous because we cannot speak of symmetry where we find intensification.[5]

One is reminded of Gertrude Stein's comparable comments in "Portraits and Repetitions": "A thing that seems to be exactly the same thing may seem to be a repetition but is it." "Is there repetition or is there insistence. I am inclined to believe there is no such thing as repetition. And really how can there be." "Expressing any thing there can be no repetition because the essence of that expression is insistence, and if you insist you must each time use emphasis and if you use emphasis it is not possible while anybody is alive that they should use exactly the same emphasis."[6]

Tynianov continues:

> The unity of a work is not a closed symmetrical whole, but an unfolding dynamic integrity. . . . The sensation of form in such a situation is always the sensation of flow (and therefore of change). . . . Art exists by means of this interaction or struggle.[7]

Language discovers what one might know, which in turn is always less than what language might say. We encounter some limitations of this relationship early, as children. Anything with limits can be imagined (correctly or incorrectly) as an object, by analogy with other objects—balls and rivers. Children objectify language when they render it their plaything, in jokes, puns, and riddles, or in glossolaliac chants and rhymes. They discover that words are not equal to the world, that a

5. Yurii Tynianov, "Rhythm as the Constructive Factor of Verse," in *Readings in Russian Poetics,* ed. Ladislav Matejka and Krystyna Pomorska (Ann Arbor: Michigan Slavic Contributions, 1978), 127–28.
6. Gertrude Stein, "Portraits and Repetitions," in *Gertrude Stein: Writings 1932–1946,* ed. Catharine R. Stimpson and Harriet Chessman (New York: Library of America, 1998), 292, 288.
7. Tynianov, "Rhythm as the Constructive Factor," 128.

blur of displacement, a type of parallax, exists in the relation between things (events, ideas, objects) and the words for them—a displacement producing a gap.

Among the most prevalent and persistent categories of jokes is that which identifies and makes use of the fallacious comparison of words to world and delights in the ambiguity resulting from the discrepancy:

—Why did the moron eat hay?
—To feed his hoarse voice.

—How do you get down from an elephant?
—You don't, you get down from a goose.

—Did you wake up grumpy this morning?
—No, I let him sleep.

Because we have language we find ourselves in a special and peculiar relationship to the objects, events, and situations which constitute what we imagine of the world. Language generates its own characteristics in the human psychological and spiritual conditions. Indeed, it nearly *is* our psychological condition.

This psychology is generated by the struggle between language and that which it claims to depict or express, by our overwhelming experience of the vastness and uncertainty of the world, and by what often seems to be the inadequacy of the imagination that longs to know it—and, furthermore, for the poet, the even greater inadequacy of the language that appears to describe, discuss, or disclose it. This psychology situates desire in the poem itself, or, more specifically, in poetic language, to which then we may attribute the motive for the poem.

Language is one of the principal forms our curiosity takes. It makes us restless. As Francis Ponge puts it, "Man is a curious body whose center of gravity is not in himself."[8] Instead that center of gravity seems to be located in language, by virtue of which we negotiate our mentalities and the world; off-balance, heavy at the mouth, we are pulled forward.

I am urged out rummaging into the sunshine, and the depths increase of blue above. A paper hat on a cone of water. . . . But, already, words. . . . She is lying on her stomach with one eye closed, driving a toy truck along the road she has cleared with her fingers.[9]

Language itself is never in a state of rest. Its syntax can be as complex as thought. And the experience of using it, which includes the experience of understanding it, either as speech or as writing, is inevitably active—both intellectually and emotionally. The progress of a line or sentence, or a series of lines or sentences, has spatial properties as well as temporal properties. The meaning of a word in its place derives both from the word's lateral reach, its contacts with its neighbors in a statement, and from its reach through and out of the text into the outer world, the matrix of its contemporary and historical reference. The very idea of reference is spatial: over here is word, over there is thing, at which the word is shooting amiable love-arrows. Getting from the beginning to the end of a statement is simple movement; following the connotative byways (on what Umberto Eco calls "inferential walks") is complex or compound movement.

8. Francis Ponge, "The Object Is Poetics," in *The Power of Language,* tr. Serge Gavronsky (Berkeley: University of California Press, 1979), 47.
9. Lyn Hejinian, *My Life* (Los Angeles: Sun & Moon Press, 1987), 14–15.

To identify these frames the reader has to "walk," so to speak, outside the text, in order to gather intertextual support (a quest for analogous "topoi," themes or motives). I call these interpretative moves inferential walks: they are not mere whimsical initiatives on the part of the reader, but are elicited by discursive structures and foreseen by the whole textual strategy as indispensable components of the construction.[1]

Language is productive of activity in another sense, with which anyone is familiar who experiences words as attractive, magnetic to meaning. This is one of the first things one notices, for example, in works constructed from arbitrary vocabularies generated by random or chance operations (e.g., some works by Jackson Mac Low) or from a vocabulary limited according to some other criteria unrelated to meaning (for example, Alan Davies's *a an av es,* a long poem excluding any words containing letters with ascenders or descenders, what the French call "the prisoner's convention," either because the bars are removed or because it saves paper). It is impossible to discover any string or bundle of words that is entirely free of possible narrative or psychological content. Moreover, though the "story" and "tone" of such works may be interpreted differently by different readers, nonetheless the readings differ within definite limits. While word strings are permissive, they do not license a free-for-all.

Writing develops subjects that mean the words we have for them.

Even words in storage, in the dictionary, seem frenetic with activity, as each individual entry attracts to itself other words as definition, example, and amplification. Thus, to open the dictionary at random, *mastoid* attracts *nipplelike, temporal, bone, ear,* and *behind.* Turning to *temporal* we find that the definition includes *time, space, life, world, transitory,* and *near the temples,* but, significantly, not *mastoid.* There is no entry for *nipplelike,* but the definition for *nipple* brings over *protuberance, breast, udder, the female, milk, discharge, mouthpiece,* and *nursing bottle,* but again not *mastoid,* nor *temporal,* nor *time, bone, ear, space,* or *word.* It is relevant that the exchanges are incompletely reciprocal.

and how did this happen like an excerpt
    beginning in a square white boat abob on a gray sea . . .
                    tootling of another message by the
        hacking lark . . .
as a child
               to the rescue and its spring . . .
      in a great lock of letters
        like knock look . . .
              worked by utter joy way
            think through with that in minutes
already
           slippage thinks random patterns
           through
           wishes
    I intend greed as I intend pride
      patterns of roll extend over the wish[2]

1. Umberto Eco, Introduction to *The Role of the Reader* (Bloomington: Indiana University Press, 1979), 32. This book was of great help to me as I was considering the ideas expressed in this essay; I was especially interested in Eco's emphasis on generation (creativity on the part of both writer and reader) and the polygendered impulses active in it.
2. Lyn Hejinian, *Writing Is an Aid to Memory* (Los Angeles: Sun & Moon Press, 1996), parts 2 and 12.

The "rage to know" is one expression of the restlessness engendered by language. "As long as man keeps hearing words / He's sure that there's a meaning somewhere," as Mephistopheles points out in Goethe's *Faust*.[3]

It's in the nature of language to encourage and, in part, to justify such Faustian longings.[4] The notion that language is the means and medium for attaining knowledge and, concomitantly, power is, of course, old. The knowledge toward which we seem to be driven by language, or which language seems to promise, is inherently sacred as well as secular, redemptive as well as satisfying. The *nomina sint numina* position (that there is an essential identity between name and thing, that the real nature of a thing is immanent and present in its name, that nouns are numinous) suggests that it is possible to find a language which will meet its object with perfect identity. If this were the case, we could, in speaking or in writing, achieve the "at oneness" with the universe, at least in its particulars, that is the condition of complete and perfect knowing.

But if in the Edenic scenario we acquired knowledge of the animals by naming them, it was not by virtue of any numinous immanence in the name but because Adam was a taxonomist. He distinguished the individual animals, discovered the concept of categories, and then organized the various species according to their different functions and relationships in the system. What the "naming" provides is structure, not individual words.

As Benjamin Lee Whorf has pointed out, "Every language is a vast pattern-system, different from others, in which are culturally ordained the forms and categories by which the personality not only communicates, but also analyses nature, notices or neglects types of relationship and phenomena, channels his reasoning, and builds the house of his consciousness." In this same essay, apparently his last (written in 1941), titled "Language, Mind, Reality," Whorf goes on to express what seem to be stirrings of a religious motivation: "What I have called patterns are basic in a really cosmic sense." There is a "PREMONITION IN LANGUAGE of the unknown, vaster world." The idea

> is too drastic to be penned up in a catch phrase. I would rather leave it un-
> named. It is the view that a noumenal world—a world of hyperspace, of higher
> dimensions—awaits discovery by all the sciences [linguistics being one of them]
> which it will unite and unify, awaits discovery under its first aspect of a realm
> of PATTERNED RELATIONS, inconceivably manifold and yet bearing a recogniz-
> able affinity to the rich and systematic organization of LANGUAGE.[5]

It is as if what I've been calling, from Faust, the "rage to know," which is in some respects a libidinous drive, seeks also a redemptive value from language. Both are appropriate to the Faustian legend.

Coming in part out of Freudian psychoanalytic theory, especially in France, is a body of feminist thought that is even more explicit in its identification of language with power and knowledge—a power and knowledge that is political, psychological, and aesthetic—and that is a site specifically of desire. The project for

3. Johann Wolfgang von Goethe, *Goethe's Faust, Part One*, tr. Randall Jarrell (New York: Farrar, Straus & Giroux, 1976), 137.
4. This idea is reiterated in *My Life*, one of the several forms of repetition in that work. (See *My Life*, 46).
5. Benjamin Lee Whorf, *Language, Thought, and Reality* (Cambridge, Mass.: MIT Press, 1956), 252, 248, 247–248.

these French feminist writers has been to direct their attention to "language and the unconscious, not as separate entities, but language as a passageway, and the only one, to the unconscious, to that which has been repressed and which would, if allowed to rise, disrupt the established symbolic order, what Jacques Lacan has dubbed the Law of the Father."[6]

If the established symbolic order is the "Law of the Father," and it is discovered to be not only repressive but false, distorted by the *illogicality* of bias, then the new symbolic order is to be a "woman's language," corresponding to a woman's desire.

Luce Irigaray writes:

> But woman has sex organs just about everywhere. She experiences pleasure almost everywhere. Even without speaking of the hysterization of her entire body, one can say that the geography of her pleasure is much more diversified, more multiple in its differences, more complex, more subtle, than is imagined. . . . "She" is indefinitely other in herself. That is undoubtedly the reason she is called temperamental, incomprehensible, perturbed, capricious—not to mention her language in which "she" goes off in all directions.[7]

"A feminine textual body is recognized by the fact that it is always endless, without ending," says Hélène Cixous: "There's no closure, it doesn't stop."[8]

The narrow definition of desire, the identification of desire solely with sexuality, and the literalness of the genital model for a woman's language that some of these writers insist on may be problematic. The desire that is stirred by language is located most interestingly within language itself—as a desire to say, a desire to create the subject by saying, and as a pervasive doubt very like jealousy that springs from the impossibility of satisfying these yearnings. This desire resembles Wordsworth's "underthirst / Of vigor seldom utterly allayed."[9] And it is explicit in Carla Harryman's "Realism":

> When I'm eating this I want food. . . . The I expands. The individual is caught in a devouring machine, but she shines like the lone star on the horizon when we enter her thoughts, when she expounds on the immensity of her condition, the subject of the problem which interests nature.[1]

If language induces a yearning for comprehension, for perfect and complete expression, it also guards against it. Thus Faust complains:

> It is written: "In the beginning was the Word!"
> Already I have to stop! Who'll help me on?
> It is impossible to put such trust in the Word![2]

6. Elaine Marks, in *Signs* 3, no. 4 (Summer 1978), 835.
7. Luce Irigaray, "This sex which is not one," 103.
8. Hélène Cixous, "Castration or Decapitation?" in *Signs* 7, no. 1 (Autumn 1981), 53.
9. William Wordsworth, "The Prelude" (1850 version), Book VI, lines 558–559, in *William Wordsworth: The Prelude 1799, 1805, 1850*, ed. Jonathan Wordsworth, M. H. Abrams, and Stephen Gill (New York: W. W. Norton & Company, 1979), 215.
1. Carla Harryman, "Realism," in *Animal Instincts* (Berkeley: This Press, 1989), 106.
2. Goethe, *Goethe's Faust, Part One*, 61.

This is a recurrent element in the argument of the lyric: "Alack, what poverty my Muse brings forth . . ."; "Those lines that I before have writ do lie . . ."; "For we / Have eyes to wonder but lack tongues to praise. . . ."[3]

In the gap between what one wants to say (or what one perceives there is to say) and what one can say (what is sayable), words provide for a collaboration and a desertion. We delight in our sensuous involvement with the materials of language, we long to join words to the world—to close the gap between ourselves and things—and we suffer from doubt and anxiety because of our inability to do so.

Yet the incapacity of language to match the world permits us to distinguish our ideas and ourselves from the world and things in it from each other. The undifferentiated is one mass, the differentiated is multiple. The (unimaginable) complete text, the text that contains everything, would in fact be a closed text. It would be insufferable.

A central activity of poetic language is formal. In being formal, in making form distinct, it opens—makes variousness and multiplicity and possibility articulate and clear. While failing in the attempt to match the world, we discover structure, distinction, the integrity and separateness of things. As Bob Perelman writes:

> At the sound of my voice
> I spoke and, egged on
> By the discrepancy, wrote
> The rest out as poetry.[4]

1983

---

3. Lines excised from Shakespeare's Sonnets, nos. 102, 115, and 106.
4. Bob Perelman, "My One Voice," in *Primer* (Berkeley: This Press, 1981), 11.

◄ LOUISE GLÜCK ►
(B. 1943)

Born in New York City, Louise Elisabeth Glück (pronounced "Glick") grew up on Long Island. Her father was a successful businessman who had unfulfilled dreams of being a writer. In "Education of the Poet," Glück observes, "Both my parents admired intellectual accomplishment; my mother, in particular, revered creative gifts." As to her own literary development, Glück remarks, "I read early, and wanted, from a very early age, to speak in return. When, as a child, I read Shakespeare's songs, or later, Blake and Yeats and Keats and Eliot, I did not feel exiled, marginal. I felt, rather, that this was the tradition of my language: *my* tradition, as English was my language. My inheritance. My wealth." In the same autobiographical essay, Glück notes the impact of psychoanalysis on her thinking.

After beginning her undergraduate education at Sarah Lawrence College, Glück transferred to Columbia University. There she eventually studied with Stanley Kunitz, to whom she would dedicate her first collection of poems, *Firstborn* (1968). She has since taught at Goddard College, the University of California at Los Angeles, Harvard, Brandeis, and since 1984 at Williams College in Massachusetts. Among the many awards her work has received are the National Book Critics Circle Award and the Pulitzer Prize. Her early collections include *The House on the Marshland* (1975); *Descending Figure* (1980), which she called her favorite among the early books; *The Triumph of Achilles* (1985); and *Ararat* (1990).

Glück's early work flirts with surrealism and occasionally employs grotesque imagery but already displays the austere and deliberate manner for which her poetry is now known. She slowly but unmistakably perfected a deeply expressive lyric style in which emotion seems simultaneously repressed and evoked. Though autobiography—in subjects like divorce and family life—enters her poems, Glück is characteristically concerned with universalizing from personal experience. She often pursues a problem she has set in terms of grammar or subject matter, or images derived from mythological archetypes. She has also quite frequently adopted personae, from the voice of a figure in a painting to that of a wildflower. Critics have noted the plainness of her diction while praising her subtle uses of sound echoes and off-rhymes. They have called her "direct" in her intimacy, yet have also noted a mysterious and philosophical quality in her work, a kind of distance, probing and provocative.

In Glück's later books like *The Wild Iris* (1992), *Meadowlands* (1996), *Vita Nova* (1999), and *The Seven Ages* (2001), a kind of metaphysical yearning emerges. Her introduction to *The Best American Poetry 1993* begins: "The world is complete without us. Intolerable fact. To which the poet responds by rebelling, wanting to prove otherwise." A collection of Glück's essays, *Proofs and Theories,* appeared in 1994. "I wrote these essays as I would poems," she states in the volume's "Author's Note." Like her poetry, her critical prose is concise, compressed, and evocative and her approach skeptical and fierce.

<hr />

DISRUPTION, HESITATION, SILENCE

In my generation, most of the poets I admire are interested in length: they want to write long lines, long stanzas, long poems, poems which cover an extended sequence of events. To all this I feel an instant objection, whose sources I'm not confident I know. Some of the sources may lie in character, in my tendency to reject all ideas I didn't think of first, which habit creates a highly charged adversarial relationship with the new. What is positive in this process is that it creates an obligation to articulate an argument.

What I share with my friends is ambition; what I dispute is its definition. I do not think that more information always makes a richer poem. I am attracted to ellipsis, to the unsaid, to suggestion, to eloquent, deliberate silence. The unsaid, for me, exerts great power: often I wish an entire poem could be made in this vocabulary. It is analogous to the unseen; for example, to the power of ruins, to works of art either damaged or incomplete. Such works inevitably allude to larger contexts; they haunt because they are not whole, though wholeness is implied: another time, a world in which they were whole, or were to have been whole, is implied. There is no moment in which their first home is felt to be the museum. A few years ago, I saw a show of Holbein drawings; most astonishing were those still in progress. Parts were entirely finished. And parts were sketched, a fluent line indicating arm or hand or hair, but the forms were not filled in. Holbein had made notes to himself: this sleeve blue, hair, auburn. The terms were other—not the color in the world, but the color in paint or chalk. What these unfinished drawings generated was a vivid sense of Holbein at work, at the sitting; to see them was to have a sense of being back in time, back in the middle of something. Certain works of art become artifacts. By works of art, I mean works in any medium. And certain works of art do not. It seems to me that what is wanted, in art, is to harness the power of the unfinished. All earthly experience is partial. Not simply because it is subjective, but because that which we do not know, of the universe, of mortality, is so much more vast than that which we do know. What is unfinished or has been destroyed participates in these mysteries. The problem is to make a whole that does not forfeit this power.

From *Proofs and Theories: Essays on Poetry* (New York: Ecco Press, 1994) 74–85.

The argument for completion, for thoroughness, for exhaustive detail, is that it makes an art more potent because more exact—a closer recreation of the real. But the cult of exhaustive detail, of data, needs scrutiny. News stories are detailed. But they don't seem, at least to me, at all real. Their thoroughness is a reprimand to imagination; and yet they don't say this is what it was to be here.

I belong, so it appears, to a generation suspicious of the lyric, of brevity, of the deception of stopped time. And impatient with beauty, which is felt to be an inducement to stupor. Certainly there is stupor everywhere; it is an obvious byproduct of anxiety. But narrative poetry, or poetry packed with information, is not the single escape from the perceived constrictions of the lyric. A number of quite different writers practice in various ways another method.

No one seems particularly to want to define the lyric. Donald Hall provides a definition which he immediately repudiates as being too general to be useful. Louis Simpson says the lyric poem is any poem expressing personal emotion rather than describing events. The opposite, in other words, of the news story. The expression of personal emotions depends, obviously, on the existence of a voice, a source of emotion. The lyric is, traditionally, intense, traditionally, also, "a moment's thought." Though it is foolish to attempt a close reading of a poem in a language one doesn't know, I want, briefly, to talk about Rilke's "Archaic Torso of Apollo" in that it is a magnificent example of lyric poetry and, as well, structurally remarkable: its last line anticipates the technique I mean to talk about.

Anticipates only because to shift terms at the end explodes a boundary but does not create, within the poem, that space which is potentially an alternative to information.

"We cannot know," Rilke says of the torso of Apollo. The unknowable is the poem's first referent, the context. And it is interesting to try to imagine the poem's arising out of another, a whole, statue. Something is lost; the poem turns a little corny, a little trite. For something whole, the act of giving directions is simple bossiness, nor is any virtuosity involved in the act of hearing such directions. What wholeness gives up is the dynamic: the mind need not rush in to fill a void. And Rilke loved his voids. In the broken thing, moreover, human agency is oddly implied: breakage, whatever its cause, is the dark complement to the act of making; the one implies the other. The thing that is broken has particular authority over the act of change.

Rilke's poem begins with the unknowable, a void located in the past. And ends with the unknown: a new, a different, life; a void projected into the future. But the impression the poem gives is no more symmetrical than is the statue: the force of the imperative is abrupt, like breakage; the swerving assaults us, implicates, challenges.

Rilke's greatness, for me, is in the making of poems which marry lyric intensity to irregularity of form. Neither Berryman nor Oppen nor Eliot seems to me much like Rilke. Yet each is, in some way, a master of not saying.

Which seems a very odd way to think of Berryman, with his high excitability and multiple personalities. A colleague of mine at Williams, Anita Sokolsky, used the word *distractedness* to describe a primary attribute of *The Dream Songs*. I like the way the word calls up a sense of bewilderedness, of childishness: in his behaviors, if not in the breadth of his suffering, Henry Pussycat is very much the precocious child, the child with the short attention span, the child keenly aware of audience.

Implicit in the idea of the lyric is the single voice: Berryman's primary disruption of the lyric is the fracturing of voice. From poem to poem, the paradigm varies: minstrel show, schizophrenia, psychoanalysis. But always one persona taking over for another, taking the stage: these are noisy poems—shattered, voluble, fragmented, desperate, dramatic, futile. The intense purpose characteristic of the lyric becomes, in Berryman, intense cross-purposes. In other words, paralysis.

The first Dream Song is as good an example as any. The poem begins with two lines of report: our speaker is someone who knows Henry from the outside ("huffy" being descriptive of behavior) and from the inside ("unappeasable"). Reasonable, then, to presume that the central figure—with a curious detachment that contains the internalized perpetual reproach of a parent—here describes himself. And reasonable, too, to anticipate consistency, if not of tone, certainly of perspective. But reason is not the long suit of dreams. If Henry, in lines one and two, is the speaker, the guiding or prevailing intelligence, then who is the "I" of line three? Friendly to the cause, adult, capable of entertaining several ideas at once ("his point" suggests the many other angles already considered). A reader encountering the first person tends to identify that pronoun with a poem's central intelligence. But the problem in *The Dream Songs,* the drama of the poems, is the absence of a firm self. The proliferating selves dramatize, they do not disguise, this absence. It is interesting, on this point, to think of Hopkins, who is in so many ways Berryman's antecedent. The sound of Berryman is like the sound of Hopkins; both poets are animated by self-disgust. But self, in Hopkins, is a miserable fixity, a pole remote from God. God is other, distant, visible in flashes, abidingly present in the world. In Berryman, there is no such sense of abiding presence. What in Hopkins are two separated halves, agonized self and remote God, are in Berryman conflated. This would seem an advantage, but is not. Hopkins was permitted reverence. The very remoteness of God, the felt division between God and self, which could become a metaphor for the division between pure good and pure evil, allowed for, perpetuated belief in, good. This separation encouraged those beliefs which support life: belief in virtue, belief in the world's essential beauty and order, belief in God's superior and embracing wisdom. There is no such reliable other in Berryman. There is no you because there is no I; no fundamental self. The stable, if anguished, relation between man and God in Hopkins has no parallel in Berryman, at least in *The Dream Songs.*

Meanwhile, in the poem, an "I" has made its debut. The ruminative tone of the third line suggests that its commentary may go on. In fact, it doesn't: the "I" is immediately absorbed into the intimate, childish rancors of lines four and five. "Do it" means *do to:* it is all things done to Henry against Henry's unknown, unknowable best interests. The very idea, which is actually Henry's, that others have such power is enough to send Henry into violent hiding. The power is vague because its agents are hazy. What exists is a sense of victimization, of jeopardy, but it is never particularly explicit. In fact, so well does Henry hide himself that, ultimately, he can't find where he is either. And the self that's hidden wakes occasionally, as in number 29, trying to account for its condition: "But never did Henry, as he thought he did, / end anyone and hack her body up / and hide the pieces, where they may be found." He looks for a crime to account for feelings: he behaves like a criminal, like someone in flight. Guilt explains flight. But so, too, does an ancient wish to protect a very fragile self.

The endless compensatory coming out and talking of *The Dream Songs* cannot change the character so formed. The last line of the first stanza is the line of fate: he should have. He didn't. Spoken by the mother, her head shaking sadly.

In terms of method, the next stanzas go on in much the same way. But there's a surprising turn in stanza three, surprising and heartbreaking. Who says "Once in a sycamore I was glad / all at the top, and I sang"? This is an "I" different from the "I" of stanza one, who sees, or the "I" of stanza two, who doesn't see. This is engagement, not commentary. This is a whole being, in behavior spontaneous, Henry-like, but in tone, calm. *The Dream Songs* search for such wholeness. But Berryman's genius, unlike Rilke's, is not expressed as longing.

The Dream Songs are quilts, collages. One way to read them is to insist on coherence, to elaborate the associative process, to pay too little attention to the gaps, the juxtapositions. We can supply what's missing, but the electricity of the poetry derives from Berryman's refusal to narrate these transformations.

Berryman at his worst, raves. No poet seems farther from that act than George Oppen. And for all the brilliant sleight of hand, for all the wit and bravura, for all the savage intelligence, the undernote of Berryman is pathos ranging to grief. The background is the abyss; the poems venture as close to the edge as possible. To some extent, this was inescapable, to some extent cultivated. In his magnificent essay on Anne Frank, Berryman writes, "We have been tracing a psychological and moral development to which, if I am right, no close parallel can be found. It took place under very special circumstances, which—let us now conclude, as she concluded—though superficially unfavorable, [were] in fact highly favorable to it; she was forced to mature, in order to survive; the hardest challenge, let's say, that a person can face without defeat is the best for him." This is noble justification as well as stunning analysis, brilliant and lucid like all the essays. Berryman, in any case, admired extreme states; control interested him very little.

It is valuable, though nearly impossible, to try to read Oppen and Berryman side by side. Nothing in Oppen feels involuntary. And yet nothing feels rigid. One impression genius fosters is that there is, beside it, no comparable mastery: no other way to sound, to think, to be. I admire both Berryman and Oppen to this degree; I regret not knowing what these two thought of each other. Berryman's meticulous need to offend everyone, to be certain that in no mind was he even briefly associated with anything even slightly conservative, mannerly, acceptable, his poignant but extremely wily egotism sometimes seems childish and limited beside Oppen. And sometimes, next to Berryman's feverish wildness, Oppen seems too lofty, too hermetic, too secure. Temperamentally, they seem to cancel one another out. And yet, like Berryman, Oppen is a master of juxtaposition. Interruption seems the wrong term; there is nothing of distractedness or disorientation in this work. Berryman's *Dream Songs* project shatteredness; Oppen's poetry, to my mind, demonstrates its opposite: a profound integrity, a self so well established, so whole, as to be invisible.

Surprisingly, Oppen's clean, austere, dynamic poetry has very few active verbs. No one uses the verb of being better—in these poems, it gives observation the aura and resonance of truth. What moves these poems is silence; in structural terms, Oppen's pauses correspond to Berryman's distractions. "Street" begins with a sighed demonstrative. There is no surprise, no histrionic excitement:

STREET

Ah these are the poor,
These are the poor—

Bergen street.

Humiliation,
Hardship . . .

Nor are they very good to each other;
It is not that. I want

An end of poverty
As much as anyone

For the sake of intelligence,
'The conquest of existence'—

It has been said, and is true

And this is real pain,
Moreover. It is terrible to see the children,

The righteous little girls;
So good, they expect to be so good. . . .

One is obliged, here, to acquiesce to what is factually present: morality, for Oppen, begins in clarity, and it is the latter which can be cultivated. Repetition prolongs the moment and threatens, briefly, to create its own, and false, order. But the dash propels the poem. A period, grammatically, would have done. But a period doesn't force motion, and part of Oppen's genius is a reluctance to conclude. His poems need this reluctance, need his suspicion of closure, in that their manner of expression is absolute.

Only one line in this poem has the force of the double stop: no enjambment, no propulsive punctuation: / "Bergen street." A recall to the specific which, in its terseness, takes on the finality of diagnosis. So final does the line seem as to make it difficult, for me, in any case, to see how the poem was even resumed. The silence that measures intervals is, in Oppen, the time it takes for information to be absorbed: there is almost never an analogous process in Berryman, as there is nothing in Oppen which resembles Berryman's aggressive parrying. Bergen street. Silence. Then the available generalizations. But these are so arranged as to construct a parallel: they follow in a vertical line after the named place so that they become, in a sense, synonyms for Bergen Street. And after the generalizations, the ruminative ellipsis. The ensuing pause contains a suppressed assertion: the poem actively resumes with a denial. This is a characteristic move in Oppen, the idea implied in being dismissed. And now, in the poem, personal response is volunteered, but the feelings of the "I" are the feelings of anyone: personal distinction is not claimed. Nor is conventional feeling held in bland contempt: reasonable, the poem suggests, to despise poverty.

One of the interesting things about this poem is the fact that, to this point, very little of the language is vivid. The poem exists in timing, in the way ideas are held in suspension, so that, by the end, what is charged becomes indisputable in context of such plainness. This is a poetry of mind, of mind processing information—not a mind incapable of response but a mind wary of premature response; a mind, that is, not hungering after sensation. I find, in Oppen, a sanity so profound as to be mysterious: this is a sound that has, for the most part, disappeared from poetry, possibly from thought.

The poem moves as a unit from the semi-colon in line six to the dash in line eleven; typical of the absorbing mind is "it has been said, and is true." But the true is not a resting place, not an epiphany. Or: this truth is not. It is incidental: the maxim is passive, the street relentless. Oppen has, in the most literal sense, an open mind, a mind resistant to closure. What is so rare in him is not that, but the simultaneous austerity and distaste for blather.

The poem refuses to project its informing intelligence. The figures beheld remain themselves, and apart. This is not insufficiency of feeling, but absence of vanity. Pain belongs, here, properly to the children, not the speaker. It may be terrible to see the children, but it is far more terrible to be the children. The speaker's detachment is his, and our, particular burden. Like someone watching *Agamemnon,* he knows what will happen. Oppen brings to what he sees integrity of two kinds: personal wholeness and probity of intent. His poem is not a campaign; he does not propose himself as the missing advocate or champion of the little girls. Whatever he does, in life, on their behalf, is not alluded to in the poem. The poem honors a boundary: the boundary of Bergen Street, the difference between the circumstances of its natives and the circumstances of the visitor. The boundary, in absolute terms, between one being and another. Bad enough for those little girls: at least let the poem not appropriate their experience.

The resources of the poem are given over to characterization of the observed: in a work so nearly devoid of modifiers, "righteous" is galvanizing. What follows is, in its repetition, parallel to the poem's first lines: a translation, a refinement, a correction. And the poem itself becomes an act of wrenching sympathy.

Oppen regularly defines things by saying what they are not. This method of creation through eradication is, for me, congenial. And I find it helpful, in trying to analyze his poetry, to say what it isn't, or what it does not do. Conspicuously, it does not impose. As the speaker's relation to the children is devoid of proprietary impulses, so that the poem seems, ultimately, to dignify the little girls, to pay homage, similarly, in relation to the reader, the poem is neither didactic nor overbearing. It is rare, almost, in my experience, peculiar to Oppen, to find such tact in combination with such intensity.

In most writing, talk is energy and stillness its opposite. But Oppen's pauses are dense with argument: they actively further the poem. When poems are difficult, it is often because their silences are complicated, hard to follow. For me, the answer to such moments is not more language.

What I am advocating is, of course, the opposite of Keats's dream of filling rifts with ore. The dream of abundance does not need another defense. The danger of that aesthetic is its tendency to produce, in lesser hands, work that is all detail and no shape. Meanwhile, economy is not admired. Economy depends on systematic withholding of the gratuitous; dispute is bound to arise over definitions of "gratuitous," but the very action of withholding is currently suspect. It is associated with rigidity, miserliness, insufficiencies; with faculties either atrophied or checked. It is a habit not admired in personal interaction, in which realm it is associated with ideas of manipulation, slyness, coldness; it is considered uniformly dangerous in governments, and so on.

The art of George Oppen is bold, severe, mysterious, intense, serene and fiercely economical. The advantage of the last, in my view, is that it promotes depth. Each turn is distilled, each movement essential. What would take the more expansive poet ten lines, Oppen does in two. That fact alone forces him to go on. Whereas the expansive poet is prone to premature linguistic satiation, by which I mean that the sense of something's having been made comes into existence too readily. The ratio of words to meaning favors words. The poem exists in its adornments. But no poem of Oppen's can be further reduced than it has already been by its maker. This means that the time it takes, as thought, is the time it requires, not the time the writer requires.

The ambitions of economy are deeply bound to the idea of form. And form, in this connection, usually appears as a chaste thing. Eliot writes:

Words, after speech, reach
Into the silence. Only by the form, the pattern
Can words or music reach
The stillness, as a Chinese jar still
Moves perpetually in its stillness.

This is late Eliot, but the dominant themes are present from the very first.

When, in "The Love Song of J. Alfred Prufrock," Prufrock asks, "Is it perfume from a dress / That makes me so digress?" the question is, itself, a kind of ruse. "Digress" suggests that some purposeful journey has been interrupted. "To stray," says the dictionary, "from the main subject." The word introduces an idea that has not, it seems, been actually present to the poem: the idea of a main subject.

"The Love Song of J. Alfred Prufrock" is a poem of pathological delay. The action of the poem is inaction, stalling. "Let us go, then, you and I, / When the evening is spread out against the sky." But Prufrock puts off starting: the second line suggests that the time proper to going, though imminent, hasn't arrived. The verbs of the poem describe an arc; they approximate an action. Let us go; there will be; I have known; how should I; would it have been—and then, dramatically, the present tense: I grow old, followed by the alternating future and past perfect. But nothing, in fact, occurs; nothing is even begun. Prufrock fears action; the poem specifically dramatizes, in its formidable hesitations, a fear of beginnings.

The poem, it is true, puts forth explanations: the casual, contemptuous dismissal of the lady, for example. But these seem screens, constructed to account for a preexisting terror. The future is impossible, the past lost. And the present a vacuum: non-action. Simply, I grow old. The refusal to take action, the permanent hesitation of standing still, has not, unfortunately, the desired effect: time does not stop.

Time is Prufrock's enemy, and Eliot's recurring subject. Time is that which mocks the idea of eternity, the stillness of the Chinese jar, a state of positive, dynamic non-change. In time, nothing achieves this stillness; nothing is incapable of being reversed. To another nature, this very fact would be an inducement to action, but long-meditated action wants to leave a mark. Indeed, it hardly matters, as Prufrock irately notes, to ask, of the overwhelming question: what is it? In a universe in which everything is in flux, nothing is final, and, to Prufrock, the authority of "overwhelming" depends on finality. Why suffer for anything less?

To begin, here, is to presume. The words recur and finally merge as the poem's agony intensifies. "Presume" is Prufrock's motif, with its suggestion of social error, of brute, clumsy will imposing itself. To venture, to dare, to take liberties. And, as well, to take on faith. To begin, you must believe in a future; motion enacts that belief. Prufrock stands to one side, out of the way of savage time, but changed anyway. The poem is all wringing of hands, its rhymes regularly sealing off options. Prufrock, in being motionless, does his best imitation of being inert: ". . . that which is only living / Can only die."

Eliot has written the masterpiece of avoidance. At the poem's center is the unsaid, the overwhelming question, the moment forced to its crisis. But Prufrock is not Lazarus; he does not tell all.

This is a dramatic poem. And the pathos of Prufrock is a subject separate from the greatness of this achievement. The poem is satire not in that Prufrock is mistaken, but in that he is inadequate to the discipline of contemplation: we can hear, almost, the very young poet cautioning himself. As a dramatic poem, the whole would dissolve were the overwhelming question elaborated. "It is impossible to say just what I mean!" This bursts from Prufrock, at a moment of frustration. But the underlying tension recurs throughout the oeuvre.

A danger of the expansive poem is that this tension is lost. Not all the poets I've talked about write specifically of this struggle. Certainly, no such strain shows in Oppen. And yet in each case some element of conquest remains, a sense of the importance of exact language, a sense of being in the presence of the crucial. There are poets I love whose work suggests infinite ease, but even in such poets, the best poems often turn on or evolve out of a misperception, something too easily seen or too readily said. Not every temperament inclines to elaboration. What I've said has been meant not to eliminate a method but to speak for the virtues of a style which inclines to the suggested over the amplified.

1994

⊷◄ MARY KINZIE ►⊷

(B. 1944)

Born in Montgomery, Alabama, Mary Kinzie earned her B.A. from North-western University in 1967 and then pursued graduate work at the Free University of Berlin and Johns Hopkins University on Fulbright and Woodrow Wilson fellowships. From Johns Hopkins University, she earned her M.A. in 1970 and her Ph.D. in 1980. Since 1975, she has taught at Northwestern, where she directs the English Department's undergraduate creative writing major. Kinzie has published five books of poetry: *The Threshold of the Year* (1982), *Summers of Vietnam and Other Poems* (1990), *Masked Women* (1990), *Autumn Eros and Other Poems* (1991), and *Ghost Ship* (1996). She developed many of her critical essays into a book-length study, *The Cure of Poetry in an Age of Prose: Moral Essays on the Poet's Calling* (1993), and collected other reviews in *The Judge Is Fury: Dislocation and Form in Poetry* (1994). Her third book of criticism, *A Poet's Guide to Poetry* (1999), is more than just a handbook of versification and poetics. In addition to introducing basic concepts, it develops an extended and challenging meditation on the arts of writing and reading poetry.

For Kinzie, the arts of poetry and literary criticism coalesce: she believes that good readers of poetry must learn to think like writers, not only through developing a knowledge of tradition and a sensitivity to the possibilities of language, but through experiencing the process of uncertainty and discovery that the poet undergoes. In *A Poet's Guide to Poetry*, she argues, "Reading, like writing, requires us to uncover a poem that is in the process of uncovering itself."

Although she often grounds her poetry in traditional forms, her deployment of form is never predictable but tends to pull against the norms of meter and rhyme scheme and unfold through complex syntax and unexpected shifts in diction. Whether writing autobiographical poetry, describing a landscape, or reframing a mythic tale, Kinzie explores the inner reaches of the psyche where knowledge—especially self-knowledge—arises through ventures into uncertain terrain. Kinzie's exacting attention to detail and skill at conveying complex states of feeling give her poems a sense of severity and strangeness even when she focuses on ordinary experiences. In *The Cure of Poetry in an Age of Prose*, Kinzie's summation of Louise Bogan's achievement reveals much about her own artistic aims. Bogan's poem, "Cassandra," Kinzie maintains, "moves the reader to extremes, as perhaps all great lyrical art must, as if to persuade us that poetry's only cure—the one concocted by its prophetic sources—is radical, a permanent alienation from ordinary life and conventional intonations."

In her criticism, Kinzie is known for thorough attention to detail and her willingness not only to make judgments about contemporary poetry, but to give an uncompromising accounting of a poet's strengths and weaknesses. For many years she reviewed books of contemporary poetry regularly for the *American Poetry Review*. During the course of reading hundreds of new poetry books, as well as through her work as a teacher, she reached the conclusions that she articulates in the following essay. After "The Rhapsodic Fallacy" was first published in the fall 1984 issue of *Salmagundi,* it stirred up controversy, and many poets and critics, agreeing or disagreeing with Kinzie's ideas, wrote responses that were published in the magazine's subsequent issue. Kinzie expanded the essay, making it the cornerstone of *The Cure of Poetry in an Age of Prose.*

◂•▸━◀▶━•▸

THE RHAPSODIC FALLACY

Contemporary poetry suffers from dryness, prosaism, and imaginative commonplace, but these are hardly its worst features. Rather, the stylistic dullness is disagreeably coarsened and made the more decadent by being a brotherly symptom of, and in fact a technical support for, the assumption (which has only strengthened in the past 150 years) that the aim of poetry is apotheosis, an ecstatic and unmediated self-consumption in the moment of perception and feeling. The flat style is thought of as a kind of private charm that protects the writer against falsehood, insuring his sincerity. But it has tended to take for granted the real content of the inner life, affecting the mannerisms of sincerity without the coherent values which that sincerity might express. The poetic has thus made an odd marriage with the prosaic, and it is this parasitic weakening of the subjective idea by an aimless prosaic experimentalism that we see in much new verse. Subjective experience is expressed as objectively derived, in a diction that is indifferent, reductive, even, on occasion, somewhat dullwitted. To judge from their practice, many poets have assumed that complexity would work against the freshness of perception. Hence, although emotion is the overriding topic, paradoxically it is not immediacy but diffuseness in diction, syntax, and argument that has manifested itself as the overriding style. To see why our culture has so confounded the poetic with the prosaic, let us step back a moment.

Most critics agree that a major begetter of a Rhapsodic Theory of poetry is Edgar Allan Poe (with two essays in particular, the defense of "The Raven" called "The Philosophy of Composition" in 1846, and "The Poetic Principle," published the year after Poe's death, in 1850). In Poe, we find articulated two modern tendencies. First, a desire for intense brevity—a desire that carries with it the belief that

From *Salmagundi* Fall 1984: 63–79. Emendations were made by the author for this volume, 2002. All footnotes are Mary Kinzie's.

intensity can be achieved only in spontaneous, fragmented utterance.[1] The second tendency adumbrated in Poe (less in the critical work than in his own practice) is the contradictory belief that the mental epic is viable. Poe has bequeathed us the long skein of excited prose about the origins and ends of the universe, which he thought of as a poem, called *Eureka* (1848), the very title of which bespeaks Poe's seizure by the drama of his own insights. The text itself lives up to Poe's claim that coherent argument is irrelevant. It proceeds by fiat and elegy to portray the coming dissolution of the cosmos as emanating from the yearning of all things to return to their union in God. Like Swedenborg a century earlier, Poe believed that all matter shared one rationale; in *Eureka* the projection from man to atom is dressed as scientific procedure in the service of the Divine, and the prose, in gorgeous surges and retards, bathes the thinker in the ebbing of his thoughts, the artist in the ecstasy that warrants his art. In fact, the thinker *is* the artist, and conversely, the artist the only philosopher. The aesthetic or poetic artifact thus fades before the experience into which the artist can plunge.

Beginning with Charles Baudelaire in 1852, the writers who took up Poe's theories and poses in the nineteenth century, or those who, like Mill and Arnold, independently corroborated Poe's opinion that the long poem on public themes was a contradiction in terms, were in fact participating in a process that not only involved weeding out the stunted and unworthy genres like civic poems and didactic verses.[2] They were also continuing the major felling of giant oak and elm from the forests of our literature. "One after another," as A. D. Hope says,[3] "the great forms disappear; the remaining forms proliferate and hypertrophy and display increasing eccentricity and lack of centre." The following poem expresses something of the current attitude:

I like it when
Achilles
Gets killed
And even his buddy Patroclus—
And that hothead Hector—
And the whole Greek and Trojan
Jeunesse dorée
Is more or less
Expertly slaughtered
So there's finally

1. According to Edgar Wind, it was A. C. Bradley in his *Oxford Lectures on Poetry* (1909) who was the first to link Poe's denigration of the long poem to the logic of fragmentation also at work in many major Romantic poems. Wind further traces the cult of the fragment through the French and German Symbolists. Edgar Wind, *Art and Anarchy* (New York: Alfred A. Knopf, 1964), pp. 35–51 and 150.
2. W. H. Auden would ask us to excuse the exaggeration in Poe's ideas on brevity by considering the audience to which these ideas were communicated: "Poe's condemnation of the long poem and of the didactic or true poem is essentially a demand that the poets of his time be themselves and admit that epic themes and intellectual or moral ideas did not in fact excite their poetic faculties and that what really interested them were emotions of melancholy, nostalgia, puzzled yearning, and the like that could find their proper expression in neither epic nor epigram but in lyrics of moderate length. Poe was forced to attack all long poems on principle, to be unfair, for example, to *Paradise Lost* or *An Essay on Criticism*, in order to shake the preconceived notions of poets and public that to be important a poet must write long poems and give bardic advice." "Introduction" to Edgar Allan Poe, *Selected Prose, Poetry and 'Eureka'*, ed. W. H. Auden (New York: Holt, Rinehart and Winston, 1950), p. xii.
3. Alec Derwent Hope, "The Discursive Mode: Reflections on the Ecology of Poetry," *The Cave and the Spring: Essays on Poetry* (Chicago: Univ. Chicago Press, 1965), p. 2.

Peace and quiet
(The gods having momentarily
Shut up)
One can hear
A bird sing
And a daughter ask her mother
Whether she can go to the well
And of course she can
By that lovely little path
That winds through
The olive orchard[4]

The poet breaks the proscenium, first to accommodate a Holden Caulfield type of vernacular ("I like it when" something or other happens; "his buddy Patroclus"; "hothead Hector"), then to allow himself to assemble counterproofs of his own cleverness ("Jeunesse dorée"; the fastidious adverb "expertly" for the rugged "slaughtered"; the self-congratulatory deftness of the indirect discourse, "And of course she can"); and finally the proscenium of the major idea of literary tradition is broken to permit the child to enter, and with it, the nameless, the sentimental, the unheroic, and the everyday.

Not only have we now eliminated from the available repertory of literary responses those forms associated with the eighteenth century, formal satire, familiar epistle, georgic, and pastoral, but also those associated with the Middle Ages and Renaissance, allegory, philosophical poem, epic, and verse drama and tragedy, until nothing is left for us now but a kind of low lyrical shrub whose roots are quick-forming, but shallow. This ecological metaphor is beautifully developed by A. D. Hope in the essay from which I quoted a moment ago, where he describes as follows "the sparse and monotonous vegetation of the arid steppe: little poems of reflection, brief comments, interior monologues, sharp critical barks and hisses, songs that never become articulate; earnestness that lacks the enchantment of truth, and frivolity that disgusts by its absence of charm."[5]

Another critic reminds us that in cutting away all but this meagre foliage of the immediate, descriptive-rhapsodic cameo, the nineteenth- and twentieth-century poets were in effect not only erasing their own literary past: they were making themselves over into types of untaught, innocent children again. What the nineteenth-century poets achieved for us, says Geoffrey Tillotson, was a language in which we could address the startlingly individual quality of each unique moment. But while a certain freshness is not to be gainsaid, what was increasingly missing in their practice was any sense of hierarchy, propriety, literary order.[6] So today, form, trope, and diction have been democratized, levelled, subjected to the mechanism of the lowest common denominator—which is to say that rhetoric has been flattened to the standard of idle conversation in an era in which the art of conversation has been scrubbed clean of art and gentleness.[7]

---

4. Charles Simic, "My Weariness of Epic Proportions," *Austerities* (New York: George Braziller, 1982), p. 50.
5. Hope, p. 3.
6. Geoffrey Tillotson, "Eighteenth-Century Poetic Diction," *Essays and Studies,* xxv (1939), 62.
7. The eighteenth-century view is thus closed to us, since verse was then seen as the heightening of educated conversation. See Donald Davie, *Purity of Diction in English Verse* [1952] (London: Routledge & Kegan Paul, 1967), pp. 1–28.

Free verse has been the great equalizer, the great democratizer of poetic speech, liberating it to utter the small impression in homely language, but at the same time creating its own built-in obstacle to the registering of leisurely and complex idea, and that obstacle is the ad hoc proscription on rhythm—the requirement that prosody, and the arguments that the prosody might bear, need to be recreated spontaneously and energetically at every point.

Furthermore, free verse marks the last stop before verse proceeds into the flatlands of prose. But prose is not practiced today with anything like the sophistication of Bacon, Browne, and Johnson. The current generations of writers in America have less command over, because less acquaintance with, the reasoning, the rhetoric, and the distinctions that were basic equipment for poets in the great ages of prose, the seventeenth and eighteenth centuries. We are even beginning to lose sight of the differences between high style and low style. As a result, to ask as Ezra Pound did that poetry be at least as well written as prose is no longer to insist on the excellence of either kind of writing.

We must also recognize that the reduction of poetic possibility to the brief compass of the free-verse lyric entails the loss (and I mean the literary *and* cultural loss) of the very keystone of logic, namely the art of making the transition—the art of inference and connection, the art of modulation and (hence) surprise. When poems not only set themselves at a uniform pitch, but also contract themselves to recurrent, predictable five- or ten-line climaxes, pretty soon the surprises do not surprise us any more. The new prosaic-lyrical effusion is organized to get us into and out of the poem with extraordinary rapidity and no lasting effects.

Behind this enormous literary levelling that began in the early nineteenth century was also the shift away from the notion that art was supposed to reflect the truth, whether the truth of nature, in which case we are dealing with one or another of the Mimetic Theories of poetry; or the truth of beliefs, in which case the poem was a Pragmatic tool toward engendering belief in the reader. Instead of the idea that poetry was supposed to imitate reality in nature or in the ethical realm, there emerged the idea that poetry was supposed to express idea, feeling, and the inmost being of the poet.[8]

William Wordsworth was the most eloquent and influential of the Expressive Theorists before Poe. It was Wordsworth who called the proper ground of the poem "the spontaneous overflow of powerful feelings," thus elevating the expressive

---

8. Meyer H. Abrams labels the four main schools the Mimetic, Pragmatic, Expressive, and Objective in his article on "Poetry, Theories of" in the *Princeton Encyclopedia of Poetry and Poetics,* ed. Preminger, Warnke, and Hardison (Princeton, N.J.: Princeton Univ. Press, 1965), pp. 640–48. Timothy Steele gives a different reason than Abrams's (and Wordsworth's) for the casting off of mimetic and pragmatic functions: ". . . by the end of the eighteenth century, Kant had given, in the system of his three critiques, philosophical legitimacy to the study of aesthetics. In the three critiques, it will be remembered, Kant divided the faculties of the mind into pure reason, practical reason, and judgment, and he identified the first of these with The True (metaphysics), the second of these with The Good and The Useful (ethics), and the third with The Beautiful (aesthetics and teleology). This division liberated art from the demands of ethical evaluation and moral purpose in much the same manner that the sciences had earlier been liberated from the weight of ecclesiastical imperatives and obsolete theory. And increasingly in the nineteenth century, one finds artists and critics contending that art is, like science, an essentially autonomous enterprise." Steele, "Sciences of Sentiment: Art as Science in the Modern Period," unpublished manuscript, p. 5. Since the writing of that essay in 1983, Timothy Steele subsequently articulated at much greater length Kant's relation to the practice of modern poets in "Free Verse and Aestheticism," chap. 4 of *Missing Measures: Modern Poetry and the Revolt Against Meter* (Fayetteville: University of Arkansas Press, 1990), pp. 171–223.

criterion from the periphery of the poem into its center. Feeling was no longer result, but origin of the work of poetic art. The reader would not be given nature and the world, but the poet's responses to them. The "growth of a poet's mind," as Wordsworth subtitled *The Prelude* (1805), is a series of striking moments during which the poet-speaker stands (usually in the open air) *transfixed* by his insights— insights, we should add, that he owes in part to the landscapes to which he has imaginatively returned. Since "feeling overflows into words," as Meyer Abrams points out, Expressive Theorists from Wordsworth to I. A. Richards tend "to give to the nature and standards of poetic diction, or 'language,' the systematic priority which earlier critics had given to plot, character, and considerations of form." "Truth to nature," Abrams concludes, "has been replaced by sincerity," or "the *air* of truth."[9]

In their exclusive and proprietary relation to language, Expressive Theorists have helped promote the paradox of modern letters, facilitating the double treatment of words as both ordinary *and* mysterious, clear *and* turbid. Words are at once more transparent to experience than ever before, because less prepossessing and ornate, as in the work of the Imagists, and simultaneously far more dense than any of the verbal ornaments devised by Lyly or Pope, because in the work of some influential modern poets words are reverenced as powers in an almost magical way; consider the curious fact that, although unrelated on every other conceivable dimension, Gertrude Stein and Gerard Manley Hopkins resemble one another in their tendency to make words obstreperous, stubborn in the mouth, thing-like in the mind.

Between these two word-habits in our century, the treating of words as transparent, and as dense, the Orphic attitude on the one hand and the Hermetic on the other,[1] or, one could say, between the utilization of words subjectively and objectively, modern art has arranged a peculiar interdependency. Some poets, like Wallace Stevens, may begin in whimsy and wordplay early in their careers, and end it behind the most transparent of linguistic veils. Others, like T. S. Eliot, base their aesthetic upon a continual oscillation, within the given poem, between the two attitudes, the Orphic or transparent taking turns with the Hermetic or self-conscious. Eliot also brings into the modern poem the language of the lie—the dullness of the clerk, the hot shabbiness of office and *Stube,* the broken ends of distracted conversation in several languages. It is in *The Waste Land* (1922) that the little typist assesses her love-making in these starkly unembellished syllables, "Well now that's done: and I'm glad it's over." This transparent realism stands out against the heavily brocaded ground of literary and religious lament.

A third poet, William Carlos Williams, comes to the task of expression in language with a single-minded fervor. He praises Gertrude Stein for "disinfecting" literature: "It's the words, the words we need to get back to, words washed clean."[2] And in Williams's own poems we frequently glimpse the scrubbed haloes shining about the words themselves:

9. Abrams, p. 644, my emphasis.
1. The terms are Gerald Bruns's, *Modern Poetry and the Idea of Language* (New Haven: Yale Univ. Press, 1974), *passim.*
2. "A 1 Pound Stein," *Selected Essays of William Carlos Williams* (New York: New Directions, 1954), pp. 162, 163.

Between Walls

the back wings
of the

hospital where
nothing

will grow lie
cinders

in which shine
the broken

pieces of a green
bottle[3]

The abruptness of this poem has an extraordinarily pleasing finish, the word (*and* the thing) made shiny, plain, whole, and absolute, all the while social significance hums in the background ("the back wings of the hospital where nothing will grow")—where, in other words, our social order's health cases are deposited like empties; where our discards languish. Carlos Williams gives a shifting transparency to the linguistic "thing" that he has made so preternaturally dense. To phrase this paradox another way, Williams objectifies words, and hence baffles his impulse to make them transparent and get rid of them entirely.

After disinfecting literature, Williams busily sets to, adorning words with color and moral opinion again. The green bottle, the red wheelbarrow, the sheet of brown paper, the plums in the icebox, the hind paw in the empty flowerpot, the fleshpale smoke from the yellow chimney, and the red brick monastery beside the polluted stream, are all images that have been stamped twice into the wax of memory—once, visually, owing to the exactness of Williams's diction, and next, formally, owing to the kind and amount of white space that isolates word from word. Williams bequeathed to Denise Levertov and Robert Creeley something of his outstanding genius for breaking the short free-verse line. But in later poets his trick has, I think, been exhausted. What began in brio ends in mechanization. The concreteness of William Carlos Williams degenerates into the stolid, dull, and, above all, repetitious materialism of Marvin Bell.

* * *

Now that we have come down with a thump to the present time, we might look at some examples of current earnestness and frivolity with a clearer sense of origins and of the sheer weight of the "tradition" that impresses itself on poetic practice. For it's not as if the myriad composers of poetry in this country had conspired in their own dullness without the considerable tutelage and support of the readers and critics and teachers of poetry. The Rhapsodic Fallacy is committed by writers only with the consent of those who read literature, which is to say, with the consent of that cultural environment that includes and excludes material from works according to shared expectations about the good poem's contours. Although the Rhapsodic Fallacy holds strong emotion to be the overriding human bond and

3. William Carlos Williams, "Between Walls," *Selected Poems* (New York: New Directions, 1969), p. 84.

index of striving, it also permits the poet to keep this material peripheral, promissory, in reserve. So widespread is the assumption that "melancholy, nostalgia, puzzled yearning, and the like"[4] are central issues, that one need only, it would appear, nod to these emotions as one passes through the poem. Meaning is thereby alluded to in a fashion that suggests both conventionality and enciphering.

Under the general convention of the prosaic-rhapsodic, we can distinguish three main contemporary substyles. In some sense, these three substyles are permeable to each other, and the modulations between them automatic. I take the Objective Style to be the easiest to recognize, if not to master.[5] Next comes the more sophisticated voice-play involved in the Mixed Ironic Style. Finally, I would recognize an adjustment of the Objective Style to reveal phenomena with features of the demonic or surreal (this technique of adjustment we might call the Innocuous Surreal Style).

The Objective Style is determined by the cumulative effect of a string of brief, bland declarative sentences, its verbs often copulas, or intransitives, or at least semantically static. The speaker is static, too: often solitary, in an empty landscape or interior, and the mood produced one of nondescript anxiety. Many of the statements of this typical poem hint at disembodied alternatives: if something *remains* clear, or hard, or bare, it suggests that we had expected it *not* to remain so, hence the fact that it does so must constitute either a small victory or a species of pride in the tenacity of such a reduced and unpropitious state bravely faced by the self. A poem in the Objective Style favors a persona who is all presence, with no past; lacking memory, the speaker confronts the items of the moment as if they were inherently symbolic and assumed personified powers: *Light* can *insist* on what it illumines; *water* can *hint* that it will spill or quench (or fail to do so); *cupboards* can *remain shut,* with a pointed bias against us; *grass* can *teem* or *languish* in a realm of will indifferent to us, but with an inkling of our helplessness. For the Objective Style makes an *object* of the self; the persona becomes a helpless perceiving-machine, but one in which the patterns of personality have little part to play.

Nor is the kind of metaphoricity we find in the Objective Style derived from abstraction or verifiable statement: This is not a poetry of concepts. Although the poems skim too lightly over particulars to reflect actual experience, its themes are not persuasively general, either. Perhaps for either particularity or generality, a real and various consciousness must be at work, whereas the objective poem generalizes eccentric perceptions, ascribing to the world the limited faculties of immediate sensation and daydream. Poems of this type insinuate anxiety, yes; some recognition that the routine of nature is weary or open to bursts of human feeling; and some disappointment that the few objects in the typically reduced landscapes now glower or extinguish—apparently meaningfully, but finally ambiguously. Needless to say, social or mental relations have no place here.

The tools of the Objective Style—juxtaposition, portent, non sequitur, and passivity—can be endlessly manipulated. Here is an example of a quasi-realistic approach:

> Czechoslovakia, the smell.
> Of turned earth, the house

---

4. See page 388, note 2.
5. Indeed, Robert von Hallberg cheerfully asserts that what he calls the "Bare Style" of poets like W. S. Merwin and Mark Strand is actually further proof of the health of the audience for poetry in America; owing to the ease with which it is consumed, von Hallberg implies, this poetry makes itself accessible to greater numbers. *American Poetry and Culture 1945–1980* (Cambridge, Mass.: Harvard University Press, 1985), chap. 1, "Audience, Canon," particularly pp. 10–21.

at field's edge.
I know these things.
There was diphtheria,
a child lost. The small grave
is circled with small white stones.
The osprey inhabits the marshes,
the stork is common, portentous.
The forests go on forever.
There will be men killed there.[6]

The noncommittal passivity of the Objective Style claims for itself a kind of repor-
torial honesty ("I know these things"), and, in the context or reportage or guide-
book-writing, the non sequiturs tease up deeper implications, so that the smell of
the earth and the death of the child and the ospreys in the marshes seem causally
connected to each other and to the greater adult deaths in an Eastern Communist
state. The loose method of inference here, however, seems as dubious as the methods of the unmentioned regime, and the remote omen of the deaths to come gains
no authority from the argument of the poem, which falls into deadened hearsay
and melodrama.

To write a poem in the second of the prosaic-rhapsodic substyles, namely the
Mixed Ironic Style, one selects the electronic chip that programs into the work a
stylistic agitation that at first feels rich, sensitive, conscious, attentive to response.
But in fact the Mixed Ironic Style is conscious only of its own circuitry; immediacy
and confidentiality are themselves disguises. The work of one poet in particular exploits an almost obsessive promiscuity of styles and attitudes:

The first year was like icing.
Then the cake started to show through.
Which was fine, too, except you forget the direction [you're taking.
Suddenly you are interested in some new thing
And can't tell how you got here. Then there is [confusion
Even out of happiness, like a smoke—
The words get heavy, some topple over, you break [others.
And outlines disappear once again.

Heck, it's anybody's story . . .

Thus, John Ashbery in a recent issue of the *New York Review of Books.*[7] Ashbery
avidly works into his poems the jargon of a composite, hypothetical character
who might have gone to high school in the early 1950s:

Heck, it's anybody's story,
A sentimental journey—"gonna take a sentimental [journey,"
And we do, but you wake up under the table of [a dream:
You are that dream, and it is the seventh layer of you.

6. Catherine Rutan, "Woman in the Rain," *Georgia Review* (Spring 1981), p. 124.
7. John Ashbery, "More Pleasant Adventures," *New York Review of Books* (31 March 1983), p. 10.

Reading Ashbery, one could imagine that one is listening to a ceaseless patter almost out of earshot; the message comes back distorted, the predicates blurred, some nouns exchanged, so that only the fossil impressions of the intensives and temporal adverbs and the adversatives still stand out. His art is at once sprightly, and depressing; he has subjected the hopelessly prosaic to his uncanny radioactive energy, while at the same time he undermines feeling by an irony so tight and dispassionate that it, too, is nightmarish. This is T. S. Eliot's "extinction of personality" carried out in the service, not of a great literary heritage, but of a tawdry and dangerously sterile commercial commonplace. Ashbery is the passive bard of a period in which the insipid has turned into the heavily toxic.

This congress between the toxic and the insipid makes one, first, pity many poets who seem to be written by their own mannerisms. Consider the desire shown in so many contemporary poems to leap from objective detail to moral rapture, to express the perceptual in ethical terms, and to make the inadvertent memory universal and proscriptive. Meditative, discursive, and comradely urges were never more in need of help from, which is also to say self-censorship from, older models of literary decorum. Imagine what Samuel Johnson would say about the following case of self-indulgence, with its specious emotive build-up of landscape items as if they *produced* the memory of the father whipping the sister, and with its fatuous pun on "sawing":

> These mornings in green mountains
> When the air burned off blue
>
> . . .
>
> Mornings I can imagine the men
> still go out along the Blue Ridge
> to handcut trees—summer and winter,
>
> hickory and oak, sycamore and maple.
> Nineteen forty-something-or-other.
> I still see my father
> sawing on my sister with a whip.
> Virginia green. Sometimes when you love someone
>
> you think of pain—how to forgive
> what is almost past memory.
> All you can remember is the name,
> some place you have in mind
> where all the blue smoke, all the ghost water collects.[8]

Surely, if at first we pity such posturing, our next immediate impulse is to condemn it, for this is poetry that fibs about its purposes and origins, which are purely self-congratulatory (note the fussy portentousness of the list of trees) and tell us nothing whatever about what it means to forgive. Such lines make us wonder at the writer's understanding of the term, and I, for one, would rather not find myself in a position

---

8. Stanley Plumly, "Virginia Beach," *APR* (March/April 1980), p. 15.

to be forgiven by such a human being, since the gesture has no moral contour except that of an autocratic will. Yet despite the unwholesome insinuations masked by the speaker's blandness, the excerpt above, with its tarnished halo of ethical concern, represents a central type of contemporary ironic memoir.

The other direction taken by the Mixed Ironic Style is a more experimental form of discursiveness.

LANDFALL

The sun rises on an uncertain shore;
loons float off to port.
This morning I'll take my new palaver out
and try it on the pilgrims.
        . . .
Some way can be found, a frame that clips nicely.
        . . .
. . . the chart speaks not only to the wise.
We go, always and ever,
in an expensive circlet homeward.[9]

One can see why Ashbery, who chose this poem for a portfolio of younger poets in a magazine, should have found the experiment appealing: he himself might have been the originator of that jazzy and self-conscious cool in phrases like "my new palaver," "a frame that clips nicely," "plain as paste," and "an expensive circlet" (which I keep reading as *expansive circle*—a mistake the poem encourages because it has used metaphors of shores, maps, and a spatial geography rather than money and jewelry). Although geographical setting is at work here, it is not realistic, and does not ground the speaker temperamentally or verbally. In other words, the factual layer of the poem can be violated at will.

In the final extension of the Rhapsodic Fallacy into innocuous, whimsical Surrealism, the factual surface can be violated as often and as abruptly as there are brief inconsequential declarative sentences to tinker with. Some Surreal prosaists depend on relentless shock, as in this excerpt from a dramatic monologue spoken by the virgin martyr St. Lucy:

I think the erotic
is not sexual, only when you're lucky.
That's where the path forks. It's not the riddle
of desire that interests me; it is the riddle
of good hands, chervil in a windowbox,
the white pages of a book, someone says
I'm tired, someone turning on the light.
        . . .
Emptiness
is strict; that pleases me. I do cry out.
Like everyone else, I thrash, am splayed.
Oh, oh, oh, oh. Eyes full of wonder.
Guernica. Ulysses on the beach.

9. Chuck Rosenberg, "Landfall," *APR* (March/April 1981), p. 33.

> . . .
> I'd rather walk the city in the rain.
> Dog shit, traffic accidents. Whatever God
> there is dismembered in his Chevy.
> A different order of religious awe:
> agony & meat, everything plain afterwards.[1]

The violation of this poem's realistic surface is accomplished by further intrusions of exaggerated and rapid-fire realism, not unlike Eliot's method in *The Waste Land*. But the pronouncements, made in the pouting manner of a child, are distinctively post-modern, as are the curt, fragmented style and the ever-potent claims: *this interests me; that pleases me.*

"It is an old story," says another poet, who has specialized in the Muted Innocuous Surreal, "the way it happens / sometimes in winter, sometimes not." Contemporary Surrealists are uncomfortably tied to the idea of landscape and season; externals are partially internalized but, again, with the selective gauge we noticed in the Objective Style, whereby things and gestures are frozen, arrested prior to the completion of their significance. The poet of the "old story" goes on: "the misfortunes come . . . their wooden wings bruising the air."[2] The world of the Surrealists today would seem to be populated by enormous installations of heroic statuary; huge caryatids of doom and oblivion; winged, acephalous bodies; great three-dimensional volumes of oppressive loss whose medium is the fluidity, blankness, and paralysis of the dormant state:

> All night, though dead, they stir.
> All night toward an unknown invitation
> The children reach, like boats
> Toward open sea, but are moored against it.
> They test their tethers. They rock
> And rock in a bloodless sleep.
>   . . .
> All night we seem to hear their breathings
> and longings, a shattered colonnade around us.[3]

Or, again in sleep, the adults share with these limbo children a hypnagogic flattening of experience, language, and particularity; the woman of the next excerpt sleepwalks heavy, nay, monumental, toward the logical end of the rhapsodic-prosaic style:

> The stars madden, and satellites hum silently
> Where no sound can awaken a sleeper. She dreams
> A language which cannot trouble her, a vocabulary
>
> Without voice. She has forgotten the ugly grammar,
> The deformed sentences. She has forgotten
> The irregularities of memory, the unknown knowns,

---

1. Robert Hass, "Santa Lucia," *Praise* (New York: Ecco Press, 1979), pp. 22–23.
2. Mark Strand, "The Room," *Darker* (New York: Atheneum, 1979), p. 9.
3. William Logan, "Children," *Sad-Faced Men* (Boston: David R. Godine, 1982), p. 2.

The can-no-longer-remembers, the slow impeachment
Of experience. She rises, stunned and serene,
Toward the promise of nothing.[4]

The brooding melancholy and trance of inwardness, which Edgar Allan Poe urged his countrymen to substitute for didactic verses, have been explored with sedulous abandon in American poetry. The "promise of nothing" is the logical end of the Rhapsodic program, nor are its plodding rehearsals particularly unpleasant; they affect one rather like the sounds of someone working away at three low notes on a bass viol.

But there may be one last worse type in store for us—the Comic Surreal, where absurdity is embraced and then forgotten.

Stuffed against the coat
her breasts want to be naked.
They bloom there
as though they lived in the tropics.
In some other life she traveled light.
In some other life she slipped away at dawn
scarcely disturbing the thick branches.[5]

The most disturbing feature of this stanza is perhaps that it was clearly devised as a kind of technically neutral, unrigorous experiment with manner that the literary decorum of the day allows. It is neither sufficiently manic nor sufficiently purified of romantic narrative elements to be "authentic" surrealism, yet it was not intended to be funny, and is deaf to its own fatuity.

The great difficulty, finally, with the Rhapsodic Fallacy is precisely that it nourishes such aimlessness, such provisionality, such nonsense. It has no standards to impose, no goals to hold out before the writer, not even the goal of rapturous utterance, inasmuch as the effusive does not need to be thorough or even central to be assumed operative in the poem. Neither does the Fallacy permit the poet to evaluate or improve himself, because it denies the validity or possibility of shared standards of judgment, and holds subjective effusion pre-eminent. This illogic at last imprisons both poet and critic, who have come to circle each other like dead stars, and the novice writer as well, who learns from their empty orbiting very little about good literature. For although they may present no significant barriers to genius, neither do the assumptions and techniques that cooperate in the kind of monotonic poetry we have examined do anything, it seems to me, to encourage, or positively enable, great thought or great poetry.[6]

[1984] 2002

---

4. "In Sleep," ibid., p. 3.
5. Leslie Ullmann, "The Woman at the Desk," *Natural Histories* (New Haven: Yale Univ. Press/Yale Younger Poets, 1979), p. 25.
6. A longer version of this essay that considers the role of idiom and error in contemporary verse along with discussions of the work of Gary Snyder, Jorie Graham, and James Wright, appears in my 1993 book from the University of Chicago Press, *The Cure of Poetry in an Age of Prose: Moral Essays on the Poet's Calling*, pp. 1–26.

SHIRLEY GEOK-LIN LIM
(B. 1944)

Shirley Geok-lin Lim was born in the small town of Malacca, Malaysia. Her childhood was difficult. Lim's Malay mother abandoned the family when Lim was eight years old, leaving her Chinese father—a failed businessman who became a paralegal—to raise her and her five brothers. Lim's father was an avid reader, and his interests soon rubbed off on his daughter. "Growing up when I did," Lim recalled, "there weren't many other recreational alternatives, and I had a pretty unhappy childhood. Reading was a huge solace, retreat, escape. I was a really obsessive reader." Although her first language was Malay and her second the Hokkin dialect of Chinese, Lim could read English by age six. She began devouring fairy tales and, later, novels and poetry (especially Tennyson and the Georgian poets). Living under the British colonial system, she attended a missionary convent school run by Irish nuns. By age ten Lim had a poem published in the *Malacca Times*. Soon after she discovered a book on versification and poetic technique that sparked her interest in poetic form. Lim won a federal scholarship to the University of Malaya, where she earned a B.A. in English in 1969. Immigrating then to America, she studied with J. V. Cunningham at Brandeis University, earning a Ph.D. in British and American literature in 1973.

Lim's first collection, *Crossing the Peninsula and Other Poems* (1980), earned the Commonwealth Poetry Prize. (She was the first woman and the first Asian to receive the award.) She has won two American Book Awards, one for coediting *The Forbidden Stitch: An Asian-American Women's Anthology* (1989) and the other for her memoir *Among the White Moon Faces: An Asian-American Memoir of Homelands* (1996). Lim has published collections of short fiction, a novel, and numerous books of poetry, including *Monsoon History: Selected Poems* (1994) and *What the Fortune Teller Didn't Say* (1998). She married Charles Bozerman in 1972 and has a son. Lim is currently a professor of English and chair of women's studies at the University of California, Santa Barbara.

THE SCARLET BREWER
AND THE VOICE OF THE COLONIZED

I was eleven when I had my first poetry reading. Sister Finigan read my poem to my absent mother aloud to the Standard Six class. Rumors went around that my essay on a day in the life of a cock had been read to the senior students, the Form Five class in the new building across the street. When I was twelve and a Form One student in one of the ground floor classrooms in the new building, I had a poem published in the *Malacca Times*. I received ten Malaysian dollars for it and immediately spent the entire sum on noodles, ice-cream, sour plums, and dried orange peel which I shared with my second brother who had mailed the poem for me. Do all writers find their beginnings in such minor triumphs, hedged by school-day tyrannies, poverty, and the almost palpable presence of a community?

At twelve, the inchoate desire to write poetry that probably characterizes the unhappy childhoods of many withdrawn insatiable readers focused itself on a book. Somewhere among the Convent School's mildewed books sent by missionary agents in Ireland was a red linen-bound copy of R. F. Brewer's *The Art of Versification and the Technicalities of Poetry*. In fact, in later life I had misremembered the book, confusing it with George Saintsbury's better known *Historical Manual of English Prosody*. Before writing this essay on intellectual memory, I walked along the library stacks in search of the 1910 edition of Saintsbury's *History*. Instead I found the unevenly aged scarlet cloth-cover of Brewer's book and recognized it immediately, despite the almost thirty-five intervening years.

Published in 1931, this University of California copy is almost an exact replica of the one the twelve-year-old child took to bed with her. I remember the heavy yellowing paper with its uneven cut edges, the ornate character of the large print, the skinnier italics, and the plainer appearance of the reduced print used for the verse selections. Especially, I remember the magisterial categorization. Under "Kinds of Poetry," Lyric divides into Ode, Ballad, Hymn and Song, and Elegy; then there are Epic or Heroic, Dramatic, Descriptive, Didactic, the Sonnet and the Epigram. Who would undertake today to lay before us such a simple and grand sweep of poetry, a sweep that ignores *vers libre,* the major domain of the idiosyncratic and of the American transatlantic speaking voice? No wonder as a university woman I had suppressed memory of Brewer and chose instead to reconstruct the more liberal Saintsbury as my saint of poetic form.

Yet Saintsbury was himself influenced by Brewer, whose work he lists in his bibliography. This scarlet book of my childhood had first been issued in 1869 as *Manual of English Poetry* (the only book in Saintsbury's bibliography with the word "Manual" in its title, indicating perhaps its prominent influence on Saintsbury's later historical study, *Historical Manual of English Prosody*). Brewer's *Manual* was enlarged and reissued as *Orthometry* in 1893, and it was this late nineteenth-century version, essentially the same except in a new scarlet suit, that had enthralled me in my precocious preadolescence.

From *The Intimate Critique,* ed. Diane P. Freedman, Olivia Frey, and Frances Murphy Zauhar (Durham, North Carolina: Duke University Press, 1993) 191–195.

Remembering the many books that have found a permanent home in my life, I suddenly see myself as a basket case. Reliquaries held sacred by British imperialists are scattered like altar figures in a shambling cavern, one lit by faith as much as by skepticism. Shakespeare's plays, every single one of them, published in tissue-thin paper in a collected edition that somehow found its way to the school library. I remember best the poems that filled the back of the volume, although to an Asian child in the tropics, "When icicles hang on the wall / And Dick the shepherd blows his nail" must remain at best exotic words on the page. For me, English words, lines of English poetry, seemed to glow in the brain even in the brightest of languid steamy afternoons.

There were also, in a book-poor community, numerous copies of Everyman's Classics and Oxford University Press World Classics, among them Oliver Goldsmith's *The Deserted Village, The Poetical Works of Gray and Collins*, and Lord Alfred Tennyson's *Selected Poems*. These were required Senior Cambridge Examination texts in the 1940s and 1950s, part of that British literature canon schoolchildren in every British colony would have to master if they hoped to succeed in the colonial administration. Ibo and Yoruba, Ghanaian and Egyptian, Tamil, Punjabi, Bengali, Ceylonese, Burmese, Malay, and Chinese studied this canon in order to get on in the British Empire. We studied mysterious volumes in which alien humans wandered through mossy churchyards, stood under strange trees called elms and yewtrees, suffered from dark, cold, gloom, and chills, and hailed "the splendour of the sun" (*Poems of Lord Alfred Tennyson* 242). Pacing the walled garden of the Buddhist temple to which I escaped from the disheveled two bedroom shack in which my five brothers and I barely breathed, in the near ninety degree glare of the equatorial sun from which there was no escape until swift night at 6 P.M., I somehow made out the sturdy figures of the English language under the encrustments of Victorian ethnocentric sentimentality.

That is, thinking hard now through layers of early colonized consciousness—the girl-child saw something in the poems beyond the cultural differences that eluded her imagination. This something was what Brewer's *Orthometry* made manifest for me: the mysterious English poetry of the British imperialists was laid bare for me in this revolutionary red book as the bones of craft. Brewer's book of forms demythologized once and for all that literary culture the English taught colonized native children to memorize and fear. Through Brewer, Gray's stanzas written in a country churchyard lost their awesome alienness. Deconstructed as prosody, they reemerged as iambic pentameters in rhymed quatrains, or as Brewer categorizes them, "Four heroics rhyming alternately . . . [to] constitute the Elegiac stanza" (73).

The simple naming of craft as craft unweighted the imperialism in English poetry and sent it floating deliriously within my grasp. What Brewer's *Art of Versification* proved to me was that the English language was not a natural possession of the English people; like me, like every governed subject of King George V, English was also a language that the English had to learn. English poets learned from other poets; there were versions, variations, imitations, parodies; they borrowed the rondel, the rondeau, and the sestina from the French and the Italians. English poems were not acts of inspired imagination issuing spontaneously from English genius and yielding their meaning only to like spirits. Instead they were mindful things constructed out of reading, observation, care, learning, and play with language and form. According to Brewer's late nineteenth-century primer, English poetry was socially constructed, not innately inherent in race and genius. The respect for craft that breathes in a book of forms, as in Karl Shapiro's *Prosody Handbook,* is also the respect for any reader who will study it.

The clarifying idea that an English poem can be understood because it is written as language using known traditions of expression was revolutionary in a time when literature teachers arriving fresh from Cambridge and Oxford warned students against studying English literature. Was it Mr. Piggott or Mr. Price and does it matter who said with helpful concern, "You haven't grown up in the British Isles—it's impossible for you to get the idioms of the Lake District to appreciate Wordsworth." Or Scottish dialect to understand Burns. Midlands speech for Hardy. British history for Shakespeare. English gentility for Austen. In short, although we were compelled to study this foreign literature and were judged civilized by our ability to write in this foreign language about this foreign literature, the iron bar Mr. Piggott, Mr. Price, and all the other colonial university teachers raised before us was that English literature was really only for the English people.

The triple bind of force-fed colonial literature, cultural imperialism, and denigration of ability has only begun to loosen in ex-British colonies. But iron and bondage will produce their own kind of revenge. Today, generations of colonial peoples are writing in English, warping it into their own instruments, producing other traditions, the way the Miltonic sonnet evolved from the Petrarchan Italian, the way that Marilyn Hacker's sonnets evolve from the English. Wole Soyinka, Chinua Achebe, Bessie Head, Narudin Farrah, R. K. Narayan, Salman Rushdie, Bharati Mukherjee—these are the illustrious non-English names that appear in English-language literature from Africa, India, Pakistan. But the postcolonial canon is more than those admitted by Anglos into their mainstream. It is the numerous nodes of writing in English produced by local national writers, read perhaps only by their local national audiences, the entire rhizomous planet of minorities, as Deleuze and Guattari would argue, replacing the hegemonic and hierarchical world view of the imperialists.

To my young mind, Brewer's *Orthometry* displayed the human skeleton of poetry; it deflated the Occidental Mystique of English Culture and offered in its place a material body of social language, although one mediated through measures of syllables, interruptions of caesura, waverings between perfect and imperfect rhymes.

I can no longer read the scarlet Brewer with the intense pleasure of a child discovering the secret of adult power. Brewer's choice of lines and stanzas come too heavily freighted now with my own adult sense of power, the solid materially inclined intelligence occluding the mere sensory motions of sound and music. Brewer, I see all too clearly, was a Victorian patriarch. While he approached poetry seriously, it was for him a moral and emotional helpmate, a feminine sublime, the way repressed men want their wives to be: full of good feeling, good judgment, beautiful shape. His selected passages expressed narrowly prescribed ideals of elevated emotion and noble thought: "There is a pleasure in the pathless woods" [Byron, cited in Brewer 182]; "Small service is true service, while it lasts: / Of friends, however humble, scorn not one; / The daisy by the shadow that it casts, / Protects the lingering dewdrop from the sun" [Wordsworth, cited in Brewer 142]. Through bitter intelligence, I see how Brewer took strong poems and inevitably extracted their safest pulp. No wonder then that after twelve, I never returned to the book again.

Instead, arriving in the United States of America in 1969, I have not stopped learning more about the malleability of English poetry, particularly in its American manifestations. I have learned to enjoy the American appetite for the novel and casual, and find the many accents in U.S. poetry an ongoing destabilizing yet regenerative force. The authoritative command of forms I had so admired as a young colonial reader now serves a different purpose: as a shaping illusion that continues to illuminate the marvelous differences between individual poems and the closed forms they are patterned on, refer to, play against, or have abandoned. The irony in the term "closed form" is that linguistic and poetic strategies in good poetry work precisely to enliven the closure, to break the form apart in little variable units of sound, rhythm, syntax; in larger movements of image, idea, feeling; in cross-grained repetitions of letters and words; constituting the seemingly infinite range and patterning of human utterance. Unlike the categories provided in Brewer's *Manual,* the diversity in American poetry lies beyond that of forms. Because they are embedded in a profoundly ideological manner in U.S. culture, American poetic traditions understand that forms are never closed: potential in any form are elements that threaten its fragmentation and thus make it new. America taught me poetry lessons that cannot be contained in a book of forms.

Why then have I picked this antiquarian volume as a foundational piece in my biography of mind? Probably to remind myself that a colonized childhood is composed of strange accidents of isolation and community; that, like Robinson Crusoe on a deserted island, a chest can wash to shore and we can find unexpected help— a book, published in Edinburgh in 1931 and read by the loneliest child in Malacca (or so I imagined myself to be), and leading her to believe that the English language could be as much hers as anyone's. Claiming English as my own was my first step out of the iron cage and into a voice, and who is to say it is not my language and not my voice?

References

Brewer, R. F. *The Art of Versification and the Technicalities of Poetry.* Edinburgh: John Grant, 1931.

Deleuze, Gilles, and Felix Guattari. "What Is a Minor Literature?" *Mississippi Review* 11, no. 3 (1983): 13–33.

Gray, Thomas. *The Poetical Works of Gray and Collins.* Ed. Austin Lane Poole. London: Oxford University Press, 1950.

Saintsbury, George. *Historical Manual of English Prosody.* 1st pub. 1910. New York: Schocken, 1966.

Shapiro, Karl, and Robert Beum. *A Prosody Handbook.* New York: Harper & Row, 1965.

Tennyson, Alfred. *Poems of Lord Alfred Tennyson.* Oxford: London, 1950.

1993, 2002

RON SILLIMAN
(B. 1946)

A leading proponent and practitioner of Language Poetry, Ron Silliman was born in Pasco, Washington, and grew up in Northern California. He once recalled that there were few cultural amenities in his family's home; yet by the age of eighteen he was publishing poems in magazines. After high school, his education was sporadic, a curious fact in the life of a poet whose theories seemingly demand an academic audience. He attended Merritt College in Oakland, San Francisco State University, and the University of California at Berkeley, but never completed a degree. Although he has worked at several colleges and universities, both as a poet and an administrator, his more recent jobs have been nonacademic. For years he worked as the managing editor of *Computer Land*. In 1995 he moved to Pennsylvania where he works as a computer market analyst, while continuing to write at a prolific pace.

Silliman's poetic stance has been influenced by such figures as Gertrude Stein, Ezra Pound, William Carlos Williams, and Jack Spicer. Although he has experimented with different prosodies in his many books, his fundamental project has been an assault on conventional poetic values along broadly poststructuralist lines, especially by rejecting conventional concepts of value and meaning. A committed leftist and former editor of the *Socialist Review*, Silliman associates his efforts to deconstruct poetic hierarchies with social egalitarianism. Yet his revolutionary attack on the literary status quo has found its most positive reception in the heart of the literary establishment, university English departments, where poststructuralist thinking has most deeply taken root.

Silliman's work is not concerned with aural structure or verbal musicality as traditionally conceived, but with visual and conceptual prosodies. His book, *Nox* (1974), for example, presents readers with pages divided into a simple grid, with a word or linguistic fragment in each quadrant of the page. The impact of the work is primarily visual and conceptual, as each text creates a field of interpretations and squarely denies efforts to impose narrative or discursive meaning.

Silliman's most ambitious project appears to be concerned with language at its most minute level. Since 1979 he has been writing *The Alphabet*, a multi–volume work with a book-length poem for each letter of the alphabet, each book published without concern for conventional sequence. This approach has been called "formalist and conceptual" by critic T. C. Marshall, and while this is literally true, that sober assessment perhaps misses some of the sincere and inspired mischief in Silliman's tactics.

As a critic, Silliman has written essays that employ the intricate academic discourse of late twentieth-century literary theory. A case in point is his " 'Postmodernism': Sign For and Struggle, the Struggle for the Sign" (1987), which backs up its methodical case with copious footnotes. Despite his leftist politics, Silliman rejects a populist approach in both his prose style and methodology. Rather, his thinking and procedures owe much to the elitist avant-garde of the Modernist era, and his work seems consciously addressed to a vanguard of fellow progressive experimentalists. Underlying all of this work is a philosophical turn of mind, controversial in its resistance to the emotions and its refusal of transparent language. His most famous theoretical text is "The New Sentence" (1987), which envisions the paragraph and the sentence, rather than the stanza and the line, as the basis of poetry.

Whatever cogency underlies his denial of cogency, Silliman's work stands as a challenge to most commonly held ideas about language and poetry. His abstract language is a far cry from the demotic energy of Ezra Pound's early Modernist manifestos, but Silliman's earnest and imaginative means of assertion reveals the same passion for radical reform of the art.

◄►──◄►──◄►

THE POLITICAL ECONOMY OF POETRY

Poems both are and are not commodities. It is the very partialness of this determination that makes possible much of the confusion among poets, particularly on the left, as to the nature of their participation in (including, perhaps, opposition to) commodity capitalism through the process of making art. Any commodity is necessarily an object and has a physical existence, even if this aspect is no more than the vibrating vocal chords of a sound poet. But not all objects are commodities. That which exists in nature and has a use, such as water, is a good—the hiker comes to the stream and drinks. Only that which is *produced* for its utility achieves the status of product (the water is piped to a metropolitan reservoir and filtered). Of products, only those that are *made for exchange* (and specifically exchange for money) become commodities (Perrier).

The writer who composes a work and reveals it to no one, keeping it instead confined to her notebook, nonetheless has created a product that possesses real use value (part of which may be in the writing process) for its lone consumer. Likewise, two poets trading photocopies of their latest works are exchanging products. And even to the extent that a small press edition of a book of poems may

Originally published in *L=A=N=G=U=A=G=E* 4 (1981), ed. Charles Bernstein and Bruce Andrews. All footnotes are Ron Silliman's.

have a certain portion of its run set aside for the author in lieu of royalties, and that many of those copies will be given away, it also will suffer a divided identity.

Yet books and texts do not exist at quite the same level, nor are they produced by exactly the same people. Further muddying the situation is the subsidization, however minimal, in most of the English-speaking nations of both writers and publications by the state. To what degree can we use the term *commodity* to describe a book sold in a store when its publisher has no hope of recouping original costs, and when these losses will be at least partly absorbed by a third party? Is its commodification nothing more than a strategy for maximum circulation, so that the volume might achieve a greater product-function? Should government patronage be seen as a metaconsumption, in which what is purchased is not textual, but simply the existence of poets and poetry as an ornament to the national culture?

Perhaps, but more important to the equation is the simple presence of consumption, for the role it plays, however dimly perceived by individual authors, in motivating the productions of texts *for exchange.* It was just this that Laura Riding discovered in her 1926 essay "T. E. Hulme, the New Barbarism, & Gertrude Stein," when she complained of "the forced professionalization of poetry."[1] The poet who writes with the idea of having her poems published, of having them collected into books and distributed through stores and direct mail purchases (which may at this point be the larger sector of the market), has inescapably been drawn into the creation of commodities.

The book, *a commodity,* radically alters the composition and potential size of an audience. Yet, although literary theory since the time of the New Critics has done much to elaborate the possible meanings in a given text, it has remained essentially silent about the relations of the social features of any actual, particular audience in the creation of such meanings. This absence banishes any serious consideration of the ideological component, which is reduced instead to a question of the politics of the writer or those of individual characters (an example would be Terry Eagleton's discussion of George Eliot in *Criticism and Ideology*).[2]

The role of the reader in the determination of a poem's ideological content is neither abstract nor beyond the scope of feasible examination. The question is contextual, not textual. As early as 1929, V. N. Voloshinov wrote:

> The actual reality of language-speech is not the abstract system of linguistic forms, not the isolated monologic utterance, and not the psychophysiological act of its implementation, but the social event of verbal interaction implemented in an utterance or utterances.
>
> Thus, verbal interaction is the basic reality of language. . . . A book, i.e., *a verbal performance in print,* is also an element of verbal communication. It is something discussable in actual, real-life dialogue, but aside from that, it is calculated for active perception, involving attentive reading and inner responsiveness, and for organized, *printed* reaction . . . (book reviews, critical surveys, defining influence on subsequent books, and so on). Moreover, a verbal performance of this kind also inevitably orients itself with respect to previous performances in the same sphere, both those by the same author and those by

1. Laura Riding [= Jackson], *Contemporaries and Snobs* (London: Cape, 1928), 123–99.
2. Terry Eagleton, *Criticism and Ideology* (New York: Verso, 1978), 110–24.

other authors. It inevitably takes its point of departure from some particular state of affairs. . . . Thus the printed verbal performance engages, as it were, in ideological colloquy of large scale: it responds to something, objects to something, affirms something, anticipates possible responses and objections, seeks support, and so on.

Any utterance, no matter how weighty and complete in and of itself, *is only a moment in the continuous process of verbal communication.* But that continuous verbal communication is, in turn, itself only a moment in the continuous, all-inclusive, generative process of a given social collective. . . . *Verbal communication can never be understood and explained outside of this connection with a concrete situation.*[3]

Contrast Voloshinov's perspective with that of New Critics René Wellek and Austin Warren: "the real problem must be conceived as a structure of norms, realized only partially in the experience of its many readers." Their argument in *Theory of Literature* (1949) is a thorough assault on all contextual approaches:

What is the "real" poem; where should we look for it; how does it exist . . . ?

One of the most common and oldest answers is the view that a poem is an "artefact," an object of the same nature as a piece of sculpture or a painting. Thus the work of art is considered identical with the black lines of ink on white paper or parchment or, if we think of a Babylonian poem, with the grooves in the brick. Obviously this answer is quite unsatisfactory. There is, first of all, the huge oral "literature." There are poems or stories which have never been fixed in writing and still continue to exist. Thus the lines in black ink are merely a method of recording a poem which must be conceived as existing elsewhere. If we destroy the writing or even all copies of a printed book we still may not destroy the poem. . . . Besides, not every printing is considered by us, the readers, a correct printing of a poem. The very fact that we are able to correct printer's errors in a text which we might not have read before or, in some rare cases, restore the genuine meaning of the text shows that we do not consider the printed lines as the genuine poem. Thus we have shown that the poem (or any literary work of art) can exist outside its printed version and that the printed artefact contains many elements which we all must consider as not included in the genuine poem.[4]

While the Saussurean bias against writing as anything more than a shadow of speech is evident enough in this classic passage, more telling (at least for its impact on subsequent literary theory) is the demand of a single aspect of the work that can be elevated to the status of *genuine.* In the cause of textual analysis, Wellek and Warren succeeded in delegitimating the fuller study of literature as a total social process.

This is not to be confused with the dialectical method of moving from the concrete to the abstract, from the printed poem to its social context, in order to identify principles and structures with which to return to concrete practice. Wellek and Warren's idealization of the text is a complete rupture, achieved by a stylistic sleight of hand (writing is only a record of speech, yet oral work is only literature in quotes, severing the text from any material finality). This dematerialization

3. V. N. Voloshinov, *Marxism and the Philosophy of Language,* trans. Latislav Matejka and I. R. Titunik (New York: Seminar Press, 1973), 94–95.
4. René Wellek and Austin Warren, *Theory of Literature* (New York: Harcourt Brace, 1949), 142–43.

conspires to make "possible the continuity of literary tradition" and "increase the unity . . . of works of art" by banishing investigations of difference at other levels.

The career of William Carlos Williams demonstrates the real consequences of those aspects of literary production and consumption that New Criticism would dismiss. Many young poets today feel that his finest work is to be found in *Spring & All* and the other books composed between 1920 and 1932. Yet several of the "New American" poets of the 1950s are on record as having been primarily influenced by Williams's 1944 collection *The Wedge*. This means that young writers perceive the stamp of Williams's example, teaching, and prestige on the work of their immediate predecessors as having a value other than that presumed by those somewhat older poets. A poet who bears that mark heavily, such as Lew Welch, is apt to become marginalized by the process.

Spring & All was not available in the 1950s, though the poems in it were included (in an altered order) in *The Collected Earlier Poems*. To be certain, the texts themselves did not change, but their inaccessibility blocked communication, and by the time Harvey Brown's Frontier Press brought them back to a possible public, the audience itself had been transformed: in addition to their having experienced a greatly expanded educational system in the 1960s, a war in Vietnam that had already gone sour, and the familiarity with psychedelics, the new readers of *Spring & All* had often already assimilated the work of Olson, O'Hara, Creeley, and others.

An even clearer example of the literary (and therefore social) difference of different editions can be found in Jim Carroll's *Basketball Diaries,* a teenage memoir of sex, drugs, and rock-and-roll that over fifteen years went through piecemeal appearances in little poetry magazines, a slick small press edition, and finally emerged as a mass market paperback—reviewed and even excerpted in the nation's *sports* pages. At one end of this spectrum is a group of readers who found in Carroll a natural, even primitive, tough-lyric prose style, embodying many of the principles held by writers associated with the Saint Mark's Church in New York and articulated most forcefully by Ted Berrigan. At the other end is a group of readers who probably have never heard of Ted Berrigan and for whom the considerations of style, without which the *Diaries* would never have been printed, are utterly beside the point.

Even in cases, such as live performance, where the author is present, different audiences will receive and interpret a given work differently. In a talk given at San Francisco's 80 Langton Street, Robert Glück offers this example:

> At several Movement readings I was interested to see members of the audience come up afterwards and say where the writer had got it right (yes, that's my life) and where the writer had got it wrong. I want to contrast this with the audience that admires writing as if it were a piece of Georgian silver, goods to be consumed. Of course this depends on an identification with a community, a shared ideology. For example, I read a story at a gay reading about being "queer-bashed." The audience responded throughout with shouts of encouragement and acknowledgement. Afterwards people told me I got it right. I read the same story to an appreciative and polite university audience, and afterwards people told me they admired my transitions. To a certain extent, my story registered only in terms of form.[5]

5. Robert Glück, "Caricature" (unpublished manuscript), 21.

Although Glück foregrounds here the role of context, he implicitly reproduces the Wellek-Warren presumption of "correctness," merely substituting a preferred definition (one that avoids addressing the *political* question of what is accomplished by correctness: the delegitimization of something, and by fiat, not argument). His characterization of an "audience that admires writing as if it were a piece of Georgian silver" is in fact incorrect, because he omits the fact that the second group's response is conditioned by their identification with Glück *as a writer* (and/or as an intellectual *because* he writes). What is shared is not the experience of homophobic violence but the problems of a craft.

What can be communicated through any literary production depends on which codes are shared with its audience. The potential contents of the text are only actualized according to their reception, which depends on the social composition of the receivers. The work of Clark Coolidge, for example, might seem opaque and forbidding at a gay reading, for the same reason that a Japanese speaker cannot communicate with an Italian: no codes are shared from which to translate from word to meaning. There may be several people at a gay reading who are as interested as Coolidge in geology, bebop, Salvador Dali, weather, and even the same kinds of writing problems, but these concerns are not what bring people to such an event.

The social composition of its audience is the primary context of any writing. Context determines (and is determined by) the motives of the readers as well as their experience, their history, that is, their particular set of possible codes. Context determines the actual, real-life consumption of the literary product, without which communication of a message (formal, substantive, ideological) cannot occur. It tells us very little to know only that one group was a "gay reading" and the other a "university audience." A school with a large English department and a creative writing major is entirely different from a school focusing on science and agriculture. A reading to a graduate-level class in rhetoric is not the same as another to the general student body.

It is here, at the question of context, a place that does not even exist within the system of Wellek and Warren, that both Riding and Glück complain in their very different ways of the "forced professionalization" of poetry. We can see here also that the "continuity of literary tradition" and the "unity . . . of works of art" is not a partial truth but a calculated fabrication that expresses, more clearly than its authors could have known, the ideology of late capitalism. Their "us, the readers," able to determine a "correct printing of a poem" and capable of restoring "the genuine meaning of the text," is not just any reader, but a particular one, unnamed, with a particular education and occupation. Glück's argument (although it fails to distinguish between the worker's concern for the quality and manufacture of her product and the attitude of a collector of Georgian silver) is an improvement to the degree that his naming of a "best reader" at least acknowledges the existence of other audiences.

The New Critics, however, were not solely responsible for the illusion of a "continuity of literary tradition" made possible by the banishment of other readers. Their task was to give this mirage a cloak of critical respectability. Wellek and Warren's comments, it should be noted, came during the long four-and-one-half-decade period (1911–1955) when the number of book titles published in the United States per year remained relatively static at under 12,000, in spite of the emergence of large corporate publishing firms, while membership in the Modern

Language Association (MLA) rose from 1,047 to 8,453.[6] In short, the rise of a professional caste of "specialized" or, more accurately, bureaucratized readers occurred precisely at the moment when a new set of dynamics, characterized by such concepts as market position, penetration, and share, began to reorganize the distribution of what had for a long time been a fixed output. Thus corporate collaboration with the leadership of this new caste at least appeared to offer commanding control over the future of the market itself.

It was, more than anything else, the affluence of the United States after the Second World War that kept this "promise" from being met. New offset printing technology lowered the cost of book production, permitting the large publishers to further segment their markets and realize profits from an increased diversity of titles, while simultaneously enabling a dramatic expansion in the number of small, independent producers. Similarly, post-Sputnik higher education brought new masses into what had previously been the terrain of a more homogeneous, class-determined few. Membership in the MLA (itself much more diversified) was to peak in 1971 at 31,356, while the number of book titles published per year in 1980 exceeded 40,000.[7] Finally, beginning with the creation of the Literature Panel of the National Endowment for the Arts in 1966, state subsidies for poets and the publication of poetry became active forces in the decentralization of literature. The rise of the "New American" poetries and their successors, as well as that of writing coming out of the women's movement and from ethnic and sexual minority communities, can be viewed as a consequence of these social and technological transformations, each of which, in turn, is grounded in economic circumstance.

Yet, even with subsidies, there is not enough capital in the entire poetry industry to directly support poets and publishers. This partly determines who will be poets and at what period of their lives poets are more apt to be active and publish. More important, however, this means that nearly all poets will turn elsewhere to make a living. Thus poets as a group have a wide range of jobs. This in turn means both that poets see work (and the politics of the workplace) in a nonuniform manner and from a variety of perspectives and that they are less likely to perceive poetry as work (at least in the sense of the politics that would extend from that perception). It also partly explains why so much of the discussion of the politics of literature has been fixated on the lone aspect of content.

"Professional" poets include individuals who come from the entire spectrum of economic classes. The actual number of those who might accurately be described as bourgeois is small, and it is speculative to suggest that it exceeds the 2 percent figure that holds for the general U.S. population. The neobeatnik/neodada/street poet scene that manifests itself in every major urban center, on the other hand, might be characterized by the lumpen orientation of many of its participants. But the vast majority of poets fall in between. While many are traditionally working class and while there may be a somewhat higher concentration of classically defined petty bourgeois than in the general American economy, a significant concentration of poets falls into a category that the late Nicos Poulantzas called the New Petty Bourgeoisie:

6. J. Kendrick Noble, Jr., "Books," in *Who Owns the Media*, ed. Benjamin Compaine (New York: Harmony, 1979), 257; "Conventions and Membership," *PMLA* 99.3 (1984): 456.
7. The 1996 total was 140,000.

This is also where the current devaluation of educational certificates and attainments is most important, given the significance that these have on the labour market and for the promotion chances of these agents. It can be seen in the currently massive occupation of subaltern posts by agents whose educational qualifications led them to have different aspirations. In actual fact, this is the fraction into which young people holding devalued university degrees gravitate on a massive scale. It leads to the various forms of disguised unemployment that ravages this fraction: various forms of illegal work, vacation work, temporary and auxiliary work. These affect all those fractions with an objectively proletarian polarization, but are particularly pronounced in this case.[8]

Poets, for obvious reasons, tend to look at "disguised unemployment" as time to write, which partly explains their gravitation to part-time service sector jobs, such as clerking in bookstores or proofreading for publishers and law firms. Poulantzas also notes that "It now seems, however, as if the last few years have seen the development, in the majority of capitalist countries, of an actual mental labour reserve army, over and above any cyclical phenomena."[9]

Poulantzas, however, has a very restricted class model, considering mental work and service sector employment to be unproductive and therefore excluded from the working class as such (although conceding the "objectively proletarian polarization"). Still, the description, especially with regard to underutilized education and partial employment, is a close fit to the lives of many American poets under forty.

Erik Olin Wright, one of Poulantzas's most vigorous critics, uses a more complex model in which this same group is categorized as working class yet with a strong degree of contradiction as to class allegiance. Noting that more than 30 percent of economically active Americans had, by 1969, come into the "unproductive mental" labor sector, Wright notes that "The contradictory locations around the boundary of the working class represent positions which do have a real interest in socialism, yet simultaneously gain certain real privileges directly from capitalist relations of production."[1]

Situated within these complex and sometimes contradictory economic relations, the social organization of contemporary poetry occurs in two primary structures: the *network* and the *scene*. The scene is specific to a place. A network, by definition, is transgeographic. Neither mode ever exists in a pure form. Networks typically involve scene subgroupings, while many scenes (although not all) build toward network formations. Individuals may, and often do, belong to more than one of these informal organizations at a time. Both types are essentially fluid and fragile. As the Black Mountain poets and others have demonstrated, it is possible for literary tendencies to move through both models at different stages in their development.

Critical to the distinction between these structures are the methods of communication available to their members. A sociology of poetry, noting, for example, that a reading series requires far less start-up capital than either a book or magazine, or that the face-to-face interactions that take place in such settings seldom demand

8. Nicos Poulantzas, *Classes in Contemporary Capitalism,* trans. David Fernbach (New York: Verso, 1978), 323.
9. Ibid., 311.
1. Erik Olin Wright, *Class, Crisis, and the State* (New York: Verso, 1979), 108–09.

the initiative needed to begin a serious, long-distance correspondence with a stranger, would correlate such implications with the class backgrounds and orientations of both writers and readers, real and potential alike. Yet, if such a sociology is not to fall prey to technological determinism, it must ask not simply which methods of interaction are in use but, more important, to what end. Because capital, of which there is so little in poetry, is necessary for the elements of network formation, competition exists between networks and scenes. Underneath lie a hidden assumption of the hierarchical ordering of these groups and the idea that one can be the dominant or hegemonic formation according to some definition, at least for a period of time. Definitions vary, but major components include monetary rewards, prestige (often called influence), and the capacity to have one's work permanently in print and being taught.

Here the role of trade publishing and its allies is completely clear. Trade presses may produce less than 4 percent of all poetry titles, but in an anthology such as *The American Poetry Anthology* they represent 54 percent of all books used as sources for the collection.[2] University presses contributed another 31 percent. Nearly half of the remaining small press books come from Ecco Press, the editor's own imprint.

Trade publishing is the metanetwork of American poetry. It is the contemporary manifestation of the academic network for which Wellek and Warren argued more than thirty years ago, and university employment remains a primary social feature. But, because this is the network that is aligned with capital, it can and does incorporate poets from other groups on a token basis. While this serves to give them much broader distribution, they in turn legitimate the metanetwork, masking to some degree its very network structure.

This alliance with capital yields another major advantage: the relative efficiency of trade distribution virtually guarantees its predominance on college course reading lists, *which is the largest single market for books of poetry,* with 2,500 colleges and 200 writing programs in North America.

So long as capital, in the form of corporate publishers, can substantially determine the distribution of poetry in its major market, and so long as Daniel Halpern can call a collection of their network *The American Poetry Anthology* without challenge, this type of hegemony is not apt to be broken. The competition between other networks and scenes amounts to little more than jockeying for the token slots in the metanetwork.

But this is neither the only mode of hegemony nor necessarily the most important. Here the question is not whether a poet will be read in five or fifty or five hundred years, but whether that poet can and will be read by individuals *able and willing to act* on their increased understanding of the world as a result of the communication. A poetics for which the ultimate motive is nothing more than the maintenance of its own social position within a status quo reaches such an audience only insofar as it fosters no action whatsoever. The inclusion of blacks and feminists in the Halpern anthology functions precisely to keep the readers of those poets from questioning the presence of the white male college teachers who dominate the book.

2. Daniel Halpern, ed., *The American Poetry Anthology* (New York: Avon, 1975).

What a consciously oppositional writer such as Robert Glück fails to consider when he dismisses one of his audiences in favor of the other is that their social composition is not identical. Any definition of response needs to be tailored accordingly. In part, this problem may reflect Glück's own overlapping membership in each community. It is, however, a major characteristic of the social codes of just those formations most often apt to attend a college reading not to know or speak their own name. In labeling that audience as consumers, Glück forgets that consumption *for further production* is a moment of production itself—it *is* action. It is through the question of transitions, for example, that the "seamlessness" (i.e., the "natural" or "inevitable" quality) of perceived reality, including that of the "continuity of literary tradition," might be revealed as the affect of a partisan ideological construct. A construct, in fact, which might also yield, as parallel states of "the inevitable," the social omnipotence of capital and the relative superiority of bourgeois (as distinct from economic) democracy as a method for governance in an imperfect world.

Still, just identifying Glück's university audience as a coalition of writers, teachers, and specialized readers falls short of connecting them to the larger social orders of which they are a strategic fragment. This self-invisibility has parallels throughout contemporary life. It has only been through the struggle of nonwhites, of women, and of gays that the white male heterosexual has come into recognition of his own, pervasive presence. In poetry, there continues to be a radical break between those networks and scenes that are organized by and around the codes of oppressed peoples and those other "purely aesthetic" schools. In fact, the aesthetics of those latter schools is a direct result of ideological struggle, both between networks and scenes and within them. It is characteristic of the class situation of those schools that this struggle is carried on *in other (aesthetic) terms*.

Poetry in America reflects struggle carried out, unfortunately, in an unorganized and often individualistic manner. This struggle is as much one between audiences as it is between poets (or, to be precise, it is one between social formations, including, but never limited to, economic classes, from which audiences are composed around individual authors). It is class war—and more—conducted through the normal social mechanisms of verse. The primary ideological message of poetry lies not in its explicit content, political though that may be, but in the *attitude toward reception* it demands of the reader. It is this "attitude toward information" that is carried forward by the recipient. It is this attitude that forms the basis for a response to other information, not necessarily literary, in the text. And, beyond the poem, in the world.

1981

TIMOTHY STEELE
(B. 1948)

One of the foremost practitioners of formal verse in the United States today, Timothy Reid Steele was born in Burlington, Vermont. Since the late sixties, however, when he entered Stanford University, his life and work have been rooted in California. When he took his B.A. at Stanford in 1970, the English department was still very much under the influence of the poet-critic Yvor Winters and his disciples. Steele then went to Brandeis University, where he did graduate work with one of Winters's strongest advocates, J. V. Cunningham, earning his Ph.D. in 1977. Steele returned to Stanford twice—first as a Stegner Fellow (1972–1973) and later as a lecturer (1975–1977). He has taught at California State University, Los Angeles, since 1987. Steele's first brief marriage ended in divorce. In 1979 he married Victoria Erpelding.

The mark of strong teachers like Winters and Cunningham reveals itself in Steele's skill with meter, his lucid style, and his tendency toward rationalism. He has even published epigrammatic verse. But unlike Cunningham's epigrams, his poems tend not to reflect bitter personal difficulties. Rather, like another mentor, Richard Wilbur, Steele often conveys a sense of the joy and awe of living. This is not to say that there is no sadness in his poems, only that Steele's emotions are usually hidden beneath burnished verbal surfaces.

The title of Steele's first book, *Uncertainties and Rest* (1979), suggests something of his dual vision in which the poet's formal poise becomes a stay against undeniable transience. Although the book was respectfully reviewed, it seemed to many an anomaly in a world where most poets had abandoned rhyme and meter. At about this time, the term "New Formalism" began to enter critical parlance, and Steele has since been identified with that movement. Like many other poets given this distinction, Steele has found the term misleading. "Meter's always been around for anyone wishing to explore it," he remarked, "the only true New Formalist in English is Geoffrey Chaucer." His next small book, *The Prudent Heart* (1983), was followed by more chapbooks and then a very successful full-length volume, *Sapphics Against Anger* (1986), where again form was perceived as a way of living with one's human passions. *The Color Wheel* (1994) was followed by

Sapphics and Uncertainties: Poems 1970–1986 (1995), which reprinted, and slightly corrected, his first two volumes.

As a critic, Timothy Steele has had a major impact by articulating a revisionist view of twentieth-century American poetry. His contrarian views were first presented in his scholarly treatise, *Missing Measures: Modern Poetry and the Revolt against Meter* (1990), a careful argument for the viability of meter that places his subject in the Modernist revolution. Steele has also published one of the most comprehensive textbooks on poetic technique: *All the Fun's in How You Say a Thing: An Explication of Meter and Versification* (1999). In these books, as well as in his superb edition of *The Poems of J. V. Cunningham* (1997), Steele's methodical scholarship makes him an indispensable literary historian.

⊸•─◄▶─•⊷

TRADITION AND REVOLUTION:
THE MODERN MOVEMENT AND FREE VERSE

Free verse is possibly the most significant legacy of the revolution in poetry that occurred in the first quarter of the twentieth century. A kind of free verse had existed earlier; in our language, the King James Psalms and the "stave-prose poetry" (to use George Saintsbury's term) of James Macpherson's Ossianic epics, William Blake's "Prophetic Books," Martin Tupper's *Proverbial Philosophy,* and Walt Whitman's *Leaves of Grass* can be adduced as examples of proto-vers libre. But it was the theory and practice of Ford Madox Ford, Ezra Pound, T. S. Eliot, and others that made free verse a dominant medium for English and American poetry. In an interview in *Antaeus* in 1978, Stanley Kunitz remarks: "Non-metrical verse has swept the field, so that there is no longer any real adversary from the metricians." Though Kunitz may be overstating the case, his assessment of prevailing practice is accurate: most contemporary verse is not metrical.

Having now some distance on the revolution, we would do well to examine the ideas with which its leaders explained it and free verse. One of the most crucial of these ideas is that the modern revolution is essentially like earlier revolutions. The modern movement's leaders commonly argue, that is, that theirs is a rebellion against an antiquated idiom and is, as such, the rebellion that "modernists" of all ages have had to undertake to keep poetry engaged with the speech and life of its time. Free verse, according to this argument, does not represent a rejection of traditional poetic discipline, but is an innovation of the sort that necessarily accompanies changes in style and taste.

In one respect, this argument is valid. Poetic conventions evolve, flourish, and eventually turn stale with use. When their art suffers a period of decline, it is only right that poets should try to revive it. This is what good poets have always done; this is what Ford, Pound, Eliot, and their followers were doing when they urged

Originally published in *Southwest Review* 70.3 (Summer 1985). Collected in *Missing Measures: Modern Poetry and the Revolt Against Meter* (Fayetteville, Arkansas: University of Arkansas Press, 1990). Emendations by the author for this volume, 2002.

that the styles of Victorian verse had grown creaky and run-down and needed to be replaced by an idiom better equipped to treat modern life.

In another respect, however, the argument is not so sound. In its advocacy of non-metrical poetry, the modern revolution differed from former revolutions. It differed from that which Euripides led against Aeschylean style and from that which Horace led against the literary excesses of his day; and it differed from—to speak of Eliot's favorite examples—the revolution Dryden led against Cleveland and the metaphysicals and the revolution Wordsworth led against the neo-classicists. To be sure, earlier revolutions had sometimes entailed the elevation of certain verse forms at the expense of once-prominent ones. Wordsworth and the romantics, for instance, cultivated the sonnet, ballad stanzas, and blank verse—forms relatively neglected by the previous age—and mostly shunned the balanced couplet, in which much of the poetry of the previous age had been composed. Yet Wordsworth did not argue, as the twentieth-century modernists did, that abandoning meter was a suitable means of reforming the faults of his predecessors. Indeed, historically considered, free verse is singular, in that, until the twentieth century, nearly all Western poetry is informed by the distinction, memorably enunciated by Aristotle (*Rhetoric*, 3.8.1–3), that prose is organized in the general patterns and periods of rhythm (*rhythmos*) and poetry in the specifically and regularly ordered rhythmical units of meter (*metron*).

The modern movement's leaders seem not to have comprehended or admitted the singularity of free verse, nor has its singularity been sufficiently appreciated by subsequent poets and critics. In this essay, I will try to clarify the nature of the modern movement and free verse. I will do this by examining what Ford, Pound, and Eliot said about their revolution and by comparing their remarks with those of earlier literary innovators. In conclusion, I will discuss the legacy of the modern movement and the implications, for current poetic practice, of the triumph and diffusion of free verse.

I will begin with Eliot. Though anticipated and influenced by Ford and Pound, Eliot became the most public and prestigious spokesman for the modern movement, and he consequently received opportunity and encouragement to expound the movement in a more systematic fashion than his co-revolutionaries. Eliot's views of the modern movement and free verse appear most tellingly in two lectures delivered in the 1940s, "The Music of Poetry" and the second of his Milton papers.

In the Milton lecture, Eliot sounds the theme that the modern revolution is like the earlier revolutions conducted by Dryden and Wordsworth and involves an effort to empty poetry of hot air and to relate poetry meaningfully to contemporary speech:

> I have on several occasions suggested, that the important changes in the idiom of English verse which are represented by the names of Dryden and Wordsworth, may be characterized as successful attempts to escape from a poetic idiom which had ceased to have a relation to contemporary speech. This is the sense of Wordsworth's Prefaces. By the beginning of the present century another revolution in idiom—and such revolutions bring with them an alteration of metric, a new appeal to the ear—was due.

It is important to note here two things. First, Eliot associates "idiom" with "metric." He frequently makes this connection, as, for instance, when he remarks in his 1951

"Poetry and Drama" essay that *Murder in the Cathedral* was too ceremonial to suggest a basis for a truly modern verse drama: "Here, then, were two problems left unsolved: that of the idiom and that of the metric (it is really one and the same problem)." Second, he asserts that, in literary revolutions, an alteration of idiom entails an alteration of metric.

Eliot's association of idiom and metric is questionable. Though what poets say is related to the way in which they say it, idiom and metric are different. Idiom is immediate and fluid; it changes from generation to generation and can even vary among different groups of contemporaries speaking the same language. Meter, on the other hand, is much less local. It is an abstraction; it comprises a measure or measures by means of which speech can be organized into rhythmical patterns. Poets far apart in time can use the same meter. Though Shakespeare and Wordsworth represent different eras, idioms, and outlooks, both employ the iambic pentameter. Indeed, different languages can share the same meters. For instance, Greek and Latin share the dactylic hexameter, and Russian, German, and English share the iambic tetrameter.

Also questionable is Eliot's assertion that alterations of idiom inevitably bring alterations of metric. This is not borne out by the testimony of literary history, certainly not by the testimony Eliot cites. Wordsworth, throughout the revolution he spearheaded, defended the virtues of meter as earnestly as he decried the vices of "poetic diction." Even as he sought to bring to poetry fresh and timely speech, he advocated casting it in time-honored metrical forms.

To put the matter more comprehensively and to anticipate issues we will explore shortly, the leaders of the modern literary revolution objected, with the best of intentions, to the diction and subject matter of Victorian verse. Yet they identified the vague and over-decorative lyricality of Victorian poetry with the metrical system which the Victorians had used but which was not itself Victorian, having been used for centuries by a variety of poets working in a variety of styles. Hence, the modernists came to feel that meter was outmoded in the same way that Victorian style was, and came to believe that to break with the latter they would need to break with the former as well. Nor did it occur to them that they might be throwing the baby out with the bath water, since the conflation of metric and idiom somewhat obscured the radical character of their move away from meter. The conflation made them see free verse less as a prosodic issue than as merely one aspect of a broader question of stylistic reform.

Discussing the objectives he and his early associates entertained, Eliot goes on to say, in his Milton lecture, that they wanted to create a poetry which spoke unaffectedly. They wanted to create a poetry that possessed the immediacy of good prose and that took its subjects and vocabulary not from dated canons of taste, but straight from modern life and speech, regardless of their "non-poetic" qualities:

> It was one of our tenets that verse should have the virtues of prose, that diction should become assimilated to cultivated contemporary speech, before aspiring to the elevation of poetry. Another tenet was that the subject-matter and the imagery of poetry should be extended to topics and objects related to the life of a modern man or woman, that we were to seek the non-poetic, to seek even material refractory to transmutation into poetry, and words and phrases which had not been used in poetry before.

In "The Music of Poetry," Eliot advances arguments like those in his Milton paper. Here, too, Eliot characterizes the modern movement as "a period of search for a proper modern colloquial idiom," and contends that the modern revolution is identical to the revolutions of Dryden and Wordsworth: "Every revolution in poetry is apt to be, and sometimes to announce itself to be a return to common speech. That is the revolution which Wordsworth announced in his prefaces, and he was right: but the same revolution had been carried out a century before by Oldham, Waller, Denham and Dryden; and the same revolution was due again something over a century later."

In addition to speaking of the modern movement in general, Eliot speaks in this essay of free verse in particular, and he makes two interesting points. One is that the free verse he and his fellow experimentalists wrote expressed simply a desire for poetic reform. Free verse embodied, Eliot says, not a rejection of poetic discipline, but a dissatisfaction with moribund procedures. "Only a bad poet could welcome free verse as a liberation from form," Eliot affirms. "It was a revolt against dead form, and a preparation for new form or for the renewal of the old."

A second point Eliot urges is that those who worry that the vogue for free verse may undermine poetic craft are misguided to the extent that they fail to see that the distinction between metrical and non-metrical verse is unimportant compared to the more profound distinction between good writing and bad:

> As for "free verse," I expressed my view twenty-five years ago by saying that no verse is free for the man who wants to do a good job. No one has better cause to know than I, that a great deal of bad prose has been written under the name of free verse; though whether its authors wrote bad prose or bad verse, or bad verse in one style or in another, seems to me a matter of indifference.

Other leaders of the modern movement embody attitudes we find in Eliot. This is especially true of Ford Madox Ford. Though mainly remembered today for his novels, Ford began writing free verse in the 1890s, and in the first quarter of the twentieth century, he could rightly claim to be, as he puts it in his *Thus to Revisit,* a volume of reminiscences published in 1921, "the doyen of living writers of *Vers Libre* in English."

Ford's views about the modern movement and free verse appear in his preface to his *Collected Poems* of 1911, in an essay entitled "The Battle of the Poets" in *Thus to Revisit,* and in some notes for a lecture on vers libre that he delivered in the 1920s in New York City and that Frank MacShane has preserved in his *Critical Writings of Ford Madox Ford.* As does Eliot, Ford emphasizes that the modern revolution was a protest against the outmoded idiom of Victorian verse. In his preface to his *Collected Poems,* he discusses the literary revolt which began with his generation and says: "What worried and exasperated us in the poems of the late Lord Tennyson, the late Lewis Morris, the late William Morris, the late—well, whom you like—is not their choice of subject, it is their imitative handling of matter, of words, it is their derivative attitude." Ford develops this theme in *Thus to Revisit,* in which he tells us that, when as a young writer he analyzed the Victorians, he came to the conclusion that their faults resulted from lofty attitudinizing and that poetry, if it was to recover from these faults, had to be brought back down to earth and into touch with the solid, workmanlike qualities of good prose. "I had to make for myself the discovery that verse must be at least as well written as prose if it is to be poetry," Ford remarks. "The Victorians killed the verse side of poetry because, intent on the contemplation of their own moral importance, they allowed their sentences to become intolerably long, backboneless, and without construction."

For Ford, as for Eliot, the importance of prose qualities in verse extends to specific issues of diction and subject. Not only must poetry achieve a clarity of meaning and structure comparable to that of prose; poetry must also speak in contemporary terms and address contemporary material. In *Thus to Revisit,* Ford says that by 1898 he had worked out a "formula" for writing poems, and his formula closely resembles the "tenets" Eliot mentions in his Milton essay. The individual articles of the formula, Ford writes, were

> that a poem must be compounded of observation of the everyday life that surrounded us; that it must be written in exactly the same vocabulary as that which one used for one's prose; that, if it were to be in verse, it must attack some subject that needed a slightly more marmoreal treatment than is expedient for the paragraph of a novel; that, if it were to be rhymed, the rhyme must never lead to the introduction of unnecessary thought; and lastly, that no exigency of meter must interfere with the personal cadence of the writer's mind or the pressure of the recorded emotion.

The faith which Ford attached to these articles is obvious in his preface to his *Collected Poems,* where he characterizes his verse as having "one unflinching aim—to register my own times in terms of my own time." And Ford relates this "unflinching aim" to earlier poetic revolutions, arguing, no less forcefully than Eliot, that he and poets like him are thus performing a function good poets have always performed. They are connecting poetry to the real life of its era: "I would rather read a picture in verse of the emotions and environment of a Goodge Street anarchist than recapture what songs the sirens sang. That after all was what François Villon was doing for the life of his day."

About free verse, Ford makes points much like those Eliot makes about it. In *Thus to Revisit,* for instance, Ford speaks of Imagism (of which he was one of the eleven charter members represented in Pound's *Des Imagistes* anthology of 1914), and he urges that imagistic vers libre is a rebellion against the rhetorical vices of the Victorians: "The work is free of the polysyllabic, honey-dripping and derivative adjectives that, distinguishing the works of most of their contemporaries, makes nineteenth-century poetry as a whole seem greasy and 'close,' like the air of a room." Ford also argues, in his lecture on vers libre, that free verse expresses the desire for (to return to Eliot's phrase) "a proper modern colloquial idiom." Perhaps recalling Wordsworth's definition of a Poet "as a man speaking to men," Ford asserts that "if a man cannot talk like an educated gentleman about things that matter in direct and simple English let him hold his tongue." Ford then cites Wordsworth's pentameter, "Shine, Poet! in thy place, and be content," and comments: "That is really what vers libre is. It is an attempt to let personalities express themselves more genuinely than they have lately done."

Many of the ideas we find in Eliot and Ford appear also in Pound. For Pound, too, the modern revolution represents an overthrowing of lax style, and shows, in this regard, a healthy resemblance to earlier revolutions. In his "Retrospect" essay, published in *Pavannes and Divisions* in 1918 but incorporating materials which had been printed earlier in periodicals, Pound looks back on the beginnings of

Imagism and free verse, and suggests that they were a salutary protest against the poetry of the nineteenth century, a period he describes as being "a rather blurry, messy sort of a period, a rather sentimentalistic, mannerish sort of a period." Pound tells us that when he, H.D., and Richard Aldington decided in 1912 to form a group dedicated to revitalizing poetry, they adopted as their first principle, "direct treatment of the 'thing' whether subjective or objective"; and in Pound's mind, this is exactly the principle earlier poets embraced when they forged new styles. "In the art of Daniel and Cavalcanti," Pound says in the same essay, "I have seen that precision which I miss in the Victorians, that explicit rendering, be it of external nature or of emotion. Their testimony is of the eyewitness, their symptoms are first hand." Speaking of the modern movement, Pound adds: "As to Twentieth century poetry, and the poetry which I expect to see written during the next decade or so, it will, I think, move against poppy-cock, it will be harder and saner. . . . At least for myself, I want it so, austere, direct, free from emotional slither."

In his 1913 essay, "The Serious Artist," Pound sounds similar themes. Alluding to Stendhal's remark that prose (specifically, the prose of the serious novelist) "is concerned with giving a clear and precise idea of the movements of the spirit," Pound urges that modern poetry must adopt the same objective. In advocating this "new sort" of poetry, Pound tells us, he is really doing nothing except advocating an "old sort," a poetry with the requisite sharpness and immediacy to engage a worthy audience:

> And if we cannot attain to such a poetry, *noi altri poeti*, for God's sake let us shut up. Let us "give up, go down," etcetera, let us acknowledge that our art, like the art of dancing in armour, is out of date and out of fashion. Or let us go to our ignominious ends knowing that we have strained at the cords, that we have spent our strength in trying to pave the way for a new sort of poetic art—it is not a new sort but an old sort—but let us know that we have tried to make it more nearly possible for our successors to recapture this art. To write a poetry that can be carried as a communication between intelligent men.

Pound also stresses, with Eliot and Ford, that poetry will not recover from its Victorian maladies unless it secures the virtues of good prose. Pound makes this point not only in "The Serious Artist," but also in his 1929 "How to Read" essay, in which he observes that in the nineteenth century "the serious art of writing 'went over to prose.'" The modern poet must in consequence emulate, Pound urges, the scrupulosity and careful workmanship of the modern novelist if poetry is to recover a central position in imaginative literature. No less emphatic on this subject is Pound's 1914 article for *Poetry* on Ford's verse. Here, Pound praises Ford for trying to bring the language of verse up to date; and he argues that, if modern poets wish to refresh their art, they would do well to follow Ford's attempt to integrate real speech and real life into poetry. Pound hails Ford's "On Heaven" as the "best poem yet written in 'the twentieth century fashion,'" and concludes his consideration of Ford by saying: "I find him significant and revolutionary because of his insistence upon clarity and precision, upon the prose tradition; in brief, upon efficient writing—even in verse."

With respect to free verse, Pound presents ideas similar to Eliot's and Ford's. Indeed, the clearest portion of the "Re Vers Libre" section of Pound's "Retrospect" essay is the one-sentence paragraph, "Eliot has said the thing very well when he said, 'No *vers* is *libre* for the man who wants to do a good job.'" Pound also cites

Eliot's dictum in his review of *Prufrock and Other Observations for Poetry* in 1917, and here Pound suggests, as Eliot does, that distinctions between formal and free verse are insignificant compared to distinctions between good and bad writing. "Conviction as to the rightness or wrongness of *vers libre*," says Pound at the start of that section of his review devoted to Eliot's versification, "is no guarantee of a poet." This notion in turn appears to underlie the "Credo" section of the "Retrospect" essay, in which Pound affirms, evidently referring to formal and free verse: "I believe in technique as the test of a man's sincerity, in law when it is ascertainable; in the trampling down of every convention that impedes or obscures the determination of the law, or the precise rendering of the impulse."

Most literary revolutions are led, as the modern one was, by poets who feel that poetry has grown pompous and must be refashioned so that it can speak directly and truly of life. Yet in breaking with traditional meter to achieve reformation, the modern movement is unique. To establish both the way the modern revolution resembled earlier revolutions and the way it differed from them in its identification of outmoded idiom with meter and in its advocacy of a poetry "free" of conventional versification, we should now turn to the two ancient literary innovators mentioned above, Euripides and Horace, and to the two English ones to whom Eliot appeals, Dryden and Wordsworth.

Though Euripides did not engage (as far as we know) in literary criticism, the fact that he consciously revolutionized tragedy at the end of the fifth century B.C. is borne out in the testimony of subsequent ancient writers. It is equally apparent that the two traits that most marked his innovations are traits we associate with the twentieth-century modernists. First, Euripides objected to the heroic model of previous tragedy and insisted on presenting his characters and their world in a "realistic" manner, however much such a presentation involved what traditionalists considered to be qualities inappropriate to tragic drama. Second, he rejected the elevated rhetoric that had characterized tragic style since Aeschylus' time and wrote rather in a style incorporating the ordinary speech of his day. The first of these traits is noted by, among others, Dio Chrysostom (*Oration,* 52) and Diogenes Laertius (*Lives,* 4.5.6 [Crantor]). It is noted as well by Aristotle (*Poetics,* 1460b33–34), who records that "Sophocles said that he portrayed people as they ought to be and Euripides portrayed them as they are." The second of these traits, the colloquial novelty of Euripides' diction, receives comment from Longinus (*On the Sublime,* 40.2) and from Aristotle (*Rhetoric,* 3.2.5) in his discussion of art-which-hides-art. "Art is cleverly concealed when the speaker chooses his words from ordinary language (*eiothuias dialektou*) and puts them together like Euripides, who was the first to show the way."

Even if we lacked the evidence of such commentators, we would still have testimony about Euripides' innovations and about the controversy they excited. This additional testimony is supplied by Aristophanes' *Frogs,* which provides perhaps the earliest extended examination of a literary revolution and several lines of which, interestingly, Ford uses as an epigraph to "The Battle of the Poets" essay in *Thus to Revisit.* The second half of *The Frogs* consists of a formal debate, with Dionysus serving as judge, between Aeschylus and Euripides—the former cast in the role of the somewhat stodgy defender of older conventions, the latter cast in the role of the wily and newfangled parvenu. The debate takes place at Pluto's palace in Hades, where Aeschylus, who has long occupied the honorary Chair of Tragedy, finds his position challenged by the arrival of the recently deceased Euripides. (Aristophanes' play was first staged in 405 B.C., the year after Euripides' death.) And the charges which Euripides levels at the older Aeschylus, and the terms with which Euripides justifies his own innovations, strikingly resemble statements made by the leaders of the modern revolution in poetry.

For example, Euripides criticizes Aeschylus as bombastic (*kompophakelorremona*, "boast-bundle-phrased") (839) and argues that Aeschylus' tragedies are works of an overly poetical impostor (*alazon*) (907ff.). So inflated is Aeschylus' style, Euripides says (926), that it is at times downright unintelligible (*agnota*); and he alleges that, under Aeschylus' influence, tragedy grew into a state of sickly bloating (*oidousan*), which, however, has since been alleviated by strong doses of modernity (939ff.). "When I took over Tragedy from you," Euripides' remarks run in David Barrett's translation, "the poor creature was in a dreadful state. Fatty degeneration of the Art. All swollen up with high-falutin' diction. I soon got her weight down, though: put her on a diet of particles, with a little finely chopped logic (taken peripatetically), and a special decoction of dialectic, cooked up from books and strained to facilitate digestion."

As for his own "new" style, Euripides boasts that he did not rely on the grandiose and fabulous (959). Instead, "I wrote about familiar things (*oikeia pragmat' eisagon*), things the audience knew about." Nor did he bludgeon the audience with big words or befuddle them with resonant obscurities; no, he spoke in "human terms" (*phrazein anthropeios*, "language man to man") (1058). Euripides adds that he avoided inane ornament or "padding" (*stoiben*) (1178) and that his writing was "clear" (*saphes*) and "subtle" (*leptos*). Indeed, when Euripides speaks of the way he "reduced" tragedy (941), the term he employs, *ischnana*, indicates not only "spare," but suggests the *ischnos charakter* of the classical plain style itself, of which he was one of the founders. That Euripides ultimately loses the debate—Dionysus favoring Aeschylus because he is a sounder ethical guide than his more stylistically sophisticated rival—does not concern us here. What is important is the similarity between Euripides' ideas and practices and those of such modern innovators as Eliot, Ford, and Pound.

Issues like those raised by Euripides' work appear in Horace's literary epistles. It would be wrong to call Horace a Euripidean figure, since Horace repeatedly urges that poetry should possess both moral concern and technical finesse, and he seeks to heal the kinds of breaches between ethics and aesthetics depicted in *The Frogs*. Nevertheless, Horace staunchly opposes the literary conservatism of his time. As he says in his epistle to Augustus, "I am impatient that any work is censured, not because it is thought to be coarse or inelegant in style, but because it is modern (*nuper*). . . . If novelty (*novitas*) had been as offensive to the Greeks as it is to us, what in these days would be ancient?" (*Epistles*, 2.1.76–77; 90–91).

Horace insists furthermore that poetry should assimilate contemporary usage. Poetic diction is not, he urges, a static and time-hallowed dialect. It must change as language changes and must stay related to living speech. For instance, in the second of his Epistles to Julius Flores (2.2), Horace contends (115–19) that the poet is at liberty to renew and alter the language of verse when the need arises: "Terms long lost in darkness the good poet will unearth for the people's use and bring into the light. . . . New ones he will adopt which Use has fathered and brought forth (*quae genitor produxerit usus*)." And he expiates on this point in Epistle 2.3, *The Art of Poetry*: "All mortal things shall perish, much less shall the glory and glamour of speech endure and live. Many terms that have fallen out of use shall be born again, and those shall fall that are now in repute, if Usage so will it (*si volet usus*), in whose hands lies the judgment, the right and the rule of speech" (68–72).

In *The Art of Poetry*, Horace also contends, as does Eliot in his Milton essay, that periodic renovations of poetic diction are necessary and healthy for verse. Just as Eliot speaks of the modernists' desire to employ "words and phrases which had not been used in poetry before," so Horace affirms: "If haply one must betoken abstruse things by novel terms, you will have a chance to fashion words never heard of by the kilted Cethegi [ancient Romans], and license will be granted, if used with modesty; while words, though new and of recent make, will win acceptance, if they spring from a Greek fount and are drawn therefrom but sparingly" (48–53). And in the same way that Eliot maintains, in his essay on Swinburne, that a poet should be free to seek language "to digest and express new objects, new groups of objects, new feelings, new aspects," so Horace urges that poets should be allowed to import into their works novel terms to treat contemporary subjects: "And why should I be grudged the right of adding, if I can, my little fund, when the tongue of Cato and of Ennius has enriched our mother-speech and brought to light new terms (*nova nomina*) for things? It has ever been, and ever will be, permitted to issue words stamped with the mint-mark of the day" (55–59).

Horace's attitudes resemble those of the twentieth-century modernists in another respect. As well as resisting stultified idiom, he urges that prosaic speech can be serviceably deployed in verse and that plain diction, adroitly controlled, is preferable to a continually elevated style. In an early satire (1.4), he explicitly refers to his diction as being "akin to prose (*sermoni propriora*)" (42), and comments that if his satirical poems were deprived of their "regular beat and rhythm (*tempora certa modosque*)" (58), they would scarcely retain any poetic features whatever. Though such remarks may sound self-deprecatory, they are also partly ironic; and in the more mature setting of *The Art of Poetry*, Horace argues that when simple speech possesses *iunctura* (a skillful weaving together of words), *calliditas* (an artful dexterity of arrangement), and *urbanitas* (an engaging refinement of manner), it can achieve effects unattainable in a grander manner. It can deal, without exaggeration or affectation, with life as it is actually lived.

Discussing dramatic writing specifically, Horace contends in *The Art of Poetry* that the poet who masters the tools of his trade should then "look to life and manners for a model, and draw from thence living words (*viva voces*)." Such a poetry may seem "without force and art (*sine pondere et arte*)," but it nevertheless "gives the people more delight and holds them better than verses void of thought, and sonorous trifles (*verses inopes rerum nugaeque canorae*)" (318–23). Speaking, in an earlier passage, of the quality of *iunctura*, Horace makes much the same argument in a more personal manner: "My aim shall be poetry so moulded from the familiar that anybody may hope for the same success, may sweat much and yet toil in vain when attempting the same: such is the power of order and connexion, such the beauty that may crown the commonplace" (240–43).

Horace appreciates the middle and high styles, skillfully used; for that matter, he employs them himself in his *Odes*. Yet he seems to share Eliot's view that "diction should become assimilated to cultivated contemporary speech, before aspiring to the elevation of poetry." Until one can manage plain diction well, one will not be able to ascend to the middle or high style.

Dryden, too, prizes an unaffected and contemporary poetic idiom. Indeed, this aspect of Dryden provides the governing theme of the three BBC lectures on Dryden which Eliot delivered in 1931 and in which Eliot observed: "What Dryden did, in fact, was to reform the language, and devise a natural, conversational style of speech in verse in place of an artificial and decadent one. . . . He restored English verse to the condition of speech."

Dryden's concern with naturalness appears in two of his earliest and best-known critical pieces, his 1664 dedication of *The Rival Ladies* to the Earl of Orrery and his *Essay of Dramatic Poetry*, which was composed in 1665/66 and published in 1668. In his dedication to *The Rival Ladies*, Dryden advocates a poetry that has "the negligence of prose." Dryden is using the term "negligence," we should note, not in the sense of "carelessness," but in the sense in which Cicero uses the word in his definition of the plain style—in the sense of "uncosmetically attractive." "There is such a thing even as a careful negligence (*neglegentia*)," writes Cicero. "Just as some women are said to be handsomer when unadorned—this very lack of ornament becomes them—so this plain style gives pleasure even when unembellished: there is something in both cases which lends greater charm, but without showing itself" (*Orator*, 78). Inasmuch as *The Rival Ladies* is not only in meter, but in rhyme, and inasmuch as some critics of Dryden's day were arguing that rhymed dramatic verse was stilted, Dryden is interested in making the point that rhyme can be harmonized with, as he puts it, "ordinary speaking." Infelicities may occur, Dryden concedes, when a poet uses rhyme ineptly. When rhyme is expertly employed, however, "the first word in the verse seems to beget the second, and that the next, till that becomes the last word in the line which, in the negligence of prose, would be so." And when used in this happy manner, Dryden continues, "rhyme has all the advantages of prose besides its own."

The virtues of natural style are discussed at greater length in the *Essay of Dramatic Poesy*. Among the many topics the four disputants in the dialogue examine are the condition of English verse in the immediately preceding age and the direction in which contemporary verse might profitably move. And Eugenius, one of the two characters who voice Dryden's views, makes statements resembling those made by Eliot, Ford, and Pound. For one thing, Eugenius argues that the metaphysical poetry so popular with the previous generation is hopelessly affected. Speaking of John Cleveland's work, Eugenius suggests that using words in an odd or distorted manner may be permissible on occasion, but "to do this always, and never be able to write a line without it, though it may be admired by some few pedants, will not pass" with discriminating readers. Eugenius then contrasts truly fine writing, which speaks "easily" (without peculiarity or strain) to a wide audience, with Cleveland's: "Wit is best conveyed to us in the most easy language; and is most to be admired when a great thought comes dressed in words so commonly received that it is understood by the meanest apprehensions, as the best meat is the most easily digested; but we cannot read a verse of Cleveland's without making a face at it, as if every word were a pill to swallow: he gives us many times a hard nut to break our teeth, without a kernel for our pains."

In another section of the dialogue, Eugenius takes a position not unlike one Pound takes in his "Retrospect" essay. This involves the argument that the innovations of newer writers like Waller and Denham are not seditious assaults on the art of poetry, but are instead a healthy reaction against the vices of a worn-out mode; and it is noteworthy that at this juncture no one else in the dialogue, not even the hidebound and cantankerous Crites, opposes Eugenius. On the contrary, Dryden reports, "Every one was willing to acknowledge how much our poesy is improved by the happiness of some writers yet living, who first taught us to mould our thoughts into easy and significant words, to retrench the superfluities of expression, and to make our rhyme so properly a part of the verse that it should never mislead the sense, but itself be led and governed by it."

As well as recommending naturalness of style and (to use Pound's phrase) "efficient writing" in verse, Dryden is a champion of the literature of his nation and his time. Much of the *Essay of Dramatic Poesy* concerns the Quarrel of the Ancients and the Moderns, which had begun in Italy in the fifteenth century and which continued in England and France down into the eighteenth; and Dryden, though respectful of the achievements of the Greeks and Romans, defends the claims of the moderns. Modern English dramatists especially, Dryden feels, deserve credit for the originality of their plots and the "just and lively image of human nature" they present. Eugenius and his ally (for the most part) Neander point out that ancient playwrights recycled the same stories again and again, and did not exhibit the entertaining and realistic varieties of mood found in many modern dramas. And if it would be an exaggeration to portray Dryden's views in terms of the Poundian program of "Make It New," he nevertheless values the contemporary in many of the ways that Pound, Eliot, and Ford do.

Before moving to the final section of this essay, I will briefly consider Wordsworth. In the preface to the second edition of *Lyrical Ballads*, Wordsworth announces that his work is a reaction against "the gaudiness and inane phraseology of many modern writers" and against "POETIC DICTION," which he characterizes as "arbitrary and capricious habits of expression." Such habits, he suggests, are connected with another literary vice, this being the turning aside from real experience in order "to trick out or to elevate nature." Of his own poetry, Wordsworth says that his object in writing it was "to choose incidents and situations from common life, and to relate or describe them, throughout, as far as was possible in a selection of language really used by men." Wordsworth also informs us that his verse involves a belief that "ordinary things should be presented to the mind." And the poet should not dwell, Wordsworth adds, in a private lexicon and among a circumscribed set of "poetical" subjects. Rather, the poet's work should partake of a "general sympathy," and the poet must remember that "Poets do not write for Poets alone, but for men."

Wordsworth also contends in his preface that the language of poetry should be related to the language of fine prose. He asserts of verse that "the language, though naturally arranged, and according to the strict laws of metre, does not differ from that of prose." Moreover, he argues "that not only the language of a large portion of every good poem, even of the most elevated character, must necessarily, except with reference to the metre, in no respect differ from that of good prose, but likewise that some of the most interesting parts of the best poems will be found to be strictly the language of prose when prose is well written." And toward the end of this part of his preface, he remarks: "We will go further. It may be safely affirmed, that there neither is, nor can be, an essential difference between the language of prose and metrical composition."

As with other innovators we have been examining, Wordsworth wants to write cleanly and honestly. Of his verse in general, he says: "I have at all times endeavoured to look steadily at my subject; consequently, there is I hope in these poems little falsehood of description, and my ideas are expressed in language fitted to their respective importance." The aim is true speech—a poetry that, free of mannerism and posturing, communicates clearly and energetically with readers.

If a reader of Roman poetry had fallen asleep in 45 B.C. and had awakened twenty-five years later to find at his bedside Horace's *Epodes* and the first three books of *Odes,* he might well have been astonished on unrolling the scrolls. The poet's material and presentation of it would have seemed most unusual. Yet the reader would have recognized the verse forms and could have traced in his mind their continuity all the way back to the misty beginnings of Greek lyric. Likewise, if an English reader had fallen asleep in 1775 and had awakened a quarter of a century later to find the *Lyrical Ballads,* he might well have been startled by the subject and style of "Tintern Abbey" or "Her Eyes Are Wild." He would, however, have had no difficulty determining that the first was in conventional blank verse and the second mainly in conventional rhymed iambic tetrameters. If a reader had fallen asleep in 1900 and had awakened in 1925 to find Ford's *To All the Dead,* Eliot's *Waste Land,* and Pound's *Draft of XVI Cantos,* he would likely have been very confused by the versification of the poems.

This break with traditional versification is what most distinguishes the modern movement, in its technical aspect at any rate. Like earlier revolutionaries, those of the twentieth century urged that poetry should shed worn-out idiom and should embody the virtues of lively colloquial speech and genuine thought and feeling. But earlier revolutionaries did not urge, to cite Ford once more, "that no exigency of meter must interfere with the personal cadence of the writer's mind or the pressure of the recorded emotion." Euripides' metrical virtuosity is legendary. Even in the astrophic monodies of his late plays (parodied by Aristophanes in *Frogs* 1331ff.), one can follow, line by line, what Euripides is doing prosodically. Horace, however innovative in his treatment of his subject matter, is a master of conventional craft. "My own delight," he says, "is to shut up words in feet (*me pedibus delectat claudere verba*)" (*Satires,* 2.1.28). To speak of Villon, to whom Ford and Pound both refer as a model, he is shockingly original; yet he writes in forms—*ballades* and *rondeaux*—that are extremely strict and that had been bequeathed to him by earlier poets like Deschamps and Machaut.

The same circumstance applies to Dryden and Wordsworth. Though a defender of modern practices, Dryden emphasizes the value of metrical composition. In fact, a common theme of his essays, dedications, and prefaces is that those who have difficulty writing naturally in verse should blame themselves and not the medium. In his dedication to *The Rival Ladies,* Dryden admits that rhyme can result in awkwardness, but adds that it does so only "when the poet either makes a vicious choice of words, or places them, for rhyme sake, so unnaturally as no man would in ordinary speaking." This argument occurs as well in the *Essay of Dramatic Poetry,* in which Neander comments that "the necessity of a rhyme never forces any but bad or lazy writers to say what they would not otherwise." That Dryden himself, later in his career, abandoned the use of rhyme in his dramatic works, is not of consequence in the present context, for he makes analogous arguments about unrhymed metrical composition. For instance, in the section of the *Essay* in which Neander discusses rhyme, he also cites a line of blank verse containing two clumsy inversions, "I heaven invoke, and strong resistance make," and remarks: "You would think me very ridiculous if I should accuse the stubbornness of blank verse for this, and not rather the stiffness of the poet." Dryden's attitude about meter seems to be summarized in a statement he makes in a *Defense* that he wrote of his *Essay* in the wake of Robert Howard's attack on it. "I have observed," says Dryden, "that none have been violent against verse, but such only as have not attempted it, or have succeeded ill in their attempt."

Wordsworth, too, defends meter, and in his preface to *Lyrical Ballads* he eloquently explains its function. He distinguishes the beneficial artifice of meter from the harmful factitiousness of "POETIC DICTION." The latter, he argues, creates a barrier between reader and poet, but the former establishes a healthy bond between them:

> The distinction of metre is regular and uniform, and not, like that which is produced by what is usually called POETIC DICTION, arbitrary, and subject to infinite caprices upon which no calculation whatever can be made. In the one case, the Reader is utterly at the mercy of the Poet, respecting what imagery, or diction he may choose to connect with the passion, whereas, in the other, the metre obeys certain laws, to which the Poet and Reader both willingly submit because they are certain, and because no interference is made by them with the passion, but such as the concurring testimony of ages has shown to heighten and improve the pleasure which co-exists with it.

Wordsworth also explores "the charm which, by the consent of all nations, is acknowledged to exist in metrical language." He discusses the happy effects of meter for the reader—the "small, but continual and regular impulses of pleasurable surprise from the metrical arrangement" and "the pleasure which the mind derives from the perception of similitude in dissimilitude." And Wordsworth speaks of the magical paradox of successful metrical composition: it is speech which is natural, yet which, at the same time, is ordered within and played off against the norm of a fixed line: "Now the music of harmonious metrical language, the sense of difficulty overcome, and the blind association of pleasure which has been previously received from works of rhyme or metre of the same or similar construction, an indistinct perception perpetually renewed of language closely resembling that of real life, and yet, in the circumstance of metre, differing from it so widely—all these imperceptibly make up a complex feeling of delight."

In view of the statements of Dryden and Wordsworth, we may find it hard to comprehend how Eliot could repeatedly justify vers libre by appealing to their authority. In a broader sense, we may find it difficult to comprehend how the twentieth-century modernists could argue that their revolution, which developed and expressed itself—practically speaking—through free verse, was just like earlier literary revolutions. Admittedly, the modernists' enterprise was, at least in its initial stages, polemical. They wanted their views heard and their verse published and read. And, like all polemicists, they may have tended to avail themselves of evidence that supported their cause and to have suppressed evidence that did not. Yet this is neither a complete nor a fair explanation of their use of the past and their desire, which was without doubt sincere, to reform poetry. We must therefore surmise that there existed additional factors, specific to the modern period, that helped give rise to free verse. Before concluding, I should like to note of several of these.

One is the influence of the modern physical sciences on our culture. Evident as early as the seventeenth century, this influence grows pervasive as a result of the technological triumphs of the nineteenth and early twentieth centuries. Increasingly in this period, one comes across the idea that art is not making the advances that science is and that art should model its methods on those of science so that it, too, can achieve demonstrable, quantitative "progress." This idea is in turn productive of the notion that art should be "experimental" and that the artist should aspire to "breakthroughs" and "discoveries." Because many of the achievements of modern science resulted from inventions or refinements of apparatus, artists of the late nineteenth and early twentieth centuries came more and more to seek novelties of technique. Pound in particular reflects the influence of the modern physical sciences, in that his literary criticism is saturated with scientific and pseudo-scientific terminology. "THE IDEOGRAM METHOD OR THE METHOD OF SCIENCE" is, for instance, the rallying cry of his *ABC of Reading*, and he apparently believed that, in heaping together the miscellaneous materials of his *Cantos*, he was following the procedure of a biologist collecting data.

Art has always been capable of novelty, but traditionally its novelty has resided in its subject matter—the ever-changing manners and morals of human beings and their societies. Then, too, art has always and necessarily shared certain values—clear-sightedness, rigor, honesty—with science. However, the tendency to model art on science and to assert that each generation of artists should do something technically new is a feature distinctly of the modern period. It is also a feature that would encourage poets to try unprecedented procedures, such as writing verse without meter.

Another factor that helped shape and sanction free verse is the development of "Aesthetics." We use the term today in discussing issues throughout literary history; I used the term in comparing Horace and Euripides. But the term did not even exist in its current sense until Alexander Gottlieb Baumgarten adopted it in 1735. And not until the end of the eighteenth century, when Kant elaborated his system of three Critiques—isolating thereby the Beautiful (Judgment) from the True (Pure Reason) and the Good (Practical Reason)—was there a philosophical scheme within which art could claim independence from reason and ethics, and from, by extension, its own history. One argument Eliot, Ford, and Pound all make about their movement is that it involved, as Eliot says in his music essay, "an insistence upon the inner unity which is unique to every poem, against the outer unity which is typical." If every poem is regarded, as Eliot suggests, as an object with a unique inner unity or autonomy, it follows that every poem can have or create its own individual prosody.

Aestheticism encouraged the development of free verse in another respect. In elevating music, as the "purest" of the arts, writers in the aesthetic tradition helped produce a climate of opinion in which literary and visual artists aspired to musicality. The thesis of Eliot's music essay is that poetry has or can have a musical structure and that such a structure is superior to a metrical structure. As for Ford and Pound, they both explain free verse in terms of music, actually construing the vers libre line with eighth-notes, quarter-notes, and half-notes—Ford doing this in his preface to his *Collected Poems* and Pound in his "Tradition" essay. In this connection, Pou's famous remark that the poet should "compose in the sequence of the musical phrase, not in sequence of a metronome" is doubly significant. First, it indicates the degree to which music has, for Pound, supplanted meter as the measure of verse. Second, it suggests the degree to which meter (the root word of metronome) has come to be viewed as monotonous and inferior.

Another factor that contributed to the development of free verse is the rise and triumph of the modern novel. Though traditions of prose fiction go back at least as far as Aesop, from the time of Homer to the eighteenth century, the fiction of prestige is largely metrical. Not until the nineteenth century do we, when thinking of the finest fiction writers of the age, think to a great extent of prose writers. A constant theme of modern poets is that verse has lost much material to prose fiction and that if poetry is to recover that material, it must assimilate characteristics of the novel. In this context, Ford and Pound's assertion that verse must be at least as well-written as prose could be readily translated into the notion that verse should be written as the novel is written—without meter.

I should also mention a point J. V. Cunningham raises in an interview in the Fall 1985 issue of the *Iowa Review*. In one respect, the modernists did not understand traditional meter and confused it with a method of reading and scanning that developed in the schools in the nineteenth century. This method, which is still reflected in some textbooks, involves speaking verse lines in a heavily sing-song fashion to bring out their metrical identity:

The *hare* limped *tremb*ling *through* the *froz*en *grass*

Such reading clarifies the normative structure of the line, but obliterates natural degrees of relative speech stress within it. This method of reading sounds awful, to boot, and can produce the feeling, as Cunningham suggests it did, that metrical composition is rigid or wooden.

This appears to have happened with Pound. His remarks about the metronome, and his related imperative, "Don't chop your stuff into separate iambs," are salutary so far as they remind poets that it is incumbent on them to give their verse rhythmical life. Yet such remarks also misconstrue English metrical practice, as does Pound's characterization, in his "Treatise on Metre" in the *ABC of Reading*, of the iambic pentameter as "ti tum ti tum ti tum ti tum ti tum . . . from which every departure is treated as an exception." Good poets do not compose foot by foot, and, given that any complete articulation in English has one and only one primarily stressed syllable and a number of syllables receiving varying degrees of lesser stress, it would be rather difficult to write a "metronomic" line in English—a line, that is, of light and heavy syllables of perfectly equivalent alternating weight. Pound's ti-tumming accounts for the analytic norm of the pentameter line and for the way a student might scan or read the line to bring out its metrical identity. But the ti-tumming does not account for the infinite varieties of rhythmical modulation (and they are not "exceptions") that can exist within the conventional pentameter. Here, for example, are pentameters from poems of Shakespeare, Dryden, Jane Austen, Robert Frost, and Thom Gunn:

Prosperity's the very bond of love
Thou last great prophet of tautology
The day commemorative of my birth
Snow falling and night falling fast, oh, fast
Resisting, by embracing, nothingness

Each of these lines is orthodox, yet each has, within that orthodoxy, a personal rhythm. The method of reading and scanning to which Cunningham refers, however, obscures this quality of English meter, and Cunningham is no doubt correct in observing that the understandable hostility to the method came to be directed at meter itself.

Whatever one feels about the modern experimental movement, one should probably be concerned about its legacy. Ford, Eliot, Pound and their followers hoped that free verse would lead, in short order, to a new prosody or to a revival of traditional prosody. Yet though their revolution triumphed, no new prosody emerged, nor is it surprising that it did not. Such a development would have required the creation of a new language or a radical alteration of the existing grammatical and morphological structures of English. Metrical systems must suit the languages they serve. Iambic meters are so prevalent in English verse because they accommodate a wide range of native speech rhythm, not because a cabal of poets decided, one evening seven or eight centuries ago, to write in them.

Neither has there been, in the wake of the modern movement, a general revival of metrical composition. To be sure, a minority of poets have continued to work in meter, and there have been periodic attempts to recover traditional versification as a significant element or option of poetic practice. However, metrical understanding has declined from generation to generation. William Carlos Williams, in a 1932 letter to Kay Boyle, spoke of "the present moment" as "a formless interim," but the interim has been prolonged until it has taken on the character of a chronic condition.

For these reasons, we should perhaps be skeptical of Eliot's contention that metrical considerations are negligible when compared with the broader question of good and bad writing. As true as it is that meter alone will never produce a fine poem, even a weak poet who writes in meter keeps its traditions alive. If, however, good and bad poets alike devote themselves largely or exclusively to free verse, all sense of meter may eventually be lost.

This would be a tragedy. Fine metrical composition offers a singular appeal to the ear, mind, and memory, and can create all sorts of pleasurable symmetries and surprises. With the bass line of meter, poets can register shades of accent and tone with a sensitivity unattainable in other media; and by playing grammatical units off or against metrical ones, poets can achieve all sorts of wonderful semantic coincidences and contrasts. Even such moralistic critics of meter as Plato have acknowledged how enchanting skillful metrical arrangement is. Further, meter can give a poem a resistant grace and power. Reading a sonnet of Shakespeare, Keats, Louise Bogan, or Countee Cullen, or a metered poem by an excellent contemporary poet like Richard Wilbur or Philip Larkin, one has the bracing sense that such work is built to last. Finally, free verse will suffer—will run the risk of degenerating into mere lineated prose—if the metrical tradition declines any further. For free verse to be genuinely free, it needs something to be free from.

Eliot grew to recognize these dangers. In his 1944 lecture on Samuel Johnson, he comments uneasily on "the riot of individual styles" in modern verse, and adds, in words that anticipate what has transpired in our day: "Originality, when it becomes the only, or the most prized virtue of poetry, may cease to be a virtue at all; and when several poets, and their respective groups of admirers, cease to have in common any standards of versification, any identity of taste or of tenets of belief, criticism may decline to an advertisement of preference." And closing his Milton essay of 1947, he remarks: "We cannot, in literature, any more than in the rest of life, live in a perpetual state of revolution"; and warning against "a progressive deterioration" in poetry, he asks his audience to reflect that "a monotony of unscannable verse fatigues the attention even more quickly than a monotony of exact feet."

Were Eliot alive today, he might well feel these anxieties even more keenly. He and his co-revolutionaries had a valid quarrel with the nineteenth century. They rebelled with specific goals in view. Their experiments had a purpose. Poetry needed fresh air and fresh views. Now, however, the styles and attitudes of the nineteenth century have long since vanished, and the great majority of contemporary poets seem to be recycling the novelties of the early twentieth century. Free verse has its own values, achievements, and resources. It has enriched poetry and can continue to enrich it. But it is not sufficient, by itself, to sustain poetry as an art—as a pursuit that has compositional principles that transcend the concerns and inclinations of this or that practitioner of it. If poetry is to retain its vitality into the new millennium, poets will have to recover the metrical tradition and to restore the age-old dialectic between prosodic rule and individual expression.

Author's Note. For this essay, I have used standard editions of the writers discussed, the Loeb Classical Library editions in the case of most of the ancient writers. I have consulted W. B. Stanford's edition of *The Frogs* (London: MacMillan, 1958) and C. O. Brink's edition of the *Ars Poetica* (Cambridge: Cambridge University Press, 1971), and I should like to acknowledge particular debts to both these editors, not only for the careful texts they prepared, but for the illuminating commentaries that accompany the texts.

[1985], 1990, 2002

◂ JULIA ALVAREZ ▸
(B. 1950)

Born in New York City, Julia Alvarez spent her childhood in the Dominican Republic until 1960, when her family returned to New York, exiled because of her father's participation in a plot to overthrow the dictator Rafael Trujillo. In the Dominican Republic, Alvarez attended the Carol Morgan School. All the classes were taught in English, and even before immigrating to the United States she felt the cultural tensions that she would explore in her writing. Her knowledge of English could not lessen the feelings of displacement and awkwardness that she experienced after she and her family fled to New York. "Overnight, we lost everything," she remembers, " a homeland, an extended family, a culture, and . . . the language I felt at home in."

Yet Alvarez was nonetheless attracted to books, and her teachers encouraged her gift for storytelling. After graduation from high school in 1967, she attended Connecticut College for two years and then transferred to Middlebury College, where she graduated summa cum laude in 1971. She went on to earn an M.F.A. from Syracuse University in 1975. Married and divorced twice in her twenties, she spent her years after graduation from Syracuse moving from university to university, earning her living on one-year teaching appointments. In fifteen years Alvarez had eighteen addresses. Stability finally came with the publication of her first poetry book, *Homecoming*, in 1984, the advent of a tenured job at Middlebury College in 1988, and a third marriage in 1989. Since resettling in Middlebury, she has published novels, additional books of poetry, and a book of essays, *Something to Declare* (1998).

Alvarez's widely read novels—*How the García Girls Lost Their Accents* (1991), *In the Time of the Butterflies* (1994), *¡Yo!* (1996), and *In the Name of Salome* (2000)—are often autobiographical, and like her poetry, they explore her dual cultural heritage. In her essay "Of Maids and Other Muses" she contemplates her sources of inspiration, finding them in the tradition of English and American poetry, and above all in her Latin heritage, especially among the women who encouraged her during her childhood:

English was my second language. I was a newcomer in this literature, tradition, way of making meaning. And so I overcompensated for my feeling of literary and linguistic insecurity by making myself learn and master everything I could about the tradition. There is a saying in the old country that the traitor always wears the best patriot uniform.

Alvarez's poetry often concerns domestic matters distinguished by her unaffected use of traditional forms, as in the sonnet sequence "33" written when the poet was thirty-three years old. *The Homecoming* uses as its epigraph a statement from the Polish poet Czeslaw Milosz: "Language is the only homeland." And in *The Other Side/El Otro Lado* (1995) Alvarez uses both of her languages and multiple forms to explore the complexities of her family heritage.

"So Much Depends," the essay reprinted below, appeared in Alvarez's prose collection *Something to Declare* (1998). As that title suggests, the essays are about borders and immigration, bilinguality and divided loyalties, speech and silence. Here Alvarez mixes memoir with literary criticism, reading William Carlos Williams as one key to *becoming* American.

◂◦▸━━◀━━◂◦▸

SO MUCH DEPENDS

I remember discovering William Carlos Williams's poetry in my anthology of American literature over twenty-five years ago. It was love at first sight:

So much depends
upon

a red wheel
barrow

glazed with rain
water

beside the white
chickens.

"What a curious syntactic structure," our teacher noted, " 'So much depends . . .' So much *what* is depending on the wheelbarrow and the chickens?"

But the syntax seemed familiar to me. I had heard a similar expression all my life, *todo depende*. Everything depended on, well, something else. It was our Spanish form of "maybe."

Scanning a collection of his poetry in the library, I found a half-dozen Spanish titles—even a volume named *Al Que Quiere!* But there was no mention in my anthology of the why of these Hispanicisms. It was only later that I came to find out

Originally published as "On Finding a Latino Voice," *Washington Post Book World* 14 May 1995. Collected in *Something to Declare* (Chapel Hill, North Carolina: Algonquin Books of Chapel Hill, 1998) 163–170.

that William Carlos Williams was—as he would be termed today—"a Hispanic American writer."

His mother was Puerto Rican—upper-class Puerto Rican with a Paris education, but still. . . . She married an Englishman who seems to have lived everywhere, including some years in the Dominican Republic, my homeland. The two moved to Rutherford, New Jersey, where they raised their two sons. Growing up, William Carlos never had a close association with Puerto Rico. In fact, he did not see the islands until he was almost sixty and had a deep longing to try to understand what his own roots really were. His was an American boyhood indeed, but with the powerful and sometimes baffling presence of his mother, who spoke Spanish in the home and who terrified and embarrassed her sons by going into trances and speaking to her Caribbean dead, especially while she played the organ during Unitarian church services. Williams did not phrase or even seem to understand his divided loyalties in terms of ethnicity. Still, as a first-generation American, he often felt "the islandness in him, his separateness," as his biographer Whittemore has described it.

His friend Ezra Pound didn't help things. "What the hell do you a blooming foreigner know about the place," Pound taunted. "My dear boy, you have never felt the swoop of the PEEraries." But it was Pound who jumped ship and fled to Europe in search of classical models. Williams stayed, in New Jersey, and struggled to set down "the good old U.S.A."

As an adolescent immigrant, I, like Williams, wanted to be an American, period. I was embarrassed by the ethnicity that rendered me colorful and an object of derision to those who would not have me be a part of their culture, at least not without paying the dues of becoming like them. And I was encouraged to assimilate by my parents and teachers, by the media and the texts I studied in school, none of which addressed the issues I was facing in my secret soul. So much of who I was seemed to have no place in this world and culture—and so I started to have a secret life, which no doubt contributed to my becoming a writer.

My family did not move into a comunidad in this country, where a concentration of Dominicans or Latinos would have kept alive and affirmed the values and customs, the traditions and language that were an increasingly hidden part of me. Jamaica Estates was a pretentious—back then, anyway—area in Queens for solidly middle-class families and for up-and-coming white European immigrants—many Germans, some Italians, some Jews, and a couple of us Hispanics.

My father did have the other comunidad in his work life. Every morning he left the Estates for his Centro Médico in a Latino area in Brooklyn, a place my mother called, "a bad neighborhood." The summers I worked at his office, I drove with him through block after block of brick apartment buildings bracketed by intricate fire escapes, a city of concrete. But the lively and populous street life was a lot more enticing than the lonely, deserted lawns back in Queens. At the Centro Médico the nurses were all Dominicans or Puerto Ricans with sometimes an Argentinian or Chilean lording it over us with her Castillian lisp and blond hair. No matter. Papi was boss, and I was la hija del doctor. His patients brought me pastelitos and dulce leche. The guys flirted with me, tossing out their piropos. ("Ay, look at those curves, and my brakes are shot!") I loved the place, though I admit, too, that I was very aware of my difference. At night, we drove back home to a welcome of sprinklers waving their wands of water over our lookalike lawns. We were of another class, in other words, a difference that was signaled the minute I walked into our house and my mother instructed me to wash my hands. "You don't know what germs you picked up over there."

But any comunidad we might have joined would have been temporary anyway. Worried about the poor reception and instruction we were receiving at the local school, my mother got scholarships for us to go away to school. We were cast adrift in the explosion of American culture on campuses in the late sixties and early seventies. Ethnicity was in. My classmates smoked weed from Mexico and Colombia and hitchhiked down the Pan American highway and joined the Peace Corps after college to expiate the sins of their country against underdeveloped and overexploited countries like, yes, the Dominican Republic. More than once I was asked to bear witness to this exploitation, and I, the least victimized of Dominicans, obliged. I was claiming my roots, my Dominicanness with a vengeance.

But what I needed was to put together my Dominican and American selves. An uncle who lived in New York gave me a piece of advice embedded in an observation: "The problem with you girls is that you were raised thinking you could go back to where you came from. Don't you see, you're here to stay?"

He was right; we were here to stay. But the problem was that American culture, as we had experienced it until then, had left us out, and so we felt we had to give up being Dominicans to be Americans. Perhaps in an earlier wave of immigration that would have sufficed—a good enough tradeoff, to leave your old country behind for the privilege of being a part of this one. But we were not satisfied with that. The melting pot was spilling over, and even Americans were claiming and proclaiming, not just their rights, but the integrity of their identities: Black is Beautiful, women's rights, gay rights.

What finally bridged these two worlds for me was writing. But for many years, I didn't have a vocabulary or context to write about the issues I had faced or was facing. Even after I discovered female models and found my own voice as a woman writer, I did not allow my "foreignness" to show. I didn't know it could be done. I had never seen it done. I had, in fact, been told it couldn't be done. One summer at Bread Loaf, a poet stated categorically that one could write poetry only in the language in which one had first said *Mother*. Thank God, I had the example of William Carlos Williams to ward off some of the radical self-doubt this comment engendered.

How I discovered a way into my bicultural, bilingual experience was paradoxically not through a Hispanic American writer, but an Asian American one. Soon after it came out, I remember picking up *The Woman Warrior* by Maxine Hong Kingston. I gobbled up the book, and then went back to the first page and read it through again. She addressed the duality of her experience, the Babel of voices in her head, the confusions and pressures of being a Chinese American female. It could be done!

With her as my model, I set out to write about my own experience as a Dominican American. And now that I had a name for what I had been experiencing, I could begin to understand it as not just my personal problem. I combed the bookstores and libraries. I discovered Latino writers I had never heard of: Piri Thomas, Ernesto Galarza, Rudolfo Anaya, José Antonio Villareal, Gary Soto. But I could not find any women among these early Latino writers.

The eighties changed all that. In 1983, Alma Gómez, Cherríe Moraga, and Mariana Romo-Carmona came out with *Cuentos: Stories by Latinas*. It was an uneven collection, but the introduction, titled "Testimonio," was like a clarion call:

> We need una literatura that testifies to our lives, provides acknowledgement of who we are: an exiled people, a migrant people, mujeres en la lucha. . . .
>   What hurts is the discovery of the measure of our silence. How deep it runs. How many of us are indeed caught, unreconciled between two languages, two political poles, and suffer the insecurities of that straddling.

The very next year Sandra Cisneros published her collection of linked stories, *The House on Mango Street;* Ana Castillo published her book of poems, *Women Are Not Roses;* I published *Homecoming*. At Bread Loaf, I met Judith Ortiz Cofer and heard her read poems and stories that would soon find their way into her books of poems, stories, and essays, and her novel *The Line of the Sun*. Lorna Dee Cervantes, Cherríe Moraga, Helena María Viramontes, Denise Chavez. Suddenly there was a whole group of us, a tradition forming, a dialogue going on. And why not? If Hemingway and his buddies could have their Paris group, and the Black Mountain poets their school, why couldn't we Latinos and Latinas have our own made-in-the-U.S.A. boom?

Still, I get nervous when people ask me to define myself as a writer. I hear the cage of a definition close around me with its "Latino subject matter," "Latino style," "Latino concerns." I find that the best way to define myself is through the stories and poems that do not limit me to a simple label, a choice. Maybe after years of feeling caught between being a "real Dominican" and being American, I shy away from simplistic choices that will leave out an important part of who I am or what my work is about.

Certainly none of us serious writers of Latino origin want to be a mere flash in the literary pan. We want to write good books that touch and move all our readers, not just those of our own particular ethnic background. We want our work to become part of the great body of all that has been thought and felt and written by writers of different cultures, languages, experiences, classes, races.

At last I found a comunidad in the word that I had never found in a neighborhood in this country. By writing powerfully about our Latino culture, we are forging a tradition and creating a literature that will widen and enrich the existing canon. So much depends upon our feeling that we have a right and responsibility to do this.

1998

DANA GIOIA
(B. 1950)

Michael Dana Gioia (pronounced JOY-a) was born in Los Angeles, the oldest child in a working-class family of Italian, Mexican, and Native American heritage. His father, Michael Gioia, was a cabdriver who later owned a shoe store. His mother, Dorothy Ortiz, was a telephone operator. "I was raised in a tightly-knit Sicilian family," he once told an interviewer. "We lived in a triplex next to another triplex. Five of these six apartments were occupied by relatives. Conversations among adults were usually in their Sicilian dialect." In the same interview Gioia recalled his Catholic education: "I was in the last generation that experienced Latin as a living language." Although he was expelled three times from his all-boys Catholic high school for bad conduct, Gioia graduated in 1969 as valedictorian.

Receiving a scholarship to Stanford, Gioia became the first person in his family to attend college. At Stanford he wrote music and book reviews for the *Stanford Daily* and later edited the literary magazine, *Sequoia*. He also spent his sophomore year in Vienna, Austria, studying German and music. After taking his B.A. with highest honors in 1973, he went to Harvard, earning an M.A. in comparative literature in 1975, and studied with two influential poet-teachers, Robert Fitzgerald and Elizabeth Bishop, as well as the critics Northrop Frye and Edward Said. At Harvard Gioia decided his ambitions to be a writer had little to do with an academic career. Leaving the doctoral program, he returned to Stanford to earn an M.B.A. "I am probably the only person in history," he has remarked, "who went to Stanford Business School to be a poet." Moving to New York after graduation in 1977, Gioia worked for the next fifteen years as an executive for General Foods, eventually becoming a vice president. In 1980 he married Mary Hiecke, whom he had met at business school.

Despite his arduous career, Gioia devoted several hours a night to writing poetry and essays. His poems, essays, reviews, and memoirs gradually appeared in such magazines as the *Hudson Review, Poetry,* and the *New Yorker.* His first full-length collection of poems, *Daily Horoscope,* appeared in 1986. Although the book contained poems in both free verse and metrical forms, Gioia's formal work caught the attention of critics who began debating the merits of what they termed the "New Formalism," and the volume was widely reviewed—winning both high praise and bitter condemnation from different poetic camps.

In 1987 the sudden death in infancy of his first son compelled Gioia to stop writing for nearly a year. When he resumed, he composed the darkly personal lyrics and narratives that made up his second collection, *The Gods of Winter* (1991), which was also published in England where it was chosen as the main selection by the Poetry Book Society. A decade passed before the publication of his third book of poems, *Interrogations at Noon* (2001), along with his verse libretto for *Nosferatu* (2001), an opera by neoromantic composer Alva Henderson.

In 1992 Gioia left business to become a full-time writer. Although he has occasionally taught as a visiting poet at universities and colleges, including Johns Hopkins, Wesleyan, Sarah Lawrence, Mercer, and Colorado College, he has never taken a full-time academic appointment. Instead, he has modeled his new life after the careers of public intellectuals of an earlier era—writing, reviewing, editing, and lecturing. In 1996 he returned to California and now lives in Santa Rosa. Since leaving the business world, Gioia has published many other books, including translations from Italian, German, and Latin and numerous anthologies he has coauthored with the poets X. J. Kennedy and R. S. Gwynn. He is also the music critic for *San Francisco* magazine and a commentator on American culture for BBC Radio.

To many readers Gioia is best known as an iconoclastic literary critic. When his essay "Can Poetry Matter?" first appeared in the *Atlantic Monthly* in 1991, it ignited an international debate on poetry's place in contemporary culture. Gioia's assertion that poets had contributed to their own cultural marginalization and his hope for a broad and diverse readership for contemporary poetry would reverberate in American letters for the rest of the decade. The essay later became the title piece of his critical book, *Can Poetry Matter? Essays on Poetry and American Culture* (1992), which also contained studies on Wallace Stevens, Robinson Jeffers, Weldon Kees, T. S. Eliot, Elizabeth Bishop, Donald Justice, and other poets.

CAN POETRY MATTER?

American poetry now belongs to a subculture. No longer part of the mainstream of artistic and intellectual life, it has become the specialized occupation of a relatively small and isolated group. Little of the frenetic activity it generates ever reaches outside that closed group. As a class, poets are not without cultural status. Like priests in a town of agnostics, they still command a certain residual prestige. But as individual artists they are almost invisible.

What makes the situation of contemporary poetry particularly surprising is that it comes at a moment of unprecedented expansion for the art. There have never

Originally published in *Atlantic Monthly* 5 (Apr. 1991). Collected in *Can Poetry Matter? Essays on Poetry and American Culture* (St. Paul, Minnesota: Graywolf Press, 1992) 1–24.

before been so many new books of poetry published, so many anthologies or literary magazines. Never has it been so easy to earn a living as a poet. There are now several thousand college-level jobs in teaching creative writing, and many more at the primary and secondary levels. Congress has even instituted the position of poet laureate, as have twenty-five states. One also finds a complex network of public subvention for poets, funded by federal, state, and local agencies, augmented by private support in the form of foundation fellowships, prizes, and subsidized retreats. There has also never before been so much published criticism about contemporary poetry; it fills dozens of literary newsletters and scholarly journals.

The proliferation of new poetry and poetry programs is astounding by any historical measure. Just under a thousand new collections of verse are published each year, in addition to a myriad of new poems printed in magazines both small and large. No one knows how many poetry readings take place each year, but surely the total must run into the tens of thousands. And there are now about 200 graduate creative writing programs in the United States, and more than a thousand undergraduate ones. With an average of ten poetry students in each graduate section, these programs alone will produce about 20,000 accredited professional poets over the next decade. From such statistics an observer might easily conclude that we live in the golden age of American poetry.

But the poetry boom has been a distressingly confined phenomenon. Decades of public and private funding have created a large professional class for the production and reception of new poetry, comprising legions of teachers, graduate students, editors, publishers, and administrators. Based mostly in universities, these groups have gradually become the primary audience for contemporary verse. Consequently, the energy of American poetry, which was once directed outward, is now increasingly focused inward. Reputations are made and rewards distributed within the poetry subculture. To adapt Russell Jacoby's definition of contemporary academic renown from *The Last Intellectuals,* a "famous" poet now means someone famous only to other poets. But there are enough poets to make that local fame relatively meaningful. Not long ago, "only poets read poetry" was meant as damning criticism. Now it is a proven marketing strategy.

The situation has become a paradox, a Zen riddle of cultural sociology. Over the past half century, as American poetry's specialist audience has steadily expanded, its general readership has declined. Moreover, the engines that have driven poetry's institutional success—the explosion of academic writing programs, the proliferation of subsidized magazines and presses, the emergence of a creative writing career track, and the migration of American literary culture to the university—have unwittingly contributed to its disappearance from public view.

To the average reader, the proposition that poetry's audience has declined may seem self-evident. It is symptomatic of the art's current isolation that within the subculture such notions are often rejected. Like chamber-of-commerce representatives from Parnassus, poetry boosters offer impressive recitations of the numerical growth of publications, programs, and professorships. Given the bullish statistics on poetry's material expansion, how does one demonstrate that its intellectual and spiritual influence has eroded? One cannot easily marshal numbers, but to any candid observer the evidence throughout the world of ideas and letters seems inescapable.

Daily newspapers no longer review poetry. There is, in fact, little coverage of poetry or poets in the general press. From 1984 until this year the National Book

Awards dropped poetry as a category. Leading critics rarely review it. In fact, virtually no one reviews it except other poets. Almost no popular collections of contemporary poetry are available except those, like the *Norton Anthology*, targeting an academic audience. It seems, in short, as if the large audience that still exists for quality fiction hardly notices poetry. A reader familiar with the novels of Joyce Carol Oates, John Updike, or John Barth may not even recognize the names of Gwendolyn Brooks, Gary Snyder, or W. D. Snodgrass.

One can see a microcosm of poetry's current position by studying its coverage in the *New York Times*. Virtually never reviewed in the daily edition, new poetry is intermittently discussed in the Sunday *Book Review*, but almost always in group reviews where three books are briefly considered together. Whereas a new novel or biography is reviewed on or around its publication date, a new collection by an important poet like Donald Hall or David Ignatow might wait up to a year for a notice. Or it might never be reviewed at all. Henry Taylor's *The Flying Change* was reviewed only after it had won the Pulitzer Prize. Rodney Jones's *Transparent Gestures* was reviewed months after it had won the National Book Critics Circle Award. Rita Dove's Pulitzer Prize–winning *Thomas and Beulah* was not reviewed by the *Times* at all.

Poetry reviewing is no better anywhere else, and generally it is much worse. The *New York Times* only reflects the opinion that although there is a great deal of poetry around, none of it matters very much to readers, publishers, or advertisers— to anyone, that is, except other poets. For most newspapers and magazines, poetry has become a literary commodity intended less to be read than to be noted with approval. Most editors run poems and poetry reviews the way a prosperous Montana rancher might keep a few buffalo around—not to eat the endangered creatures but to display them for tradition's sake.

Arguments about the decline of poetry's cultural importance are not new. In American letters they date back to the nineteenth century. But the modern debate might be said to have begun in 1934, when Edmund Wilson published the first version of his controversial essay "Is Verse a Dying Technique?" Surveying literary history, Wilson noted that verse's role had grown increasingly narrow since the eighteenth century. In particular, Romanticism's emphasis on intensity made poetry seem so "fleeting and quintessential" that eventually it dwindled into a mainly lyric medium. As verse—which had previously been a popular medium for narrative, satire, drama, even history and scientific speculation—retreated into lyric, prose usurped much of its cultural territory. Truly ambitious writers eventually had no choice but to write in prose. The future of great literature, Wilson speculated, belonged almost entirely to prose.

Wilson was a capable analyst of literary trends. His skeptical assessment of poetry's place in modern letters has been frequently attacked and qualified over the past half century, but it has never been convincingly dismissed. His argument set the ground rules for all subsequent defenders of contemporary poetry. It also provided the starting point for later iconoclasts, such as Delmore Schwartz, Leslie Fiedler, and Christopher Clausen. The most recent and celebrated of these revisionists is Joseph Epstein, whose mordant 1988 critique "Who Killed Poetry?" first appeared in *Commentary* and was reprinted in an extravagantly acrimonious symposium in *AWP Chronicle* (the journal of the Associated Writing Programs). Not coincidentally, Epstein's title pays a double homage to Wilson's essay—first by mimicking the interrogative form of the original title, second by employing its metaphor of death.

Epstein essentially updated Wilson's argument, but with important differences. Whereas Wilson looked on the decline of poetry's cultural position as a gradual process spanning three centuries, Epstein focused on the past few decades. He contrasted the major achievements of the Modernists—the generation of Eliot and Stevens, which led poetry from moribund Romanticism into the twentieth century—with what he felt were the minor accomplishments of the present practitioners. The Modernists, Epstein maintained, were artists who worked from a broad cultural vision. Contemporary writers were "poetry professionals," who operated within the closed world of the university. Wilson blamed poetry's plight on historical forces; Epstein indicted the poets themselves and the institutions they had helped create, especially creative writing programs. A brilliant polemicist, Epstein intended his essay to be incendiary, and it did ignite an explosion of criticism. No recent essay on American poetry has generated so many immediate responses in literary journals. And certainly none has drawn so much violently negative criticism from poets themselves. To date at least thirty writers have responded in print. Henry Taylor published two rebuttals.

Poets are justifiably sensitive to arguments that poetry has declined in cultural importance, because journalists and reviewers have used such arguments simplistically to declare all contemporary verse irrelevant. Usually the less a critic knows about verse the more readily he or she dismisses it. It is no coincidence, I think, that the two most persuasive essays on poetry's presumed demise were written by outstanding critics of fiction, neither of whom has written extensively about contemporary poetry. It is too soon to judge the accuracy of Epstein's essay, but a literary historian would find Wilson's timing ironic. As Wilson finished his famous essay, Robert Frost, Wallace Stevens, T. S. Eliot, Ezra Pound, Marianne Moore, E. E. Cummings, Robinson Jeffers, H. D. (Hilda Doolittle), Robert Graves, W. H. Auden, Archibald MacLeish, Basil Bunting, and others were writing some of their finest poems, which, encompassing history, politics, economics, religion, and philosophy, are among the most culturally inclusive in the history of the language. At the same time, a new generation, which would include Robert Lowell, Elizabeth Bishop, Philip Larkin, Randall Jarrell, Dylan Thomas, A. D. Hope, and others, was just breaking into print. Wilson himself later admitted that the emergence of a versatile and ambitious poet like Auden contradicted several points of his argument. But if Wilson's prophecies were sometimes inaccurate, his sense of poetry's overall situation was depressingly astute. Even if great poetry continues to be written, it has retreated from the center of literary life. Though supported by a loyal coterie, poetry has lost the confidence that it speaks to and for the general culture.

One sees evidence of poetry's diminished stature even within the thriving subculture. The established rituals of the poetry world—the readings, small magazines, workshops, and conferences—exhibit a surprising number of self-imposed limitations. Why, for example, does poetry mix so seldom with music, dance, or theater? At most readings the program consists of verse only—and usually only verse by that night's author. Forty years ago, when Dylan Thomas read, he spent half the program reciting other poets' work. Hardly a self-effacing man, he was nevertheless humble before his art. Today most readings are celebrations less of poetry than of the author's ego. No wonder the audience for such events usually consists entirely of poets, would-be poets, and friends of the author.

Several dozen journals now exist that print only verse. They don't publish literary reviews, just page after page of freshly minted poems. The heart sinks to see so many poems crammed so tightly together, like downcast immigrants in steerage. One can easily miss a radiant poem amid the many lackluster ones. It takes tremendous effort to read these small magazines with openness and attention. Few people bother, generally not even the magazines' contributors. The indifference to poetry in the mass media has created a monster of the opposite kind—journals that love poetry not wisely but too well.

Until about thirty years ago most poetry appeared in magazines that addressed a nonspecialist audience on a range of subjects. Poetry vied for the reader's interest along with political journalism, humor, fiction, and reviews—a competition that proved healthy for all the genres. A poem that didn't command the reader's attention wasn't considered much of a poem. Editors chose verse that they felt would appeal to their particular audiences, and the diversity of magazines assured that a variety of poetry appeared. The early *Kenyon Review* published Robert Lowell's poems next to critical essays and literary reviews. The old *New Yorker* showcased Ogden Nash between cartoons and short stories.

A few general-interest magazines, such as the *New Republic* and the *New Yorker,* still publish poetry in every issue, but, significantly, none except the *Nation* still reviews it regularly. Some poetry appears in the handful of small magazines and quarterlies that consistently discuss a broad cultural agenda with nonspecialist readers, such as the *Threepenny Review,* the *New Criterion,* and the *Hudson Review.* But most poetry is published in journals that address an insular audience of literary professionals, mainly teachers of creative writing and their students. A few of these, such as *American Poetry Review* and *AWP Chronicle,* have moderately large circulations. Many more have negligble readerships. But size is not the problem. The problem is their complacency or resignation about existing only in and for a subculture.

What are the characteristics of a poetry-subculture publication? First, the one subject it addresses is current American literature (supplemented perhaps by a few translations of poets who have already been widely translated). Second, if it prints anything other than poetry, that is usually short fiction. Third, if it runs discursive prose, the essays and reviews are overwhelmingly positive. If it publishes an interview, the tone will be unabashedly reverent toward the author. For these journals critical prose exists not to provide a disinterested perspective on new books but to publicize them. Quite often there are manifest personal connections between the reviewers and the authors they discuss. If occasionally a negative review is published, it will be openly sectarian, rejecting an aesthetic that the magazine has already condemned. The unspoken editorial rule seems to be, Never surprise or annoy the readers; they are, after all, mainly our friends and colleagues.

By abandoning the hard work of evaluation, the poetry subculture demeans its own art. Since there are too many new poetry collections appearing each year for anyone to evaluate, the reader must rely on the candor and discernment of reviewers to recommend the best books. But the general press has largely abandoned this task, and the specialized press has grown so overprotective of poetry that it is reluctant to make harsh judgments. In his book *American Poetry: Wildness and Domesticity,* Robert Bly has accurately described the corrosive effect of this critical boosterism:

> We have an odd situation: although more bad poetry is being published now than
> ever before in American history, most of the reviews are positive. Critics say, "I
> never attack what is bad, all that will take care of itself," . . . but the country is full

of young poets and readers who are confused by seeing mediocre poetry praised, or never attacked, and who end up doubting their own critical perceptions.

A clubby feeling also typifies most recent anthologies of contemporary poetry. Although these collections represent themselves as trustworthy guides to the best new poetry, they are not compiled for readers outside the academy. More than one editor has discovered that the best way to get an anthology assigned is to include work by the poets who teach the courses. Compiled in the spirit of congenial opportunism, many of these anthologies give the impression that literary quality is a concept that neither an editor nor a reader should take too seriously.

The 1985 *Morrow Anthology of Younger American Poets,* for example, is not so much a selective literary collection as a comprehensive directory of creative-writing teachers (it even offers a photo of each author). Running nearly 800 pages, the volume presents no fewer than 104 important young poets, virtually all of whom teach creative writing. The editorial principle governing selection seems to have been the fear of leaving out some influential colleague. The book does contain a few strong and original poems, but they are surrounded by so many undistinguished exercises that one wonders if the good work got there by design or simply by random sampling. In the drearier patches one suspects that perhaps the book was never truly meant to be read, only assigned.

And that is the real issue. The poetry subculture no longer assumes that all published poems will be read. Like their colleagues in other academic departments, poetry professionals must publish, for purposes of both job security and career advancement. The more they publish, the faster they progress. If they do not publish, or wait too long, their economic futures are in grave jeopardy.

In art, of course, everyone agrees that quality and not quantity matters. Some authors survive on the basis of a single unforgettable poem—Edmund Waller's "Go, lovely rose," for example, or Edwin Markham's "The Man With the Hoe," which was made famous by being reprinted in hundreds of newspapers—an unthinkable occurrence today. But bureaucracies, by their very nature, have difficulty measuring something as intangible as literary quality. When institutions evaluate creative artists for employment or promotion, they still must find some seemingly objective means to do so. As the critic Bruce Bawer has observed,

> A poem is, after all, a fragile thing, and its intrinsic worth, or lack thereof, is a frighteningly subjective consideration; but fellowships, grants, degrees, appointments, and publications are objective facts. They are quantifiable; they can be listed on a résumé.

Poets serious about making careers in institutions understand that the criteria for success are primarily quantitative. They must publish as much as possible as quickly as possible. The slow maturation of genuine creativity looks like laziness to a committee. Wallace Stevens was forty-three when his first book appeared. Robert Frost was thirty-nine. Today these sluggards would be unemployable.

The proliferation of literary journals and presses over the past thirty years has been a response less to an increased appetite for poetry among the public than to the desperate need of writing teachers for professional validation. Like subsidized farming that grows food no one wants, a poetry industry has been created to serve the interests of the producers and not the consumers. And in the process the integrity of the art has been betrayed. Of course, no poet is allowed to admit this in public. The cultural credibility of the professional poetry establishment depends on maintaining a polite hypocrisy. Millions of dollars in public and private funding are at stake. Luckily, no one outside the subculture cares enough to press the point very far. No Woodward and Bernstein will ever investigate a cover-up by members of the Associated Writing Programs.

The new poet makes a living not by publishing literary work but by providing specialized educational services. Most likely he or she either works for or aspires to work for a large institution—usually a state-run enterprise, such as a school district, a college, or a university (or lately even a hospital or prison)—teaching others how to write poetry or, at the highest levels, how to teach others how to write poetry.

To look at the issue in strictly economic terms, most contemporary poets have been alienated from their original cultural function. As Marx maintained and few economists have disputed, changes in a class's economic function eventually transform its values and behavior. In poetry's case, the socioeconomic changes have led to a divided literary culture: the superabundance of poetry within a small class and the impoverishment outside it. One might even say that outside the classroom—where society demands that the two groups interact—poets and the common reader are no longer on speaking terms.

The divorce of poetry from the educated reader has had another, more pernicious result. Seeing so much mediocre verse not only published but praised, slogging through so many dull anthologies and small magazines, most readers—even sophisticated ones like Joseph Epstein—now assume that no significant new poetry is being written. This public skepticism represents the final isolation of verse as an art form in contemporary society.

The irony is that this skepticism comes in a period of genuine achievement. Gresham's Law, that bad coinage drives out good, only half applies to current poetry. The sheer mass of mediocrity may have frightened away most readers, but it has not yet driven talented writers from the field. Anyone patient enough to weed through the tangle of contemporary work finds an impressive and diverse range of new poetry. Adrienne Rich, for example, despite her often overbearing polemics, is a major poet by any standard. The best work of Donald Justice, Anthony Hecht, Donald Hall, James Merrill, Louis Simpson, William Stafford, and Richard Wilbur—to mention only writers of the older generation—can hold its own against anything in the national literature. One might also add Sylvia Plath and James Wright, two strong poets of the same generation who died early. America is also a country rich in émigré poetry, as major writers like Czeslaw Milosz, Nina Cassian, Derek Walcott, Joseph Brodsky, and Thom Gunn demonstrate.

Without a role in the broader culture, however, talented poets lack the confidence to create public speech. Occasionally a writer links up rewardingly to a social or political movement. Rich, for example, has used feminism to expand the vision of her work. Robert Bly wrote his finest poetry to protest the Vietnam War. His sense of addressing a large and diverse audience added humor, breadth, and humanity to his previously minimalist verse. But it is a difficult task to marry the Muse happily to politics. Consequently, most contemporary poets, knowing that they are virtually invisible in the larger culture, focus on the more intimate forms of lyric and meditative verse. (And a few loners, like X. J. Kennedy and John Updike, turn their genius to the critically disreputable demimonde of light verse and children's poetry.) Therefore, although current American poetry has not often excelled in public forms like political or satiric verse, it has nonetheless produced personal poems of unsurpassed beauty and power. Despite its manifest excellence, this new work has not found a public beyond the poetry subculture, because the traditional machinery of transmission—the reliable reviewing, honest criticism, and selective anthologies—has broken down. The audience that once made Frost and Eliot, Cummings and Millay, part of its cultural vision remains out of reach. Today Walt Whitman's challenge "To have great poets, there must be great audiences, too" reads like an indictment.

To maintain their activities, subcultures usually require institutions, since the general society does not share their interests. Nudists flock to "nature camps" to express their unfettered lifestyle. Monks remain in monasteries to protect their austere ideals. As long as poets belonged to a broader class of artists and intellectuals, they centered their lives in urban bohemias, where they maintained a distrustful independence from institutions. Once poets began moving into universities, they abandoned the working-class heterogeneity of Greenwich Village and North Beach for the professional homogeneity of academia.

At first they existed on the fringes of English departments, which was probably healthy. Without advanced degrees or formal career paths, poets were recognized as special creatures. They were allowed—like aboriginal chieftains visiting an anthropologist's campsite—to behave according to their own laws. But as the demand for creative writing grew, the poet's job expanded from merely literary to administrative duties. At the university's urging, these self-trained writers designed history's first institutional curricula for young poets. Creative writing evolved from occasional courses taught within the English department into its own undergraduate major or graduate-degree program. Writers fashioned their academic specialty in the image of other university studies. As the new writing departments multiplied, the new professionals patterned their infrastructure—job titles, journals, annual conventions, organizations—according to the standards not of urban bohemia but of educational institutions. Out of the professional networks this educational expansion created, the subculture of poetry was born.

Initially, the multiplication of creative writing programs must have been a dizzyingly happy affair. Poets who had scraped by in bohemia or had spent their early adulthood fighting the Second World War suddenly secured stable, well-paying jobs. Writers who had never earned much public attention found themselves surrounded by eager students. Poets who had been too poor to travel flew from campus to campus and from conference to conference, to speak before audiences of their peers. As Wilfrid Sheed once described a moment in John Berryman's career, "Through the burgeoning university network, it was suddenly possible to think of oneself as a national poet, even if the nation turned out to consist entirely of English Departments." The bright postwar world promised a renaissance for American poetry.

In material terms that promise has been fulfilled beyond the dreams of anyone in Berryman's Depression-scarred generation. Poets now occupy niches at every level of academia, from a few sumptuously endowed chairs with six-figure salaries to the more numerous part-time stints that pay roughly the same as Burger King. But even at minimum wage, teaching poetry earns more than writing it ever did. Before the creative writing boom, being a poet usually meant living in genteel poverty or worse. While the sacrifices poetry demanded caused much individual suffering, the rigors of serving Milton's "thankless Muse" also delivered the collective cultural benefit of frightening away all but committed artists.

Today poetry is a modestly upwardly mobile, middle-class profession—not as lucrative as waste management or dermatology but several big steps above the squalor of bohemia. Only a philistine would romanticize the blissfully banished artistic poverty of yesteryear. But a clear-eyed observer must also recognize that by opening the poet's trade to all applicants and by employing writers to do something other than write, institutions have changed the social and economic identity of the poet from artist to educator. In social terms the identification of poet with teacher is now complete. The first question one poet now asks another upon being introduced is "Where do you teach?" The problem is not that poets teach. The campus is not a bad place for a poet to work. It's just a bad place for all poets to work. Society suffers by losing the imagination and vitality that poets brought to public culture. Poetry suffers when literary standards are forced to conform to institutional ones.

Even within the university contemporary poetry now exists as a subculture. The teaching poet finds that he or she has little in common with academic colleagues. The academic study of literature over the past twenty-five years has veered off in a theoretical direction with which most imaginative writers have little sympathy or familiarity. Thirty years ago detractors of creative writing programs predicted that poets in universities would become enmeshed in literary criticism and scholarship. This prophecy has proved spectacularly wrong. Poets have created enclaves in the academy almost entirely separate from their critical colleagues. They write less criticism than they did before entering the academy. Pressed to keep up with the plethora of new poetry, small magazines, professional journals, and anthologies, they are frequently also less well read in the literature of the past. Their peers in the English department generally read less contemporary poetry and more literary theory. In many departments writers and literary theorists are openly at war. Bringing the two groups under one roof has paradoxically made each more territorial. Isolated even within the university, the poet, whose true subject is the whole of human existence, has reluctantly become an educational specialist.

To understand how radically the social situation of the American poet has changed, one need only compare today with fifty years ago. In 1940, with the notable exception of Robert Frost, few poets were working in colleges unless, like Mark Van Doren and Yvor Winters, they taught traditional academic subjects. The only creative writing program was an experiment begun a few years earlier at the University of Iowa. The modernists exemplified the options that poets had for making a living. They could enter middle-class professions, as had T. S. Eliot (a banker turned publisher), Wallace Stevens (a corporate insurance lawyer), and William Carlos Williams (a pediatrician). Or they could live in bohemia supporting themselves as artists, as, in different ways, did Ezra Pound, E. E. Cummings, and Marianne Moore. If the city proved unattractive, they could, like Robinson Jeffers, scrape by in a rural arts colony like Carmel, California. Or they might become farmers, like the young Robert Frost.

Most often poets supported themselves as editors or reviewers, actively taking part in the artistic and intellectual life of their time. Archibald MacLeish was an editor and writer at *Fortune*. James Agee reviewed movies for *Time* and the *Nation*, and eventually wrote screenplays for Hollywood. Randall Jarrell reviewed books.

Weldon Kees wrote about jazz and modern art. Delmore Schwartz reviewed everything. Even poets who eventually took up academic careers spent intellectually broadening apprenticeships in literary journalism. The young Robert Hayden covered music and theater for Michigan's black press. R. P. Blackmur, who never completed high school, reviewed books for *Hound & Horn* before teaching at Princeton. Occasionally a poet might supplement his or her income by giving a reading or lecture, but these occasions were rare. Robinson Jeffers, for example, was fifty-four when he gave his first public reading. For most poets, the sustaining medium was not the classroom or the podium but the written word.

If poets supported themselves by writing, it was mainly by writing prose. Paying outlets for poetry were limited. Beyond a few national magazines, which generally preferred light verse or political satire, there were at any one time only a few dozen journals that published a significant amount of poetry. The emergence of a serious new quarterly like *Partisan Review* or *Furioso* was an event of real importance, and a small but dedicated audience eagerly looked forward to each issue. If people could not afford to buy copies, they borrowed them or visited public libraries. As for books of poetry, if one excludes vanity press editions, fewer than a hundred new titles were published each year. But the books that did appear were reviewed in daily newspapers as well as magazines and quarterlies. A focused monthly like *Poetry* could cover virtually the entire field.

Reviewers fifty years ago were by today's standards extraordinarily tough. They said exactly what they thought, even about their most influential contemporaries. Listen, for example, to Randall Jarrell's description of a book by the famous anthologist Oscar Williams: it "gave the impression of having been written on a typewriter by a typewriter." That remark kept Jarrell out of subsequent Williams anthologies, but he did not hesitate to publish it. Or consider Jarrell's assessment of Archibald MacLeish's public poem *America Was Promises:* it "might have been devised by a YMCA secretary at a home for the mentally deficient." Or read Weldon Kees's one-sentence review of Muriel Rukeyser's *Wake Island*—"There's one thing you can say about Muriel: she's not lazy." But these same reviewers could write generously about poets they admired, as Jarrell did about Elizabeth Bishop, and Kees about Wallace Stevens. Their praise mattered, because readers knew it did not come lightly.

The reviewers of fifty years ago knew that their primary loyalty must lie not with their fellow poets or publishers but with the reader. Consequently they reported their reactions with scrupulous honesty, even when their opinions might lose them literary allies and writing assignments. In discussing new poetry they addressed a wide community of educated readers. Without talking down to their audience, they cultivated a public idiom. Prizing clarity and accessibility, they avoided specialist jargon and pedantic displays of scholarship. They also tried, as serious intellectuals should but specialists often do not, to relate what was happening in poetry to social, political, and artistic trends. They charged modern poetry with cultural importance and made it the focal point of their intellectual discourse.

Ill-paid, overworked, and underappreciated, this argumentative group of "practical" critics, all of them poets, accomplished remarkable things. They defined the canon of Modernist poetry, established methods to analyze verse of extraordinary difficulty, and identified the new mid-century generation of American poets (Lowell, Roethke, Bishop, Berryman, and others) that still dominates our literary consciousness. Whatever one thinks of their literary canon or critical principles, one must admire the intellectual energy and sheer determination of these critics, who developed as writers without grants or permanent faculty positions, often while working precariously on free-lance assignments. They represent a high point in American intellectual life. Even fifty years later their names still command more authority than those of all but a few contemporary critics. A short roll call would include John Berryman, R. P. Blackmur, Louise Bogan, John Ciardi, Horace Gregory, Langston Hughes, Randall Jarrell, Weldon Kees, Kenneth Rexroth, Delmore Schwartz, Karl Shapiro, Allen Tate, and Yvor Winters. Although contemporary poetry has its boosters and publicists, it has no group of comparable dedication and talent able to address the general literary community.

Like all genuine intellectuals, these critics were visionary. They believed that if modern poets did not have an audience, they could create one. And gradually they did. It was not a mass audience; few American poets of any period have enjoyed a direct relationship with the general public. It was a cross-section of artists and intellectuals, including scientists, clergymen, educators, lawyers, and, of course, writers. This group constituted a literary intelligentsia, made up mainly of nonspecialists, who took poetry as seriously as fiction and drama. Recently Donald Hall and other critics have questioned the size of this audience by citing the low average sales of a volume of new verse by an established poet during the period (usually under a thousand copies). But these skeptics do not understand how poetry was read then.

America was a smaller, less affluent country in 1940, with about half its current population and one sixth its current real GNP. In those pre-paperback days of the late Depression neither readers nor libraries could afford to buy as many books as they do today. Nor was there a large captive audience of creative writing students who bought books of contemporary poetry for classroom use. Readers usually bought poetry in two forms—in an occasional *Collected Poems* by a leading author, or in anthologies. The comprehensive collections of writers like Frost, Eliot, Auden, Jeffers, Wylie, and Millay sold very well, were frequently reprinted, and stayed perpetually in print. (Today most *Collected Poems* disappear after one printing.) Occasionally a book of new poems would capture the public's fancy. Edwin Arlington Robinson's *Tristram* (1927) became a Literary Guild selection. Frost's *A Further Range* sold 50,000 copies as a 1936 Book-of-the-Month Club selection. But people knew poetry mainly from anthologies, which they not only bought but also read, with curiosity and attention.

Louis Untermeyer's *Modern American Poetry*, first published in 1919, was frequently revised to keep it up to date and was a perennial best-seller. My 1942 edition, for example, had been reprinted five times by 1945. My edition of Oscar Williams's *A Pocket Book of Modern Poetry* had been reprinted nineteen times in fourteen years. Untermeyer and Williams prided themselves on keeping their anthologies broad-based and timely. They tried to represent the best of what was being published. Each edition added new poems and poets and dropped older ones. The public appreciated their efforts. Poetry anthologies were an indispensable part of any serious reader's library. Random House's popular Modern Library series, for example, included not one but two anthologies—Selden Rodman's *A New Anthology of Modern Poetry* and Conrad Aiken's *Twentieth-Century American Poetry*. All these collections were read and reread by a diverse public. Favorite poems were memorized. Difficult authors like Eliot and Thomas were actively discussed and debated. Poetry mattered outside the classroom.

Today these general readers constitute the audience that poetry has lost. United by intelligence and curiosity, this heterogeneous group cuts across lines of race, class, age, and occupation. Representing our cultural intelligentsia, they are the people who support the arts—who buy classical and jazz records; who attend foreign films, serious theater, opera, symphony, and dance; who read quality fiction and biographies; who listen to public radio and subscribe to the best journals. (They are also often the parents who read poetry to their children and remember, once upon a time in college or high school or kindergarten, liking it themselves.) No one knows the size of this community, but even if one accepts the conservative estimate that it accounts for only two percent of the U.S. population, it still represent a potential audience of almost five million readers. However healthy poetry may appear within its professional subculture, it has lost this larger audience, who represent poetry's bridge to the general culture.

But why should anyone but a poet care about the problems of American poetry? What possible relevance does this archaic art form have to contemporary society? In a better world, poetry would need no justification beyond the sheer splendor of its own existence. As Wallace Stevens once observed, "The purpose of poetry is to contribute to man's happiness." Children know this essential truth when they ask to hear their favorite nursery rhymes again and again. Aesthetic pleasure needs no justification, because a life without such pleasure is one not worth living.

But the rest of society has mostly forgotten the value of poetry. To the general reader, discussions about the state of poetry sound like the debating of foreign politics by émigrés in a seedy café. Or, as Cyril Connolly more bitterly described it, "Poets arguing about modern poetry: jackals snarling over a dried-up well." Anyone who hopes to broaden poetry's audience—critic, teacher, librarian, poet, or lonely literary amateur—faces a daunting challenge. How does one persuade justly skeptical readers, in terms they can understand and appreciate, that poetry still matters?

A passage in William Carlos Williams's "Asphodel, That Greeny Flower" provides a possible starting point. Written toward the end of the author's life, after he had been partly paralyzed by a stroke, the lines sum up the hard lessons about poetry and audience that Williams had learned over years of dedication to both poetry and medicine. He wrote,

> My heart rouses
>   thinking to bring you news
>   of something
> that concerns you
>   and concerns many men. Look at
>   what passes for the new.
> You will not find it there but in
>   despised poems.
>   It is difficult
> to get the news from poems
>   yet men die miserably every day
>   for lack
> of what is found there.

Williams understood poetry's human value but had no illusions about the difficulties his contemporaries faced in trying to engage the audience that needed the art most desperately. To regain poetry's readership one must begin by meeting Williams's challenge to find what "concerns many men," not simply what concerns poets.

There are at least two reasons why the situation of poetry matters to the entire intellectual community. The first involves the role of language in a free society. Poetry is the art of using words charged with their utmost meaning. A society whose intellectual leaders lose the skill to shape, appreciate, and understand the power of language will become the slaves of those who retain it—be they politicians, preachers, copywriters, or newscasters. The public responsibility of poetry has been pointed out repeatedly by modern writers. Even the arch-symbolist Stéphane Mallarmé praised the poet's central mission to "purify the words of the tribe." And Ezra Pound warned that

> Good writers are those who keep the language efficient. That is to say, keep it accurate, keep it clear. It doesn't matter whether a good writer wants to be useful or whether the bad writer wants to do harm. . . .
> If a nation's literature declines, the nation atrophies and decays.

Or, as George Orwell wrote after the Second World War, "One ought to recognize that the present political chaos is connected with the decay of language. . . ." Poetry is not the entire solution to keeping the nation's language clear and honest, but one is hard pressed to imagine a country's citizens improving the health of its language while abandoning poetry.

The second reason why the situation of poetry matters to all intellectuals is that poetry is not alone among the arts in its marginal position. If the audience for poetry has declined into a subculture of specialists, so too have the audiences for most contemporary art forms, from serious drama to jazz. The unprecedented fragmentation of American high culture during the past half century has left most arts in isolation from one another as well as from the general audience. Contemporary classical music scarcely exists as a living art outside university departments and conservatories. Jazz, which once commanded a broad popular audience, has become the semiprivate domain of aficionados and musicians. (Today even influential jazz innovators cannot find places to perform in many metropolitan centers—and for an improvisatory art the inability to perform is a crippling liability.) Much serious drama is now confined to the margins of American theater, where it is seen only by actors, aspiring actors, playwrights, and a few diehard fans. Only the visual arts, perhaps because of their financial glamour and upper-class support, have largely escaped the decline in public attention.

The most serious question for the future of American culture is whether the arts will continue to exist in isolation and decline into subsidized academic specialties or whether some possibility of rapprochement with the educated public remains. Each of the arts must face the challenge separately, and no art faces more towering obstacles than poetry. Given the decline of literacy, the proliferation of other media, the crisis in humanities education, the collapse of critical standards, and the sheer weight of past failures, how can poets possibly succeed in being heard? Wouldn't it take a miracle?

Toward the end of her life Marianne Moore wrote a short poem called "O To Be a Dragon." This poem recalled the biblical dream in which the Lord appeared to

King Solomon and said, "Ask what I shall give thee." Solomon wished for a wise and understanding heart. Moore's wish is harder to summarize. Her poem reads,

> If I, like Solomon, . . .
> could have my wish—
>
> my wish—O to be a dragon,
> a symbol of the power of Heaven—of silkworm
> size or immense; at times invisible.
> Felicitous phenomenon!

Moore got her wish. She became, as all genuine poets do, "a symbol of the power of Heaven." She succeeded in what Robert Frost called "the utmost of ambition"—namely, "to lodge a few poems where they will be hard to get rid of." She is permanently part of the "felicitous phenomenon" of American literature.

So wishes can come true—even extravagant ones. If I, like Marianne Moore, could have my wish, and I, like Solomon, could have the self-control not to wish for myself, I would wish that poetry could again become a part of American public culture. I don't think this is impossible. All it would require is that poets and poetry teachers take more responsibility for bringing their art to the public. I will close with six modest proposals for how this dream might come true.

1. *When poets give public readings, they should spend part of every program reciting other people's work*—preferably poems they admire by writers they do not know personally. Readings should be celebrations of poetry in general, not merely of the featured author's work.
2. *When arts administrators plan public readings, they should avoid the standard subculture format of poetry only.* Mix poetry with the other arts, especially music. Plan evenings honoring dead or foreign writers. Combine short critical lectures with poetry performances. Such combinations would attract an audience from beyond the poetry world without compromising quality.
3. *Poets need to write prose about poetry more often, more candidly, and more effectively.* Poets must recapture the attention of the broader intellectual community by writing for nonspecialist publications. They must also avoid the jargon of contemporary academic criticism and write in a public idiom. Finally, poets must regain the reader's trust by candidly admitting what they don't like as well as promoting what they like. Professional courtesy has no place in literary journalism.
4. *Poets who compile anthologies—or even reading lists—should be scrupulously honest in including only poems they genuinely admire.* Anthologies are poetry's gateway to the general culture. They should not be used as pork barrels for the creative-writing trade. An art expands its audience by presenting masterpieces, not mediocrity. Anthologies should be compiled to move, delight, and instruct readers, not to flatter the writing teachers who assign books. Poet-anthologists must never trade the Muse's property for professional favors.
5. *Poetry teachers, especially at the high-school and undergraduate levels, should spend less time on analysis and more on performance.* Poetry needs to be liberated from literary criticism. Poems should be memorized, recited, and performed. The sheer joy of the art must be emphasized. The pleasure of performance is what first attracts children to poetry, the sensual excitement of speaking and hearing the words of the poem. Performance was also the teaching

technique that kept poetry vital for centuries. Maybe it also holds the key to poetry's future.

6. *Finally, poets and arts administrators should use radio to expand the art's audience.* Poetry is an aural medium, and thus ideally suited to radio. A little imaginative programming at the hundreds of college and public-supported radio
stations could bring poetry to millions of listeners. Some programming exists,
but it is stuck mostly in the standard subculture format of living poets reading
their own work. Mixing poetry with music on classical and jazz stations or creating innovative talk-radio formats could reestablish a direct relationship between poetry and the general audience.

The history of art tells the same story over and over. As art forms develop, they establish conventions that guide creation, performance, instruction, even analysis.
But eventually these conventions grow stale. They begin to stand between the art
and its audience. Although much wonderful poetry is being written, the American
poetry establishment is locked into a series of exhausted conventions—outmoded
ways of presenting, discussing, editing, and teaching poetry. Educational institutions have codified them into a stifling bureaucratic etiquette that enervates the art.
These conventions may once have made sense, but today they imprison poetry in
an intellectual ghetto.

It is time to experiment, time to leave the well-ordered but stuffy classroom,
time to restore a vulgar vitality to poetry and unleash the energy now trapped in the
subculture. There is nothing to lose. Society has already told us that poetry is dead.
Let's build a funeral pyre out of the desiccated conventions piled around us and
watch the ancient, spangle-feathered, unkillable phoenix rise from the ashes.

1992

WILLIAM LOGAN
(B. 1950)

William Logan was born in Boston, Massachusetts, the son of a marketing executive and a realtor. His family moved several times, from Boston to Pittsburgh and then to Long Island where Logan attended high school. He was educated at Yale (B.A. 1972) and the University of Iowa (M.F.A. 1975), where he studied with Donald Justice. After leaving Iowa, Logan worked as a critic, reviewing both fiction and poetry. Since 1983 he has been director of creative writing at the University of Florida in Gainesville, where he lives with the poet Debora Greger. The couple also keep a house in Cambridge, England, where they spend their summers.

Logan's first collection was a chapbook, *Dream of Dying* (1980). Written in the high style with dense wordplay, frequent allusions, and sharply pointed phrasing, Logan's poems have from the start approached personal subject matter as if armed. They overtly distrust the confessional territory most American poets take for granted. Often his poems use other people's lives—including those of historical figures—for their personal expressive ends. The poets he has most admired have often been Englishmen— W. H. Auden, Philip Larkin, and Geoffrey Hill—or Americans whose aesthetic is impersonal, like Justice and Amy Clampitt. There is something essentially dark and sorrowfully stoic about his sensibility, which is evident even from the titles of his five full-length collections of verse: *Sad-Faced Men* (1982), *Difficulty* (1985), *Sullen Weedy Lakes* (1988), *Vain Empires* (1995), and *Night Battle* (1999).

Despite his poetic accomplishments, Logan is far better known as America's most astringent critic and book reviewer. Like one of his literary heroes, Randall Jarrell, Logan is often more passionate in his prose than in his verse. Parsimonious with praise and savage with his wit, he is fiercely independent in his opinions, willing to alienate any constituency. Poet-critic Robert McDowell has accurately summed up Logan's position: "I have heard writers refer to him as 'the most hated man in American poetry,' a title one could be proud of in this time of fawning and favor-trading." Even poets who have been "Loganized," to use a private parlance among poets, by having their work raked over his fiery wit, usually admit his intelligence if not his taste. His two critical collections are *All the Rage: Prose on Poetry 1976–1992* (1998) and *Reputations of the Tongue: On Poets and Poetry* (1999). He also coedited (with Dana Gioia) the critical festschrift, *Certain Solitudes: On the Poetry of Donald Justice* (1997). Logan contributes a regular "Verse Chronicle" to the *New Criterion*.

Although Logan has written an enormous number of book reviews and pieces on individual poets, he has published only a handful of essays on general poetic topics. "Four or Five Motions toward a Poetics" was first published in the *Sewanee Review*. In this far-ranging piece, Logan considers four aspects of the contract between reader and poem. The terms he uses for these are "trust," "valence," "gesture and expression," and "armature." What gives a good poem its "seductive power,"? he asks. What allows a poet to earn "the vulnerability of his reader"?

◄•►———◄◄►———•►

FOUR OR FIVE MOTIONS TOWARD A POETICS

Like scenes from Tiepolo's Punchinello, the scenes of reading are a complication of masquerades (a complication that masquerades), and when we read we feel inducted into mysteries we have no name for. Often a sense of meaning, of the conveyance of intentions, lies half known, half intuited, just beyond the edge of the eye. If certain experiences in poetry do not have a name, by describing them I want to be obliged less for the taxonomy of a mystery than for exploring uncharted country. These are not very good names, but the name matters less than extending a finger in the right direction. "Objective correlative" is a clumsy and ridiculous name; but its use is as purposeful as saying *aardvark* or *beetle,* and that was Adam's task.

Trust. Violation of the contract between reader and poem is a violation of trust. Trust not merely names the intimate understanding of the terms the poem sets out, or the temporary credit every author is afforded until betrayed by the language (minor authors are betrayed line by line). Trust might be called significant authority within attending possibility. It is the poem's ability to proceed without distracting the reader with clumsiness of technique, while offering benefit to the reader's imagination equal to or exceeding the energy expended in reading. Trust is therefore the aroused interest (excitation of the reader's comprehending sympathies) achieved within a controlled momentum (the forward drive or narrative of the lines, aided where present by technical supports like meter and enjambment). Trust is that allowance we give to the unsayable as it is said.

When trust falters, the reasons may include provision of irrelevant matter, missed opportunities, lapel-pulling, comedies of tone, corruptions of diction, solecism, redundancy, tedium, inconsistency, sentiment, cliché, pointless obscurity, the whole panoply of which bad poetry is composed and the abyss good poetry struggles to avoid and into which it occasionally descends. What is remarkable about good poetry is how rarely we remember there *are* such disasters: in trust we forget

Published in *Sewanee Review* 107.2 (Spring 1999): 244–259. All notes are William Logan's.

disasters can occur, even if the poetry at hand never reaches the highest level of the art. Bad poetry is not a disaster waiting to happen: it is a disaster reborn every minute in the collapse of trust.

Where an author has earned the vulnerability of his reader, the reader will allow risks far beyond what he would afford a writer more expedient (or less skillful) in his authority. In such intimacy the major author may reach an apprehension beyond that of the minor author. The disasters in Whitman are everywhere sensed by the reader even when warded off by the verse, though in the verse the disasters are just as often fondly embraced. The reader never enjoys trust in his verse (except of a perverse kind)—instead the reader lives in numbed astonishment at the bad and hapless gratitude for the good. Milton is a different matter.

> When I consider how my light is spent
>   Ere half my days, in this dark world and wide,
>   And that one talent which is death to hide
>   Lodged with me useless, though my soul more bent
> To serve therewith my Maker, and present
>   My true account, lest he returning chide;
>   "Doth God exact day-labor, light denied?"
>   I fondly ask; but Patience to prevent
> That murmur, soon replies, "God doth not need
>   Either man's work or his own gifts; who best
>   Bear his mild yoke, they serve him best. His state
> Is kingly. Thousands at his bidding speed
>   And post o'er land and ocean without rest:
>   They also serve who only stand and wait."

The opening of this sonnet creates a little nest of signification, and our burrowing into its intentions while keeping the exact meaning in suspension is the action of trust. The poem must justify those significances, each against the others; and our willingness to permit that slow untangling (akin to the unveilings of meter, its intricate substitutions and balancings) is the measure and condition of trust. In a sonnet such trust moves within the language as well as the form, and appropriately Milton's sonnet concerns a matter of trust at the highest level of faith.

These lines were written in the years before *Paradise Lost*. Milton may recently have gone blind. He may have lost his inspiration. There is a difference for the conduct of the poem between physical infirmity imposed and artistic ability withdrawn, but the question is undecidable; at least, it has never been decided by critics. The conduct of trust—the conviction in the elaborating character of the language—allows such conflicting interpretations to exist in mutual apprehension, without the poem's deciding on one or the other. Either blindness (of sight or insight) is a particular of loss.

The ambiguity of the opening is mirrored by a series of linguistic ambiguities. "Spent" may mean exhausted through overwork or squandered (there is little sense of care here). This is, after all, a poem partly about money (the pun informs Wordsworth's "getting and spending"): "that one talent" refers to the parable in Matthew 25 of the man who gives his servants various sums before "traveling into a far country." Two servants invest their talents and double them. The third buries his single talent for fear of losing it. Digging it up for his returning master, he is called wicked and slothful and cast "into the outer darkness."

Our modern sense of "talent" derives from the ancient coin through the medium of this very parable: the language bifurcates thematically (toward artistic as well as monetary squander) without forcing the previous ambiguities into alignment. The specie or medium of exchange exists in a shadowy realm behind the artistry, and vice versa; and whether we take the one as symbol or the other as action makes no difference to the losses the poem was built to confide. That each supports the ambiguities is a provision of trust.

The trust required between poem and reader is partly a fiction of biblical knowledge: the poem will be obscure without a working comprehension of St. Matthew that once could be taken for granted. To that extent trust is threatened by cultural change or cultural error. But the second half of the poem offers revision: its imagery associates more conveniently with the parable of the vineyard in Matthew 20.

A householder hires laborers at a penny a day and through the day continues to hire at the same rate, some workers even about "the eleventh hour." When at evening they're all paid the same penny for toil in the vineyard, those who have sweated through "the heat of the day" protest. The sonnet's "day-labor," its "murmur" darkly echoing the laborers who "murmured against the goodman of the house," the final line's "stand and wait" that finds acknowledging repose in those "standing idle in the market place"—these are exactions of a richly insinuating language. Christ's vineyard is the visible symbol of the kingdom of heaven, entrance to which must be the unstated longing of the poem—a man who makes nothing of his gifts can hardly guarantee himself access to the God of those gifts. Milton's answer is that the parable of the talents is mistaken.

The poem like the parable implies a mystery: the mystery of Milton's disorder, like the mystery of his anxiety, is subordinate to the mystery of the desire of God. The ambiguities conceal that mystery in one parable in order to reveal it—in sidelong interpretative fashion—through another. Christ, oldest among hermeneutic interpreters, said in Matthew 13: "Therefore speak I to them in parables: because they seeing see not; and hearing they hear not, and neither do they understand." The language beneath Milton's disorder is a language of concealment, blindness, outer darkness, and a far country—language troubled in the quarrel of Milton's quibble: can God exact day-labor from those in endless night?

When the householder came to the market again late in the day and still found men "standing idle," he said, "Why stand ye here all the day idle?" They replied, "Because no man hath hired us." It is these men who later received their reward first, received their penny though they had toiled least, and they who become the subject of the lesson: that "the last shall be first," that "many be called, but few chosen."

God does not need the gifts he himself devised—this is Milton's radical answer to his own dilemma. The justice of the poem, the fulfillment of the potential whose exhaustion or waste the poet questions, is the *bearing* up under the burden of the mystery (here sonnet again echoes parable, some laborers having "borne the burden and heat of the day"—but see Christ's words in Matthew 11: "My yoke is easy, and my burden is light"). Those who stand and wait also serve their role, a more difficult role because seemingly so empty and unrewarding.

Milton's sonnet is a strange act of self-consolation, but the poem is itself a triumph of the exactions of trust—its very existence shows the talent has *not* been hidden. The poem, as a perfected object, answers the anxiety about the effect of blindness (imaginative or physical) or artistry, and is therefore a model of the purposes of trust: to convey the reader through a series of alternatives without forcing him to choose alternatives, its action itself a triumph over loss of faith. In this, trust is the reader's account of a negative capability. Milton's gratitude for the answer was *Paradise Lost*.

Trust is also a matter of assumptions left unquestioned. Part of the drama of trust is our willingness to listen to a man frame his analysis in accord with his supernatural beliefs, without his seeming to have access to the voices of heaven (only the voice of Patience, from whatever realm Patience inhabits). Trust allows a man to question his faith, and receive an answer in faith, without our breaking into nervous laughter; indeed, with our being moved in the process.

Valence. The emotional complex of any poem is affected by matters formal as well as intimate. If the lyric is a voice it is also the articulation of voice, calculated to the extent it is conditioned by rhetoric. When at the end of her villanelle "One Art" Elizabeth Bishop writes, "It's evident / the art of losing's not too hard to master / though it may look like (*Write* it!) like disaster," the imperative is the final goading toward losses hard to contemplate, a way of marking her hesitation (while overcoming the hesitation) to write the very word most difficult to admit. The sudden irruption of the author's voice within her voice measures the violence of the denial. Here the parenthesis is very much what Coleridge called it—a "drama of reason."

None of these torsions would be as effective had the form of the villanelle not *compelled* that "disaster" be the word written, that this be its final and necessary repetition—the poem could not end otherwise. Valence is the portion of meaning for which the form alone is responsible, and within the armory of valence we may include meter (and the various effects of rhythm),[1] rhyme with all the partial rhymes of assonance and consonance, and the repetitions or returns of form (most significantly, the closure of form), whether traditional or ad hoc. That the contribution of some of these may be arguable does not make them negligible. Meaning in a poem is slippery, often a function of effects of voice barely registered. Valence is where meaning inheres in form.

"Visits to St. Elizabeths" offers a striking instance of the formal contribution to effect. Where the poem is an idea, part of its meaning lies in the instance of its construction; and here the meaning is contemplated by the underlying nursery rhyme: the incremental additions of "The House That Jack Built" constitute a narrative. The poem is partly composed of, partly an editorial about, the reduction of Pound to a childlike state.[2]

This is the house of Bedlam.

This is the man
that lies in the house of Bedlam.

This is the time
of the tragic man
that lies in the house of Bedlam.

---

1. Note how beautifully Bishop handles the repetition in that final line—this is an example of the plasticity of pentameter. *Like* in the first instance is a down-in-the-mouth, unstressed acknowledgment of the unsaid; when repeated it is a shout. The stress emphasizes the anxiety as well as the telling shock of the forced comparison. In such cases valence is the meaning *only* form makes possible.
2. The house of Bedlam is a grim reminder of linguistic contortion, important given Pound's diatribes against Jews—it is the collapsed and misunderstood pronunciation of what was once the house of Bethlehem, the Hospital of St. Mary of Bethlehem.

This is a wristwatch
telling the time
of the talkative man
that lies in the house of Bedlam.

This is a sailor
wearing the watch
that tells the time
of the honored man
that lies in the house of Bedlam.

This is the roadstead all of board
reached by the sailor
wearing the watch
that tells the time
of the old, brave man
that lies in the house of Bedlam. . . .

The form conducts the meaning in collusive ways. The dozen stanzas, each one line longer than the last, record a succession of visits (the number a timely reminder of time in a poem in which watches are important): at each visit a new perception must be added, a deepening regression of the view—we see time before the wristwatch, the watch before the sailor. The stanzas represent a darkening acquaintance with the condition of madness as well as a failure of consolation in the face of madness.

That the poem *is* in essence a nursery rhyme gives the whole exercise a childlike, inconsequential air (this is a valence at work). In a nursery rhyme Pound would be a moral innocent, a victim of the hapless operation of fate.[3] Bishop toys with the inevitability of the form: each visit penetrates further the defenses of madness, as well as the defense of madness by which Pound escaped trial for treason. A moral innocent cannot be guilty of treason.

The form specifies the repetition, but stanza by stanza Bishop deceives the expectation of form by slightly varying the prior lines. Pound each time acquires new character, becoming by turns *tragic; talkative; honored; old, brave; cranky; cruel.* (Pound is never named in the poem, and this extra-literary identification renders him a figure nearly anonymous.) These variations lie within the sing-song monotony of the form, the monotony of the days and years in which Pound is incarcerated (after the opening, every stanza ends with the same flat epitaph: *lies* has an informing ambiguity here). Each of the adjectives adds to the portrait, but some subtract from the humanity—he is finally *tedious* and even *wretched* (the sequence of adjectives is important to their meaning). The penultimate pair, *the poet, the man,* suggests how divided Pound is as a figure. The other characters are referred to by the relative pronoun "that," not "who"—they are no better off than the objects.

Each visit shows the man in a new guise, but all these guises still don't make a whole man: they make a man of fragments, a shattered personality. These are the insights of form, what form and the poet's adaptation allow—valence is not just

---

3. The house that Jack, or jackboots, built? The language can be taken too far; but it invites being taken too far, because nursery rhymes trade in the outlandish and may conceal the fossils of political raillery. There was an old woman who lived in . . . a jackboot.

what form effects, but the use of form for effect. "The House That Jack Built" is a comic concatenation of accident, "Visits to St. Elizabeths" a melancholy series of discoveries, melancholy last in its failure to become the nursery rhyme that gave it shape. If Pound's self-entrapment could be treated as pure comedy, the poem would seem less like a spiderweb.

This is the soldier home from the war.
These are the years and the walls and the door
that shut on a boy that pats the floor
to see if the world is round or flat.
This is a Jew in a newspaper hat
that dances carefully down the ward,
walking the plank of a coffin board
with the crazy sailor
that shows his watch
that tells the time
of the wretched man
that lies in the house of Bedlam.

Pound's is one tragedy among others. The variations permit Bishop a narrative latitude: the mad boy, the mad Jew, and the mad sailor have their own stories (even Jews are susceptible to madness—Pound is locked up with the object of his prejudice). These modulations over the stability of form operate like the permissible variations in meter, and not only in their content but in their kind affect the emotional structure of the poem.

The form proposing the monotony that is the character of madness also offers the ground against which character may be construed. Without the form, madness would not have possessed the same descent into the repetitive intensity of the particular (the repetitions almost a form of rage, in emphasis, or mockery, or frustration), as well as the variations that invent Pound's character and the opposing and critical views of character. The nursery rhyme is a formal as well as tonal restraint, but Bishop takes advantage in each instance of the limitations of form: the form admits the accusation as well as the analysis. Each aspect contributes to meaning, and the sum of their contributions—what the form itself adds to the meaning— may be called its valence. If the substance of emotion is often deeper than what is said, it is deeper because it exploits the various opportunities form provides.

Gesture and Expression. Gesture is the visual or metaphorical representation of an object—it may be a description, a characteristic, a color, a posture. Expression is a gesture to which significance has been added. Every expression begins as a gesture, but every gesture is not an expression (poetry is filled with gestures that are not expressions). All objects in a poem make gestures.[4]

4. Marvell's *vegetable love* is an act of expression, *vegetable* compressing and giving translucence to much in the poem. It doesn't particularly matter that Williams's wheelbarrow is red—red is a visual gesture. Where the poet tries too hard to make an expression of a gesture, the result is comic overstatement or editorializing. The idea of gesture perhaps unconsciously borrows from Kenneth Burke's distinction between motion and action—an action is a motion with purpose. R. P. Blackmur uses the term *gesture* in different context. Gesture, for Blackmur, is the successful deployment of language to mean more than it says (for what it does in addition to words): "Gesture, in language, is the outward and characteristic play of inward and imaged meaning. It is that play of meaningfulness among words which cannot be defined in the formulas in the dictionary."

A sufficiently subtle criticism may draw an expression from every gesture, but as readers we are aware that in the work of many poets everything remains a gesture and nothing becomes an expression. An expression must depend, not just on the underlying flux of meaning the poem is constructed to convey, but on how each gesture fits the fabric of the form. When the seen is seeing alone, gesture is vacant; gesture is the empty form of the visual.

> Earth has not anything to show more fair:
> Dull would he be of soul who could pass by
> A sight so touching in its majesty:
> This City now doth, like a garment, wear
> The beauty of the morning; silent, bare,
> Ships, towers, domes, theatres, and temples lie
> Open unto the fields, and to the sky;
> All bright and glittering in the smokeless air.
> Never did sun more beautifully steep
> In his first splendor, valley, rock, or hill;
> Ne'er saw I, never felt, a calm so deep!
> The river glideth at his own sweet will:
> Dear God! the very houses seem asleep;
> And all that mighty heart is lying still!

Wordsworth's sonnet is a striking use of expression because each object makes such a small visual imprint. The objects are presented but scarcely described, and so depend to an unusual degree on the structure of meaning for their translation into significance. It is an unusual poem to begin with—for Wordsworth, at any rate—because in praise of the city. Wordsworth was not Johnson: he would not have felt a man tired of London was tired of life. The advantage of not being superior to your material is that you are allowed to adopt a stance of innocence.

The poem describes the city in its glory, but also registers the condition under which the city may assume such glory. Wordsworth is obviously surprised to find the city has any majesty at all—that the civilization of this world can attain the heavenly splendor reserved in his mind for the landscape. It is perhaps as a heavenly city that "Ships, towers, domes, theatres, and temples" assume a memory hauntingly biblical. The ships of Tarshish (very frequent in the Old Testament), the towers and temples of Jerusalem (and the domes of Muslim occupation, or the great dome of St. Peter's in Rome)—these are objects with more than secular definition. Those curious temples might be Christopher Wren's churches or the Inner Temple and Outer Temple of barristers. (Wordsworth specifies *temples*, not *churches*, which would have had the same metrical profile; but it is the heightened language that is biblical. Lawyers would suggest a mocking irony the poem does not possess.) *Theater* is mentioned twice in Acts—even theaters partake of Christian martyrology.

Such suggestiveness might be enough to establish those architectural gestures as an expression of meaning; but meaning must be disciplined elsewhere, and here the poet must create his expression by cunning indirection. The religious character of the imagery might not have been a prospect aroused had the poet not conjured "soul" in the second line, followed closely by "majesty." The sun rises "in his first splendour," a dawn that might be the first dawn (one of the small expressions of the poem, the list of city sights is itself a landscape, imitating the country of "valley, rock, or hill"). These hints in language are subsumed by the sudden exclamation of the penultimate line—"Dear God!" Wordsworth says. If this is not a city on a hill, it is a city whose splendors are compared to a hill.

The invocation of the deity for such a sight, just a city in the stillness of dawn, might seem blasphemous; but it serves two rhetorical ends, measuring the poet's surprise at his own reaction and delighting in the ways of a Maker for whom civilization might be a final form of glory. He was, after all, a raiser-up of temples. The final line has been prepared in the earlier personification, the city wearing the garment of morning (compare Shakespeare's "morn in russet mantle clad"). The image of houses seemingly asleep might close with the city itself asleep, but the line goes a great deal further. The city's heart cannot be lying still unless the city is dead.[5] If our attention has been prepared by the biblical cast to previous lines, we cannot help recalling the tale of Lazarus, a Lazarus who must each dawn be returned to the living.

The visual gestures are thereby consumed by an expression of meaning not isolated within those gestures alone, but prepared by the intentions of the form, the biblical underpinning to the imagery, and the contrastive nature of this particular poem set against all the praise Wordsworth had lavished on landscape. There is a final matter. Wordsworth must remain true to his own nature, a nature out of nature. For this man of the country, there was only one moment the city could be so beautiful—it had to be devoid of people.

Armature. The armature is the technical framework of the poem, consisting of the organization of meter, rhyme, or inherited form (the sonnet, say) and the organic structure of syntax and sentence (rhythm is the organic expression of meter). These latter modes of organization might be called the responsive form—the aspects not predicated by formal scaffolding. The armature includes the method of argument, the way sentences cohere or fail to cohere in progression. We might call this the poem's reasoning.

The articulation of argument might be charted from the purely logical (stopping short, perhaps, of mathematical formulae, though always with the sense of "if x, then y") to the merely associative (where beyond lies the aleatory or dissociative). No doubt many poems have a range of such logics, perhaps coexisting at different levels of organization. The deployment of reason might be suggested by saying that Shakespeare's sonnets are lyrical and logical but that Auden's are lyrical and associative, that *The Ring and the Book* is narrative and logical but that Browning's monologues, like the border ballads, are narrative and associative. The associative is the inductive response to deductive logic; in the associative, steps are left out. Modern poetry depends heavily on the capacity of the reader's intuition, his ability to bridge gaps of expression: our poetry is now excessively tolerant of the aleatory, not because we are untrained in logic, but because we are no longer willing to dismiss the illogical, or the autistic, as the inartistic.

Poems once reveled in a different organization: cunning logics exist in narrative even beneath a progression of events. In the first book of *Don Juan,* Byron sets for the reader a trap deeper than narrative. As far back as stanza 79, Julia has been thinking of platonic love.

5. Compare John Donne's letter to Lady Mrs. Bridget White: "Your going away hath made London a dead carkasse. A Tearm and a Court do a little spice and embalme it, and keep it from putrefaction, but the soul went away in you: and I think the onely reason why the plague is somewhat slackend is because the place is dead already, and no body left worth the killing. Wheresoever you are, there is London enough. . . ." And wherever Wordsworth was, there was landscape enough.

113

The sun set, and up rose the yellow moon:
    The Devil's in the moon for mischief; they
Who called her chaste, methinks, began too soon
    Their nomenclature; there is not a day,
The longest, not the twenty-first of June,
    Sees half the business in a wicked way,
On which three single hours of moonshine smile—
And then she looks so modest all the while!

114

There is a dangerous silence in that hour,
    A stillness, which leaves room for the full soul
To open all itself, without the power
    Of calling wholly back its self-control;
The silver light which, hallowing tree and tower,
    Sheds beauty and deep softness o'er the whole,
Breathes also to the heart, and o'er it throws
A loving languor, which is not repose.

115

And Julia sate with Juan, half embraced
    And half retiring from the glowing arm,
Which trembled like the bosom where 'twas placed;
    Yet still she must have thought there was no harm,
Or else 'twere easy to withdraw her waist;
    But then the situation had its charm,
And then—God knows what next—I can't go on;
I'm almost sorry that I e'er begun.

116

O Plato! Plato! you have paved the way,
    With your confounded fantasies, to more
Immoral conduct by the fancied sway
    Your system feigns o'er the controlless core
Of human hearts, than all the long array
    Of poets and romancers:—You're a bore,
A charlatan, a coxcomb—and have been,
At best, no better than a go-between.

117

And Julia's voice was lost, except in sighs,
    Until too late for useful conversation;
The tears were gushing from her gentle eyes,
    I wish, indeed, they had not had occasion;
But who, alas, can love, and then be wise?
    Not that Remorse did not oppose Temptation;
A little still she strove, and much repented,
And whispering "I will ne'er consent"—consented.

The opening opposition broods over the romantic oppositions below, the
moon's chaste exterior having all too symbolic significance for the woman whose

story is slowly exposed. Here, and in the following lines about loss of self-control, we witness the command of logical form—the action must be prepared in the narrative, and otherwise ambiguous modes of character first attended in the argument. Every advance is conditioned in the landscape of argument.

The poem therefore proceeds as a series of fulfilled propositions (it is a poem about a proposition, which makes it all the wittier). Julia is the moon-faced witness to her own chaste undoing: the loss of self-control is proposed by the poet before engaged in the meter. (The other way around and arguments would become morals.) The situation through three stanzas proceeds in just such a methodic way—and then Byron overthrows all expectation. He can't go on—he must—he can't. It's an old actor's ploy, but with it he has seduced the reader. The reader's expectation is heightened, as in any seduction, by delay. Byron's digression, his curse upon philosophers, is as calculated a device as the chapters on cetology with which Melville retards the action in *Moby-Dick*.

I can't go on is of course exactly what a girl might say—and the point of the seduction is that what we say and what we do often conspire in their opposition (it is these contraries of character that compose the initial proposition, the dark longing that underlies the moon's modest exterior). That philosophers and not poets are responsible for immorality is a charming thing for a poet to say, especially when using his accusations only to extend and intensify a poetic seduction. That the seduction is of the fictional woman as well as the actual reader is not a matter of philosophy. The poor philosopher here *is* only the go-between, between stanzas 115 and 117. A philosopher might invent lovers who shout Plato! Plato! in their ecstasies.

Much wit is properly self-referential, which is often what we mean by depth. Julia's voice is lost, and once lost is useless—here silence betrays, but by the end of the stanza even language betrays her. When we betray something, we reveal it to use the sense against itself; Julia's betrayal of one nature only reveals another, where love is an ignorance embraced and knowledge an insolence endured. There is a final little flurry of withholding, while the mighty abstractions Remorse and Temptation grapple with each other; and then comes that beautifully poised final line, rhyming significantly with *repented*. Here *ne'er consent* suddenly and irrevocably topples over into *consented*. Desire finally defeats the desire of language: language is only the conscious denial of an unconscious wish. The power of that wish, like the manner by which it has been achieved over a series of obstacles and objections, is largely the power of the logical armature whose propositions the seduction has fulfilled. The seduction is remorseless, at least on the seducer's part. We have unconsciously been given a picture, perhaps even consciously become the object, of Byronic seduction.

It is not in nostalgia that one might view the armature of such stringent reasoning—as well as gesture and expression, valence, and trust—as offering certain rigors of pleasure beyond those provided in the permissions of current verse. There is, after all, a great deal of seductive power in the saying of a name. To name these aspects of a poetics of reading is not to exhaust the complications of reading, but to push toward consciousness various elopements or escapements by which reading is often unconsciously consummated. We read as if asleep, but such a poetics is how we dream.

1999

➤◄ RITA DOVE ►◄

(B. 1952)

AND

MARILYN NELSON

(B. 1946)

In a memoir of her family life and early career, Rita Dove recalled, "Both sets of grandparents were blue-collar workers who had moved Up North as part of the Great Migration of rural southern blacks to the northern urban centers during the 1910s and '20s. My parents were the first in their working-class families to achieve advanced degrees." Growing up middle-class in Akron, Ohio, Dove and her three siblings learned that they were "expected to carry 'the prize'—the respect that had been earned—a little further along the line." With time, Dove became aware that class and race had provided hardships for both her parents and her grandparents, but she herself met strong encouragement for her talents. One supportive high school teacher took her to a book signing by poet John Ciardi, an event that helped Dove realize her own interest in writing.

Dove matriculated at Ohio's Miami University, graduating summa cum laude in 1973. A Fulbright Fellowship to Germany (1974–75) broadened her sense of language, culture, and history. On her return to the United States, while pursuing her M.F.A. at the Iowa Writers' Workshop, she met the German novelist Fred Viebahn. They were married in 1979 and have a daughter, Aviva.

The poetry Dove would write over the next decades would explore the themes of personal and national history, travel and language, motherhood and domesticity. Her first full-length collection, *The Yellow House on the Corner*, appeared in 1980, followed by *Museum* (1983), and a collection of short stories, *Fifth Sunday* (1985). It was her third collection of poems, *Thomas and Beulah* (1986), a sequence of lyrics based on the lives of her maternal grandparents, that proved a critical breakthrough. Championed by new advocates of narrative poetry, as well as established critics like Helen

Vendler, it won the Pulitzer Prize and established Rita Dove, at age thirty-five, as one of her generation's most visible poets.

Although Dove's poetry squarely faces issues of race in America, she has never felt that this was her only subject and has openly expressed a desire to speak for humanity in broader terms. The public success of *Thomas and Beulah* enabled her to move from her first teaching position in Arizona to a chair at the University of Virginia and to gain increased public notice not only as a poet, but as an advocate of poetry. From 1993 to 1995 she served as the youngest-ever and first African American poet laureate of the United States.

Her important collections after *Thomas and Beulah* include *Grace Notes* (1989), *Selected Poems* (1993), *Mother Love* (1995), a book dedicated to her daughter that melds personal experience with Greek mythology, and *On the Bus with Rosa Parks* (1999). Dove has also published a novel, *Through the Ivory Gate* (1992), and a successful verse drama, *The Darker Face of the Earth* (1994), in which she reimagines the tragedy of Oedipus in the antebellum South.

Well known as a poet of formal grace and narrative breadth, Marilyn Nelson has also brought quiet but undeniable power to poems of social conviction and spirituality. Born in Cleveland, Ohio, the eldest child of an air force officer and a schoolteacher, Nelson and her family moved often throughout her childhood. The necessity of making friends in varied circumstances may have contributed to the compassion and humor of her work. Her father was one of the Tuskegee Airmen, a famous African American squadron, and her mother's family had preserved its stories from slave times on down. Her legacy was thus one of pride in the face of adversity. When she was born her father drove a cab while her mother studied toward an M.A., but when the Korean War broke out her father was recalled to active service. Thereafter, Nelson and her younger siblings moved constantly— to Maine, California, and many points between. They were often the only black family on base, and Nelson grew up bookish and relatively protected from racism, although she experienced a few incidents that shocked her into an awareness of the prejudice most African Americans faced.

Nelson finished high school in Sacramento, California, then attended the University of California, Davis, where she took her B.A. in 1968. By that time she was also involved in the antiwar and civil rights movements, developing spiritual and political convictions that remain important to her. While working toward an M.A. at the University of Pennsylvania, she met her first husband, Erdmann Waniek. After they married, she taught in Oregon while he pursued his doctorate, then the two lived in Denmark and later Minnesota, where they both taught at St. Olaf College while Nelson worked toward her Ph.D. at the University of Minnesota. The couple eventually divorced, and in 1978 Nelson began teaching at the University of Connecticut, Storrs. With her second husband, scholar Roger Wilkenfield, she had a son and daughter.

Her first book of poems, *For the Body* (1978), which was published under the name Marilyn Nelson Waniek, involved personal and familial subjects, while her second, *Mama's Promises* (1985), grew out of an attempt to create a "black feminist theology." In her third book, *The Homeplace* (1990), Nelson went back to family stories, retelling them in sequences of lyrics, both in free and fixed forms. This book, which was a finalist for the National Book Award, established Nelson (still publishing under the name Waniek) as one of the most assured and compassionate voices of her generation. She followed it with *Magnificat* (1994), a more overtly spiritual book in which she introduced her character Abba Jacob, a Benedictine monk. She also made translations from Euripides and Rilke. Nelson's *The Fields of Praise: New and Selected Poems* (1997), another finalist for the National Book Award and winner of the Poets' Prize, revisited earlier collections but removed many of her poems from their original sequences. Author or translator of several books for children, Nelson has recently published *Carver, A Life in Poems* (2001), a sequence of poems for younger readers that is also compelling reading for adults.

Dove and Nelson collaborated on their article "A Black Rainbow: Modern Afro-American Poetry" for Robert McDowell's critical anthology, *Poetry after Modernism* (1991). In this ambitious article Dove and Nelson survey the changing course of "Black American" poetry across the twentieth century, examining its achievements, controversies, and challenges as it first confronted and then entered "the white mainstream." The article originally ended with a long interview-format dialogue between Dove and Nelson, which has been omitted from this anthology.

<hr/>

A BLACK RAINBOW: MODERN AFRO-AMERICAN POETRY

The number of Afro-American poets represented in major anthologies is relatively small; three or four may appear here and there, but to discover others one must seek out the anthologies of Black literature or find individual volumes of poetry. Literary politics have a great deal to do with social politics. Confined to a literary ghetto for many of the same reasons Blacks have been confined to physical ghettos, Black poets have created their own tradition, rooted in a song fundamentally different from its white counterpart. Modern Black poetry is nourished by the work of earlier Black poets, and draws much of its sustenance from the folk sources which have nurtured the race since slavery. These sources include Black music, Black speech, the Black church, and the guerrilla techniques of survival—irony, concealment, double entendre, and fable.

The most pervasive influence on modern Black poetry has been the idea of the audience. Black poets bear witness to the oft-quoted observation by W. E. B. DuBois that the Black American "ever feels his twoness." That "twoness" can be seen in the work of poets as a division in their address to their Black and white audiences. Most approach this division by choosing to address one or the other

From *Poetry after Modernism*, ed. Robert McDowell (Ashland, Oregon: Story Line Press, 1991) 142–46. All footnotes are Rita Dove's and Marilyn Nelson's.

group; a few choose to combine their audiences, overlooking the differences between them in a hopeful attempt to speak to the whole of the American people.

The idea of the audience has affected Black poetry in several ways: one is in the choice of language. As the work of the troubled turn-of-the-century poet Paul Laurence Dunbar demonstrated, the Black poet must consciously choose to write either in the standard English preferred by the white audience, or in what Dunbar called the "broken tongue" of dialect or colloquialism. Early in this century, Black poets tended to alternate between the two modes. The work of later poets, most especially those of the Amiri Baraka generation, continues this tendency.

Choice of language is related to a second aspect of the Black poet's view of the audience. The readership of poetry in the United States is very small; to address oneself to only a portion of that already small audience is to limit oneself severely. Those Black poets who address the Black audience often resolve this problem by writing poems intended to be performed, rather than silently read. The older tradition of the *griot,* or storyteller, has been kept very much alive by poets who perform their works on street corners, at political gatherings, anywhere they can find an audience willing to listen. Indeed, the oral nature of much Black poetry is one of its strongest identifying characteristics, and one of the reasons critics and teachers often find it difficult to discuss more than the sociological backgrounds of individual poems.

Performance poetry directed primarily to a Black audience often lacks literary polish. Free of metaphor, of simile, of literary allusion, this poetry relies to a large extent on an extra-literary convention traditional in the Black community: that of call-and-response. The poet, in the role of the caller, expects—even demands—the audience to respond verbally (or at least vocally) to words, intonations, and associations familiar to the community. As the traditional Black preacher expects the congregation to respond, the performance poet requires a sort of "Amen reaction" from the Black audience. This response is a vital part of the poem, although it is not expressed in the text itself.

Modern Black poetry has, from its beginnings in the Harlem Renaissance, incorporated elements of Black music. The blues and jazz poems of Langston Hughes, the ballads of Sterling Brown, Margaret Walker, and Gwendolyn Brooks, the gospel-song righteousness of Carolyn Rodgers's poems: all of these bear witness to the influence of Black music. Clarence Major, in his introduction to *The New Black Poetry,* points out another, less obvious influence: the emphasis of "the *beat* as opposed to anything melodic." Black poets often strive for syncopation in metrical verse, and even loose free verse by Black poets often achieves jazzlike rhythmic effects. Both Langston Hughes and the Black Arts poets of the Sixties and early Seventies learned to "worry the line" like blues singers; instead of the literary references of generic poetry, Black poetry tends to allude to spirituals, the blues, and jazz, often going so far as to mention specific jazz musicians or pop singers by name, as if to insure the place of poetry in that richest tradition of Black culture.

Of the other elements of Black culture which make their way into Black poetry, the breath units of the inspired sermon and the tenacity of faith—if not in Christianity's God, at least in the possibility of an improved future, often expressed in revolutionary terms—can be discerned. In a long and persuasive introduction to *Understanding the New Black Poetry,* Stephen Henderson enumerates several elements of what he describes as "elegant Black linguistic gesture": these include the use of virtuoso naming and enumerating, of virtuoso free-rhyming, of hyperbolic or understated imagery, of metaphysical imagery, and of compression.[1] In her *Negro Digest* essay, "Black Poetry—Where It's At," Carolyn Rodgers adds to the list the use of "signifying" (hyperbolic insult, often describing one's adversary's Mama), of "shouting" (verbal harangue) and of "du-wah dittybop bebop" (which defies explanation).[2] The spoken virtuosity of many Black poets is one way they call up audience response: It's difficult for a Black audience to hear a signifying competition or a talented shouter lay down his rap without adding, "Sock it to 'em," "Right on," or simply, "Amen!"

While many critics argue the existence of one or several Black themes, a most appropriate and encompassing understanding of theme recognizes the sense of mission shared by Black poets. Dismissing the idea that poetry does nothing, many Black poets have persistently believed that poems are tools of power. A sense of cultural responsibility prompts them to affirm the place of poetry in the struggle against social injustice. This is not to say that there is a party line of Black poetry; rather, this poetry insists that it will be heard or read by individuals who are a part of a real, larger social and political community. Whether they address Black or white audiences, Black poets, as Amiri Baraka points out, "can't go anywhere without an awareness of the hurt / the white man has put on the people. Any people."[3] Taking the side of the people, Black poetry offers them a description of life's possibilities. Even when it addresses political problems, social injustice, or personal pain, its tonal character tends to be enlivening. It draws inspiration from the survival of Black people in a hostile world and from the survival of their faith in a dream.

1991

1. Stephen Henderson, *Understanding the New Black Poetry: Black Speech and Black Music as Poetic References* (New York: Wm. Morrow & Co., 1973).
2. Carolyn Rodgers, "The New Black Poetry: Where It's At," *Negro Digest*, Vol. XVII, (1969), pp. 7–16.
3. Amiri Baraka, "Jitterbugs," *The Selected Poetry of Amiri Baraka / LeRoi Jones* (New York: Wm. Morrow & Co., 1979), p. 93.

ALICE FULTON
(B. 1952)

Alice Fulton was born and raised in Troy, New York. She earned her B.A. in creative writing in 1978 from New York Empire State College and her M.F.A. in 1982 from Cornell University, where she studied with A. R. Ammons. In the late 1970s she worked briefly for an advertising firm in New York City, and in 1980 she married Hank De Leo, a painter. In 1983 she began teaching at the University of Michigan. After *Dance Script with Electric Ballerina* (1983), her first book, she published four more poetry collections— *Palladium* (1986), *Powers of Congress* (1990), *Sensual Math* (1995), and *Felt* (2001)—and a book of essays, *Feeling as a Foreign Language: The Good Strangeness of Poetry* (1999). Among her many awards, she has received a prestigious MacArthur Foundation grant.

In her drive to freshen poetic diction, avoid cliché and sentimentality, and create "skewed domains" in her poetry, Fulton has distinguished herself as one of the most original American poets writing today. She has succeeded in challenging not only assumptions about gender roles, but also the assumptions underlying current modes of poetry such as the autobiographical, first person lyric or the experimental "Language Poem." Rather than follow any prescriptive method for writing, she mixes her techniques, so that poems of hers that appear to be autobiographical are often concerned with how the mind comes to terms with experience through language, and poems that call attention to her linguistic virtuosity through puns and sudden shifts of diction are never abstract products of the mind, but invest themselves in feeling and celebrate the quirky details that she observes in the world around her.

Although many of the poems from *Dance Script with Electric Ballerina* refer to details of her Catholic girlhood, she has voiced skepticism about autobiographical poetry, pointing out that such poems are constructs whose pose of sincerity readers rarely question. Her later books have tended more and more toward emphasizing texture and variety of language and poses that call attention to themselves as poses—dramatic monologue, poems in which several voices arise and often contradict one another, and active enjambments that make words do double duty as different parts of speech.

In particular, she often refuses to gender her speakers, forcing her readers to reconsider their assumptions about what constitutes male or female identity. Like the Language Poets, Fulton is interested in linguistic play and artifice, and also in critical theory and philosophy, although the theories most evident in her poetry and essays are those of science and mathematics. Like her teacher, A. R. Ammons, she often develops analogies drawn from these fields to explain her poetics. Fulton has criticized the narrow emotional range of contemporary poetry: "Poems of 'desire' or loss are the safest, least vulnerable poems imaginable these days. It is far riskier, more vulnerable, to allow contrarian feelings: humiliation, vulgarity, perversity, humor, et cetera—than to express loss." Whether in her poetry or her essays, Fulton's contrarian stances have tried to occupy the "inbetween" spaces. Her work defies categories and continually averts predictable solutions, so that, in accordance with the title of her essay collection, she achieves the "good strangeness" that she seeks.

◦—◀▶—◦

OF FORMAL, FREE, AND FRACTAL VERSE: SINGING THE BODY ECLECTIC

For the past three years, there's been a critical outburst against the "formlessness" of much contemporary poetry. This critical bias defines and defends a narrow notion of form, based largely on a poem's use of regular meter. J. V. Cunningham defined form more generously as "that which remains the same when everything else is changed. . . . The form of the simple declarative sentence in English is the same in each of its realizations." Hence, by changing the content of any free verse poem while retaining (for example) its irregular meter and stanzaic length, one can show its form. And if a poem's particular, irregular shape were used again and again, this form eventually might be given a name, such as "sonnet."

It seems to me that good free and formal verse have a lot in common. In fact, I'd venture to say that both are successful in proportion to their approximation of one another. Often, a metered poem contains several lines so irregular we might as well call them free. The poems of Donne, Blake, Dickinson, and Hopkins are frequently polyrhythmic, and substitutions of one metrical foot for another are common in both classical and romance verse forms. We know that perfectly regular rhythm is a sure sedative to the ear. It follows that the variations rather than the regularities of metered verse give the work of its great practitioners a signature charm. On the other hand, vers libre frequently contains an underlying beat that comes close to regular measure. Richard D. Cureton, writing on the prosody of free verse, observes: "If we are interested in the rhythmic structure of a poetic text, the appropriate question is not *Is this text rhythmic?* but *At what level and to what degree is this text rhythmic?*"

Regular meter is pleasing because we can readily anticipate the rhythm of the lines to come. The pleasure lies in having our expectations fulfilled. Irregular

Originally published in *Poetry East* 20–21 (Fall 1986). Collected in *Conversant Essays: Contemporary Poets on Poetry,* ed. James McCorkle (Detroit: Wayne State University Press, 1990) 185–193.

meter, on the other hand, pleases because it delivers something unforeseen, though, in retrospect, well-prepared for. Free verse is most compelling when most rhythmic: the poet must shape the irregular rhythms of language to underscore, contradict, or in some way reinforce the poem's content. Occasional lapses into regular meter frame the more jagged lines and help the reader appreciate their unpredictable music. For example, when a long iambic line is followed by a spondee or two, the rhythms are thrown into high relief. It's a little like placing a swatch of red next to a swatch of green: when juxtaposed these complements increase each other's vibrancy.

Prosody provides a comprehensive means of discussing traditional metered verse. But free verse is seldom subjected to any such systematic analysis in our literary magazines. There is, however, an insightful and growing body of literature by scholars of prosody, linguistics, and musicology on the rhythms of free verse. I think of Stephen Cushman's new book *Williams and the Meaning of Measure* (which in advancing our understanding of Williams' prosody advances our understanding of free verse); Charles O. Hartman's *Free Verse, An Essay on Prosody;* Cooper and Meyer's work on musical rhythm; linguist Ray Jackendoff's model of hierarchical structure in language as applied to music; David Stein and David Gil's linguistic insights concerning prosodic structures; phonologist Elizabeth Selkirk's study of the relationship between sound and structure; Donald Westling's syntactic theory of enjambment, which he calls "grammetric scissoring"; and Richard D. Cureton's analysis of the "myths and muddles" of traditional scansion. However, to judge from their opinions, many of the critics, essayists, and poets holding forth in our literary journals are unaware of such studies and, consequently, of any of the newer theories of prosody. As reviewers, they are content to describe the content of the poems and praise the poet's skillful use of blank verse. If the poet does not write in blank verse or in any of the more obvious metrical forms, the poems simply are not scanned. It's as if the reader, upon scanning two lines and finding dissimilar rhythms, gives up the search and regards the poem as a formless mass of words. I'd argue, however, that all poems have shape—whether it's pleasing or perceptible to the reader is something else. It's time that we, as poets, readers, and critics, begin to discern and analyze the subtle, governing structures of free verse and to talk more about its operative tropes.

Rather than placing the emphasis upon the formal devices of regular rhythm and meter, why not consider the whole panoply of design and pattern? As J. V. Cunningham noted, "A poem is a convergency of forms. It is the coincidence of forms that locks in the poem." Prosody is too specific an instrument to describe all the pattern-making possibilities of verse. To devote our analytical energy and aesthetic passion solely to metrical form is to deny the existence (and importance) of the myriad structural options available. At the very least, responsible formal analysis must define the details it chooses to disregard.

What are some of the formal schemes awaiting our investigation? As a beginning, we might look at the smaller linguistic units that influence or enlarge a text, such as allusions, puns, apostrophe, and pronouns with their function of insinuating gender. Or we could dissect the poem's larger governing organization: its rhetorical questions, conceits, virtuoso listings, registers of diction, and lineations. Cushman effectively argues that Williams wrote a prosody of enjambment, a counterpointing of visual line and syntactic unit. We might analyze the poem's enjambment within a syntactic-grammatical context or consider its use of resistant or resolved line-breaks. As Cureton notes, enjambments alone can dramatize the "curve of emotion" in the text, from relaxation to tension to resolution. It's also important to consider the poem's visual form on the page, which changes the way we hear words. Is the use of white space mimetic, abstract, or temporal; do such effects serve to emphasize or to defamiliarize the line? We also should be attentive to the poem's use of reiterative devices such as epanalepsis (ending a sentence with its own opening words—*Leaves of Grass* has many examples), refrain, chorus, or repetend (a repetition that occurs irregularly or partially, as in Delmore Schwartz's poem "Do the Others Speak of Me, Mockingly, Maliciously"). And, as Jonathan Holden has pointed out, we can regard many contemporary poems as analogues that borrow their form from letters, horoscopes, television listings, fugues, etc. The deep logic of a poem may be based upon such concepts as the microcosm moving toward macrocosm; the linkage of opposites (oxymoron); stasis; dynamism; and equilibrium. Because English, unlike the Romance languages, does not contain a multitude of rhymes, we need to appreciate and make use of aural difference rather than similitude. French and Spanish poetry can afford to value endings, which contribute so much to the irregular texture and attendant richness of our language. With this in mind, we might consider the orchestration of verse through echo (assonance, consonance, irregular rhyme, front rhyme, half-rhyme, accords, and so on). It's also interesting to analyze the operative rhetorical strategies, such as paralipsis (a passing over with brief mention in order to emphasize the suggestiveness of what was omitted) and parataxis (placing words or phrases next to one another without coordinating connections). In rhythm, we could turn our attention to the use of accentual or syllabic verse, to irregular meter that enforces content (i.e., the tension of strong-stress rhythms or the relaxation of pyrrhic, atonic lines). If we wish to be more ambitious, Cureton's theory of hierarchical scansion provides a formal mechanism for representing comparable rhythmic shapes at different linguistic levels. (The major levels are narrative, syntactic, and phonological.) We also could consider the formal devices of asyndeton (omission of conjunctions, common in the work of Ammons or Swenson, for example) and its opposite, polysyndeton (repetition of conjunctions).

The last two devices, though opposite in principle, both have the effect of making the content more vivacious and emphatic. In fact, I hope that discussion of form will lead to considerations of content. Without this obligation, formalism becomes a comfortable means of avoiding responsibility for what is being said. It's safer to speak of metrical finesse or blunders than to appraise the subjects poets choose. In too many reviews, I find lengthy *descriptions* of content, which do little more than paraphrase. Descriptive criticism is fine as a place to begin, but few critics go on to question why particular subjects continue to be chosen (while other topics suffer poetic banishment). Brave criticism might ask what is this subject's value to me, as reader? And, what world views, values, or secular mythologies are implicit in the poet's stance? Surely we must consider the cultural assumptions questioned or supported by the text, as well as the style in which these concerns are voiced.

Quantum physics teaches us that the act of measuring changes what is being measured. It follows that the act of measuring language (by putting it into regular meter) must change what is being said. Part of the resistance toward metered verse is coupled with a belief that passion or sincerity evaporates when the poet takes to counting stresses and feet. I'd contend that the content of metered poems can, at times, take on a greater urgency by means of a regular rhythm. The exigencies of form foster such careful choices that each word can become a palimpsest of implication. In fact, I value the qualities of rhythm and multidimensional language in all poetry, whether the meter is regular or not. If it is true (and I'm not sure it is) that the poetry of social commitment is often written in irregular meters, perhaps this is because the poets write from a tradition other than that of English prosody. We should respect the richness of such cultural contexts. It is ethnocentric to regard traditional English prosody as the one sure means of writing poetry. Such a stance also fails to consider the changes our language underwent in becoming American.

Several critics have lamented the repose of free verse into stylistic plainness. Mary Kinzie has even coined a new literary term, "the rhapsodic fallacy," which speaks to the problem. Kinzie's position is too complex to summarize here, but the rhapsodic fallacy describes, in part, the equation of a prosaic style with authenticity of engagement. The observation is an important one. Have we forgotten that the plain-style represents a conscious aesthetic choice, rather than a simple outpouring of pure feeling? The word "style" itself points to language as a selective construct. As such, flat style poetry is no more "sincere" or "engaged" than are the constructs of metered verse. And when the majority of poets choose to write in a given style, one suspects it is becoming a convention, as well as an artful device. (However, free verse is not to be equated with plain style or any other calcified aesthetic. If it were, there would be nothing free about it.) Perhaps readers are bored by the plethora of poems in simple language; perhaps they feel manipulated by the poet's guileless pose. As solution to the monotony of flat style poetry, Mary Kinzie calls for a return to "those forms associated with the eighteenth century: formal satire, familiar epistle, georgic, pastoral." Lamenting the blurring of high and low styles into "the low lyrical shrub" that is contemporary poetry, she would have poets write in clearly delineated genres. This stance supposes that by segregating high style from low and by restricting subject one may write "heart-piercing" poetry, to borrow Kinzie's adjective. But hearts are subjective entities, steadfast only in their refusal to be reliably pierced by aesthetic programs—that's the great thing about them! They remain willful little blobs, despite our best efforts at persuasion.

Robert Hillyer's *In Pursuit of Poetry* classifies the language of verse into two styles: "the rhetorical, heightened and dignified, and the conversational, informal and familiar. . . . Each has its dangers as well as its virtues; the first may become bombastic, the second prosaic." I don't agree that the language of verse falls neatly into binary registers of diction. If so, where would Chaucer or Shakespeare land in the aesthetic shakedown, combining as they do, the dignified with the familiar, the high with the low? To my mind, great work is large enough to include a multiplicity of styles, tones, and subjects. However, our attention for the moment is on the two styles Hillyer describes, rather than the wide diversity of work he excludes. I think his description of the dangers common to high and low style holds true. Poets are just as likely to write rhapsodic epics that ring false as they are to write fallacious, plain-style lyrics. If Mary Kinzie's programme should catch on, we'd undoubtedly see vast numbers of insufferable "genre" poems, written to fit the bill. Isn't this what happened in the eighteenth century?

Perhaps the impulse for simplicity began as a corrective when the formal post–World War II poem was felt to have degenerated (through imitation and overuse) into a polished veneer of language. The veneer might have been gold plate or marble, but everyone suddenly felt a yen for solid oak—or formica. And since the early 1960s the majority of poets have forsaken the primrose path for the plain one, which now begins, in its turn, to feel like an aesthetic shortcut.

In the largest terms, the search for a style is a search for a language that does justice to our knowledge of how the world works. According to one ordering of the canon, poetry has consistently reflected the world views of its age. Thus, in the Middle Ages, when everyone believed the world was created and run by a divine being, and earthquakes were viewed as a result of God's intervention (rather than of shifting plates), poetry mirrored the religious hierarchy. Dante's conception of the world as a series of spheres—the enormous heavens, the crystalline planets, the earth's elements, and the seven circles of hell—gave everyone a proper place, from king to serf. Newtonian physics replaced the hierarchical model with a physics of ordinary matter ruled by mathematical laws. And the literary climate of the early eighteenth century mirrored the harmony of a universe seen as a great, logical clock. The lawful and orderly cosmos was taken for proof of God's presence and goodness. Christian Wolff evolved the first system of German Rationalism from aspects of Newton's *Principia*. And the idea of Nature as order (prominent in *Principia*) also influenced such representative eighteenth-century literature as Pope's "Essay on Man." Later in the century, the rise of democracy, which posits an equality between parts of the social machinery, found expression in an enthusiasm for the simpler modes of folk poetry. And by the early nineteenth century, Wordsworth's "Preface to Lyrical Ballads" argued for the democratic readmission of "rustic" speech and subjects into English poetry.

Just as Newton shattered the medieval hierarchical conception of the world, modern physics has smashed Newton's mechanistic clockwork. Modernism may indeed have been a true reflection of Einstein's physics. He, after all, never accepted quantum theory and held to the old-fashioned hope that a realistic vision of the world could be congruent with the quantum facts. In his autobiography he states, "I still believe in the possibility of a model of reality—that is, of a theory which represents things themselves and not merely the probability of their occurrence." If we substitute "ideas" for "probability," we have a restatement of Williams' famous "No ideas but in things."

However, Niels Bohr's claims that there is no deep reality represents the prevailing view of contemporary quantum physics. Bohr insisted "There is no quantum world. There is only an abstract quantum description." Physicist N. David Mermin summed up Bohr's antirealist position by stating, "We now know that the moon is demonstrably not there when nobody looks." Perhaps popular literature and culture have made people aware of this and other quantum theories, such as the view that reality consists of a steadily increasing number of parallel universes; that consciousness creates reality; or that the world is twofold, consisting of potentials and actualities. Heisenberg's uncertainty principle, which forbids accurate knowledge of a quantum particle's position and momentum, is certainly well known. A truly engaged and contemporary poetry must reflect this knowledge. As a body of literature it might synthesize such disparate theories into a comprehensive metaphor for the way the world appears to us today. Or it may be that synthesis and unity are fundamentally premodern concepts. In this case, a fragmentary, diffuse literature is the perfect expression of our world knowledge. In a sense, our search for a language mirrors science's search for a quantum reality. As Nobel laureate Richard Feynman remarked, "I think it is safe to say no one understands quantum mechanics. Do not keep saying to yourself, if you can possibly avoid it, 'but how can it be like that?' Nobody knows how it can be like that." This reluctance to attempt meaning is clearly reflected in postmodernist literature and deconstructionism, where "meaning" is no longer the issue.

Perhaps it shouldn't surprise us, then, that the term *free verse* has lost its meaning and become a convenient catch-all whereby any piece of writing with wide margins may be defended as poetry. Pound's advice was to "compose in the sequence of the musical phrase, not in sequence of a metronome." He didn't say poetry should have no music at all. And founding mother Amy Lowell preferred the term "cadenced verse" to vers libre, noting that "to depart satisfactorily from a rhythm it is first necessary to have it." Frost, of course, thought that writing free verse was like playing tennis without a net. But surely the Net-Nabbing Freeform Tennis Club would waste no time in inventing another restriction. They might move the game indoors, use the walls as obstacles, and call their new sport "raquetball." In the same way, when free verse absconded with the net, it created other means of limitation. The best poets of free verse work long and hard to structure their poems. But as readers and critics, we have been slow in finding ways to discern and discuss the orders of their irregular form. But form *is* regularity, you might protest. If so, how much regularity constitutes pattern and structure?

Perfect Euclidean forms occur rather rarely in nature. Instead we find a dynamic world made up of quantities constantly changing in time, a wealth of fluctuations—such as variations in sunspots and the wobbling of the earth's axis. In 1977, the mathematician Benoit Mandelbrot observed that "twenty-five or thirty years ago, science looked at things that were regular and smooth." In contrast, he became intrigued by what are called chaotic phenomena: the occurrence of earthquakes; the way our neurons fire when we search our memories; patterns of vegetation in a swamp; price jumps in the stock market; turbulence in the weather; the distribution of galaxies; and the flooding of the Nile. Mandelbrot saw similarities in shapes so strange that fin de siècle mathematicians termed them "pathological" and "monsters." These earlier scientists never supposed that such "monstrous" shapes bore any relation to reality. Mandelbrot, on the contrary, believed they described nature much better than ideal forms. He found that certain chaotic structures (including the preceding list) contained a deep logic or pattern. In 1975, he coined the word *fractals* (from the Latin *fractus,* meaning "broken or fragmented") to describe such configurations. (Pound's injunction to "break the pentameter" is nicely implicit in the term.)

To put it simply, each part of a fractal form replicates the form of the entire structure. Increasing detail is revealed with increasing magnification, and each smaller part looks like the entire structure, turned around or tilted a bit. This isn't true of the classical Euclidean forms of lines, planes, and spheres. For example, when a segment of a circle is subjected to increasing magnification it looks increasingly like a straight line rather than a series of circles. But a fractal form has a substructure (we might say a subtext) that goes on indefinitely, without reposing into ordinary curves. The bark patterns on oak, mud cracks in a dry riverbed, a broccoli spear—these are examples of fractal forms: irregular structures containing just enough regularity so that they can be described. Such forms are, at least to my perception, quite pleasing. Like free verse, they zig and zag, spurt and dawdle, while retaining an infinite complexity of detail. (In contrast, formal verse travels at a regular pace and is less dynamic, less potentially volatile.) The fascination of these intricate forms ("the fascination of what's difficult," you might say) indicates that we don't need an obvious or regular pattern to satisfy our aesthetic or psychological needs. Nonobjective art, which often reflects the fractal patterns of nature, makes the same point. In fact, asymmetrical or turbulent composition may be the essence of twentieth-century aesthetics.

There are two kinds of fractals: geometric and random. The geometric type repeats an identical pattern at various scales. As a corollary, imagine a poem structured on the concept of the oxymoron. The linkage of opposites on the smallest scale might appear in antonymic word usage, on a larger scale in one stanza's ability to oppose or reverse the form and content of another, and at the grandest scale in the poem's overall form becoming a paradoxical or self-reflexive contradiction of content. Thus far, the poem could be a sonnet or an ode. After all, ordered forms about chaos were rather popular in the eighteenth century. But let's suppose that the poem's rhythm is also oxymoronic: that a smooth, regular line is purposefully followed by a rambunctious or jagged utterance. If repeated throughout, this juxtaposition would constitute the poem's metrical form. Random fractals, to consider another possibility, introduce some elements of chance. In the composition of poetry, this could be as simple a factor as opening a book at random and using the metrical pattern happened upon as a contributing factor in your verse.

In his essay "How Long Is the Coast of Britain?" Mandelbrot showed that a coastline, being infinitely long with all of its microscopic points and inlets, is best treated as a random fractal rather than as an approximation of a straight line. While complication is characteristic of coastlines, there is also a great degree of order in their structures, which are self-similar. A self-similar mechanism is, formally speaking, a kind of cascade, with each stage creating details smaller than those of the preceding stages. As Mandelbrot writes, "Each self-similar fractal has a very specific kind of unsmoothness, which makes it more complicated than anything in Euclid." Fractal form, then, is composed of constant digressions and interruptions in rhythm.

Scientists are just beginning to uncover all the events, things, and processes that can be described through fractals. Clouds follow fractal patterns. (Incidentally, you'll notice that the previous sentence is composed of three trochaic feet, with one extra stressed syllable at the beginning, How regular! And irregular.) Since fractals can be illustrated by means of computer graphics, it's possible to *see* the basic fractal properties in all their intricacy and beauty.

Mandelbrot's discoveries could change the way we look at the world and, by extension, the way we look at poetry. Certainly the discovery of order within the turbulent forms of nature should encourage us to search for patterns within the turbulent forms of art. Fractal form may allow a more precise measure of those poetic shapes that aren't governed by the strategies of prosody. Though it's been around for over one hundred years (if one counts Whitman), in regard to free verse we're a little like primitive people who've never seen a two-dimensional image and can't, at first, ascertain that the shapes in photographs from faces or bodies. We must develop our ability to recognize subtle, hidden, and original patterns as the time-honored (and more obvious) metrical orders of prosody. And we might pay more attention to the irregularities of traditional formal verse, the freedoms and deviations within a context of similitude and correctness. (After all, deviance can't exist without an orderly context from which to differ.)

Since "free verse" has become a misnomer, perhaps we could use the irregular yet beautifully structured forms of nature as analogue and call the poetry of irregular form *fractal verse*. Its aesthetic might derive from the structural limitations of self-similar fractal form. I offer the following as a tentative exploration of fractal precepts: any line when examined closely (or magnified) will reveal itself to be as richly detailed as was the larger poem from which it was taken; the poem will contain an infinite regression of details, a nesting of pattern within pattern (an endless imbedding of the shape into itself, recalling Tennyson's idea of the inner infinity); digression, interruption, fragmentation, and lack of continuity will be regarded as formal functions rather than lapses into formlessness; all directions of motion and rhythm will be equally probable (isotropy); the past positions of motion, or the preceding metrical pattern, will not necessarily affect the poem's future evolution (independence).

Poems are linguistic models of the world's working. Now our knowledge of form includes the new concept of manageable chaos, along with the ancient categories of order and chaos. If order is represented by the simple Euclidean shapes of nature and by metered verse, chaos might be analogous to failed free verse and gibberish. (It's somehow reassuring that chaos is still with us, evident in natural forms that show no underlying pattern.) And manageable chaos or fractal form might find its corollary in fractal poetry. One thing seems certain: our verse should be free to sing the wildly harmonious structures that surround and delight us, the body eclectic, where geography ends and pebbles begin.

1986

REFERENCES

Abrams, M. H., ed. *The Norton Anthology of English Literature,* Volume 1. New York: W. W. Norton, 1979.

Breslin, Paul, Alan Shapiro, Stephen Yenser, Marjorie Perloff, Julia Randall, and Bonnie Costello. "Responses to Mary Kinzie's 'The Rhapsodic Fallacy.'" *Salmagundi,* no. 67 (1985):135–153.

Cooper, Grosvenor, and Leonard Meyer. *The Rhythmic Structure of Music.* Chicago: University of Chicago Press, 1960.

Cunningham, J. V. "The Problem of Form." *Shenandoah* 35:113–116.

Cureton, Richard D. "The 'Measures' of 'Free Verse.'" *William Carlos Williams Review,* forthcoming.

———. "Traditional Scansions: Myths and Muddles." *Journal of Literary Semantics,* Vol. 15, no. 3 (1986):171–208.

———. "Rhythm: A Multilevel Analysis." *Style* 19(2) pp. 242–57.

Diggory, Terence. "Two Responses to Mary Kinzie: I: Dr. Johnson on the Arid Steppe." *Salmagundi,* no. 65 (1984):80–85.

Gardner, Martin. "Mathematical Games." *Scientific American,* December 1976, p. 124, and April 1978, p. 16.

Hartman, Charles O. *Free Verse, An Essay on Prosody.* Princeton: Princeton University Press, 1986.

Herbert, Nick. *Quantum Reality.* Garden City, N.Y.: Anchor Press/Doubleday, 1985.

Hillyer, Robert Silliman. *In Pursuit of Poetry.* New York: McGraw-Hill, 1960.

Hofstadter, Douglas R. "Metamagical Themas." *Scientific American,* November 1981, p. 22.

Holden, Jonathan. "Postmodern Poetic Form: A Theory." In *Poetics: Essays on the Art of Poetry,* ed. P. Mariani and G. Murphy, pp. 13–34. Green Harbor, Mass.: Tendril, 1984.

Jackendoff, Ray, and Fred Lerdahl. *A Deep Parallel Between Music and Language.* Bloomington: Indiana University Linguistics Club, 1980.

Kinzie, Mary. "The Rhapsodic Fallacy." *Salmagundi,* no. 65 (1984):63–79.

———. "Learning to Speak." *Salmagundi,* no. 67 (1985):154–162.

Leithauser, Brad. "Metrical Illiteracy." *The New Criterion,* January 1983, pp. 41–46.

Lerdahl, Ray, and Fred Jackendoff. *A Generative Theory of Tonal Music.* Cambridge, Mass.: MIT Press, 1983.

Mandelbrot, Benoit. *Fractals: Form, Chance, and Dimension.* San Francosco: W. H. Freeman, 1977.

———. *The Fractual Geometry of Nature.* San Francisco: W. H. Freeman, 1982.

———. "Fractals and the Geometry of Nature." In *1981 Yearbook of Science and the Future,* Encyclopaedia Britannica.

McDermott, Jeanne. "Geometric Forms Known as Fractals Find Sense in Chaos." *Smithsonian,* December 1983, p. 110.

Molesworth, Charles. "Two Responses to Mary Kinzie: II: Sleeping Beside the Muse: Formalism and the Conditions of Contemporary Poetry." *Salmagundi,* no. 65 (1984):86–96.

Preminger, Alex, ed. *Princeton Encyclopedia of Poetry.* Princeton: Princeton University Press, 1974.

Selkirk, Elizabeth O. *Phonology and Syntax: The Relations Between Sound and Structure.* Cambridge, Mass.: MIT Press, 1984.

Stahl, E. L., and W. E. Yuill. *German Literature of the Eighteenth and Nineteenth Centuries.* London: Cresset Press, 1970.

Stein, David, and Davil Gil. "Prosodic Structures and Prosodic Markers." *Theoretical Linguistics* 7:173–240.

Westling, Donald. *The New Poetries: Poetic Form Since Coleridge and Wordsworth.* London and Toronto: Associated University Presses, 1985.

CHRISTIAN WIMAN
(B. 1966)

Born in Abilene, Texas, Christian Wiman was raised in the small oil town of Synder, and the imagery of Wiman's poetry reflects the flat, dry landscape of his native region. He attended Washington and Lee University in Virginia where be became an All-American tennis player who helped win for his school the national championship. Graduating in 1988, Wiman spent the next seven years traveling while mastering the craft of writing. He taught English at the Prague School of Economics in the Czech Republic and worked as a translator in Mexico City. In 1992 he won a Wallace Stegner Fellowship to Stanford where in 1996 he became the Jones Lecturer in Poetry. He also lived in England and Guatemala. In 1998 his first book, *The Long Home,* won the Nicholas Roerich Prize in poetry. He has taught at Lynchburg College in Virginia and is currently on the faculty at Northwestern University in Evanston, Illinois.

Wiman is one of the most eloquent and authoritative poetry critics of his generation. His essays and reviews have appeared in *Poetry, Sewanee Review,* and the *Hudson Review.* He has also reviewed widely for newspapers, especially the *Dallas Morning News* and *Austin American-Statesman.* The experience of poetry, he has written, "is to be given an image of life that you have lost or long dreamed of, to hear as sound something of the farthest sorrows that you are, and to know in that moment that what you've been given is not enough."

Wiman's criticism is learned without ever seeming academic. Tough-minded and skeptical, he ponders his topics by framing them carefully in larger issues. Not a proponent of any critical school, Wiman nonetheless seems instinctively drawn to biographical and historical perspectives in his writing. His essay, "A Piece of Prose," which appeared in *Poetry* in 1999, examines the various reasons that contemporary poets have turned to critical prose as a medium for self-expression.

A PIECE OF PROSE

1.

Of all the many and mostly noble reasons why a poet might turn to prose, there is one which is often primary, personal, and only occasionally conscious: it staves off the silence. If, as Thomas Mann wrote, a writer is someone for whom writing is more difficult than it is for other people, a poet is someone for whom writing—in his poems, I mean—is more difficult than it is for other writers. At least it seems this ought to be the case. To write a real poem is to be made aware at once of the singularity of words and their precariousness, their "propensity to come off from reality," as Milosz puts it. For anyone who has been made so aware, the time between poems can become a time of some peril, of encroaching unreality and increasing confusion. It can seem like silence is steadily claiming everything.

Prose can be an antidote to this, at least for a while. Though I don't feel that critical ability inevitably accompanies a poetic gift, nor that all poets bear a kind of *a priori* burden to produce criticism (those who do usually know who they are), I have little patience for people who see the application of critical intelligence as somehow inimical to poetic creation. It's true that a poem can't be an illustration of an idea, that a too scrupulous attention to one's own means and modes of creation can result in paralysis. Something like this seems to have happened to Coleridge, but it's hardly an inevitability. Ideally, the two activities should be at once intimate and separate.

"Periods of poetic activity usually end with critical awareness," Pavese writes, and the articulation of this awareness can be a way out of it, a way into whatever new and different work lies ahead. The poetry of a poet-critic is always of paramount importance, for himself, obviously, but also in a way for his audience, even if that audience is unfamiliar with the poems. The worth of a poet's critical awareness will have been determined by the truth and intensity of the poetic activity which preceded it, the depth to which he descended in his poems. (Accomplishment is usually but not necessarily an issue: it's possible to come up empty-handed but greatly changed.) The poet's own emphasis will be somewhat different. Criticism will be valuable to him only in so far as it charts the waters where he's been, enables him to move away, and equips him for the next descent.

But prose can also be mere evasion. Silence is not some negative state with regard to poetry but is in some way part of its very nature, the element out of which, with great pain, it emerges and to which, with what can sometimes seem an almost greater pain, it tries to return:

As all the Heavens were a Bell,
And Being, but an Ear,
And I, and Silence, some strange Race
Wrecked, solitary, here—

Published in *Poetry* 174.5 (Aug. 1999): 286–298.

Enduring silence is no small part of poetry's discipline, acquiring the patience to wait, knowing when not to write. There is a kind of frenetic production which conceals an essential indolence, and a writer can be at the same time prolific and mute. Prose that is written *merely* to stave off silence, then, serves roughly the same function as booze or excessive exercise. It's merely a busier, less efficient oblivion.

Don't ask me where the balance lies, somewhere between a statement once made by William Matthews—"one job of a poet is not to fall silent"—who seems to miss the point, and the late muteness of Ezra Pound, who impaled himself upon it: "In the end, silence overtook me." Not to fall silent, then, and yet to feel it, to bring something of its pure potential and finality into one's work and self without being overtaken by it: there's the goal. For me, for now, prose helps.

2.

Style is not an infallible guide to the value of a poet's prose and opinions, but it's the least fallible. That's Auden, or almost, who was himself an exemplary prose stylist. By "exemplary" I mean two things. His prose has the sort of authoritative yet intimate air that is evidence of issues engaged at a primary level, which is to say, in his own poems. The second thing is at once simpler and rarer: it gives pleasure. One ought not expect that the style of a poet's poems and prose will be indistinguishable, but I do think it's fair to expect that some of the aesthetic elements that lead to distinction in poetry—metaphorical intelligence, a sense of linguistic rhythm, enough wit and wide life to suggest that some whole person is addressing you—will make itself felt in the prose. It's going too far to hope for a prose that could, like a poem, compel and even almost convince simply by the way it sounds, but I like a writer who at least *tries.*

There are dangers in this. A writer as good as Heaney can have you thinking some lumpy, lugubrious translation of an Eastern European poet is ringing in your inner ear and setting your moral soul on fire. I don't mind this. We reveal ourselves much more deeply—both in terms of taste and character—in our enthusiasms than in our censures. The lapses passion causes are never altogether ignoble. Love, even if misguided, even if its object has been supplanted by an ideal, is always distinguishable from the cold, clinical efficiency of mere need. It's the difference between a wrongheaded but righthearted affair and—more on this when I talk about reviewing—prostitution.

Criticism is easier to write than poetry, but it shares a first imperative of that more exacting art. Poets, so long as they are poets, never lose their sense of language as a living thing, their ear for it in the one air of their own time. They use language only so long as they are living it, discovering in its historically specific depths and inflections the same small set of truths that every other poet has labored—and lived—to discover. It's all in *how* you say a thing.

Criticism is different, in that it does matter precisely *what* is being said, and good insight can occasionally survive bad style. Geoffrey Hill's criticism is an example. There are brilliant things packed away inside the perdurable prose, but getting at them can be a bit like cracking a husk coincidentally with your tooth: that's a tough nut to savor. There are, I think, more examples of good style surviving bad judgment. Think of Eliot on *Paradise Lost,* Johnson on the Metaphysicals, Yvor Winters on almost anything. We read these pieces less for their perceptions than for the lively, momentarily misguided minds at work in them, for their *styles*. Being right won't save you. Judicious dullness is like a good job of embalming: the subject is cleaned up, tastefully presented, recognizable, and *dead*.

"Writers themselves usually make the best critics," the poet Anne Stevenson has written, "because, even when wrong, they care so much about writing well." My experience as a poet makes me want to agree immediately with this. My experience as a reviewer gives me some pause. When John Hollander begins a sentence, "Before we avail ourselves of these texts," this is one reader who knows immediately that he's not going to be around long enough to avail himself of these texts. That's a joke, of course, but just barely. Hollander's book *The Work of Poetry* is probably the most meticulous and comprehensive of the twenty or so books I read through in preparation for this essay, and I certainly learned things from it. But there's a stuffiness to his style, some main charge missing. Similarly, although James Longenbach has some solid things to say about the legacies of Modernism in *Modern Poetry After Modernism,* and though his prose is always clean and readable, his tone is that of someone who can't stop looking over his shoulder. With his careful qualifications, his endless good sense, his empty term-paper rhetoric ("his strategy . . . helps to insure the future health and diversity of American literature"), he sounds less like a poet than a valedictorian.

Which raises the question: What exactly *should* a poet's prose sound like? There are random answers among the books I read through. It may have the dense, impacted quality of Christopher Middleton's (some tough nuts here), the reach and richness of Walcott's essay on Lowell. It may have the autobiographical elegance of J. D. McClatchy's essays on reading and writing, the passionate economy of the title piece in Donald Justice's book *Oblivion,* the moral seriousness of Mary Kinzie's *The Cure of Poetry in an Age of Prose.* In prose as in poetry, there is perhaps only one definite proscription for a vital style: it must make a reader feel that something is truly at stake.

The higher the stakes, the better, more durable the work. Patrick Kavanagh wrote of "dabbling in verses" until they became his life, suggesting an idea of the poet as someone who one day wades into the shallows of words and later discovers, with what is half elation, half pure panic, that the deepest currents of his life are running through them. The way one tries to reconcile that latter discovery with that initial play will be one's style. It is a reconciliation which, for the poet, must never quite occur, for the moment style becomes completely conscious, the moment it becomes applied rather than discovered, it becomes a manner.

This burden is eased considerably in the more forgiving medium of critical prose, in which one needn't reinvent an achieved style, but it isn't altogether gone. If you find that your life is in your poetry, or that you can somehow only get to your life *through* your poetry, it follows that the ideas you have about poetry will demand a similar sort of scrupulous attention to language as language. When Yeats agonizes in his *Autobiographies* over the difficulty of achieving a great prose style, he is attesting to the relationship between his poems and his prose, his language and his life. A poet's prose engages and emerges out of this relationship, this difficulty, and the style that is its means of doing so will be imprinted with the deepest currents of a particular mind, a particular life. Or not.

3.

Thus far I have been talking primarily about what I would call impractical prose, the origins of which are more internal than external, bound up with the poet's feeling for his own gift rather than with his feeling for his or poetry's place in the world. Such prose may be prompted by its occasion, but it won't be determined by it. Letters can sometimes fall in this category (Rilke, Keats, Crane), as can reviews. Eliot's famous essay on the Metaphysicals is in fact a commissioned review, though the book in question is clearly little more than a catalyst for ideas that had long been emerging in Eliot's mind. The one evaluative sentence comes almost as an afterthought.

Practical prose is almost always more ephemeral, if for no other reason than the impermanence of the books themselves. Practical criticism is a sort of oil in the engine of the literary world. It's what poets with prizes, houses, and big reading fees have learned either to avoid or practice very cannily. It's what fills the back, usually terminally boring pages of literary magazines. It's what everyone—*everyone*—disparages for being too timid, too political, too exclusive, too incestuous. Discovering you have some ability for practical criticism is like being a prospector discovering you can crack rocks on your skull. Eventually other prospectors begin to bring you rocks, for which you charge a nominal fee. No one's happy when you point out there's no gold inside, as you must almost always do, and in those rare instances when you do discover a vein of the real thing, none of its benefits accrue to you. The only definite permanent result of practicing such a talent is a massive headache.

But practical criticism can be even more important than other kinds. It can serve as a cleansing element when that aforementioned engine's begun to sputter and spew pollution, the air contaminated by habit and unconscious conventions. Great poets aren't breathing that air, but good ones are, and the health of a literary culture is in some ways more contingent upon its good poets than its great ones. One need only read through a period piece like the *Morrow Anthology of Younger Poets,* a sort of *Golden Treasury of Suburban Verse,* to see what can happen when the practical critical intelligence is in a kind of generational abeyance. History will dispense with even the most massively wrongheaded of our monuments, but it's a slower erosion than people think. When a good practical critic like Geoffrey O'Brien goes after the Morrow anthology, he exposes the soft rot at the center of some of our assumptions, and thereby helps to hasten a necessary decay.

William Logan is the best practical critic around. I sometimes disagree with his judgments fiercely, but *that* I so fiercely disagree, that his prose provokes such a response, is what makes him the best. Most criticism is like most poetry: it simply leaves you indifferent. I've seen Logan's name bring bile to the lips of the gentlest spirits, and I'd be surprised if his candor hasn't cost him a good deal. But for breadth of intelligence, an incisive style, and pure passion, I don't think he can be matched.

Good reviewing always has an edge to it. "Passions face both ways," Logan writes, and it's telling that the title of his book is *All the Rage,* that Mary Kinzie's collected reviews are called *The Judge Is Fury.* Anger, when it's the good anger, when it's for the faked emotion or failed technique (the same thing, usually) that is a deep violation of life, can hone and enhance taste. Something of the same kind of self-dissatisfaction that leads to the finding of forms in poetry—you want an order that you are not, a peace that you can't be—can lead a critic who is primarily a poet to seeing that quality in other work, and often the purest, most convincing praise is laced with an element of, if not anger exactly, at least insufficiency, self-dissatisfaction, a critic's sense that someone else has done something that he could not. It's only when one's anger is for the "literary world," when its origins are personal and mercenary, that it becomes debased, one's energies short-circuited, and the calibrations of taste distorted.

One ought to inhabit the role of reviewer without relishing it. Part of what makes Fred Chappell's prose attractive—besides the wit, readability, and sharp opinions—is his unease over the entire enterprise and his part in it. This keeps him alert, for the most part (he has a soft spot for Southerners), saves him from the boilerplate praise of most contemporary reviewers, the clichéd thinking of critics who use phrases like "bearing witness" or "subversive" or "taking risks" with the sort of gestural imprecision that ought to be anathema to a poet; the bland personality-pieces that conflate the person and the work, amiability and accomplishment.

Good reviewing is mostly the province of the young, whose occlusions can amount to a kind of strength. The cheerful broad-mindedness that can be attractive in a person, a bloodhound ability to sniff out the good in the smelliest circumstances, can ruin a reviewer. Young poets usually have some sort of passionate focus rather than range. They will miss much, will make outlandish mistakes, but when some book falls within the range of taste they have acquired, which has been largely determined by their own work, they will nail it. And it just so happens that, since major shifts in a culture's poetry are also usually the province of the young (the Romantics, the Modernists, etc.), most of what is truly innovative and new in poetry, whether it's some subtle change in the way conventions are being inhabited or a more radical assault upon those conventions, will occur within this range.

Innocence can also help. The poetry world being what it is—so small, so self-contained, so far removed from *the* world—a poet who isn't a hermit is going to suffer, both professionally and personally, from the sharpness of his opinions. Young poets may know this, but they know it as young smokers know that cigarettes cause cancer: it's pure abstraction. They'll fire from the hip for a while, partly just for the flair of it, but mostly because of a genuine, healthy contempt for complacency and the idea of a "career" in poetry. If this isn't quite the case in the la-la land of workshops and blurbs, it ought to be.

I'm not at all sure what causes or enables some poets to persist. Whatever one thinks about Logan and Chappell, or other mid-career poets who have continued to write balanced reviews (Dana Gioia, Richard Tillinghast, Mary Kinzie, Bruce Bawer), there's something admirable in this persistence. Admirable, that is, so long as one trusts the motives behind it, the sense of necessity, even almost of moral responsibility, to which both Logan and Chappell allude. Less generous motives are not difficult to imagine. It's easier to make a name for oneself as a reviewer than as a poet, though anyone who would value this lesser recognition is probably not a real poet anyway. Then, too, there are always those who are keen on accumulating "power" in the poetry world, and reviewing may be just one more means of doing so. One hardly knows what to say about this. Wielding power in the poetry world is roughly the equivalent of cutting a wide swath through your local PTA.

Public reaction may in the end be one of the strongest incentives, and not a base one. Poetry is lonely. Publish a poem in some conspicuous place and the response is not likely to be overwhelming, not likely to even *be* a response. Publish a review or essay that is at all partisan or passionate in that same place and you'll get some letters. One of these will be from someone who is clearly quite intelligent and thoughtful, and will be very gratifying. Another will come from someone you suspect has broken off from society, who likely wrote you while on a break from building his bomb shelter or foraging for dung beetles. And then you'll get the rare, cherished one that could go either way, like the letter I once received from some mad rancher down in south Texas who objected to a review I had written. "Christian Wiman!" he screamed in a letter to the editor, "What is this, a joke? Some sort of right-wing temperance group?" He meant Christian women, you see. I sent him a bottle of bourbon.

4.

The scope of a poet's prose will tell you at once something of his own and his culture's perspective of poetry's place in the world. One of the most consistent qualities of the books I read through while thinking about this piece was modesty—tonal modesty, yes, a certain levelling stylistic diffidence, but even more than that a modesty in the range of subject matter they address. The three books by non-Americans—Walcott's *What the Twilight Says,* Milosz's *Road-side Dog,* and Middleton's *Jackdaw Jiving*—make for a sharp contrast, as all of these writers are more ecumenical, more political, more *historical* than their American counterparts, who, when they do range away from specific treatments of poems or issues relating to poetry, tend to do so in the direction of personal experience.

American poets, except in the rarest instances (Adrienne Rich), and then usually only with regard to a very specific issue, don't become public intellectuals in the broadest sense of that term. It's tough to become a public intellectual when your public thinks of you as extraneous, even faintly ridiculous, but even when a poet does seem to have acquired something of a public forum—our poet laureates, for example—there's little effort to speak to broader cultural issues. The enclosed focus of most contemporary American poetry, which often seems to have resigned itself to the fact that its only readers are other poets, seems to obtain for our criticism as well. It's difficult to imagine a book like *The Captive Mind* or *The Labyrinth of Solitude* being written by a prominent American poet.

I mean that mostly by way of observation rather than criticism. Some of the strongest writing in these books I've read occurs when criticism merges with autobiography, and combining the intimately personal with the critical may be a particularly American strength. (Tellingly, this is precisely where Walcott's writing becomes weakest.) I have already mentioned McClatchy in this regard, whose autobiographical essays are at once personal and impersonal, directly confessional but very cannily crafted. C. K. Williams's concluding essay in *Poetry and Consciousness* on why he no longer reads many novels, which digresses and then focuses on what form means in a poem, is another good example of this balance.

The example of poets becoming pundits is not always, or even usually, a good one. As it happens, of the three books by non-Americans that I mentioned, only Milosz's seems to me compelling in this sense, as cultural commentary, as wisdom. American precedents aren't too promising. We could live without the sophisticated hatefulness of Eliot in *After Strange Gods,* the streetcorner rants of Pound on money. And yet all of these examples—Walcott and Middleton included—suggest an idea of what the poet's place in the world might be, and thus by extension what poetry's place in the world might be. The reach is greater, whatever has been successfully grasped, and it's hard not to see the narrowed scope of contemporary American critics as a diminished thing.

The recent rash of technical manuals on prosody is almost certainly a symptom of this attenuated scope. These manuals are by and large a salutary thing, I guess. After the train-wreck of broken-prose confessionalism, there seems to be a general heightened emphasis upon technique, an understanding that, for the best poets, technique is co-extensive with feeling, and that many of the elements associated with traditional technique must be mastered if poetry is to remain a serious art. Still, there's something disappointing in the fact that our most prominent poet of the moment, Robert Pinsky, whose first book of opinionated and partisan prose, *The Situation of Poetry,* remains interesting and useful, has produced a mild, rudimentary, mostly redundant book on the sounds of poetry. There's something frustrating in watching all of these well-established poets expend so much energy explaining dipodic meters, synaloepha, or the evolution of the pantoum. Yeats, at the death of Swinburne, declared himself King of the Cats. The battle now seems to be over who will be King of the Teachers.

This pedagogical inclination can sometimes disguise narrowed focus as enlarged scope, can substitute range of reference and taste for range of passion and experience. Part of becoming a poet is realizing that, as those shallows in which Kavanagh spoke of dabbling begin to deepen, the currents they contain are not simply of one's individual life, but of life itself, of reality beyond one's own. It is this awareness that informs the work of the truly great critics like Heaney, Eliot, Coleridge, and Dryden, and that I find missing from so much contemporary writing about poetry, which is frequently merely explanatory, concerned with *how* rather than *why* one ought to read particular poems, locating them in literature rather than life. Close readings have their uses, can anchor a criticism that has become too impressionistic and vague. Witnessing a powerful mind limit itself to the literary elements of a text can be fascinating, and yet there is for me always something a bit appalling about it as well, like watching a spider that, limb by limb, line by line, sucks the life out of some poor fly.

But there's a much subtler kind of pedagogical withdrawal. A recurrent refrain within these books I've read is the necessity for broad-mindedness, a rejection of aesthetic exclusivity, a plea for openness with regard to what poetry can be, or what it needs to be at any given moment. "I don't think any particular imperative—that poetry must become more difficult, more accessible, more formal, more disjunctive, more self-conscious—is ever very useful," Longenbach writes, largely in response to Eliot. It's a statement which, on its surface, seems pleasantly equanimical and hard to disagree with, a reformulation of negative capability, of sorts, in that for Longenbach the ideal for both the poet and critic seems to be that capacity "of being in uncertainties, Mysteries, doubts, without any irritable reaching after fact & reason." It's wrong, or at least oversimplified.

Poetry arises out of absence, a deep internal sense of wrongness, out of a mind that feels itself to be in some way cracked. An original poem is a descent into and expression of this insufficiency. Criticism, when it is written by a poet who understands the urgency involved in making poems, is usually either a careful delineation of the depths entered (Heaney), or an equally careful attempt to recast them somewhat in order to make them more manageable (Eliot). In either case, in terms of taste, historical understanding, and a feeling for what is *necessary* in poems, the criticism is going to be pitched in one particular direction. We might say that often the critic in a man must choose sides, *precisely in order that* the poet in him can go on stealing secrets from the enemy. You spend years sealing up the gaps in your uncertainty, shoring fragments of fact and reason against your ruins, all the while praying that in rare moments some ghost of that good unknowingness—call it spirit, call it the unconscious, call it God—will slip back in to save you from your best efforts. Negative capability is a good and necessary thing, but you can't *plan* on it.

Poetry, insofar as it is written by those bundles of accident and incoherence that are individual poets, demands imperatives, whether it's Eliot formulating his ideas about impersonality, difficulty, and tradition while writing his personal, aurally immediate, and altogether original poems, or Milton deploying dogma as a sort of defensive strategy against the real feeling and passion of *Paradise Lost.* Indeed, strong critical beliefs can serve roughly the same function as dogmas, which only those whose lives are as blithe and formless as their poems will dismiss out of hand. The poet can't ever embrace either, that's probably right, but the critic can and often must on his behalf. So while it's generally true that at any given moment it's not necessary that poetry be more difficult, more accessible, more formal, more disjunctive, more self-conscious than the poetry of the past, there's a way in which, for anyone whose concern is for the here and now, for the poems that are possible for us at this particular moment, this is a useless sort of truth. It's the long view of the scholar, not the immediate, urgent anxiety of the poet.

5.

Poetry's origins and courses are mysterious and, if it is to avoid becoming mechanical, merely an imitation of literature, must remain so. It ought to come as easily as leaves to a tree, Keats said, by which he meant, I think, not that it ought to come necessarily with ease but that there should be something natural about it, that it should be both a poet's life and life itself occurring somehow in language. This is why at the onset of a poem, when most possessed by it, it can seem like greatness is possible. It may not be possible for *you,* and coincidental with this immensity of potential may be the most corrosive awareness of inadequacy, but there is some greatness inherent in the act itself.

Reality doesn't need us. A poet knows this, and then, in the midst of a poem, when reality streams through the words that would hold it, doesn't quite. W. S. Di Piero, one of the best prose writers among contemporary American poets, writes of that moment when one realizes that one's "attempt to write poetry, with all its halting correctiveness and will toward coherence, is of no consequence to the starry sky." And yet it was the starry sky that occasioned the poem, perhaps, that seems to be not simply its subject but somehow *in* the poem, of it. It is a calling, we say, trying to explain this need to make things the world can do without, as if the plain givenness of reality could ever be a call, as if a poem could ever be an answer.

Prose is an altogether different order of experience, more public, less mysterious, less ultimately rewarding. I'm not sure it makes much sense to speak of "greatness" in critical prose, and the only call you're likely to get is on the telephone, some editor asking you to write something. And yet I've found it impossible to talk about prose without talking a great deal about poetry, for a poet's prose is intimately bound up with that original calling.

It can occasionally, in certain limited ways, be even more satisfying. Prose can provide a poet with a means of direct self-discovery and articulation that poetry, with its impersonal formal imperatives, in which personality and selfhood can seem to be annihilated, cannot. Poetry, feeding on singular instances of consciousness and psychological urgencies, can't afford to become a habit, and the will to remain vigilant to its occasions can be exhausting. Prose can afford to become habitual, without much damage to either the poet or his prose. There can be great comfort in this, both in terms of surviving the silences I've mentioned as well as satisfying a puritanical desire for work, work, work. In the end, though, when the work is done, any poet who is at all a poet knows it for what it is, which is something considerably less than the real work, mere means, a very careful sort of public appearance, a bit of money, maybe, a bit of a headache, probably, a piece of prose.

1999

Selected Bibliographies

JULIA ALVAREZ

Poetry
Homecoming: New and Collected Poems. New York: Plume, 1996.

Prose
In the Name of Salome. Chapel Hill, NC: Algonquin Books, 2000.
Something to Declare. Chapel Hill, NC: Algonquin Books, 1998.
YO! Chapel Hill, N. C.: Algonquin Books, 1996.
In the Time of the Butterflies. Chapel Hill, NC: Algonquin Books, 1994.
How the Garcia Girls Lost Their Accents. Chapel Hill, NC: Algonquin Books, 1991.

Critical Studies
Andreu, Alicia G. "Julia Alvarez and the Reconstruction of the Self." *Torre de Papel* (Fall 1998) 8(3): 49–56.
Varnes, Kathrine. "'Practising for the Real Me': Form and Authenticity in the Poetry of Julia Alvarez." *Antipodas: Journal of Hispanic and Galician Studies* (Victoria, Australia 1998) 10: 67–77.
Vela, Richard. "Daughter of Invention: The Poetry of Julia Alvarez." *Postscript: Publication of the Philological Association of the Carolinas* (1999) 16: 33–42.

JOHN ASHBERY

Poetry
Your Name Here: Poems. New York: Farrar, Straus, Giroux, 2000.
Girls on the Run: A Poem. New York: Farrar, Straus, Giroux, 1999.
Wakefulness. New York: Farrar, Straus, Giroux, 1998.
The Mooring of Starting Out: The First Five Books of Poetry. New York: Ecco, 1997.
Can You Hear Me, Bird. New York: Farrar, Straus, Giroux, 1995.
And the Stars Were Shining. New York: Farrar, Straus, Giroux, 1994.
Hotel Lautréamont. New York: Knopf, 1992.
Flow Chart. New York: Knopf, 1991.
Selected Poems. New York: Viking Penguin, 1985.

Prose
Other Traditions. Cambridge, Mass.: Harvard UP, 2000.
Reported Sightings: Art Chronicles, 1957–1987. Ed. David Bergman. New York: Knopf, 1989.

Bibliography
Kermani, David K. *John Ashbery: A Comprehensive Bibliography*. New York: Garland, 1976.

Critical Studies
Herd, David. *John Ashbery and American Poetry*. New York: St. Martin's, 2001.
Lehman, David, ed. *Beyond Amazement: New Essays on John Ashbery*. Ithaca, NY: Cornell UP, 1980.
Schultz, Susan M, ed. *The Tribe of John: Ashbery and Contemporary Poetry*. Tuscaloosa: U of Alabama P, 1995.
Shapiro, David. *John Ashbery: An Introduction to the Poetry*. New York: Columbia UP, 1979.
Shoptaw, John. *On the Outside Looking In: John Ashbery's Poetry*. Cambridge, MA: Harvard UP, 1994.

ROBERT BLY

Poetry
Snowbanks North of the House. New York: HarperCollins, 1999.
Morning Poems. New York: HarperCollins, 1997.
What Have I Ever Lost by Dying?: Collected Prose Poems. New York: HarperCollins, 1992.
Loving a Woman in Two Worlds. New York: Harper, 1987.
Selected Poems. New York: Harper, 1986.

Prose
The Sibling Society. Reading, Mass.: Addison Wesley, 1996.
American Poetry: Wildness and Domesticity. New York: Harper, 1990.
Iron John: A Book about Men. Reading, MA: Addison Wesley, 1990.

Translations
Lorca and Jimenez: Selected Poems. Boston: Beacon, 1997.
Machado. *I Never Wanted Fame*. Minneapolis, MN: Ally Press, 1979.
Kabir. *The Kabir Book: Forty-Four of the Ecstatic Poems of Kabir*. Boston: Beacon, 1977.
Pablo Neruda and Cesar Vallejo. *Selected Poems*. Boston: Beacon, 1971.
Knut Hamsun. *Hunger*. New York: Farrar, Straus, 1967.

Editing
William Stafford. *The Darkness around Us Is Deep: Selected Poems*. New York: HarperCollins, 1994.
The Rag and Bone Shop of the Heart: Poems for Men. With James Hillman. New York: HarperCollins, 1992.
David Ignatow. *Selected Poems*. Watertown, CN: Wesleyan UP, 1975.

Biographical and Critical Studies
Daniels, Kate and Richard Jones, eds. *On Solitude and Silence: Writings on Robert Bly*. Boston: Beacon, 1982.

Davis, William V. *Understanding Robert Bly*. Columbia, SC: U of South Carolina, 1989.

Nelson, Howard. *Robert Bly: An Introduction to the Poetry*. New York: Columbia UP, 1984.

Peseroff, Joyce, ed. *Robert Bly: When We Sleeper Awake*. Ann Arbor: U of Michigan P, 1984.

Smith, Thomas R., ed. *Walking Swiftly: Writings and Images on the Occasion of Robert Bly's 65th Birthday*. Minneapolis, MN: Ally Press, 1992.

LOUISE BOGAN

Poetry
The Blue Estuaries: Poems 1923–1968. 1968. New York: Farrar, Straus, Giroux, 1996.

Prose
Journey around My Room: The Autobiography of Louise Bogan. Ed. Ruth Limmer. New York: Viking, 1980.

What the Woman Lived: Selected Letters of Louise Bogan, 1920–1970. Ed. Ruth Limmer. New York: Harcourt, Brace, Jovanovich, 1973.

A Poet's Alphabet: Reflections on the Literary Art and Vocation. Ed. Ruth Limmer and Robert Phelps. New York: McGraw-Hill, 1970.

Achievement in American Poetry, 1900–1950. Chicago: Henry Regnery, 1951.

Bibliography
Knox, Claire E. *Louise Bogan: A Reference Source*. Metuchen, NJ: Scarecrow, 1990.

Biographical and Critical Studies
Bowles, Gloria. *Louise Bogan's Aesthetic of Limitation*. Bloomington: Indiana UP, 1987.

Collins, Martha, ed. *Critical Essays on Louise Bogan*. Boston: G. K. Hall, 1984.

Frank, Elizabeth. *Louise Bogan: A Portrait*. New York: Knopf, 1985.

Ridgeway, Jacqueline. *Louise Bogan*. Boston: Twayne, 1984.

Upton, Lee. *Repression and Release: Rereading the Poetry of Louise Bogan*. Lewisburg, Pa.: Bucknell UP, 1996.

GWENDOLYN BROOKS

Poetry
Selected Poems. New York: 1963; New York: Harper, 1999.

Blacks. Chicago: David Press, 1987; Rpt. Third World Press, 1991.

The World of Gwendolyn Brooks. New York: Harper, 1971.

Prose
Report from Part Two. Chicago: Third World Press, 1996.

Report from Part One. Detroit: Broadside Press, 1972.

Maud Martha, A Novel. New York: Harper, 1954.

Bibliography

Miller, R. Baxter. *Langston Hughes and Gwendolyn Brooks: A Reference Guide.* Boston: G. K. Hall, 1978.

Biographical and Critical Studies

Bloom, Harold, ed. *Gwendolyn Brooks (Modern Critical Views).* New York: Chelsea House, 2000.

Bolden, B. J. *Urban Rage in Bronzeville: Social Commentary in the Poetry of Gwendolyn Brooks, 1945–1960.* Chicago: Third World Press, 1998.

Kent, George. *A Life of Gwendolyn Brooks.* Lexington, KY: UP of Kentucky, 1987.

Melhem, D. H. *Gwendolyn Brooks: Poetry and the Heroic Voice.* Lexington, KY: UP of Kentucky, 1987.

Mootry, Maria K., and Gary Smith, eds. *A Life Distilled: Gwendolyn Brooks: Her Poetry and Fiction.* Urbana: U of Illinois P, 1987.

Shaw, Harry. *Gwendolyn Brooks.* Boston: Twayne, 1980.

Wright, Stephen Caldwell, ed. *On Gwendolyn Brooks: Reliant Contemplation.* Ann Arbor: U of Michigan P, 1996.

HART CRANE

Poetry

The Poems of Hart Crane. Ed. Marc Simon. New York: Liveright, 1986.

Prose

O My Land, My Friends: The Selected Letters of Hart Crane. Ed. Langdon Hammer and Brom Weber. New York: Four Walls, Eight Windows, 1997.

Hart Crane and Yvor Winters: Their Literary Correspondence. Ed. Thomas Parkinson. Berkeley: U of California P, 1978.

The Letters of Hart Crane and His Family. Ed. Thomas S. W. Lewis. New York: Columbia UP, 1974.

Bibliography

Schwartz, Joseph. *Hart Crane: A Reference Guide.* Boston: G. K. Hall, 1983.

———. *Hart Crane: An Annotated Critical Bibliography.* New York: D. Lewis, 1970.

Biographical and Critical Studies

Brown, Susan Jenkins. *Robber Rocks: Letters and Memories of Hart Crane, 1923–1932.* Middletown, Conn.: Wesleyan UP, 1969.

Edelman, Lee. *Transmemberment of Song: Hart Crane's Anatomies of Rhetoric and Desire.* Stanford, CA: Stanford UP, 1987.

Grossman, Allen. "Hart Crane and Poetry: A Consideration of Crane's Intense Poetics with Reference to 'The Return.'" *Critical Essays on Hart Crane.* Ed. David R. Clark. Boston: G. K. Hall, 1983.

Hammer, Langdon. *Hart Crane and Allen Tate: Janus Faced Modernism.* Princeton, NJ: Princeton UP, 1993.

Leibowitz, Herbert. *Hart Crane: An Introduction.* Columbia UP, 1968.

Lewis, R. W. B. *The Poetry of Hart Crane: A Critical Study.* Princeton, NJ: Princeton UP, 1967.

Mariani, Paul. *The Broken Tower: A Life of Hart Crane.* New York: Norton, 1999.

Unterecker, John. *Voyager: A Life of Hart Crane.* New York: Farrar, Straus, Giroux, 1969.

Yingling, Thomas. *Hart Crane and the Homosexual Text: New Thresholds, New Anatomies.* Chicago: U of Chicago P, 1990.

ROBERT CREELEY

Poetry
Life and Death. New York: New Directions, 1998.

Echoes. New York: New Directions, 1994.

Selected Poems. Berkeley: U of California P, 1991.

Collected Poems of Robert Creeley, 1945–1975. Berkeley: U of California P, 1982.

Prose
Collected Prose. Rev. Ed. Ed. Donald Allen and Benjamin Friedlander. McLean, IL: Dalkey Archive Press, 2001.

Irving Layton and Robert Creeley: The Complete Correspondence, 1973–1978. Ed. Ekbert Faas and Sabrina Reed. Montreal: McGill-Queen's UP, 1990.

The Collected Essays of Robert Creeley. Berkeley: U of California P, 1989.

Charles Olson and Robert Creeley: The Complete Correspondence. Ed. George F. Butterick. 10 vols. Santa Barbara, CA: Black Sparrow Press, 1980–1996.

Bibliography
Fox, Willard. *Robert Creeley, Ed Dorn, and Robert Duncan: A Reference Guide.* Boston: G. K. Hall, 1989.

Novik, Mary. *Robert Creeley: An Inventory, 1945–1970.* Kent, Ohio: Kent State UP, 1973.

Biographical and Critical Studies
Clark, Tom. *Robert Creeley and the Genius of the American Common Place: Together with the Poet's Own Autobiography.* New York: New Directions, 1993.

Edelbert, Cynthia Dubin. *Robert Creeley: A Critical Introduction.* Albuquerque: U of New Mexico P, 1978

Faas, Ekbert. *Robert Creeley: A Biography.* Hanover, NH: UP of New England, 2001.

Ford, Arthur. *Robert Creeley.* Boston: Twayne, 1978.

Terrell, Carroll F., ed. *Robert Creeley: The Poet's Workshop.* Orono, ME: National Poetry Foundation, 1984.

Wilson, John, ed. *Robert Creeley's Life and Work: A Sense of Increment.* Ann Arbor: U of Michigan P, 1987.

J. V. CUNNINGHAM

Poetry
The Poems of J. V. Cunningham. Ed. Timothy Steele. Athens: Swallow/Ohio UP, 1997.

Prose
The Collected Essays of J. V. Cunningham. Chicago: Swallow, 1976.
Tradition and Poetic Structure: Essays in Literary History and Criticism. Denver: Swallow, 1960.

Bibliography
Gullans, Charles. *A Bibliography of the Published Works of J.V. Cunningham, 1931–1988*. Florence, KY: Robert L. Barth, 1988.

Biographical and Critical Studies
Barth, R. L. *Chicago Review*. Cunningham Memorial Issue. Autumn 1985.
———. "The Vacancies of Need: Particularity in J.V. Cunningham's *To What Strangers, What Welcome*." *Southern Review* Spring 1982: 286–98.
Donoghue, Denis. *The Connoisseurs of Chaos*. New York: Macmillan, 1965.
Helmling, Steven. "J. V. Cunningham." *In Dictionary of Literary Biography*, vol. 5, Part I. Detroit: Gale, 1980: 159–65.
Pinsky, Robert. "The Poetry of J. V. Cunningham." *New Republic* January 28, 1978: 25–26, 28–29.
Sequoia. Cunningham Memorial Issue. Spring 1985.
Steele, Timothy. "An Interview with J. V. Cunningham." *Iowa Review* Fall 1985: 1–24.
Taylor, Henry. *Compulsory Figures*. Baton Rouge: Louisiana State UP, 1992: 1–17.
Winters, Yvor. *Forms of Discovery*. Denver: Swallow, 1967: 299–311.
———. *The Poetry of J. V. Cunningham*. Denver: Swallow, 1961.

RITA DOVE

Poetry
On the Bus with Rosa Parks. New York: Norton, 1999.
Mother Love: Poems. New York: Norton, 1995.
Selected Poems. New York: Pantheon, 1993.

Play
The Darker Face of the Earth. Ashland, OR: Story Line Press, 1994.

Prose
Through the Ivory Gate. New York: Pantheon, 1992.
Fifth Sunday. Baltimore, MD: Callaloo Fiction Series, 1985.

Critical Study
Vendler, Helen. *The Given and the Made: Strategies of Poetic Redefinition*. Cambridge, Mass.: Harvard UP, 1995.

ROBERT DUNCAN

Poetry
Selected Poems. Revised and enlarged edition. Ed. Robert J. Bertholf. New York: New Directions, 1997.
Ground Work II: In the Dark. New York: New Directions, 1987.
Ground Work: Before the War. New York: New Directions, 1984.
Bending the Bow. New York: New Directions, 1968.
The Years as Catches: First Poems, 1939–1946. Berkeley: Oyez Press, 1966.
Roots and Branches. New York: Scribner, 1964; Rpt. New Directions, 1969.
The Opening of the Field. New York: Grove, 1960; Rpt. New Directions, 1973.

Prose
Selected Prose. Ed. Robert. J. Bertholf. New York: New Directions, 1995.
Fictive Certainties: Essays. New York: New Directions, 1985.

Bibliography
Bertholf, Robert J. *Robert Duncan: A Descriptive Bibliography.* Santa Barbara, CA: Black Sparrow Press, 1986.
Fox, Willard. *Robert Creeley, Ed Dorn, and Robert Duncan: A Reference Guide.* Boston: G. K. Hall, 1989.

Biographical and Critical Studies
Bertholf, Robert J. and Ian W. Reid, eds. *Robert Duncan: Scales of the Marvelous.* New York: New Directions, 1979.
Davidson, Michael. "Marginality in the Margins: Robert Duncan's Textual Politics." *Contemporary Literature* 33 (Summer 1992): 275–301.
Faas, Ekbert. *Young Robert Duncan: Portrait of the Poet as Homosexual in Society.* Santa Barbara, CA: Black Sparrow Press, 1983.
Gunn, Thom. "The High Road: A Last Collection" and "Adventurous Song: Robert Duncan as Romantic Modernist." *Shelf Life: Essays, Memoirs, and an Interview.* Ann Arbor: U of Michigan P, 1993: 118–34, 129–70.
———. "Homosexuality in Robert Duncan's Poetry." *The Occasions of Poetry: Essays in Criticism and Autobiography.* Exp. ed. Ed. Clive Wilmer. San Francisco: North Point Press, 1985.
Johnson, Mark. *Robert Duncan.* Boston: Twayne, 1988.
Paul, Sherman. *The Lost America of Love: Rereading Robert Creeley, Edward Dorn, and Robert Duncan.* Baton Rouge: Louisiana State UP, 1981.

T. S. ELIOT

Poetry
The Waste Land: A Facsimile and Transcript of the Original Drafts Including the Annotations of Ezra Pound. Ed. Valerie Eliot. New York: Harcourt, 1971.
Complete Poems and Plays. New York: Harcourt, 1952.

Prose

The Letters of T. S. Eliot. Vol. 1, 1898–1922. Ed. Valerie Eliot. New York: Harcourt, 1988.
To Criticize the Critic. New York: Farrar, Straus, 1965.
The Use of Poetry and the Use of Criticism. Cambridge, MA: Harvard UP, 1932.
For Lancelot Andrewes. London: Faber, 1928.
Homage to John Dryden. London: Hogarth, 1924.
The Sacred Wood. London: Methuen, 1920.

Bibliography

Gallup, Donald. *T. S. Eliot: A Bibliography.* New York: Harcourt, 1969.

Biographical and Critical Studies

Ackroyd, Peter. *T.S. Eliot: A Life.* New York: Simon and Schuster, 1984.
Bush, Ronald. *T. S. Eliot: A Study in Character and Style.* New York: Oxford UP, 1983.
Donoghue, Denis. *Words Alone: The Poet T. S. Eliot.* New Haven: Yale UP, 2000.
Gardner, Helen. *The Art of T. S. Eliot.* New York: Dutton, 1950.
———. *The Composition of Four Quartets.* New York: Oxford UP, 1978.
Gordon, Lyndall. *Eliot's Early Years.* New York: Oxford UP, 1977.
———. *Eliot's New Life.* New York: Oxford UP, 1988.
Kenner, Hugh, ed. *T. S. Eliot: A Collection of Critical Essays.* Englewood Cliffs, NJ: Prentice-Hall, 1962.
———. *T. S. Eliot: The Invisible Poet.* New York: McDowell-Oblonsky, 1959.
Moody, A. David, ed. *The Cambridge Companion to T. S. Eliot.* New York: Cambridge UP, 1994.
Ricks, Christopher. *T. S. Eliot and Prejudice.* Berkeley: U of California, 1988.
Tate, Allen, ed. *T. S. Eliot: The Man and His Work.* New York: Delacorte, 1966.

RHINA ESPAILLAT

Poetry

Rehearsing Absence. Evansville, IN: U of Evansville P, 2001.
Mundo y Palabra/The World and the Word. Vol. 4 of *Walking to Windward: 21 New England Poets.* Durham, NH: Oyster River Press, 2001. (Bilingual chapbook)
Where Horizons Go. Kirksville, MO: Truman State UP, 1998.
Lapsing to Grace. East Lansing, MI: Bennett & Kitchel, 1992.

JACK FOLEY

Poetry

Exiles. Berkeley: Pantograph, 1996.
Adrift. Berkeley: Pantograph, 1993.
Gershwin. San Francisco: Norton Coker, 1991.
Letters/Lights—Words for Adelle. Berkeley: Mother's Hen Press, 1987.

Prose
Foley's Books. Berkeley: Pantograph, 2000.
O Powerful Western Star! Berkeley: Pantograph, 2000.
Contemporary Authors Autobiography Series. Vol. 24. Detroit: Gale, 1993: 153–81.

Translation
Some Songs by George Brassens. Seattle: Goldfish, 2001.

ROBERT FROST

Poetry
Collected Poems, Plays, and Prose. New York: Library of America, 1995.
Complete Poems of Robert Frost. New York: Holt, 1968.
Selected Poems. Introduction by Robert Graves. New York: Holt, 1963.
Collected Poems. New York: Holt, 1930.

Prose
Robert Frost on Writing. Ed. Elaine Barry. New Brunswick: Rutgers UP, 1972.
Robert Frost: Poetry and Prose. Ed. Lawrence Thompson and Edward Connery Lathem. New York: Holt, 1972
Selected Prose of Robert Frost. Ed. Hyde Cox and Edward Connery Lathem. New York: Holt 1966.

Letters
Robert Frost and Sidney Cox: Forty Years of Friendship. Ed. William R. Evans. Hanover, NH: UP of New England, 1981.
Family Letters of Robert and Elinor Frost. Ed. Arnold Grade. Albany: State U of New York P, 1972.
Selected Letters of Robert Frost. Ed. Lawrance Thompson. New York: Holt, 1964.
The Letters of Robert Frost to Louis Untermeyer. Ed. Louis Untermeyer. New York: Holt, 1963.
Robert Frost and John Bartlett: The Record of a Friendship. Ed. Margaret Bartlett Anderson. New York: Holt, 1963.

Interviews
Interviews with Robert Frost. Ed. Edward Connery Lathem. New York: Holt, 1966.

Biographical Studies
Meyers, Jeffery. *Robert Frost: A Biography.* Boston: Houghton Mifflin, 1996.
Parini, Jay. *Robert Frost: A Life.* New York: Holt, 1999.
Sergeant, Elizabeth Shepley. *Robert Frost: The Trial by Existence.* New York: Holt, 1960.
Thompson, Lawrence. *Robert Frost: The Early Years, 1874-1915.* New York: Holt, 1966.
Thompson, Lawrence. *Robert Frost: The Years of Triumph, 1915-1938.* New York: Holt, 1970.
Thompson, Lawrence, and R. H. Winnick. *Robert Frost: The Later Years, 1938–1963.* New York: Holt, 1976.

Bibliography

Mertins, Marshall Louis, and Esther Mertins. *Intervals of Robert Frost: A Critical Bibliography*. Berkeley: U of California P, 1947.

Critical Studies

Bloom, Harold, ed. *Robert Frost*. New York: Chelsea House, 1998.

Brower, Reuben A. *The Poetry of Robert Frost: Constellations of Intention*. New York: Oxford UP, 1963.

Cox, James M. *Robert Frost: A Collection of Critical Essays*. Englewood Cliffs: Prentice-Hall, 1962.

Cox, Sidney. *Swinger of Birches: A Portrait of Robert Frost*. New York: New York UP, 1957.

Cramer, Jefferey S. *Robert Frost among His Poems: A Literary Companion to the Poet's Own Biographical Contexts and Associations*. Jefferson, NC: McFarland, 1996.

Francis, Lesley Lee. *The Frost Family's Adventure in Poetry*. Columbia, MO: U of Missouri P, 1994.

Jennings, Elizabeth. *Frost*. New York: Barnes & Noble, 1966.

Kearns, Katherine. *Robert Frost and a Poetics of Appetite*. Cambridge, England: Cambridge UP, 1994.

Kilcup, Karen L. *Robert Frost and Feminine Literary Tradition*. Ann Arbor: U of Michigan P, 1998.

Lathem, Edward C., ed. *A Concordance to the Poetry of Robert Frost*. New York: Holt, 1971.

Lentriccia, Frank. *Robert Frost: Modern Poetics and the Landscapes of Self*. Durham: Duke UP, 1975.

Maxson, H. A. *On the Sonnets of Robert Frost*. Jefferson, NC: McFarland, 1997.

Nitchie, George W. *Human Values in the Poetry of Robert Frost*. Durham: Duke UP, 1960.

Poirier, Richard. *Robert Frost*. New York: Oxford UP, 1977.

Pritchard, William H. *Frost: A Literary Life Reconsidered*. New York: Oxford UP, 1984.

Richardson, Mark. *The Ordeal of Robert Frost: The Poet and His Poetic*. Chicago: U of Illinois P, 1997.

Squires, Radcliffe. *Major Themes of Robert Frost*. Ann Arbor: U of Michigan P, 1969.

Wagner, Linda Welshimer, ed. *Robert Frost: The Critical Reception*. New York: B. Franklin, 1977.

ALICE FULTON

Poetry

Felt: Poems. New York: Norton, 2001.

Sensual Math: Poems. New York: Norton, 1995.

Powers of Congress. New York: Norton, 1990.

Palladium. New York: Norton, 1986.

Dance Script with Electric Ballerina. Philadelphia: U of Pennsylvania P, 1983.

Prose

Feeling as a Foreign Language: The Good Strangeness of Poetry. St Paul, MN: Graywolf, 1999.

Critical Studies

Grosholz, Emily. "Distortion, Explosion, and Embrace: The Poetry of Alice Fulton."
Michigan Quarterly Review 34 (Spring 1995): 213–29.

Keller, Lynn. "The 'then some inbetween': Alice Fulton's Feminist Experimentalism."
American Literature 71:2 (June 1999): 311–40.

Miller, Cristanne. " 'The Erogenous Cusp': Or Intersections of Science and Gender in Alice
Fulton's Poetry." *Feminist Measures: Soundings in Poetry and Theory*. Ed. Lynn Keller
and Cristanne Miller. Ann Arbor: U of Michigan P, 1994: 317–43.

DANA GIOIA

Poetry

Interrogations at Noon. St. Paul, MN: Graywolf, 2001.
The Gods of Winter. St. Paul, MN: Graywolf, 1991.
Daily Horoscope. St. Paul, MN: Graywolf, 1986.

Prose

"Fallen Western Star: The Decline of San Francisco as a Literary Region." *Hungry
Mind Review* 52 (Winter 1999–2000): 17–21.
Can Poetry Matter? St. Paul, MN: Graywolf, 1992.

Libretto

Nosferatu. St. Paul, MN: Graywolf, 2001.

Translations

Seneca. *The Madness of Hercules*. Baltimore: Johns Hopkins UP, 1995.
Eugenio Montale. *Mottetti: Poems of Love*. St. Paul, MN: Graywolf, 1990.

Editing

The Longman Anthology of Short Fiction. With R. S. Gwynn. New York: Longman, 2001.
Certain Solitudes: On the Poetry of Donald Justice. With William Logan. Fayetteville:
U of Arkansas P, 1997.
New Italian Poets. With Michael Palma. Ashland, OR: Story Line, 1990.
Poems from Italy. With William Jay Smith. St. Paul, MN: New Rivers, 1985.
Weldon Kees. *The Ceremoney and Other Stories*. St. Paul, MN: Graywolf, 1984.

Bibliography

Hagstrom, Jack W. C., and Bill Morgan. *Dana Gioia: A Descriptive Bibliography with
Critical Essays*. Jackson, MS: Parrish House Books, 2002.

Biographical and Critical Studies

Lindner, April. *Dana Gioia*. Western Writers Series #143. Boise, ID: Boise State UP,
2000.
———. *New Formalist Poets of the American West*. Western Writers Series #149.
Boise, ID: Boise State UP, 2001.
Mason, David. *The Poetry of Life and the Life of Poetry*. Ashland, OR: Story Line,
2000.

Turco, Lewis. "Dana Gioia." In *American Poets Since World War II. Dictionary of Literary Biography,* vol. 120. Ed. R. S. Gwynn. Detroit: Gale, 1992.

Walzer, Kevin. *The Ghost of Tradition: Expansive Poetry and Postmodernism.* Ashland, OR: Story Line 1998.

LOUISE GLÜCK

Poetry

Vita Nova. New York: HarperTrade, 2001.

Meadowlands. Hopewell, NJ: Ecco Press, 1996.

The First Four Books of Poems. Hopewell, NJ: Ecco Press, 1995.

The Wild Iris. Hopewell, NJ: Ecco Press, 1992.

Ararat. Hopewell, NJ: Ecco Press, 1990.

The Triumph of Achilles. Hopewell, NJ: Ecco Press, 1985.

Prose

Proofs and Theories: Essays on Poetry. Hopewell, NJ: Ecco Press, 1994.

Critical Studies

Dodd, Elizabeth Caroline. *The Veiled Mirror and the Woman Poet: H. D., Louise Bogan, Elizabeth Bishop, and Louise Glück.* Columbia: U of Missouri P, 1992.

DONALD HALL

Poetry

Without. Boston: Houghton, 1998.

The Old Life. Boston: Houghton, 1996.

The Museum of Clear Ideas. New York: Ticknor & Fields, 1993.

Old and New Poems. New York: Ticknor & Fields, 1990.

Prose

Principal Products of Portugal. Boston: Beacon Press, 1995.

Life Work. Boston: Beacon Press, 1993.

Their Ancient Glittering Eyes. New York: Ticknor & Fields, 1992.

Poetry and Ambition. Ann Arbor: U of Michigan P, 1987.

The Weather for Poetry. Ann Arbor: U of Michigan P, 1982.

String Too Short to Be Saved. New York: Viking; Expanded edition, Boston: Godine, 1979.

Goatfoot Milktongue Twinbird. Ann Arbor: University of Michigan, 1978.

The Pleasures of Poetry. New York: Harper, 1971.

Marianne Moore: The Cage and the Animal. New York: Pegasus, 1970.

Henry Moore: The Life and Work of a Great Sculptor. New York: Harper, 1966.

Editing

Claims for Poetry. Ann Arbor: U of Michigan P, 1982.

Contemporary American Poetry. Baltimore: Penguin, 1963.

The New Poets of England and America. With Robert Pack and Louis Simpson. New York: Meridian, 1957.

Biographical and Critical Study
Rector, Liam, ed. *The Day I Was Older: Collected Writings on the Poetry of Donald Hall*. Brownsville, OR: Story Line Press, 1989.

ROBERT HAYDEN

Poetry
Collected Poems. Ed. Frederick Glaysher. New York: Liveright, 1985, 1996.

Prose
Collected Prose. Ed. Frederick Glaysher. Ann Arbor: U of Michigan P, 1984.

Editing
Kaleidoscope: Poems by American Negro Poets. New York: Harcourt Brace Jovanovich, 1967.

Biographical and Critical Studies
Feltrow, Fred M. *Robert Hayden*. Boston: Twayne, 1984.
Harper, Michael S. "Remembering Robert Hayden." *Michigan Quarterly Review* (Winter 1982): 182–86.
Hatcher, John. *From the Auroral Darkness: The Life and Poetry of Robert Hayden*. Oxford: George Ronald, 1984.
O'Brien, John. *Interviews with Black Writers*. New York: Liveright, 1973.
Williams, Pontheolla Taylor. *Robert Hayden: A Critical Analysis of His Poetry*. Champaign, IL: U of Illinois P, 1987.

LYN HEJINIAN

Poetry
The Cold of Poetry. Los Angeles: Sun & Moon Press, 1994.
The Cell. Los Angeles: Sun & Moon Press, 1992.
My Life. Providence, RI: Burning Deck, 1980. Revised and enlarged edition, Los Angeles: Sun & Moon Press, 1987.
Writing Is an Aid to Memory. Berkeley: The Figures, 1978.

Prose
The Language of Inquiry. Berkeley: University of California Press, 2000.
Oxota: A Short Russian Novel. Great Barrington, MA: The Figures, 1991.

Critical Studies
Altieri, Charles. "Lyn Hejinian and the Possibilities of Postmodernism in Poetry." *Women Poets of the Americas: Toward a Pan-American Gathering*. Ed. Jacqueline Vaught and Cordelia Chavez Candelaria. Notre Dame, IN: U of Notre Dame P, 1999: 146–55.
Armentrout, Rae. "Feminist Poetics and the Meaning of Clarity." *Artifice and Indeterminacy: An Anthology of New Poetics*. Ed. Christopher Beach. Tuscaloosa: U of Alabama P, 1998: 287–96.

Dworkin, Craig Douglas. "Penelope Reworking the Twill: Patchwork, Writing, and Lyn Hejinian's *My Life*." *Contemporary Literature* 36 (Spring 1995): 58–81.

Spahr, Juliana. "Resignifying Autobiography: Lyn Hejinian's *My Life*." *American Literature* 68 (March 1996): 139–59.

LANGSTON HUGHES

Poetry
The Collected Poems of Langston Hughes. Ed. Arnold Rampersad and David Roessel. New York: Knopf, 1994.

Prose
Short Stories of Langston Hughes. New York: Hill & Wang, 1996.

Langston Hughes and the Chicago Defender: Essays on Race, Politics, and Culture, 1942–62. Ed. Christopher C. De Santis. Urbana, IL: U of Illinois P, 1995.

I Wonder as I Wander. New York: Rinehart, 1956.

The Big Sea: An Autobiography. New York: Knopf, 1940.

Biographical and Critical Studies
Berry, Faith. *Langston Hughes, before and after Harlem*. New York: Wings, 1995.

Dunham, Montrew. *Langston Hughes: Young Black Poet*. Madison, WI: Turtleback, 1995.

Emanuel, James. *Langston Hughes*. Boston: Twayne, 1967.

Harper, Donna Sullivan. *Not So Simple: The "Semple" Stories by Langston Hughes*. Columbia: U of Missouri P, 1985.

Meltzer, Milton. *Langston Hughes: A Biography*. New York: Crowell, 1968.

Walker, Alice. *Langston Hughes, American Poet*. New York: HarperCollins, 1988.

RANDALL JARRELL

Poetry
Selected Poems, Ed. William H. Pritchard. New York: Farrar, Straus and Giroux, 1990.

Complete Poems. New York: Farrar, Straus and Giroux, 1968, 1980.

Translations
Johann Wolfgang von Goethe. *Faust, Part I*. New York: Farrar, Straus and Giroux, 1976.

———. *The Juniper Tree and Other Fairy Tales from the Brothers Grimm*. New York: Farrar, Straus and Giroux, 1973.

Jakob and Willem Grimm. *The Golden Bird and Other Fairy Tales of the Brothers Grimm*. New York: Macmillan, 1962.

Ludwig Bechstein. *The Rabbit Catcher and Other Fairy Tales of Ludwig Bechstein*. New York: Macmillan, 1962.

Ferdinand Gregorovius. *The Ghetto and the Jews of Rome*. New York: Schocken, 1948.

Prose
No Other Book: Selected Essays. Ed. Brad Leithauser. New York: HarperCollins, 1995.

Jarrell's Letters: An Autobiographical and Literary Selection. Ed. Mary Jarrell and Stuart Wright. Boston: Houghton, 1985.

Kipling, Auden & Co: Essays and Reviews 1935–1964. New York: Farrar, Straus and Giroux, 1979.
Poetry and the Age. New York: Knopf, 1953. Rpt. Noonday, 1972.
The Third Book of Criticism. New York: Farrar, Straus and Giroux, 1969.

Novels and Children's Books
Fly by Night. New York: Farrar, Straus and Giroux, 1976.
The Animal Family. New York: Pantheon, 1965.
The Bat-Poet. New York: Macmillan, 1964.
The Gingerbread Rabbit. New York: Macmillan, 1963.
Pictures from an Institution. New York: Knopf, 1954.

Biographical and Critical Studies
Ferguson, Suzanne. *The Poetry of Randall Jarrell*. Baton Rouge: Louisiana State UP, 1971.
Lowell, Robert, Peter Taylor, and Robert Penn Warren, eds. *Randall Jarrell: 1914–1965*. New York: Farrar, Straus and Giroux, 1967.
Pritchard, William H. *Randal Jarrell: A Literary Life*. New York: Farrar, Straus and Giroux, 1990.
Quinn, Sister Bernetta. *Randall Jarrell*. Boston: Twayne, 1981.
Rosenthall, M. L. *Randall Jarrell*. Minneapolis: U of Minnesota P, 1972.

ROBINSON JEFFERS

Poetry
The Selected Poetry of Robinson Jeffers. Ed. Tim Hunt. Stanford: Stanford UP, 2001.
The Collected Poetry of Robinson Jeffers. Ed. Tim Hunt. 5 vol. Stanford: Stanford UP, 1988–2002.
Selected Poems. New York: Random House, 1964.
The Selected Poetry of Robinson Jeffers. New York: Random House, 1938.

Plays
The Cretan Woman. First produced in 1954.
The Tower Beyond Tragedy. First produced in November 1950.
Medea. New York: Random House, 1946. Reprinted with *Cawdor*. New York: New Directions, 1970. First produced October 1947.

Prose
The Selected Letters of Robinson Jeffers, 1897–1962. Ed. Ann N. Ridgeway. Baltimore: Johns Hopkins UP, 1968.
Themes in My Poems. San Francisco: Book Club of California, 1956.
Poetry, Gongorism and a Thousand Years. Los Angeles: Ritchie, 1949.

Biographical and Critical Studies
Beers, Terry. *"A thousand graceful subtleties": Rhetoric in the Poetry of Robinson Jeffers*. New York: Peter Lang, 1995.
Brophy, Robert. *Robinson Jeffers*. Boise, ID: Boise State UP, 1975.
———. *Robinson Jeffers: Dimensions of a Poet*. New York: Fordham UP, 1995.

———. *Robinson Jeffers: Myth, Ritual, and Symbol in His Narrative Poems*. Cleveland: Case Western Reserve UP, 1973.

Carpenter, Frederic I. *Robinson Jeffers*. New York: Twayne, 1962.

Everson, William. *The Excesses of God: Robinson Jeffers as a Religious Figure*. Stanford: Stanford UP, 1988.

———. *Robinson Jeffers: Fragments of an Older Fury*. Berkeley: Oyez, 1968.

Karman, James, ed. *Critical Essays on Robinson Jeffers*. Boston: Hall, 1990.

———. *Robinson Jeffers: Poet of California*. Brownsville, OR: Story Line, 1995.

Squires, Radcliffe. *The Loyalties of Robinson Jeffers*. Ann Arbor: U of Michigan P, 1956.

Vardamis, Alexander. *The Critical Reputation of Robinson Jeffers*. Hamden, CT: Archon P, 1972.

Zaller, Robert. *The Cliffs of Solitude: A Reading of Robinson Jeffers*. Cambridge: Cambridge UP, 1983.

———. ed. *Centennial Essays for Robinson Jeffers*. Newark: U of Delaware P, 1991.

JAMES WELDON JOHNSON

Poetry
Poems. New York: Penguin, 2000.
God's Trombones: Seven Negro Sermons in Verse. 1927. New York: Penguin, 1990.

Poetry and Prose
The Selected Writings of James Weldon Johnson. Ed. Sondra Kathryn Wilson. New York: Oxford UP, 1995.

Prose
Black Manhattan. 1930. Salem, NH: Ayer, 1988.
The Autobiography of an Ex-Colored Man. 1927. New York: Knopf, 1979.
Along This Way: The Autobiography of James Weldon Johnson. 1933. New York: Penguin, 1990.

Editing
The Book of American Negro Poetry. 1931. San Diego: Harcourt Brace Jovanovich, 1983.
The Second Book of Negro Spirituals. New York: Viking, 1926.
The Book of American Negro Spirituals. New York: Viking, 1925.

Bibliography
Fleming, Robert E. *James Weldon Johnson and Arna Wendell Bontemps: A Reference Guide*. New York: G.K. Hall, 1978.

Biographical and Critical Studies
Fleming, Robert E. *James Weldon Johnson*. Boston: Twayne, 1987.
Levy, Eugene. *James Weldon Johnson: Black Leader, Black Voice*. Chicago: U of Chicago P, 1973.
Price, Kenneth M. and Lawrence J. Oliver, eds. *Critical Essays on James Weldon Johnson*. New York: G. K. Hall, 1997.

DONALD JUSTICE

Poetry

New and Selected Poems. New York: Knopf, 1995.

A Donald Justice Reader: Selected Poetry and Prose. Middlebury, VT: Middlebury College, 1991.

The Sunset Maker: Poems / Stories / A Memoir. New York: Atheneum, 1987.

Prose

Oblivion. Ashland, OR: Story Line, 1998.

Platonic Scripts. Ann Arbor: U of Michigan P, 1984.

Editing

Joe Bolton. *The Last Nostalgia: Poems, 1982–1990.* Fayetteville: U of Arkansas P, 1999.

The Collected Poems of Weldon Kees. Omaha: U of Nebraska P, rev. 1992.

The Collected Poems of Henri Coulette. With Robert Mezey. Fayetteville: U of Arkansas P, 1990.

Biographical and Critical Study

Gioia, Dana and William Logan, eds. *Certain Solitudes: On the Poetry of Donald Justice.* Fayetteville: U of Arkansas P, 1998.

MARY KINZIE

Poetry

Ghost Ship: Poems. New York: Knopf, 1998.

Autumn Eros and Other Poems. New York: Knopf, 1991.

Summers of Vietnam and Other Poems. Riverdale-on-Hudson, NY: Sheep Meadow P, 1990.

The Threshold of the Year. Columbia, MO: U of Missouri P, 1982.

Prose

A Poet's Guide to Poetry. Chicago: U of Chicago P, 1999.

The Judge Is Fury: Dislocation and Form in Poetry. Ann Arbor: U of Michigan P, 1994.

The Cure of Poetry in an Age of Prose: Moral Essays on the Poet's Calling. Chicago: U of Chicago P, 1993.

Editing

Tales of Arturo Vivante. Riverdale-on-Hudson, NY: Sheep Meadow Press, 1990.

The Little Magazine in America: A Documentary History. With Elliott Anderson. Yonkers, NY: Northwestern UP, 1978.

Prose for Borges. With Charles Newman. Evanston, IL: Northwestern UP, 1974.

DENISE LEVERTOV

Poetry

Poems 1972–1982. New York: New Directions, 2001.

This Great Unknowing: Last Poems. New York: New Directions, 1999.

The Life around Us: Selected Poems on Nature. New York: New Directions, 1997.

The Stream and the Sapphire: Selected Poems on Religious Themes. New York: New Directions, 1997.
Poems, 1968–1972. New York: New Directions, 1987.
Poems, 1960–1967. New York: New Directions, 1983.
Collected Earlier Poems, 1940–1960. New York: New Directions, 1979.

Prose
The Letters of Denise Levertov and William Carlos Williams. Ed. Christopher MacGowan. New York: New Directions, 1998.
Tesserae: Memories and Suppositions. New York: New Directions, 1995.
New & Selected Essays. New York: New Directions, 1992.
Light Up the Cave. New York: New Directions, 1981.
The Poet in the World. New York: New Directions, 1973.

Biographical and Critical Studies
Marten, Harry. *Understanding Denise Levertov.* Columbia, SC: U of South Carolina P, 1988.
Rexroth, Kenneth. *Assays.* New York: New Directions, 1961.
———. *With Eye and Ear.* New York: Herder & Herder, 1970.
Rodgers, Audrey T. *Denise Levertov: The Poetry of Engagement.* Rutherford, NJ: Fairleigh Dickinson UP, 1993.
Wagner, Linda W. *Denise Levertov.* New Haven: Twayne, 1967.
Wagner-Martin, Linda W., ed. *Critical Essays on Denise Levertov.* Boston: G. K. Hall, 1990.

SHIRLEY GEOK-LIN LIM

Poetry
What the Fortune Teller Didn't Say. London: West End Press, 1998.
Monsoon History: Selected Poems. London: Skoob Pacifica, 1994.
Crossing the Peninsula and Other Poems. Kuala Lumpur: Heinemann Writing in Asia Series, 1980.

Prose
Joss and Gold (a novel). New York: Feminist Press. Singapore: Times Books International, 2001.
Two Dreams: Short Stories. New York: Feminist Press, 1997.
Among the White Moon Faces: An Asian-American Memoir of Homelands. New York: Feminist Press, 1996.

WILLIAM LOGAN

Poetry
Night Battle. New York: Penguin, 1999.
Vain Empires. Boston: Godine, 1995.
Sullen Weedy Lakes. Boston: Godine, 1988.
Difficulty. Boston: Godine, 1985.

Sad-Faced Men. Boston: Godine, 1982.
Dream of Dying. Port Townsend, WA: Graywolf, 1980.

Prose
Reputations of the Tongue: On Poets and Poetry. Gainesville: U of Florida P, 1999.
All the Rage: Prose on Poetry, 1976–1992. Ann Arbor: U of Michigan P, 1998.

Editing
Certain Solitudes: On the Poetry of Donald Justice. With Dana Gioia. Fayetteville: U of Arkansas P, 1997.

AMY LOWELL

Poetry
Complete Poetical Works. Boston: Houghton Mifflin, 1955.

Prose
Poetry and Poets: Essays. Ed. Ferris Greenslet. Boston: Houghton Mifflin, 1930.

Editing
Some Imagist Poets, 1916: An Annual Anthology. Boston: Houghton Mifflin, 1916.
Some Imagist Poets, 1917: An Annual Anthology. Boston: Houghton Mifflin, 1917.

Biographical and Critical Studies
Benvenuto, Richard. *Amy Lowell.* Boston: Twayne, 1985.
Galvin, Mary E. "Imagery and Invisibility: Amy Lowell and the Erotics of Particularity." *Queer Poetics: Five Modernist Women Writers.* Westport, CT: Praeger, 1999.
Gould, Jean. *Amy: The World of Amy Lowell and the Imagist Movement.* New York: Dodd, Mead, 1975.
Ruihley, Glenn Richard. *The Thorn of a Rose: Amy Lowell Reconsidered.* Hamden, CT: Archon, 1975.

W. S. MERWIN

Poetry
The River Sound. New York: Knopf, 1999.
The Folding Cliffs. New York: Knopf, 1998.
The Vixen. New York: Knopf, 1996.
Travels. New York: Knopf, 1993.
The Rain in the Trees. New York: Knopf, 1988.
Selected Poems. New York: Atheneum, 1988.
The Compass Flower. New York: Atheneum, 1977.
The First Four Books of Poems. New York: Atheneum, 1975.
The Carrier of Ladders. New York: Atheneum, 1970.
The Lice. New York: Atheneum, 1969.
The Moving Target. New York: Atheneum, 1963.

Prose
Unframed Originals: Recollections. New York: Atheneum, 1982.
Houses and Travellers. New York: Atheneum, 1977.
The Miner's Pale Children. New York: Atheneum, 1970.

Translations
Dante Alighieri, *Purgatorio.* New York: Knopf, 2000.
East Window: The Asian Poems. Port Townsend, WA: Copper Canyon, 1998.
Selected Translations, 1968–78. New York: Atheneum, 1979.
Osip Mandelstam. *Selected Poems.* With Clarence Brown. New York: Atheneum, 1974.
Pablo Neruda. *Twenty Love Poems and a Song of Despair.* London: Cape, 1969.
Selected Translations, 1948–1968. New York: Atheneum, 1969.
Some Spanish Ballads. New York: Doubleday, 1961.
The Poem of the Cid. London: Dent, 1959.

Critical Studies
Hix, H. L. *Understanding W. S. Merwin.* Columbia, SC: U of South Carolina P, 1997.
Nelson, Cary and Ed Folsom, eds. *W. S. Merwin: Essays on the Poetry.* Urbana, IL: U of Illinois P, 1987.

MARIANNE MOORE

Poetry
Becoming Marianne Moore: Early Poems 1907–1924. Ed. Robin G. Schulze. Berkeley: U of California P, 2002.
The Complete Poems of Marianne Moore. New York: Macmillan/Viking, 1981.

Prose
The Selected Letters of Marianne Moore. Ed. Bonnie Costello, Celeste Goodrich, and Cristanne Miller. New York: Knopf, 1997.
The Complete Prose of Marianne Moore. Ed. Patricia Willis. New York: Viking, 1986.

Bibliography
Abbot, Craig S. *Marianne Moore: A Descriptive Bibliography.* Pittsburgh: U of Pittsburgh P, 1977.
———. *Marianne Moore: A Reference Guide.* Boston: G. K. Hall, 1978.

Biographical and Critical Studies
Costello, Bonnie. *Marianne Moore: Imaginary Possessions.* Cambridge, MA: Harvard UP, 1981.
Gregory, Elizabeth. *Quotation and Modern American Poetry: "Imaginary Gardens with Real Toads."* Houston: Rice UP, 1996.
Heuving, Jeanne. *"Omissions Are Not Accidents": Gender in the Art of Marianne Moore.* Detroit: Wayne State UP, 1992.
Leavell, Linda. *Marianne Moore and the Visual Arts: Prismatic Color.* Baton Rouge: Louisiana State UP, 1995.

Miller, Cristanne *Marianne Moore: Questions of Authority.* Cambridge, MA: Harvard UP, 1995.

Stapleton, Lawrence. *Marianne Moore: The Poet's Advance.* Princeton, NJ: Princeton UP, 1978.

Willia, Patricia, ed. *Marianne Moore: Woman and Poet.* Orono, ME: National Poetry Foundation, 1990.

MARILYN NELSON

Poetry
For the Body. Baton Rouge: Louisiana State U, 1978.
Mama's Promises. Baton Rouge: Louisiana State U, 1985.
The Homeplace. Baton Rouge: Louisiana State U, 1990.
Magnificat. Baton Rouge: Louisiana State U, 1994.
The Fields of Praise. Baton Rouge: Louisiana State U, 1997.
Carver: A Life in Poems. Ashville: Front Street Books, 2001.

Translation
Rasmussen, Halfden. *Hundreds of Hens and Other Poems for Children.* Minneapolis: Black Widow Press, 1982.

Contributor
"A Black Rainbow: Modern Afro-American Poetry." With Rita Dove. Poetry after Modernism. Ed. Robert McDowell. Ashland, OR: Story Line Press, 1991.
A Formal Feeling Comes: Poems in Form by Contemporary Women. Ed. Annie Finch. Ashland, OR: Story Line Press, 1994.

FRANK O'HARA

Poetry
The Collected Poems of Frank O'Hara. Ed. Donald Allen. Berkeley: U of California P, 1995.

Prose
Art Chronicles: 1954–1966. Rev. Ed. New York: Braziller, 1990.
Standing Still and Walking in New York. Bolinas, CA: Grey Fox Press, 1975.

Bibliography
Smith, Alexander, ed. *Frank O'Hara: A Comprehensive Bibliography.* New York: Garland, 1979.

Biographical and Critical Studies
Ashbery, John. Introduction. *The Collected Poems of Frank O'Hara.* New York: Knopf, 1971: vii–xi.
Ellege, Jim, ed. *Frank O'Hara: To Be True to a City.* Ann Arbor: U of Michigan P, 1990.

Ferguson, Russell. *In Memory of My Feelings: Frank O'Hara and American Art.* Los Angeles: The Museum of Contemporary Art, 1999.
Gooch, Brad. *City Poet: The Life and Times of Frank O'Hara.* New York: Knopf, 1993.
Perloff, Marjorie. *Frank O'Hara: Poet among Painters.* New York: Braziller, 1977.

CHARLES OLSON

Poetry
The Collected Poems of Charles Olson. Ed. George F. Butterick. Berkeley: U of California P, 1987.
The Maximus Poems. Ed. George F. Butterick. Berkeley: U of California P, 1983.

Prose
Collected Prose. Ed. Donald Allen and Benjamin Friedlander. Berkeley: U of California P, 1997.
Charles Olson and Robert Creeley: The Complete Correspondence. Ed. George F. Butterick. 10 vols. Santa Rosa, CA: Black Sparrow, 1980–1996.
Call Me Ishmael. New York: Reynal and Hitchcock, 1947. Rpt. Grove, 1958.

Biographical and Critical Studies
Clark, Tom. *Charles Olson: The Allegory of a Poet's Life.* Berkeley: North Atlantic, 2000.
Foley, Jack. "Projective Verse at Fifty." http://www.flashpointmag.com/projvers.htm.
Foster, Edward Halsey. *Understanding the Black Mountain Poets.* Columbia, SC: U of South Carolina P, 1995.
Maud, Ralph. *Charles Olson's Reading: A Biography.* Carbondale, IL: Southern Illinois UP, 1996.
———. *What Does Not Change: The Significance of Charles Olson's "The Kingfishers."* Madison, NJ: Fairleigh Dickinson UP, 1998.
Merrill, Thomas F. *The Poetry of Charles Olson: A Primer.* Cranbury, DE: U of DE P, 1982.

ROBERT PINSKY

Poetry
Jersey Rain. New York: Farrar, Straus and Giroux, 2000.
The Figured Wheel: New and Collected Poems, 1966–1996. New York: Farrar, Straus and Giroux, 1996.

Prose
The Sounds of Poetry: A Brief Guide. New York: Farrar, Straus and Giroux, 1998.
Poetry and the World. Hopewell, NJ: Ecco Press, 1988.
Landor's Poetry. Chicago: University of Chicago, 1968.

Translations
The Inferno of Dante: A New Verse Translation. New York: Farrar, Straus and Giroux, 1994.

Czeslaw Milosz. *The Separate Notebooks*. With Robert Hass. Hopewell, NJ: Ecco Press, 1983.

EZRA POUND

Poetry
The Collected Early Poems of Ezra Pound. New York: New Directions, 1982.
Selected Cantos of Ezra Pound. New York: New Directions: 1970.
Personnae: The Collected Poems of Ezra Pound. New York: New Directions, 1950.
Selected Poems. Edited with introduction by T. S. Eliot. London: Faber & Gwyer, 1928.

Prose
Pound-Williams: Selected Letters of Ezra Pound and William Carlos Williams. Ed. Hugh Witemeyer. New York: New Directions, 1996.
Pound/Cummings: The Correspondence of Ezra Pound and E. E. Cummings. Ed. Betty Ahearn. Ann Arbor: U of Michigan P, 1996.
Ezra Pound and James Laughlin: Selected Letters. Ed. David Gordon. New York: Norton, 1994.
Selected Letters of Ezra Pound and Louis Zukofsky. New York: New Directions, 1987.
Pound-Lewis: The Letters of Ezra Pound and Wyndham Lewis. New York: New Directions, 1985.
Ezra Pound and Dorothy Shakespear: Their Letters, 1909–1914. New York: New Directions, 1985.
Pound-Ford, The Story of a Literary Friendship: The Correspondence between Ezra Pound and Ford Madox Ford and Their Writings about Each Other. New York: New Directions, 1982.
Ezra Pound and Music: The Complete Criticsm. Ed. R. Murray Schafer. New York: New Directions, 1977.
Selected Prose, 1909–1965. Ed. William Cookson. New York: New Directions, 1973.
Pound-Joyce: The Letters of Ezra Pound to James Joyce. Ed. Forrest Read. New York: New Directions, 1967.
Literary Essays of Ezra Pound. Edited and with an introduction by T. S. Eliot. New York: New Directions, 1954.
Patria Mia. Chicago: R. F. Seymour, 1950. Published in England as *Patria Mia and The Treatise on Harmony*. London: Owen, 1962.
The Letters of Ezra Pound, 1907–1941. Ed. D. D. Paige. New York: Harcourt, 1950.
Polite Essays. London: Faber, 1937.
Jefferson and/or Mussolini. London: Nott, 1935.
Social Credit: An Impact (pamphlet). London: Nott, 1935.
Make It New. London: Faber, 1934.
ABC of Reading. New Haven: Yale UP, 1934.
How to Read. London: Harmsworth, 1931.

Translation
The Translations of Ezra Pound. Ed. Hugh Kenner. New York: New Directions, 1953. Enlarged edition published as *Translations*. New York: New Directions, 1963.

Editing

Confucius to Cummings: An Anthology of Poetry. With Marcella Spann. New York: New Directions, 1964.

Ernest Fenollosa. *The Chinese Written Character as a Medium for Poetry.* London: Nutt, 1936.

(And contributor) *Active Anthology.* London: Faber, 1933.

(And contributor) *Catholic Anthology, 1914–1915.* London: Elkin Mathews, 1915.

(And contributor) *Des Imagistes.* New York: Boni. 1914.

Bibliography

Gallup, Donald. *Ezra Pound: A Bibliography.* Charlottesville, VA: UP of Virginia, 1983.

Biographical and Critical Studies

Bacigalupo, Massimo. *The Forméd Trace: The Later Poetry of Ezra Pound.* New York: Columbia UP, 1980.

Carpenter, Humphrey. *Serious Character: The Life of Ezra Pound.* New York: Houghton Mifflin, 1988.

Chace, William M. *The Political Identities of Ezra Pound and T.S. Eliot.* Stanford: Stanford UP, 1973.

Cookson, William. *A Guide to the Cantos of Ezra Pound.* Rev. Ed. New York: Persea Books, 2002.

Davie, Donald. *Ezra Pound.* New York: Viking, 1976.

———. *Ezra Pound: Poet as Sculptor.* New York: Oxford UP, 1964.

de Rachewiltz, Mary. *Discretions.* Boston: Little, Brown, 1971.

Eliot, T. S. *Ezra Pound: His Metric and Poetry.* New York: Knopf, 1917.

Kenner, Hugh. *The Poetry of Ezra Pound.* New York: New Directions, 1951.

———. *The Pound Era.* Berkeley: U of California P, 1971.

Norman, Charles. *Ezra Pound,* revised edition. New York: Minerva, 1969.

Pratt, William, ed. *Ezra Pound, Nature and Myth.* AMS Studies in Modern Literature No. 23. New York: AMS P; 2002.

Quinn, Sister Bernetta. *Ezra Pound: An Introduction to the Poetry.* New York: Columbia UP, 1973.

Russell, Peter. *An Examination of Ezra Pound.* New York: New Directions, 1950.

Stock, Noel. *The Life of Ezra Pound.* New York: Pantheon, 1970.

Tytell, John. *Ezra Pound: The Solitary Volcano.* Anchor Books: Reprint edition 2001.

Sullivan, J. P. *Ezra Pound and Sextus Propertius: A Study in Creative Translation.* Austin: U of Texas P, 1964.

Terrell, Carroll F. *A Companion to the Cantos of Ezra Pound.* Berkeley: U of California P, 1993.

Xie, Ming, and Ming Hsieh. *Ezra Pound and the Appropriation of Chinese Poetry: Cathay, Translation, and Imagism.* New York: Garland: 1998

Yip, Wai-lim. *Ezra Pound's Cathay.* Princeton: Princeton UP, 1969.

KENNETH REXROTH

Poetry

The Complete Poems of Kenneth Rexroth. Ed. Sam Hamill and Bradford Marrow. Port Townsend, WA: Copper Canyon P, 2002.

Drama
Beyond the Mountains. New York: New Directions, 1951.

Prose
Kenneth Rexroth and James Laughlin: Selected Letters. Ed. Lee Bartlett. New York & London: Norton, 1991.
More Classics Revisited. Ed. Bradford Morrow. New York: New Directions, 1989.
World Outside the Window: The Selected Essays of Kenneth Rexroth. Ed. Bradford Morrow. New York: New Directions, 1987.
Communalism: From Its Origins to the Twentieth Century. New York: Seabury, 1974.
The Elastic Retort: Essays in Literature and Ideas. New York: Seabury, 1973.
American Poetry in the Twentieth Century. New York: Herder, 1971.
The Alternative Society: Essays from the Other World. New York: Herder, 1970.
Classics Revisited. Chicago: Quadrangle Books, 1968.
An Autobiographical Novel. Garden City, NJ: Doubleday, 1966. Revised and enlarged. Ed. Linda Hamalian. New York: New Directions, 1991.
Assays. New York: New Directions, 1961.
Bird in the Bush: Obvious Essays. New York: New Directions, 1959.

Translations
Poems from the Greek Anthology. Ann Arbor: U of Michigan P, 1962.
Thirty Spanish Poems of Love and Exile. San Francisco: City Lights, 1956.
One Hundred Poems from the Chinese. New York: New Directions, 1956.
One Hundred Poems from the Japanese. New York: New Directions, 1955.

Biographical and Critical Studies
Bartlett, Lee. *Kenneth Rexroth.* Boise, ID: Boise State UP, 1988.
Hamalian, Linda. *A Life of Kenneth Rexroth.* New York & London: Norton, 1991.

ADRIENNE RICH

Poetry
Fox, Poems 1998–2000. New York: Norton, 2001.
Midnight Salvage: Poems 1995–1998. New York: Norton, 1999.
Dark Fields of the Republic, Poems 1991–1995. New York: Norton, 1995.
Collected Early Poems, 1950–1970. New York: Norton, 1993.
An Atlas of the Difficult World: Poems 1988–1991. New York: Norton, 1991.
Time's Power: Poems, 1985–1988. New York: Norton, 1988.
Your Native Life, Your Land. New York: Norton, 1986.
The Fact of a Doorframe: Poems Selected and New, 1950–1984. New York: Norton, 1984.

Prose
Arts of the Possible: Essays and Conversations. New York: Norton, 2001.
What Is Found There: Notebooks on Poetry and Politics. New York: Norton, 1993.
Blood, Bread, and Poetry: Selected Prose, 1975–1985. New York: Norton, 1986.
Of Woman Born: Motherhood as Experience and Institution. 1975. New York: Norton, 1986.
On Lies, Secrets, and Silence: Selected Prose, 1966–1978. New York: Norton, 1979.

Critical Studies

Cooper, Jane Roberta, ed. *Reading Adrienne Rich: Reviews and Revisions, 1955–1981*. Ann Arbor: U of Michigan P, 1984.

Dickie, Margaret. *Stein, Bishop, and Rich: Lyrics of Love, War, and Place*. Chapel Hill, NC: U of North Carolina P, 1997.

Gelpi, Barbara, and Albert Gelpi, eds. *Adrienne Rich's Poetry and Prose: Poems, Prose, Reviews, and Criticism*. 2nd ed. New York: Norton, 1993.

Keyes, Claire. *The Aesthetics of Power: The Poetry of Adrienne Rich*. Athens, GA: U of Georgia P, 1986.

Templeton, Alice. *The Dream and the Dialogue: Adrienne Rich's Feminist Poetics*. Knoxville, TN: U of Tennessee P, 1994.

MURIEL RUKEYSER

Poetry

Out of Silence: Selected Poems. Ed. Kate Daniels. Evanston, IL: TriQuarterly Books, 1994.
Collected Poems. New York: McGraw-Hill, 1978.

Poetry and Prose

A Muriel Rukeyser Reader. Ed. Jan Heller Levi. New York: Norton, 1994.

Prose

The Life of Poetry. 1949. Ashfield, MA: Paris Press, 1996.
Willard Gibbs. 1942. Woodbridge, CT: Ox Bow Press, 1988.
The Traces of Thomas Hariot. New York: Random House, 1971.
One Life. New York: Simon and Schuster, 1957.

Biographical and Critical Studies

Herzog, Anne F. and Janet E. Kaufman. *"How Shall We Tell Each Other of the Poet?"*: *The Life and Writing of Muriel Rukeyser*. New York: St. Martin's, 1999.

Kertesz, Louise. *The Poetic Vision of Muriel Rukeyser*. Baton Rouge: Louisiana State UP, 1980.

RON SILLIMAN

Poetry

Xing. Buffalo, NY: Meow Press, 1996.
N/O. New York: Roof Books, 1994.
The New Sentence. New York: Roof Books, 1987.
LIT. Hartford, CT: Potes & Poets Press, 1987.
Paradise. Providence, RI: Burning Deck, 1985.
ABC. Berkeley: Tuumba Press, 1983.
Tjanting. Berkeley: Figures, 1981.
Ketjak. San Francisco: This Press, 1978.
Nox. Providence, RI: Burning Deck, 1974.

Critical Studies

Beckett, Tom, ed. *The Difficulties: Ron Silliman Issue*. Vol. 2, no. 2, 1985.

Hartley, George. *Textual Politics & the Language Poets*. Bloomington: Indiana UP, 1989.

McGann, Jerome (as Anne Mack and J. J. Rome). *"The Alphabet,* Spelt from Ron Silliman's Leaves." *South Atlantic Quarterly* 89 (Fall 1990): 736–59.

———. *Social Values and Poetic Acts: The Historical Judgment of Literary Work*. Cambridge, MA: Harvard UP, 1988: 197–220.

Perloff, Marjorie. *The Dance of the Intellect: Studies in the Poetry of the Pound Tradition*. Cambridge, MA: Cambridge UP, 1985: 215–38.

CHARLES SIMIC

Poetry

Jackstraws. New York: Harcourt, 1999.

Selected Early Poems. New York: Harcourt, 1999.

Walking the Black Cat. New York: Harcourt, 1994.

Hotel Insomnia. New York: Harcourt, 1990.

Unending Blues. New York: Harcourt, 1986.

Selected Poems, 1963–1983. New York: Braziller, 1985.

Prose

Orphan Factory. Ann Arbor: U of Michigan P, 1997.

The Unemployed Fortune-Teller. Ann Arbor: U of Michigan P, 1994.

The Uncertain Certainty. Ann Arbor: U of Michigan P, 1985.

Translations

Horse Has Six Legs: Contemporary Serbian Poetry. St. Paul, MN: Graywolf, 1992.

Tomaz Salamun. *Selected Poems*. New York: Viking, 1987.

Critical Studies

Weigl, Bruce, ed. *Charles Simic: Essays on the Poetry*. Ann Arbor: U of Michigan P, 1996.

LOUIS SIMPSON

Poetry

There You Are: Poems. Ashland, OR: Story Line P, 1995.

In the Room We Share. New York: Paragon House, 1990.

Collected Poems. New York: Paragon House, 1988.

Prose

The King My Father's Wreck. Ashland, OR: Story Line Press, 1995.

Ships Going into the Blue: Essays and Notes on Poetry. Ann Arbor: U of Michigan P, 1994.

The Character of the Poet. Ann Arbor: U of Michigan P, 1986.

A Company of Poets. Ann Arbor: U of Michigan P, 1981.

A Revolution in Taste: Studies of Dylan Thomas, Allen Ginsberg, Sylvia Plath and Robert Lowell. New York: Macmillan, 1979.
Three on the Tower: The Lives and Works of Ezra Pound, T. S. Eliot and William Carlos Williams. New York: Morrow, 1975.
James Hogg: A Critical Study. New York: St. Martin's, 1962.
Riverside Drive, New York: Atheneum, 1962.

Translations
François Villon's The Legacy & Testament. Ashland, OR: Story Line Press, 2000.
Modern Poets of France: A Bilingual Anthology. Ashland, OR: Story Line Press, 1997.

Biographical and Critical Studies
Lazer, Hank, ed. *On Louis Simpson: Depths Beyond Happiness.* Ann Arbor: U of Michigan P, 1988.
Mason, David. *The Poetry of Life and the Life of Poetry.* Ashland, OR: Story Line Press, 2000.
Moran, Ronald. *Louis Simpson.* Boston: Twayne, 1972.
Roberson, William H. *Louis Simpson: A Reference Guide.* Boston: G. K. Hall, 1972.

JACK SPICER

Poetry
Collections: *The House that Jack Built: The Collected Lectures of Jack Spicer.* Ed. Peter Gizzi. Hanover, NH: UP of New England, 1998.
The Collected Books of Jack Spicer. Ed. Robin Blaser. Santa Barbara, CA: Black Sparrow P, 1975.
Collected Poems: 1945–1946. San Francisco: White Rabbit P, 1981.

Bibliography
Keller, Larry. *Jack Spicer: A Bibliography.* Tiburon, CA: Cadmus Editions, 1985.

Biographies
Duncan, Robert. *As Testimony: The Poem & the Scene.* San Francisco: White Rabbit P, 1964.
Ellingham, Lewis, and Kevin Killian, *Poet Be Like God: Jack Spicer and the San Francisco Renaissance.* Middletown, CT: Wesleyan UP, 1998.
Foster, Edward Halsey. *Jack Spicer.* Boise, ID: Boise State UP, 1991.
Kyger, Joanne. *The Dharma Committee.* Bolinas, CA: Smithereens P, 1986.

WILLIAM STAFFORD

Poetry
The Way It Is: New and Selected Poems. St. Paul, MN: Graywolf Press, 1998.
Learning to Live in the World: Earth Poems. San Diego: Harcourt Brace, 1994.
The Darkness around Us Is Deep: Selected Poems of William Stafford. Ed. Robert Bly. New York: Harper Perennial, 1993.

Prose

Crossing Unmarked Snow: Further Views on the Writer's Vocation. Ed. Paul Merchant and Vincent Wixon. Ann Arbor: U of Michigan P, 1998.
You Must Revise Your Life. Ann Arbor: U of Michigan P, 1986.

Critical Studies

Andrews, Tom. *On William Stafford: The Worth of Local Things.* Ann Arbor: U of Michigan P, 1993.
Holden, Jonathan. *To Mark the Turn: A Reading of William Stafford's Poetry.* Lawrence, KS: U of Kansas P, 1976.
Kitchen, Judith. *Writing the World: Understanding William Stafford.* Corvallis, OR: U of Oregon P, 1999.
Pinsker, Sanford. *Three Pacific Northwest Poets: William Stafford, Richard Hugo, and David Wagoner.* Boston: Twayne, 1987.

TIMOTHY STEELE

Poetry

Sapphics and Uncertainties: Poems 1970–1986. Fayetteville: University of Arkansas, 1995.
The Color Wheel. Baltimore, MD: Johns Hopkins UP, 1994.

Prose

All the Fun's in How You Say a Thing: An Explanation of Meter and Versification. Athens: Ohio UP, 1999.
Missing Measures: Modern Poetry and the Revolt against Meter. Fayetteville: University of Arkansas, 1990.

Editing

The Poems of J. V. Cunningham. Athens: Swallow/Ohio UP, 1997.

Biographical and Critical Studies

Kennedy, X. J. *Timothy Steele. American Poets since World War II. D. L. B.* vol. 120. Ed. R. S. Gwynn, Detroit: Gale, 1992: 296–99.
Lindner, April. *New Formalist Poets of the American West.* Boise, ID: Boise State University Western Writers Series #149, 2001.
Walzer, Kevin. *The Ghost of Tradition: Expansive Poetry and Postmodernism.* Ashland, OR: Story Line Press, 1998.
———. "An Interview with Timothy Steele." *Edge City Review* 6 (September 1996): 3–6.
———. "The Poetry of Timothy Steele." *The Tennessee Quarterly* 2/3 (Winter 1996): 16–30.

GERTRUDE STEIN

Poetry and Prose

Writings 1903–1932: Q.E.D., Three Lives, Portraits and Other Short Works, The Autobiography of Alice B. Toklas. Ed. Catherine R Stimpson. New York: Library of America, 1998.

Writings 1932–1946: Stanzas in Meditation, Lectures in America, The Geographical History of America, Ida, Brewsie and Willie, other works. Ed. Catherine R. Stimpson. New York: Library of America, 1998.
Selected Writings of Gertrude Stein. 1946. Ed. Carl Van Vechten. New York: Vintage, 1990.
The Yale Gertrude Stein. Ed. Richard Kostelanetz. New Haven: Yale UP, 1980.
The Yale Edition of the Unpublished Writings of Gertrude Stein. Vols. 1–8. Ed. Carl Van Vechten. New Haven: Yale UP, 1956–1958.

Bibliography
Liston, Maureen R. *Gertrude Stein: An Annotated, Critical Bibliography.* Kent, OH: Kent State UP, 1979.

Biographical and Critical Studies
Brinnin, John Malcolm. *The Third Rose: Gertrude Stein and Her World.* Boston: Little, Brown, 1959.
DeKoven, Marianne. *A Different Language: Gertrude Stein's Experimental Writing.* Madison, WI: U of Wisconsin P, 1983.
Hoffman, Michael J. *Critical Essays on Gertrude Stein.* Boston: G. K. Hall, 1986.
Kellner, Bruce, ed. *A Gertrude Stein Companion: Content with the Example.* New York: Greenwood, 1988.
Mellow, James R. *Charmed Circle: Gertrude Stein and Company.* New York: Praeger, 1974.
Ruddick, Lisa. *Reading Gertrude Stein: Body, Text, Gnosis.* Ithaca, NY: Cornell UP, 1990.

WALLACE STEVENS

Poetry
Collected Poetry and Prose. New York: Library of America, 1997.
The Palm at the End of the Mind: Selected Poems and a Play by Wallace Stevens. Ed. Holly Stevens. New York: Knopf, 1971.
Opus Posthumous. Ed. Samuel French Morse. New York: Knopf, 1957.
The Collected Poems of Wallace Stevens. New York: Knopf, 1954.

Prose
Letters of Wallace Stevens. Ed. Holly Stevens. New York: Knopf, 1966.
The Necessary Angel: Essays on Reality and the Imagination. New York: Knopf, 1951.

Bibliography
Edelstein, J. M. *Wallace Stevens: A Descriptive Bibliography.* Pittsburgh: U of Pittsburgh P, 1973.

Biographical and Critical Studies
Bate, Milton J. *Wallace Stevens: A Mythology of Self.* Berkeley: U of California P, 1985.
Blessing, Richard Allen. *Wallace Stevens' "Whole Harmonium."* Syracuse, NY: Syracuse UP, 1970.

Brazeau, Peter. *Parts of A World: Wallace Stevens Remembered: An Oral Biography.* New York: Random House, 1983.

Brown, Ashley, and Robert S. Haller, eds. *The Achievement of Wallace Stevens.* Philadelphia: Lippincott, 1962.

Ehrenpreis, Irvin, ed. *Wallace Stevens: A Critical Anthology.* Harmondsworth, UK: Penguin, 1973.

Lensing, George. *Wallace Stevens and the Seasons.* Baton Rouge: Louisiana State UP, 2001.

Litz, A. Walton. *Introspective Voyager: The Poetic Development of Wallace Stevens.* New York: Oxford UP, 1972.

Morse, Samuel French. *Wallace Stevens: Poetry as Life.* New York: Pegasus, 1970.

Richardson, Joan. *Wallace Stevens: The Early Years.* New York: Morrow, 1986.

Santilli, Kristine. *Poetic Gesture: Myth, Wallace Stevens, and the Motions of Poetic Language.* New York: Routledge, 2002.

Schaum, Melita, ed. *Wallace Stevens and the Feminine.* Tuscaloosa: U of Alabama P, 1993.

Stevens, Holly. *Souvenirs and Prophecies: The Young Wallace Stevens.* New York: Knopf, 1977.

Vendler, Helen Hennessy. *On Extended Wings: Wallace Stevens' Longer Poems.* Cambridge: Harvard UP, 1969.

ANNE STEVENSON

Poetry

Granny Scarecrow. Newcastle-upon-Tyne, UK: Bloodaxe Books, 2000.
The Collected Poems of Anne Stevenson. New York: Oxford UP, 1996.

Prose

Between the Iceberg and the Ship: Selected Essays. Ann Arbor: U of Michigan P, 1998.
Five Looks at Elizabeth Bishop. London: Bellew, 1998.
Bitter Fame: A Life of Sylvia Plath. Boston: Houghton, 1989.
Elizabeth Bishop. Boston: Twayne, 1966.

Interview

Haven, Cynthia. "Anne Stevenson." http://www.cortlandreview.com/issue/14/stevenson 14.htm.

ALLEN TATE

Poetry

Collected Poems, 1919–1976. New York: Farrar, Straus, 1977.

Prose

Essays of Four Decades. Chicago: Swallow, 1968.
The Man of Letters in the Modern World: Selected Essays 1928–1955. New York: Meridian, 1955.

Reason in Madness: Critical Essays. New York: Putnam, 1941.
Reactionary Essays on Poetry and Ideas. New York: Scribner, 1936.

Biographical and Critical Studies
Bishop, Ferman. *Allen Tate.* Boston: Twayne, 1967.
Bradbury, John M. *The Fugitives: A Critical Account.* Chapel Hill: U of North Carolina P, 1958.
Dupree, Robert S. *Allen Tate and the Augustinian Imagination.* Baton Rouge: Louisiana State UP, 1983.
Hammer, Langdon. *Hart Crane & Allen Tate: Janus-Faced Modernism.* Princeton, NJ: Princeton UP, 1993.
Squires, Radcliffe. *Allen Tate: A Literary Biography.* New York: Bobbs-Merrill, 1971.
———, ed. *Allen Tate and His Work: Critical Evaluations.* Minneapolis: U of Minnesota P, 1972.

WILLIAM CARLOS WILLIAMS

Poetry
Paterson. Rev. ed. Ed. Christopher MacGowan. New York: New Directions, 1992.
The Collected Poems of William Carlos Williams. Vols. 1 and 2. Ed. A. Walton Litz and Christopher MacGowan. New York: New Directions, 1986.

Prose
Imaginations: Five Experimental Prose Pieces. Ed. Webster Schott. New York: New Directions, 1970.
Selected Essays of William Carlos Williams. 1954. New York: New Directions, 1969.
In the American Grain. 1925. New York: New Directions, 1956.

Bibliography
Wagner, Linda W. *William Carlos Williams: A Reference Guide.* Boston: G. K. Hall, 1978.

Biographical and Critical Studies
Axelrod, Stephen Gould, and Helen Deese, eds. *Critical Essays on Williams Carlos Williams.* Boston: G. K. Hall, 1995.
Breslin, James E. *William Carlos Williams: An American Artist.* New York: Oxford UP, 1970.
Cushman, Stephen. *William Carlos Williams and the Meaning of Measure.* New Haven: Yale UP, 1985.
Mariani, Paul. *William Carlos Williams: A New World Naked.* New York: McGraw-Hill, 1981.
Rapp, Carl. *Williams Carlos Williams and Romantic Idealism.* Hanover, NH: UP of New England, 1984.

CHRISTIAN WIMAN

Poetry
The Long Home. Ashland, OR: Story Line Press, 1998.

YVOR WINTERS

Poetry

The Collected Poems of Yvor Winters. Manchester, UK: Carcanet New P, 1978. Republished as *The Poetry of Yvor Winters.* Athens, OH: Swallow, 1980.

The Early Poems of Yvor Winters, 1920–28. Denver: Swallow, 1966.

Collected Poems. Denver: Swallow, 1952, rev. 1960. London: Routledge & Kegan Paul, 1962.

Prose

Uncollected Essays and Reviews. Ed. Francis Murphy. Chicago: Swallow, 1973.

Forms of Discovery: Critical and Historical Essays on the Forms of the Short Poem in English. Chicago: Swallow, 1967.

On Modern Poets: Stevens, Eliot, Ransom, Crane, Hopkins, Frost. Cleveland & New York: Meridian/ World, 1959.

The Function of Criticism. Denver: Swallow, 1957.

In Defense of Reason. New York: Swallow & William Morrow, 1947. London: Routledge & Kegan Paul, 1960.

Edwin Arlington Robinson. Norfolk, CT: New Directions, 1946. Rev. ed., New York: New Directions, 1971.

Editing

Quest for Reality. Ed. Winters and Kenneth Fields. Chicago: Swallow, 1969.

Poets of the Pacific. Second Series. Stanford: Stanford UP, 1949.

Twelve Poets of the Pacific. New York: New Directions, 1937.

Bibliography

Lohf, Kenneth A., and Eugene P. Sheehy. *Yvor Winters: A Bibliography.* Denver: Swallow, 1959.

Powell, Grosvenor. *Yvor Winters: An Annotated Bibliography, 1919–1982.* Metuchen, NJ: Scarecrow P, 1983.

Critical Studies

Isaacs, Elizabeth. *An Introduction to the Poetry of Yvor Winters.* Chicago: Swallow, 1981.

Parkinson, Thomas. *Hart Crane and Yvor Winters: Their Literary Correspondence.* Berkeley: U of California P, 1978.

Powell, Grosvenor. *Language as Being in the Poetry of Yvor Winters.* Baton Rouge: Louisiana State UP, 1980.

LOUIS ZUKOFSKY

Poetry

Complete Short Poetry. Baltimore, Md.: Johns Hopkins UP, 1991.

"A." 1978. Baltimore, Md.: Johns Hopkins UP, 1993.

Prose

Prepositions+: The Collected Critical Essays. Ed. Mark Scroggins. Hanover, NH: UP of New England/Wesleyan UP, 2000.

A Test of Poetry. Hanover, NH: UP of New England/Wesleyan UP, 2000.

Bibliography
Zukofsky, Celia Thaew. *A Bibliography of Louis Zukofsky.* Santa Barbara: Black Sparrow Press, 1969.

Biographical and Critical Studies
Ahearn, Barry. *Zukofsky's "A": An Introduction.* Berkeley: U of California P, 1983.
Scroggins, Mark. *Louis Zukofsky and the Poetry of Knowledge.* Tuscaloosa: U of Alabama P, 1998.
———. ed. *Upper Limit Music: The Writing of Louis Zukofsky.* Tuscaloosa: U of Alabama P, 1997.
Stanley, Sandra Kumamoto. *Louis Zukofsky and the Transformation of Modern American Poetics.* Berkeley: U of California P, 1994.
Terrell, Clark. *Louis Zukofsky: Man and Poet.* Orono, ME: National Poetry Foundation, 1979.

Acknowledgments

JULIA ALVAREZ "So Much Depends" from *Something to Declare,* Algonquin Books of Chapel Hill, 1998. Copyright © 1982, 1998 by Julia Alvarez. Originally published under the title "On Finding a Latino Voice," *Washington Post Book World,* May 14, 1999. Reprinted by permission of Susan Bergholz Literary Services, New York. All rights reserved.

JOHN ASHBERY "The Invisible Avant-Garde" by John Ashbery. Copyright © 1968 by John Ashbery. Reprinted by permission of Georges Borchardt, Inc.

ROBERT BLY "A Wrong Turning in American Poetry" from *American Poetry: Wilderness and Domesticity* by Robert Bly. Copyright © 1990 by Robert Bly. Reprinted by permission of HarperCollins Publishers Inc.

LOUISE BOGAN "The Springs of Poetry" from *The New Republic,* December 5, 1923. Reprinted with the permission of Mary Kinzie, executor of the literary estate of Louise Bogan.

GWENDOLYN BROOKS "The New Black" from *Report from Part One* by Gwendolyn Brooks, Detroit: Broadside Press, 1972. Copyright © 1972 by Gwendolyn Brooks. Reprinted by permission of the publisher.

HART CRANE "General Aims and Theories" from *The Complete Poems and Selected Letters and Prose of Hart Crane,* edited by Brom Weber. Copyright © 1933, 1958, 1966 by Liveright Publishing Corporation. Copyright © 1952 by Brom Weber. Used by permission of Liveright Publishing Corporation.

ROBERT CREELEY "To Define" and "Poems Are a Complex" by Robert Creeley from *The Collected Essays of Robert Creeley.* Copyright © 1989 The Regents of the University of California.

J. V. CUNNINGHAM "The Problem of Form" from *The Collected Essays of J. V. Cunningham.* Copyright © 1976 The Swallow Press Inc. Reprinted with the permission of Ohio UP/Swallow Press, Athens, Ohio.

RITA DOVE AND MARILYN NELSON "A Black Rainbow: Modern Afro-American Poetry" from *Poetry After Modernism,* Story Line Press, 1998. Copyright © 1998 Rita Dove and Marilyn Nelson. Reprinted by permission of the authors.

ROBERT DUNCAN "The Homosexual in Society" by Robert Duncan from *A Selected Prose,* edited by Robert J. Bertholf. Copyright © 1968 by Robert Duncan. Reprinted by permission of New Directions Publishing Corporation.

RHINA ESPAILLAT "Bilingual/Bilingue" from *Where Horizons Go: Poems by Rhina Espaillat,* Kirksville, Mo.: Truman State UP, 1998. Reprinted by permission of the publisher.

JACK FOLEY "'What about All This . . .': Speculations on Poetry and My Relationship to It" from *O Powerful Western Star* by Jack Foley, Pantograph Press. Copyright © 2000 by Jack Foley. Reprinted by permission of Pantograph Press.

ROBERT FROST   "The Sound of Sense: A Letter to John T. Bartlett" from *Selected Letters of Robert Frost,* edited by Lawrence Thompson. Compilation © 1964 by Lawrence Thompson and Henry Holt & Co. "The Figure a Poem Makes" from *Selected Prose of Robert Frost,* edited by Hyde Cox and Edward Connery Lathem. Copyright © 1939,1967 by Henry Holt and Co. Reprinted by permission of Henry Holt and Company, LLC.

ALICE FULTON   "Of Formal, Free, and Fractal Verse: Singing the Body Electric" from *Feeling as a Foreign Language* by Alice Fulton. Copyright © 1999 by Alice Fulton. Reprinted with permission of Graywolf Press, Saint Paul, Minnesota. This essay was originally published in 1986 by *Poetry East* in a slightly different version.

DANA GIOIA   "Can Poetry Matter?" from *Can Poetry Matter?* by Dana Gioia. Copyright © 1992 by Dana Gioia. Reprinted with permission of Graywolf Press, Saint Paul, Minnesota.

LOUISE GLÜCK   "Disruption, Hesitation, Silence" from *Proofs and Theories: Essays on Poetry* by Louise Glück. Copyright © 1994 by Louise Gluck. Reprinted by permission of HarperCollins Publishers Inc.

DONALD HALL   "Poetry and Ambition" by Donald Hall. First published in *The Kenyon Review*—New Series, Fall 1983, Vol. V., No. 4. Copyright © 1983 by Donald Hall. Reprinted by permission of the author.

ROBERT HAYDEN   "Introduction" from *Kaleidoscope: Poems by American Negro Poets* by Robert Hayden. Copyright © 1967 by Harcourt, Inc. and renewed 1995 by Maia Patillo. Reprinted by permission of the publisher.

LYN HEJINIAN   "The Rejection of Closure" from *The Language of Inquiry* by Lyn Hejinian. Copyright © 2000 The Regents of the University of California. Reprinted with permission from the publisher.

LANGSTON HUGHES   "The Negro Artist and the Racial Mountain" by Langston Hughes. First published in *The Nation.* Copyright © 1926 by Langston Hughes. Reprinted by permission of Harold Ober Associates Incorporated.

RANDALL JARRELL   "The Obscurity of the Poet" from *Poetry and the Age* by Randall Jarrell. Copyright © 1953 by Randall Jarrell. Reprinted by permission of Mary Jarrell, Executor of the Estate of Randall Jarrell.

ROBINSON JEFFERS   "Poetry, Gongorism and a Thousand Years" from *The Collected Poetry of Robinson Jeffers: Poetry 1903–1920, Prose, and Unpublished Writings,* edited by Tim Hunt. Copyright © 1948 Robinson Jeffers; editorial matter © 2000 by the Board of Trustees of the Leland Stanford Jr. University. Used with the permission of Stanford UP, www.sup.org.

DONALD JUSTICE   "Meters and Memory" from *Oblivion: On Writers & Writing* by Donald Justice. Published with permission of the author and Storyline Press (www.storylinepress.com).

MARY KINZIE   "The Rhapsodic Fallacy" by Mary Kinzie. Copyright © 2002 by Mary Kinzie. Reprinted by permission of the author.

DENISE LEVERTOV   "Some Notes on Organic Form" from *New and Selected Essays* by Denise Levertov. Copyright © 1973 by Denise Levertov. Reprinted by permission of New Directions Publishing Corporation.

SHIRLEY GEOK-LIN LIM   "The Scarlet Brewer and the Voice of the Colonized" by Shirley Geok-Lin Lim. Copyright © 2002 by Shirley Geok-Lin Lim.

WILLIAM LOGAN   "Four or Five Motions toward a Poetics" by William Logan. First published in *The Sewanee Review,* Vol. CVII, no. 2, Spring 1999. Copyright © 1999 by William Logan. Reprinted by permission of the author.

W. S. MERWIN   "An Open Form" by W. S. Merwin. Copyright © 1969 W. S. Merwin. Reprinted by permission of The Andrew Wylie Agency, New York.

MARIANNE MOORE   "Indiosyncrasy and Technique" from *A Marianne Moore Reader.* Copyright © 1958 University of California Press.

FRANK O'HARA   "Personism: A Manifesto." First published in *The New American Poetry* by Donald Allen. "Ave Maria" from *The Collected Poems of Frank O'Hara,* New York: Alfred A. Knopf, 1971. Reprinted by permission of Maureen Granville-Smith, Administratrix of the Estate of Frank O'Hara.

CHARLES OLSON   "Projective Verse" from *Selected Writings of Charles Olson.* Copyright © 1951, 1966 by Charles Olson. Reprinted by permission of New Directions Publishing Corp.

GEORGE OPPEN   "Street" from *Collected Poems* by George Oppen. Copyright © 1975 by George Oppen. Reprinted by permission of New Directions Publishing Corp.

ROBERT PINSKY   "Responsibilities of the Poet" from *Poetry and the World* by Robert Pinsky. Copyright © 1988 by Robert Pinsky. Reprinted by permission of HarperCollins Inc.

EZRA POUND   "How to Read" from *The Literary Essays of Ezra Pound* by Ezra Pound. Copyright © 1935 by Ezra Pound. Reprinted by permission of New Directions Publishing Corporation.

KENNETH REXROTH   "The Art of the Beat Generation" from *World Outside the Window: Selected Essays* by Kenneth Rexroth. Copyright © 1957 by Kenneth Rexroth. Reprinted by permission of New Directions Publishing Corp.

ADRIENNE RICH   " 'When We Dead Awaken': Writing as Re-Vision" from *Arts of the Possible: Essays and Conversations* by Adrienne Rich. Copyright © 2001 Adrienne Rich; From *Collected Early Poems: 1950–1970* by Adrienne Rich: "Aunt Jennifer's Tigers" Copyright © 1993, 1951 by Adrienne Rich, "The Loser" Copyright © 1993, 1967, 1963 by Adrienne Rich, the lines from "Snapshots of a Daughter-in-Law" Copyright © 1993, 1967, 1963 by Adrienne Rich, "Onion" Copyright © 1993 by Adrienne Rich Copyright © 1969 by W. W. Norton & Company, Inc., "Planetarium" Copyright © 1993 by Adrienne Rich, Copyright © 1971 by W. W. Norton & Company, Inc. Used by permission of the author and W. W. Norton & Company, Inc.

MURIEL RUKEYSER   Excerpt from *The Life of Poetry* by Muriel Rukeyser. Copyright © 1996 by Paris Press, Ashfield, Mass. First published in *The Intimate Critique,* edited by Diane P. Freedman, Oliver Frey and Frances Murphy Zanhar, Duke UP, 1993.

RON SILLIMAN   "The Political Economy of Poetry" by Ron Silliman. Copyright © Ron Silliman 1981, 1982, 1995, 2002.

CHARLES SIMIC   "My Weariness of Epic Proportions" from *Charles Simic: Selected Early Poems* by Charles Simic. Copyright © 1999 by Charles Simic. Reprinted by permission of George Braziller, Inc. "Negative Capability and Its Children" by Charles Simic. Copyright © 1978 Charles Simic.

LOUIS SIMPSON   "Reflections on Narrative Poetry" from *A Company of Poets* by Louis Simpson, University of Michigan Press, 1981. Reprinted with permission of the publisher.

JACK SPICER   "On Spoken Poetry" by Jack Spicer from *The House that Jack Built: The Collected Letters of Jack Spicer.* Copyright © 1998 by Peter Gizz and the Estate of Jack Spicer. Reprinted by permission of Wesleyan UP.

WILLIAM STAFFORD   "Some Arguments Against Good Diction" from *Writing the Australian Crawl* by William Stafford, University of Michigan Press, 1978. Reprinted by permission of Kim Stafford and the publisher.

TIMOTHY STEELE   "Tradition and Revolution: The Modern Movement and Free Verse" by Timothy Steele. First published in *Southwest Review,* Summer 1985, vol. 70, no. 3. Copyright © 1985 by Timothy Steele. Reprinted by permission of the author.

GERTRUDE STEIN   "Composition as Explanation" from *Selected Writings of Gertrude Stein,* edited by Carl Van Vechten. Copyright © 1946 by Random House, Inc. Used by permission of Random House, Inc.

WALLACE STEVENS   "The Noble Rider and the Sound of Words" from *The Necessary Angel*   by Wallace Stevens. Copyright © 1951 by Wallace Stevens. Used by permission of Alfred A. Knopf, a division of Random House, Inc.

ANNE STEVENSON   "Writing as a Woman" by Anne Stevenson from *Women Writing and Women Writing About Women,* edited by Mary Jacobus, Barnes and Noble Books, 1979. Reprinted by permission of the author and Taylor & Francis, London.

ALLEN TATE   "Tension in Poetry" from *Collected Essays* by Allen Tate. Copyright © 1959 by Allen Tate. Reprinted by permission of Helen Tate, Literary Executrix of the Estate of Allen Tate.

WILLIAM CARLOS WILLIAMS   "Between Walls" from *Collected Poems: 1909–1939, Volume I* by William Carlos Williams. Copyright © 1938 by New Directions Publishing Corp.; "A New Measure" from *In the American Grain: Essays by William Carlos Williams* by William Carlos Williams. Copyright © 1933 by William Carlos Williams; "The Poem as a Field of Action" from *Selected Essays of William Carlos Williams* by William Carlos Williams. Copyright © 1954 by William Carlos Williams. Reprinted by permission of New Directions Publishing Corp.

CHRISTIAN WIMAN   "A Piece of Prose" by Christian Wiman. First published in *Poetry,* August 1999. Copyright © 1999 by The Modern Poetry Association. Reprinted by permission of the Editor of *Poetry* and the author.

YVOR WINTERS   Foreword to "The Testament of a Stone" from *Yvor Winters: Uncollected Essays and Reviews,* edited by Francis Murphy, Swallow Press, 1973. Reprinted with the permission of Ohio UP/Swallow Press, Athens, Ohio.

LOUIS ZUKOFSKY   "An Objective" by Louis Zukofsky from *Prepositions: The Collected Critical Essays of Louis Zukofsky.* Copyright © 2001 by Paul Zukofsky. Reprinted by permission of Wesleyan University Press.

Index of Authors and Titles